Lincoln's Tragic Pragmatism

Lincoln's Tragic Pragmatism

LINCOLN, DOUGLAS, AND MORAL CONFLICT

JOHN BURT

THE BELKNAP PRESS OF
HARVARD UNIVERSITY PRESS
Cambridge, Massachusetts
London, England   2013

Library of Congress Cataloging-in-Publication Data
Burt, John, 1955–
    Lincoln's tragic pragmatism : Lincoln, Douglas, and moral conflict /
John Burt.
        p.   cm.
    Includes bibliographical references and index.
    ISBN 978-0-674-05018-1 (alk. paper)
        1. Lincoln-Douglas Debates, Ill., 1858.   2. Lincoln, Abraham, 1809–
1865—Political and social views.   3. Lincoln, Abraham, 1809–1865—
Ethics.   4. Douglas, Stephen A. (Stephen Arnold), 1813–1861—Political and
social views.   5. Douglas, Stephen A. (Stephen Arnold), 1813–1861—
Ethics.   6. Democracy—Moral and ethical aspects—United States.
7. Slavery—Moral and ethical aspects—United States—History—19th
century.   I. Title.
E457.4.B97   2013
973.7092—dc23   2012011267

For Jo Anne and Denisa, with love

Contents

Preface

Anyone who has read *Middlemarch* will probably remember feeling a touch of sadness as the novel drew to its conclusion. The sadness is not sadness about the plot, since the novel ends as happily as any text driven by Eliot's skepticism about human nature could have ended. The sadness is that, having spent perhaps a month invested in it, loving its characters, wondering about their fates, living in imagination in their town, the reader knows that one will have to leave the world of that book and never again enter it in quite the same way. Completing this book gives me something of the same experience. I have lived in this book for so long that the thought of saying "Go, not-so-little-book" is a source of complex feelings.

In retrospect, it was my good fortune to have spent so long a time with this book as I have. First of all, of course, I had its company to enjoy for many years. Second, writing a book over a long time forced me to break myself of the habit of looking for present-day parallels to what was happening in the book, since all too many of my examples, set in the days of the elder President Bush and of President Clinton, began to need explanatory footnotes to make sense to present-day readers. Most of all, however, I am grateful to have worked long enough on this book to have seen the main ideas change as I began to grasp them better. Many of the arguments of this book may still be wrong, but they are certainly better considered than they would have been had I finished this book on my original schedule.

Two conclusions that I did not anticipate drawing, one of them surprising, the other repellent, have emerged out of my rethinking and rewriting this book, each of which might prove controversial, since neither of them is in accord with prevailing views of Lincoln and antebellum politics. First, the surprising one: Lincoln had chosen commitments whose entailments included racially equal citizenship years before he explicitly advocated such a thing, indeed while he actively denied having made such a commitment.

When Lincoln argued in his 1854 Peoria speech that slavery must be kept out of Kansas on primarily moral grounds, rather than merely because the people of Kansas do not want it, that argument made straightforward practical and moral sense, because how the struggle in Kansas would turn out could not then have been clear. The people who would reject or demand slavery were not yet in Kansas, and it was not obvious which side would win the footrace for control of the territory's institutions that the Kansas-Nebraska Act had set off.

I have wondered why Lincoln persisted making this argument in the fall of 1858, after the people of Kansas, the one western territory where slavery might have imaginably had a chance of establishing itself, had decisively rejected it. Why stir up a possibly inflammatory quarrel over an issue in which one had already practically speaking had one's way? Why should it have mattered to Lincoln, once it became clear that slavery would not go into Kansas in any event, whether moral reasons or other reasons kept it out? Why insist that Kansas not only choose the right outcome but for the right reasons? I had inclined to the generally held view that Lincoln's motives in 1858 were expedient ones: Douglas having unexpectedly emerged as a significant Free Soil political leader as a result of his opposition to the fraudulent Lecompton Constitution (which would have forced slavery into Kansas against the will of its people), Lincoln wished to shape his platform so as to keep Douglas from entering his party and taking a leadership position, as eastern Republicans like Seward were encouraging him to do. Douglas could take a Free Soil position about Kansas so long as he could say that in doing so he was merely respecting the will of the people of Kansas, but he could not do so if the test of his convictions was a willingness to denounce slavery in a straightforward way as an evil.

I had expected to make a similar argument about Lincoln's embrace of the "slave power conspiracy theory," advanced in the "House Divided" speech, which depicted Douglas, with breathtaking implausibility, as part of a national conspiracy to force slavery back into the free states. I intended to hold that this argument was also a purely expedient one, intended to prevent Douglas from reaping among Republicans what little political benefit might have fallen to him from opposing the Lecompton Constitution, an act that had already destroyed his future in the Democratic Party. This account of Lincoln's motives had a plausible ring, but I have come to see it as mistaken. Another reading of the slave power conspiracy argument (advanced by Harry Jaffa, for instance) holds that the territories in fact did remain open to slavery despite the decisive defeat of slavery in Kansas, and so Douglas's position really did pose a threat to the future of the free states. This view of the argument is more favorable to Lincoln, but I have come to hold that it is not completely plausible either.

I wound up advancing a different view of Lincoln's motivations in maintaining the moral arguments of the Peoria speech after the free state victory in Kansas, holding that Lincoln argued that way because of his allegiance to certain fundamental values among whose consequences was his ultimate commitment to seeking citizenship for black people. To see how this argument works, consider how, in 1862, in choosing his main arguments for emancipation, Lincoln did not emphasize that emancipation would bring the war to the economy of the South, or that emancipation would strike at the root cause of the war, but argued instead that emancipation would clear the way for military service by former slaves.

Putting his argument this way had obvious advantages. First, it undeniably derived from the concrete military necessities Lincoln felt he could invoke in order to end slavery. Before the adoption of the Thirteenth Amendment, Lincoln and his federal government had no power to end slavery in the slave states except on grounds of military necessity. It may or may not have served a military interest to break the economic mainspring of the South, or to provoke a slave insurrection, but the likelihood is that quavering public opinion in the border states would have quailed before reaching for this kind of expedient, and doing so might have provoked secession in the border states. Indeed, fear that Missouri, Kentucky, Delaware, or, worst of all, Maryland would secede constrained Lincoln to making only the most cautious moves against slavery until after the battle of Antietam, which put the question of Maryland's secession to rest. But nobody could deny, by the summer of 1862, the urgent need for more soldiers, and in making the argument turn on military necessity Lincoln both evaded a possible challenge to his action from Chief Justice Taney and put the onus on opponents of emancipation to come up with an alternative source of soldiers if they foreclosed this one.

Second, Lincoln's method made emancipation irreversible. If one frees slaves to make economic war, one may enslave them again to rebuild the economy of a restored Union. But one can never re-enslave people into whose hands one has put rifles.

Finally, by putting former slaves in uniform, in asking them to value the res publica beyond all private interests, even beyond their own lives, Lincoln had put the Republic in a situation in which it would ultimately have to recognize their sacrifice on the Republic's behalf in the way the Republic recognizes the sacrifices others have made for it, which is to say, by ushering in a new birth of freedom. The introduction of near-universal military service in all the nations of the West during the last half of the nineteenth century has been linked by John Keegan to the broadening of the franchise; throughout this period the vote followed the uniform, as Lincoln well understood, and only extraordinary repression and violence at the end of Reconstruction kept it from doing so for former slaves in the United States. In choosing this apparently modest argument about enlistment over more morally and politically charismatic ones, Lincoln chose the one ground for emancipation most likely to make a case for black citizenship later. Perhaps he did not have a plan for black citizenship in mind; but even if his repeated and insistent denials about entertaining that ambition are more than mere rhetorical misdirection, he unerringly chose the course that would raise the pressure for citizenship, and articulated the meaning of the war in language that is comprehensible only if racial equality is understood to be among the aims of the war.

That Lincoln made commitments in the summer of 1862 that could be redeemed only by establishing black citizenship is not an entirely new claim; LaWanda Cox made a persuasive argument that Lincoln had such an intention twenty-five years ago, and Allen Guelzo and Richard Striner have made similar arguments more recently. For me, the committed step in the process was taken not in 1862 but in 1858. I have come to believe that Lincoln chose to reject the purely political case for free soil (that the people of the territories do not want slavery) in favor of the moral case (that slavery is wrong in principle) despite the fact that the purely political case had already won the day in Kansas and despite the fact that the moral case was under the immediate circumstances an inflammatory one, because that moral case was the argument most suited to making a case for the moral equality of black and white, and thus the argument most suited to making the case for black citizenship later. The purely political case does not have racial equality as an implication, since it is not in the nature of majority will to seek rights for "discrete and insular minorities" that the majority has a stake in stigmatizing. Lincoln repeatedly and plausibly denied having an investment in racial equality when Douglas accused him of it, and in the tangle of his complicated motives and necessities I would hesitate to say that he had a mature plan for racial equality, but racial equality was within the penumbra of his intentions, and he had chosen, even in the face of the recognition that what he chose had a political cost (a cost that included his defeat in the close election in 1858), a course of argument that would lend that idea of racial equality magnetic force.

The repellent conclusion I found myself drawing is a little less out of the mainstream of historical thought about the antebellum era. For a long time it has been off limits to speculate about the inevitability of civil war over slavery in the United States, since doing so invites too much in the way of tea-leaf reading and question-begging. But the fact remains that except for Haiti, no other new world society had to go to war to end slavery, and in some of those other slave societies slavery was at least as well established and as brutal as in the United States. I have gradually come to the conclusion, recently drawn also by William Freehling in the second volume of *The Road to Disunion* (2007), that what made the slavery problem insoluble by any means short of war was democracy itself. Nowhere else did the slaveholders have a full say in the future of slavery, and nowhere else were the slaveholders able, through political organization, to foreclose all of the measures that might have weakened their hold upon the political agenda. Nowhere else, also, did democracy itself present to slaveholders, both in the Union as a whole and within the individual slave states, such a threat to slavery that the slaveholders, by resorting to loyalty politics, conformity

politics, blackmail, and plain physical bullying, had to subvert democracy or lose their footing. Democracy both made it possible for slavery
to resist destruction (to the point of civil war) and made it inevitable
that a fight to the death over slavery would occur. I had not expected to
draw this conclusion, and I still regard it with misgivings. But it has
become one of the key arguments of my book.

Acknowledgments

My first acknowledgments are to the three foundations that supported me at different stages during the composition of this book. A fellowship from the John Simon Guggenheim Foundation in 1997, and another from the American Council of Learned Societies in 1998, supported much of my research and enabled me to write much of a first draft of this book. A resident fellowship at the Susan and Donald Newhouse Center for the Humanities at Wellesley College in 2006 enabled me to reshape this project from the beginning, and this book was largely written at Wellesley. I am grateful also for a grant from Brandeis University, and its then Dean, Adam Jaffe, which enabled me to work at Wellesley for an entire year.

Portions of Chapter 2 appeared as "Liberalism's Hope and Despair: Lincoln's Peoria Speech of 1854," *Social Research*, vol. 66 no. 2 (Summer 1999): 679–707 (www.socres.org). Part of Chapter 7 appeared as "Lincoln's *Dred Scott:* Contesting the Declaration of Independence," in *Lincoln and Cultural Value*, a special issue of *American Literary History*, vol. 21, no. 4 (2009): 730–751.

At the Brandeis English Department I shared pieces of this project, and batted around ideas, with Timo Gilmore, William Flesch, Eugene Goodheart, Laura Quinney, Caren Irr, and David Sherman; and from the History and Philosophy Departments I had thoughtful help from Mark Hulliung, Jane Kamensky, David Hackett Fisher, and Andreas

Teuber; Stephen Whitfield and Jerry Cohen from the American Studies Department were also constant interlocutors. I had illuminating commentary also from Hubert Zapf of the Lehrstuhl für Amerikanistik at the University of Augsburg. At Wellesley, Tim Peltason, who read and commented on all of what I wrote there, was an invaluable resource, and an insightful critic. Lara Friedenfels, a crosser of disciplinary boundaries herself, encouraged me to believe that the way my book veered between philosophy, history, and literary criticism was a strength, not a weakness. Jim Kloppenberg encouraged me to see the Lincoln-Douglas debates against the context of the history of liberalism, and gave me a great deal of patient and insightful advice. At Wellesley I also had the generous advice of Suzy Anger, Alexis Boylan, Carolyn Finney, Anjali Prabhu, Kalpana Seshadri, and Lakshmi Srinivas. My graduate school mentors John Hollander and Harold Bloom have often helped me clarify my thinking on this project over the years. Henry Bolter and Rich Young of Brookline Public Schools and the Seeking Justice program spent many an afternoon with me thinking the issues of this book through. Rev. Stephen Kendrick of the First Church in Boston, Unitarian-Universalist, the author of a fine study of Lincoln and Frederick Douglass (I'm writing about the "other" Douglas), spent a memorable Sunday morning with me having an open discussion about Lincoln with his congregation. I also had much help and advice from members of the Robert Penn Warren Circle, especially James A. Grimshaw, William Bedford Clark, Randy Hendricks, Randolph Runyon, and James A. Perkins. I had an extremely helpful correspondence with William Miller and with William W. Freehling, both of whom encouraged me to see some Lincoln texts in a controversial way. I am also grateful for very careful and thoughtful readings of some of my drafts by Anthony Hutchison, Daniel W. Hamilton, Robert A. Ferguson, and, most of all, Gordon Hutner. My research assistants Luigi Juarez, Erin Erhart, Jon Sudholt, and Kurt Cavender have combed through this text repeatedly looking for errors and repetitions. My three anonymous readers at Harvard University Press gave me truly invaluable criticism and kept me from making some very serious mistakes. And I am grateful also for the patience and support of my editors at Harvard University Press, Lindsay Waters and John Kulka, and my very careful copyeditors, Ellen Lohman and John Donohue. I had the benefit of careful reading and thoughtful comments by my brothers, Richard and Frank Burt. Finally, I am grateful to my daughter, Denisa, who has grown up with Lincoln as an invisible but demanding member of our family, and to my wife, Jo Anne Preston, who encouraged me at many points when I thought this project would never see completion and who has patiently and wisely helped me see it through. I can't thank you enough, darling.

CHAPTER I

Introduction: Implicitness and Moral Conflict

1.1 Negative Capability

The aim of this book is to discern in the 1858 Lincoln-Douglas debates part of the unwritten political philosophical tradition that has shaped American political practices. More specifically, the aim of this book is to see both Lincoln and Douglas, even as they campaigned against each other with votes in mind, as articulating views about how moral conflicts should go on in a liberal republic, and about how to behave when a moral conflict strains the persuasive engagements upon which liberal government depends. The problems each posed to the other were philosophical problems, not merely partisan ones, and the issues debated by Lincoln and Douglas continued to inform the speeches and policies of Lincoln's presidency, long after Douglas, having reconciled with Lincoln in the aftermath of Fort Sumter, wore himself to death raising troops for the Union army.

Although the debate centers on Lincoln and Douglas, other voices will matter too. Madison and Jefferson will be heard above all, Madison in the tenth *Federalist* describing a worldly method for engaging in and containing political conflict, a method that the moral conflict over slavery put under pressure, and Jefferson articulating the key issue of the conflict—the meaning of equality—while backing away from its implications. Clay and Jackson, the opposed giants, will also cast a long shadow over these debates, Clay as Lincoln's party leader and beau ideal, until Douglas made a successful argument that he was more the heir of Clay's compromising politics than Lincoln was, Jackson as the animating spirit of Douglas's party, and the chief exponent of its racism, until Lincoln, facing down secession, learned to stand in the place Jackson had stood facing down nullification. Other thinkers of Lincoln and Douglas's own generation lay out positions on the flanks of theirs— Charles Sumner and Frederick Douglass staking out more morally earnest ground about slavery than Lincoln dared to claim, John C. Calhoun, James Henry Hammond, and Alexander Stephens making clear just what the alternative position was to Douglas's. But the center of this book will always be the arguments Lincoln and Douglas had with each other.

With the possible exception of Rawls, the United States has not produced political philosophers to articulate the meaning of its example; it has no Marx, no Hobbes, no Plato. But it has a robust tradition of workaday political writing and oratory, from the *Federalist Papers* through the Second Reply to Hayne to the Pueblo speech, the "Four Freedoms" speech, and the "I Have a Dream" speech, in which an implicit political philosophy of some power is articulated in practice. The Lincoln-Douglas debates, along with earlier speeches of Lincoln, such as the Lyceum and Peoria speeches, and later speeches, such as the Gettysburg Address and the two Inaugural Addresses, are central contributions to that tradition, a tradition in which immediate political concerns shed philosophical light, not merely practical light, upon the ruling ideals that shape the politics of the United States. Indeed, the Lincoln-Douglas debates develop some of these key ideals in ways only situated practice can do, bringing out of the shadows of implicitness consequences of these ideals that do not lend themselves to development by the usual philosophical methods of construction from first principles and analysis of concepts.

One of the reasons that the key themes of the American political tradition cannot be fully developed philosophically by construction from first principles is that they have inexhaustible inwardness, by which I mean that they commit those who honor them to entailments they could not have anticipated when the commitments were made, entailments that sometimes were even explicitly denied by those who made the commitment.

The classic example of this is the set of promises with which Jefferson prefaced the Declaration of Independence, which Lincoln correctly saw entailed the end of slavery (even if many of the Founders themselves did not) and which, as succeeding generations have come to see (but as Lincoln, perhaps with strategic disingenuousness, did not profess to see) also committed the Republic to a multiracial vision of citizenship. The meaning of those promises continues to unfold, and their furthest implications have yet to be brought to light. Few of them could have been in the focal consciousness of the Founders. But to deny being bound by the entailments of such values is probably a more destructive misreading of the Founders' intentions than to acknowledge being bound by them, intentions being complex things. Jefferson, as Lincoln argued, both did and did not will the end of slavery. Lincoln both did and did not will racial equality. Both were in a position to deny embracing those intentions, and their denials may not have been entirely strategic. But both also, in the tangle of intuitions and doubts one finds in the penumbra where human willing happens, did indeed will both things, and willed them more deeply than they willed their own denials.

Implicit commitments like these, only darkly understood even by those who made them, have the kind of depth that makes it an open question whether they are something *chosen* or *given*, whether they are expressions of conscious agency or the unchosen and inevitable realizations of character and destiny. They are, in Lincoln's phrase, a *proposition* a republic is designed to test, but they are also, again in Lincoln's phrase, a *history* the Republic cannot escape. The ruling values of the constitutional order, what H. L. A. Hart would call their *concepts*, restlessly and endlessly become, because they are saturated with an implicitness that no particular development of them, no *conception*, suffices to exhaust. Only concrete political exigencies force these entailments out of the shadows of latency, where they prepare the way for yet further entailments, unanticipated until they become urgent but inevitable once they do. It is because concepts are implicit that they become, and it is also because they are implicit that it is only historical experience, not simple rationality, that articulates their becoming. Indeed, since we become aware of concepts only by the pressure they put upon fraught political particulars, we may not experience concepts (unlike conceptions) in propositional forms at all, but rather in the form of an urgent but inarticulate rebuke to the intuitions, much like the Socratic daimon.

Because concepts are implicit, they are susceptible of contradictory developments into conceptions, and so intractable conflicts among them are inevitable. Because concepts are implicit, and because we have no reason to assume that they must all sort with each other, we must expect experience lived in their light to be fraught with tragic conflicts among the concepts themselves. Because concepts are implicit, our conceptions have inevitably betrayed them, by failing to embrace the entailments we dimly sensed but could not bring ourselves to acknowledge, and by failing to imagine the further entailments we were not in a position to anticipate. All three of these kinds of conflict leave none of us in a position free of complicity in things of which we have reason to be ashamed. This mutual imbrication of half-submerged values and half-acknowledged complicities is most fully articulated in Lincoln's Second Inaugural Address. We are always, Lincoln implies, partly in the dark about our own values and aims (and even about our own motives), perhaps seeing them through a haze of self-love, perhaps fearing to face their implications, entangled as we are not only in mixed motives and self-deception but also in the primary contradictions of the concepts themselves, so that we are never in a position to act simply and with clean hands, but are always dirtied with unacknowledged wrongs that threaten to discredit us entirely.

Lincoln approached the problem of the authority of principles by vesting them in unspoken and unarticulable concepts that underlie democratic practices but are not exhausted by them, and that continue, from their implicit space, to generate entailments that could not have been envisioned by those who first gave themselves to those concepts. I will call this "the implicitness of concepts." Loyalty to the Founders is not expressed by repetition of their practices, but by allowing one's self to be rebuked by the promises they knew they could not keep but made anyway. I will call this "reverse Burkeanism." When one wishes to keep the promises the Founders committed their nation to, one always discovers that the exigencies of history unfold new demands out of those concepts, demands our generation has also almost inevitably failed. These demands are imperative and absolute, yet we are also required to practice the art of the possible in realizing them, always wagering that our compromises will not somehow compromise them. I will call this "tragic pragmatism." These three themes characterize Lincoln's response to the political crisis over slavery and race that issued in, but was not ended by, the Civil War.

Tragic pragmatism is characteristic of Lincoln's analysis of the political conflicts of his own era. It also casts some light onto the political conflicts of our own era. It is an open question whether it casts light upon the general predicament of liberal democracy as well. Lincoln never had to answer this question directly, because he argued that American democracy was the proving ground for liberal democracy everywhere, and that however much the American understanding depended upon the specific contingencies of American history and culture, it offered a lesson that would bear on the fate of other attempts at liberal democracy. Unlike Lincoln, who did not live in a world in which there were many other examples of liberal democracy, I have to leave open the question of whether what Niebuhr called "the irony of American History" is also the irony of liberal democracy itself, because it is in fact an open question, which I cannot but pose, but which nobody really can answer.

This book is not quite a work of history. But it is also not quite a work of political philosophy either. The idea of implicitness commits me to a form that is not political history, but requires knowledge about it, and is not political theory, but requires access to the world of abstractions that discipline provides. The idea of implicitness motivates the view that concrete political experiences are ways of proving political ideas on the pulse, of discovering the form of life they embody. Interpretation of implicit political values, this is to say, requires what Keats called "negative capability," the key interpretive skill of the literary critic, and the key creative skill of the artist who seeks to create imaginatively living characters and imaginatively coherent plots. It is not only the scholar who must use negative capability to come to terms with implicitness; the implicitness of concepts also requires negative capability from the political agents who interpret those values, from judges and officeholders, and, for that matter, from citizens as well.

To seek a grounded view of the meaning of political ideas is not precisely the same thing as to historicize those ideas, to use a current scholarly term of art. To historicize political ideas is to see them as interventions in the concrete struggles of their time and place. Clearly the desire to see ideas in a historicized way is a sound one. But historicization comes with temptations. To see ideas as interventions in concrete political struggles raises the temptation to see all argument as merely strategic, as merely a way one faction may gain some kind of advantage over another. It is to see those ideas not only as *conditioned* by the struggles in which they are deployed, but as *constituted* by them, as if the chief thing that matters about an idea is not what it means but which side it advanced.

To historicize an idea also raises the temptation to see that idea as only meaningful to its own time and place. Scholars have long made merry with the naive prejudice that moral ideas are universal unitary essences, available in the same way to all people everywhere throughout history. And that merriness tempts them to the view that moral ideas may have no meaning at all outside their specific circumstances, which is to say, may have no meaning at all for *us*. Key terms do change meaning over time, and a key value of the nineteenth century may well be, if not incomprehensible to the twenty-first century (since to historicize a value is precisely to provide the interpretive context under which it once had meaning), at least something that the twenty-first century is under no obligation to take seriously as a value. To make that kind of assumption does not close off the past to us—it is still available as an object of interpretation. But it does close off the past as a live source of meaning, because we can judge that kind of past, but it cannot judge us.

That kind of historicization seems to me to fail to take ideas with full seriousness as ideas, because to take an idea seriously as an idea is to remain open to its rebuke, to remain aware that we in the here and now are still somehow implicated in it. I do not want to assume, in Leo Strauss's caustic phrase about historicism, that we can learn a great deal *about* the past but nothing *from* it. That said, I also do not want to assume, as Strauss sometimes seems to, that it is possible for a disciplined reader to articulate the teaching of a political text all the way to the bottom, since so often a powerful idea is grasped only in an intuitive way, surrounded by a penumbra of implications that stretch off into shadow. The meaning of political idea is not exhausted by the here and now in which it was articulated. But we only know the meaning of political ideas once we have lived our way into them.

I also do not want to say that understanding the relationship between a political abstraction and a concrete political struggle is simply a matter of understanding how that abstraction is to be applied, as if actual history were merely instances of a general rule. This book will turn on disputes about the meaning of a number of ideals: first of all the ideal of equality, and the ideal of moral autonomy, which between them are the ideals of political freedom. This book will also turn on a number of fraught questions about what kind of issue is within the pale of reasonable dispute and what kind of issue is outside of it, when a dispute is within the horizon of dealmaking and persuasion, and when it can be settled only by violence, and what are the risks of being too quick, or too slow, to draw a line in the sand. These ideas are ineluctably normative ones, and they are normative for us no less than they were for the political class of the 1850s. How these ideals are to be cashed out in actions under the particular circumstances of the 1850s United States is not always an easy question, and what at first might seem to be subtle distinctions—should slavery be kept out of Kansas only because the people do not want to have it, or should it be kept out of Kansas because it is morally wrong?—lead one down very different historical paths, and lead in the direction of profoundly different moralities.

Now it is certainly true that no idea dictates how it applies in the here and now, and applying ideas requires a seasoned judgment that one obtains only by somehow growing one's way into a capacity for it. At the same time, ideas are also meant as a critique of that seasoned judgment, and one never uses judgment without the recognition that it will always be partly wrong, will always partly falsify the idea it attempts to embody, and therefore judgment needs the continuous reflective review of ideas. A seasoned judgment refines insights into the meaning of ideas, but ideas allow us to criticize "seasoned judgment" when it shades from what Kant calls the "*sensus communis*" into unexamined dogmatism. Judgment and ideas refine each other in what John Rawls calls a process of "reflective equilibrium," bringing out, under the pressure of concrete political conflicts, implicit entailments of ideas, consequences of promises we have already made but have not yet had to face.[1]

Aristotle used the term "phronesis" to convey his sense that no knowledge of principles, however disciplined, however rigorous, suffices to enable one to cash those principles out in actual living. Aristotle means by phronesis an intuitive know-how, guided by principles but not dictated by them, about how one lives out a life in the light of those principles. Phronesis involves a feel for particulars and a feel for nuance and qualification. It by nature resists being formalized. Phronesis is always a matter of *knowing how*, not a matter of *knowing that*, and for that reason it is a species of knowing into which one can be initiated or apprenticed but that one cannot describe in an explicit or rule-bound way. Like every variety of expert knowledge, phronesis is essentially imprecise, which is not to say that the rule of phronesis is the rule of anything goes. Phronesis is intuitive but principled in exactly the way that any act of judgment, such as connoisseurship, is intuitive but principled. Phronesis provides some of those humanizing prejudices that prevent one from being maddened by too dazzling an insight into the highest truth. But phronesis also demands the review of reflection upon practices, lest one be swamped in those practices and made a prisoner by their unexamined assumptions. Phronesis is an assay of political ideas, a way to prove them upon the pulse (again in Keats's phrase), a way to comprehend their meaning from the inside. Workaday political texts have the virtue that political philosophy from first principles sometimes lacks, which is recognizing the phronetic dimension of political ideas.

What we seek in workaday political texts of some depth, such as the Lincoln-Douglas debates or the *Federalist Papers*, is not merely a practical insight into how guiding values are applied, but philosophical insights into what those ideas mean when we attempt to live them out under circumstances where we always practically resist facing up to the meaning of those ideas, and where they continually unfold new layers of obligation that are binding upon us but that were obscure to us when we bound ourselves to them. Furthermore, one sees in workaday texts like the Lincoln-Douglas debates what key political themes amount to when they are illuminated by moments in which they come into tragic contradiction among themselves. Only by seeing the key values of political life under the pressure of the phronetic demands of actual political conflicts can one see the way in which political philosophy makes itself open to specifically tragic kinds of knowing. It is the nature of phronesis to disenchant intoxicating political ideas. But Lincoln's own development of phronesis, the tragic pragmatism one sees in the Second Inaugural Address, enables one to turn the disenchanted knowledge of political values seen at moments of irreconcilable conflict into wisdom.

Although I have tried to do justice to both philosophy and history, while perhaps doing not quite either, this book is not entirely idiosyncratic or without precedent. A similar attempt to write a situated philosophy, or a philosophically aware history, was carried out by Hannah Arendt in such books as *On Revolution* (1962), or for that matter in *The Origins of Totalitarianism* (1951). In different ways, David Donald's *Lincoln* (1995), Michael Lind's *What Lincoln Believed* (2004), and William Lee Miller's *Lincoln's Virtues* (2002) and *President Lincoln: The Duty of a Statesman* (2008) exemplify the balance between philosophical abstraction and historical particulars I have sought. I view my book as a contribution to literary criticism, in the vein of Harry Jaffa's *Crisis of the House Divided* (1959), or of John Channing Briggs's *Lincoln's Speeches Reconsidered* (2005), in that I hope to bring to my study a literary critic's respect for the nuances and suggestions of a particular text, and a literary critic's sense of the vexed relationship between the abstractions and the particulars.

I am of course deeply indebted to the historical scholarship of the Civil War era, most especially to the intellectual and political accounts of Lincoln and his era by Don Fehrenbacher, and by Douglas's biographer Robert Johannsen, and to recent book-length analyses of particular Lincoln speeches by Garry Wills, Ronald White, Harold Holzer, and Lewis Lehrman. The Lincoln-Douglas debates have recently been the subjects of keen and detailed political analysis by William C. Harris, and, most particularly, by Allen Guelzo, both of whose books have more of a political and historical focus than this book has. Closer in spirit to this book is David Zarefsky's keenly insightful *Lincoln, Douglas, and Slavery in the Crucible of Public Debate* (1990), which, informed by the rhetorical theories of Chaim Perelman and others, pays careful attention to the back and forth of the arguments, how Lincoln and Douglas employ their available persuasive resources against each other.

The ultimate model for this book, however, and its ultimate antagonist, is Harry Jaffa's great book *Crisis of the House Divided* (1959) and its sequel *A New Birth of Freedom* (2000). Like Jaffa, in this book I seek to engage in historically situated philosophy without assuming that philosophical truths are completely the prisoners of their own age. Like Jaffa, I seek to clarify the meaning of concrete political speeches by turning to great philosophers the historical agents cannot have deeply studied—Plato and Strauss in Jaffa's case, Kant and Rawls in mine. Like Jaffa, I see the central issue to be whether moral conflicts in a democratic polity must be faced as moral conflicts or whether they can be made more tractable by treating them as something else. Unlike Jaffa, I see the philosophical antecedents of both Lincoln and Douglas within the liberal tradition, and connect them with Kant, Madison, and Tocqueville rather than with Plato and Aristotle. Also, unlike Jaffa, I do not think Lincoln overpowers Douglas on every point or that Douglas represents a kind of hybrid of Thrasymachus and Neville Chamberlain.

The method of this book is more literary than historical, in that it confines itself to commentaries on the literary sources, the speeches and letters of the principals, and relies very little upon other kinds of historical evidence such as witness testimony, statistics, private papers, or newspaper reports. But if the method is literary-critical, it is, I hope, at least historically informed literary criticism.

1.2 Liberalism and Moral Conflict

The hope of liberal politics is that it can establish a tradition of fair dealing among people of different interests and views. At a minimum, when liberalism moves us to recognize that we usually have overlapping values, and overlapping stakes, even with those with whom we are at the moment in conflict, it makes it worth our while to deal with each other fairly.[2] But the hope of liberal politics is more than this: it is that the habit of insight into the situations of other people that dealmaking and compromise encourage in us will move us to treat the tradition of fair dealing as itself a common interest and as the basis of a common moral life, a moral life that values principled engagements across lines of difference. The ultimate hope of liberalism is that we will approach even our adversary dealings with each other not merely opportunistically, as occasions to talk our interlocutors out of more of what we want from them, but in a political spirit, as part of an investment in a structure of fairness that is an object of interest in its own right rather than merely a means of satisfying other interests. Interest may be a motivation for politics, but a polis life, which involves the moral investments of different people in each other, is its purpose.

The term "overlapping values" needs to be defined more precisely. To a first approximation, it means a common agreement upon morally acceptable ground rules, and also upon those public values that are necessary for a public square to be maintained among us. But the requirement of an overlapping consensus about public values does not mean that all parties must accept those values for the same reasons; evangelical Christians and secular Socialists may have different reasons for valuing freedom of speech or equal citizenship, but that difference does not matter as long as they both value them as strongly.

There is a further question about whether an overlapping consensus must specify all the same values for all parties, that all parties must recognize all the same public values in order to engage in public reason with each other. Might it be possible that common values are a tangled fabric of connection that holds itself together but does not radiate from a common center? Must an overlapping consensus cover a space held in common by all of the circles of the Venn diagram, or is it enough that all of the circles overlap many of the others? The first view, I think, was Lincoln's view, and Rawls's view as well. The second view was Douglas's view. And the argument between Lincoln and Douglas, particularly after the Illinois campaign, during their rematch in Ohio in 1859, was whether Douglas's version of an overlapping consensus could be sustained. Of course, Douglas was not wrestling with a philosophical problem in 1859 so much as scrambling to find some arrangement, any arrangement, that would keep the Union together in the face of conflicts over almost every imaginable issue. Douglas was trying to hold a Union together in which only an increasingly strained habit of dealing with each other survived, most of the key common values, the better angels of our nature, having been already frayed to shreds by the conflict. Even so, Douglas's question was not only a practical one.

It is common to think of large-scale cultural difference as the despair of liberalism, and to assume that liberalism is a kind of folkway that is available only in the West or in its cultural colonies. But cultural difference has been not the problem, but the enabling precondition of liberalism since the end of the Wars of Religion (and indeed, wherever people seek a modus vivendi among different traditions, they invent something like liberalism). It is probably therefore a mistake to think of cultural difference as itself generally setting the limits to the availability of liberalism. Even the view that certain strongly held habits of life and belief (such as Islamic or Christian belief) render a liberal political order impossible is probably also a mistake, at least so far as purely political (as opposed to cultural) liberalism is concerned.[3]

The suitability or unsuitability of liberal political regimes for particular places is not in any way an obvious function of the strength or
weakness of certain traditions of belief, but a function of unhappy local histories of conflict among particular groups. Indeed, many of the
bitterest ethnic or religious conflicts of the modern era have occurred
between peoples who in fact have a great deal in common with each
other, people who suffer what Freud called the narcissism of small differences. But even these kinds of conflicts are not inevitably beyond
the reach of liberal methods. The limit of liberalism is not cultural
conflict among different kinds of people, or conflict between liberal
and nonliberal regimes, but certain kinds of moral conflict within liberal regimes that put key liberal values at odds with each other.

When conflicts merely concern interests, liberal politics has a long
and largely successful record of mediating them. One might at first
believe that it would have similar success with moral conflicts, especially if one is in the habit of treating moral conflicts merely as interest
conflicts in disguise, a habit that in many circles has the unearned prestige of superior realism. But conflicts over values, because they involve
issues of identity and often bear about them the electric tang of moral
panic, do not lend themselves to dealmaking politics in the same
straightforward way that interest conflicts do. This is not to say, however, that liberalism inevitably fails in cases of moral conflict. Nor is it
even to say that the depth of the conflict is a measure of whether liberal
methods will fail or succeed, as if liberal methods can succeed only in
cases where nobody really cares about the outcome. The failure or success of liberal methods to mediate moral conflicts is not in any obvious
way a function of the importance of the moral stake; where liberalism
fails it fails not because of the importance of the issue it seeks to address, but because the detailed local history of the political conflict over
it exposes some of the inner strains within liberal traditions.

My aim here is to examine the means that American political culture, a political culture committed to an ethos of compromise and
dealmaking, brings to bear upon deep moral conflicts that can be neither evaded nor compromised away. In treating the political crisis over
slavery and race during the 1850s as a moral conflict, I do not deny that
it was also a political conflict of a traditional sort, concerned with power
and control over resources, nor do I deny that the moral conflicts were
always entangled with the political and economic conflicts that are the

traditional matter of politics. I do not deny that the moral claims brought by each side were in many ways flawed by self-serving and illusion and wishful thinking, not to mention racism and greed. But I do say, and it is not controversial to say, that the special edge of the conflicts of the 1850s had to do with both sides' awareness of the moral stakes between them, and how their political culture could mediate or resolve or evade deep moral conflicts was an issue explicitly fought out by the major political figures of that era.

It is not, or not only, because of the blunders of the politicians of that era that they were to unable to resolve the conflict over slavery, nor is their failure an inevitable consequence of the magnitude of the evil of slavery or of the scale of the interests involved in its behalf. The failure of the politics of the 1850s had to do with insoluble ironies in the central concepts of liberal politics, insoluble ironies that might lead some to despair of liberal politics generally but that led Lincoln to discover liberalism's tragic dimension.

Liberal politics is preeminently politics by discussion, as Isaiah Berlin called it. The authority of the arrangements liberal politics seeks to invent is chiefly a function of the consent those arrangements are able to win from people with conflicting interests and views. The authority of consent is different from the authority of principle: I am bound to the dictates of an arrangement of consent because I have agreed to it, not because it is right, and right matters in a culture of consent only insofar as one has been able to persuade all parties to be bound by it.[4] Right does matter in a culture of consent—cultures of consent are not amoral joint-stock companies for trading in pepper and slaves—but right only matters in behind-the-scenes ways, as a source of the telling arguments to common values to which mutually morally engaged opponents make persuasive resort. In a culture of consent, morality matters as a means of persuasion, but where it extends beyond persuasion, it is an instrument of tyranny, although perhaps of high-minded tyranny.

These arrangements of consent are available only to those who are willing to yield something to get something, to trade one issue for another, to accept half a loaf in the hope of getting the rest another day. Such arrangements are of course possible only if one has enough detachment from one's agenda that one can mortgage a part for the whole, the present for the future. They are not possible if one is so urgently invested in one's own position that one cannot make prudent compromises about it. One can engage in dealmaking only if one believes that in no particular case is one's entire position at risk, that on particular issues there is always room to bend, that there is no particular stake one should be unwilling to trade away if it came down to it, except if there are enough other particular stakes to be traded away on other issues to make it still worth my opponent's while to cut a deal with me. That is to say, I can afford to make nonnegotiable demands only if I have other, negotiable, issues about which to engage in logrolling.

The politics of consent functions best in the political culture Madison described in the tenth *Federalist*, a culture in which people with heterogeneous interests that conflict with each other along many different lines are motivated to deal fairly with each other because those who are their opponents on one issue may be their allies on the next. I must treat political minorities fairly because I can anticipate circumstances under which I will be in one. I must treat opponents in general with fairness because I may need their friendship later over other issues, or even over this one, should circumstances change in such a way as to move them in my direction.

The politics of consent functions much less well under conditions of polarized ideological conflict, in which every issue inscribes deeper lines of division in the same place and in which side issues, which under less fraught conditions provide means of mediating and moderating some larger quarrel, become instead mere theaters of proxy war over the main issue. A political culture of detached and worldly negotiation is also possible only if one has enough respect for one's opponents to imagine that they too may press claims against one, and that one should refrain as much as possible from the temptation to drive them to the wall, to demand from them, in Carl Becker's famous words of fifty years ago, a fatal sacrifice of vital interests.

Liberal democratic cultures value dealmaking and compromise because they see legitimacy as a product of the interaction of consent and principle. The rule of consent alone is mob rule, and the rule of principle alone is a kind of absolutist tyranny; for principle to weigh in politics, it must win consent from people of conflicting views. One consequence of this requirement is that what is politically legitimate and what is ethically required may not necessarily be the same thing, because what the conscience demands and what it has been able to persuade others to accept may not be the same thing.

Conscience may command me, but it must persuade you, because I cannot will for you unless I subject you. And if I attempt to subject you, then I have left the world of politics and entered the world of violence, where victory goes to the strong, not to the good. Even if I enter the world of violence in the defense of the idea that justice is not merely another name for the will of the stronger, once I enter the world of violence, I have entered a world governed in fact by the will of the stronger; indeed, by risking violence in the name of an ideal, I enter the very world in which that ideal is least likely to survive. Under the pressure of the moral and political crisis over slavery, tensions between consent and principle strained even the relatively weak forms of consensus politics required to maintain liberalism. Both Lincoln and Douglas sought, in different ways, to work out the relationship between principle and consent in liberal politics, and neither was fully successful in enabling liberal politics to mediate the conflict over slavery. The quarrel between them casts light upon the relationship between morality and politics that bear on a large number of present-day issues.

Liberalism has always been defined in ways that underestimate its moral and religious commitments. When it has not been seen as merely a rationalization for private acquisitiveness in a market economy, as what C. B. Macpherson (1962) calls "possessive individualism," liberalism has been described, most memorably by Michael Sandel (1982), as a retreat from the ambition to discover a moral foundation for a common life, as an agreement to settle for fairness and mutual tolerance made by those who have neither the power nor the stomach to impose their vision of the good upon their society.

Against this view, I argue that liberalism is an expression of the conviction that citizens have a crucial moral investment in each other's ethical freedom, and of the conviction that a habit of moral deliberation with people of other views is necessary to preserve one from the futility and self-destruction that always follow from an uncritical adherence to one's own governing values.[5]

Much criticism of liberalism turns, I think, on a limited idea of its genealogy. Liberalism has often been seen as taking its origin from (and taking its limitations from) the capitalist ethos, so that the rights-bearing citizen is simply the translation into political terms of the *homo economicus*, an atomic individual concerned with appropriating as much property to his private possession as he can manage, and essentially divorced from public concerns of any kind. This version of liberalism is a cartoon parody. And, as a cartoon, it dims out other parts of the painting. For one thing, it is not even a particularly plausible account of the political behavior of actual people in a liberal society. More plausible, to my mind, is Bruce Ackerman's concept of the "private citizen," who is, unlike the "pure privatist," not merely a rational maximizer of his interests, but someone with an intermittent and hazy attention to the public world, but who at some moments of emergency comes to clarity about the meaning and requirements of his own agency.[6]

Liberal individualism arises from the concern with inwardness as the source of agency in the theology of the radical Reformation, which itself has connections with but is not identical to the spirit of capitalism. It also depends upon a concept of moral autonomy that has religious aspects but worked itself out chiefly in the political conflicts of the Wars of Religion, and issued in the theory of toleration that emerged out of those wars. The theory of toleration was a theory about the meaning of moral autonomy: compulsion on religious matters should be renounced because religious professions made under threat of death are by nature inauthentic, and to demand such professions corrodes the values the demand is meant to enforce.[7] Liberalism's roots go not only into capitalism but also into the radical Reformation, and into the Enlightenment regime of toleration that came into being as a response to the Wars of Religion that the Reformation provoked.[8]

Critics of liberalism, most importantly Michael Sandel and Alasdair MacIntyre, see in liberalism a backing-away from moral issues, perhaps even a desire for neutrality about those issues. This of course is Jaffa's, and behind that, Strauss's critique of liberalism too. In the 1990s this sense that there was something morally squishy about liberalism expressed itself in the effort to define an alternative republican philosophy grounded in the Italian Renaissance's understanding of the classical politics of public virtue, which was to be contrasted with the modern politics of fairness and duty.[9]

In Lincoln studies the theme of "liberalism and republicanism" has played out in Sandel's argument that the liberal attempt to "bracket" values or to recuse liberalism from quarrels over values, which Sandel attributes to Rawls's *A Theory of Justice* (1971), is reflected in Douglas's position in the Lincoln-Douglas debates, and Lincoln's position, in turn, reflects the values of Sandel's own republican communalism. Rawls's reply, in *Political Liberalism* (1993), was that Douglas's position cannot be considered a liberal one, since parties who stand behind a veil of ignorance that prevents them from knowing what position in the society they are projecting they would themselves occupy (which is what Sandel had in mind when he argued that Rawls required liberals to bracket their values) could not conceivably choose to design for themselves a slave society, since they might themselves wind up being slaves in that society. I view Rawls's reply to Sandel as conclusive, but I also think that neither of them, in their hurry to cast themselves as Lincoln and their opponent as Douglas, really quite understood what Douglas's position actually was. For my own view on this, see section 6.3 below.

Liberalism is a consequence of the recognition that values become values, rather than moral obsessions, only when they are worked out in a network of principled engagements. For all of the rough-and-tumble politics of the 1858 campaign, the Lincoln-Douglas debates are not only an example of the kind of persuasive engagement that distinguishes values from moral obsessions but also an examination (on Douglas's side) of the circumstances under which values begin to behave like moral obsessions and an examination (on Lincoln's side) of the circumstances under which attempts to restrain the futility and self-destructiveness to which values are subject compromise their status as values at all. In other words, Lincoln and Douglas are both concerned, if in opposite ways, with the ways in which liberal regimes, under strains that separate their guiding values from each other, begin to transform themselves into nonliberal regimes.

When Charles Sumner announced that he was not in politics but in morals, he understood himself to be saying that the tendencies of those two professions pulled in opposite directions. The rule of God matters more than the rule of the majority, and to enter into political compromises with those with whom one is in deep and intractable moral conflict is inevitably to compromise one's own moral standing. Certainly this view has undeniable attractions. Many things are beyond the reach, or ought to be beyond the reach, of political bargaining among reasonable and decent people, and certainly slavery would be high on anybody's list of such things. Dealmaking and compromise are only for those things that are within the moral pale, and to treat certain outrageous things as if they were within that pale, one wants to say, is already to have fatally surrendered one's own moral position. When politics asks us to deal with institutions that are beyond the moral pale, it asks us, it appears, to place politics above morality, and nobody wants to do such a thing.

The ironies to which this position is subject are obvious enough to be sketched in a few sentences. When one draws a moral line in the sand, one does so in the faith that public life should be something other than merely a contest for power. One does this as a way to reject the Thrasymachean claim that right is an illusion, that what we call justice is in fact nothing more than the will of the stronger. Yet once one has drawn a line in the sand, one has no choice but to engage in a contest of force with those who are on the other side of that line. A stance of moral stringency is morally exhilarating and rhetorically attractive. But the stringent idealist projects himself or herself into a world in which the issue will be decided by force, and contests of force are tests not of which side is right but of which side is strong. A stringently ethical politics seems inevitably to become a kind of crusader politics, a politics that kills what it loves through the very excess of that love.

Politics can serve an ethical aim, it seems, only if it treats those ethical aims with detachment, but that detachment seems to deny those ethical claims the urgency they deserve. That detachment is the source of the other side of the double-bind of 1850s politics. If one wishes to engage in a politics that does not destroy what it loves, one must treat moral imperatives as somehow not really imperative at all, as something about which people and political institutions have perfect freedom of choice. A moral order has no authority except under conditions of choice, and I compel others to adopt my views only by imperiling the authority of those views. At the same time, either moral imperatives have compelling force or they are not moral imperatives. In moments of intense moral conflict the two key features of moral autonomy, the fact that ethics gives binding law and the fact that ethical acts must be free, face each other in stark contradiction.

Under the normal conditions of moral argument, I may make persuasive recourse to claims about transcendent things if by doing so I can make an appeal to my opponent's own key values. If I am able to do this I am able to win my opponent's unforced consent and thus to do justice to both aspects of moral autonomy. Even if I do not in fact bring my opponent over to my views, I am capable of remaining morally engaged with him by arguing on the basis of an overlapping consensus of values. Under these circumstances the idea of transcendence serves two related purposes. When directed against the opponent, the idea of transcendence is an appeal to the opponent's best self, a way to resolve a conflict by making a commanding appeal to a shared value. We need not know whether or not that value is an absolute value, so long as it roots itself in a deeper level of abstraction than our immediate quarrel, and so long as we share it and recognize its power. When directed against one's self, the idea of transcendence mostly serves to remind us that we may indeed not already have the last word about the things that matter most to us, that, in some way we are unable to anticipate, our opponent may yet be able to fairly rebuke us in the name of our own values. Here again, we need not specify exactly what such a transcendent value is; we need only be aware that so long as we remain persuasively engaged with the other side, the other side may yet cast a light on something deep and common to each of us. This vision of transcendence does not amount to dogmatic clinging to a prejudice, but to a kind of healthy skepticism: however deeply I may think I have gone, it remains possible that somebody else may have gone more deeply, and for that reason I should hesitate to assume that the story of my moral conflict with you is one whose conclusion I already know. Under conditions of intense moral conflict, however, I am no longer able to appeal to shared key values, and my use of ideas about transcendence in that case might well reduce to the justifications I provide myself before resorting to force.

One might think it possible to restore persuasive engagement among such enemies by refraining from resort to moral absolutes when they can only be used in this inflammatory way. But if I really must make this concession thoroughly, I must treat all my values as if they were only private obsessions, and I must treat all public issues as if they were only conflicts over interests (with values being perhaps only a slightly irrational kind of interest). And if I treat public issues as only conflicts over interests, then the shape of the res publica is a function only of the outcome of contests of force, and I have no reason to accord those outcomes moral respect. If, as the price of engagement with people of different views, I soften my commitment to my key values, then I have nothing with which to defend my position if my opponent wishes to raise the price of my engagement with him. Indeed, once I soften my commitments I have also softened my resistance to giving

way to him, because my opponent knows there is nothing I will not
trade away if I have to.

The reader may recognize these positions as versions of those taken
by Lincoln and Douglas, respectively, against each other. Both men, in
the summer of 1858, sought ways to prevent the extension of slavery
into the western territories, and both sought to do so without provoking the South into secession. Each made against the other arguments
of the kind I have just sketched in, and each was aware that the other's
arguments were telling. Neither fully succumbed to the temptations
inherent in their positions. Lincoln never adopted a destructive crusader politics, and Douglas neither adopted expediency politics nor
ultimately allowed himself to be driven to the wall by his slaveholding
opponents.[10] Neither was able to hold off war either, but of course what
the outcome would be was not entirely up to them, since neither anticipated just how intransigent the fire-eaters were becoming, and neither
anticipated how adroitly the fire-eaters would outmaneuver their moderate opposition in the South, something that it seems likely would
have happened even had Lincoln and Douglas not both, in their different ways, played into the fire-eaters' hands.

Douglas is not the villain of this book, although I hope I see his flaws,
especially his virulent and passionate racism, with sufficient clarity.
Douglas's most telling argument in the summer of 1858 was a practical
one: since economic and geographical factors have already decided
that the western territories will ultimately all enter the Union as free
states anyway, it is needless, as well as risky, to inflame the resentment
of the slave states by explicitly prohibiting slavery in the territories.
Douglas (somewhat unfairly) saw Lincoln in the "House Divided"
speech as all but calling for war, a war that Lincoln could not have been
certain he would win, and that, whoever won, would possibly transform
American political culture in the unanticipated and ugly ways mass
violence always risks. Douglas's deepest vulnerability, which Lincoln
exploited, was that in rejecting a moral politics that struck him as inflammatory, he retreated to a kind of interest politics which, while not
obviously amoral, nevertheless stood on a slippery slope down to naked expediency. If moral imperatives are to be treated with the same
provisionalness that interests are, then, as Harry Jaffa argued years ago,
what won't one bargain away if one has to? Those who, like Douglas,
are constrained by the necessity of maintaining a culture of deal-

making and compromise can often be driven to the wall by those who are not.

The ethical politics that Lincoln advances as an alternative seems at first more attractive. But it too stood on a slippery slope, one that leads down to crusader politics, that imagines its opponents as less than human, and that is for that reason capable of almost anything and often winds up destroying what it aims to serve. Further, crusader politics cannot free itself from a humiliating delusion in which it cannot distinguish its own wishes and interests from divine commands. Crusader politics is not finally any more characteristic of Lincoln than expediency politics was of Douglas, but neither could convincingly resist the charge the other made. Both, indeed, worked hard to assume the other's grounds, but each, tragically, prevented the other from making a persuasive appeal to those grounds, and neither party could break out of the impasses in which both ethical politics and interest politics found themselves. Only in the Second Inaugural did Lincoln arrive at a convincing vision of the relationship between ethical and political obligation, arguing that political acts are matters of intense ethical moment but that whenever we believe that our purposes are aligned with God's we have deluded ourselves and turned our values to the service of folly and worse.

The interest of the political crisis of the 1850s is that both of the obvious alternatives, to keep dealing despite everything or to spring at each other's throats and have at it, seem obviously fatal. The particular interest of Lincoln and Douglas is that both of them seem to realize that the available positions are all impossible. Neither takes a position of apocalyptic moral stringency, and neither takes a position of craven expediency, although each accuses the other of doing one of these things. The differences between their positions is subtle but telling—more subtle, I argue, than most critics have seen, but telling enough that each of them finds themselves on the opposite slippery slope.

To see the way the political crisis of the 1850s pulled apart some of the key values upon which liberalism depends will require examining a number of concrete political conflicts in considerable detail. From Lincoln's point of view, what transformed the conflict over slavery from a sectional conflict about what to do about slavery while one waits for its extinction into a world-historical conflict over the soul of democracy was Douglas's Kansas-Nebraska Act of 1854. Therefore, this book

will open with a very detailed account of that act, and of the development of the policy Douglas will call "Popular Sovereignty in the Territories" in the quarrels over slavery in the seven years before 1854. I
hope to show that Douglas's position was not as obviously pro-Southern
as it has been received to be; it was an ambiguous position (fatally so),
and he intended it to be ambiguous.

As the conflict in Kansas that Douglas unintentionally set off inten-
sified, Lincoln came to the view that Douglas's policy was intended not
only to force slavery into all of the western territories but also to force
slavery back into the free states. The first of these views is arguable,
but false; the second is nonsense. The question to be asked about Lincoln's conspiracy theories is not whether they had a grain of truth but
what light they cast upon Lincoln's other convictions and, given that
even Lincoln seems to have believed such things, what light they cast
upon the state of the conflict.

Douglas also put forward an implausible conspiracy theory, arguing
that Lincoln sought to whip up sectional hostility in order to ride to the
leadership of a sectional party strong enough to rule the entire Union
without any support in the opposing section. Douglas's theory was also
not only false but ludicrous. But it raised an important question about
the nature of political parties: should the parties have ideological unity,
and therefore be able to claim to be organizations vitalized by principle, or should they each be a congeries of conflicting interests, so that,
at the price of inconsistency, they can win power only by working out a
factional compromise that would constrain the political process toward
the middle ground? Douglas's view of what parties should be had implications for his views about what political conflict should be, since the
alternative to a politics of disorderly and overlapping factions seemed to
him to be a politics of conflicting fanaticisms.

Both Lincoln's and Douglas's positions were threatened by Chief
Justice Taney's opinion in the 1857 *Dred Scott* case, although Douglas
tried, with some disingenuousness, to interpret his way out of the corner Taney had put him in. My argument is that Lincoln's and Douglas's responses to Taney's decision resemble each other more closely
than most interpreters have seen, in that each sought ways to preserve
a space for politics and dealmaking in the face of the Court's attempt
to close off that space in the name of what it took to be constitutional
principle. Both Lincoln's and Douglas's strategies continue to have

some relevance even in cases where the Court's claim to constitutional principle is less strained than it was in the *Dred Scott* case.

The arguments they had used against each other shaped, but also constrained, the arguments available to them on the larger political stage in 1859 and 1860. Douglas, for instance, wound up using against Buchanan and his proxies many of the arguments Lincoln had used against Douglas himself. By 1860, betrayed by the southern faction of his party, and shocked by the slide toward secession, Douglas saw his views and Lincoln's views begin to converge. In the Cooper Union and First Inaugural speeches, while he sharpened his policy differences with Douglas, and avoided making fatal concessions on the issue of slavery in the territories, Lincoln also sought a kind of persuasive engagement with the South that was in some tension with the more confrontational stance he had taken in the summer of 1858. He also sought a way to engage in moral confrontation without breaking persuasive engagement, finding only in his Second Inaugural Address a satisfactory response to Douglas's charge that brandishing a moral principle is equivalent to brandishing a stick.

There is an asymmetry in this book that needs explaining. It takes a topic in the intellectual history of liberalism in the antebellum era. But it concerns only the perspective of two northern Unionists—in fact, two Unionists from Springfield, Illinois. Even among northerners, its perspective is limited—many key figures, such as Kent, Story, Parker, Bushnell, Spooner, Garrison, or Douglass, are either excluded or included only glancingly. But the absence of a southern point of view would seem to be more crucial.

Certainly the political operating assumptions of most ordinary southerners were liberal in the same way that the operating assumptions of ordinary northerners were. They venerated the same Revolutionary heroes, spoke in the same clichés on the Fourth of July, quoted and interpreted the same founding documents, and professed allegiance to the same parties, parties that were, until the crisis of the 1850s, both national in scope despite having regional bases of power. South Carolina was always a bit of an exception, imagining itself the only pure heir of the republican tradition, and resisting for the most part the democratization of the franchise in the Jacksonian era. In the South as in the North the democratization of the franchise coincided with a crescendo of popular racism, and in both sections the rise of *herrenvolk* democracy, the belief that a strident insistence upon racial difference could restrain or at least conceal class conflicts in the white community, was the central political consequence of the rise of American democracy under Jackson and his heirs.[11] Indeed, it was a common investment in *herrenvolk* democracy that bound together the very disparate factions that made up the antebellum Democratic Party, the white, largely Catholic working class of the North, the hardscrabble, nonslaveholding yeomen of the upland South, and the slaveholders of the lowland South.

But for the intellectual leaders of the South, for Calhoun, or Fitzhugh, or Hammond, it was a different story. Was the thought of these men part of a liberal political tradition? I think the jury is still out on this question. David Ericson has made a case that however deviant the thought of the southern theorists was, it was still within the liberal orbit. Eugene Genovese has long made an impressive case that southern intellectual traditions articulated an alternative to liberalism, and to modernism.[12] For me, it is William Freehling's treatment in the two volumes of his *The Road to Disunion* that most captures the strangeness of these texts, how, for instance, they insist that *herrenvolk* democracy makes all white people equal, while insisting that all societies are founded upon subjection of their laboring class, which presumably includes nonslaveholding whites. The principal constraint of all these texts, that no matter what else they did they had to make racialized slavery foundational to their vision of society, could not but distort them. Indeed, looking closely at these texts confirms Freehling's insight that there was a fundamental incompatibility between slavery and democracy. The idea that there is something crank about these texts, how they are hostile to liberalism but do not really propose alternatives to liberalism in the way that the nineteenth century Right did in Europe, was articulated long ago by Louis Hartz, who noted among other things the tension between these texts' nominal respect for Burkean tradition and nominal distaste for abstract novelties on the one hand, and on the other hand the fantastic, Rube Goldberg quality of the structures of government they tended to elaborate. This book gives extended readings of texts by Calhoun, Hammond, and Stephens, but it never treats them as elaborating theories that have anything to do with liberalism; these theories are always seen as threats to liberalism.

Lincoln offers an example of moral depth and subtlety that is hard to find elsewhere in American politics or for that matter in American literature. He embodies those values that Reinhold Niebuhr long ago lamented the lack of in American culture, the ability to balance a prophetic sense of ethical mission with a tragic sense of the ironies of politics and history. Lincoln's final position, in the Second Inaugural, evinces an ethical generosity toward his enemies that arises from a mature sense of the moral complicity experienced by all fallen and finite beings. Lincoln provides a model for moral agency in a complex world in which one must make one's way among various half-understood alternatives, none of which leave one's hands very clean. This tragic sensibility differentiates Lincoln from figures like Emerson, Thoreau, and Parker, who had a clearer vision of the moral stakes involved than Lincoln himself did but who also sometimes showed that moral narcissism, that inability to conceive the humanity of one's opponents, that comes from being on the right side. It differentiates Lincoln as well from figures like Hawthorne and (less clearly) Melville, whose ironic moral consciousness lent itself to passivity, to special pleading, and to evasive bad faith. Next to both Emerson and Hawthorne, Lincoln's virtues shine out, especially his mysterious ability to retain the power of acting, sometimes in a ruthless and violent way, while never losing sight both of the moral compromises of his own position and of the moral humanity of his enemies. Lincoln had that hardest to understand of gifts, the ability to fight a great war without self-delusion, without self-congratulation, without truculent self-righteousness, and, most of all, without destroying through uncritical love the values in whose name he waged the war.

To maintain this position, Lincoln had to hold both love and rage at arm's length. Lincoln had to resist the attractions of rage, its promise of cutting the Gordian knot of complexity and complicity, and its promise of cathartic regeneration through violence. Lincoln had also to resist the attractions of love. Love's virtues, the recognition of ultimate human kinship and the ability to see the world through the eyes of (and comprehend the moral claims of) one's enemies, are closely tied to love's vices, its temptation to moral relativism and to adopting a policy of surrender in cases of intractable moral conflict. It is the ability to negotiate these contradictions that is celebrated in the Second Inaugural, at once the greatest elegy and the most profound political speech in the American tradition.

The study of the political crisis of the 1850s may not yield policy for contemporary problems. But it can yield whatever is at the end of the downward path that runs from suffering to wisdom, that path first glimpsed by Aeschylus, who, like many who surveyed politics then and now, saw enough of the ways in which intractable wrongs breed endless chains of consequences to wonder what the end of things would be.

CHAPTER 2

Lincoln's Peoria Speech of 1854

2.1 The Debate over the Kansas-Nebraska Act

The speech Lincoln gave against the Kansas-Nebraska Act in Peoria on October 16, 1854, was a reprise of a speech he had given in Springfield on October 4. The measure had been proposed by Douglas on January 4 and not passed by Congress until May, so Lincoln's response was the product of long meditation. Lincoln's response was the response of an old Whig, not of the Republican he was to become over the next two years, and it was quite different from the response of the "Independent Democrats" Sumner, Chase, and Giddings, who had published their own heated, even inflammatory, attack upon the bill before Douglas had even given it its final form. Although Lincoln had been desultorily active in the Scott campaign in 1852 and had published an editorial critical of the Kansas-Nebraska Act in the summer of 1854, these speeches mark Lincoln's serious return to political life after the end of his term in Congress, and in them one hears for the first time the characteristic themes of Lincoln's mature political thought and the characteristic music of his rhetoric.[1]

The chief aim of the Kansas-Nebraska Act was to organize a territorial government for the unorganized regions (excepting Oklahoma) of the Louisiana Purchase, what is now most of the states of Kansas, Nebraska, Colorado, Wyoming, North and South Dakota, and

Montana. Douglas had been attempting to organize a government for this region since 1845. Early historians such as James Ford Rhodes at the turn of the century took for granted a sinister interpretation of Douglas's motives in the 1854 act, taking Sumner's view of it as an attempt to create new slave states in the western territories in order to advance Douglas's own presidential ambitions by currying favor in the South. A slightly later generation took Douglas's motives to be less sinister but venal, arguing that Douglas was seeking to make possible a transcontinental railroad that would have its eastern terminus in Illinois, preferably in some region where he himself owned property. (Douglas owned the land where the University of Chicago is now.)[2] My own view is that there is no reason not to take Douglas at his own word when he said that organizing governments, any governments he could persuade Congress to accept, was his aim. Most of the transmississippian west had territorial governments organized by him, and many of the states of that region were shepherded to statehood under his auspices.[3]

The territories were theaters of proxy war over slavery throughout the four decades before the Civil War, because the existence of slavery in the states themselves was not an open question, constitutionally speaking, before the Thirteenth Amendment, and those who opposed slavery but were unwilling to risk the Union by pressing for immediate abolition felt they could compromise the economic vitality of slavery by preventing it from expanding into the territories, while those who favored slavery usually favored expanding it into the territories.[4]

Before 1854, the status of slavery in the territory of the Louisiana Purchase, which included what would be the area of the Kansas-Nebraska Act, was settled by the first Missouri Compromise of 1820, which, among other things, prohibited slavery in the region north of the 36° 30' line, the southern border of Missouri. The problem of the future of the Mexican Cession, acquired by the United States from Mexico at the end of the Mexican War, enflamed this conflict anew, provoking a long struggle between those who (with President Polk) wished to extend the 36° 30' line across to the Pacific, those who (with almost all of the northern Whigs, and many of the northern Democrats) supported the Wilmot Proviso, which applied the anti-slavery language of Jefferson's 1787 Northwest Ordinance to the Mexican Cession,[5] and those who (with John C. Calhoun) denied that the federal government had power to abolish slavery even in the territories and demanded that the entire region be organized on a slaveholding basis.

Polk's plan is the easiest to explain, but also the easiest to dispose of. In choosing the 36° 30′ line, Polk had chosen a line of demarcation already known to American politics. That line, however, was intended to apply only to the land purchased from France at the time of the Louisiana Purchase, and was not intended in 1820 as a guideline to determine the fates of lands that were not then and might not ever be under American control. Furthermore, that line was chosen when most of the territory under U.S. control to which it might apply was north of it. The line was intended as a concession to free state interests, in order to make the admission of Missouri as a slave state more palatable. But a very large proportion of the land taken from Mexico by the treaty of Guadalupe Hidalgo was south of that line, so after the Mexican War that line would seem not to represent a concession to the free states so much as a landgrab by the slave states. Finally, if the line were understood as a boundary between slavery and freedom no matter how the United States might subsequently acquire territory, the existence of that line would represent a standing temptation to expansionist warfare aimed at bringing the rest of Mexico, and perhaps the rest of Central America (where American freebooters such as William Walker continued to attempt to build empires for themselves), into the Union as slave states.

Calhoun's theory, also advanced after Calhoun's death by Jefferson Davis, was that the territories were not the property of the American people collectively but the joint property of the several states, and that therefore, in administering the territories, the federal government must do nothing that would jeopardize the interests of the slaveholding states in those territories. To advance this theory, Calhoun had to empty the language in the Constitution giving the Congress "Power to dispose of and make all needful Rules and Regulations respecting the Territory or other Property belonging to the United States." Calhoun argued that this language did not apply to the territories, but only to unorganized land owned by the United States (such as harbor islands). In practice Calhoun's doctrine meant that all territories would have to be organized upon a slaveholding basis, although Calhoun continued, for fig-leaf purposes, to insist that the final status of those territories would be settled only at the time they submitted state constitutions to

Congress and petitioned for admission to the Union, long after slavery had taken deep root in the territory in question. Many northerners thought of the Calhoun-Davis view as a self-seeking invention of recent vintage, but in fact the view had strong currency in the South back to the time of the Missouri Compromise, and even James Madison, who supported the compromise and admired the Northwest Ordinance, was not certain that the Calhoun-Davis view did not have a constitutional case, although Madison opposed that case.[6]

Calhoun's embrace of this theory considerably antedated his famous exposition of it during the Wilmot Proviso crisis in February 1847. Calhoun had originally proposed his joint sovereignty theory in a series of resolutions he introduced in the Senate on December 27, 1837. The immediate context did not have to do with the status of slavery in the territories, but with the status of slavery in the District of Columbia. Now there is not really much doubt that the Founders intended Congress to have control over the status of slavery in the territories, as Lincoln was to demonstrate in the Cooper Union speech. But the case for congressional control over slavery in the District of Columbia was even stronger, since Congress was given the power "to exercise exclusive legislation in all cases whatsoever" concerning the District. The immediate issue was what to do with petitions from citizens regarding slavery in the District. Up to this time, these petitions had been dealt with in the traditional way Congress deals with issues it does not wish to face, by sentencing them to the limbo of a committee that will never act upon them. But Calhoun and his allies, principally James Henry Hammond of South Carolina and Henry Wise of Virginia, demanded more than this, since even receiving the petition and tabling it seemed to them to recognize that it was an issue upon which Congress might have acted had it chosen to do so. The mere admission that the future of slavery anywhere could even be discussed openly in the halls of Congress seemed to Hammond an invitation to servile insurrection. Calhoun and Hammond sought to silence public criticism of slavery in Congress entirely, treating even tabling anti-slavery petitions as a matter so serious as to justify the threat of immediate secession.[7]

To do this, supporters of the gag rule had to argue that the issue of slavery in the District of Columbia, and in the territories, raised grave constitutional issues, notably the issue of depriving citizens of property without due process of law. Calhoun understood "due process" here as what would later be called (particularly when protection of the rights of corporations to exploit their workers was concerned) "substantive due process," which is to say that such property cannot be taken away by the process of ordinary lawmaking or ordinary regulation, but only by criminal trial, since the presumption of the slaveholder's right to his or her human property trumps any public aim Congress might have in regulating that property.[8] Calhoun's claim was rather stronger even than this, in that the right to property was held not only by the individual slaveholder but also by the slave states, which had rights in the District of Columbia and in the territories that the federal government could not override. Calhoun's argument was designed to allow slaveholders to have it both ways: slavery, as a state institution, could not be interfered with by the federal government, but since the slave states were stakeholders in the federal government, the federal government was required to make the protection of slavery in the territories and in the District of Columbia a federal matter. Calhoun in 1837 had already put the Republic onto the rails that would lead it toward the train wreck that destroyed the Democratic Party in 1860, and the Union itself a year later.

The Wilmot Proviso position had complicated origins in the internal divisions of the Democratic Party, and in particular, like the northern position during the Missouri crisis, in the internal divisions of the Democratic Party of New York. The primary motive among the sponsors of the Wilmot Proviso in August 1846, as in the case of their counterparts during the Missouri crisis, was straightforward opposition to the expansion of slavery, but it was the strains within the Democratic Party that gave the proviso its particular cast and occasion. Intraparty tensions among Democratic factions had escalated during Polk's presidency on account of his supplanting of Martin Van Buren as leader of the party over the issue of annexation of Texas, which Van Buren had opposed, and the animus behind the Wilmot Proviso, although probably not the principle of nonextension of slavery that the proviso embodied, derived from the resentment of Van Buren's supporters against Polk's displacement of their leader nationally, and from their resentment against the favor Polk showed to Van Buren's rivals in the New York Democratic Party in his patronage appointments.

Van Buren had assumed that the 1844 election would pit him against Henry Clay. Each, aware of the danger the annexation of Texas would pose to the stability of the Republic, had published letters on the same day advising against the immediate annexation of Texas (although Clay hedged and fudged about it). The result was a party coup d'état against Van Buren at the 1844 Democratic National Convention, a coup organized mostly by Robert J. Walker of Mississippi, who later figured as the governor of Kansas Territory during the Lecompton struggle. Van Buren had the support of a simple majority of delegates, but Walker resurrected an old rule requiring a two-thirds majority for nomination, raising a road block for Van Buren, who faced determined minority opposition from the South. Polk, a relative unknown, defeated Van Buren for the Democratic nomination on the eighth ballot, winning the presidency on a platform of aggressive expansionism both south (Texas) and north (Oregon).

Once in office, Polk was aware of the danger of alienating the supporters of his party's traditional standard bearer. However, Polk's attempt to mollify the Van Buren or "Barnburner" faction by appointing Benjamin F. Butler to his cabinet failed, and Polk wound up appointing William Marcy, Van Buren's in-state "Hunker" rival, in Butler's place.[9] Polk gave Van Buren's supporters reason to believe that he had proscribed them, and that there would not be a place in the Democratic Party for anyone who had doubts about the annexation of Texas. Hostility to Polk's patronage strategy, this is to say, was not merely a reflection of disappointed factional ambitions, but also fear of domination of the party by politicians, some of them northern, who sought to advance the interests of the slave power.

Part of the intransigence of Democratic supporters of the Wilmot Proviso also had to do with their anger about the way the economic policies of the Democratic Party were increasingly being taken hostage by slaveholders and made to serve a slaveholding agenda. Polk's support of the low Walker tariff, authored by the engineer of Van Buren's defeat, persuaded the Wilmot Proviso supporters that the economic interests of northern Democrats (who, in Wilmot's Pennsylvania at least, like northern Whigs, favored protective tariffs) were to be sacrificed to southern interests. This is not to say that Wilmot Proviso Democrats were motivated by the tariff rather than by hostility to slavery, but rather that resentment over the tariff gave added sharpness to their feelings of betrayal—they had supported the Mexican War— over the slavery question.[10] Historians of the generation between the wars often argued that the sectional quarrels of the antebellum era were really only about the tariff and that the slavery issue was only a pretext. In fact, the reverse seems to be the case. The tariff was an issue because a low tariff strengthened the hands of slaveholders against their opponents. And, as Calhoun had argued at the time of the Nullification crisis, a federal government that had the power to impose a protective tariff also had the power to abolish slavery. The tariff, like so much else, was a theater of proxy war over slavery.[11]

Although the South took the Wilmot Proviso as an assault aimed at its key interest, the proviso's supporters thought of it as a defensive measure, protecting them against an unintended consequence (a flood of new slave states, whose values and interests alike would oppose their own) of a war they had favored. That is why the Wilmot Proviso was initiated by pro-war Democrats, not by anti-slavery Whigs, who had opposed the Mexican War from the beginning. Many of these Democrats would temporarily leave the party in 1848, following Van Buren into the short-lived Free Soil Party.

In 1850, at the time of the Compromise of 1850, and again in 1854, at the time of the Kansas-Nebraska Act, Douglas embraced a doctrine distinct from the Wilmot Proviso, from the Calhoun-Davis theory, and from the extension of the Missouri Compromise line. Douglas's proposals for Utah and New Mexico in 1850, the "Popular Sovereignty" (or, less sympathetically, "Squatter Sovereignty") position, had been articulated by Lewis Cass in the famous December 1847 letter to A. O. P. Nicholson that probably cost Cass the 1848 presidential election. The position was studiedly ambiguous. All sides agreed that the doctrine meant that the two territories could choose for themselves whether to enter the Union with or without slavery, inscribing their choice on the matter in the state constitutions they would send to Congress for approval at the time of admission to the Union. But there was ambiguity about whether the territories could choose to prohibit slavery before they sought admission as states. Douglas felt that his 1850 bill provided that the territorial governments, even before they proposed state constitutions and applied for admission to the Union, could prohibit or permit slavery as they wished, beginning as soon as they had population enough for them to organize a territorial legislature.[12] The language of his bill was ambiguous enough, however, that the Calhounite reading, that the territorial governments could not abolish slavery on their own (since the territories were the joint property of the states) and had to permit slavery until they had a chance to abolish it at the moment of their admission to the Union as states, could still be advanced as a version of the popular sovereignty doctrine, although of course the point of this interpretation was to prevent the prohibition of slavery until facts on the ground had foreclosed the option of doing so.

There is a further twist in the ambiguity of the popular sovereignty position, because it is unclear whether it is merely a matter of policy, adopted for reasons of political prudence by a Congress that might have taken some other course, or whether it is a matter of constitutional mandate, adopted because all of the alternative policies are unconstitutional. Clearly Cass and Dickinson and for that matter Douglas were moved to their position for prudential reasons, and wanted to regard popular sovereignty as a policy rather than as a constitutional command. But it was the tendency of all disputes in the antebellum era to become "constitutionalized," as each side wished to use the Constitution to rule competing interpretations completely out of the public square. Popular sovereignty had to be constitutionalized to defend it from the supporters of the Calhoun-Davis view, which was constitutionalized from the beginning, and Cass adopted this strategy in the Nicholson letter. Now constitutionalization was a game that anyone could play, but few moves in that game could count as more deft than the slaveholder insistence that the clauses in the Constitution giving the federal government power over the territories did not refer to the territories, exactly, but only to the unorganized land owned by the United States. Douglas and other popular sovereignty advocates wound up adopting this rather forced position as well, since it enabled them to steal a point from at least one of their opponents. But the gambit could have been as available to the Wilmot Proviso advocates as well, since if Congress cannot make laws about slavery in the territories, then it cannot establish it, or provide slave codes, or any of the other legal machinery of slavery, for the territories either. Even the joint sovereignty thesis itself could have played out differently, since the free states also were stakeholders in the territories, with vulnerable interests there. Indeed, Lincoln himself argued just this in the Peoria speech, and the argument had been advanced on the anti-slavery side as early as the debate over Missouri.

Constitutionalizing the popular sovereignty doctrine had another unfortunate consequence, in that if the federal government could not act in the territories, its agents could not either. This is of course exactly the argument Chief Justice Taney will make in the *Dred Scott* decision. There is a possible reply to this, and one that occurred to Douglas, which is that the federal government often creates agents that do things that it cannot itself do, since it after all does admit new states, which do things the federal government cannot do (such as abolish slavery). But this argument is complicated by the fact that in many ways the territorial legislature is not merely a weaker state legislature but a creature of the federal government, since its governor is appointed and its laws are subject to federal review.[13]

The meaning of the popular sovereignty position also must be seen in the context of the contemporary conflict over the status of slavery during the period *before* territorial governments were organized. Douglas held that in the Mexican Cession, Mexican law, which prohibited slavery, applied until the territorial governments chose to repeal it.[14] Legal precedents stretching back to the *Somerset* case in the eighteenth century had held that the right to property in slaves could never be established by natural law, and that slavery could only be legal where there was positive law establishing it. In defiance of this precedent, most southern Democrats argued that slavery had legal standing in the territories even in the absence of a positive law establishing it, since the shamefaced and evasive language concerning slavery in the Constitution seemed to them to amount to a positive law establishing slavery rather than, as it seems to everyone without an interest in seeing it otherwise, a mere concession to the necessity of recognizing slavery where it existed already.[15]

The purported ambiguity of the popular sovereignty position should be seen, however, in the context of the original use of the strategy during the debate over the organization of Oregon Territory in 1847–1848. In the years from the Oregon debates in 1847 to the Kansas-Nebraska Act of 1854, Douglas faced increasingly intransigent opposition from supporters of the Calhoun-Davis view within his party, and he was hard put to prevent southern Democratic extremists from imposing slavery upon such unlikely places as Minnesota and Oregon. Indeed, the doctrine of popular sovereignty in the territories was invented (by New York senator Daniel S. Dickinson six months before Cass's

Nicholson letter) to forestall a fire-eater attempt to force slavery into
Oregon, which was organizing a territorial government and which
wished to keep slavery out. Seen in that context, the ambiguity about
when the territory is to decide its future with regard to slavery seems
to be entirely a retrospective confabulation by pro-slavery politicians.
Nobody doubted in 1847, at the time of the Oregon debate, that Oregon Territory was supposed to decide the slavery issue for itself, and
although Cass's Nicholson letter is ambiguous about whether he intended to let the territorial legislatures in the Mexican Cession decide
the slavery issue for themselves, Cass also felt that it was very unlikely
that slavery could survive there, and argued that the Constitution forbade the federal government from imposing it there.[16] The meaning of
the popular sovereignty position is slightly different in Oregon, which
had already made its intention to reject slavery clear, from its meaning
in the Mexican Cession, where most people assumed that slavery could
not prosper, but where nevertheless the question of which way the
territories would choose to go was still in some sense an open one.[17]
The debate over Oregon overlapped the early stages of the debate
over the Mexican Cession, and the meaning of popular sovereignty
took its cast, in southern eyes at least, from how it was employed during the Oregon debate.

From the time of the Oregon and Mexican Cession debates Douglas
had no sympathy at all for the Calhoun-Davis view of slavery in the
territories:

> What share has the South of the Territories? or the North? or any
> other geographical division unknown to the Constitution? I answer,
> none—none at all. The Territories belong to the United States as one
> people, one nation, and are to be disposed of for the common benefit
> of all, according to the principles of the Constitution. Each State, as a
> member of the Confederacy, has a right to a voice concerning the rules
> and regulations for the government of the Territories, but the differ-
> ent sections—North, South, East, and West—have no such right. It is
> no violation of the Southern rights to prohibit slavery, nor of North-
> ern rights to leave the people to decide the question for themselves.[18]

During the Oregon debates, Douglas, then in the House, at first
favored the view that slavery was already prohibited in Oregon by the

Northwest Ordinance. New York's Preston King, on February 15, 1847, had attempted to use the Wilmot Proviso's language, which was the Northwest Ordinance's language, to keep slavery out of Oregon. Many southerners were willing to concede that slavery should not go to Oregon, but they claimed that the only grounds for doing this would be the Missouri Compromise. Their motivation was to give some color to their proposal to extend the 36° 30' line across the Mexican Cession, a policy that would give them control over a very large piece of Utah and New Mexico Territories, and so northern congressmen, seeing through the subterfuge, voted down an amendment, proposed by Armistead Burt of South Carolina, prohibiting slavery in Oregon on account of Oregon being north of the 36° 30' line.[19] The failure of Burt's subterfuge provoked Calhoun to deliver on February 19, 1847, a very intransigent version of the Calhoun-Davis joint property theory, a version that included in its very language a not-very-oblique threat of secession:[20]

> *Resolved*, That the territories of the United States belong to the several States composing this Union, and are held by them as their joint and common property.
>
> *Resolved*, That Congress, as the joint agent and representative of the States of this Union, has no right to make any law, or do any act whatever, that shall directly, or by its effects, make any discrimination between the States of this Union, by which any of them shall be deprived of its full and equal right in any territory of the United States, acquired or to be acquired.
>
> *Resolved*, That the enactment of any law, which should directly, or by its effects, deprive the citizens of any of the States of this Union from emigrating, with their property, into any of the territories of the United States, will make such discrimination, and would, therefore, be a violation of the constitution and the rights of the States from which such citizens emigrated, and in derogation of that perfect equality which belongs to them as members of this Union—and would tend directly to subvert the Union itself.
>
> *Resolved*, That it is a fundamental principle in our political creed, that a people, in forming a constitution, have the unconditional right to form and adopt the government which they may think best calculated to secure their liberty, prosperity, and happiness; and that, in

conformity thereto, no other condition is imposed by the Federal
Constitution on a State, in order to be admitted into this Union, except that its constitution shall be republican; and that the imposition
of any other by Congress would not only be in violation of the constitution, but in direct conflict with the principle on which our political system rests.[21]

Calhoun also made an oblique attack upon the preamble of the Declaration of Independence, adumbrating a speech he would give on June
27, 1848, as the Oregon debate was drawing to a close:

> Now, Sir, what is proposed? It is proposed, from a vague, indefinite,
> erroneous, and most dangerous conception of private individual
> liberty, to overrule this great common liberty which a people have
> of framing their own constitution! Sir, the right of framing self-
> government on the part of individuals is not near so easily to be estab-
> lished by any course of reasoning, as the right of a community or State
> to self-government. And yet, Sir, there are men of such delicate feeling
> on the subject of liberty—men who cannot possibly bear what they
> call slavery in one section of the country—although not so much slav-
> ery, as an institution indispensable for the good of both races—men so
> squeamish on this point, that they are ready to strike down the higher
> right of a community to govern themselves, in order to maintain the
> absolute right of individuals in every possible condition to govern
> themselves.[22]

This threat seems to have spooked everybody. Douglas was ready, as a
way to end to an increasingly heated argument, to retreat to Burt's Missouri Compromise Line position, and it was to forestall this concession
that Dickinson invented the popular sovereignty argument.[23] Dickinson
had some help in doing this from the settlers in Oregon, who, having
found a copy of the Iowa territorial statutes, organized a territorial government for themselves on a free state basis and petitioned Congress to
recognize it. Dickinson's argument, and the fact that the people of
Oregon had already decided the issue for themselves, persuaded Douglas to come over to the popular sovereignty view.

Now Daniel S. Dickinson was the leader of the anti–Van Buren
"Hunker" faction of the New York Democratic Party, and later led the

so-called Hard faction, which opposed reconciliation with former Free Soilers who wished to reenter the Democratic Party after the failure of Van Buren's 1848 Free Soil ticket, so his argument could be read as an attack on the Van Burenite Wilmot Proviso.[24] But in his immediate context Dickinson seems to have been shoring up Douglas against the South, not embarrassing Van Buren by currying favor there.[25] Cass's adoption of the popular sovereignty position as a party line, by contrast, was intended to outflank Calhoun and to divide his southern supporters, and so his motivations for embracing popular sovereignty seem to be different from Dickinson's: Dickinson sought to shore up a collapsing North, Cass to divide the South. (Cass had, like Franklin Pierce and like Millard Fillmore—who even once had kind words to say about abolition—earlier been a supporter of the Wilmot Proviso.)[26]

Cass's attempt to divide southern Democrats into pro- and anti-Calhoun factions did not at first seem to be promising, since whatever doubts southern Democrats may have had about the joint property theory (a minority doctrine among them in 1847, although probably a majority doctrine by 1850), they nevertheless could have been stampeded into supporting that theory by Calhoun's playing of the sectional-loyalty card. Calhoun's supporters, however, overplayed their hand. When Virginian Thomas Ritchie, the editor of the administration organ, the *Washington Union*, denounced Calhoun's doctrine, Florida senator David Yulee had him banned from the Senate floor, which enabled moderate southerners, with uncharacteristic success, to rally their forces. Southern hard-liners, panicked by the Dickinson-Cass-Douglas popular sovereignty argument, tried variously to press for a federal law positively legalizing slavery in the Mexican Cession (a strategy they would revive against Douglas in 1860) or to argue that the Constitution provided legal cover for slavery in the Mexican Cession already (the argument that "the Constitution follows the flag"). But neither they nor the supporters of the Wilmot Proviso, nor the supporters of the extension of the Missouri Compromise line, nor the supporters of popular sovereignty were able to have their way or construct a binding deal with supporters of other positions.

The result of the impasse was a series of failed compromises over the last years of the Polk administration. Finally Delaware Whig senator John M. Clayton proposed to separate the Oregon and Mexican

Cession questions, allowing Oregon to organize a free territorial government on a popular sovereignty basis, and punting the question of
the status of slavery in the Mexican Cession to the courts.[27]

What exactly the strategy of moving the question to the courts meant
is open to question, since it seemed to have meant opposite things even
to the same people. Clayton seems to have intended his position to be a
way to fudge the question, to try to avoid giving any answer at all because every possible answer was inflammatory. In his hands reference
to the Court was a desperate way to attempt to hold the Whig Party
together, for if northern Whigs succeeded in enabling the federal government to prevent slavery from going to the Mexican Cession by en-
acting the Wilmot Proviso, or if southern Whigs succeeded in resolving the question in favor of the joint sovereignty theory, the party
would come apart, but if each side could simply hold their collective
breath while the Court deliberated, the party could survive at least as
long as it took for the Court to make up its mind. Clayton's position
was tenable only so long as the Supreme Court either did not hand
down any decision or handed down a muddy one. It might not have
been a failed strategy—the muddy delays and half-measures adopted by
the Burger Court did successfully mediate conflicts over affirmative
action, for example, by giving neither side much. But it was the fate in
the antebellum era of every attempt to use ambiguity to make compromise possible to exacerbate the conflict it was supposed to evade, since
each side took its view of the matter as a promise made to it by the
other, and each side's hotheads, seeking clarity, always managed to outflank their moderates, who, recognizing that the problems facing them
were in fact intractable if directly faced, sought only safety by means of
postponement, half-measures, and smoke.

By contrast with the Whigs, the Democrats, so long as the question
was the power of the federal government over slavery in the territories,
looked for a firm decision, one that would destroy the Whig Party
however it came down. But they too punted a decision to the Court—
the question of whether the territorial legislature had the power to
decide the future of slavery or whether only the territorial constitutional convention had that power—and they too did so mostly as a
way to whistle through the graveyard while they hoped that something might come along to enable their own fragile coalition to survive.
They simultaneously looked to the Court to draw a line in the sand

(against the northern Whigs, then against the Republicans) and to paper over their own differences with platitudes. Douglas clearly did intend the territorial legislatures to make the decision about slavery. But as it became clearer to him as the 1850s progressed that his party could not survive resolving this question either way, he became cagier and cagier about saying so directly, pressing his own view implicitly, and hoping that events would play out his way. Put on the spot in the cases of the Chase Amendment and the Toombs bill (both to be discussed in Chapter 3), he eluded making direct statements of the case in the law, which postponed the destruction of his party, but also enabled Lincoln in the "House Divided" speech and in the 1858 debates to raise doubt about whether Douglas really supported popular sovereignty after all.

Clayton was perhaps lucky that he did not get what he wanted, if the consequences, ten years later, of the legal decision he asked for are any indication. The Clayton Compromise, like so many other proposals at the end of the Polk administration, collapsed under the burden of its own ambiguities and wishful thinking.[28]

Another of the last-minute compromises was a December 11, 1848 bill by Douglas, with Polk's support, to admit the entire Mexican Cession immediately as a single state on a popular sovereignty basis. This might avoid the application of the Wilmot Proviso to the Mexican Cession, but only by admitting the entire region as, most probably, a free state. Morrison discusses the complexities of this last-ditch compromise, noting that both the fire-eaters and the Free Soilers thought of the bill as a trick designed to favor the other.[29] It should be noted that this desperate improvisation rather resembles the policy Taylor would seek to impose during the next year, a policy that has usually been taken to be an anti-slavery one. During the Polk administration, Douglas flirted with several ways of dealing with slavery in the territories, from extending the 36° 30' line, to admitting the entire region at once, to the Dickinson-Cass popular sovereignty position. The first of these three positions—as Lincoln reminded his hearers in the "House Divided" speech and during the debates—was a nominally pro-slavery one; the second became, in after years, a nominally anti-slavery one; and the third position was, in the Polk administration if not in the Pierce administration, an ambiguous one. Douglas's shifting of tack during the Polk administration argues to me that his primary motive even in

1854 was the creation of territorial governments for regions that need government, and to that end he was willing to adopt almost any policy (excepting the Calhoun-Davis joint sovereignty policy) for which he could cobble together a majority.

Failing to get any compromise proposal through, Polk passed the question of the Mexican Cession to his successor, but signed a bill allowing Oregon to be organized as a free territory, a decision that persuaded those southerners who were not already alienated by the Democrats' nomination of Lewis Cass (who after all had designed the popular sovereignty position for use against them) to vote for Zachary Taylor, who, in office, although a slaveholder from Louisiana, turned out to be one of the more anti-slavery presidents between Jefferson and Lincoln.

The solution to the impasse between these views in 1850 is usually credited to Henry Clay and Daniel Webster. Douglas himself gave the credit to Lewis Cass, the nominal leader of the Democratic Party in 1850. But the resolution of the struggle over the Mexican Cession, called the Compromise of 1850, was actually for the most part Douglas's own work. We think of the Compromise of 1850 as a package deal, offering the South the Fugitive Slave Act (and the assumption of the national debt of the Republic of Texas) in exchange for the admission of California as a free state (which would change the balance of power in the Senate, shifting it forever against the South), the resolution of the Texas boundary in favor of New Mexico, the abolition of the slave trade in Washington, D.C., and a discreet silence about the future status of slavery in the Utah and New Mexico Territories.[30] Only about a quarter of the senators and representatives supported the compromise as a package deal, and the compromisers were chiefly the increasingly desperate minority factions of the two parties, southern Whigs and northern Democrats. (Only four congressmen from what would be the Confederate states actually supported the compromise as a package.) As a deal, the compromise had gone down to defeat on a series of shockingly opportunistic votes by hard-core factionalists of both sides.[31] Douglas salvaged the compromise only by separating its provisions, with the compromisers and the northern Whigs providing a majority for the North-favoring measures, and the compromisers and the southern Democrats providing a majority for the South-favoring measures.

The portions of the compromise dealing with slavery in the territories also were all Douglas's work, and the language for those bills was taken from proposals Douglas had made in the previous session. The compromisers had taken Douglas's bills, he said, and simply put a wafer between them to hold them together.[32] The Fugitive Slave Act, however, was not Douglas's work, having been proposed by Virginia senator James Mason. Douglas had little to say about it during the congressional debates, and indeed was absent from Congress during this portion of the debates and missed the formal vote, although presumably like Webster and Clay he swallowed hard before supporting it, and he defended it vigorously before a hostile audience in Chicago during a stormy meeting in October 1850, where he—mistakenly—argued that it did not suspend the right of habeas corpus, but also conceded that it did not sufficiently provide for the protection of the innocent and the free.[33]

The result of Douglas's management was a compromise that neither side felt much allegiance to as a compromise, and each side was constantly on the lookout for ways to blame the other for breaking it, so that they themselves could do so.[34]

The complicated history of popular sovereignty as a strategy in the Polk administration should affect how one judges Douglas's embrace of it during the Pierce administration. At the very least, that history makes it unclear whether it was a pro-slavery or an anti-slavery strategy, since the hotheads in each section assumed it was a trick aimed at undermining them. Despite this history, as late as the fall of 1853 Douglas was still attempting to organize the Nebraska lands on a free territory basis, as the first Missouri Compromise required him to do. In January 1854 Douglas made a series of fatal concessions, and because those concessions were perhaps the most fraught and disastrous moves ever made by an American politician, they demand to be presented in a step-by-step way.

Arguing that the popular sovereignty position adopted for Utah and New Mexico had changed the political landscape, Douglas brought in the Nebraska bill (not yet separating Kansas and Nebraska) with language from the Compromise of 1850 allowing the region to choose or reject slavery at the time of admission. At this time he noted that many figures from the South doubted the constitutionality of the Missouri Compromise, but his language was specifically designed to duck that question either way. And indeed, since the states formed from the

Nebraska Territory, once they became states, could have done whatever they wished about slavery in any event, it is hard to see exactly what this bill promised other than a sympathetic hearing from the North in the event that the constitutional conventions in the territories wound up submitting pro-slavery constitutions and a sympathetic hearing from the South in the event that they submitted anti-slavery constitutions.

Given the state of politics at that time, even this may have been wishful thinking. The slave states had made it difficult to organize Oregon Territory on a free basis, although there was no case for slavery to be made there. And the free states had resisted the entry of Arkansas as a slave state into the Union, although on the basis of the Missouri Compromise Arkansas was slated to become a slave state. Douglas repeatedly reminded his anti-slavery critics, who insisted after 1854 upon the sacredness of the Missouri Compromise, that many of them had already violated the spirit of that compromise during the Arkansas debates in 1836, and were thus scarcely in any position to criticize him for overturning it in 1854.[35]

Southerners read this first form of Douglas's bill as implicitly prohibiting slavery in the territories before the adoption of a state constitution. On January 10, under pressure from a cabal of southern Democrats including Senators Atchison, Mason, Hunter, and Butler—all Washington, D.C., housemates, by the way, the famous "F Street Mess"—Douglas (under the pretense of correcting a typographical error in his original bill) added an additional fourteenth section to the bill, giving (as he thought) the territorial legislature the power to act on slavery, and including his famous sentence arguing that the intent of the bill was neither to legislate slavery in nor to legislate it out, but to leave the territories perfectly free to form their institutions in their own way.

It was this second version of the bill that provoked the initial firestorm of criticism, although since Chase, Sumner and Giddings's "Appeal of the Independent Democrats" did not in fact see print until it had reached yet another, third form, that fact might be obscured. The Chase appeal denounced the bill as "a gross violation of a sacred pledge; as a criminal betrayal of precious rights; as part and parcel of an atrocious plot to exclude from a vast unoccupied region immigrants from the Old World and free laborers from our own States, and convert it into a dreary region of despotism, inhabited by masters and slaves."

This denunciation undoubtedly hardened Douglas's mind about the bill, particularly since Chase had, with a show of friendship, asked him to postpone the debate for a few days so that he could think about it, a few days that Chase used to rush his rather personal denunciation of Douglas into print.[36]

What Chase and company did not see was that the concession the January 10 version offered was a very ambiguous one, because although the bill gave the territorial legislature power to legislate on slavery, it also assumed that the Missouri Compromise prohibition would remain in force until the legislature acted, which is to say that the legislature that would be called upon to decide the fate of slavery in those territories would be made up of nonslaveholders. Perhaps the F Street Mess counted on their ability to rush, extralegally, a large enough number of slaveholders into the territory to have their way. Douglas certainly bet the opposite way. Each hoped to be able to skate very quickly over the patch of thin ice.

They were prevented from doing so by Senator Archibald Dixon of Kentucky, a moderate Whig, who sat in Clay's seat in the Senate and looked forward ineffectually to the day when slavery might depart his state. His motives in stressing the risk to the South of the January 10 bill are hard to figure. William Freehling and Allan Nevins both believe that he was looking to revive the fortunes of his party in the South by showing that Whigs too could take a hard line.[37] It was a fatal miscalculation, because he underestimated the Democrats' ability to raise the stakes higher than the Whigs could follow them. The fire-eaters seized upon this issue as a kind of knife to the throat of the Union, and they were able to capitalize upon northern hostility to Douglas's bill in order to transform the struggle into an identity politics contest about who would be disloyal to the South and who would stand up for it come what may. The fire-eaters were in principle opposed to the popular sovereignty position (committed as they were to their joint property theory), and were not enthusiastic about Douglas's bill. Indeed, advanced fire-eater opinion from the beginning treated popular sovereignty as a kind of cat's-paw aimed at securing the aims of the Wilmot Proviso. But they used it ruthlessly to destroy the last shred of legitimacy the Whig Party had south of the Mason-Dixon line, and the hostility Douglas's bill provoked at the North gave them a very strong hand in doing so.

Douglas tried for some days to duck the challenge Senator Dixon's argument proposed, but after a long carriage ride with Dixon on January 15 he conceded, and on January 22 he forced the explicit repeal of the 36° 30' provision of the Missouri Compromise down the throat of the bewildered President Pierce. Conceivably had Chase or some more reputable like-minded person striven in private with Douglas, Douglas might have bent the other way. In 1858, when Douglas began to waver about opposing the English Compromise in favor of the fraudulent Lecompton Constitution for Kansas, his protégé David Broderick of California took him aside and told him that if Douglas supported the English bill he (Douglas) might as well "go out into the street and blow his brains out." Douglas did ultimately oppose the English bill. And, as we have just seen, Douglas wavered about the Oregon question, and might have allowed Oregon to be given a free territorial government at the price of giving legitimacy to the idea of extending the Missouri Compromise line, had not Dickinson given him some backbone. This time, however, it was Dixon who knew how to handle Douglas, and Chase knew only how to infuriate Douglas but not how to beat him. From January 22 the die was cast, and at least the several-years-long guerrilla war in Bleeding Kansas, if not the Civil War itself, became inevitable, as the Free Soil and pro-slavery factions fought for control over the territory.

The simplest way to describe Douglas's error would be to say that he seems to have assumed that only southerners would be so foolish as to whip themselves into a fury over a symbolic issue. He never for a moment believed that slavery could survive in Kansas, Missouri Compromise or no Missouri Compromise. At the time of the Compromise of 1850, he had spoken of the inevitability that seventeen new free states would arise from the Mexican Cession and the rest of the Louisiana Purchase, and that no new slave states would arise. He had also predicted on the floor of the Senate in 1849 that slavery's days in Delaware, Maryland, Virginia, Kentucky, and Missouri were numbered.[38] As far as Douglas was concerned, the conflict over Kansas was, in the language of the postwar Republican politician James G. Blaine, a quarrel about "an imaginary Negro in an impossible place."[39]

Douglas, like Lincoln, felt that the vitality of slavery depended upon its ability to expand. But he felt that prohibiting the expansion of slavery by fiat would enflame sectional resentments. Popular sovereignty enflamed them even more, especially once it became clear in 1858 that, by almost nine-to-one margins, settlers in Kansas opposed slavery. But Douglas felt that the South would accept a practical defeat so long as it was accorded a symbolic victory, and that the North would accept a symbolic defeat so long as it was accorded a practical victory. Both guesses were wrong.

Douglas may well have been wrong about whether slavery could have expanded into Kansas. It is true that Kansas is too dry and cold for cotton. But it is not too dry and cold, at least in the river valleys, for hemp, the chief slave-grown crop of Kentucky and Missouri. Certainly David Atchison, who was from western Missouri, where slavery was stronger than in the east of the state, felt that slave agriculture could cross the state line, and Jefferson Davis and many other southerners agreed with him, as did Lincoln.

Kansas may yet have become a very marginal slave state like Delaware, or for that matter Missouri. Now large-scale expansion of plantation slavery into the dry regions west of the hundredth meridian, where high-value, labor-intensive crops would not grow, seems unlikely to me. But other forms of slavery may yet have been viable there. Perhaps something like the peonage that prevailed in dry areas of Mexico might have succeeded marginally. Perhaps slaves could have been made to work mines. They did, for instance, work in the Tredegar Iron Works in Richmond, and did a great deal of skilled labor in the shipbuilding trades in Baltimore. On the other hand, the fact that the South did not in the slavery era spin or weave very much of its own cotton but did a great deal of both after emancipation is evidence for the view that slaveholders did not feel that using their slaves as factory workers rather than as agricultural workers represented a good investment.[40] Once the competition with slave agriculture for capital was over, a great deal of cotton began to be spun in the South, so much so in fact that the great northern weaving centers of Lowell and Lawrence were impoverished by the competition.[41]

Except for outliers like George Fitzhugh, those who sought to advance slavery did not have the kind of economies in which enslaved miners or enslaved factory workers are a part in ideological focus when they thought about slavery. And the case of Baltimore is usually cited not as an example of the power of slavery to expand into new regions of the economy but as a sign of how shaky slavery was becoming in

Maryland. On this issue, as on so much else, the experience of Maryland was so anomalous that it provided South Carolina–style pro-slavery ideologues with as many occasions for discomfort as for cheer.

On balance, my view is that it is unlikely slavery could have gone much farther west than a few counties into Kansas without becoming something else. But the fight over slavery in the territories was not avoidable even if its outcome was inevitable, because it was a proxy war anyway, a place for both sides to fight out a conflict in which the real stakes were elsewhere.

Slaveholders must completely dominate the politics of any republic of which they are a part, and so long as the United States had any pretenses to democracy there was bound to be a conflict over slavery, since the slaveholders, to protect themselves from that democracy, would ultimately have to keep raising the stakes until they demanded something that even supine free state politicians like the northern Democrats could not surrender. Possession of Kansas was itself, I think, not something in which either side had a crucial objective stake. But both sides were spoiling for a fight, and Kansas was available.

Douglas's argument was not merely a geographical one about temperature and rainfall, although Lincoln consistently portrayed it is if that were all there was to it. Douglas allowed Lincoln to do so, because it allowed Douglas cover for his position that something other than the fiat of the central government will keep slavery out of Kansas. Douglas's argument was a sociological one, not a geographical one. Douglas was aware that the kind of people who would be looking to move to the dry plains of Kansas (as opposed to the better lands of south Texas) would be yeoman nonslaveholders from the South who would be moving there to escape the competition from slave labor and from the presence of black people. In an earlier generation, such people would have taken slaves to new territories and painfully aped the ways of the kinds of people who looked down on them in the established slave states. (Thomas Sutpen in William Faulkner's *Absalom! Absalom!* is such a man.) But because the rise in the price of slaves since the closure of the international slave trade had made such people unable to own slaves, yeoman emigrants became the kind of anti-slavery racists that Eugene Berwanger describes, people who hated slavery and black people about equally.[42] These were the kind of people who settled California and Oregon (who wrote free state constitutions under popular sovereignty conditions), and who for that matter had earlier settled southern Illinois. They were the kind of people who in fact did settle Kansas, despite everything, and, like their counterparts in Illinois, wrote a free state constitution that forbade the entry of free blacks into the state.[43] Douglas had intended to give such people a powerful incentive, in the form of what we now call the Homestead Act, which Douglas originated in 1849, although it did not become law until 1862, the year after his death. This act can only have been, and can only have been intended to be, a deathblow to slavery, and that is why Douglas was never able to pass it.[44]

The point of this summary is that Douglas in 1854 was not fighting an avant-garde action on behalf of the slave power conspiracy, but a rearguard action against the Calhounite joint property position.[45] Lincoln might not have known that in 1854. He could not have missed it in 1858, but he chose to ignore it.

On his own side, Douglas seems to have been tone-deaf, as Allan Nevins called him fifty years ago, about the cost of moral compromises. People are willing to take a loss in the hopes of reaping a gain when the stake is money, and Douglas seems to have thought that people—well, northerners anyway—could easily make the same kind of detached prudential calculations about moral issues. The problem is this: when I give up money to make money, I still know how much money means to me. But when I give up right to advance right, I am likely to lose sight of how valuable right is to me, or even perhaps what it is. The ethos of moral dealmaking is in some ways an attractive one, but its risk is that engaging in that dealmaking may make what matters to one less and less clear, less and less worth the struggle. When Lincoln accuses Douglas of weakening the commitment in the public mind to hostility to slavery, he partly accuses Douglas of being part of the slave power conspiracy. But Lincoln's charge has another meaning, and a more plausible one. For if one is to be always willing to deal with one's enemy where one finds him, and with what is ready to hand, one might well begin to lose one's grip on just what matters. The problem in a nutshell is that we cannot know in advance what Douglas would not have conceded if he had been pressed hard enough and ruthlessly enough for concessions. When the break came, from the struggle over the fraudulent pro-slavery Lecompton Constitution in Kansas in 1857 to the outbreak of war four years later, Douglas stood firm. But many people of his views did not, and knowing the details of those views does not predict how such people will turn.

2.2 Making and Breaking Deals in 1850 and in 1854

Douglas's later account of the debates concerning the Kansas-Nebraska Act is so loaded that it is hard to imagine that even he believed it. Douglas began with a reprise of the negotiations that led to the Compromise of 1850. He treated the compromise as the platforms of both major parties in 1852 pretended to treat it, as a thorough settlement of the issue of slavery in the territories in all of its aspects. Furthermore, he treated his own Kansas-Nebraska Act as if it were so consistent with the principles of the Compromise of 1850 that only interested men conniving for power, and seeking ways to overturn the compromise in order to kick up the fuss that would yield them that power, could have opposed it. Now most historians think that it was Douglas, not his opponents, who overturned the Compromise of 1850, so making sense of Douglas's argument here will require a certain suspension of disbelief.

The Democratic Party included a ringing endorsement of the compromise in its 1852 platform, and the divided Whig Party also included a less-than-ringing endorsement after an angry debate on the question. Southern Whigs had wished to renominate Millard Fillmore on a platform endorsing the compromise; northern Whigs had wanted to run Winfield Scott on a platform opposing the compromise. The party compromised by nominating Scott on a pro-compromise platform, a solution that pleased nobody. Indeed, one of the many issues over which the hapless Winfield Scott came to grief in the 1852 campaign was ambiguity about whether or not he sincerely endorsed his party's pro-compromise platform ("I accept the nomination with the resolutions attached," he had written in his acceptance letter). Lincoln's speech to the Scott Club includes a devastatingly funny attack on Douglas's claim that Scott's endorsement of the compromise was ambiguous. Douglas had argued that that "with" meant that Scott took notice of the resolutions but did not really endorse them. Lincoln took several speeches of Douglas's own and substituted "with" with some of the phrases Douglas suggested Scott might really have had in mind ("although I oppose," "although I defy," "although I spit upon"), with hilarious results. But the endorsement really *was* ambiguous, and the Whig Party really was divided about how enthusiastically to support the Compromise of 1850.

Lincoln's own support of the compromise was not ambiguous; he even supported the Fugitive Slave Act, on exactly the grounds Webster had taken in the Seventh of March speech, as the price of a bargain that came out on balance for freedom.

Scott's opponent, the even more hapless Franklin Pierce, elected on a pro-compromise platform (with an official campaign biography written by Nathaniel Hawthorne, his Bowdoin College friend), inaugurated his presidency by undermining the compromise, spurning compromisers in his appointments, and promoting instead an odd congeries of fire-eaters and former Free Soilers. Pierce's very cabinet appointments indicate how unstable the political situation was. The destruction of the Whig Party, accidentally set in motion by Douglas's Kansas-Nebraska Act, set off a profound and far-reaching reorganization of the party system. But even within the Democratic Party, Free Soilers and fire-eaters were itching to have at each other. With only loyalty to the incompetent Pierce keeping the party together, it is easy to see how the fracturing of the Whig Party would also destabilize the Democratic Party, and cause it to lose the Free Soil faction to a new party, even if that new party did not exist in 1852, and even if there was the further misadventure of the American Party to go through before that new party could gain its footing.

Lincoln was aware that Pierce sought to draw support not only from compromisers (his Scott Club speech includes some very grudging praise of Douglas for his role in the compromise), but also from opponents of the compromise, from southerners who had gone to the Nashville Convention in 1850 to press for secession, to Barnburner Free Soilers who had left the Democratic Party in 1848 to support Van Buren and Adams and the short-lived Free Soil Party. When Lincoln baited race he almost always did so defensively (as a way to preempt race baiting by Douglas, typically).[46] The Scott Club speech is one of the few occasions in which Lincoln baited race maliciously and aggressively. It was news to me, until I read this passage, that Pierce loathed the Fugitive Slave Act, although I did know that Pierce had briefly supported the Wilmot Proviso.[47] The passage Lincoln refers to has never surfaced. It may even be a complete fabrication.

> The indispensable necessity with the democrats of getting these New York free soil votes, to my mind, explains why they nominated a man who "loathes the Fugitive Slave Law." In December or January last Gen. Pierce made a speech, in which, according to two different

news paper reports, published at the time in his vicinity and never questioned by him or anyone else till after the nomination, he publicly declared his loathing of the Slave law. Now we shall allow ourselves to be very green, if we conclude the democratic convention did not know of this when they nominated him. On the contrary, its supposed efficacy to win free soil votes, was the very thing that secured his nomination. His southern allies will continue to bluster and pretend to disbelieve the report, but they would not, for any consideration, have him to contradict it. And he will not contradict it—mark me, he will not contradict it. I see by the despatches he has already written a letter on the subject; but I have not seen the letter, or any quotation from it. When we shall see it, we shall also see it does not contradict the report—that is, it will not specifically deny the charge that he declared his loathing for the Fugitive Slave Law. I know it will not, because I know the necessity of the party will not permit it to be done. The letter will deal in generalities, and will be framed with a view of having it to pass at the South for a denial; but the specific point will not be made and met.

And this being the necessity of the party, and its action and attitude in relation to it, is it not particularly bright in Judge Douglas to stand up before a slave-holding audience, and make flings at the Whigs about free soil and abolition! Why Pierce's only chance for presidency, is to be born into it, as a cross between New York old hunkerism, and free soilism, the latter predominating in the offspring. Marryat, in some one of his books, describes the sailors, weighing anchor, and singing:

> "Sally is a bright Mullatter,
>   Oh Sally Brown—
> Pretty gal, but can't get at her,
>   Oh, Sally Brown."

Now, should Pierce ever be President, he will, politically speaking, not only be a mulatto; but he will be a good deal darker one than Sally Brown. (1:297)[48]

Pierce's cabinet may already have been divided on the slavery issue, and of course the issue was hardly as quiescent as both Lincoln and

Douglas claimed it was in the course of the debates. There was the little issue of the Fugitive Slave Act, for instance, and the numerous inflammatory attempts to enforce it, and to resist its enforcement. And there was the hue and cry over the publication of Harriet Beecher Stowe's *Uncle Tom's Cabin* in 1852, which, in the probably apocryphal story, prompted Lincoln to ask Stowe, upon meeting her during his presidency, if she was "the little woman who made this great war." Both Lincoln and Douglas wanted to treat the crisis as beginning with the Kansas-Nebraska Act, Lincoln because he saw Douglas's legislation as kicking over the apple cart, Douglas because he saw opposition to that act as the fruit of a conspiracy. But however many ways the slavery issue may have claimed urgent attention in the four years between the Compromise of 1850 and the Kansas-Nebraska Act, it is true that the Kansas issue brought a completely new urgency to the conflict.

The nuance that matters here is the question of whether the Kansas-Nebraska Act was an abrogation of the Compromise of 1850 or an extension of it. Historians have always argued the former, and it is hard to make the case any other way; but the question remains whether Douglas had any rationale, other than the desire to engage in ruthless spin, for arguing otherwise.

Douglas's explicit argument was that the adoption of the popular sovereignty policy for New Mexico and Utah Territories had changed the political landscape and made that the default position for any new territory. The position on the issue that Lincoln sketched out in the Peoria speech is the only plausible one: that as far as the territories were concerned, the status quo involved a patchwork of incompatible theories applied to different territories as the result of different deals. So, for instance, the territories of the Old Northwest were reserved for free territory status by the Northwest Ordinance, voted on both in the Confederation Congress and in the First Congress by many of the same people, North and South, who had written the territories clauses in the Constitution that Calhoun and his allies tried to read with such interpretive will to power. The territories of the Old Southwest had been ceded by Georgia and North Carolina with an explicit promise that slavery would not be prohibited in them, so they were de facto developed as slave territories, although the laws in force there were technically popular sovereignty laws. Florida and "West Florida" were acquired on the same basis. Of the territories of the Louisiana Purchase, Louisiana and Arkansas were organized as slave states because slavery preexisted there, Missouri was admitted as a slave state by the Missouri Compromise, and the rest of the territories north of the 36° 30′ line were to be organized as free territories under the provisions of the same bill. The Pacific Northwest was organized on a free territory basis, after a confused argument about whether Congress was doing this because it was north of the 36° 30′ line or not (because those territories were not part of the Louisiana Purchase, to which the Missouri Compromise applied) or because (as Douglas argued) the Northwest Ordinance applied there (it did not) or because the people of the territory simply did not want it. Finally, the Mexican Cession was organized on a popular sovereignty basis, with the exception of California, which was admitted as a free state on popular sovereignty grounds, by the Compromise of 1850.[49]

Douglas noted in one of his first speeches on the Kansas-Nebraska Act, his speech of January 30, 1854, that popular sovereignty had already guaranteed freedom for Oregon, and for California. He was quite explicit from the beginning that he expected the same outcome in Kansas:

> When settlers rush in—when labor becomes plenty, and therefore cheap, in that climate, with its productions—it is worse than folly to think of its being a slaveholding country. I do not believe there is a man in Congress who thinks it could be permanently a slaveholding country. I have no idea that it could. All I have to say on that subject is, that when you create them into a territory, you thereby acknowledge that they ought to be considered a distinct political organization. And when you give them in addition a legislature, you thereby confess that they are competent to exercise the powers of legislation. If they wish slavery, they have a right to it. If they do not want it, they will not have it, and you should not attempt to force it upon them.[50]

Lincoln was quite right that the adoption of popular sovereignty for the Mexican Cession did nothing to change the status of what would become Kansas Territory, because the status of Kansas had been settled by the Missouri Compromise. Douglas's argument to the contrary seems to be handwaving at best and rationalization at worst. Certainly, as Lincoln pointed out, a large number of northern supporters of the Compromise of 1850 would not have supported it if they had known that repeal of the 36° 30′ provision of the Missouri Compromise was part of the deal. Douglas had, after all, been attempting to organize the Kansas and Nebraska land on a free territory basis as late as 1853. The best argument Douglas could make for abandoning that attempt was the practical one, the argument that whatever the Missouri Compromise may have stated, the slave states had the votes (and had been using them) to prevent the organization of territorial governments for Kansas and Nebraska, and organizing governments for those regions was a matter of urgent necessity. That is not a completely principled defense, but it is one that has the advantage of pragmatism, realism, and attention to the most urgent practical necessities, which most people think of as Douglas's chief virtues.

Douglas argued that the agreement to adopt the popular sovereignty solution for New Mexico and Utah somehow invalidated the Missouri Compromise's use of the 36° 30′ line in the Louisiana Purchase. Lincoln was right to treat this as fishy. But Douglas did not invent this argument in 1854. He was arguing this way in 1850, most famously in the speech Douglas in Chicago gave just after the compromise when he argued down a hostile audience.[51]

Douglas further argued that the supporters of the Wilmot Proviso, in refusing to extend the 36° 30′ line across the Mexican Cession to the Pacific, had invalidated it as a demarcation in the Louisiana Purchase. He argued also that they had invalidated the compromise as well by opposing the admission of Arkansas as a slave state, which should have had a free ride under the principles of the compromise, and by trumping up a case against the admission of Missouri as a slave state as early as 1821, the occasion of the "second Missouri Compromise."[52] This argument, too, Lincoln rightly saw as fishy, comparing it to the claim that if one does not build onto a house then one has somehow forfeited that house. But Douglas was right to argue that when the slave states balked at organizing Kansas as a free territory under the Missouri Compromise restriction they were not behaving terribly differently from the way the free states had behaved in 1821.

The pragmatic claim that repealing the 36° 30′ line provision of the Missouri Compromise, combined with the proviso that slavery could not prosper in Kansas anyway, was the only way to organize territorial

governments in the face of southern opposition was probably Douglas's strongest argument, and, for that matter, probably also renders
his actual motivations. But Douglas also argued that his position was
not only consistent and principled but in the spirit of the Compromise
of 1850. Why did he make this claim?

For one thing, Douglas could claim that the politicians who most opposed him about the Kansas-Nebraska Act were opponents of the Compromise of 1850 to begin with, and thus were in no position to speak of
its meaning or treat it as a sacred compact that Douglas, who was after
all both the principal author of the compromise and the manager of its
adoption, had shattered. As Douglas had said at the time:

> They talk about the bill being a violation of the compromise mea-
> sures of 1850. Who can show me a man in either house of Congress
> who was in favor of those compromise measures in 1850, and who is
> not now in favor of leaving the people of Nebraska and Kansas to do
> as they please upon the subject of slavery, according to the principle
> of my bill? Is there one? If so I have not heard of him. The tornado
> has been raised by abolitionists, and by abolitionists alone.[53]

Douglas was probably right about who his opponents were (remembering how the compromise was reached), although he was wrong
in Lincoln's case. Certainly Chase, Sumner, and Giddings, the most
vociferous opponents of the Kansas-Nebraska Act, were no sympathizers with the Compromise of 1850. And Douglas knew how people
behave when they have made a deal they begrudge: his speeches during the spring of 1854 were full of examples of how northern politicians who signed onto the Missouri Compromise spent years trying
to evade it, and only discovered that it was something to revere when
Douglas sought to repeal it.[54] Indeed, as Douglas pointed out in a letter responding to a protest from thirty-five Chicago clergymen about
the Kansas-Nebraska Act, many of those who gave speeches about the
sacredness of the compact enshrined in the Missouri Compromise
had been doing their best to subvert the Fugitive Slave Act, which was
the product of exactly the same kind of deal.[55] Douglas treated anti-
slavery northerners who had in fact opposed the Compromise of 1850
as looking for ways to subvert it, in just the way he accused their earlier moral equivalents of seeking to subvert the Missouri Compro-

mise from the beginning. But the fact that the opponents did not favor the compromise to begin with, and may in fact have been looking for grounds to break it, does not really matter if they interpreted the meaning of the Compromise of 1850 about the territorial question correctly, which they did.

Douglas was moved chiefly by an appreciation of the depth of the crisis that had preceded the Compromise of 1850; the threat to the Union then had altered the whole political world, and his belief that the popular sovereignty solution to the Utah and New Mexico problems had changed everything was at least sincere, his attempts to introduce free soil territorial bills for the Nebraska Territory in 1853 notwithstanding, for those attempts, like Douglas's attempt to admit the entire Mexican Cession as a single free state, were the products of practical concessions to political realities. Left to himself, Douglas had argued, he would always have chosen to let the voters of the territories themselves determine their fate.

The most interesting position in the development of Douglas's views was the one he held in the brief period between his original submission of the bill and his "correction," his explicit repeal of the Missouri Compromise line. For this period he chose to treat the Missouri Compromise prohibition of slavery north of the 36° 30′ line the way he had treated the Mexican law prohibiting slavery in the Mexican Cession, as a valid law that later law can supersede (as opposed to an invalid law to be repealed because of its constitutional flaws, the southern view). Before his fateful carriage ride with Senator Dixon, Douglas sought, in his own words, to neither affirm nor repeal the eighth section of the Missouri act.[56] Douglas's language in the bill gives a clear statement of his intention, to seek a more general solution that would not so much repeal as transcend the Missouri Compromise. Referring back to the Compromise of 1850, Douglas argued:

> [Those acts] were intended to have a far more comprehensive and enduring effect than the mere adjustment of the difficulties arising out of the recent acquisition of Mexican territory. They were designed to establish certain great principles, which would not only furnish adequate remedies for existing evils, but, in all time to come, avoid the perils of similar agitation, by withdrawing the question of slavery from the halls of Congress and the political arena, and committing it

to the arbitrament of those who were immediately interested in, and
alone responsible for its consequences.[57]

Up to the moment the territorial legislature itself votes slavery in,
under this reading, the Missouri Compromise restriction still applies.
Until Douglas caved to Dixon and the F Street Mess, his view of the
default position for Kansas was that it would still be a free territory.
Douglas was cornered into conceding support for explicit repeal, and
in making that concession he violated the inner logic of his own position. The distinction was lost on the authors of the "Appeal of the Independent Democrats," who treated both Douglas's original version
and the explicit repeal negotiated with Dixon as the same thing.
  Douglas's case involved treating not only the Compromise of 1850
but also the original compromises of 1820–1821 as establishing a principle meant to be applied in future cases. (Lincoln treated neither case
as establishing a principle, seeing each as applying only to the immediate case at hand, to the Louisiana Purchase and to the Mexican Cession, respectively.) As a principle for future cases, Douglas argued, the
36° 30′ line had already been discredited by Congress's refusal to extend
it across the Mexican Cession, and, more particularly, by the entry of
California as a free state. The other available general principles, the
Wilmot Proviso and the Calhoun-Davis joint property theory, were
nonstarters, because each was absolutely unacceptable to the other
section, and in Douglas's mind support of either of those positions
amounted to agitation for civil war. If the aim was to seek a general rule,
and one that therefore must be applied generally (even to the Louisiana
Purchase), popular sovereignty had obvious advantages over the other
available principles. And to argue, as Lincoln did, that the Compromise of 1850 established no general rule was also to argue that the key
issues have to be argued de novo every time new territories are to be
organized, which was, in Douglas's view, to reopen inflammatory debates that would threaten the union seventeen more times (since Douglas estimated that the West would make up seventeen new states).
Douglas was not crazy to seek to avoid that. But he was crazy to think
that popular sovereignty would be a less inflammatory position than
the Wilmot Proviso or the Davis-Calhoun position. Douglas's error
was not in breaking the compromises of 1820–1821, but in failing to
see that the solution he proposed would set off a brushfire civil war in

every new territory as armed settlers struggled to control the institutions of each territory while it was being formed.

Douglas argued that at least popular sovereignty applies a consistent rule everywhere, and consistently invokes the same kind of authority, the agency of the deliberative bodies that rule the territories. The outcome of this method would perhaps produce a heterogeneous patchwork of outcomes—with some territories slave and some free. But the alternative produces not only a patchwork of outcomes but a patchwork of authorities: the people of some territories can choose for themselves whether there will be slavery or not in the territory, and the people of other territories are foreclosed from doing so by Congress, which has ruled slavery either in, as in the Old Southwest, or out, as in the Old Northwest. A principled solution can produce a patchwork of outcomes, but no principled solution can depend upon a patchwork of kinds of authorities. Douglas's argument is that if the Compromise of 1850 really *is* to be a compromise, it must put forward a consistent principle; if it does not, it is not a compromise but a modus vivendi arrangement. The chief problem with this argument is that the Compromise of 1850 really *was* only a modus vivendi arrangement, as Douglas himself, who put it together by separating its provisions to work a compromise in a situation where only about a quarter of the Congress really wanted to compromise, was in a better position than anyone else to know.

What is the key difference between a modus vivendi arrangement and a true compromise? The former is a kind of armistice. It reflects the balance of power at the moment it is drawn. Neither side has any principled reason to respect the fact that the line is drawn where it is, because the fact that the line is where it is is only a consequence of the momentary equilibrium of forces. Had one side been stronger, the line would have been drawn differently. Indeed, each can claim to have made the deal under duress, since each side, if it had been capable of doing so, if it had not been subject to the threat of violence from the other side, would have driven the other side to the wall, and each side agreed to the arrangement only in order to prevent itself from being driven to the wall. Should one side become stronger than the other, it has no principled reason to respect the existing arrangement, because, in the first place, that arrangement is the work of force, not of principle, and their agreement to the arrangement was merely a recognition of reality, not an agreement upon principle, and, in the second place, such realities as the balance of force change over time. Modus vivendi arrangements are ad hoc, and they deserve the respect ad hoc arrangements are able to earn (it is better to keep them, for instance, than to risk the chaos that would ensue otherwise, unless you are pretty sure how the alternative would come out), but they do not earn much more respect than that. A compromise, by contrast, invokes a principle that each side would have reason to respect, and that principle gives the compromise sturdiness even in the face of changes in the balance of power.[58]

To imagine that the Compromise of 1850, or indeed any of the arrangements about slavery in the antebellum era, could ever have been more than a modus vivendi agreement is wishful thinking. Ever since 1820, or maybe since 1787 itself, politicians had regularly announced comprehensive settlements of the slavery issue, and had argued, as Van Buren did repeatedly, that the conflict would just go away if we all just kept our mouths shut about it. And they were always wrong. Douglas himself should have seen this most of all, since the hallmark of all of his thinking is a realistic understanding that modus vivendi solutions are about as much as one can ask of intractable conflicts, and that a politician has done well if he has persuaded mortal enemies to put off killing each other for a few days.

Perhaps what upset Douglas about the opposition to the Kansas-Nebraska Act was not that it denied that the Compromise of 1850 was a comprehensive settlement, because it was not, but that it overturned the pretending rhetoric that might, perhaps, have enabled the Republic to whistle its way through the graveyard. Douglas's argument here, like Lincoln's argument against Douglas later, was an argument about the effect taking certain kinds of position in public might have on the public mood. Only this pretending rhetoric was the grounds of consistency between the Compromise of 1850 and the Kansas-Nebraska Act; they share a grounding in the wishful thinking of the sectional minority factions of both of the major parties, the southern Whigs and the northern Democrats. To those groups, and those groups alone, the two bills were continuous.

Ultimately Douglas's claim to have inherited the mantle of Clay as a compromiser is an ironic one, for the key element of the compromise Douglas pushed through in 1854 was the repeal of the key element of Clay's own compromises of 1820 and 1821. But Douglas's claim to the mantle of Clay was not entirely bogus. What he inherited from Clay, however, was not the specific principles upon which Clay's compromises were built, but Clay's skill at improvising temporary solutions to intractable problems. In turning from improvised bargains to confrontations, however principled and however reasonable and moderate the position he maintained in that confrontation, Lincoln really did surrender the mantle of Clay to Douglas. It was Douglas, not the anti-Nebraska politicians, who broke up the ad hoc arrangement called the Compromise of 1850. But it was the anti-Nebraska men who broke up the tradition of seeking ad hoc compromises, and for that reason Douglas's charge against them, although wrong, was not completely without traction. Of course it was not only north of the Mason-Dixon line that powerful politicians gave up on ad hoc compromises; indeed, it is fair to say that the South gave up on such compromises before the North did; if the South made concessions in 1850, bending to the inevitable about California, for instance, it is hard to see what concessions it made in 1854 or after. After 1858 the position of compromising politicians became increasingly difficult, becoming finally, in the failed Crittenden Compromise, or the Washington Peace Conference of 1861, or Douglas's own bizarre Customs Union plan, not only impossible but ridiculous.

Both Lincoln and Douglas sought some kind of accommodation with the South. Lincoln sought a principled compromise. To find a principled compromise, fair terms of cooperation rooted in deep concepts, requires what Rawls calls an overlapping consensus about shared basic political principles, deep value commitments which each side adopts within the horizon of its own moral views and for its own reasons, while recognizing that the other has made the same commitments for its own reasons. It is not clear that such a consensus could be reached with those who not only embraced a "positive good" view of slavery but also demanded, as a condition for remaining part of the Republic, the ability to dominate its political institutions to ensure the protection of slavery. Douglas, by contrast, sought only an ad hoc modus vivendi rooted in prevailing conceptions. But to maintain this required a commitment on both sides to sustain the habit of negotiation. And this habit cannot be sustained with people who cannot accept defeat even on the terms they themselves had specified, as had happened in Kansas. Sustaining the habit of negotiation further requires both sides to understand that escalating the conflict to the point of war is riskier to them than making a deal, however shaky, however shabby.

Both sides, the North and the South, habituated to impressing their own home folks by raising the stakes with each other, became dulled to the reality of what a violent conflict between them would mean. And the slaveholders, in particular, accustomed to forcing their opponents to back down in every conflict, came to feel that when shouting gave way to shooting, having the upper hand would come easily to them. This is why the mere inability to accept a simple electoral defeat in the election of 1860 moved them to dissolve the Union. Compromises dirty the hands, and require everybody to satisfy themselves with morally shady and practically incomplete half-measures. In rushing to war, each side rejoiced; each side believed it had finally cut the Gordian knot of mere politics, and, purified by the prospect of glorious violence, had found a bracing moral clarity. Everybody, in the North and in the South, except for William T. Sherman, who was briefly hospitalized as delusional for thinking otherwise, felt that the war would be over by its first Christmas. The habit of political one-upsmanship blinded them all to the moral horror of war.

2.3 Lincoln's Chief Arguments

When Douglas traveled back to Illinois in the late summer of 1854 to defend the Kansas-Nebraska Act, he said that he could have traveled the entire way by the light of his own burning effigy. In Chicago on September 1, where four years earlier he had successfully won over a hostile audience to support the Compromise of 1850, he was shouted down by the crowd and was unable to give his speech. In Springfield, the neutral territory between the anti-slavery northern counties of Illinois and the pro-southern (if not pro-slavery) counties of Little Egypt at the southern tip of the state, he was able to make his speech. But Lincoln, whom he had refused to debate, rose at the end of the speech and announced he would reply the next day. Accepting the inevitable, Douglas agreed to allow Lincoln to reply to him when next he spoke, a few days later at Peoria, on condition that Douglas himself have a few minutes rebuttal at the end. Lincoln readily agreed to this, he humorously admits in the opening paragraphs, since it assured him that the Democrats in the audience would stay to hear his own speech, if only for the pleasure of hearing Douglas flay him once it was over.

Lincoln's Peoria speech opened with a disavowal of the kinds of personal attacks upon Douglas that were the focus of the "Appeal of the Independent Democrats" (and would be the focus of Lincoln's own "House Divided" speech four years later). His motive was partly a political one, in that he wished to dissociate himself from the kind of radicalism that would cost him a hearing from voters in Central Illinois. But he was also motivated by his ideas about what kinds of argument are fair game and what kinds of views one is allowed to take about one's opponent's position. He wanted not only to dissociate the cause of free soil in the territories from the cause of abolition in the states but also to affirm that his position was a national position, not merely a reflection of a northern sectional agenda, and that he would come to grips with his opponents fairly, without special pleading and without self-righteousness:

> I wish further to say, that I do not propose to question the patriotism, or to assail the motives of any man, or class of men; but rather to strictly confine myself to the naked merits of the question.
>
> I also wish to be no less than National in all the positions I may take; and whenever I take ground which others have thought, or may think, narrow, sectional and dangerous to the Union, I hope to give a reason, which will appear sufficient, at least to some, why I think differently.
>
> And, as this subject is no other, than part and parcel of the larger general question of domestic-slavery, I wish to MAKE and to KEEP the distinction between the EXISTING institution, and the EXTENSION of it, so broad, and so clear, that no honest man can misunderstand me, and no dishonest one, successfully misrepresent me. (1:308)

In making the distinction between toleration of slavery where it exists already and hostility to its extension into the territories, Lincoln constructed an ideal slaveholder by whom his speech might imaginably be overheard, a slaveholder who stood within Lincoln's own horizon of persuadability. Not all slaveholders stood within Lincoln's horizon of persuadability. The slaveholder who believed, with Calhoun, that slavery is a positive good did not. But Lincoln was unwilling

to assume that the positive good position was characteristic of slaveholders as a whole.[59] To address this idealized slaveholder, Lincoln had
to give up the idea that the slaveholder was, qua slaveholder, an evildoer with a demonic agenda, and had to see at least some kinds of slaveholder as people with moral capacities and values not far different
from his own. This idealized slaveholder, a figure whom Lincoln recognized as being a member of his own moral species, was the slaveholder
who hated slavery in principle but did not see any immediately available
practical way to end it. He had in mind some of the great Virginians of
the Revolutionary generation, Washington, Madison, and Jefferson,
and their non-Virginian successors, men such as Henry Clay and John
Crittenden (and for that matter Zachary Taylor), who represented the
road not taken for southern politics. While it is easy to stigmatize such
men as lacking the moral force to take the South down a difficult road,
as loving peace and ease more than right, it is important to remember
that such persons were often themselves prisoners of necessity, of debt,
for instance, and of the inability to imagine that former slaves and
their masters might ever be able to live together on terms of political
and social equality. Thomas Jefferson may, thinking of slavery in a famous passage, have trembled for his country when he reflected that
God is just, but he also described himself and people like him as having, in his famous phrase, "a wolf by the ears."

The key theme for Lincoln is that the conditions for freedom are
easily lost and not easily recovered. It is not merely that as a master one
learns habits of brutality and repression that make one incapable of
democracy. It is also that the master, because slavery is perpetually
under threat, must perpetually defend it by threats, must perpetually
demonstrate who is master, both to the slaves and to the nonslaveholders, so that the master is a kind of slave to his mastery. Slaveholding,
like alcohol, binds master as well as slave upon the wheel of necessity,
and the polis life is available only under conditions where necessity is
at bay. The slaveholder, like the alcoholic, has surrendered himself to a
kind of necessity against which even his best intentions are ineffectual.
But the man who has surrendered to necessity is nevertheless a far different figure from the demonic, sexually aggressive, and endlessly re-
sourceful figure one sees in Stowe's Simon Legree:

> Before proceeding, let me say I think I have no prejudice against
> the Southern people. They are just what we would be in their situ-

ation. If slavery did not now exist amongst them, they would not introduce it. If it did now exist amongst us, we should not instantly give it up. This I believe of the masses north and south. Doubtless there are individuals, on both sides, who would not hold slaves under any circumstances; and others who would gladly introduce slavery anew, if it were out of existence. We know that some southern men do free their slaves, go north, and become tip-top abolitionists; while some northern ones go south, and become most cruel slave-masters.

When southern people tell us they are no more responsible for the origin of slavery, than we; I acknowledge the fact. When it is said that the institution exists; and that it is very difficult to get rid of it, in any satisfactory way, I can understand and appreciate the saying. I surely will not blame them for not doing what I should not know how to do myself. If all earthly power were given me, I should not know what to do, as to the existing institution. (1:315–316)

Lincoln's proposals on this score were very feeble indeed—chiefly the emigration of freed slaves to Liberia, that last resort of wishful thinkers (like Madison, or Clay, or Stowe) who wished to somehow rid their country of slaves and of black people in one breath.[60] Even twenty-two years before this, the most promising emancipation movement in Virginia, which came within a few votes of ending slavery in the Old Dominion, had come to grief on the recognition that Liberian emigration—or rather, deportation—was neither practicable nor decent. But the point is that Lincoln was fully aware of the inadequacy of this response, and he presented it not as a possible course of action but as evidence of his bewilderment, bewilderment he shared with the decent among his slaveholding opponents:

My first impulse would be to free all the slaves, and send them to Liberia,—to their own native land. But a moment's reflection would convince me, that whatever of high hope, (as I think there is) there may be in this, in the long run, its sudden execution is impossible. If they were all landed there in a day, they would all perish in the next ten days; and there are not surplus shipping and surplus money enough in the world to carry them there in many times ten days. What then? Free them all, and keep them among us as underlings? Is it quite certain that this betters their condition? I think I would not hold one

in slavery, at any rate; yet the point is not clear enough for me to denounce people upon. (1:316)

It is puzzling that Lincoln was not certain that even keeping freedmen underfoot as a kind of permanent underclass was at least an improvement over keeping them under the power of the lash and the
patroller. We want to say that there ought to be other choices—equality,
for instance—but the point is that it is extremely hard to imagine giving power to those whom you have given reason to hate you. That those
whom one has subjected and repressed really do have reason for this
hate does not make the act of handing power over to them any easier,
and indeed the thought of the anger and desire for revenge that would
seem to be the natural concomitant of repression would provoke nightmares enough to make a common life difficult even without paranoid
fantasies and a demonic vision of the otherness the other. Given this,
the surprise is not how vicious the postwar world of Jim Crow and
Lynch law was, but that it was not far worse. Lincoln certainly thought
it might be.

Lincoln was also aware of the intractable problem of racist feelings,
including his own. The passage I am about to quote is still often cited
as exhibit A in the debunking case against Lincoln. And indeed, the
actual positive content of Lincoln's racism here is not far different from
Douglas's and has some of the same policy implications. But there is a
key difference in tone between Lincoln's avowals here and the more
gleeful claims of the same kind made by Douglas, and that is that Lincoln was not proud of his racism, only realistic about its power and
intractability. Racism seemed irrational to Lincoln, but he knew the
pull of that irrationality because he felt it. To concede that an irrational
feeling is intractable is not to argue that it is rational or right. Lincoln
did not use the depth of these feelings as an excuse for leaving them to-
tally untouched but cautiously suggested ways to modify those feelings
gradually. This is far different from the use other people made of the
assumption that widespread racism made it impossible to imagine how
white people could outgrow it. For instance, Justice Taney's claim, in his
Dred Scott opinion, that black people have no rights that white people
are bound to respect was not meant as a representation of his own
views (indeed, he deplored those views) but of what he—mistakenly—
took to be the views of the Founders. Taney argued that these views

are reprehensible, but that since no constitutional acts have been taken to change the order they established, they still have legal force, reprehensible as they are. Lincoln's view pulled in precisely the opposite direction. Indeed, even his confession of his own ugly racial feelings had something of the air of a strategic concession to it, as if Lincoln were attempting to wheedle the members of his Illinois audience, not just the out-of-state slaveholders, out of their own racism. He used toward them the tone one uses when speaking to a strange dog. The power of irrational feeling, like the act of holding slaves, binds people to necessity and weakens their capacity for freedom. As in the case of slavery itself, Lincoln sees the futility of a direct assault upon these things that corrode the public life. But to concede that is not to concede that they need always triumph, or that they cannot be weakened at the margins until they begin to give way at the center. Lincoln's hostility to racism was a more cautious version of his already very cautious hostility to slavery:

> What next? Free them, and make them politically and socially, our equals? My own feelings will not admit of this; and if mine would, we well know that those of the great mass of white people will not. Whether this feeling accords with justice and sound judgment, is not the sole question, if indeed, it is any part of it. A universal feeling, whether well or ill-founded, can not be safely disregarded. We can not, then, make them equals. It does seem to me that systems of gradual emancipation might be adopted; but for their tardiness in this, I will not undertake to judge our brethren of the south. (1:316)

Lincoln could afford sympathy with this idealized slaveholder because that figure had already made the crucial concession that slavery is wrong and must ultimately be abolished. Lincoln found this concession in the language of the Declaration of Independence, whose preamble he saw as making commitments that are incompatible with the persistence of slavery. Lincoln was willing to concede that the Founders were unable to make good on the promises contained in that document. But he argued that the Founders wanted to make sure that the promise they made would not be forgotten, that it would stand as a reminder to them of unfinished business, and that for all of the ways the Founders had compromised themselves in the design of the federal

Constitution, even there they had adopted pointedly evasive and shame-faced language such as "the importation or migration of persons" for the slave trade, and avoided the use of the word "slave" even where it was glaringly obvious that slavery was the subject. It was the Virginia legis-lature, after all, not just Thomas Jefferson, that insisted upon the prohi-bition of slavery in the Old Northwest at the time of the Northwest Ordinance, under the Articles of Confederation. And, Lincoln argued, it was only because slavery had already planted itself there that Virginia did not insist upon the same thing for Kentucky, North Carolina for Tennessee, and Georgia and South Carolina for the Old Southwest.[61]

Attacking Douglas's contention that allowing the territories to decide for themselves about slavery was simply allowing them the right to self-government, Lincoln invoked the language of the Declaration about what self-government means. But Lincoln used "self-government" to describe a kind of government that the Founders did not in fact establish. Neither Lincoln nor Douglas was obviously right about what the Found-ers intended, because what the Founders intended was an open question even to them. Douglas described the state they set up, but Lincoln de-scribed the meaning of that state. Douglas described their conception, Lincoln their concept.[62] That said, Lincoln's attack upon the idea that self-government includes the right to enslave other people is a devastat-ing one:

> The doctrine of self government is right—absolutely and eternally right—but it has no just application, as here attempted. Or perhaps I should rather say that whether it has such just application depends upon whether a negro is *not* or *is* a man. If he is *not* a man, why in that case, he who *is* a man may, as a matter of self government, do just as he pleases with him. But if the negro *is* a man, is it not to that extent, a total destruction of self-government, to say that he too shall not govern *himself?* When the white man governs himself that is self-government; but when he governs himself, and also governs *another* man, that is more than self-government—that is despotism. If the negro is a *man*, why then my ancient faith teaches me that "all men are created equal;" and that there can be no moral right in connec-tion with one man's making a slave of another.
>
> Judge Douglas frequently, with bitter irony and sarcasm, para-phrases our argument by saying "The white people of Nebraska are

good enough to govern themselves, *but they are not good enough to govern a few miserable negroes!!*"

Well I doubt not that the people of Nebraska are, and will continue to be as good as the average of people elsewhere. I do not say the contrary. What I do say is, that no man is good enough to govern another man, *without that other's consent.* I say this is the leading principle—the sheet anchor of American republicanism. (1:328)

Lincoln saw the Declaration of Independence as making promises of equality that the Founders were not in a position to keep but wished their successors to remember. The promise has two aspects: first, that one can claim only the freedom one is willing to recognize in others, and one is free only insofar as one shares that freedom with others in a culture of persuasion and consent; second, that to the extent one denies the freedom of others, one loses it for one's self. The master is enslaved by his mastery, and is bound by the necessities that go with preserving mastery. The master's bondage also has two aspects—he is unable to stop being a master (to the extent that once slavery is permitted in a society it is very difficult to root it out), and he must continually defend his mastery (as the master class was obliged to do, whether against threats from the free states such as the tariff or the admission of free territories, or from the slaves themselves, whom the masters imagined, even as they insisted that their slaves loved them, were nevertheless continually plotting their deaths).[63] As Lincoln would point out in 1859 in a letter to Henry L. Pierce, "This is a world of compensations; and he who would *be* no slave must consent to *have* no slave. Those who deny freedom to others, deserve it not for themselves; and, under a just God, can not long retain it" (2:19).

The promise of equality is not only a moral promise like other moral promises but a promise of a special kind, having a foundational relationship to the idea of self-rule, and for that reason the argument that the state cannot afford to decide moral questions about which the people are divided does not apply to the promise of equality. About many kinds of moral promise, some of great weight, politics cannot be asked to impose a solution so long as the people are divided about them. Douglas argued, in a famous letter to a group of Chicago clergymen who wrote to criticize the Kansas-Nebraska Act on moral grounds, that there are many issues, some involving even the fate of

one's immortal soul, that free republics will just have to agree to disagree about if they are to remain free republics.[64] But the promise of
equality has a power that many other kinds of moral claim do not have,
because the reciprocity it demands is at the heart of democratic political ideals, and democracy cannot be maintained without it. The power
of the promise of equality arises from its centrality to the democratic
ethos, not from sources in transcendence. This is how the promise of
equality differs from other kinds of moral requirement—that one worship a particular God in a particular way may be demanded by the
Almighty, and the salvation not only of the soul but of the world may
hang on it, but salvation is not of itself a political value. Equality by
contrast is an essentially political value, and the existence of freedom
itself hangs on respect for equality; a democratic regime need not (and
should not) attempt to settle the question of what the one best religion
is, but it cannot survive as a democratic regime if it fundamentally
betrays the values that define it as such a regime.

The boundaries of the promise of equality are not specified, and for
that reason it continues to unfold new layers of obligation. This claim,
that some political promises are saturated with entailments that those
who make them may not be able to make good on, is pressed by Lincoln
into an even stronger view: that in politics one makes certain kinds of
value commitments without fully knowing what their entailments are,
that only much later do we know the meaning of the things we have
promised, and indeed, we find ourselves often to have promised things
we would have denied were in our intentions when we made the promise. Political values have the kind of implicitness that people do. They
have stories that are not over and turn in unanticipated directions that
nevertheless seem to have inevitability in retrospect. If pressed, the
Founders would perhaps have denied that "All men are created equal"
or that "they are endowed by their Creator with certain inalienable
rights" committed them to abolition, or to political rights for women.
Indeed, had an issue been made of those things at the time, the Declaration would probably not have passed (if the fight over Jefferson's denunciation of slavery in the original draft of the Declaration is any
sign). But it is not merely an exercise in strong misreading or special
pleading to argue that the Founders committed themselves in those
words. And it is not hard to apply the same case to Lincoln himself, to
argue that his opposition to slavery is phrased in terms that commit

him to the political and social equality of the races, despite his passionate and explicit disavowal of that commitment when Douglas pressed
him about it. Charged political agreements are of course strategically
ambiguous, otherwise agreement will not happen; but they also are full
of implicitness, and their entailments keep emerging as an unanticipated but startling rebuke from a better self.

Lincoln cannot but have been aware that the kind of slaveholder he
had imagined had been losing ground in the South to the kind of slaveholder who believed that slavery is a positive good. Lincoln addressed
the "positive good" slaveholder by doubting whether he really meant
what he said. If slavery were a positive good, Lincoln argued, then why
did slaveholders share the northern enthusiasm to abolish the international slave trade? (He did not foresee how Breckinridge's supporters
would call for reviving that trade in 1860.) If the slave were merely a
species of domestic animal, then why did slaveholders treat slave dealers
as repugnant creatures? They did not think of horse dealers or cattle
dealers in these terms:

> Now, I admit this is perfectly logical, if there is no difference be-
> tween hogs and negroes. But while you thus require me to deny the
> humanity of the negro, I wish to ask whether you of the south your-
> selves, have ever been willing to do as much? It is kindly provided
> that of all those who come into the world, only a small percentage
> are natural tyrants. That percentage is no larger in the slave States
> than in the free. The great majority, south as well as north, have hu-
> man sympathies, of which they can no more divest themselves than
> they can of their sensibility to physical pain. These sympathies in
> the bosoms of the southern people, manifest in many ways, their
> sense of the wrong of slavery, and their consciousness that, after all,
> there is humanity in the negro. If they deny this, let me address them
> a few plain questions. In 1820 you joined the north, almost unani-
> mously, in declaring the African slave trade piracy, and in annexing
> to it the punishment of death. Why did you do this? If you did not
> feel that it was wrong, why did you join in providing that men should
> be hung for it? The practice was no more than bringing wild negroes
> from Africa, to sell to such as would buy them. But you never thought
> of hanging men for catching and selling wild horses, wild buffaloes
> or wild bears.

Again, you have amongst you, a sneaking individual, of the class of native tyrants, known as the "SLAVE-DEALER." He watches your necessities, and crawls up to buy your slave, at a speculating price. If you cannot help it, you sell to him; but if you can help it, you drive him from your door. You despise him utterly. You do not recognize him as a friend, or even as an honest man. Your children must not play with his; they may rollick freely with the little negroes, but not with the "slave-dealers" children. If you are obliged to deal with him, you try to get through the job without so much as touching him. It is common with you to join hands with the men you meet; but with the slave dealer you avoid the ceremony—instinctively shrinking from the snaky contact. If he grows rich and retires from business, you still remember him, and still keep up the ban of non-intercourse upon him and his family. Now why is this? You do not so treat the man who deals in corn, cattle or tobacco. (1:326)

The "positive good" advocates were fond of invoking the claim that slaves are species of property like any other. They were attracted to this formula because it appears to be sweeping, and compact, and it puts an end to argument. It has the sound of apodictic certainty, and those who brandish it gain from it an air of unhesitant self-confidence. A brandished formula like this gives one the sense of having settled the subject; it also gives one rhetorically the ability to close the door on messy concessions and negotiations. The value of show-stopping replies in an uncertain world is perhaps so high that we often embrace them even when they in fact falsify what our convictions really are. That is the force of Lincoln's argument here: that the brandished reply was false to the actual convictions it was invoked to defend. What the slaveholders denied in resorting to such formulas was the implicitness of their own convictions. Convictions with implicitness are vulnerable convictions, and it is all too human to feel that it is better to swear to a lie than to concede that. I call this rejection of one's own implicitness in the name of rhetorical firmness "the suicidally apodictic." I call it suicidal because it pays more attention to the appearance of force of one's own side than to the actual convictions that side stands for. It is suicidal also because it demands a similar response. The South was not alone in wielding suicidally apodictic statements, and such statements tend to ratchet each other up in a kind of *Wechselwirkung* that ought to be familiar to anyone who has ever found himself enmeshed in an argumentative economy of reciprocated vituperation. To reject the implicitness of other people is ultimately to render political life with them hopeless. But to reject one's own implicitness is worse, for it is an instance of what Kierkegaard calls a despair so deep that it cannot recognize itself as despair.

Given Lincoln's generosity to the imagined slaveholder, his first entry into his quarrel with Douglas was surprisingly harsh, which is not to say that it is unjust:

> This *declared* indifference, but as I must think, covert *real* zeal for the spread of slavery, I can not but hate. I hate it because of the monstrous injustice of slavery itself. I hate it because it deprives our republican example of its just influence in the world—enables the enemies of free institutions, with plausibility, to taunt us as hypocrites—causes the real friends of freedom to doubt our sincerity, and especially because it forces so many really good men amongst ourselves into an open war with the very fundamental principles of civil liberty—criticizing the Declaration of Independence, and insisting that there is no right principle of action but *interest*. (1:315)

Now Douglas had said nothing against the Declaration of Independence, although he assumed that the Founders meant it only to apply to white men. But pro-slavery ideologues like Calhoun, Dew, Harper, and Fitzhugh consistently treated the Declaration as wild and dangerous nonsense, whether applied to racial inequality or to any other form of inequality, and Lincoln saw Douglas's popular sovereignty position as providing intellectual cover for such a position, however differently Douglas himself interpreted the Declaration. Even more startling was the way Lincoln tied criticism of the Declaration to the notion that "there is no right principle of action but interest." Douglas did not really believe that either, so we must resist the temptation to see the debate as a replay of the first book of the *Republic*, with Lincoln himself as Socrates and Douglas as Thrasymachus. But there is a way in which Lincoln is right. Douglas saw himself not as an amoral fixer with an eye out for his political advantage, nor even, although he sometimes talked this way, as a cynic who thought of all moral arguments as disguised ways of advancing economic interests. He saw himself, instead, as a prudent maker of fair-minded deals among people with different values and different interests. The ethos of fair-minded dealmaking is not an obviously amoral one. But it is an ethos that carries moral risks.[65]

Douglas's key motivation in the concessions he made in January 1854 was to gather enough southern votes to organize a government for Kansas and Nebraska Territories without conceding the region to the Calhoun-Davis understanding of the status of slavery in the territories. He felt that the risk of opening the two territories to the possibility of slavery was a prudent concession for a free state politician to make, because he felt that the odds were that the territories would ultimately be organized on a free basis, and that the South could not justly complain if it was shut out of those territories after having been given every opportunity to gain them. Douglas was moved by his understanding of the requirements of persuasive engagement—that persuasive engagement with your opponents requires two things: first, the concession that sometimes you can be defeated and that your world will not end because of it, and second, the promise that you will not make too much of your victories.

Concerning the first feature of persuasive engagement, Douglas signified his willingness to accept defeat if it is really in the cards by accepting the outcome of the struggle in Kansas, whatever it would be. He was free to do this because he had a pretty good idea already that the outcome would be in his favor. But he did not see himself required to give the South even odds, only not to load the dice. Douglas believed in turn that he could persuade the South to accept defeat in Kansas so long as it was not the federal government that imposed that defeat. But as it happened, the southerner who would accept that defeat under even the most favorable circumstances was becoming as rare as the idealized Jeffersonian southerner of Lincoln's imagination. The slaveholders' unwillingness to accept even a fair defeat most gives color to the notion, increasingly credible in northern circles, that the South was involved in a slave power conspiracy aimed at subverting their governments. If you view every defeat, as the South did, as a threat to your vital interests, then you must rule or ruin, and you cannot share a free government with people whom you can never afford to lose to. Neither the North nor the South was willing to accept any kind of defeat in Kansas under any circumstances; for this reason they could not remain in persuasive engagement with each other, and even

Douglas could not ultimately remain in persuasive engagement with either side.

Concerning the second feature of persuasive engagement, the promise not to drive your opponents to the wall in the event of victory over them, Douglas's prognostications about the geography and sociology of the territories were intended to let nature, rather than the dictation of his own section (or perhaps moral hostility to slavery), take the responsibility for the failure of slavery in Kansas; Douglas meant popular sovereignty to be a way to mark his own side's voluntary restraint about using its political dominance in a threatening way. Douglas asked the North to prudently restrain its hostility to slavery; as a northern politician he also asked his section to prudently restrain its power in the national government. He may not, himself, have had much moral hostility to slavery that he had to restrain. But he did have a sense of his section's power, and of how that section's interests might be better served by using that power with discretion. The two things are quite different, but the calculation would have worked the same way on either basis. (This is why, once it became clear that Kansas would indeed choose to exclude slavery, political figures who were much more willing to stand in public against slavery itself than Douglas was, people like Greeley and Seward, were tempted by Douglas's position. It seemed to them to be a way to secure a moral aim without making politically inflammatory moral arguments.)

Lincoln's promise not to abolish slavery in the states where it already existed was also meant to be a promise that he would not use his moral advantage as a pretext to drive his opponents to the wall. But only the older type of slaveholder, who thought of slavery as an evil that could not be rooted out immediately but that should be put in the way of ultimate extinction, could have seen Lincoln's act as that kind of promise. To those who believed that slavery was a positive good, and that it must either expand or die, Lincoln's concession was no concession at all. But to those people Douglas's concession was no concession either, since it would have resulted in the same outcome, the failure of slavery in the territories.

Douglas's act, in his own view, was a willingness to renounce using an inflammatory weapon in the course of a contest he already knew (or rather, believed) he would win by other means. Lincoln was not so sure that the matters-of-fact of geography and sociology pointed to an anti-slavery victory in Kansas, since it is on the same latitude as Illinois, and slavery was strong in the counties of Missouri closest to the Kansas border. Lincoln saw slavery as economically robust and politically aggressive, capable, by its own force, of establishing itself so deeply that it could not be pulled out once it became rooted. After all, even if slavery could not have survived in Kansas in 1854, which Lincoln did not concede, slavery had in the preceding generation been given, in other regions where it was assumed it would not prosper, a powerful new lease on life by the invention of the cotton gin. Should some practical equivalent of the cotton gin have arisen to give slavery new possibilities, Douglas's position would have been a losing one, and Lincoln was not willing to run the risk, particularly since slavery did not have to be terribly well established to have a chokehold over the political institutions of a territory or a state, as the example of the power of slavery in lightly enslaved Missouri should demonstrate.

What Lincoln was most afraid of in the Peoria speech was not that slavery would establish itself in Kansas but that the "positive good" theory about slavery would gain such standing that those who opposed slavery but did not want to go to war about it would be forced to treat slavery as if it were a matter of moral indifference, an interest like an economic interest to be traded off against other interests with which it might be in conflict. That the "positive good" view was gaining ground can be measured by the extent to which a moral critique of slavery, once shared even by slaveholders, became a style of argument so inflammatory that those who were not immediately ready for violence were put under pressure to cease to press such a critique. And Douglas indeed did refuse to press that critique.

What Lincoln feared was that the pressure of the "positive good" argument may drive moral motives out of politics, so that political questions will always be decided by nonmoral things like force or money or geography. Now Douglas did speak as if money and geography would decide the slavery question, and had already decided it in Kansas. But it is possible to argue that Lincoln was wrong in claiming that Douglas had no moral motives, that what Douglas did was to refrain, for strategic purposes, from making moral arguments. At the very least, Douglas intended to use popular sovereignty as a device to persuade the South to accept what he took to be its inevitable defeat in the territories. Had slavery been kept out by a moral fiat, the slaveholding states could complain, Douglas feared, that they had been shut out of a say in the future of the nation and treated as a kind of subject province rather than as members of the polis community. Under popular sovereignty, Douglas felt that he could reply to this claim by arguing that the slave states had been given a fair chance to have their way in the territories, but, having fairly lost out there, should accept their defeat.

In saying that Douglas expected that Kansas would become a free territory, and that he sought ways to persuade the South to accept the inevitable outcome there, I am not arguing that Douglas opposed slavery. Historians of an earlier generation such as George Fort Milton and Gerald Capers, on the basis of private recollections published long after Douglas's death, did argue that Douglas privately opposed slavery. His best biographer, Robert Johannsen, argues that that testimony, with all of its problems, probably does reflect his private feelings.[66] But Douglas was never a public opponent of slavery, although he became in 1860 and 1861 a public opponent of the slave power.

Douglas did not intend the Kansas-Nebraska Act as a covert blow against slavery (although his southern opponents from 1858 on increasingly came to adopt this view). But he did expect Kansas to be populated by white independent farmers who would go there to escape the domination of slaveholders and the competition of slaves, people who did not seek to abolish slavery but did not want to live in a slave state either. And he sought, by means of what later was called the Homestead Act, to secure the interests of such people in the western territories. Such people could go in several directions, either following anti-slavery racists such as Montgomery Blair into the Republican Party or remaining as Union-loyal, non-Copperhead Democrats who were willing to fight secession and to oppose the slave power's domination of the Republic but not to crusade against slavery, people who might not have wished slavery upon their own states but who opposed pressing for emancipation in the South.

Hostility to slaveholder bullying eventually transformed Douglas himself, particularly after Fort Sumter, into a War Democrat. During the 1860 presidential campaign, Jefferson Davis proposed a scheme whereby all three anti-Lincoln candidates would withdraw in favor of some other candidate, possibly Mayor Horatio Seymour of New York. Douglas would have none of this. Approached about another scheme to keep Lincoln from getting an electoral vote majority, and deciding the question in the House, where the by-state voting would give the South more power, Douglas promised to throw the election to Lincoln rather than stand for such a course.[67] On the night after the attack on Fort Sumter, Douglas met with Lincoln, and proposed that he call for 200,000 volunteers to put down the Confederacy, rather than the 75,000 Lincoln had planned on calling, remarking with some bitterness of the seceders, "You do not know the dishonest purposes of these men as I do."[68] Of Lincoln at this time, he remarked to a friend, "I've known Mr. Lincoln a longer time than you have, or than the country has. He'll come out all right, and we will all stand by him."[69] Douglas, indeed, went rather further in support of Lincoln than other Democrats did, who still hoped that a weaker response to the attack on Fort Sumter might at least prevent the upper South from seceding. In his final speech, in Illinois, regretting how often he had bent to mollify the South, Douglas referred to secession as a "crime against constitutional freedom, and the hopes of the friends of freedom throughout the wide world," and, breathing fire, proclaimed that the shortest way to peace "is the most stupendous and unanimous preparation for war."[70]

Douglas's ultimate transformation involved a revolution in convictions. From a grudging or negligent acceptance of slavery as the price of union, and from an alliance with slaveholders in order to support the stability of the Union, War Democrats like Douglas came to view the slaveholders themselves as threats to the Union. It is a step, but a big one, from viewing the power of slaveholders as a threat to the Union to viewing slavery itself as a threat to the Union. Many War Democrats did take this step, but we do not know, because of his early death, whether Douglas would have been one of them. Many non-Copperhead Democrats did not take this step, however, continuing to chase the fantasy of restoring "the Union as it was" straight through the 1864 election, in which they were forced into an uneasy and ultimately suicidal alliance with the Copperheads. But Douglas spent the last few months of his life in a rage against the secessionists; while it is plausible to imagine him being hostile to emancipation and as seeking to restore "the Union as it was," it is hard to imagine him ever mending fences with the Copperheads.[71]

Even those Democrats who did move from opposition to slaveholder tyranny to opposition to slavery, and we cannot say whether Douglas would have gone even that far, often did so tentatively, and thus never made the further step of embracing racial equality. Once the actual attempt at secession was defeated, the racism of this kind of northern Democrat trumped everything else, and they entered into the practical alliance with the former slaveholders that ultimately destroyed Reconstruction.[72]

Certainly in 1854 Douglas was by no stretch of the imagination an anti-slavery politician. If Douglas in 1854 sought anything beyond merely whatever territorial government in Kansas he could get the votes in Congress to establish, he sought not to advance the interests of the slaveholders or to strike a blow against slavery but to advance the interests of people like his constituents in Illinois, people who were southern in their cultural allegiances and southern in their racism but who also did not want to concede the domination of their state to slaveholders. By 1858, though, his arguments had attractions for some opponents of slavery, and, with some help from influential eastern Republicans, Douglas did seek to draw some anti-slavery racist Democrats, who had been drifting to the Republicans, to his side.[73] His opposition to the Lecompton fraud in Kansas had made him, de facto, a formidable practical opponent of the extension of slavery into the territories, and to the extent that the future of slavery depended upon extension, a practical, although not an ideological, opponent of slavery itself. Unlike the Republicans, he was careful never to go on the public record against slavery, but even the Republicans went no further than nonextension, although they intended, as perhaps Douglas did not, nonextension to be a positive blow against the cultural and economic vitality of slavery. Whether or not Douglas had anti-slavery motivations, Seward and Greeley argued, Douglas's views had a practical anti-slavery force.

By 1858 Seward and Greeley saw Douglas, whatever his private moral views were about slavery (which we know to have been ambivalent), as pursuing a functionally anti-slavery course which, in order to be successful, required him to disavow having moral anti-slavery motives. Renouncing moral arguments under those circumstances could have a strategic moral purpose, although those purposes could more fairly be attributed to Seward and Greeley than to Douglas. But why not, in the crooked timber of actual human motivations, attribute something like this to Douglas himself? Certainly after 1857 the slaveholders themselves took Douglas to be an opponent not only of the slave power but of slavery. And perhaps Douglas really did have moral motives he not only never avowed publicly but also never really acknowledged privately. It is plausible to argue that the ferocity of his opposition to the Lecompton fraud arose in part from unacknowledged hostility to slavery itself, something kept down until circumstances let it break out. Douglas's anti-southern rage during the descent to war is what one characteristically feels once one is betrayed by an ally in whose interest one has been, in Lincoln's phrase, crucifying one's feelings. Harsh exigencies do have a way to clarify one's ambivalences and bringing unacknowledged commitments into focus.[74]

The strategy of renouncing moral arguments to serve a moral purpose involves a large moral risk: if one may have moral motives but cannot bring moral arguments into the public arena, one may be forced not only to pretend but to behave as if there is no right public principle of action but interest. For if the price of political engagements with others is a promise to lay one's moral objections to one side, one can of course be held to that promise, in which case one might as well have conceded that one's moral motives were only sentimental illusions. If one must act on the basis of the assumption that one cannot press in public a disputed moral agenda about slavery, it does not matter that one is merely pretending to let that agenda go, for then one can give one's self no good reason to oppose slavery anywhere, and can be forced to argue that just as states can decide the issue of the morality of slavery for themselves, so persons can, and if any one person wishes to hold a slave, no other can say him nay: "If you don't like slavery, then don't hold slaves," the bumper sticker of 1854 might have read.

At first this argument seems rather a stretch. After all, an anti-slavery voter tempted by Douglas's arguments would have known perfectly well what his moral motives were, and those motives would not have lost their force if he confined himself to nonmoral arguments so long as those arguments, even if they are economic rather than moral arguments, continued to be aimed at ultimately securing the moral outcome he sought. But Lincoln's argument was that to confine one's self to a particular style of argument is to establish a particular kind of public self-consciousness. Refraining from moral critique, Lincoln felt, would harden the public mind to the injustice of slavery. The risk was twofold. First, in making a moral sacrifice to secure a moral aim, one risks clouding one's sense of the depth of the moral issue. The issue is hard enough when one must dirty one's hands to serve a moral end, as, say, supporters of the Compromise of 1850 had to do. But it is harder still when one has to pretend that the issue is not a moral one at all. Second, in treating moral stakes as commensurable with other stakes, one risks the distinction between a moral value and a monetary one. Dealmaking often involves trade-offs on collateral issues—you can have your tariff reduction if I get my harbor dredged—but it is hard to treat some moral issue as collateral to a nonmoral one, to say that you get to have slavery if I get to build my railroad.

As a Whig, Lincoln felt that liberal regimes require for their support a deeply ingrained and only partly conscious structure of habits and feelings, without which liberal regimes are unstable. As a Democrat, Douglas was less committed to the idea that liberal regimes require the support of deeply ingrained cultural habits, and for this reason the idea that his strategic retreat from moral argument might have a corrupting effect on the public mind was mystifying to him.[75]

Even though liberal regimes, on the Whiggish view of them, depend upon the widespread prevalence of particular habits of thought, they cannot impose those habits of thought by force of law. One might think of it this way: our government now can legally repress some public forms of racism—no matter how much a white restaurant owner hates black people, he or she must serve them. But our government cannot make that restaurant owner *like* black people, and if too many people become like that restaurant owner, our government will be unable to secure racial equality.[76] A liberal regime must not only shape public institutions, but must also shape the public mind. But it cannot compel the public mind, and if the public mind sets in a particular unwholesome direction it will have no choice but to give way.

Exactly what means a liberal regime may use to secure the cultural preconditions of its stability is of course an exquisite question. There is a strain of liberal thought that argues that liberal regimes must adopt a position of strict neutrality about moral issues that divide the people. This is of course Douglas's view, and it is (in some readings of his work) the view of the earlier Rawls. Lincoln's view is the view of the later Rawls, that liberal regimes need not adopt a position of strict neutrality about every moral conflict, but must promise to refrain from using the repressive power of the state to foreclose such conflicts by force. It is perfectly appropriate for liberal regimes to use the persuasive resources of a public culture against values that, if they triumphed, would make liberal regimes impossible, but those resources do not include the police.

It is the numbing effect upon the public mind of Douglas's treatment of moral reservations as if they were matters of taste and choice, his treatment of the conflict over slavery as a traditional political conflict over interests, that is at the heart of Lincoln's critique of Douglas's strategy. Lincoln's description of the slippery slope upon which Douglas stands is stern but just:

> But you say this question should be left to the people of Nebraska, because they are more particularly interested. If this be the rule, you must leave it to each individual to say for himself whether he will have slaves. What better moral right have thirty-one citizens of Nebraska to say, that the thirty-second shall not hold slaves, than the people of the thirty-one States have to say that slavery shall not go into the thirty-second State at all?
>
> But if it is a sacred right for the people of Nebraska to take and hold slaves there, it is equally their sacred right to buy them where they can buy them cheapest; and that undoubtedly will be on the coast of Africa; provided you will consent to not hang them for going there to buy them. You must remove this restriction too, from the sacred right of self-government. I am aware you say that taking slaves from the States to Nebraska, does not make slaves of freemen; but the African slave-trader can say just as much. He does not catch free negroes and bring them here. He finds them already slaves in the hands of their black captors, and he honestly buys them at the rate of about a red cotton handkerchief a head. This is very cheap, and it is a great abridgement of the sacred right of self-government to hang men for engaging in this profitable trade! (1:330)

Douglas proposed popular sovereignty because, in leaving the question of slavery to be settled by the matters of fact of sociology and geography, he believed that doctrine allowed him to secure a moral aim— the establishment of a free state government in Kansas and the seventeen other states that he felt would follow the lead of Kansas—without adopting moral arguments that in context were inflammatory. But what seemed to Douglas a matter of easily affordable moral generosity seemed to Lincoln a fatal moral concession. Douglas did not really believe (even though he sometimes says as much) that "there is no right principle of action but interest." But his generous restraint of his own moral judgment, exercised in the interest of maintaining persuasive engagement with those who have different moral ideas, forced him to behave as if he did believe such a thing.

That allowing the people of Kansas to choose for themselves whether or not to permit slavery there also commits one to allowing the reopening of the African slave trade seems also at first to be rather a stretch. Douglas nowhere proposed such a thing, and spent considerable effort in 1860 resisting such proposals when Breckinridge's supporters advanced them. (Indeed, after having made a campaign issue of it in 1860, the slaveholders of the seceding Confederacy nevertheless in its constitution forbade reopening the African slave trade.)[77]

But the charge Lincoln made here about the African slave trade was not entirely unfair. Douglas may have quailed at the idea of reopening the African slave trade because, however he argued about slavery when the issue was the fate of slavery in the territories, he never was able to completely give in to the idea that slaves are ordinary property like any other. But his attempt to treat the future of slavery as an entirely economic matter would seem to lead him in that direction. Revulsion against reopening the slave trade and treating the slavery problem as only a question of economics are contradictory tendencies, and Douglas's revulsion reveals among other things that his use of economic arguments to substitute for moral ones was a pretense, adopted to defuse the conflict but not in fact a reflection of his actual convictions. Adopting an argument because it seems trumping, and because it forecloses opposition, is not the same thing as adopting an argument as an expression of conviction, because it is possible to do only so long as one does not have to face up to the consequences of adopting that position consistently. In putting aside his revulsion far enough to treat slavery in purely economic terms, Douglas risked blunting the revulsion in the popular mind against engaging in brutal forms of economic realism like the slave trade, and prepared the public mind calmly to accept things he himself would have been opposed to had he looked at them directly. For in leaving the slavery question to be solved by matters of fact of sociology, geography, politics, and economics, Douglas, while seeking to leave the matter to the individual moral agency of voters and the collective moral agency of Kansas, also in fact wound up replacing moral agency altogether with economic rationality. To treat the slavery issue in economic terms is to concede that it is essentially an issue about property, and to treat the slavery issue as an issue about property is to concede almost everything to the slaveholders, who after all wanted nothing so badly as to be able to see slaves only as a kind of property like any other.

Two very different propositions, "The fate of slavery in Kansas should be settled by the people of Kansas" and "The fate of slavery in Kansas will be settled by rainfall and profitability," were often somehow conflated in Douglas's mind, perhaps because he hesitated to imagine that the people of one region may indeed adopt a different collective morality from those of another, and so retreated to the view that what separated pro-slavery and anti-slavery regions must have been just that slavery could be made to pay in one region and could not be made to pay in another. Douglas was not a consistent or self-critical thinker, and in his mind what we might think of as contradictory ideas, the idea that a political outcome is the upshot of individual moral choice summed into collective moral agency and deliberation and the idea that a political outcome is the upshot of economic rationality, tended to shade into each other.

If it is the sacred right of individuals to exercise their choice in markets, and if any restraint upon that right is tyranny, then indeed what *does* prevent the reestablishment of the slave trade? Certainly not market forces. For even when both the United States and Britain treated engaging in the African slave trade as a capital offense, as piracy, in the words of the 1820 U.S. law against it, the slave trade was lucrative enough that captains from New York and Portland were willing to take part in it.[78] Market fundamentalism really does come down to a version of the claim that justice is really only the will of the stronger, in that it places something other than practical reason at the center of the moral life. And in treating the slavery question as something to be resolved by something other than practical reason, by market forces, Douglas abetted, although he probably did not intend to do so, the triumph of market fundamentalism over moral agency.

Now Douglas did not really believe what Thrasymachus does any more than he believed in the divine right of kings (something Lincoln will accuse him of in the 1858 debates), but his prudential reasons moved him to behave as if he did, and that concession cannot help but cloud the issue of just how much moral ideas really meant to him. Douglas's concession, in leaving the outcome of moral conflicts to matters of fact, was a fatal concession not only because the matters of fact may turn out unpredictably but also because turning to matters of fact to settle moral conflicts falsifies the nature of those conflicts. We have no reason to accord moral respect to the outcomes of natural processes, because those outcomes are the happen-so of laws other than those of morality. To behave otherwise is to subordinate the moral identity that makes us human to natural processes, to dissolve practical reason in the metabolism of nature, to build altars to a bloody necessity tricked out as a beautiful one.

Slavery, this is to say, subjects the polities where it exists to a kind of fatality. Slavery is a kind of force that people or groups of people hold over each other. As a kind of force it is subject to the necessities of force. Slaveholding is a kind of trap door through which polities fall into depths out of which they cannot climb by their own power. The defenders of popular sovereignty argued that decisions about slavery, like other decisions, should be the object of free choice by those who actually stand at the moral crossroads. This vision of free choice is defensible only so long as one can imagine that freely choosing whether or not to deprive others of freedom has no effect upon one's own capacity for freedom. But it is the tendency of slavery to corrupt free institutions, because it is very difficult to undo what it has already done and root out slavery once it is already established, and the force of that necessity brings in its train other consequences that corrupt democratic rule, from the extensive and ugly police regulations required to keep slavery going, to the inevitability with which slavery corrupts the economic and cultural status of free labor and drives out the yeomen who would practice free labor, to the disproportionate power slaveholders demand and are given in the polities where they are a force.

The fatality of slavery is that by freely choosing to introduce it, I make it impossible for my descendants to freely choose to remove it, and I commit them to an endless contest of force with their slaves and with nonslaveholders.

Another important objection to this application of the right of self-government, is that it enables the first FEW, to deprive the succeeding MANY, of a free exercise of the right of self government. The first few

may get slavery IN, and the subsequent many cannot easily get it OUT.
How common is the remark now in the slave States—"If we were only
clear of our slaves, how much better it would be for us." They are actually deprived of the privilege of governing themselves as they would,
by the action of a very few, in the beginning. The same thing was true
of the whole nation at the time our constitution was formed. (1:330)

Much later, in a speech at Kalamazoo on August 27, 1856, Lincoln
had plausibly described how even a few slaveholders, without engaging
in any particularly devious or tyrannical political practices—such as the
supporters of slavery actually did engage in in Kansas—could dominate
the political machinery of the new territory and fix slavery so deeply
there that later generations could not get rid of it:

We will suppose that there are ten men who go into Kansas to settle.
Nine of these are opposed to slavery. One has ten slaves. The slaveholder is a good man in other respects; he is a good neighbor, and being a wealthy man, he is enabled to do the others many neighborly
kindnesses. They like the man, though they don't like the system by
which he holds his fellow-men in bondage. And here let me say, that in
intellectual and physical structure, our Southern brethren do not differ from us. They are, like us, subject to passions, and it is only their
odious institution of slavery, that makes the breach between us. These
ten men of whom I was speaking, live together three or four years;
they intermarry; their family ties are strengthened. And who wonders that in time, the people learn to look upon slavery with complacency? This is the way in which slavery is planted, and gains so firm a
foothold. I think this is a strong card that the Nebraska party have
played, and won upon, in this game. (1:377)

In an editorial in the *Illinois Journal*, published shortly before the Peoria speech, on September 11, 1854, Lincoln had put it this way, referring
to John Calhoun, whom he had debated on the subject two days previously, the same John Calhoun who would later be the pro-slavery
surveyor-general of Kansas Territory (and who had, in a former life in
Illinois, hired Lincoln as a subordinate):

To illustrate the case—Abraham Lincoln has a fine meadow, containing beautiful springs of water, and well fenced, which John Calhoun

had agreed with Abraham (originally owning the land in common) should be his, and the agreement had been consummated in the most solemn manner, regarded by both as sacred. John Calhoun, however, in the course of time, had become owner of an extensive herd of cattle—the prairie grass had become dried up and there was no convenient water to be had. John Calhoun then looks with a longing eye on Lincoln's meadow, and goes to it and throws down the fences, and exposes it to the ravages of his starving and famishing cattle. "You rascal," says Lincoln, "what have you done? what do you do this for?" "Oh," replies Calhoun, "everything is right. I have taken down your fence; but nothing more. It is my true intent and meaning not to drive my cattle into your meadow, nor to exclude them therefrom, but to leave them perfectly free to form their own notions of the feed, and to direct their movements in their own way!" (1:306)

Even the Kansas-Nebraska Act itself, conceived as an exercise in agency, as something that would license the people of Kansas to arrange their own affairs their own way, has a kind of fatality about it:

The people are to decide the question of slavery for themselves; but WHEN they are to decide; or HOW they are to decide; or whether, when the question is once decided, it is to remain so, or is it to be subject to an indefinite succession of new trials, the law does not say, Is it to be decided by the first dozen settlers who arrive there? or is it to await the arrival of a hundred? Is it to be decided by a vote of the people? or a vote of the legislature? or, indeed by a vote of any sort? To these questions, the law gives no answer. There is a mystery about this; for when a member proposed to give the legislature express authority to exclude slavery, it was hooted down by the friends of the bill. This fact is worth remembering. Some yankees, in the east, are sending emigrants to Nebraska, to exclude slavery from it; and, so far as I can judge, they expect the question to be decided by voting, in some way or other. But the Missourians are awake too. They are within a stone's throw of the contested ground. They hold meetings, and pass resolutions, in which not the slightest allusion to voting is made. They resolve that slavery already exists in the territory; that more shall go there; that they, remaining in Missouri will protect it; and that abolitionists shall be hung, or driven away. Through all this, bowie-knives and six-shooters are seen plainly enough; but never a glimpse of the

ballot-box. And, really, what is to be the result of this? Each party
WITHIN, having numerous and determined backers WITHOUT, is it not
probable that the contest will come to blows, and bloodshed? Could
there be a more apt invention to bring about collision and violence, on
the slavery question, than this Nebraska project is? I do not charge, or
believe, that such was intended by Congress; but if they had literally
formed a ring, and placed champions within it to fight out the controversy, the fight could be no more likely to come off than it is. And if
this fight should begin, is it likely to take a very peaceful, Union-saving
turn? Will not the first drop of blood so shed, be the real knell of the
Union? (1:334–335)

The best argument against the Kansas-Nebraska Act was not that it
was part of a design to sneak slavery into Kansas, but that by inviting
the opposing parties to enter into a footrace to determine the future of
the territory it could not help but enflame the conflict it was meant to
solve. Why Douglas never saw this is still a puzzle. It was pretty clear
to Lincoln in the Peoria speech. It would seem to be obvious to anybody. "Will not the first drop of blood so shed, be the real knell of the
Union?" All too truly. Popular sovereignty, through what Harry Jaffa
calls the intoxication of the will, is the means by which freedom bends
itself back into fate.

2.4 The Irony of American History

Douglas renounced moral language because he felt that it was inflammatory. He invented, in place of the inflammatory language of
moral dispute, a less inflammatory language of geography and sociology: Kansas will be free anyway because of the dictates of climate
and culture, and the South would be wiser to accept that than to resist it. This position is morally coherent only so long as the happen-
so of climate and culture advances a moral agenda one in fact holds
on other grounds, that is, only so far as the climate of Kansas will in
fact keep slavery out of the territory. This dependency ties the outcome of morally charged events to processes that in fact are not part
of a moral economy: if Kansas were wetter or warmer, one would
have to concede it to slavery. This dependency, that is to say, enslaves
practical reason to natural destiny, which is contrary to the work of

practical reason, which is to establish the moral autonomy of persons and of polities.

Despite what he sometimes said, it did matter to Douglas which side won out in Kansas, just as it mattered to him which side had already won out in Illinois. But in pretending that the outcome would be only the consequence of natural forces, or only the outcome of a contest of political force, he deprived himself of the resources of moral argument at a time when they became increasingly necessary. If I recuse myself from moral conflicts, even if I do have a moral aim and feel fairly certain of having my way with it, I nevertheless can fairly be said to have treated the power of moral ideas merely as a function of their ability to win out in a contest of force or in a contest of forces of nature, and this is to concede, in the face of my own moral agenda, that there are no moral ideas, and that justice really is only the will of the stronger. If I must treat justice only as if it were the will of the stronger, I transform by that act, no matter what moral motives bring me to it, contests between moral opponents into contests of force. And I deprive my victory in such a contest, if I win it, of its moral authority, because the outcome of contests of force has no claim to moral authority.

The other position, however, has an equally fatal flaw, for in an enflamed dispute I take a moral hard line, I transform that contest into a contest of force, and again we enter a world in which justice has no force, a world governed only by the will of the stronger. Lincoln was no more the stringent idealist, no more Shakespeare's Angelo, than Douglas was Thrasymachus, and Douglas's attempts to describe him that way were no less unfair than Lincoln's own parodies of Douglas's position. But both had already made fatal concessions. For whether one recuses one's self from a moral claim or presses it with however many qualifications, each position risks ushering us into a world in which outcomes are determined by contests of force.

Does historical irony amount to despair about the ability of liberal regimes to weather fraught moral conflicts? It certainly amounts to recognition that a general and repeatable solution to the problem of intractable moral conflict is likely to continue to evade us. But we have no reason to believe that war over slavery was inevitable merely because of the intensity of the evil of slavery or the magnitude of the interests or forces arrayed on its behalf. For intractable and bloody moral conflicts over religious issues in which the highest stakes seemed to be at risk, conflicts that, like the conflict over slavery, involved enormous secular interests as well, were also pressing in the era when liberalism came into being. Deep and intractable moral conflicts were among the problems liberalism was designed to manage, and recognition of how high the price of the failure to manage those conflicts would be was among the motivations that made liberalism attractive in the first place. So the fact that a moral conflict is deep is not itself an argument that the conflict must evade the attempts of liberal politics to mediate it.

Managing a deep moral conflict is not, however, likely to be a matter of discovering some global solution to it, which all sides will immediately recognize themselves as bound to accept. For it is a sad fact of human nature that when we discover a deep regulative principle that ought to govern the conflict at hand, when we climb to a higher level of abstraction in order to discover a commanding appeal to a common value shared with our opponents, we usually use that principle to sharpen rather than to resolve the conflict, because in enflamed situations the temptations such principles offer us to argue that our opponents are completely beyond the moral pale (and are therefore not people with whom we should have to engage in dealmaking) are rhetorically irresistible. Because we so often transform what ought to be a common principle into a private weapon, we should not count on discovering a principle deeper than our conflict that we might use to regulate it.

But if it is unwise to seek a global resolution to a conflict, it is possible to make local arrangements which, once made, pave the way for other local arrangements, which in turn pave the way for a global resolution that appears unimaginable at the beginning. A resolution to a deep moral conflict, this is to say, is more likely to arise from a strategy of seeking slightly irrational, ad hoc, catch-as-catch-can bargains whose chief attraction is that they are less disastrous than a failure to engage in dealmaking would be, a strategy that is closer to Douglas's strategy in 1854 than to Lincoln's, did not Douglas, with unerring instinct, never fail to choose means that would enflame the very conflicts he was trying to smooth over.

To form the basis of a stable political order, however, something more than a modus vivendi is necessary; for one thing, it is necessary to persuade one's self that the concessions one is prepared to offer in the name of a modus vivendi do not amount to a fatal moral sacrifice. One cannot always know in advance which moral sacrifices are fatal ones. Douglas's sacrifices did not seem fatal to him, and indeed, in his own case, since he did not allow himself to be forced into deeper and deeper concessions by increasing resistance from the fire-eaters, the sacrifices he offered were not in fact fatal, although other politicians might have shown less resistance, and the sacrifices he offered arguably did offer the South an invitation to raise the stakes. Ultimately, the disaster of the Kansas-Nebraska Act was not that it encouraged the supporters of freedom in the territories to give up their moral convictions in the name of supporting popular sovereignty in Kansas (as Lincoln said it might) but that it unintentionally encouraged the settlers of Kansas to settle their differences with each other by force, which in turn enflamed the conflict the Kansas-Nebraska Act was designed to evade, making it necessary for each side to demand more and more stringent concessions and to be less and less willing to offer its own. The four years of civil conflict in Kansas so hardened sectional divisions that by the summer of 1858, when the people of Kansas had made their wishes clear by coming out overwhelmingly against slavery in their region, the major politicians of the South were no longer unwilling to abide by the bargain that Douglas had made with them in good faith.

Enflamed moral conflicts only lend themselves to modus vivendi solutions. Modus vivendi solutions involve moral sacrifices whose depth is never fully obvious when we make them, because we cannot tell in advance how making them will change our minds, whether they will weaken our moral fiber by bending it or will strengthen our moral position by enabling us to skate over the thin ice to a safer place. The moral sacrifice of modus vivendi politics such as Douglas's is a wager. We cannot know whether that sacrifice was worth it merely by knowing how high the stakes were. We can only know whether the sacrifice was worth it once we know whether it enabled us to establish a habit of successful dealmaking with our opponents, from which something more than a mere modus vivendi may ultimately be expected. We cannot know whether our sacrifice was foolish or wise until later, because the success of our strategy is a function of whether our opponent is willing to respond in kind, which is something that is in our opponent's power and not in our own.

A stable political order must finally rest not on a modus vivendi but on common political if not moral values, on something like the common political vision that Lincoln argues that North and South do, in their good moments, really share. But we do not discover those values merely by invoking the better angels of our nature. We discover them only after a history of successful dealmaking persuades us that we were not fools to have taken moral risks with each other. Douglas's modus vivendi solution in 1854, seen from within its own premises, was more promising than it has usually been taken to be. But it could redeem that promise only if it enabled both sides to move to a common moral position that was not merely a modus vivendi, to a position, this is to say, that is ultimately closer to Lincoln's than to Douglas's. I think it is still an open question whether that transition was possible or not. But it would have had to have used a modus vivendi compromise that was better than the Kansas-Nebraska Act, which tempted the Border Ruffians and the Jayhawkers to settle their differences with Bowie knives, and forced each side nationally into a position where compromise became no longer possible.

The irony of history is that it turns on moral wagers whose wisdom cannot be clear when they are made, moral wagers that risk not only one's outcome but also one's moral standing. Douglas's risk in 1854 turned out to be a losing one, and he paid not only a prudential but a moral price for it. Lincoln in 1861 was forced to make a similar wager, that the violence of a great civil war would not so unhinge the Republic that even a victory would cost it its soul. As he argues in the Second Inaugural, he could have known at the time neither whether his act was prudent nor whether it was ultimately speaking moral, not only because he could not know whether his side would win the war, or only because he could not know whether the justice of his cause would ultimately outweigh the mixed motives, self-serving, and self-deceit that inevitably attend all human acts, but also because he could not know to what extent his moral purposes would inevitably be transformed by the ugliness and brutality that war always involves. Warmaking was also a great wager, a leap of faith comparable to that of another Abraham, a leap made, like that other Abraham's, in the face of irony.

This irony is a function not only of the concrete historical situation of the political crisis of the 1850s, but of tensions within the concept of practical reason that under pressure rise to the level of stark contradictions. It is the work of practical reason to give binding law. But the element of practical reason is freedom. If the persuasive resources available to us are unable to win the uncoerced consent of the other to a dictate of practical reason, the only alternative to us is force, which, however, cares nothing for practical reason. Except in a tradition of persuasive engagement, which in the 1850s had already become strained, moral proclamations reduce to incitements to violence, and freedom reduces to contests of violence.

The binding dictate of right and the unforced consent of the will to right are always at the point of disengagement from each other. Lincoln did not stand for tyrannizing right, and Douglas did not stand for tyrannizing will. But neither could keep right and will aligned, and neither knew how to restore persuasive engagement once it became discredited. Democratic polities will often come to grief over moral conflicts, because moral issues cannot be decided by votes, and a moralizing tyranny destroys moral autonomy. We cannot know in advance whether we will find a way out of this contradiction, although we know of similar occasions in which others have managed to do so. Neither Lincoln nor Douglas could find such a way out, although both knew it was a contradiction, and both, with considerable force of mind and even considerable intellectual integrity, tried as hard as they could. The consequence of their failure was that 623,000 Americans killed each other. But that did not solve the problem either.

CHAPTER 3

Lincoln's Conspiracy Charge

*T*HE "HOUSE DIVIDED" SPEECH, given on June 16, 1858, in Springfield, was Lincoln's formal acceptance of the Republican nomination for the Senate. The speech was strikingly different, in strategy, in the way it conceived of the opponents it was aimed against, and in tone, from the Peoria speech, both for its truculence—uncharacteristic of Lincoln—and for the breathtaking implausibility of its central charge, its claim that Douglas was a party to a conspiracy to force slavery into every part of the Union, the free states as much as the territories. Lincoln continued to press, even to sharpen, this absurd charge throughout the 1858 campaign. Now perhaps if one were already predisposed to think the worst of Douglas, one might say that there were circumstances enough to give color to this charge, but they do not in fact survive much examination. The question remains, however, whether Lincoln pressed that charge only for strategic reasons, using it to advance his own candidacy even though he knew it was false, or whether the political climate was noxious enough that even Lincoln, no fool and no paranoid, actually believed such stuff.

Beyond the concrete allegation, Lincoln's conspiracy charge, like Douglas's conspiracy charge, was driven more by fear about what the political world might be in the process of becoming than by the particulars of imaginary conspiracies. As Douglas's charge ultimately reflected his fear that an ideological, no-holds-barred, all-or-nothing style of politics would make persuasive engagement, never mind compromise, between political opponents impossible, so Lincoln's charge ultimately reflected his fear of a politics in which only interest appeals, not moral appeals, would be allowed to have persuasive force, a kind of politics in which right really does become only the will of the stronger. If the "House Divided" speech seemed designed to make Douglas's underlying fear plausible, so Douglas's speeches of that spring and summer, even his speeches against imposing slavery upon Kansas, gave plausibility to Lincoln's underlying fear.

3.1 The "House Divided" Metaphor

The "House Divided" metaphor might lead one to anticipate that the argument of the speech would be that the slavery problem was so deep that it would continue to make the United States politically unstable until slavery was abolished. That argument, of course, was perfectly plausible, both in its own day and now. But that was not the argument Lincoln devoted the speech to developing.

The speech was mostly invested in developing two different sorts of conspiracy theory, one of them plausible, one of them implausible. Both are versions of what is called the slave power conspiracy theory. The larger-scale, and more plausible, argument, which I will call the "general" slave power conspiracy theory, was sketched out in the opening paragraphs of the speech. That argument held that it is in the nature of slavery itself, as an economic, social, and political institution, to entrain the entire society around itself. The general slave power conspiracy theory argued that the political logic of slave societies dictates that slaveholders must always, in defense of slavery, seek to dominate any republic in which they play a part. The consequence for America is that the slave states must inevitably seek to subvert the political order of the Republic or resign themselves to the death of slavery.

This general slave power conspiracy argument may not have been entirely a confabulation of what Richard Hofstadter called "the paranoid style," since there really is a fundamental incompatibility between slavery and democracy that committed the slave states to a destabilizing and ultimately suicidal quest for mastery of the Republic, even if, as historians now believe, it was slavery that made the Republic possible in the first place.

A more concrete version of the general slave power conspiracy theory might have argued that the slave power actually was meditating a
plan to force slavery back into the free states. There is no plausible evidence that the politicians of the slave states were pursuing such an aim
in 1858. However, it could be argued that if the slaveholders had to
seek mastery of the Republic in order to defend slavery, a realistic view
of their situation would have dictated that sooner or later they would
have had to attempt to nationalize slavery. That said, one can use arguments about the threats that one ideology must *sooner or later* pose
to another to prove almost anything, and arguments of that kind are
often self-fulfilling prophecies.

The main charge of the speech was more specific than this, and more
problematic. Lincoln devoted most of the "House Divided" speech to
the claim that Stephen Douglas, in concert with Presidents Pierce and
Buchanan and with Chief Justice Taney, had since some time before
1854 been engineering not only the establishment of slavery in the remaining western territories but also the reintroduction of slavery into
all of the free states by judicial fiat. Lincoln developed what I will call
the "special" slave power conspiracy theory in considerable detail, and
most of his evidence was extremely flimsy.[1]

The opening lines of the speech appear to state the general slave
power conspiracy theory:

> If we could first know *where* we are, and *whither* we are tending, we
> could then better judge *what* to do, and *how* to do it.
>
> We are now far into the *fifth* year, since a policy was initiated, with
> the *avowed* object, and *confident* promise, of putting an end to slavery
> agitation.
>
> Under the operation of that policy, that agitation has not only, *not
> ceased*, but has *constantly augmented.*
>
> In *my* opinion, it *will* not cease, until a *crisis* shall have been
> reached, and passed.
>
> "A house divided against itself cannot stand."
>
> I believe this government cannot endure, permanently half *slave*
> and half *free*.
>
> I do not expect the Union to be *dissolved*—I do not expect the
> house to *fall*—but I *do* expect it will cease to be divided.
>
> It will become *all* one thing or *all* the other.

> Either the *opponents* of slavery, will arrest the further spread of it,
> and place it where the public mind shall rest in the belief that it is in
> the course of ultimate extinction; or its *advocates* will push it forward,
> till it shall become alike lawful in *all* the States, *old* as well as *new*—
> *North* as well as *South*. (1:426)

The first thing to notice about this grand opening is that it poses a dichotomy under which only the two extreme possibilities, total victory by the free states and total victory by the slave power, are imaginable, and any ambivalent or dealmaking strategy short of pursuit of complete domination amounts at best to surrender and at worst to a scheme of betrayal.

Two different kinds of people invested themselves in ambivalent strategies about slavery of the kind that this argument is designed to rule out, and Lincoln's metaphor was as likely to threaten as to persuade each kind. North of the Mason-Dixon line, Lincoln's argument was aimed at those who opposed slavery, or at least the extension of slavery into the territories, but who might not have been ready to initiate a high-stakes confrontation that might endanger the Union. Lincoln put such people on notice that their timidity itself endangers the Union and also makes them pragmatic allies (if not covert agents) of the slave power. The argument was aimed chiefly, of course, at anti-slavery followers of Douglas, who were prepared to draw the line over the Lecompton Constitution but not prepared to confront slavery in a more sweeping way. But it also posed challenges for what was left of the Whig Party, and for conservative Republicans of the kind who might have supported Bates or McLean, to whom it offered a stark choice of no-holds-barred confrontation or abject submission in language about equally likely to nerve them to action or to cause their nerve to fail.

Allen Guelzo argues that Lincoln sought a strategy that would play well both in the hardmindedly anti-slavery counties of Illinois's northern tier and in the more guardedly anti-slavery regions of the "Whig Belt" in the center of the state.[2] Posing this challenge to the anti-slavery Whigs and conservative Republicans upon whom the election turned had the virtue of drawing the issue with Douglas clearly, at the price, as Guelzo points out, of possibly scaring them over to Douglas's side. The aim was to draw the line starkly enough to appeal to the anti-slavery voters in the northern counties, and to nerve the conservative

Republicans in the Whig Belt to face a confrontation that may have been inevitable anyway (but also pushing relatively moderate policy proposals to soothe their fears about embracing anti-slavery radicalism), while at the same time forcing out the anti-Lecompton Democrats whom Lincoln did not wish to welcome into the Republican Party.[3]

South of the Mason-Dixon line, Lincoln's argument was addressed to moderate slaveholders like Joshua Speed, or for that matter Thomas Jefferson, who disliked slavery but could not imagine a (to them) satisfactory way to end it. Slaveholders like Speed were faced in the "House Divided" speech with a stark choice of slavery or Union. Here again Lincoln's argument seems to be about equally likely to scare away its audience as to persuade it. The rhetoric was threatening enough to such slaveholders if they believed its central dichotomy, for it said to them, in effect, "Choose your side, once and for all, and immediately, and damn the risks." But it was even more threatening to them if they believed that Lincoln was wrong about the starkness and immediacy of the choice faced by the Union. I may not think a confrontation is inevitable, but if you do, and you come to power, you may well make that confrontation inevitable anyway.

Ambivalent slaveholders like Speed, Lincoln argued, must seek either an all-free Union, forcing their ambivalences in one direction, or an all-slave Union (but perhaps not this Union), forcing their ambivalences in the other. The same choices, although in a stronger form of course, faced those slaveholders like Alexander Stephens who believed that slavery was a positive good but who also did not wish to destroy the Union they shared with nonslaveholders. Under this kind of pressure, Speed's kind of slaveholder may just have thrown his lot in with the Union, as Speed in fact did. But Stephens's kind of slaveholder was just as likely to find himself, as Stephens himself did, driven against his inclinations into the secessionist camp.

The second thing to notice about the opening passage is that Lincoln's argument changed how one must conceive of the slaveholder and of the quarrels one might have with him. If the only choice really was between an all-free or an all-slave Union, then one could not treat the slaveholder as one might have treated other political agents, as someone with whom one could strike bargains, taking half the loaf today in hope of a better deal tomorrow, trading a concession in one area for a concession in another, since every concession under those circumstances could only be a fatal concession. If what the slaveholders really sought, whatever they might have said about it, was domination of the Union, rather than, say, the best deal they could work out in the ongoing dance of confrontation and concession, then they could no longer safely be approached with ordinary political worldliness.

In the Peoria speech Lincoln had engaged an imagined opponent, the slaveholder who was morally uncomfortable about slavery but could not see his way clear to ending slavery, and to that figure Lincoln offered a politics of accommodation and pragmatic adjustment, so mediating the ultimate extinction of slavery as to largely dissipate emancipation's threat to the interests of existing slaveholders. The repetition in the "House Divided" speech of the theme of the ultimate extinction, rather than the immediate abolition, of slavery seems to promise the same politics of pragmatic adjustment that was embraced in the Peoria speech. But the "House Divided" speech could not in fact offer that kind of politics, because it did not imagine an opponent with whom that kind of politics could be practiced. One cannot engage in ordinary worldly negotiation when the issues can only be decided in an all-or-nothing way. And one especially cannot do so if one's opponents are demonic ghouls hatching plots against you. Once you fling that kind of charge, there is no going back.

The third thing to notice about the opening charge is that it was inflammatory, because it described a situation in which the free states were under the kind of radical threat to which they could only respond by threatening in their turn. One's opponents never fail to understand, once you announce that you understand yourself to be under mortal threat *from* them, that you intend to be a mortal threat *to* them. Certainly most southern politicians understood this, since they had themselves been employing precisely this brinksmanship strategy for thirty-eight years.

Exactly how confrontational the "House Divided" speech was intended to be, even in putting forward the general rather than the specific conspiracy charge, becomes clear when one examines Lincoln's earlier use of the same logic in his letter to George Robertson of August 15, 1855. This letter was written during that period when Lincoln was mulling joining the new Republican Party. The famous letter to Joshua Speed, also discussed in section 4.1 below, in which Lincoln described himself, despairing of the Whig Party's future, as still a Whig,

was written only nine days later, and Lincoln had, only four days before, somewhat coyly rebuffed a feeler from Owen Lovejoy about joining the Republican Party.

Robertson, like Speed, was a cautious, upper-South opponent of slavery. Visiting Springfield while Lincoln was away, he had left for Lincoln a copy of his speeches and papers, in which Lincoln found an 1819
speech against the extension of slavery. The letter opens essentially as a
thank-you note for the present, and, like all good thank-you notes, begins with a characterization of what was special about the gift:

> It was new to me that the exact question which led to the Missouri
> compromise, had arisen before it arose in regard to Missouri; and
> that you had taken so prominent a part in it. Your short, but able and
> patriotic speech upon that occasion, has not been improved upon since,
> by those holding the same views; and, with all the lights you then had,
> the views you took appear to me as very reasonable. (1:359)

Lincoln might have left it there, with the note of gratitude to an
old campaigner in his own cause. But he could not help taking a confrontational tone with nominally anti-slavery Kentuckians who had let
Clay's last attempt to abolish slavery in Kentucky, in 1849, go down to
failure. The letter to Robertson has some of the same frustrated tone
as his letter to Speed a few days later, to whom he also said, in effect, if
you dislike slavery, then why have you not done anything about it
when you have had a chance?

Lincoln did not merely treat Robertson as a survival of a morally
better, more hostile to slavery, generation of southerner. He treated
him as someone who, through fatuous wishful thinking, has lost his
resolution and let harder-minded southerners get the better of him. It
is hard not to hear the asperity in the next few sentences:

> You are not a friend of slavery in the abstract. In that speech you
> spoke of *"the peaceful extinction of slavery"* and used other expressions
> indicating your belief that the thing was, at some time, to have an
> end. Since then we have had thirty six years of experience; and this
> experience has demonstrated, I think, that there is no peaceful ex-
> tinction of slavery in prospect for us. The signal failure of Henry
> Clay, and other good and great men, in 1849, to effect any thing in

favor of gradual emancipation in Kentucky, together with a thousand other signs, extinguishes that hope utterly. On the question of liberty, as a principle, we are not what we have been. When we were the political slaves of King George, and wanted to be free, we called the maxim that "all men are created equal" a self evident truth; but now when we have grown fat, and have lost all dread of being slaves ourselves, we have become so greedy to be *masters* that we call the same maxim "a self-evident lie." The fourth of July has not quite dwindled away; it is still a great day—*for burning fire-crackers!!!* (1:359)

The last sentence about the Fourth of July shares some of the same bitterness of Frederick Douglass's famous oration about "your Fourth of July." And it shares some of the rhetoric of Lincoln's own 1838 Lyceum speech about the decline in the love of freedom since the days of the Founders.[4] Grammatically, the edge of the anger seems to be directed at "we," which is to say, at we Americans of the current generation who have lost sight of the meaning of the Declaration of Independence. But, as so often when we passionately rebuke a *we*, what we really are trying to rebuke is a *you*. "You are not a friend of slavery in the abstract. (But you never take any concrete measure against it.) You speak of *the peaceful extinction of slavery*. (But you let Clay's attempts to end it go down to defeat.)" It is not just Americans in general who are "so greedy to be *masters*." It is nominally anti-slavery southerners like Robertson and Speed, who have allowed their opponents to get away with treating "all men are created equal" as if it were "a self-evident lie." Lincoln does not accuse Robertson of losing faith in the Declaration of Independence. But he does accuse him of allowing people who treat the promises of the Declaration as self-evident lies to dominate the public agenda.

The August 24, 1855, letter to Speed considerably sharpens the impatience, accusing Speed of hypocrisy (in that he will avow in a private letter what he will not avow in public), of cowardice (in that he will not face down the loyalty politics pressures that have beaten down the better judgment of many, maybe even most, southerners), of complicity in violent repression of freedom (in being unwilling to support anyone for office who does not publicly promise to back up the lynch-law Stringfellow and the other Border Ruffians have been imposing in order to secure minority tyranny in Kansas by Missouri slaveholders), and, coming right to the edge of unforgivable insult, of being a kind of slave:

You say if Kansas fairly votes herself a free state, as a christian you will rather rejoice at it. All decent slave-holders *talk* that way; and I do not doubt their candor. But they never *vote* that way. Although in a private letter, or conversation, you will express your preference that Kansas shall be free, you would vote for no man for Congress who would say the same thing publicly. No such man could be elected from any district in any slave-state. You think Stringfellow & Co ought to be hung; and yet, at the next presidential election you will vote for the exact type and representative of Stringfellow. The slave-breeders and slave-traders, are a small, odious and detested class, among you; and yet in politics, they dictate the course of all of you, and are as completely your masters, as you are the masters of your own negroes. (1:363)

As in the Speed letter, where Lincoln had unfavorably compared American democracy to Russian autocracy, where at least despotism can be taken pure, without the base alloy of hypocrisy, so in the Robertson letter, America merely seems a less honest Russia:

So far as peaceful, voluntary emancipation is concerned, the condition of the negro slave in America, scarcely less terrible to the contemplation of a free mind, is now as fixed, and hopeless of change for the better, as that of the lost souls of the finally impenitent. The Autocrat of all the Russias will resign his crown, and proclaim his subjects free republicans sooner than will our American masters voluntarily give up their slaves. (1:359–360)

The never-stated but strongly implied conclusion of the Robertson letter is not only that nominally anti-slavery southerners are a hopeless lot but also that only bloodshed will free the slaves: "Our political problem now is "Can we, as a nation, continue together *permanently—forever*—half slave, and half free?" The problem is too mighty for me. May God, in his mercy, superintend the solution" (1:360).

It is hard to take the piety of that last qualification seriously. At best it is a throwing-up of hands at the question: this one is just too hard for me, so God, if there is one, will conveniently have to step in and solve it for us. But the phrase also invites the ominous consideration of just how God might plan to superintend that solution, in which case "May

God superintend the solution" is a euphemism, exactly like Locke's euphemistic claim that those who oppose tyrants must make an "appeal to heaven," by which he meant an appeal to arms. That is the context of Lincoln's early use of the logic of the "House Divided" speech—an impatient and bitter confrontation, and not with the fire-eaters or with those who thought of slavery as a positive good, but with decent-minded southerners whom Lincoln knew certainly knew better than to defend slavery but about whom he felt he no longer had any option other than to give them up to their fate. The reason that the division of the "House Divided" must issue in an irrepressible conflict is that moderately anti-slavery southerners are either halfhearted in their opposition, or entirely ineffectual in putting that opposition into action, and no reliance can be placed upon them even to take the most cautious and minimal actions against slavery in their own states or to resist the most brutally repressive designs of the slave power against the free states. The meaning of the "House Divided" figure is that there are no decent southerners to rely upon in any aspect of the quarrel over slavery, and the campaign against slavery, and against the strangulation of northern liberty by the slave power, is something northern politicians will have to manage entirely on their own, without the help of moderate southerners, and without consulting those moderate southerners' interests. If moderate southerners saw the "House Divided" speech as a kind of opening of hostilities, it is because deep down, in its emotional logic if not in its policy prescriptions, it was one.

Lincoln defended the "House Divided" speech by arguing that it merely put forward a prediction, that its arguments were in the indicative rather than in the optative mood: the conflict between free states and slave states will continue until the entire Union goes either one way or the other. In a speech he gave at Springfield on July 17, 1858, defending the "House Divided" speech against Douglas's strictures, Lincoln remarked: "I did not express my *wish* on anything. In that passage I indicated no wish or purpose of my own I simply expressed my *expectation*. Cannot the Judge [Douglas] perceive the distinction between a *purpose* and an *expectation?* I have often expressed an expectation to die, but I have never expressed a *wish* to die" (1:470).

The proposition may be true, but the defense is not honest. If, during the Berlin crisis of the late 1940s, President Truman had announced that the conflict between communism and capitalism was so intractable that it would continue to escalate until one of the two systems was wiped off the face of the earth, communists would not have to be subject to Stalin's paranoia to see the statement as threatening, no matter whether the statement were phrased as a mere prediction, and no matter whether it was in fact true. Lincoln's argument was uncharacteristically disingenuous and, moreover, politically incoherent, because it was just threatening enough to set the already-hysterical South on edge, and just pacific enough to prevent the North from nerving itself to face the conflict. As strategy, the only word for this is fatuous.

3.2 The Unfolding of the Bleeding Kansas War

Both sides had poised themselves for a hand-to-hand struggle in Kansas, and each side overestimated the organizational powers of the other. Eli Thayer's New England Emigrant Aid Company, which did found the town of Lawrence, sent about 1,650 settlers to Kansas during the years of its greatest activity, but many of these settlers did not remain long in the territory.[5] Despite wide press coverage, prominent stockholders, vocal public support, and a great deal of hype, firm anti-slavery settlers from the upper North amounted to only 16 percent of the Kansas population by 1860. "Beecher's Bibles," the Sharps rifles the New England Emigrant Aid Company sent with their settlers for self-protection, stirred up patriotic feeling in the North and fear and rage in the South, but in fact Thayer's men were never in a position to determine the outcome of the course of events.

Thayer's Deep South counterpart, Jefferson Buford of Eufala, Alabama, promised subsidies for emigrants to Kansas from the Deep South, and managed in 1856 to bring to Kansas 400 settlers who brought their own rifles and left the actual Bibles Buford had equipped them with on the Missouri River steamboats. But mostly Buford's effort was the occasion for fiery speeches by prominent windbags pro and con (depending on the section), and Buford and his associates lost their investments to little purpose. Only about 13.5 percent of the 1860 settlers of Kansas came from the Deep South. In the final analysis pro-slavery emigration to Kansas, where the future of slavery was anything but secure and where the land was of questionable use for growing slave crops, was a far riskier proposition than emigration to Texas, where fortunes could still be made and where slavery was already well established.

Most settlers to Kansas (about 65 percent) came from the border states, and although they tended to oppose slavery, they also were strongly hostile to blacks and, like their counterparts in Illinois, sought to exclude free blacks from the territory. If the New England emigrants were represented by their leader, the future governor Charles Robinson, who opposed the exclusion of free blacks (and favored suffrage for women), the border state contingent can be represented by his bitter rival, the pugnacious and (at that time) virulently racist free state militia leader Jim Lane.[6] Lane as a Democratic Indiana congressman had in fact voted for the Kansas-Nebraska Act, and came to Kansas as a Douglas Democrat. The settlers he represented opposed slavery but were drawn to Kansas by the opportunities for new farmland, for land speculation, and for development generally that brought other settlers to the plains and to the West. They opposed slavery because they felt that slave labor degraded their own labor. And for all their opposition to slavery, they were often straight-out negrophobes. Their free state racism was not terribly different from that of the settlers of Oregon and California, and, given the chance, they might have become typical Douglas supporters.

More formidable than the Deep South proponents of slavery were pro-slavery politicians from Missouri such as editor Benjamin F. Stringfellow and Senator David Atchison. Slavery was weak in Missouri as a whole but strong in the counties along the Missouri River and in the half-dozen counties along the Kansas border. The relative weakness of slavery in Missouri accounts somewhat for the violent rhetoric and ruthless behavior of Atchison and his supporters, since they were perpetually in a state of hysterical panic.[7] They used their inflammatory rhetoric to encourage the foundation of armed militias such as the Platte County Self-Defensive Association, the Kickapoo Rangers, and the Blue Lodge, who promised to kill abolitionist settlers in Kansas and did manage, through their control of the ferry crossings, to intimidate and otherwise prevent suspected opponents of slavery from entering the territory.[8]

The federal appointees Pierce sent to the territory were mixed characters. The first governor, Andrew Reeder, was a nobody with very limited experience. He was, however, committed to neutrality on the slavery question, a commitment nobody on either side believed he took seriously. The first chief justice, Samuel Lecompte, was a pro-slavery zealot of the most ruthless and unprincipled kind.[9] The surveyor-general of the Land Office, John Calhoun, who earlier in Illinois had employed the young Abraham Lincoln as a surveyor, had been appointed as a way to toss Douglas's supporters a bone of patronage, but became in the end a potent ally of Lecompte against Douglas.[10]

The first elections Reeder supervised in the territory were highly flawed. Reeder knew that there would be a problem with voters whose claims to residence in the territory were shaky. When he was approached by a pro-slavery delegation about moving the first territorial elections up (so that they could steal a march on anti-slavery settlers), he told the leader of the delegation, one F. Gwinner, that he had the man's land claim in his pocket, a three of diamonds playing card with the words "Gwinner's Claim—October 21 1854" scrawled upon it that Reeder's aide had found while hunting. Reeder quipped that Gwinner should have played a higher card, since anyone with the four of diamonds could jump his claim. But his meaning was clear: only people who actually live in Kansas should vote there.[11] The election for delegate to Congress on November 29, 1854, elected John Whitfield, the pro-slavery candidate, by a margin of 2,258 to 305, in an election in which there were 1,700 bogus pro-slavery votes and considerable intimidation of free state voters as well.[12] Reeder protested the fraud, but did not set aside the election.

The elections for the territorial legislature on the next March 30 were considerably more corrupt, with election judges being driven from their posts by threat of lynching. In Bloomington, the pro-slavery mob, led by Samuel Jones, a livery stable keeper from Weston, Missouri, and later the pro-slavery sheriff of Douglas County, managed, after breaking windows and brandishing pistols in the faces of the election judges, to make off with the ballot box itself. In Leavenworth, five times the number of people recorded in the census cast their votes. Altogether nearly 5,000 of the 6,000 votes cast in that election (at a time when there were fewer than 3,000 registered voters in the territory) were fraudulent, and the free staters, kept from the ballot by fear and force, boycotted the election, as they did every election until the election for the final territorial legislature in 1857 and the ratification election for the Lecompton Constitution the next year.[13]

Reeder did not, however, overturn the election results but merely declared the results invalid in a few of the most flagrantly corrupted precincts.[14] This hardly satisfied the free staters, but it was enough for the slave staters to cry to Washington for Reeder's head, which Pierce promptly gave them (moved partly by news of shady land speculations on Reeder's part), replacing him with the more compliant Wilson Shannon on August 16. In the post-election hubbub, scuffles broke out, some of them deadly, and boxes of Beecher's Bibles, and even a small howitzer, began to arrive in Lawrence. Reeder himself, transformed into a free state politician, remained in the territory, twice contesting Whitfield's seat as delegate, and twice losing in fraudulent elections.

The pro-slavery legislature passed laws making any public criticism of slavery, whether in print or by speech, including the mere denial that Kansas was a slave territory, a felony punishable by two years imprisonment, and made assisting in the escape of a fugitive slave punishable by death. It also provided that all citizens had to swear an oath to support the Fugitive Slave Act, and that in any case concerning slavery, no free soiler could sit on the jury.[15] The law also provided for the suppression of anti-slavery newspapers, a law aimed at the opposition newspapers in Lawrence.

On August 14, 1855, free staters, alarmed by the fraudulent March elections, had begun to organize their own government, ultimately calling a constitutional convention that met in Topeka on October 23 to draft the free state Topeka Constitution. Like their pro-slavery counterparts, the elections concerning the Topeka government involved only their own partisans: the Topeka Constitution was "ratified" on December 15, 1855, by a vote of 1,731 to 46, with only a small fraction of the state's inhabitants voting.

From this point there were two governments in Kansas, each elected only by their own voters: on one hand, the Topeka government of the anti-slavery state-in-waiting, which appointed state officers but, aware that it could not act as a state legislature until the Topeka Constitution was accepted by Congress, refrained from actually passing new laws for the state, and on the other hand the pro-slavery territorial government, which passed flamingly undemocratic laws for the territory.[16] The pro-slavery government met first in Pawnee (where Reeder had directed it to meet, because he owned property there), then in Shawnee Mission, and finally, from the spring of 1856, in Lecompton, a town named after Samuel Lecompte himself.

Governor Shannon treated the Topeka government as an illegal revolutionary conspiracy, and Pierce and for that matter Douglas followed

Shannon's lead, saying to the Free Soilers in Congress, "We believe that you organised all the difficulties, and are justly responsible for the consequences. . . . We believe there never would have been any trouble in Kansas but for your efforts, and they were for political objects."[17] Shannon sought opportunities to confront the free staters and to assert the power of his government. By contrast, the free staters' Governor Robinson, while rejecting the authority of the pro-slavery territorial legislature, realized that whichever side initiated violent conflict with the other would lose by it nationally, and did his best to keep his partisans reined in until the sack of Lawrence in 1856 enabled Jim Lane and John Brown to take the bit in their teeth.

The most important confrontation in late 1855 between free state and pro-slavery forces was known as the "Wakarusa War." The precipitating event was a land dispute that had nothing particular to do with the slavery issue. When the land dispute escalated, the fact that the opponents were on opposite sides of the slavery question suddenly became the only thing that mattered. On November 21 a free state settler was murdered, and his friends organized a vigilance committee, which burned the houses of a few pro-slavery settlers. The notorious Sheriff Jones, with a posse, arrested the leader of the vigilantes, one Jacob Branson, and then had to give him up to an angry crowd that whisked him to the safety of Lawrence, where the thick-walled Free State Hotel, with loopholes for rifles, seemed more like a fortress than like a lodging. Governor Shannon, arguing that he was facing an armed attempt to overthrow the government, unsuccessfully begged President Pierce to send in federal troops to subdue Lawrence, but did manage to get a couple of thousand Missourians under arms on the banks of the Wakarusa under the command of Sheriff Jones.

Shannon was spooked by his own unruly militia, particularly after a trigger-happy scouting party murdered a free state settler named Thomas Barber on December 6 as he left Lawrence for home. On the other side, Robinson, in the besieged Lawrence, had his doubts whether the Branson case was really worth a test of force. Ultimately, leaders on both sides backed down, with Robinson surrendering Branson but not acknowledging the authority of the Shawnee Mission government. Shannon also, hearing that the free staters feared that their opponents encamped at the Wakarusa might not actually disband, agreement or not (although they had in fact already disbanded), allowed Robinson to organize his own militia for the defense of the town, a decision that caused the pro-slavery men to see him as a traitor, and the free state men to see him as a fool.

Somewhat belatedly, President Pierce jumped into the quarrel between the rival governments in a special message on January 24, 1856, labeling the Topeka Constitution movement a treasonable conspiracy, threatening to suppress it with federal troops, blaming the deaths of Thomas Barber and of Reese Brown (a free state militia leader hatcheted to death while in the custody of the Kickapoo Rangers on January 16) on abolitionist provocation, and announcing that the irregularities in the election of the Shawnee Mission government did not compromise its legitimacy.

Douglas chimed in with similar language on March 12, seeing the acts of the Border Ruffians as chiefly defensive in character, and describing the New England Emigrant Aid Company as a "vast moneyed corporation," seeking to impose its will by lucre.[18] Douglas in fact had contempt for both sides in Kansas, though he was always, throughout 1856, quite a bit harder on the free state party.[19] But Douglas also on March 17 set in motion an effort to make a fresh constitutional start in Kansas, with a new census, a constitutional convention, and a promise of admission to the Union. Douglas's proposal set off several months of wrangling in the Senate, where it was derailed by the sack of Lawrence and the assault upon Senator Sumner in May.

Seward and his allies countered Douglas's plan with a proposal to admit Kansas immediately under the Topeka Constitution, a plan that passed the House but failed in the Senate. In the debate over Seward's motion, Douglas noted that the Topeka Constitution had been (like the Shawnee Mission legislature) voted upon in a loaded election in which only its partisans voted. And, somewhat strangely given his own racial views, he took the Topeka Constitution to task for its racism, jeering at the idea that the "especial friends of the Negro" would seek to deny blacks the right "to enter, live or breathe, in the proposed State of Kansas."[20] Moreover, when the Topeka Constitution was brought to Congress by Jim Lane, Douglas found the document fishy, since it was full of handwritten interpolations and excisions (deleting, for instance, the language excluding free blacks from the state, which Douglas knew had been approved by the Topeka Constitution's supporters in a separate vote), and all of the signatures were written in the same hand.[21]

It was in support of this effort to adopt the Topeka Constitution that Charles Sumner delivered his famous "Crime against Kansas" oration on May 19 and 20, to which Congressman Preston Brooks, believing that Sumner had cast sexual aspersions on his uncle, Senator Andrew Butler of South Carolina, responded by beating Sumner senseless at his desk with a cane on May 22.

Douglas's behavior during the lead-up to the assault upon Sumner gave plausibility to the worst views his opponents might have had of him. His response to Sumner's oration (which abused Douglas in personal language almost as harsh as Sumner had used against Senator Butler, Brooks's uncle) inadvertently did far worse. During the speech, Douglas had taken exception to the "lasciviousness and obscenity" of Sumner's personal attacks, and was heard to mutter "That damn fool will get himself killed by some other damn fool." This set off a slanging match between Douglas and Sumner, who rose to interrupt:

> "He has crowned the audacity of this debate by venturing to rise here and calumniate me. . . . I say, also, to that Senator, and I wish him to bear it in mind, that no person with the upright form of man can be allowed—[Hesitation]"
>
> "Say it," urged Douglas.
>
> "I will say it—no person with the upright form of man can be allowed, without violation of all decency, to switch out from his tongue the perpetual stench of offensive personality. . . . The noisome, squat, and nameless animal, to which I now refer, is not a proper model for an American Senator. Will the Senator from Illinois take notice?"
>
> "I will," Douglas replied, "and therefore will not imitate you, sir."
>
> "Mr. President, again the Senator has switched his tongue, and again he fills the senate with its offensive odor."[22]

After the speech Douglas asked, almost presciently, "Is it his object to provoke some of us to kick him as we would a dog in the street, that he may get sympathy upon the just chastisement?"[23] During the actual assault upon Sumner, Douglas was falsely reported to have restrained lawmakers from coming to Sumner's defense.[24] Douglas had also, falsely, been accused of saying of the free staters, "We will subdue you."[25] All this made perfect sense to those who, like Lincoln, were ready to believe the worst about Douglas in any event. But Douglas's hostility to the Topeka government, and for that matter his hostility to anti-slavery movements generally, does not suffice to prove that he actively sought to force slavery into Kansas, never mind to force it back into the free states. Indeed, his March 17 bill rather argues the contrary, that he sought simply to assure that the people of Kansas would rule it themselves.

Douglas's March 17 proposal for a constitutional convention in Kansas was in many ways weaker than the Toombs bill's proposal in June. For one thing, Douglas did not propose immediate admission of Kansas as a state, but admission only when Kansas's population reached 93,000, the number required for a representative in Congress. And he did not explicitly demand submission of the Constitution to the people for ratification (although Douglas probably took for granted—mistakenly, as it turned out—that a ratification election was understood by all sides to be a matter of course). Worst of all, his bill left the administration of the territory in the meantime in the hands of the pro-slavery government. The Toombs bill, on the other hand, proposed an honest census not administered by the territorial government, proposed immediate admission to the Union with Kansas's current population, and offered no role for the territorial legislature in the admission and constitution-making process. It also, cleverly, set the date for the election for delegates to the constitutional convention to be Election Day 1856, a move that would have pretty much eliminated interference from Missourians, who would have had their own elections to attend to. (Whether the constitution called for by the Toombs bill would have been ratified by the people of Kansas was a subject of acute disagreement between Lincoln and Douglas during the 1858 campaign, as we shall see in section 3.4 below, but Douglas assumed that it would be submitted for ratification even if the bill did not call for it in so many words.) The Toombs bill was a response to the revulsion against the caning of Sumner and the sack of Lawrence, and it represented an attempt by the more clearheaded pro-slavery politicians to retreat from a position about Kansas that events had made it impossible for them to defend. Despite the shady pro-slavery reputation of its author, the Toombs bill was probably the fairest-minded proposal to let the people of Kansas decide the issue for themselves to come out of either side of the contest.

Douglas's actions appear less sinister if one does not assume that the free staters had the upper hand numerically from the beginning. Most historians now believe that the pro-slavery forces would have won the election for territorial delegate, and probably the first election for the territorial legislature too, even without fraud and intimidation, although the Republican-dominated Howard Commission, traveling around the territory at the time of the sack of Lawrence, found enough evidence of fraud in the 1855 elections to make the argument that the Topeka government had the better claim to legitimacy.[26]

Fraud and intimidation were anyway staples of elections in the South and West until the secret ballot came in, with each party attempting to use its drunken bullies to keep the other party from voting. Douglas was wrong not to object to the fraud, but not crazy in seeing it as not much different from how elections were handled in most of the antebellum Union. Of course there is, as Douglas was about to discover, a difference in scale between the typical nineteenth-century electoral irregularities and what went on in Kansas. But the rivalry between the Democrats and the Americans in 1850s Baltimore was about as violent, and the elections about as corrupt, as anything that happened in Kansas.

It has become traditional to describe the Lecompton government, with all its flaws, as a merely formally legitimate government, a minority government with the force of law and the support of the federal government behind it, like the government of Rhode Island at the time of the Dorr Rebellion in 1842. The picture is slightly different if it is seen instead as a (temporary) majority government, in which case it is easy to understand how Douglas might have been hostile to the free staters in Lawrence and Topeka. That said, it is traditional in democracies that when the majority changes hands, so does the power, which of course is something the pro-slavery government in Kansas never contemplated. Nevertheless, the point is that few governments tolerate armed rival governments in their area of jurisdiction.

Douglas's views about which side had the right in Kansas began to change in the early months of 1857, when on the basis of his correspondence with people on the scene in Kansas, he came to the conclusion that the supporters of slavery in Kansas had become a minority, and that they must no longer be allowed to dominate the territorial government.[27] In Douglas's defense it could not have been completely clear which government actually had popular support until that time. But once it did become clear, he exerted himself to limit the power of the Lecompton government to shape the course of events leading to the admission of Kansas. It seems to have occurred to nobody on either side of the aisle that Douglas meant what he said about majority rule.

What made Douglas's position untenable was a confluence of inflammatory events both in Washington and in Kansas in the late spring of 1856, of which the assault upon Sumner on May 22 was only one part.

In the weeks prior to the assault on Sumner, the confrontations between the free staters at Lawrence and Sheriff Jones had escalated dramatically. Seeking again to confront the free state authorities, Jones on April 19 had attempted to arrest one S. N. Wood, one of the principals in the rescue of Branson back at the time of the Wakarusa War. After Jones and his posse had been twice heaved out of town, he returned on April 23 with a party of U.S. Dragoons, who managed to arrest several of Wood's protectors, but not Wood himself. Some hothead in the crowd wounded Jones in his tent that night with a shot, and this caused Robinson to fear for his town. While Sheriff Jones gathered his forces to subdue Lawrence, Robinson and former governor Reeder slipped out of the town, in fear of their lives, but were captured. Meanwhile pro-slavery militia killed free staters on thin pretexts around the territory, as Lawrence prepared to be besieged.

On May 5 Judge Lecompte had the chief free state officials indicted, and designated the Free State Hotel and the two Lawrence newspapers as public nuisances. On May 21, backed by about 500 militiamen, Jones again entered the town, ready to take his revenge. No sooner had Jones brought in the militiamen, including Senator Atchison himself, than they began to destroy the Free State Hotel, to destroy the presses of the *Kansas Free State* and the *Lawrence Herald of Freedom*, and to plunder one of the private houses of the town. Atchison wheeled up a cannon to destroy the hotel, but was too drunk to hit the building, which indeed even withstood explosives placed in its basement, although ultimately the rioters did destroy it with fire. (One curious absentee in all this was Governor Shannon, whom nobody on either side seems to have either consulted or counted on.) Nobody was killed, however, except one Border Ruffian unlucky enough to be struck by a dislodged chunk of the Free State Hotel. The sack of Lawrence, ultimately, was more an opera buffa skirmish than a battle.

The revenge taken by John Brown and his party on the 24th for the sack of Lawrence on the 21st, and for the caning of Sumner on the

22nd, was somewhat more substantial. Brown and his confederates attacked five pro-slavery settlers (not slaveholders) in their cabins near Pottawatomie Creek, killed them, and dismembered them with broadswords. It must be remembered that Brown was a freelancer who never took orders from the likes of Governor Robinson, but Jones and Lecompte, on the other hand, were acting in the name of the territorial government, and in Lecompte's case in the name of the federal government as well. Brown had actually offered his services to Robinson at the time of the Wakarusa War, proposing an immediate attack upon the Border Ruffian camp. But he left in disgust after Robinson expressed no enthusiasm for this proposal. In fact, Brown's whole strategy of striking the fear of God into his opponents was at odds with Robinson's strategy in Kansas of putting the onus of aggression on the pro-slavery side. Among the people whom Brown sought to compel by acts of dramatic violence, then, were the free staters themselves, whom he thought might be more capable of showing backbone if someone bloodied their hands. (The same might be said of Brown's motives during the Harper's Ferry raid: he wished to force the hand of sympathizers who were reluctant to shed blood, by shedding blood in ways they could not escape responsibility for.)

The Pottawatomie killings sowed the wind and reaped the whirlwind in Kansas, setting off a series of skirmishes that Governor Robinson, jailed at the time of the sack of Lawrence, was unable to put an end to. Many of these involved freelancers, including Brown's men, who on June 2 tricked a larger detachment of territorial militia led by H. C. Pate into surrendering at Black Jack, and Jim Lane, who shook off his nominal subordination to the Topeka government. Larger, and more confused, partisan battles took place at Osawatomie on August 7, at Franklin on August 12, and at Fort Titus on August 16. Through all this the U.S. troops, under the command of Colonel Edwin V. Sumner, the senator's cousin, ineffectually dispersed pro-slavery militias (who immediately regrouped), and read Governor Shannon's proclamations to audiences who took them as seriously as the comet took the Pope's bull against it.

Shannon having ignominiously fled the territory, Colonel Sumner found himself in charge. He impetuously broke up the free state legislature at the points of bayonets when it attempted to meet in Topeka on July 4. (One wonders what the colonel's cousin thought of this move.)

Sumner's act, ironically, turned out tremendously to the free staters' advantage, since it gave color to their claim that the federal government was dead set on forcing slavery into Kansas. This was embarrassing to Pierce, whose party was on thinning ice north of the Mason-Dixon line, and Pierce was forced to replace Sumner with General Persifor Smith. Pierce also intervened to prevent Judge Lecompte from trying the imprisoned governors Robinson and Reeder for treason (as the price of Republican cooperation in passing a military funding bill), and, aware of how disastrously the public relations battle was playing out for the Democrats, tried to retreat from the strategy of confrontation with the Topeka government, a retreat that undercut Pierce in the South without winning him any credibility in the North.[28]

Shannon's successor, John W. Geary (formerly the first mayor of San Francisco), sought, with the military backing of Smith, to align himself with neither of the two governments and to keep both sides within bounds. This evenhanded vigilance suppressed political violence in Kansas for the next year. Geary attempted a delicate dance of confrontation and accommodation with the Topeka government, holding back from striking them so long as they did not themselves pass laws or supplant the Lecompton government's officials, a restraint to which Robinson, if not Lane, was committed anyway. Geary was a loyal Democrat of Douglas's stripe, and thought of himself as saving the Democratic Party both in Kansas, where he hoped to provide popular sovereignty as Douglas imagined it, and nationally, where he hoped to vindicate the party's reputation in the face of allegations of catering to slavery.

Geary's administration was subverted by the pro-slavery politicians whom Geary unsuccessfully sought to replace. The Lecompton legislature compounded the insult by repudiating Geary's (and Pierce's) strategy of seeking a modus vivendi with the Topeka government, passing a law aimed at the officers of that government declaring "insurrection against the territorial authorities" a capital offense. The next time they arrested Charles Robinson, this is to say, they would have a rope handy.

Among Geary's last acts, before throwing up his hands in frustration and resigning, was a fruitless veto of the Lecompton legislature's plan to hold a constitutional convention to be led by none other than John Calhoun. Geary objected to the seedy territorial officials the legislature had picked to supervise the elections to the Lecompton Convention, and objected even more to the fact that the bill did not require

any ratification vote for the resulting constitution. Aware that they had
lost the majority, and that the Lecompton Convention might be their
last chance to secure Kansas for slavery, the legislature drew a line in
the sand.[29] Geary would not be the only decent-enough, neutral-
minded politician to smell a rat in the Lecompton Convention.

3.3 Douglas and the Lecompton Constitution

Given how things turned out, it is surprising that President Buchanan's
first moves about the Kansas question were promising ones. To replace
Geary, Buchanan appointed, at Douglas's suggestion, a figure of genuine stature whom we have met before, Robert J. Walker of Mississippi,
who promised that the slavery issue in Kansas would be decided by, as
he wrote to his sister on April 6, 1857, a "a *full* and *fair* vote of a *majority*
of the people of Kansas."[30] Douglas had been alarmed by the Lecompton government's treatment of Geary, and by their loaded plans for a
constitutional convention, so he sought Walker's appointment hoping
that Walker would have the strength to keep the Lecomptonites in
hand.[31]

In his inaugural address, Walker had proclaimed that "in no contingency will Congress admit Kansas as a slave state or free state, unless
a majority of the people shall first have fairly and freely decided this
question for themselves by a direct vote on the adoption of the Constitution, excluding all fraud or violence."[32] Walker's language promised,
as clearly as language can, that he intended to include the free staters
fairly in any political arrangement, and that he intended to keep fraudulent votes from Missouri out.

Walker did not, however, start the process de novo. For instance, he
let stand the very biased census conducted by the Lecompton government, which listed Lawrence as having no inhabitants at all.[33] He also
let stand the plan for elections for delegates to the convention that the
Lecompton government (using its own corrupt election officials) had
already set in motion. Walker was aware that these flaws might compromise the constitution the Lecompton Convention was called to write.
A fair vote about ratification, Walker felt, would rectify any of the flaws
in the convention.

Walker also made no secret of his understanding that the free staters
would handily win any fair election in the territory, and that climate
had already foreclosed slavery's future in Kansas.[34] Even as he argued

that climate would prevent slavery in Kansas, however, Walker railed against the "treason and fanaticism of abolition" and, strangely (considering his own racial views), denounced the hypocrisy of the Topeka Constitution's language prohibiting the entry of free blacks into the state. Like Geary, he assumed that the free staters were for the most part not Republicans (whom he said were outnumbered by Democrats by two to one), but free state Democrats, who had a large majority over pro-slavery Democrats, and he expected that these Democrats would control the institutions of the new state.[35] Given his imagined constituency of racist free state Democrats, his jeering at abolitionism and at the emissaries of the New England Emigrant Aid Company does not necessarily contradict his hostility to the Border Ruffians and their chiefs at Lecompton.

Walker's key aim was to persuade free staters to vote in the June 15 elections for delegates to the upcoming Lecompton Convention. Walker's attempts to assuage the doubts and court the friendship of free state leaders like Robinson and Lane earned him nothing. Southern Democrats denounced him as a sectional traitor, and newspapers all over the South began calling for his removal, but the free staters still boycotted the June 15 elections, and an overwhelmingly pro-slavery convention, which would begin to meet in Lecompton in September, was elected by a very small number of voters, with even the transitory Missourians for the most part staying home. All told, only some 2,200 ballots were cast in this election, out of a registered voting population of 9,251, and an adult white male population of about 20,000.[36] Buchanan initially—another surprise—backed Walker firmly, promising him privately on July 12 (but at the same time making no public statement), "On the question of submitting the constitution to the *bona fide* resident settlers of Kansas, I am willing to stand or fall."[37] Douglas, perhaps not seeing that popular ratification of the constitution would become an issue, took the position that if the free staters chose to boycott the election for delegates to the convention, they would have nobody to blame but themselves if Kansas were to become a slave state. He probably intended this remark more as a rebuke of the free staters than as a defense of the Lecompton Constitution, since it still mattered to him that the actual majority actually rule.[38]

Buoyed by what he thought was the administration's support, Walker persuaded the free state voters to take part in the October 1857 elections for a new territorial legislature. These elections, like the others, were marked by fraudulent votes. But this time the frauds were so egregious that Walker had to intervene. In Oxford, a Johnson County hamlet with six houses, 1,628 pro-slavery votes had been submitted. Free state representatives, searching for the election judges there, found that they had decamped (if they ever existed at all). Coming to investigate, Walker and his secretary Frederick Stanton found a fifty-foot-long scroll with 1,601 names all in the same handwriting, all in alphabetical order, 1,500 of them from the city directory of Cincinnati. (Local suspicions centered on John Calhoun, the surveyor-general, as the author of this fraud.)[39] McGee County, with fewer than 100 voters, and which had submitted only 12 votes in the elections for delegates to the Lecompton Convention, had cast 1,266 votes.[40] Walker rightly decided that he could not stand for this. But not having the ability to mount another election, or to investigate each individual vote, he simply chose to put aside the results in these places, which turned the outcome of the election in favor of the free staters. Predictably, southern newspapers and politicians denounced Walker's intervention in this case as a tyrannous usurpation, and in the face of this high-decibel abuse Buchanan changed front. Facing pressure closer to home from Judge Sterling Cato, who threatened Walker with a writ of mandamus requiring him to certify the elections (including the fraudulent ballots at Oxford and McGee), and from Sheriff Jones, who threatened Stanton with a pistol, both Walker and Stanton stood their ground.

Meanwhile, the Lecompton conventioneers, sensing that their moment was passing, chose a desperate if ruthless strategy. In the document itself, they adopted language arguing that the right of property, and particularly property in slaves, was prior to all government, and therefore could not be interfered with by government, a striking interpretation of the meaning of the *Dred Scott* case, and one that gives color to Lincoln's notion that a "second *Dred Scott* case" legalizing slavery everywhere was in the offing. The instrument also could not be amended for seven years, and its provisions establishing slavery could not be amended at all.[41] The Lecomptonites chose also to bypass a ratification election by the voters of the territory, submitting their constitution directly to Congress. And they dissolved the newly elected territorial legislature, which was dominated by free staters, taking the affairs of the territory out of the hands of Governor Walker and placing them in the hands of the president of the convention, John Calhoun.[42]

Henry Martin, Buchanan's agent, was in the basement of the building during the convention, ostensibly checking land records but in fact keeping track of the doings of the Lecomptonites behind Walker's back. Realizing that the convention's strategy could only backfire, Martin sought to persuade the delegates to seek a ratification vote. Calhoun, invoking, ironically as it turned out, the name of Stephen Douglas, persuaded the convention to reconsider the ratification issue by pushing a very devious ratification strategy, in which the choice would not be to vote the constitution up or down, but to vote for either the constitution "with slavery" or the constitution "without slavery."[43] The last phrase needs some explanation, because voting in the Lecompton Constitution "without slavery" would not in fact have ended slavery in Kansas. Those who were already enslaved in Kansas (not very many, about 200 slaves) would have remained slaves forever, and so would their progeny.[44] This bogus ratification election, overseen by Calhoun, was scheduled for December 21, and, free staters rightly choosing to boycott it, the pro-slavery version won handily, 6,226 to 569.

Calhoun's partial submission strategy, while not what Buchanan had hoped for, nevertheless won Buchanan's approval (since, he argued, submission was the convention's business, not his), and, through Martin, Buchanan endorsed the strategy without bothering to apprise the governor he had appointed about what he had done. Walker was outraged, and traveled to Washington to lobby against the Lecompton Constitution, stopping in Chicago first to bring the bad news to Douglas, who shared Walker's views. Douglas's choice to adopt a confrontational strategy over the Lecompton Constitution was the turning point of his career. In Kansas, Frederick Stanton, acting for Walker, called into session the newly elected legislature, now with a free state majority, which set up its own ratification vote on the constitution as a whole for January 4, 1858, and, assuming that the Lecompton Constitution would be defeated, called for the Topeka Constitution to be resubmitted to Congress. For doing this, Stanton was cashiered and replaced with James Denver, who eventually succeeded Walker as governor. The ratification election Stanton and the new territorial legislature managed proved as problematic as the Lecompton Convention's version, since only the free staters turned out to vote on January 4, 1858.

When the Lecompton Constitution "with slavery" won the convention-sponsored December 21 election (with, as usual, a large number of the votes being problematic), the stakes were raised on the issue all over the Union, since the slave state politicians felt they had taken a position from which they could no longer safely retreat. On January 4, the same day that the free state voters rejected the Lecompton Constitution by a margin of about 10,000 to 200, Kansas also voted to elect new state officers and a new legislature under the Lecompton Constitution. After the usual highjinks (this time among other things involving John Calhoun hiding a box of returns in a candle box under a woodpile) the free staters wound up winning control even of the new legislature, which met at Lawrence.[45] Calhoun's refusal to certify the results of the January 4 state elections was the last straw for Buchanan, who belatedly ejected that sorry ex-friend of both Lincoln and Douglas.

Despite the rejection of the Lecompton Constitution in the election arranged by the territorial legislature, and despite even the victory of the free state forces both in the elections for the territorial legislature arranged by Stanton and Walker and in the elections for the new state legislature under the Lecompton Constitution, the problem of what to do about the Lecompton Constitution remained before Congress, and pro-slavery partisans insisted that the Lecompton Constitution had been sufficiently "ratified" in the Calhoun-controlled elections of December 21. Buchanan's decision to attempt to force this constitution down the throats of Kansans, despite their rejection of it on January 4, could not but be taken as evidence for the worst conspiracy theories about his motives, and about southern motives. In his special message to Congress in February 1858, he had declared:

> Kansas is therefore at this moment as much a slave state as Georgia and South Carolina. Without this the equality of the sovereign states composing the Union would be violated, and the use and enjoyment of a territory acquired by the common treasure of all the States would be closed against the people and property of nearly one-half the members of the confederacy.[46]

When Douglas confronted Buchanan personally on December 2, Buchanan attempted to force Douglas into line by threats, reminding him of what had happened to Democrats who opposed Andrew Jackson during the Bank War: "Mr. Douglas, I desire you to remember that no Democrat ever yet differed from the Administration of his own choice without being crushed. Beware of the fate of Tallmadge and Rives." Douglas was not to be spoken to in this high-handed way by a man he had helped make president: "Mr. President, I wish you to remember that General Jackson is dead."[47]

If the behavior of Jones, Calhoun, and Stringfellow can be written off as the antics of corrupt hayseeds, the behavior of Congress during the debates over the Lecompton Constitution cannot be so defended. The conflict, even by the low standards of antebellum Congresses, was squalid, punctuated by a brawl between South Carolina's Laurence Keitt and Pennsylvania Republican Galusha Grow (once David Wilmot's law partner) over the momentous issue of whether Grow could set foot on the "Democratic" side of the House. In the commotion Mississippi congressman William Barksdale lost his wig, and only his happening to put it on his head backward, which provoked fight-ending hilarity, prevented this incident from becoming another version of the assault upon Sumner, proving Marx's famous adage about how tragedy is often repeated as farce.

Douglas rejected the Lecompton Constitution as a perversion of his doctrine of popular sovereignty, a "system of trickery and jugglery to defeat the fair expression of the will of the people" (to quote his speech in the Senate of December 9). But only four of the twelve northern Democrats were willing to defy Buchanan with Douglas in the Senate, giving Buchanan a narrow victory, although those who did vote to accept the Lecompton Constitution formally rejected its provisions against amendment, and cut the enormous land grant the state had awarded itself from federal lands (sixteen million acres) by about three quarters.

While the settlers back in Kansas braced for another round of violence (and while the free state territorial legislature, taking a page from its pro-slavery predecessors, passed but could not sustain a bill making it a capital offense to take office under the Lecompton Constitution),[48] debate shifted over to the House of Representatives, where Pennsylvania congressman William Montgomery picked up a proposal Kentucky's John J. Crittenden had failed to persuade the Senate to pass, calling for an entirely new ratification election. This bill expressed Douglas's convictions exactly, and he was gratified when most House Republicans, reasoning that despite its embrace of popular sovereignty it also would have had the practical effect of killing off the Lecompton Constitution, supported the Crittenden-Montgomery bill. Senate Republicans did not take the same view, so this idea, like Crittenden's original proposal, came to nothing. (During the debates, as we shall see in section 4.6 below, Douglas cited this widespread support of the Crittenden-Montgomery bill as evidence that Democrats and Republicans could make common cause, and that Republicans could embrace popular sovereignty without making a fatal sacrifice of position.) Douglas's anti-Lecompton allies in the House did have enough votes, in alliance with the Republicans, to prevent the Lecompton Constitution from becoming law.

Meanwhile in Kansas, opinions among the free staters divided, with Robinson arguing that it might be best to accept, and then transform, the Lecompton Constitution, since it provided a short route to statehood, and more radical spirits calling a new constitutional convention which, meeting in Leavenworth at the end of March, wrote a new free state constitution, removing the Topeka Constitution's prohibition of settlement by free blacks, giving blacks a vote in the ratification election, and calling for a referendum on black suffrage more generally. Although this constitution was embraced by Seward on its arrival in Washington, Congress never acted upon it, and the Leavenworth Constitution represented not only a constitutional dead end but a racial road not taken.[49]

On April 21, Congressman William English of Indiana, who opposed the Lecompton Constitution but did not wish to break with Buchanan, proposed a devious and somewhat unfair version of the Crittenden-Montgomery bill known as the English Compromise. The bill did not propose a ratification election in so many words. But it used the rejection of the Lecompton Constitution's land grant proposal as a pretext for a vote on it: the voters of Kansas would be asked either to accept the Lecompton Constitution with a much-reduced land grant or to reject it, at the price of having to wait before applying for statehood again until their population had risen to the number required for a congressional district (which would have required a threefold growth of population in the territory).

Douglas opposed the English Compromise, recalling how Napoleon put it to his troops at the time of his election as First Consul: "Now, my soldiers, you are to go to the election and vote freely just as you please.

If you vote for Napoleon, all is well; vote against him, and you are to be instantly shot."[50] But its supporters were able to peel away just enough of Douglas's supporters to prevail in the House by a vote of 112 to 103 on April 30.[51] Douglas and two other Senate Democrats continued to oppose the bill in the Senate but were defeated by a vote of 31 to 22.

The referendum called for under the English Compromise was held on August 2, 1858, and the Lecompton Constitution was defeated by a vote of 11,300 to 1,788.[52] Lincoln had given the "House Divided" speech on June 16, and would meet Douglas at Ottawa on August 21. The Kansas issue, still alive at the time of the "House Divided" speech, was moot by the time the Lincoln-Douglas debates began, and indeed, since Douglas had opposed the Lecompton Constitution from the beginning and had long conceded the victory of the free state forces in Kansas, the practical issue, if not the philosophical issue, between Lincoln and Douglas had been moot for months, although Lincoln continued to revisit the conflict in search of evidence to support his conspiracy charge.

The rejection of the Lecompton Constitution, and for that matter the admission of Kansas to statehood under the Wyandotte Constitution in the waning days of the Buchanan administration—the resignation of southern politicians in the wake of secession had changed the balance of power in Congress even before Lincoln took office—did not end the suffering in Bleeding Kansas. An ongoing guerrilla war between free state outriders led by James Montgomery (who fought federal dragoons at Yellow Paint in late April) and pro-slavery outriders led by Charles Hamilton (who massacred free state settlers at the Marais des Cygnes on May 19) kept the cycle of outrage and reprisal (usually upon people who had nothing to do with the original outrage) going straight through the Civil War years. John Brown returned to Kansas, running a party of slaves from Missouri to freedom in January 1859. Even former governor Shannon had a role to play in the endgame in Kansas, defending Dr. John Doy, who was convicted of aiding runaway slaves in Missouri in March 1859 but rescued from prison by a free state mob. The conflicts back and forth between Kansas and Missouri culminated, but did not end, in the Lawrence Massacre in 1863, and in the depopulation of western Missouri called for by Lincoln in the infamous Order Number 11.

3.4 Lincoln's Evidence

"Stephen, Franklin, Roger, and James"

Although the fate of Kansas had for all practical purposes been decided by the time Lincoln delivered the "House Divided" speech, the lessons of the Kansas struggle—that the slaveholders were capable of anything, and the northern Democrats were capable of defending anything that slaveholders did—weighed more in Lincoln's mind than the outcome of the specific struggle. This was one reason why Lincoln raised the stakes, moving from the struggle in Kansas, which was over except for the killing, to the general and special slave power conspiracy theories, which were still live if partially false issues. Now it was unlikely that southern politicians ever actually imagined they would be in a position to force slavery back into the free states. But they did, nevertheless, seek to repress even unstated reservations about slavery in the minds of nonslaveholders, and this desire to shout down unstated second thoughts, when combined with an accurate sense that slavery really had become politically vulnerable, committed the southern master class to demanding ever more dramatic surrenders from their allies, who could never quite be submissive enough, no matter how deeply they bowed down. Lincoln understood, and Douglas did not, that the slave power would never long be satisfied with any compromise. This is why, just as southern opinion-formers were denouncing Douglas as an apostate to their cause, Lincoln was almost able to make good on his forced and hyperbolic case that he remained their lackey.

In the opening lines of the "House Divided" speech, Lincoln saw Douglas as a leading actor in a repetitive drama in which northern politicians offered futile and increasingly fatal sacrifices of principle to appease the slave power: "We are now far into the *fifth* year, since a policy was initiated, with the *avowed* object, and *confident* promise, of putting an end to slavery agitation" (1:426).

The policy Lincoln described here was of course the Kansas-Nebraska Act, introduced by Douglas in January 1854. Lincoln described that policy as having the "avowed object of putting an end to slavery agitation." Two things about that sentence need comment. The first is the implication of the word "avowed." The word suggests that there were other, unavowed purposes of the Kansas-Nebraska Act, such as opening

Kansas and the other territories to the expansion of slavery (a suggestion that might have occurred to any opponent of slavery), or forcing slavery back into the free states (a suggestion largely cooked up by Lincoln in this speech).

That the purpose of the Kansas-Nebraska Act was to "put an end to slavery agitation" is also a claim that requires comment. "Putting an end to slavery agitation" would more fairly be described as one of the intended *consequences* of the act, but it could not be described as its central *purpose*. That purpose, at least as Douglas conceived of it, was to provide a pattern for new territorial governments which would avoid the Scylla of the Wilmot Proviso–style federal prohibition of slavery and the Charybdis of the Calhoun-Davis position, both of which amounted, as far as Douglas was concerned, to declarations of sectional war. Lincoln did not describe the problem in language Douglas would have recognized, because he did not credit Douglas with attempting to solve the problem of the future of slavery in the territories, only with trying to silence debate about slavery generally.

Lincoln alluded here to the common assumption, on the Democratic side of the aisle, that the slavery issue would simply go away if the abolitionists just stopped making a fuss about it. This was certainly Buchanan's view, and it was Douglas's also, who never publicly conceded that the abolitionists were anything more than troublemakers, and tended to argue that the conflicts over slavery were entirely the product of abolitionist meddling. Indeed, the Democratic approach to abolitionists was to seek to repress them, either through popular intimidation or through legal harassment.

Lincoln was quite correct to argue that Douglas could hardly have chosen a less effective means of quieting controversy over slavery than the Kansas-Nebraska Act. The course of the quasi war in Kansas gave a great deal of color to the claim that the aim of the act was to enable slavery to establish itself in Kansas, and perhaps in the other western territories. It certainly showed that the Border Ruffians and their supporters all over the South never intended to engage in fair dealing, since they could not accept a fair defeat in Kansas even after having enjoyed many unfair advantages there. But even the sordid history of Bleeding Kansas does not give much color to the claim that the Kansas-Nebraska Act was always intended to make slavery "alike lawful in *all* the States, *old* as well as *new—North* as well as *South*."

Lincoln made the hop, skip, and jump from the argument about the future of Kansas, to the general slave power conspiracy argument, to the specific conspiracy argument against Douglas, so deftly that one might not notice that the process involved several leaps in the dark. Lincoln noted the undeniable fact that the struggle over slavery had only become more intense since the Kansas-Nebraska Act was passed. From this he concluded—and here is the first leap—that that struggle would not cease becoming more intense until the Union became either entirely free of slavery or entirely slaveholding. Then, in order to show that there was a "tendency" in current politics toward an entirely slaveholding Republic, Lincoln introduced—here is the second leap— the evidence of Douglas's plot to invalidate the emancipation laws of the free states, as if evidence of the tendency of politics to turn in a general direction were the same thing as evidence of a particular conspiracy to subvert the political order:

> In *my* opinion, it *will* not cease, until a *crisis* shall have been reached, and passed.
>
> "A house divided against itself cannot stand."
>
> I believe this government cannot endure, permanently half *slave* and half *free*.
>
> I do not expect the Union to be *dissolved*—I do not expect the house to *fall*—but I *do* expect it will cease to be divided.
>
> It will become *all* one thing or *all* the other.
>
> Either the *opponents* of slavery, will arrest the further spread of it, and place it where the public mind shall rest in the belief that it is in the course of ultimate extinction; or its *advocates* will push it forward, till it shall become alike lawful in *all* the States, *old* as well as *new*— *North* as well as *South*.
>
> Have we no *tendency* to the latter condition?
>
> Let any one who doubts, carefully contemplate that now almost complete legal combination—piece of *machinery* so to speak— compounded of the Nebraska doctrine, and the Dred Scott decision. Let him consider not only *what work* the machinery is adapted to do, and *how well* adapted; but also, let him study the *history* of its construction, and trace, if he can, or rather *fail*, if he can, to trace the evidence of design and concert of action, among its chief architects, from the beginning. (1:426)

The argument that followed elaborated the idea that there was a "concert of action" between "Stephen, Franklin, Roger, and James" aimed at undermining the legal status of emancipation in the free states. Stephen Douglas initiated the conspiracy, by authoring the Kansas-Nebraska Act. President Pierce forwarded the conspiracy not only by signing the act but also by attempting to manipulate the institutions of Kansas Territory in favor of slavery by ignoring the obvious illegalities involved in early territorial elections and by treating the minority pro-slavery government as the legitimate one. Chief Justice Taney, in the *Dred Scott* decision, turned the conspiracy toward its more general aim, making a claim about the sanctity of (slave) property in such a way as to make the arguments against the prohibition of slavery in the territories also serve as arguments against emancipation in the states, since both acts would involve interventions against the right to property, a right which, in pro-slavery minds, was both prior to and higher than the government. President Buchanan forwarded the conspiracy in a twofold way. First, he colluded in making the *Dred Scott* decision a sweeping one, not only, in his inaugural address, announcing his "cheerful submission" to the decision beforehand (pretending that he did not know what the decision would be) but also in applying pressure to the Court behind the scenes to make a broad rather than a cautious decision, a decision that would determine not only whether residence in a free territory worked the emancipation of slaves taken to those territories but also the question of whether blacks could ever have federal citizenship rights, and whether the federal government, or even the territorial legislatures, could prohibit slavery in the territories. (This is the weakest link in the argument, since it requires one to show that Douglas introduced the concept of popular sovereignty over slavery in the territories knowing in advance that the Supreme Court would rule that it was unconstitutional.) Buchanan's sotto voce conversation with Taney during his inauguration was widely felt at the time to be evidence of his collusion in Taney's decision. It was not such evidence, but the charge was in substance true on other grounds. Buchanan did not engage in any direct manipulation of Taney, but he did correspond with Justices Catron and Grier, asking for a broad rather than a narrow decision, and received from them assurances that a broad decision was in the works. Whatever he whispered with Taney on the stand on Inauguration Day 1857, he did not learn from him then the substance of the decision, because he already knew it.

Pierce's public statements did give some color to Lincoln's charge that the *Dred Scott* decision was somehow preconcerted between the Pierce administration and the Court, although in fact no such thing happened. In his last speech as president, as Lincoln pointed out, Pierce had gloated over the victory of his party in 1856, taking it as an endorsement of the Kansas-Nebraska Act, which, in repealing the Missouri Compromise, had removed "an objectionable enactment, unconstitutional in effect and injurious in terms to a large portion of the States."[53] Pierce's gloating included the argument that the Court had ruled that the 36° 30′ line drawn by the first Missouri Compromise was unconstitutional. It had, of course, done no such thing yet, although it was about to. According to James Simon, Pierce had taken an advisory opinion by his attorney general, Caleb Cushing, as an opinion from the Court, although what it really was was an accurate prediction of how the Court would decide the issue.[54] Pierce wanted the Court to rule as it did, and expected the Court to rule as it did, but he did not conspire with the Court to produce the ruling.

Also lending some traction to Lincoln's charges was the fact that the Court appeared to delay giving its opinion in the *Dred Scott* case until safely after the 1856 election. Whether the Court actually did delay the decision in order to help Buchanan is another matter.[55] To make time for this delay, Lincoln maintained, Douglas had been arguing (particularly when asked directly about it by the anti-slavery senator from Illinois, Lyman Trumbull) that the status of slavery in the territories was a matter for the Court to decide, and therefore something about which neither party should have anything to say. Douglas does not in fact seem to have had any idea what the Court would actually decide. His answer seems to have been more a way to fudge a question he could no longer politically afford to give any direct answer to than a way to carry water for the Court. But Lincoln did not see it that way. The effect of Douglas's evasions, Lincoln argued, was twofold. First, it removed public outrage in the North against the *Dred Scott* decision from the political calculus in 1856, helping to ensure that James Buchanan would squeak by to a narrow victory over John C. Frémont. Second, it enabled Buchanan, once in office, to argue that the 1856 election was a ratification of the *Dred Scott* decision. Now it might not seem to make sense that votes one was afraid of scaring away by the decision would be, once given, understood to be votes for that decision. After all, voters who would have been driven away by the decision can hardly be called supporters of it. But all seems to be fair in politics, and Buchanan did in fact interpret his election that way.

Buchanan's reply took a curious form. The noted chemist and Yale professor Benjamin Silliman issued a public letter to the president, taking him to task for sending Governor Robert J. Walker to Kansas with a military force to suppress the free state forces there. Although Silliman and the other signers were wrong about Walker, they were certainly right about the Border Ruffians, who, in the words of Silliman's diary, sought to "enforce against the people of Kansas, the cruel and wicked code of laws inflicted upon them by an invasion from Missouri, creating a false and unauthorized legislature."[56]

Buchanan's reply to the Silliman letter, his public letter of August 15, 1857, was remarkable for its mendacity even in a mendacious presidency like Buchanan's. The president denied that there was any taint of illegitimacy surrounding the pro-slavery territorial government. Indeed, it was the free staters that he stigmatized as lawless and seditious rebels. Knowing that Silliman and the other signers were from Connecticut, Buchanan could not help comparing the free staters to the supporters of the Hartford Convention, at which, in the hubbub surrounding the War of 1812, the secession of New England was meditated—and this despite the fact that in his early career Buchanan himself had been a Federalist.[57] Further, with a great parade of innocence, Buchanan wondered how anyone, ever, could have entertained a shadow of the belief that anybody, anywhere, had the power to keep slavery out of the territories. How anybody ever doubted the right of the South to carry slavery into Kansas was "a mystery," he said, as if the divine right of slaveholders had been a commonplace accepted for generations rather than something Buchanan had himself just made up. Buchanan's fatuous and amoral reply to the Silliman letter gave color to Lincoln's suspicions about his conduct. Now there is no question that Buchanan did not have it in mind to force slavery back into the free states. But had the Court issued what Lincoln calls the "second *Dred Scott* decision," it is genuinely uncertain how Buchanan would have responded. By contrast, there is no uncertainty about how Douglas would have responded.

Lincoln allowed an ingenious metaphor—one that seems to grow from his earlier metaphor about the "architects" of the plan—to make his case for him:

We can not absolutely *know* that all these exact adaptations are the
result of preconcert. But when we see a lot of framed timbers, different portions of which we know have been gotten out at different times
and places and by different workmen—Stephen, Franklin, Roger and
James, for instance—and when we see these timbers joined together,
and see they exactly make the frame of a house or a mill, all the ten-
ons and mortices exactly fitting, and all the lengths and proportions
of the different pieces exactly adapted to their respective places, and
not a piece too many or too few—not omitting even scaffolding—or,
if a single piece be lacking, we can see the place in the frame exactly
fitted and prepared to yet bring such piece in—in *such* a case, we find
it impossible to not *believe* that Stephen and Franklin and Roger
and James all understood one another from the beginning, and all
worked upon a common *plan* or *draft* drawn up before the first lick
was struck. (1:431)

There were two key themes in the design metaphor. The first was
that the parts of the design were adapted to each other in ways that only
a prearrangement could account for. The mortise of one timber somehow exactly fits the tenon of the timber it is to be joined with, and each
timber is just long enough make all the angles square and all the parallels straight. When the Kansas-Nebraska Act was written, this is to say,
language was included in the act that was designed to seem unexcep-
tionable at the time, and not unconnected with the outward purpose of
the act, but that laid the groundwork for aspects of the *Dred Scott* decision, which some who supported the act would not have supported had
they known the ultimate intent of the language. Something was planted
in the language of the bill, this is to say, that appeared to be consistent
with the popular sovereignty doctrine, but which actually provided the
archimedean point for the overthrow of that doctrine at the hands of
supporters of the Calhoun-Davis joint sovereignty doctrine. Such an
interpretation may be contrary to the intentions of many of the legislators who voted for the bill, but, since the bill was passed with that language in it, they would find themselves as bound by that language as
they would have been had it been in their focal intention.

The dupes of Douglas's scheme, that is to say, were in the position of
those characters in folktales who inadvertently say magic words. Lincoln was not crazy to think that Douglas might pull a "magic words"

trick. After all, the burden of Lincoln's argument about the Kansas-Nebraska Act in the Peoria speech was that Douglas had done just that, that he had wrenched consent for popular sovereignty in the Louisiana Purchase from language endorsing popular sovereignty in the Mexican Cession. On the other side of the aisle, Douglas feared a "magic words" argument from Lincoln as well, in which he would use Jefferson's language from the Declaration of Independence to secure civil and political rights for black people. A "magic words" argument, this is to say, is an argument from implicitness viewed from the other end of the telescope.

The second theme was that by examining the design as it has already been realized, one can predict the next step of the design. If one sees three timbers arranged in a square, one can predict that a fourth timber will complete the square, particularly if there are already mortises carved in the two timbers to which it will be joined. It is this second theme that carried the main charge of Lincoln's argument, because the missing timber was the "second *Dred Scott* decision," which, Lincoln predicted, would claim that just as slaveholders cannot be deprived of their (human) property when they enter a territory, so they cannot be deprived of their (human) property when they enter a state. This reading of the Fifth Amendment's prohibition of depriving a person "of life, liberty, or property, without due process of law" may be strained, but it is hardly the only strained reading of that amendment in the history of the Constitution, and in the *Lochner* era (and increasingly in our own era) strained readings of that clause, readings designed to limit the rights of actual persons and to enlarge the rights of corporations, were the rule, not the exception.

Now on its face Lincoln's theory about concert of action was implausible, because in the first place, as Douglas repeatedly pointed out, James Buchanan was minister to England at the time of the Kansas-Nebraska Act and played no part in its adoption (indeed, that was why he was able to become a more plausible candidate for the Democratic nomination in 1856 than Douglas, who was discredited in northern eyes by the controversy over the Kansas-Nebraska Act and by the electoral disaster it had wrought for the Democrats in the northern states). Buchanan had kept a discreet silence about the act while in England, so that he would not have to take political responsibility for Douglas's blunders, while at the same time he accepted his party's Cincinnati Platform of 1856, which endorsed the act, in language that fudged the difference between the Douglas and Calhoun-Davis interpretations of it.[58]

Second, Douglas himself was hardly an opponent of the idea that territorial legislatures could decide the slavery issue for themselves. Lincoln evaded this rather large problem with his conspiracy theory by treating Douglas's doctrine as always no more than window-dressing, a position Douglas adopted to serve a temporary expedient purpose (lulling the North into complacency about the fate of slavery in Kansas, apparently—but if that was the purpose, few expedients were ever less successful than the Kansas-Nebraska Act was). Popular sovereignty was a position designed to be overruled by the Supreme Court, Lincoln argued, once it had served its purpose of diverting northern attention. Douglas adopted it, this is to say, only as a way to misdirect northern attention, and his real aim was something else.

One crucial difficulty with this view was the fact that Douglas was in a death-struggle with Buchanan over precisely this issue, and within days of Lincoln's delivering the speech, his views in Kansas had won out, with the voters in Kansas decisively choosing to wait until they had enough population for a congressional district rather than accept admission to the Union under the pro-slavery Lecompton Constitution. Lincoln was forced by the Buchanan-Douglas quarrel to minimize the significance of the struggle over the Lecompton Constitution; indeed he went further than this, completely distorting its meaning, treating the Buchanan-Douglas struggle as a mere dispute about tactics, which is, to say the least, not how subsequent generations of historians have taken it.

In his rejoinder at Ottawa, Douglas treated the elegance of Lincoln's metaphor with derision, seeing it as a rhetorical paste-gem, the kind of thing that nowadays candidates have political consultants to write for them. Of Lincoln's "folly and nonsense about Stephen, and Franklin, and Roger, and Bob, and James," Douglas remarked:

> He studied that out, prepared that one sentence with the greatest care, committed it to memory, and put it in his first Springfield speech, and now he carries that speech around and reads that sentence to show how pretty it is. [Laughter.] His vanity is wounded because I will not go into that beautiful figure of his about the building of a house. [Renewed laughter.] All I have to say is, that I am not green enough to let him make a charge which he acknowledges he does not know to be

true, and then take up my time in answering it, when I know it to be false and nobody else knows it to be true. [Cheers.] (1:533)

About the key feature of the conspiracy theory—the supposed articulation between the Kansas-Nebraska Act and the *Dred Scott* decision, Douglas in the Charleston debate has a truly devastating reply:

I called his attention to the fact that at the time the Nebraska bill was introduced, there was no such case as the Dred Scott case pending in the Supreme Court, nor was it brought there for years afterwards, and hence that it was impossible there could have been any such conspiracy between the Judges the Supreme Court and the other parties involved. (1:660)

It is fairer to say that the case fell into the hands of a court that was looking for some case to use in order to make its point than it is to say that the case was got up for that purpose from the beginning. But that the Supreme Court was spoiling to issue a ruling like *Dred Scott* is better proof of the general slave power conspiracy theory, the theory that slaveholders must rule or be ruined, than of the specific one, that Douglas and Pierce and Taney and Buchanan were planning the outcome all along. Further, how the Court might decide questions about slavery in the territories might not have been obvious to everybody in the late 1840s, when Delaware senator John M. Clayton, no pro-slavery radical (indeed, the only senator from a slave state to cast a vote for the Wilmot Proviso) began arguing that the issue should be passed to the Court, and Douglas's statements in the middle 1850s sound to me more like Clayton's wishful buck-passing than like the maturing of a conspiracy.

Now exactly what the status of Lincoln's charge was in his own mind is a bit of a question. At Clinton on June 27, Douglas, replying to this charge from the "House Divided" speech, had noted that he had never "had any talk with Judge Taney or the President of the United States with regard to the Dred Scott decision before it was made." Lincoln's reply to this at Ottawa was tricky: "What if Judge Douglas never did talk with Chief Justice Taney and the President, before the Dred Scott decision was made, does it follow that he could not have had as perfect an understanding without talking, as with it?" (1:518). Or perhaps Douglas could, after all, prove that he had no knowledge of the conspiracy—that does not prove, to Lincoln, anyway, that there was no conspiracy in which Douglas had a part to play:

> And now, I ask, even if he [Douglas] has done so [claimed that he "neither had any knowledge, information, or belief in the existence of such a conspiracy"] have not I a right to *prove it on him*, and to offer the evidence of more than two witnesses, by whom to prove it; and if the evidence proves the existence of the conspiracy, does not his broad answer denying all only show that he was *used* by the conspirators, and was not a *leader* of them. [Vociferous cheering.] (1:519)

Of course, it proved no such thing. To prove that Douglas was used by a conspiracy, you first have to prove that there was a conspiracy. The burden of proof was still on Lincoln to establish a conspiracy, and all he really had to go on was a well-connected story, and the ability to call on a general and well-earned suspicion of southern motives. (The line about the "more than two witnesses" is strange also; one gains from that line a lightning insight into the world of nineteenth-century legal pettifogging).

One of the odder rhetorical moves of the debates followed, in which Lincoln denied that he *knew* there was a conspiracy between Stephen, Franklin, Roger, and James, claiming only that he *believed* it. All this is in reply to a stricture Douglas applied in the Clinton speech, in which he said of Lincoln that "the man who makes a charge without knowing it to be true, falsifies as much as he who knowingly tells a falsehood." Now Douglas here had come to the brink of making a charge he did not really want to follow through on, since directly calling someone a liar in public was in some eyes grounds for a duel, and Douglas not only did not want to engage in any such thing but had also spent part of the Clinton speech maintaining that he had no personal quarrel with Lincoln, whom he had always found to be a "kind, amiable, intelligent gentleman." Douglas was so dumbfounded by the conspiracy charge that rather than describe it as a barefaced lie he assumed that Lincoln must have made it in jest: "I did not answer the charge [of conspiracy] before, for the reason that I did not suppose there was a man in America with a heart so corrupt as to believe such a charge could be true. I have too much respect for Mr. Lincoln to suppose he is serious in making the charge" (1:521).

Lincoln had to retreat to the claim that he was not speaking about what he *knew* but only about what he *believed*. What Lincoln apparently meant was that he was not actually making a charge that there was a conspiracy, only announcing that he believed there was one. One might wonder whether this makes much difference, although Lincoln came back to this nondistinction so repeatedly in the course of the debates that he seemed to imagine that he could make such nonsense into a commonplace by sufficient repetition:

> Now, in regard to his reminding me of the moral rule that persons who tell what they do not know to be true, falsify as much as those who knowingly tell falsehoods. I remember the rule, and it must be borne in mind that in what I have read to you, I do not say that I *know* such a conspiracy to exist. To that I reply, *I believe it.* If the Judge says that I do *not* believe it, then *he* says what *he* does not know, and falls within his own rule, that he who asserts a thing which he does not know to be true, falsifies as much as he who knowingly tells a falsehood. (1:519)

It is hard to find any other remark in all of Lincoln's public utterances that matches this one for pure silliness. In this exchange each hurls, but denies that he is doing so, a high-energy charge: Lincoln, that Douglas is conspiring against the free states; Douglas, that Lincoln's charge is an infamous lie. Nowadays we do not have to engage in these kinds of gyrations to press infamous lies without taking responsibility for them; we merely have "527" committees with which we can pretend to have no official connection do all our dirty work for us.

The "Or State" Phrase

The first step of the concerted action Lincoln saw Douglas as being a principal agent in was of course not the Kansas-Nebraska Act, but the floating of the doctrine of popular sovereignty during the debates over the Compromise of 1850, and during the Oregon debates of 1847–1848. The idea here is that even at the time of the Oregon debate, Douglas was preparing not only the Kansas-Nebraska Act, but the *Dred Scott* decision, and the hypothetical "second *Dred Scott* decision," which would overthrow the abolition of slavery in the free states:

The new year of 1854 found slavery excluded from more than half the States by State Constitutions, and from most of the national territory by congressional prohibition.

Four days later, commenced the struggle, which ended in repealing that congressional prohibition.

This opened all the national territory to slavery, and was the first point gained.

But, so far, *Congress* only, had acted; and an *indorsement* by the people, *real* or apparent, was indispensable, to *save* the point already gained, and give chance for more.

This necessity had not been overlooked; but had been provided for, as well as might be, in the notable argument of *"squatter sovereignty,"* otherwise called *"sacred right of self government,"* which latter phrase, though expressive of the only rightful basis of any government, was so perverted in this attempted use of it as to amount to just this: That if any *one* man, choose to enslave *another,* no *third* man shall be allowed to object.

That argument was incorporated into the Nebraska bill itself, in the language which follows: *"It being the true intent and meaning of this act not to legislate slavery into any Territory or state, nor to exclude it therefrom; but to leave the people thereof perfectly free to form and regulate their domestic institutions in their own way, subject only to the Constitution of the United States."*

Then opened the roar of loose declamation in favor of "Squatter Sovereignty," and "Sacred right of self-government."

"But," said opposition members, "let us be more specific—let us *amend* the bill so as to expressly declare that the people of the territory may exclude slavery." "Not we," said the friends of the measure; and down they voted the amendment. (1:427)

The argument here is rather subtle, and many of the points are made indirectly. In its broadest terms, the argument is that the popular sovereignty position was introduced in order to open all of the national territory to slavery, and the 1856 election was contrived so as to amount to an endorsement not only of the principle of popular sovereignty but also of opening all of the territories to slavery, or, more pointedly, of ensuring that all of the territories would be organized on a slaveholding basis.

Lincoln's philosophical critique of the doctrine of popular sovereignty is familiar, and echoes the argument he had made in the Peoria
speech, that whatever the meaning of freedom is, it cannot include the
freedom to deprive other people of freedom, and that governing another people without their consent is not something that can be covered by the concept of "self-government."

Lincoln's political critique of the doctrine of popular sovereignty is
new. In the Peoria speech, he had argued that popular sovereignty
would have bad effects upon the cultural prerequisites for freedom,
hardening people's hearts to the essential injustice of slavery, and accus-
toming people to making brutal arrangements about it under cover of
ordinary political dealmaking, since the way such dealmaking goes on
systematically keeps the brutality of the deal out of sight for the principals. But in the "House Divided" speech, Lincoln argued that popular
sovereignty had been planted in law long beforehand in order to prepare
for a later use unanticipated by the people but envisaged by the projec-
tors of the doctrine. The doctrine was elaborated in 1847, ostensibly to
justify organization of Oregon Territory on a free basis, in order to lay
the groundwork for use of the same concept to give cover for the organization of New Mexico and Utah Territories on an unknown basis and
of Kansas Territory on a slaveholding one. It was a kind of poison pill,
which free staters on the Oregon question were deceived into swallow-
ing. When Lincoln argued that the "necessity had not been overlooked,
but had been provided for," he meant that the use of popular sovereignty
as a way to force slavery in the territories not only down the throats of
the free states but also down the throats of the people of the territories
themselves had been anticipated not only in 1850, but as far back as 1847,
when it had served an apparently opposite purpose. It is fair to say that
this is a loaded reading of the doctrine, and one that is contradicted by
the legislative history of the popular sovereignty position both in 1847
and in 1850, although it may describe the motivations of some of the
supporters of popular sovereignty in 1854.

Lincoln cited Douglas's language from his January 10, 1854, version of the bill about the intention of the Kansas-Nebraska Act. Lincoln's reading of the key sentence, whose plain prose sense is that the
Kansas-Nebraska Act leaves the future of slavery in Kansas Territory
up to the people of Kansas Territory, systematically inverted the sentence's meaning; in fact, Lincoln intended to argue that in signing

onto the argument of that sentence, the supporters of the bill were endorsing exactly the opposite of what they thought they were endorsing.

Consider how Lincoln read the first half of Douglas's sentence: "It
being the true intent and meaning of this act not to legislate slavery
into any Territory or state, nor to exclude it therefrom." Lincoln read a
dark significance into the "or state" phrase of that clause, arguing that
it means that when the Supreme Court has determined that the Kansas-
Nebraska Act does indeed legislate slavery into any territory, it also
legislates it into any state as well:

> It should not be overlooked that, by the Nebraska Bill, the people of
> a *State*, as well as a *Territory*, were to be left *"perfectly free," "subject only
> to the Constitution."*
>
> Why mention a *State?* They were legislating for *territories*, and not
> *for* or *about* States. Certainly the people of a State *are* and *ought to be*
> subject to the Constitution of the United States; but why is mention of
> this *lugged* into this merely *territorial* law? Why are the people of a *ter-
> ritory* and the people of a *State* therein *lumped* together, and their rela-
> tion to the Constitution therein treated as being *precisely* the same?
>
> While the opinion of *the Court*, by Chief Justice Taney, in the
> Dred Scott case and the separate opinions of all the concurring
> judges, expressly declare that the Constitution of the United States
> neither permits Congress nor a Territorial legislature to exclude
> slavery from any United States territory, they all *omit* to declare
> whether or not the same Constitution permits a *state*, or the people
> of a State, to exclude it.
>
> Possibly this is a mere *omission;* but who can be *quite* sure, if McLean
> or Curtis had sought to get into the opinion a declaration of unlim-
> ited power in the people of a *state* to exclude slavery from their limits,
> just as Chase and Macy sought to get such declaration, in behalf of
> the people of a Territory, into the Nebraska Bill—I ask, who can be
> quite *sure* that it would not have been voted down in the one case as it
> had been in the other?
>
> The nearest approach to the point of declaring the power of a
> State over slavery is made by Judge Nelson. He approaches it more
> than once, using the precise idea, and *almost* the language, too, of the
> Nebraska Act. On one occasion, his exact language is, "except in
> cases where the power is restrained by the Constitution of the United

States the law of the State is supreme over the subject of slavery within its jurisdiction."

In what *cases* the power of the *states* is so restrained by the United States Constitution is left an *open* question, precisely as the same question, as to the restraint on the power of the *territories*, was left open in the Nebraska Act. Put *that* and *that* together, and we have another nice little niche which we may ere long see filled with another Supreme Court decision declaring that the Constitution of the United States does not permit a *state* to exclude slavery from its limits.

And this may especially be expected if the doctrine of "care not whether slavery be voted *down* or voted *up*," shall gain upon the public mind sufficiently to give promise that such a decision can be maintained when made. (1:431–432)

Lincoln's argument was as follows: the Kansas-Nebraska Act was supposed to be concerned only with slavery in two territories, and slavery in the states was not a subject of debate in Congress at that time, so the only reason language about states was shoehorned into the bill was to provide a pretext for applying whatever counterintuitive interpretation the Court chose to force from the bill concerning the territories to the states as well. So if, for instance, the Court were to decide that the territories did not have the power to forbid slavery, because doing so would interfere with the property rights of slaveholders, the Court could make the same argument about the power of state governments to forbid slavery.

This reading of the "or state" phrase was nonsensical. It may be true that the aim of the act was to provide a territorial government for Kansas, but it was also intended that Kansas should eventually become a state. The reason Douglas included the "or state" phrase was to ensure that however the people of Kansas Territory decided the slavery issue, their wishes would be respected when it came time for Kansas to apply for statehood. This is of course precisely the issue he wound up fighting Buchanan over in Kansas. And it had earlier been the issue when California applied for statehood, and for that matter when Missouri did also. Besides, if the Court really were to use an argument about the sacredness of property rights to attack emancipation in the free states, they would not have needed anything from the Kansas-Nebraska Act to make that case anyway.

Lincoln's supporting evidence is forced as well. The fact that Chase and Macy were unable to pass an amendment to the Kansas-Nebraska Act explicitly giving the territorial legislatures the power to prohibit slavery is not by any stretch of the imagination evidence for the argument that since Chief Justice Taney's opinion in the *Dred Scott* case did not explicitly specify that states had the power to abolish slavery that Taney intended to deny that power. Nor is Justice Nelson's concession that the states' power over slavery is restrained by the Constitution of the United States evidence of a plan to use a forced reading of the Constitution to reimpose slavery in the states. Nelson's language, which is mostly just a pious commonplace, was principally aimed at preventing the states from nullifying the Fugitive Slave Act. And given Nelson's own weak and limited concurrence in the *Dred Scott* case itself, Nelson's language is a pretty unlikely foundation to build a conspiracy case upon.

In his rejoinder, Douglas makes short work of Lincoln's argument, pointing out the obvious meaning of his language. He also catches Lincoln in a cleft stick. One of the questions he had put to Lincoln during his own speech was whether he stood pledged against the admission of any more slave states whatsoever. The "platform" from which Douglas quoted during that speech, which he thought was a state Republican platform adopted in Lincoln's presence (and which turned out to be a county platform with which Lincoln had nothing to do), had called for this, and Douglas knew that if he could tie Lincoln to it, it would cost him votes among cautious former Whigs, but if he could make Lincoln repudiate it, it would also cost him the enthusiasm of some of his most committed supporters. Lincoln at Ottawa was clearly rattled by Douglas's questions, and did not answer them until the Freeport debate, where he wound up threading the needle by saying that he would, with great reluctance, support the entry of a new slave state, on the rather unrealistic condition that that state must have had no slavery during the entire period of its existence as a territory. This was a politically effective answer, but it left the main question unanswered, which is the question of what Lincoln would have done had the slaveholders in Kansas won the footrace for control of Kansas as completely and as convincingly as the free staters turned out to win it. Both possible answers to that question would have posed difficulties for Lincoln, but despite repeated pressure from

Douglas he never did address it. Douglas assumed that everyone knew very well that had the slaveholders convincingly won the footrace over Kansas Lincoln would have opposed its admission, and Douglas was quite right, in the course of ridiculing Lincoln's argument about the "or state" phrase, to ridicule Lincoln's disingenuousness about the larger issue:

> Mr. Lincoln wants to know why the word "state," as well as "territory," was put into the Nebraska Bill! I will tell him. It was put there to meet just such false arguments as he has been adducing. [Laughter.] That first, not only the people of the Territories should do as they pleased, but that when they come to be admitted as States, they should come into the Union with or without slavery, as the people determined. I meant to knock in the head this Abolition doctrine of Mr. Lincoln's, that there shall be no more slave States, even if the people want them. [Tremendous applause.] And it does not do for him to say, or for any other Black Republican to say, that there is nobody in favor of the doctrine of no more slave States, and that nobody wants to interfere with the right of the people to do as they please. What was the origin of the Missouri difficulty and the Missouri compromise? The people of Missouri formed a constitution as a slave State, and asked admission into the Union, but the Free Soil party of the North being in a majority, refused to admit her because she had slavery as one of her institutions. Hence this first slavery agitation arose upon a State and not upon a Territory, and yet Mr. Lincoln does not know why the word State was placed in the Kansas Nebraska bill. [Great laughter and applause.] (1:534–535)

"Subject Only to the Constitution"

Lincoln engaged in similar interpretative will to power about the second half of Douglas's sentence, the requirement that whatever ways the territorial governments or the states choose to regulate slavery be "subject to the Constitution of the United States." This apparently benign requirement seemed to Lincoln to be the thin edge of the wedge, enabling a loaded reading of the Constitution to establish a pro-slavery hegemony over territories and states alike.

The charge is articulated in the "House Divided" speech:

"Subject to the Constitution of the United States," neither *Congress* nor a *Territorial Legislature* can exclude slavery from any United States territory.

This point is made in order that individual men may *fill up* the territories with slaves, without danger of losing them as property, and thus enhance the chances of *permanency* to the institution through all the future. (1:429)

The idea here is that the Kansas-Nebraska Act had provided that the territorial legislatures could prohibit slavery only if the Constitution allowed them to do so, but Douglas knew all along that the Taney Court would rule that the Constitution did not allow any such thing. The promise about popular sovereignty had been intended from the beginning as a misdirection to disguise the fact that the act actually imposed the Calhoun-Davis doctrine upon the territories. As Lincoln went on to argue in the "House Divided" speech:

Several things will *now* appear less *dark* and *mysterious* than they did *when* they were transpiring. The people were to be left "perfectly free," "subject only to the Constitution." What the *Constitution* had to do with it, outsiders could not *then* see. Plainly enough *now*, it was an exactly fitted *niche* for the Dred Scott decision to afterward come in and declare the *perfect freedom* of the people to be just no freedom at all. (1:430)

If this is the niche that fits the *Dred Scott* case into the Kansas-Nebraska Act, it is a pretty shallow one, and just about anything could fit into it. Did Lincoln expect that the settlers of Kansas would be subject to the Constitution only if the Kansas-Nebraska Act said they were? Douglas's earlier invocation of the Constitution did not lay the groundwork for Taney's loaded and sinister reading of the Constitution. It was no more than a whiff of pious incense designed to fumigate a bad-smelling law, not part of a plan to subvert his own doctrine of popular sovereignty. Indeed, Douglas resisted Taney's attack on popular sovereignty vigorously, despite his repeated show of submission to the authority of the *Dred Scott* decision.

Lincoln's charge is given color, however, not only by the loaded way pro-slavery apologists interpreted the Constitution, but also the way they appropriated the very term "Constitution." They used the phrase "the Constitution follows the flag," for instance, to assert that the default state in the Mexican Cession favored slavery, despite standing Mexican law to the contrary, and despite a long legal tradition that slavery requires positive law to become legal and thus cannot be a default condition. "The Constitution follows the flag" meant that the Constitution, of itself, provided the legal protection necessary to make slavery the default state of territories. This, in turn, meant that the Calhoun-Davis joint sovereignty theory was as sacred a feature of the Constitution as the First Amendment or the separation of powers. The word "Constitution" meant something loaded to southern ears, roughly in the way the word "freedom" does to present-day conservatives (meaning not freedom of conscience, with the implied necessity of toleration of political dissent, but free market economics, with the implied necessity of tolerating exploitative practices by those with economic power).[59]

Behind that view of the Constitution was the doctrine Lincoln and Douglas both had reason to fear, the doctrine that slaves are ordinary property, and that political bodies are prohibited (both by natural law and by the Fifth Amendment) from taking a high-handed stance about property. This is of course the very doctrine that Lincoln argued that the doctrine of popular sovereignty was designed to advance. But Lincoln had this exactly backward, since popular sovereignty was concocted precisely in order to circumvent the challenge of the Calhoun-Davis view; it was certainly not a stalking horse for that view. And Douglas resisted the idea that natural law or the Fifth Amendment protected the right of slaveholders to property in slaves in the territories just as strongly as Lincoln did.

The Chase Amendment

Lincoln also made a similar, but more complex, case regarding the failed Chase Amendment to the Kansas-Nebraska Act, which expressly declared that the territorial government may exclude slavery. Lincoln was quite correct that Douglas and his supporters voted the Chase Amendment down, but quite wrong about their motives in doing so. The first mention of the Chase Amendment in the "House Divided" speech was simple and direct:

Then opened the roar of loose declamation in favor of "Squatter
Sovereignty," and "Sacred right of self-government."

"But," said opposition members, "let us be more specific—let us
amend the bill so as to expressly declare that the people of the territory may exclude slavery." "Not we," said the friends of the measure;
and down they voted the amendment. (1:427)

The history of the amendment is rather more complicated than
that, and the details of its legislative history were a subject of hot dispute during the 1858 debates. Douglas, both in 1854 and in 1858, insisted that his unamended language already clearly enough gave the
territorial legislatures power over slavery, with or without Chase's addition. If that were true, Lincoln argued, then why reject an amendment that merely stated that intention explicitly? Lincoln hinted that
there was a second, darker meaning in the rejection of the Chase
Amendment, and that is that it was necessary for the amendment to be
rejected for the loaded phrase "subject only to the Constitution" to do
the work the conspirators designed it to do:

> It will throw additional light on the latter, to go back, and run the
> mind over the string of historical facts already stated. Several things
> will *now* appear less *dark* and *mysterious* than they did *when* they were
> transpiring. The people were to be left "perfectly free," "subject only
> to the Constitution." What the *Constitution* had to do with it, outsid-
> ers could not *then* see. Plainly enough *now*, it was an exactly fitted
> *niche*, for the Dred Scott decision to afterward come in, and declare
> the *perfect freedom* of the people to be just no freedom at all.
>
> Why was the amendment, expressly declaring the right of the
> people, voted down? Plainly enough *now:* the adoption of it would
> have spoiled the niche for the Dred Scott decision. (1:430–431)

Lincoln's view was that had the Kansas-Nebraska Act included the
Chase Amendment, it would have been more difficult for Chief Justice Taney to issue his attack upon the doctrine of popular sovereignty. But is there any reason to believe that Taney would have been
inhibited by such language? Why should Taney have felt any com-
punction about treating the Kansas-Nebraska Act as brusquely as he
had treated the Missouri Compromise, especially since he did in fact

brush aside crucial features of that act in the *Dred Scott* decision as it stands?

In the passage we have quoted above, Lincoln made a further argument that the lack of language in the *Dred Scott* decision itself similar to the language of the Chase Amendment, language reaffirming the idea that the *states* themselves have power to choose or to reject slavery for themselves, was the niche into which the "second *Dred Scott* decision," forcing slavery back into the free states, was to be fitted.

Lincoln's suggestion was that had McLean or Curtis, the dissenters in the *Dred Scott* case, attempted to use Chase-like language about the states, then Taney would have been forced to play his card about the states in *Dred Scott I* rather than in the hypothetical *Dred Scott II*. As the lack of the Chase Amendment facilitated *Dred Scott I*, so the lack of Chase-like language in *Dred Scott I* would facilitate *Dred Scott II*.

This claim was also a stretch. But Lincoln's argument brings to mind a long-running argument about the Court's deliberations in the case. The Court had originally assigned Justice Nelson, of New York, to write the majority decision. Nelson had planned to write a minimal decision that would have ducked the most fraught issue in the case, the question of whether the federal government had the power to abolish slavery in the territories. Nelson had sought to argue, on the basis of the holding in the case of *Strader v. Graham* (1851), that the question of whether Scott's residence in the free territory of Minnesota and the free state of Illinois emancipated him had become a moot one upon his return to Missouri, because if Missouri law held that slavery "reattached" to him upon his return to the state, Missouri law would control the case. But the opinion was reassigned to Taney himself, who of course took a more aggressive approach.

Defenders of Taney long argued that he was moved to reassign the opinion by hearing that Justices McLean and Curtis were planning to write detailed dissents to the ruling. The burden of this theory, of course, is that the anti-slavery justices themselves somehow provoked Taney into writing a more sweeping decision. But Taney also was under pressure, via Buchanan's correspondence with Justices Catron and Grier, to provide a broader opinion than the one Nelson was writing, and most historians now do not believe that McLean and Curtis have any responsibility for provoking Taney to write the decision in the way he did, although Taney did treat McLean and Curtis with exceptional

peevishness during and after the deliberations, indicating that their
dissents did in fact get under his skin.[60] Lincoln could not have known
this back story about the deliberations at the time he wrote the "House
Divided" speech, but the kind of reaction he anticipated from Taney if
McLean and Curtis had reaffirmed the right of states to end slavery
within their own borders resembles the kind of reaction earlier historians attributed to Taney in his composition of the decision as a whole.

Douglas's reply to the Chase Amendment argument, in his rejoinder
at Ottawa, argues that the amendment was, in the first place, unnecessary, and in the second, set up as a kind of trap, because it specified that
the people of a territory could outlaw slavery but not that they could
legalize it:

> Mr. Lincoln wants to know why I voted against Mr. Chase's amend-
> ment to the Nebraska Bill. I will tell him. In the first place, the bill
> already conferred all the power which Congress had, by giving the
> people the whole power over the subject. Chase offered a proviso that
> they might abolish slavery, which by implication would convey the
> idea that they could prohibit by not introducing that institution. Gen.
> Cass asked him to modify his amendment, so as to provide that the
> people might either prohibit or introduce slavery, and thus make it
> fair and equal. Chase refused to so modify his proviso, and then Gen.
> Cass and all the rest of us, voted it down. [Immense cheering.] These
> facts appear on the journals and debates of Congress, where Mr. Lin-
> coln found the charge, and if he had told the whole truth, there would
> have been no necessity for me to occupy your time in explaining the
> matter. [Laughter and applause.] (1:534)

One might defend Douglas's act here as a way to preserve constructive ambiguity about the meaning of the act. But that ambiguity comes
in two kinds, only one of which is defensible. The first kind, which
promised (and yielded) only trouble for Douglas and for the Union, was
ambiguity about when the territory was supposed to exercise its choice
about the subject of slavery (during the period of territorial government
or only upon submission of a state constitution to Congress for approval). An agreement based upon ambiguity about an issue so central
to the bill is not really an agreement at all. But there is another kind
of ambiguity, which involves allowing people to support something so

long as they do not have to come out and phrase their support in so many words. Border state southerners, for instance, could support Douglas's language, but not Chase's, even though the two proposals actually mean the same thing, because Chase's language requires them to make a public statement in a way that might prove costly to them at the ballot box. They would have rejected Chase's language for exactly the same reason Chase rejected Cass's language: Cass's language would not have really changed the meaning of Chase's amendment, but it would have required Chase to put his name to language allowing a territory to adopt slavery, something he was committed never to do.

When Lincoln returned to the subject of the Chase Amendment in the Freeport debate, he added one interesting detail, the idea that Cass's motion was not intended to clarify the meaning of the underlying bill, but simply to box Chase out from offering his own amendment:

> The men, who were determined that that amendment should not get into the bill and spoil the place where the Dred Scott decision was to come in, sought an excuse to get rid of it somewhere. One of these ways—one of these excuses—was to ask Chase to add to his proposed amendment a provision that the people might *introduce* slavery if they wanted to. They very well knew Chase would do no such thing—that Mr. Chase was one of the men differing from them on the broad principle of his insisting that freedom was *better* than slavery—a man who would not consent to enact a law, penned with his own hand, by which he was made to recognize slavery on the one hand and liberty on the other as *precisely equal;* and when they insisted on his doing this, they very well knew they insisted on that which he would not for a moment think of doing, and that they were only bluffing him. (1:547)

The proof, according to Lincoln, that Cass's move was only a bluff is that the Nebraska men did not choose to vote in Chase's amendment and then vote in Cass's (the procedure parliamentary rules would have required of them). Even on its face this is a losing argument, because it provides no reason why Cass should have had to swallow hard at voting for something he disagreed with while letting Chase off from doing the same. When Douglas replied to Lincoln at Freeport on this issue, he pointed out, with a great deal of plausibility, that Chase had, as Chase himself said, proposed the amendment precisely for the purpose of having it rejected, so that he and his allies could make political hay about it. Douglas was well aware of how this kind of thing works in the Senate, and in our own day it is common enough for one side to set up a tangle of procedural votes for the sole purpose of putting their opposition on record as being against something they do not really oppose or on record as for something they would not dream of supporting.

Douglas also had more particular reasons for opposing the Chase Amendment. In the first place, putting the matter so explicitly, even with Cass's language added, may have done to the bill roughly what the "omnibus" strategy did during the debates over the Compromise of 1850. That strategy did make clear that the compromise was to be thought of as a package deal, in which each side had to give in order to take. But factionalists on either side were not willing to be seen by their supporters as giving way on anything, and the result of the omnibus strategy was only to ally the opponents of the bill on both sides against it. Douglas's strategy of separating the different parts of the Compromise of 1850 had a twofold effect. First, it roped in opponents of compromise, who had to vote for the parts of the deal that favored their section, while giving the balance of power to the desperate minority that in fact wanted to make a compromise. But, second, it also provided those who wanted compromise but needed political cover with the ability to support compromise without having to acknowledge in public that that was what they did, because Douglas's strategy turned up enough votes for each measure that such politicians would not need to pluck up their courage and cast votes that may cost them support at home.

By contrast, the parliamentary move Lincoln proposed would, in particular, have raised ugly memories of just how the omnibus came to crash. Some of the same strategies that destroyed the omnibus bill were in play in the debate over the Kansas-Nebraska Act, and some of them lent credibility to Lincoln's own conspiracy charges against Douglas, even though those charges are false.

The details of the conflict in 1850 worked out this way. In the last week of July 1850, Maine senator James Bradbury had proposed a compromise solution to the problem of the boundary of Texas, referring the issue to a commission appointed by the federal government and the government of Texas. On July 29, Senator William Dawson of Georgia managed to pass an amendment prohibiting New Mexico from exercising jurisdiction east of the Rio Grande (Texas claimed New Mexico up to the Rio Grande) until the commission reported, giving de facto control of the majority of the population of New Mexico to Texas. Recognizing that this amendment was contrary to the purposes of the compromise, James A. Pearce, the Whig senator from Maryland, sought for a way to remove the Dawson Amendment. Pearce was persuaded to remove all of the portions of the omnibus bill pertaining to New Mexico, then move an entirely new section of the bill with his own language. Pearce had fallen into a trap, since many of those who had voted for his motion to remove the New Mexico portions of the bill voted against his substitute. Immediately two southern Democrats, David Yulee of Florida and David Atchison of Missouri, successfully removed the provisions concerning Texas and California from the bill, leaving only the organization of Utah Territory remaining in the bill, thus effectively dismantling the omnibus. What was shocking about the votes on July 29 is that all of these bills were carried by an alliance of northern Whigs and southern Democrats, senators who had no ideological principle in common except hostility to compromise on any terms. The decision of the northern Whigs, in particular, to vote for the Yulee and Atchison Bills (the latter denying a free state constitution to California) can only be described as nakedly opportunistic.[61]

One thing that Lincoln, making his slave power conspiracy charge against Douglas, faulted Douglas for is his not falling into a trap during the negotiations over the Kansas-Nebraska Act like that the anti-compromisers on both sides set for Pearce in 1850. Had proponents of the bill adopted Chase's language, the only way to include Cass's language as well would have been to adopt a strategy like Pearce's, which would have enabled those who opposed the Kansas-Nebraska Act on anti-slavery grounds, and those who opposed it because it gave credibility to popular sovereignty at the expense of the Calhoun-Davis doctrine, to unite to defeat it.

Even without the "Pearce trap" there were fatal problems with the strategy Lincoln faulted Douglas for not adopting. First, it asked southern Whigs to make a vote suicidal to them, since asking them to support the Chase Amendment would have given an opening to fire-eater Democrats to continue the destruction of the Whig Party in the South. Chase and his allies, by contrast, may have been asked by this strategy to accept a bad-smelling compromise, but they were not subject to the same kind of loyalty pressure that the southern Whigs were, because they were themselves the ones playing the sectional loyalty card. Second, even the Democratic coalition was too fragile to keep itself together for such a maneuver. The strategy Lincoln faults Douglas for not adopting asked of the Democrats a kind of worldliness that Lincoln exempted the Republicans from having to exercise, and it required the southern Whigs and the northern Democrats to risk their survival, while asking nothing from northern Whigs other than that they dirty their hands.

Douglas did not undermine the Chase Amendment in order to prepare the way for making slavery national. He did it to avoid a legislative trap such as every senator experiences in the course of complex lawmaking. To avoid the trap, he had to make moves that gave color to Lincoln's charges. But because he was avoiding a trap, it is clear that those charges were false.

The Toombs Bill

In the Charleston debate, Lincoln and Douglas argued about the Toombs bill, an 1856 attempt to admit Kansas as a state. If anything, Lincoln's charges about the Toombs bill are less plausible than his charges about the Chase Amendment. But Lincoln persisted in making the charges long after they had worn out their credibility, and with a vituperativeness that was uncharacteristic of him.

After the disastrous conflicts of May 1856, congressional Democrats realized that it was crucial for them to resolve the future of Kansas Territory in such a way as to remove stories about violence there (and for that matter about violence on the Senate floor) from the headlines. Douglas already in March had proposed a bill allowing Kansas to call a constitutional convention as soon as it had the minimum number of inhabitants required for a congressional district. In late June, Robert Toombs proposed a substitute measure enabling Kansas to call its convention without waiting for the population to grow, allowing Kansas to elect a constitutional convention in November 1856, with the idea that Congress would be able to admit Kansas as a state before adjourning in March 1857.

Now Republicans had reason to regard with suspicion any proposal that issued from the Pierce administration, which had backed the pro-slavery government in Kansas and turned a blind eye to the shady electoral practices that installed the government. And nobody might have expected a fair compromise proposal about Kansas to bear the name of Robert Toombs. But in fact, the Democrats had done quite a bit to make their bill attractive. For one thing, they proposed to brush aside both the Lecompton government and the anti-slavery Topeka government and begin the process from scratch. For another thing, they were prepared to conduct a census to determine who really was an inhabitant of Kansas, in order to prevent the influx of one-day citizens from Missouri from determining the outcome of the elections for delegates to the convention. (Holding the election for delegates to the constitutional convention on the day of the 1856 presidential election also would keep down interference by Missourians.) They were willing to allow settlers who had been driven from the territory—they had in mind anti-slavery settlers—to return to cast their votes. They repealed many of the most objectionable laws that the pro-slavery territorial government had passed, laws aimed at legally harassing anti-slavery settlers. And they proposed appointing five federal commissioners to make sure that the elections to the constitutional convention were honestly conducted. When the Republicans, well remembering the character of the men Pierce had been sending to represent the federal government in Kansas, argued that the commissioners themselves might try to tilt the results in favor of slavery, backers of the bill gave them private assurances about who would be sent.

The Democrats' aim in the Toombs bill was not only to provide a solution to the Kansas problem but to put the Republicans on the spot about resisting that solution. They knew that it was to the Republicans' advantage to keep the Kansas issue at a boil, and they sought a way to point that out to the general public. (As Douglas said at the time, "All these gentlemen want is to get up murder and bloodshed in Kansas for political effect. They do not mean that there shall be peace until after the presidential election.")[62] And they knew that rather than risk a new constitution, the Republicans would attempt to impose the Topeka Constitution, which the Topeka government, which probably by this time represented the majority of the inhabitants but was procedurally illegitimate, had already forwarded to Congress. The Toombs bill wound up passing the Senate in July, but was brushed aside in the Republican-dominated House, and never became law.

The Toombs bill had several fatal flaws. One involved an amendment from Lyman Trumbull, the anti-Nebraska Democrat-turned-
Republican who outmaneuvered Lincoln in the Senate election of 1855,
conferring on the territorial government of Kansas the power to abolish slavery. The aim here, as with the Chase Amendment, was to put
Douglas in a bind. Douglas's reply was threefold: first, that the amendment was redundant, since it did not confer on Kansas Territory any
power that the Kansas-Nebraska Act had not already given it; second,
that the amendment was irrelevant, because the Toombs bill concerned
the admission of Kansas as a state, not its powers as a territory; and
third, that the question of what kind of power territorial governments
had over slavery was a question for the courts. The last two answers are
of course contradictory, since Douglas had to insist simultaneously that
he understood that the Kansas-Nebraska Act did give this power to the
legislatures (and that whatever pro-slavery politicians had to say about
"subject only to the Constitution" or "all rightful subjects of legislation" amounted—as it did—only to hocus pocus), and that the Supreme
Court still had to rule on this subject. The contradiction mirrors the
tensions of Douglas's political aim, which was to try to advance his own
view of the powers of territorial governments without breaking the
Democratic coalition. And the arguments about this amendment simply replay those that had already been made about the Chase Amendment back in 1854.

The second flaw was that the Toombs bill did not specify in so many
words that the state constitution it provided for would be subject to a
direct ratification vote by the people of Kansas. But neither did Seward's
bill accepting the Topeka Constitution. Curiously, the issue of the apparent failure of the Toombs bill to call for a ratification vote was not
raised by Trumbull during the debates over the bill, but only came up
two years later, in a speech at Alton in August 1858, in which Trumbull
charged that Douglas had removed language from the Toombs bill requiring submission of the new constitution for ratification of Congress,
and was a principal in "a plot entered into to have a Constitution
formed for Kansas, and put in force, without giving the people an opportunity to vote upon it" (1:639).

It is curious that Trumbull waited two years to make this charge,
since he was looking for ways to derail the Toombs bill in 1856, and
making a case about the absence of a requirement for ratification would

have been easy if it had really been felt to be an issue at that time. Trumbull also cited, as evidence for his charge, the claim by the Buchanan Democratic senator Bigler of Pennsylvania that "it was agreed among them that it was best not to have a provision for submitting the Constitution to a vote of the people after it should be formed" (1:639), and that after his conference with Douglas the bill came back to the Senate with the clause referring to submission to the people stricken out, and another clause added that would prevent submission to the people. Now Bigler also did not make these claims until Senate speeches on December 9 and 21, 1857. Bigler's story is suspect on its face because, as a supporter of the Lecompton Constitution, he would have wanted to argue that opposition to ratification was a part of the plan for the bill from the beginning, and that opposition to ratification was a Democratic policy of long standing, embraced even by Douglas before personal ambition led him to challenge Buchanan. The key point is that there was not debate in the Senate on this issue in 1856, which in itself casts suspicion on Bigler's story, since the Republicans would certainly have made hay on the issue then if there had been anything to it. But Trumbull made no hay in 1856 either about the absence of language requiring ratification or about removal of such language from the bill. (That Douglas actively sought to remove ratification language from with bill would have been a stronger charge, since the mere absence of ratification language is not proof of an intention to prevent a ratification vote.) Douglas complained throughout the debates that Democrats of Buchanan's faction (the so-called Buchaneers or Danites) were cooperating with the Republicans in Illinois (as indeed they were), and little has so much of the smell of the Buchaneer-Republican alliance as Bigler and Trumbull's collusion on this charge.

When Douglas, replying to Trumbull's charge at his own speech in Jacksonville, referred to the charge as a "forgery from beginning to end," he of course had in mind that he had put his career on the line not only about letting territorial legislatures rule about slavery but also specifically about requiring the constitutions of new states to be ratified by their people. Lincoln spent a half-dozen tedious pages treating Douglas's remark as if it were a formal charge of forgery, asking him to prove whether or not what Bigler had said in December 1857 really was in the *Congressional Record*. But Lincoln had no evidence at all from 1856 about this question and he had no evidence from 1856 about what was or was not in the original drafts of the bill. Lincoln seemed to be simply engaging in the familiar lawyer's strategy of pounding the table when he finds himself unable to pound either the facts or the law.

Douglas's reply in his Jacksonville speech to Trumbull's charge is pretty categorical:

> I will ask the Senator to show me an intimation, from any one member of the Senate, in the whole debate on the Toombs Bill, and in the Union, from any quarter, that the Constitution was not to be submitted to the people. I will venture to say that on all sides of the chamber it was so understood at the time. If the opponents of the bill had understood it was not, they would have made the point on it; and if they had made it, we should certainly have yielded to it, and put in the clause. That is a discovery made since the President found out that it was not safe to take it for granted that that would be done, which ought in fairness to have been done. (1:648)

Lincoln also quoted (at second hand again, from Trumbull) a second defense by Douglas, which he believed was inconsistent with the first: "That the bill was silent on this subject was true, and my attention was called to that about the time it was passed; and I took the fair construction to be, that powers not delegated were reserved, and that of course the Constitution would be submitted to the people" (1:648).

I have to confess that I do not see that very much can be made of the inconsistency between these passages. Douglas conceded that the lack of a ratification vote may have been mentioned, but it is obvious that no great fuss was made about it at the time by either side, and it is equally obvious that Douglas stood first and last for ratification.

Lincoln also built a case on language in the Toombs bill that "until the complete execution of this act there shall be no election in said Territory" (1:644). This looked to Lincoln and Trumbull like the proverbial smoking gun. But the clause did not refer to a ratification election, but to the election of a new territorial legislature. Pro-slavery sorts were very nervous that anti-slavery voters might abandon their strategy of boycotting flawed elections and turn out in numbers to elect a new legislature, and the bill sought to prevent this legislature from being elected. Now in fact this language was removed from the Toombs bill on Douglas's motion, as Lincoln conceded, and Lincoln did not have any evidence that it was initially included on Douglas's behest, although he insinuated that repeatedly. Lincoln treats evidence that in fact exculpates Douglas as if it were evidence of guilt.

As the story played out in Kansas, as we have seen, Governor Walker, after failing to persuade the free staters to participate in the elections for delegates to what became the Lecompton Convention, did persuade them to vote in elections for a new legislature, which the free staters won. The pro-slavery strategy from this point was to try to prevent the new free state territorial government from being recognized, from calling for ratification elections, from behaving, this is to say, as a government. (Hammond's "Mud-Sill" speech, discussed in section 6.5 below, gives a sample of the kind of contortions those who took this position were reduced to.) But Douglas supported the new territorial government, and supported ratification, and always did. It is hard to see how anyone not already committed to Lincoln could have been persuaded by arguments of the caliber he used here.

Lincoln's charges contain in their very making their own refutation. When Douglas got to speak for himself at Charleston, he made very short work of them. First, he made clear the falsity of Bigler's invention about the supposed ratification clause in the Toombs bill, noting that Trumbull was in the hall when he (Douglas) publicly took Bigler apart on the Senate floor, and that Trumbull did not rise to Bigler's defense. Douglas went on to remark that even Toombs himself said that no ratification clause was removed from his bill, because it never included one in the first place. Douglas further argued that the standing assumption was that the constitution called for in the Toombs bill would indeed be subject to ratification:

> I wish you to bear in mind that up to the time of the introduction of the Toombs Bill, and after its introduction, there had never been an act of Congress for the admission of a new State which contained a clause requiring its Constitution to be submitted to the people. The general rule made the law silent on the subject, taking it for granted that the people would demand and compel a popular vote on the ratification of their Constitution. Such was the general rule under Washington, Jefferson, Madison, Jackson and Polk, under the Whig Presidents and the Democratic Presidents from the beginning of the Government down, and nobody dreamed that an effort would ever be

made to abuse the power thus confided to the people of a Territory. For this reason our attention was not called to the fact of whether there was or was not a clause in the Toombs Bill compelling submission, but it was taken for granted that the Constitution would be submitted to the people whether the law compelled it or not. (1:655)

Douglas's historical premises were mistaken: many states, including Illinois, were admitted to the Union without formal popular ratification of their constitutions. But the point is clear: Douglas himself always supported ratification, and did not even understand that it might have been a controversial issue. In fact, Douglas's defense was sometimes a bit sloppy, because the language he cited from his committee report on the Toombs bill, language that he thought of as proving beyond doubt that he stood for ratification, could in fact (with a little forcing) be taken as referring only to the election of a constitutional convention:

In the opinion of your Committee, whenever a Constitution shall be formed in any Territory, preparatory to its admission into the Union as a State, justice, the genius of our institutions, the whole theory of our republican system, imperatively demand that the voice of the people shall be fairly expressed, and their will embodied in that fundamental law, without fraud, or violence, or intimidation, or any other improper or unlawful influence, and subject to no other restrictions than those imposed by the Constitution of the United States. (1:656–657)

Indeed, the passage in the Toombs bill that Trumbull had taken to be about submission of the constitution as a whole was in fact merely about the land grant from the federal government that went with it:

The printed copy of the bill which Mr. Lincoln held up before you, and which he pretends contains such a clause, merely contains a clause requiring a submission of the land grant, and *there is no clause in it requiring a submission of the constitution.* Mr. Lincoln cannot find such a clause in it. My report shows that we took it for granted that the people would require a submission of the Constitution, and secure it for themselves. There never was a clause in the Toombs Bill requiring the Constitution to be submitted; Trumbull knew it at the time, and his speech made on the night of its passage discloses the fact that he knew it was silent on the subject. (1:657)

Lincoln did in fact know that the language in question referred to the land grant, not to the constitution, but he argued that there was no way to subject the one to a vote without subjecting the other. In the very summer of the English Compromise, this was a strange argument to make.

Having spent most of the Charleston debate on the issue—the non-issue—of whether the Toombs bill, which never became law anyway, did or did not seek to determine the will of the people of Kansas about their proposed constitution, Lincoln let this part of his case lapse, and moved in the Galesburg debate onto more promising ground.

The Reply to the Washington Union

One of the stranger turns in Lincoln's development of his conspiracy case against Douglas is his use of a speech in which Douglas made against President Buchanan essentially the same charges that Lincoln made against Douglas. In the Ottawa debate, Douglas had expressed astonishment about being charged with conspiracy to reintroduce slavery into the free states. Douglas hesitated, he said, to respond to the charges Lincoln made in the "House Divided" speech because he "did not suppose there was a man in America with a heart so corrupt as to believe such a charge could be true. I have too much respect for Mr. Lincoln to suppose he is serious in making the charge" (1:521).

In the immediate context of the Ottawa speech, Lincoln's quotation of Douglas's attack upon Buchanan (or rather, Buchanan's proxy, the editor of the *Washington Union*, the house organ of Buchanan's government) is meant to say that Douglas did indeed know of people who do not think of charges such as those Lincoln had just made as crazy, since Douglas himself had made substantially the same charge.

What Douglas was responding to was the *Union*'s announcement of the provisions of the Lecompton Constitution on November 18, 1857, an announcement made on the day before the *Union* and the administration came out in its support. The argument was indeed a startling one for an administration organ (the interpolated paragraphs are from

Douglas's speech in the Senate of March 22, 1858, in which he responded to the article in the *Union*):

> KANSAS AND HER CONSTITUTION—The vexed question is settled. The problem is solved. The dead point of danger is passed. All serious trouble to Kansas affairs is over and gone.
>
> And a column, nearly, of the same sort. Then, when you come to look into the Lecompton Constitution, you find the same doctrine incorporated in it which was put forth editorially in the Union. What is it?
>
> ARTICLE 7, *Section* 1. The right of property is before and higher than any Constitutional sanction; and the right of the owner of a slave to such slave and its increase is the same and as inviolable as the right of the owner of any property whatever.
>
> Then in the schedule is a provision that the Constitution may be amended after 1864 by a two-thirds vote.
>
> But no alteration shall be made to affect the right of property in the ownership of slaves. (1:522)

What is striking about the text from the Lecompton Constitution is the way it seems to quote the nightmares of the most paranoid antislavery politicians. The right of white people to own slaves is "before and higher than any Constitutional sanction." It has the sanction of a law higher than the Constitution, a pro-slavery version of a Garrisonian higher law, something dictated by God, something higher than the highest political authority. The slaveholder's right includes his property not only in the slave but also in that slave's increase, in that slave's children on down through the generations.

Douglas's summary of the *Union*'s argument reads rather like Lincoln's own indictment of Douglas:

> Mr. President, you here find several distinct propositions advanced boldly by the Washington *Union* editorially, and apparently *authoritatively*, and any man who questions any of them is denounced as an Abolitionist, a Freesoiler, a fanatic. The propositions are, first, that the primary object of all government at its original institution is the protection of person and property; second, that the Constitution of the United States declares that the citizens of each State shall be en-

titled to all the privileges and immunities of citizens in the several States; and that, therefore, thirdly, all State laws, whether organic or otherwise, which prohibit the citizens of one State from settling in another with their slave property, and especially declaring it forfeited, are direct violations of the original intention of the Government and Constitution of the United States; and, fourth, that the emancipation of the slaves of the Northern States was a gross outrage on the rights of property, inasmuch as it was involuntarily done on the part of the owner. (1:522)

Douglas's judgment about this doctrine is also not far from Lincoln's:

When I saw that article in the *Union* of the 17th of November, followed by the glorification of the Lecompton Constitution on the 18th of November, and this clause in the Constitution asserting the doctrine that a State has no right to prohibit slavery within its limits, I saw that there was a *fatal blow* being struck at the sovereignty of the States of this Union. (1:523)

Indeed, Douglas's response says enough about how he feels about the prospect of the nationalization of slavery:

This attempt now to establish the doctrine that a free State has no power to prohibit slavery, that our emancipation acts were unconstitutional and void, that they were outrages on the rights of property, that slavery is national and not local, that it goes everywhere under the Constitution of the United States, and yet is higher than the Constitution . . . will not be tolerated.[63]

What Douglas was responding to was of course exactly the logic of the "second *Dred Scott* decision" Lincoln feared may be in the offing. There was a slight difference between the "second *Dred Scott* case" Douglas described in his attack upon the *Washington Union* and the case Lincoln described in the "House Divided" speech and in the debates, in that the case Douglas mentioned turns on a matter of prepolitical higher-law right, whereas the case Lincoln mentioned turns merely on the idea that slave property is distinctly protected in the federal Constitution.

Lincoln describes his version of the "second *Dred Scott* case" this way during the Galesburg debate:

> The essence of the Dred Scott case is compressed into the sentence which I will now read: "Now, as we have already said in an earlier part of this opinion, upon a different point, the right of property in a slave is distinctly and expressly affirmed in the Constitution." I repeat it, *"The right of property in a slave is distinctly and expressly affirmed in the Constitution!"* What is it to be "affirmed" in the Constitution? Made firm in the Constitution—so made that it cannot be separated from the Constitution without breaking the Constitution—durable as the Constitution, and part of the Constitution. Now, remembering the provision of the Constitution which I have read, affirming that that instrument is the supreme law of the land; that the Judges of every State shall be bound by it, any law or Constitution of any State to the contrary notwithstanding; that the right of property in a slave is affirmed in that Constitution, is made, formed into, and cannot be separated from it without breaking it; durable as the instrument; part of the instrument;—what follows as a short and even syllogistic argument from it? I think it follows, and I submit to the consideration of men capable of arguing, whether as I state it, in syllogistic form, the argument has any fault in it?
>
> Nothing in the Constitution or laws of any State can destroy a right distinctly and expressly affirmed in the Constitution of the United States.
>
> The right of property in a slave is distinctly and expressly affirmed in the Constitution of the United States.
>
> Therefore, nothing in the Constitution or laws of any State can destroy the right of property in a slave. (1:713–716)

There is a shade of difference between Douglas's presentation of this case and Lincoln's. Both saw the same aim—providing grounds for attacking emancipation in the free states. Both saw some of the same means—an argument about the sanctity of property. But the case Douglas feared is a higher-law case, a case founded in a pre-political notion of rights, and the case Lincoln feared is a constitutional case, founded in language purportedly in the Constitution that distinctly affirms the right of property in slaves.

In Douglas's mind, what separated these cases may have been a distinction without a difference. Douglas was in the habit of seeing a constitutional case as having the same kind of trumping power one might assign to a higher-law case. And indeed, usually Douglas treated higher-law cases in their pure form as little more than incitements to bloodshed—notice how often citations from the Bible by his opponents seem to set him off. But there is a difference between the two kinds of case. A higher-law case is a prelude to a revolutionary confrontation between those who follow it and those who break it. It forms the basis of an "appeal to heaven" such as Locke described in the *Second Treatise of Government* and such as Jefferson proposed in the Declaration of Independence. But a constitutional case forms the basis of an episode of lawmaking, in that it subjects a polity to a settlement of an issue about which it has already made the underlying principle clear. A constitutional case may cause an upheaval, but a higher-law case may cause a revolution.

A second thing to notice in the passage is that at Galesburg Lincoln did not use Douglas's speech against the *Washington Union* to argue that Douglas was somehow in the conspiracy so much as to argue that if the Supreme Court *were* to do what both of them feared it might, Douglas would be in a rather weak position to oppose it. First, Douglas had argued that support or opposition to slavery is not a moral choice so much as either an economic one or a choice best left to personal moral discretion, as if choices about slavery were matters of taste or of interest rather than of principle, and thus he would be in a weak position to draw a moral line in the sand about it. This argument, in my view, is a weak one, and does not predict what Douglas actually did in 1860 and 1861. Second, Douglas had argued that citizens have a responsibility to accept the ipse dixit of the Supreme Court, and that any attempt to quarrel with the grounds or the holding of a decision amounts to an anarchist challenge to the constitutional order. Douglas did play this card, but its force was rhetorical; Douglas sought no less than Lincoln did to forestall some parts of Taney's opinion, although he did not think that on those points Taney spoke for the Court.[64]

Lincoln's arguments do not quite get to the heart of the charge. The question, after all, is what Douglas would do if the Court did in fact issue such a decision:

The third question which Mr. Lincoln presented is, if the Supreme Court of the United States shall decide that a State of this Union cannot exclude slavery from its own limits, will I submit to it? I am amazed that Lincoln should ask such a question. ["A school boy knows better."] Yes, a school-boy does know better. Mr. Lincoln's object is to cast an imputation upon the Supreme Court. He knows that there never was but one man in America, claiming any degree of intelligence or decency, who ever for a moment pretended such a thing. It is true that the Washington *Union*, in an article published on the 17th of last December, did put forth that doctrine, and I denounced the article on the floor of the Senate, in a speech which Mr. Lincoln now pretends was against the President. The *Union* had claimed that slavery had a right to go into the free States, and that any provision in the Constitution or laws of the free States to the contrary were null and void. I denounced it in the Senate, as I said before, and I was the first man who did. Lincoln's friends, Trumbull, and Seward, and Hale, and Wilson, land the whole Black Republican side of the Senate, were silent. They left it to me to denounce it. [Cheers.] And what was the reply made to me on that occasion? Mr. Toombs, of Georgia, got up and undertook to lecture me on the ground that I ought not to have deemed the article worthy of notice, and ought not to have replied to it; that there was not one man, woman or child south of the Potomac, in any slave State, who did not repudiate any such pretension. (1:553–554)

Douglas was probably not play-acting when he says that he could not imagine the Supreme Court making the "second *Dred Scott* decision"; the charge seemed so astounding he could barely comprehend it. (In fact, it contradicted the sense of what Lincoln would call "the public mind." It so went against the grain of public tradition that Douglas could not come to grips with it.) That seems to be why he cited the uncharacteristically reassuring speech by Toombs on the subject.

When Douglas said at the Quincy debate that such a decision was inconceivable, a voice in the crowd said, "The same thing was said about the Dred Scott decision before it passed" (1:755–756). Harry Jaffa famously compared this voice to "the voice of History." Does Douglas's sincere incredulity about Lincoln's charge concerning the "second *Dred Scott* case" square with his own charges against the *Washington*

Union? Lincoln obviously did not think so: he believed that Douglas saw the same threat he did, and had chosen to ignore it. But there is a shade of difference in hearing an outrageous argument from a newspaper, even from an administration organ, and hearing the same argument from the Supreme Court. And it is quite possible that Wendell was running a little ahead even of Buchanan on the subject. It seems most likely that Douglas was aware of the currency of the argument he responded to among southern *ultras*, and sought to fire a warning shot across Buchanan's bow to warn him away from taking the administration down such a road. That was not quite the same thing as saying that the course was so irrational that it is inconceivable. But it was also not quite the same thing as seeing an imminent conspiracy about to come to fruition.

There is an odd postscript to the argument with the *Washington Union* in the Quincy debate. The editor of the *Union* had been launching conspiracy charges of his own against Douglas. The *Union* had taken umbrage at the Freeport Doctrine, Douglas's argument that since slavery could not prosper without extensive police and economic legislation to support it, a territory could effectively keep slavery out, even if it could not formally outlaw it, by refusing to pass the necessary legislation. To the editors, that proved that Douglas had all along been scheming in the interests of the free states, and that popular sovereignty was a ruse Douglas adopted in order to make the slave states drop their guard. Douglas was in the ironic position of being accused, on the basis of precisely the same evidence, of exactly opposite conspiratorial intentions.

Douglas quoted the editorial against him with a certain amount of relish, since it accused him, in tones of shock and outrage, of holding positions he not only never made any secret of but was in fact proud of:

> The Washington *Union* there charges me with the monstrous crime of now proclaiming on the stump, the same doctrine that I carried out in 1850, by supporting Clay's Compromise measures. The *Union* also charges that I am now proclaiming the same doctrine that I did in 1854 in support of the Kansas and Nebraska bill. It is shocked that I should now stand where I stood in 1850, when I was supported by Clay, Webster, Cass, and the great men of that day, and where I stood in 1854, and in 1856, when Mr. Buchanan was elected President. It goes

on to prove and succeeds in proving, from my speeches in Congress on Clay's Compromise measures, that I held the same doctrines at that time that I do now, and then proves that by the Kansas and Nebraska bill I advanced the same doctrine that I now advance. It remarks:

"So much for the course taken by Judge Douglas on the Compromises of 1850. The record shows, beyond the possibility of cavil or dispute, that he expressly intended in those bills to give the Territorial Legislatures power to exclude slavery. How stands his record in the memorable session of 1854, with reference to the Kansas-Nebraska bill itself? We shall not overhaul the votes that were given on that notable measure. Our space will not afford it. We have his own words, however, delivered in his speech closing the great debate on that bill on the night of March 3, 1854, to show that *he meant* to do in 1854 precisely what *he had meant* to do in 1850." (1:758–759)

The *Union* even pressed its own version of the "or State" and "subject to the Constitution" arguments, noting that in 1850 the Utah and New Mexico Bills first came to the Committee on Territories with language prohibiting the territorial legislatures from acting on slavery in any way. Presumably the authors of this language held that only a constitutional convention, not a territorial legislature, could make decisions about slavery. Douglas specifically and vociferously objected to this provision, and had it removed from the bills, and argued at the time that removing this language would give the territorial legislatures power over slavery. This fight did not recur during the debates over the Kansas-Nebraska Act in 1854, but, says the *Union*, Douglas's care to include in that act language identical to his earlier language about Utah and New Mexico is proof that he wanted the earlier debate to be remembered, and wanted the earlier conclusion to be drawn. The *Union* charged, in other words, that Douglas had laid a trap for supporters of the Calhoun-Davis joint sovereignty argument, giving them in the Kansas-Nebraska Act explicit language ambiguous enough to support their reading, but also writing that language in such a way as to recall a historical context hostile to the Calhoun-Davis view. Douglas had waltzed them, this is to say, into giving away the store. One almost wishes that the *Union*'s charges were completely true.

3.5 *Dred Scott* II

Douglas did not think there was any imminent threat of a decision nationalizing slavery coming even from the Taney Court. But Lincoln took that threat very seriously, and made it the keystone of his case against Douglas. Is there reason to believe that the threat Lincoln described from the Taney Court was a serious one?

The hypothetical "second *Dred Scott* case" could have taken either of two courses. The *Somerset* case, as we shall see below, had held that slavery could not have the protection of natural law, but could be established by positive law. A "second *Dred Scott* case" could have conceded the *Somerset* case's reading of natural law but have argued that the Constitution established legal protection of slavery in positive law, and that therefore property in slaves would be protected by the Fifth Amendment even in the free states. This version would make slavery national by arguing that the Constitution gave slavery the same status it gives other varieties of property. (This is the version Lincoln feared.) Or a hypothetical "second *Dred Scott* case" could have directly attacked the *Somerset* case by arguing that slave property is not a special category of property but an ordinary kind of property fully in keeping with natural law, and thus worthy of the kind of transcendent protection given to ordinary property both in natural law and in the federal Constitution. (This is the version Douglas feared.)

Historians have often found in *Lemmon v. New York*, which was decided by the New York Court of Appeals in 1860, a case that, had it been brought before the Supreme Court in time, might have been Lincoln's "second *Dred Scott* case." The Lemmon case involved eight slaves who were brought in November 1852 to New York City aboard the steamer *Richmond City* in transit with their master from Virginia to Texas. Because New York did not recognize the right of masters to pass through its territory with their slaves, New York Superior Court Justice Elijah Paine set the Lemmon slaves free. Richard Sewell (1976) and Paul Finkelman (1981), among others, have argued that overturning Paine's decision would have given the Taney Court an opportunity to either attack or undermine the emancipation statutes of the free states.

Overturning Paine's decision would not of itself have forced slavery into the free states, since *Lemmon* on its face turned on issues about transit through a free state with slaves, not about long-term residence

in a free state with slaves, of domicile. New York had abolished sojourning and transit rights in 1841, taking the position (in high *Somerset* style) that the first footstep a slave took on the soil of New York effected that slave's emancipation. An attack on the New York decision
by the Supreme Court could have more easily focused on the 1841
repeal of transit than on the 1817 abolition of slavery. It would have
taken considerable wrenching to transform the *Lemmon* case into the
"second *Dred Scott* case" Lincoln and Douglas argued about. But perhaps even a more modest version of the *Lemmon* decision aimed only at
the 1841 transit statute might have worn the 1817 emancipation statute
around the edges by raising questions about just how long one has to
remain in the state with slaves before sojourning with slaves becomes
domicile with slaves. And questions about what to do about slaves who
escaped from sojourning masters might also have required New York
to elaborate some of the legal and institutional structures of slave states.
Finally, it could have eroded free state use of the *Somerset* precedent by
inventing, as the federal courts were already inclined to do, a federal
right to transit with slaves that would have trumped any free state statute, thus making slavery to that extent a creature of federal positive law,
immune to the strictures in *Somerset*.

   If the *Lemmon* case scenario seems strained, it must be remembered
that few people would have believed the Court capable of what it did
in *Dred Scott* had they not actually done it, just as the heckler in the
Lincoln-Douglas debates pointed out. Furthermore, just as the *Lemmon* case offered an easy way out of confrontation, through the distinction between transit and domicile, so *Dred Scott* had also offered
two easy ways out, first, through a minimal decision based on the
Strader case (which Justice Nelson had originally prepared as the majority decision) or second, through a decision arguing that since Scott
himself did not have standing to sue (since he did not have the rights
of a U.S. citizen) that the rest of the case was moot. The court in *Dred
Scott* sought out the confrontation the case produced, although perhaps it also felt that it had been asked to settle the territorial issue and
could not evade it.[65]

   To use the *Lemmon* case as an attack on emancipation in the free
states would require a somewhat more reckless urge for no-holds-
barred confrontation than the *Dred Scott* case had required, since the
status of slavery in the free states was not an urgently lobbied issue for

slaveholders in the 1850s in the way that the status of slavery in the territories was.

That said, there was a great deal of contemporary fear, not only from professional conspiracy theorists but also from sober legal minds, that the *Lemmon* case would be used as the "second *Dred Scott* case" Lincoln described, and probably the majority of recent historians (including even Fehrenbacher) take the *Lemmon* case scenario very seriously.[66] George Templeton Strong, the level-headed, conservative attorney whose diary enables one to take the pulse of respectable northern opinion during the war years, wrote in November 1860:

> If we accede to Southern exactions, we must re-open the slave trade with all its horrors, establish a Slave Code for the territories, and acquiesce in a decision of the United States Supreme Court in the Lemmon Case that will entitle every Southerner to bring his slaves into New York and Massachusetts and keep them there. We must confess that our federal government exists chiefly for the sake of Nigger owners. I can't do that. Rather let South Carolina and Georgia secede. We will coerce and punish the traitorous seceders if we can; but if we can't, we are well rid of them.[67]

As early as 1855 Judge Samuel A. Foot of the New York Supreme Court had warned of the dire consequences that might arise from a Supreme Court opinion in the *Lemmon* case, and by 1858 he was warning that such a decision would, changing the Constitution, "turn this nation into a great slaveholding republic."[68] Henry Wilson alluded to the *Lemmon* case as a "second *Dred Scott* decision" in a speech in the Senate in February 1858.[69] Lyman Trumbull, during the summer of the 1858 campaign, warned: "There is now a case pending, known as the 'Lemmon Case,' and when the country gets prepared to receive the decision, you will probably hear again from the Supreme Court of the United States, the doctrine announced, that under the Constitution Slavery goes into all the States of the Union."[70]

It is worth speculating, even if it involves a certain amount of tea-leaf reading, how the judges who decided the first *Dred Scott* might have decided the second. Certainly Justices McLean and Curtis would not have supported a decision to nationalize slavery. But Curtis resigned from the Court just after *Dred Scott*, incensed at how Taney treated

him, and President Buchanan appointed Maine lawyer Nathan Clifford
to take his place. Clifford was a pro-slavery Democrat who believed in
a firm separation between state and federal authority. Those two allegiances would have been in conflict in the *Lemmon* case, since it would
have overturned New York's right to decide the legality of slavery within
its boundaries, and nobody can say for certain how Clifford would have
voted. But it is safe to say that if "pro-slavery" means "willing to defend
slavery in the slave states," it does not necessarily stretch so far as to favor reintroducing slavery into Maine.

It is likely that the two other justices from free states, Nelson, from
New York, and Grier, from Pennsylvania, would not have voted to
nationalize slavery either. Nelson's opinion in *Dred Scott* opposed the
Court's attack on the Missouri Compromise, so an attack on emancipation in the free states from him seems unlikely. He did, however, in
his opinion in *Dred Scott*, obliquely refer to the *Lemmon* case, and from
his remarks it is clear that he would have overturned New York's position in that case, applying the distinction between domicile and transit
to New York. But allowing a master right of transit through a free state
with slaves is not quite the same thing as reintroducing slavery into
that state. Nelson's language in the last paragraph of his opinion can
be forced into a threat of something stronger, and indeed Finkelman
reads it straightforwardly as just that kind of threat, but to me that
reading seems unlikely:

> A question has been alluded to, on the argument, namely, the right of
> the master with his slave of transit into or through a free State, on
> business or commercial pursuits, or in the exercise of a Federal right,
> or the discharge of a Federal duty, being a citizen of the United States,
> which is not before us. This question depends upon different consider-
> ations and principles from the one in hand, and turns upon the rights
> and privileges secured to a common citizen of the republic under the
> Constitution of the United States. When that question arises, we shall
> be prepared to decide it.[71]

Nelson's role in the deliberations over *Dred Scott* was to try to push
the Court into making a modest decision, to decide against Scott on
the basis of the *Strader* decision, without raising either the question of
whether blacks can sue in federal court or whether the federal govern-

ment can prohibit slavery in the territories. His effort, this is to say, was to dispose of the case without reaching for a controversial decision. Nelson was no bomb-thrower, and however he may have decided on the question of transit through free states with slaves, he would have resisted a sweeping *Lemmon* decision just as he resisted a sweeping *Dred Scott* decision. It is a very far stretch to see a threat to the emancipation laws of the free states in his last sentence.

Grier supported the attack on the Missouri Compromise restriction late in the game, and reluctantly, because he did not want the majority to rule on purely sectional lines if it was going to strike down the Missouri Compromise restriction anyway (and in his correspondence with Buchanan he tried to separate his views from those of the true pro-slavery radicals, Wayne, Taney, Daniel, and Campbell). It is doubtful those same motivations could have led him to reintroduce slavery into his own Pennsylvania.[72]

On the other side, only Justice Daniel, a crank and a fanatic, would have been a sure bet, although Justice Campbell, who ultimately supported secession, may have supported nationalization as well. But the question of how Campbell would have ruled is complicated by his own reasoning in *Dred Scott*, since he argued that the federal government could wield "no power over the subject of slavery within the States." This meant that if only federal law prohibited slavery, the master's property rights would trump that law even in the free states, but the free states' own emancipation laws would still remain in force, since the states had sovereign authority, something that the putative "second *Dred Scott* case" would have to deny.

Justices Catron and Wayne had decided *Dred Scott*–like cases earlier in their careers in different ways, and both, although from seceding states, remained loyal to the Union during the war at some cost to themselves, so it is not clear how they would have voted. Wayne took a hard line in *Dred Scott*—he was really the only one of the concurring justices who agreed with Taney down the line, and historians used to believe that a great deal of Taney's opinion was actually Wayne's work—so it is possible, although not certain, he would also have taken a hard line in a "second *Dred Scott* case."[73]

In his opinion in *Dred Scott*, Catron attacked the constitutionality of the Missouri Compromise restriction, but he defended the constitutionality of the Northwest Ordinance, arguing that the prohibition of slavery there was the act of Virginia (not of the Confederation Congress) and that in accepting that prohibition as the price of accepting cession of Virginia's claim to those lands, the Confederation Congress was in effect making a treaty and was bound by the obligations it had to Virginia. Since Catron's decision depended upon his recognition that Virginia had the right to abolish slavery, it would not make sense for him to deny that New York also had that right. And what made the Missouri Compromise restriction unconstitutional for Catron was not that Congress lacked the power to govern the territories, but that prohibiting slavery in the Louisiana Purchase was contrary to the treaty with France by which the United States had acquired the territory. Furthermore, as Fehrenbacher has shown, Catron believed that the portions of Taney's decision dealing with black citizenship were dictum.[74] Finally, since Catron, like Nelson, seems to have felt that had Scott remained in Illinois he would unquestionably have been free, and only his return to Missouri subjected him (sort of) to reattachment, he does not seem to have any intention of questioning Illinois's right to be a free state.

Even how Taney would have voted in this case is not completely certain, though given his Lear-on-the-Heath rage after the *Dred Scott* decision provoked the controversy it was certain to provoke, it is hard to say that anything would have been beyond him. A switch by any one of these last three would have made the *Dred Scott II* scenario impossible.

But the gravamen of Lincoln's charge was not finally that Douglas was a party to the conspiracy, but that Douglas's arguments could not prevent such a judicial revolution by the slave power should the pro-slavery Supreme Court decide to attempt it. Nor does he anticipate that *Dred Scott II* would be immediately decided by the existing court; rather, he expects the slaveholders might lay the groundwork for such a case over a period of decades, much as he himself planned to lay the groundwork for the end of slavery over a period of decades, so that a decision that might have seemed outrageous in 1858 would seem obvious in, say, 1880. No matter how angry Douglas and his immediate allies might be about the use of the Fifth Amendment to nationalize slavery, Lincoln argued, they would have already drained away the reservoir of specifically moral outrage that would be needed to resist that use; if the Douglasites choose to see politics as a matter of economics, personal choice, and power, rather than as a matter of justice grounded in some deep stratum of conviction, they will be in no position to resist the particularly brilliant coup the slave power might pull off by having its way in the *Lemmon* case, because only a moral vision of politics, not a popular sovereignty vision of politics, gives durable grounds for that resistance. And indeed, Lincoln went on to argue, by encouraging people to see politics as only about economics, personal choice, and power, the Douglasites have inadvertently prepared the way for the victory of the slave power, by depriving the people of the moral resources they would need to oppose the slave power firmly.

It is worth wondering whether even this argument is a plausible one. It is true that Douglas's popular sovereignty grounds provide weaker arguments against slavery than Lincoln's moral ones. But it is not true that Douglas, by (ambiguously, for all his blunt language) defending the first *Dred Scott* decision, had foreclosed the ability to resist the hypothetical "second *Dred Scott* decision" represented by the *Lemmon* case. Lincoln had argued that since Douglas had trained the public mind to accept the *Thus saith the Lord* of the Taney court in the *Dred Scott* case, he would therefore be in no position to do anything but preach the same kind of abject submission to the Court's ruling in the "second *Dred Scott* case." Now in the first place, despite much handwaving on Douglas's part about it, Douglas's actual response to *Dred Scott* was far from abject, as we shall see in Chapter 7, and Douglas left himself a great deal of room both to resist the first *Dred Scott* decision (or to reshape it to the advantage of his point of view), and to resist a hypothetical "second *Dred Scott* decision" as well.

Douglas had argued against Lincoln that resistance to the will of the court in the *Dred Scott* case was anarchic resistance to the legal order, but he could not have actually believed such a thing, because he did not believe that the Court's decision had foreclosed every political riposte, and he elaborated, in the Freeport Doctrine, a far more direct and specific way to limit the reach of the decision than Lincoln ever did. Lincoln responded to the Freeport Doctrine by charging that Douglas too proposed anarchic resistance to the legal order, returning Douglas's charge against him in a form not much more credible than Douglas's original charge against Lincoln had been. Lincoln and Douglas both accused each other of attempting to subvert the legal order by resistance to the *Dred Scott* decision, whether by appointing new justices to overrule it or by evading it through the Freeport Doctrine. But both of their arguments seem strategic and disingenuous,

and neither really felt that Taney's ruling had left them in their own
case with no alternative but abject submission. Each sought to evade the
decision, and each sought to prevent the other from doing the same.
Lincoln's argument that the Freeport Doctrine represented a revival
of nullification was a stronger argument than Douglas's argument that
Lincoln's attack on the *Dred Scott* decision amounted to idealist anar-
chism. But neither argument was a very telling one, and neither argument outweighs the attempts of both politicians to work their way out
from under Taney's decision. Both looked for the cracks in *Dred Scott*,
and both would have resisted *Lemmon*.

In the second place, surely Douglas's arguments about popular sovereignty would speak to the hypothetical *Lemmon* case scenario every bit
as pointedly as Lincoln's moral arguments do. For not only would such
a ruling run in the face of decades of tradition that slavery is a matter of
state law; such a ruling would also be something that someone with a
commitment to popular sovereignty would have to oppose, since the
upshot of the case is that no deliberative body of any kind has anything
to say on the subject of slavery, and that the right to own slaves is so fundamental a right that no political body can interfere with it.

The path from *Dred Scott* to the hypothetical ruling in the *Lemmon*
case is not a direct one, and some of the legal premises of the first case
would seem to lead the second in a different direction. For the *Lemmon*
case to do the work of nationalizing slavery, it would have to overturn
the idea that the status of slavery is a function of state law. Overturning
the idea that the status of slavery is a function of state law would have
been fraught with risks, not only because overruling decades of legal
and political tradition would have been inflammatory but also because
the idea that the status of slavery is a function of state law was a key element in the slaveholder's constitutional defense of slavery.

Both Justice Scott's opinion in the Missouri Supreme Court decision in *Dred Scott v. Emerson* and several of the concurring opinions in
the U.S. Supreme Court decision in *Dred Scott v. Sandford* elided the
distinction between residence with slaves in a free state and temporary
sojourning with slaves in a free state or transit through a free state. But
they did this in cases of "reattachment," in which the purported slave
had returned to a slave state after residence in a free state, and their
opinions do not bear directly on the *Lemmon* case, since the Lemmons' slaves remained in New York. Reattachment was a decisive is-

sue, as we have just seen, for several of the justices in the majority in the *Dred Scott* case, and the reattachment issue did not play out in the same way in *Lemmon* as it did in *Dred Scott*. For one thing, the whole concept of reattachment depended upon the assumption that slavery is a state, not a national institution, since the argument that a state can "reattach" slavery to someone freed by domicile or sojourning in a free state upon that person's return to a slave state depends upon the assumption that that is a question that a slave state can decide for itself.

The ruling in the 1851 case of *Strader v. Graham* (discussed in Chapter 7) was that if a person thought of as a slave returned to the slave state after residence in a free state, and the slave state's laws held that that person remained a slave, the free state had nothing to say about it, since it is the laws of the state where the (might be) slave is actually at the moment residing that control the case.[75] The principal ruling of the case would seem to support the slaves, not the Lemmons, since it held that New York's law, not Virginia's, would decide the status of the (might be) slaves. *Strader* was a key element in the architecture of *Dred Scott*, but the Court could not decide *Lemmon* in a pro-slavery way without overruling *Strader*.

It is also true that *Dred Scott* itself overruled (or evaded) decades of legal tradition, going back to Mansfield's decision in the *Somerset* case, that residence in a free polity emancipates slaves brought to it, so perhaps the Court might have felt free to overrule its own very recent decision in the *Strader* case. But the precedent that the Taney Court overturned in *Dred Scott* was an *anti-slavery* precedent, the *Somerset* ruling. In overruling the idea that slavery is essentially a state institution, the hypothetical ruling in the *Lemmon* case would have overruled something that for years had been the main legal bulwark *defending* slavery, the idea that the legal status of slavery is a state matter and that the federal government, including the federal judiciary, is foreclosed from intervening about the legal status of slavery in the states by the independent sovereignty of the states. The Court on the hypothetical case would have overruled this precedent for pro-slavery reasons, but it would also have laid the legal groundwork for an anti-slavery counterattack in a later time.[76] It is hard to imagine that even fire-eaters would not have seen the risk of declaring that slavery is not a state institution. Douglas's incredulity that such a case could even be taken seriously says enough, I think, about whether he or his followers would be in a position to oppose the Taney Court if it were foolish or reckless enough to make such a decision.

3.6 A Living Dog Is Better than a Dead Lion

Given that Lincoln's conspiracy argument is implausible, although perhaps he had reasons to believe it, are there reasons later readers might have to take his conspiracy case seriously? The principal burden of the conspiracy case ultimately is not that Douglas was a party to the conspiracy, but that he was not the best agent to resist it. As Lincoln put it in the "House Divided" speech:

> There are those who denounce us *openly* to their *own* friends and yet whisper *us softly*, that *Senator Douglas* is the *aptest* instrument there is, with which to effect that object [defeating the attempt to make slavery national]. *They* do *not* tell us, nor has *he* told us, that he *wishes* any such object to be effected. They wish us to *infer* all from the facts, that he now has a little quarrel with the present head of the dynasty; and that he has regularly voted with us on a single point, upon which, he and we, have never differed.
>
> They remind us that *he* is a very *great man*, and that the largest of *us* are very small ones. Let this be granted. But "a *living dog* is better than a *dead lion*." Judge Douglas, if not a *dead* lion, *for this work*, is at least a *caged* and *toothless* one. How can he oppose the advances of slavery? He does not *care* anything about it. His avowed *mission is impressing* the "public heart" to *care* nothing about it. (1:432–433)

Lincoln worried in the "House Divided" speech that Douglas's doctrines would corrupt what he calls "the public mind," preparing them to accept a world in which it really is a matter of indifference whether people enslave each other or not. He meant by the public mind a great deal more than mere public opinion. He meant by it that largely unconscious body of habits, received opinions, prejudices, assumptions, allegiances, and dispositions through which we make practical sense of the political world.[77]

Lincoln puts forward an amusing definition of the public mind in his 1842 address to the Washington Temperance Society. Speaking of the possibility of using "moral influence" against alcoholism, he enter-

tains the objection that "none will disuse spirits or anything else, merely
because his neighbors do." Imagining a man who argues that "moral
influence" is not a powerful engine, he asks such a man "what compensation he will accept to go to church some Sunday and sit during the
sermon with his wife's bonnet upon his head?" There could not be a
moral or religious objection to doing such a thing; the interlocutor
would refuse to wear his wife's bonnet because he would look strange
doing so, because it would run against "the influence that *other* people's
actions have on our own actions, the strong inclination each of us feels
to do as we see all our neighbors do" (1:88). To shape the public mind is
to make drinking alcohol, or supporting slavery, as strange as wearing
one's wife's bonnet to church. Temperance and opposition to slavery are
things that might be dictated by reason. Intemperance and slavery
are things that corrupt reason. But reason cannot durably sustain itself
without the support of the public mind, without, this is to say, a set of
wholesome prejudices that clear reason's path.

To use the terms I have been developing here, the public mind is
the implicit space from which values become, from which concepts
unfold. To corrupt access to these things, by encouraging the belief
that they are largely unreal, or mere matters of preference, is to corrupt the only things that distinguish freedom—the capacity for moral
agency—from mere imprisonment in impulses, whims, and desires.
To do this is not only to make us unworthy of freedom, but to make
freedom impossible.

Lincoln elaborates upon what it means to corrupt the public mind
in a speech at Edwardsville during the 1858 campaign. Notice that it is
not just slavery, but racial inequality itself, that unfits the people for
democracy:

Now, when by all these means you have succeeded in dehumanizing
the negro; when you have put him down, and made it forever impossible for him to be but as the beasts of the field; when you have extinguished his soul, and placed him where the ray of hope is blown out
in darkness like that which broods over the spirits of the damned; are
you quite sure the demon which you have roused *will not turn and rend
you?* What constitutes the bulwark of our own liberty and independence? It is not our frowning battlements, our bristling sea coasts,
the guns of our war steamers, or the strength of our gallant and

disciplined army. These are not our reliance against a resumption of tyranny in our fair land. All of them may be turned against our liberties, without making us stronger or weaker for the struggle. Our reliance is in the *love of liberty* which God has planted in our bosoms. Our defense is in the preservation of the spirit which prizes liberty as the heritage of all men, in all lands, every where. Destroy this spirit, and you have planted the seeds of despotism around your own doors. Familiarize yourselves with the chains of bondage, and you are preparing your own limbs to wear them. Accustomed to trample on the rights of those around you, you have lost the genius of your own independence, and become the fit subjects of the first cunning tyrant who rises. And let me tell you, all these things are prepared for you with the logic of history, if the elections shall promise that the next Dred Scott decision and all future decisions will be quietly acquiesced in by the people. [Loud applause.] (1:585)

This passage also makes a deeper argument than the mere slave power conspiracy argument that Lincoln used it to support. Lincoln's conspiracy charges, like Douglas's, were wrong. But, as was also true about Douglas's charges, there were things about the opponent's acts that make the charges not altogether crazy. Douglas had, for instance, behaved in a way as to give color to the worst charges one might make against him. What is more, also like Douglas's charges against Lincoln, Lincoln's charges pointed to something true beyond the conspiracy charge itself. The Republican Party really was, as Douglas said it was, a new kind of party, and Lincoln's views, despite his denials, really did point ultimately to racial equality, just as Douglas said they did. So also, Lincoln's charge that Douglas's attempt to view the conflict over slavery in purely economic or narrowly political terms placed one on a slippery slope to expedience politics is quite true. The way to redeem Lincoln's argument from the irrationality of its conspiracy charge is to show that Lincoln was finally more deeply invested in the idea that you cannot be a master without becoming a slave, and that Douglas's politics cannot reckon with this deep truth. Furthermore, in seeing the meaning of politics finally not as a matter of justice at all, but as a matter of interest and economics, Douglas bound politics upon the wheel of nature, where it is the prisoner of nature's necessity. That is the ultimate meaning of these debates, not the slave power conspiracy.

The world Lincoln feared in the "House Divided" speech is a world that has become familiar to us. It is a world in which the human being is the plaything of natural forces, a bundle of instincts and desires, a higher primate who makes many noises that sound like moral arguments but are really only the reflection into an interior space of the urges such primates feel in external nature or external culture. It is a world in which the ideology of autonomous agency and free labor is replaced by the ideology of impersonal economic or biological law. It is a world in which actual people have merely formal equality, but the state is foreclosed, in the name of an imprisoning ideology of property, from rendering that equality meaningful, a world, this is to say, in which justice really becomes, through the adoption of social Darwinian (and classical economic) language about competition, the struggle for existence, and survival of the fittest, merely another word for the will of the stronger. It is even a world in which the "second *Dred Scott* decision" Lincoln so feared actually came to pass, except that, rather than nationalizing chattel slavery, a host of legal rulings from the *Slaughterhouse* cases through the *Lochner* and *Schechter* decisions turned the legal instruments that had been devised to bring about a new birth of freedom for actual people to the service of artificial people, of corporations, who were given the kind of substantive due process rights individuals trespassed upon by those corporations were denied. It is the world rendered in the novels of Norris, Crane, and Dreiser, and analyzed, with horrified fascination, in the last chapters of *The Education of Henry Adams*. It is a world bound in the iron cage of purely instrumental rationality, in which means are calculated but ends are "value judgments" about which reason has nothing to say. It is, in short, the modern world.

CHAPTER 4

Douglas's Conspiracy Charge

4.1 Lincoln and the Founding of the Republican Party

Douglas began the debates, in his opening speech at Ottawa on August 21, 1858, by making a false charge about the origin of the Republican Party:

> In 1854, Mr. Abraham Lincoln and Mr. Trumbull entered into an arrangement, one with the other, and each with his respective friends, to dissolve the old Whig party on the one hand, and to dissolve the old Democratic party on the other, and to connect the members of both into an Abolition party under the name and disguise of a Republican party. (1:497)

Lincoln and Trumbull, Douglas argued, had created not only a new party but a new kind of party, a purely sectional party and a purely ideological party whose ability to inflame moral outrage over slavery would give it an organizing issue of such power in the free states that the party would be able to dominate national politics without having to seek accommodation with any of its opponents or having to make pragmatic compromises across regional or ideological lines. The triumph of such a party, Douglas argued, would transform the nature of politics itself, since such a party would be motivated and energized by a rejection of the kind of mutual accommodation that is the principal work of traditional politics as Douglas saw it.

Almost everything Douglas asserted on this subject was wrong. Lincoln was not yet a Republican in 1854, although Republican activists had hopefully, but without Lincoln's permission, included his name among their number in the call for their Springfield convention in October of that year; and of course there is no evidence at all of any conspiracy with Trumbull to break up the second party system in Illinois.[1] Lincoln's politics at no point in his career was characterized by ideologically charged will to power, and he has been more often faulted for seeking accommodation with his ideological opponents than for seeking to drive them to the wall.[2] Much less did Lincoln, or the Republican Party, in 1854 or for that matter in 1860, stand in any straightforward way for the abolition of slavery, although both did believe that what they did support, the prohibition of slavery in the federal territories, would lead to slavery's demise. And Lincoln, like most Republicans in the prewar era, was on record opposing social and political equality for white and black.

Exactly when Lincoln became a Republican is a hard to define precisely, since his transition from the Whig to the Republican Party was reluctant and gradual, and he continued to entertain as a Republican most of the convictions he had held as a Whig.[3] He was in any case not among the founders of the party, and although most of his familiar themes are already present in the speech against the Kansas-Nebraska Act that he gave in Peoria on October 16, 1854, he does not seem to have completely joined the Republican Party until 1856. As late as August 24, 1855, Lincoln had written his friend Joshua Speed:

> You enquire where I now stand. That is a disputed point. I think I am a whig; but others say there are no whigs, and that I am an abolitionist. When I was at Washington I voted for the Wilmot Proviso as good as forty times, and I never heard of anyone attempting to unwhig me for that. I now do no more than oppose the *extension* of slavery. (1:360–363)

Only thirteen days before writing the Speed letter, Lincoln had rebuffed the idea, proposed to him by Owen Lovejoy, of joining an anti-Nebraska "fusion" party. He was not, in principle, opposed to the fusion

politics upon which the Republican Party was founded, but he preferred, on a catch-as-catch-can basis, to support any candidate, regardless of party, who would oppose the Kansas-Nebraska Act, to setting up
a formal party. He argued for this course in his letter to Lovejoy by
noting that the Know Nothing Party was still strong in Illinois, and
included many of his oldest political and personal friends. Many of these
Know Nothings might ultimately join a fusion or Republican Party,
since they opposed the Kansas-Nebraska Act. But they would not do so
so long as they felt that the Know Nothing Party had any hope of success. To set up a rival political organization while the Know Nothing
Party still had its organization would needlessly alienate Know Nothings whose support would be crucial to the success of any fusion party.

David Herbert Donald argues that Lincoln was not ready to become
a Republican until January 1856, and only formally entered the party at
the Bloomington convention on May 29, where he sought a platform
that would hedge the nativism issue enough to accommodate both the
ethnic Germans and the former Know Nothings.[4] Lincoln himself
dated the founding of the party as a serious, statewide political organization from that convention, and saw the earlier meetings either as tentative or as purely county affairs. (The next month, at the Republican
National Convention in Philadelphia, Lincoln received 110 votes for
vice president.) What the institutional connection is between the various organizations using the Republican name in 1854 and the party that
emerged out of the 1856 state convention was a vexed question, and one
that Douglas sought to exploit in the course of the debates, because the
earlier organizations, especially in the northern counties, adopted far
more radical platforms than the state platform of 1856.

Douglas also got a good deal play out of the issue of what the new
party tried to call itself, hence the little fillip about how Trumbull and
Lincoln drew their friends into a new party "in the name and disguise
of a Republican party" (1:497). Douglas here may have been twitting
their revival of the name of Jefferson's old party for a party closer to
Hamilton in orientation, but he was also calling attention to the difficulty the Republicans had naming themselves. Douglas noted that in
the northern counties of Illinois, settled by New Englanders, and as
firmly anti-slavery as the Connecticut Western Reserve was in northern Ohio, party meetings were convened by groups that called themselves Republican. In the middle counties such organizations tended to

call themselves "anti-Nebraska," since that name would seem less inflammatory to those who associated the name "Republican" with the more radically anti-slavery resolutions adopted in the northern counties, resolutions that typically included abolition of slavery in the District of Columbia, repeal of the 1850 Fugitive Slave Act, and abolition of the interstate slave trade, in addition to the central organizing issue of nonextension of slavery into the territories. Still farther south, in the region known as "Little Egypt," which was mostly settled from Kentucky and other slave states, Trumbull advertised the party as the "Free Democrats," who, in Douglas's phrase, "contented themselves with talking about the inexpediency of the repeal of the Missouri Compromise" (1:589).[5]

This last name seemed to Douglas to be especially deceptive, since to him it meant that the Republicans had to advertise themselves as Democrats in order to get elected, like sheep in wolves' clothing. But Trumbull had been in fact a Democrat, and "Free Democrat" is as good a name as any for an anti-slavery Democrat. The name "Free Democrat" hearkens back to the original somewhat inflammatory "Appeal of the Independent Democrats," published by Salmon Chase, Charles Sumner, and others during the debates over the Kansas-Nebraska Act, so it is not so clear to me that the name provides much protective coloration for Trumbull as a moderate anyway. And Chase and Sumner themselves were, on the older issues of tariffs and banks, aligned with the Democrats to begin with, and both of them owed their election to (somewhat disreputable) fusions with the Democrats of their states.[6] So the name "Free Democrat" was not an entirely misleading one, however annoying Douglas may have found it.[7]

Lincoln had run for Senate on the basis of the opposition to the Kansas-Nebraska Act he had articulated in the Peoria speech, but was beaten in the legislative session on February 9, 1855, by none other than Lyman Trumbull.[8] Lincoln had come in with more votes than Trumbull (44 to 5) but could not persuade a handful of anti-Nebraska Democrats (Democrats opposed to Douglas's Kansas-Nebraska Act) to vote for a Whig.[9] Pro-Nebraska Democrats despaired of reelecting their candidate, the incumbent James Shields, and were organizing a drive on behalf of the governor, Joel Matteson, who was considered anti-Nebraska, but more weakly so than either Lincoln or Trumbull.[10] To head off the election of Matteson, Lincoln threw his votes to

Trumbull, who was elected. Lincoln felt some bitterness about this course of events, and although he put on a brave face about it during the debates with Douglas, Douglas knew that Lincoln's friends felt that Trumbull had double-crossed him, and Douglas gleefully quoted, in the Jonesboro debate, resentful remarks Lincoln's ally James Matheny had made publicly about the event.

Lincoln would have run in the 1855 Senate election as a Whig, and Trumbull would have run as a Democrat, so it is not completely without reason that Trumbull's Democratic supporters would not have wished to vote for a Whig candidate, and it is also not without reason, given the moribund state of the Whig Party nationally in 1855, that the Whig legislators might have shown more flexibility about voting for Democrats who shared their views about the extension of slavery into Kansas than the Democrats did about voting for Whigs.[11] That Lincoln and Trumbull would still have formally been members of their previous parties in 1855 lends some color to Douglas's charge that Lincoln and Trumbull had worked under cover to subvert the party system in Illinois, much in the way other Democrats and Whigs did in other states during the organization of the Republican Party. But Lincoln did not run in 1855 with the intention of leading a new party, and Trumbull was hardly his ally in anything, much less in subverting the party system.

In 1856, having formally entered the party, Lincoln lobbied for the Republican presidential nomination for John McLean, the conservative Supreme Court justice from Ohio (the candidate most like an "Old Line Whig," and the candidate least likely to bring upon himself charges of sympathy with abolition), and of course he exerted himself for the presidential campaign of John Frémont.[12] (McLean went on to become one of the two dissenters from the *Dred Scott* decision the next year and was still a candidate for the Republican nomination in 1860.)

Douglas needled Lincoln repeatedly with the charge that Trumbull double-crossed him in 1855, partly of course to drive a wedge between the two politicians. He seized particularly upon the language of the Republican convention that nominated Lincoln as the party's "first and only choice":

Mr. Lincoln demands that he shall have the place intended for Trumbull, as Trumbull cheated him and got his, and Trumbull is stumping the State traducing me for the purpose of securing that position for Lincoln, in order to quiet him. ["Lincoln can never get it, &c."] It was in consequence of this arrangement that the Republican Convention was empanelled to instruct for Lincoln and nobody else, and it was on this account that they passed resolutions that he was their first, their last, and their only choice. Archy Williams was nowhere, Browning was nobody, Wentworth was not to be considered, they had no man in the Republican party for the place except Lincoln, for the reason that he demanded that they should carry out the arrangement. ["Hit him again."] (1:502)

The convention's language about their "first and only choice" was indeed strange. It must be remembered, however, that nominations by party conventions for the Senate were relatively new things in the 1850s, and in fact Illinois had never nominated a senator by convention. Lincoln's nomination was only the second time any state party convention had endorsed a candidate for the Senate.[13] Senators then were elected by the state legislature, so it is unclear exactly what being nominated by a convention meant, anyway. In worrying the convention's language calling Lincoln his party's "first, last, and only choice," Douglas was particularly interested in pressing the rumor the Democrats had been spreading that this language had been included in order to head off the legislature's giving the nomination, in a replay of the 1855 process, to the mayor of Chicago (and editor of the *Chicago Democrat*), "Long John" Wentworth, An anti-Nebraska Democrat turned Republican.[14] Probably the convention's actual motive was to rebuke eastern Republicans like Greeley and Seward, who had been pressing, because Douglas's fight against Buchanan's plan to force the pro-slavery Lecompton Constitution upon Kansas had raised the possibility that Douglas might be persuaded to change parties, for the nomination to be given to Stephen Douglas.[15]

4.2 The Reorganization of Parties

Douglas's conspiracy charge is false on its face, but in the long view not entirely false in its meaning. The Republican Party may not have originated in a conspiracy, but the language of conspiracy was the traditional language nineteenth-century people used to describe and analyze the course of history and to register trends that were the impersonal effects of large-scale causes. Lincoln himself, as we have seen, described in the "House Divided" speech large-scale events—the triumph or defeat of slavery, or the transformation of public thinking about slavery—as if they were the work of an elite conspiracy rather than the upshot of a cultural, economic, or political process. And indeed, the habit of imagining large-scale developments as the fruit of small conspiracies has a long history, and is not the exclusive property of manipulative politicians or diseased imaginations.[16]

Douglas was of course right that the new party took factions from both sides of the second party system. That itself distinguished the creation of the Republican Party from earlier episodes of party formation in the United States. The Democratic and National Republican Parties of the early Jacksonian era could each claim to be developments from within the Jeffersonian Democratic-Republican Party, reflecting that party's residual anti-development, anti-urban, anti-government "country party" ideology in the former case and its nationalist, pro-development turn in the Madison administration in the latter.[17] The Republican Party, by contrast, took factions from both of the existing parties, in an attempt to realign political conflict to turn on a different set of issues from those that had previously separated the parties.

What was different about the political realignment that created the third party system was that factions of both existing parties came together to create a new party, and that the members of that new party used their influence upon members of their former parties to revolutionize the party structure. This was a novelty of 1850s politics, and it was this novelty of a revolutionary cross-party fusion that Douglas had in mind in elaborating his conspiracy theory about the origins of the Republican Party.

The party they created was, first of all, a coalition of Conscience Whigs (which is to say, Whigs who opposed the extension of slavery) and Democrats who had supported the Wilmot Proviso (and who perhaps had briefly been members of the Free Soil Party, under Martin Van Buren, in 1848).[18] The Republican Party also included much of the American or Know Nothing Party (whose members had for the most part once been Whigs), and Democrats who might not have supported Free Soil but who opposed the Kansas-Nebraska Act. Its most radical element derived from adherents of the Liberty Party, who claimed either with William Goodell, Lysander Spooner, and Frederick Douglass that the Constitution of its own force made slavery unconstitutional or with Salmon Chase that the Constitution rigorously refused to recognize slavery at the national level, treating it as a state institution only. The Liberty Party, which sought to abolish slavery either by Court decision or by constitutional amendment, was an antislavery party in a far more serious way than either the Free Soil Party was or the Republican Party would be.[19]

Douglas's fantasy about the conspiracy that created the Republican Party gave an inflated role to the last party, doubtless because he thought the Liberty Party an unpopular fringe group whom it would be easy to stigmatize, both for its convictions and for its racially mixed membership. So Douglas imagined Lincoln and Trumbull driving their new recruits before them bound hand and foot "into the Abolition camp," where such Liberty Party figures as Salmon Chase and Frederick Douglass would "receive them and christen them in their new faith" (1:497).

What gave rise to Douglas's conspiratorial account of the origin of the Republican Party, however, was not so much that the rise of the third party system (in which a new party, taking factions from existing parties, reoriented partisan conflict around a different set of issues) is different in kind from the rise of the second party system (in which a dominant party broke in two, with the remnants of its opposition party seeking shelter mostly, but not entirely, in one of the fragments of the dominant party). What gave rise to Douglas's conspiratorial account was the fact that the third party system arose because the second party system fell victim to a bewildering and tangled set of conflicts over slavery and over nativism that even now tests the mettle of historians to make sense of. The political chaos of the 1850s, in which ordinary politicians behaving in ordinary partisan ways set loose forces they could not control, with consequences they could not anticipate, is precisely the kind of political state of affairs people attempt to make sense of with conspiracy theories. Conspiracy theories are the natural last resort political thinkers turn to when they are asked to account for stormy political events that take place at a scale larger than that of ordinary partisan conflict.

The American Party and the Whig Collapse

A sweeping transformation of the party system, such as the one that Douglas accused the Republicans of attempting, had in fact already happened earlier in the 1850s, and it had everything to do with the almost simultaneous rise of the Republicans. This transformative assault on the second party system was the work not of the Republicans, but of the American or Know Nothing Party, which really did have a conspiratorial side, both in its thinking about its opponents (whom it saw as the secret minions of Popery) and in its own internal organization (members of the fraternal lodges from which the party grew were supposed to respond "I know nothing" if they were asked about it).

The rise of the Republican Party is so entangled with the rise (and almost simultaneous fall) of the American Party that the way the two parties reacted upon each other is very hard to sort out. Nativism had been a political force since the 1830s, and the American Party elected its first congressman, Lewis Levin of Philadelphia, in 1846.[20] The turbulent history of this party, from its sudden leap to major party status in 1852, when it found itself dominating the politics of several important states and, after the 1854 midterm elections, wielding considerable power in Congress, to the equally sudden collapse of this party in 1856, when it divided over the slavery issue and never again was able to contest a national election, itself says something about the instability of 1850s politics.

The American Party's signature issue, support for a twenty-one-year probation period before immigrants could be naturalized, expressed only part of its project. The party also sought to restrict important offices to native-born Americans, and to limit voting by noncitizens in state elections. State citizenship and U.S. citizenship were different things until the passage of the Fourteenth Amendment (in fact the *Dred Scott* decision party turned on the distinction), and many states allowed noncitizens to vote if they satisfied the rather minimal residency requirements. Recent nonnaturalized immigrants from Ireland tipped the balance of power for the Democrats in Illinois in the 1830s and 1840s, for instance, and Lincoln and Douglas had opposed each other in 1839 in a case about noncitizen voting that has interesting analogies to the *Dred Scott* case.[21]

Hostility to Catholics was the main cultural agenda of the American Party. Key organizing issues for the American Party included opposition to support for Catholic schools (and other school-related issues with an anti-Catholic edge, such as support for prayer in school and for mandatory reading of the King James Bible, a requirement that provoked bloody riots in Philadelphia in 1844), resistance to the political power wielded by some important Catholic clergy (such as New York Archbishop John Hughes), and outrage at the presumed misbehavior of Archbishop Bedini, the nuncio the Pope had sent to America in 1852 to represent him (and who had helped put down the Italian Republicans in Bologna in 1849).[22]

The Bedini incident illustrates the dual nature of the American Party's commitments. On one hand, it stood for the political and cultural domination of largely poor and working-class Irish Catholic immigrants by native-born Protestants, and to that extent it stood for anti-democratic limitations on citizenship and suffrage. But in opposing Rome's subversion of Italian republicanism, and Rome's hostility to the liberal revolutions of 1848, the American Party took positions that in its own day would have been felt to be progressive and pro-democratic. The Americans were not wrong to see the nineteenth-century Catholic Church as hostile to democracy, for in Europe, although not in the United States, the church had played a powerful anti-liberal role. But it was not merely opposition to these concrete acts by Rome, or even simple national snobbery, that energized nativism so much as the belief that republican rule itself had evolved out of Protestantism, whose traditional desire to remove authority in religious matters from institutional hierarchies and to found religious experience instead in the confrontation with the divine in the individual conscience was felt to be a cultural precondition for a republican political order.

The cultural agenda of the American Party also included sympathy with temperance (an issue that never lost its anti-Catholic edge), Sabbatarianism (another issue that, for unclear reasons, never lost its anti-Catholic edge), and a general tendency to police the self-discipline of the people in order to support moral habits. They also supported laws enabling married women to own property separately from their husbands, an issue connected in the public mind with temperance (since both protected sober women from abuse by alcoholic husbands). The link between nativism and temperance was not merely a reflection of stereotypes about the drinking habits of the Irish. The Americans saw in the power of Rome something rather like the power of alcohol to corrupt and blunt the agency of the rational and self-disciplined individual conscience. Much of the party's improving agenda, and some of the American Party's nativism as well, poached on territory that had been held by the Whig Party, although important Whig leaders like William Seward had never had sympathy for nativism.

The rise of the Americans gave the coup de grâce to the Whig Party, which had clumsily tried under Winfield Scott in the 1852 presidential campaign to shed its reputation for nativism. Scott's comic attempt to describe how much pleasure he took in hearing the Irish brogue did not singlehandedly kill off the Whig Party, although it alienated the nativists without impressing the Irish. But so many dogs were in at the kill when the Whig Party went down that it is hard to sort out who bit where.

Traditionally historians have argued that it was the Kansas-Nebraska Act, although a Democratic concoction (and almost fatal to the Democrats too), that killed off the Whig Party. In the traditional account, the Whig Party, whose sectional divisions were strained over the Compromise of 1850, was fatally weakened by the debate over the Kansas-Nebraska Act. The traditional account sees the American Party as putting an end to what was by that time the mere shell of the Whig Party, but, since the American Party was in essence a diversion from the main theme of sectional politics, it was unable to survive the sectional conflicts that had destroyed the Whigs, leaving its northern adherents to become Republicans and leaving its southern adherents to carry on as a forlorn hope or to seek shelter as a faction within the Democratic Party.

The relationship among the three closely spaced political transformations—the collapse of the Whigs, the rise and fall of the Americans, and the rise of the Republicans—has still not been persuasively accounted for. More recent accounts, however, have given the American Party a far larger role in killing off the Whig Party than the traditional account did, and have argued that the three waves of political change in the years from 1852 to 1858 were somewhat separate events in which the conflict over slavery and the conflict over nativism were entangled with each other in chaotic ways.

THE KANSAS-NEBRASKA ACT AND WHIG COLLAPSE

The conflict over the Kansas-Nebraska Act reveals the way that the internal logic of the sectional conflict escalated that conflict in self-destructive ways. As we saw in Chapter 2, when Kentucky Whig Archibald Dixon persuaded Stephen Douglas to press for explicit repeal of the prohibition of slavery in Kansas and Nebraska Territories by the Missouri Compromise, he did so, among other reasons, to show that the southern Whigs could play sectional politics as well as the Democrats could. But Dixon did not understand that the southern Whigs could never win a race to the bottom with the southern Democrats on that kind of issue.

Historians of the 1930s and 1940s, such as James G. Randall or George Fort Milton, noticing the ways in which politicians like Dixon or for that matter Douglas initiated conflicts that escalated beyond their intentions and ability to control, argued that the conflict that brought about the Civil War was wholly avoidable, the work of a "blundering generation" of incompetent partisans.[23] The reckless way in which politicians like Dixon sought political advantage in the fraught atmosphere of the conflict over slavery does give some color to the claims of the "blundering generation" school about the incompetence of the political leaders of the antebellum era. But it does not necessarily support the Randall school's main claim, that the Civil War was completely and easily avoidable.[24]

The politicians of the "blundering generation" behaved in an ordinary partisan way under circumstances in which ordinary partisan conflict had unforeseen (or dimly seen) and unwished-for consequences. But it was slavery itself that made that partisan conflict in the antebellum era fraught with danger, because slavery could not survive in a society whose political institutions it did not dominate (which would seem to make a conflict between slave and free states inevitable), and because, in their quest for domination of the Republic, the slaveholders, driven by their sense of ontological threat as much as by their intramural competition to outdo each other in proofs of loyalty to their section, used their power to foreclose any policy of accommodation (which would seem to guarantee that the conflict would escalate into war). The "blundering generation" did not create the sectional tensions that underlay the war. They did not invent sectional conflict to serve their fanaticism or to serve their partisan advantage. War may well have been avoidable—slavery ended almost everywhere else without civil war—but the conditions that tended to war were not merely the creation of incompetent but ambitious politicians, and the chances of the conflict escalating into war were high, even if war was not inevitable.

The sectional tensions that broke up the Whig Party in the traditional account were felt by the Democratic Party as well. The Democratic Party proved somewhat more durable than the Whig Party, although it too came unglued a few years later, in 1860. The difference between the fates of the two parties is hard to explain. One explanation turns on the different ways the two parties experienced sectional conflict. Although southern Whigs were not for the most part as hardminded sectionalists as their Democratic counterparts were, northern Whigs were also a great deal less submissive to slave-state dictation, and this made the Whig Party less able than the Democratic Party to survive the sectional tensions the Kansas-Nebraska Act kicked up. Northern Democrats were more likely to bend to pressure from southern Democrats than southern Whigs were likely to bend to pressure from northern Whigs, because until the Lecompton crisis the sectional loyalty pressures on southern politicians were more powerful. The Democrats were the majority party, but the majority of Democrats were in the South, the minority section. Conversely the Whigs were the minority party, but were stronger in the North, the majority section. Perhaps because the North did not (until the slave power conspiracy theory took deep root, after 1856) feel itself to be under ontological threat, the Democratic minority in the North might have felt itself to have more leeway for compromise than the Whig minority in the South did, where hysterical fear for the future of slavery became deeply rooted during the 1830s. Hysterical fear for the future of slavery and adherence to the idea that slavery is a positive good ran closely together. The proposition may be a defiant response to the fear. Certainly it was no accident that the first serious defenses of slavery as a positive good—by the economist Charles R. Dew of William and Mary—were issued as a response to the nearly successful attempt to pass an emancipation law by the Virginia House of Burgesses in 1832, which attempt was itself partly a response to the Nat Turner uprising of the previous year. Also, the rise of the nativism issue itself may have helped preserve the Democratic Party's organization, since Democrats north and south opposed nativism, but the Whigs, although more sympathetic to nativism, were also divided about it in both sections, and indeed had made a costly and futile effort to reach out to foreign-born voters in the last few years of the party's life.

The Chase-Sumner-Giddings "Appeal of the Independent Democrats" had a number of unintended effects that illustrate the sectional crosscurrents that destroyed the Whig Party. By forcing northern Whigs onto firmly anti-slavery terrain, lest they be accused of abetting what the authors portrayed as a pro-slavery conspiracy, Chase and Sumner forced a break between northern and southern Whigs. Most northern Whigs probably already opposed the Kansas-Nebraska Act on anti-slavery grounds, or at least on nonextensionist grounds, being opposed to the spread of slavery into the western territories because that would give new vitality to slavery and would foreclose the development of the region by nonslaveholding white people. But whatever their private reasons for doing so, these northern Whigs could have still chosen a less confrontational way to organize against the act by opposing it in public on grounds that it would needlessly stir up sectional hostility. To oppose the Kansas-Nebraska Act because it is inflammatory was a somewhat different thing from opposing the act because it favored slavery. Southern Whigs might have taken (and had been taking) the former grounds, but they could never, in 1854 anyway, have taken the latter. By taking the former grounds, the Whigs could conceivably have organized opposition to the Kansas-Nebraska Act in a way that would have preserved their cohesion.

The appeal forced northern Whigs to take nonextensionist grounds, and to sacrifice their southern wing. Once Chase and Sumner had framed the issue as they did, even those northern Whigs who took the traditional grounds, of opposing the admission of new states if doing so would inflame quarrels over slavery, no longer had any traction in the South, because in the context of the appeal their arguments seemed disingenuous. In southern eyes it would have appeared as if these northern Whigs really were nonextensionists who adopted the traditional Whig argument about caution only for expedient reasons rather than for principled ones, as indeed they probably actually did.

Chase and Sumner also destroyed the position of southern Whigs, who were faced with the choice of appearing to be outright sectional traitors, by remaining in alliance with the northern Whigs, or of becoming second-rate entries in a loyalty-politics competition by pretending to be slightly less earnest versions of southern Democrats. Either course would destroy the Whig Party as a national organization.

This was former Massachusetts senator Robert C. Winthrop's view at the time of what Chase and Sumner did:

> [The authors of the appeal] precipitated themselves into the front ranks of the opposition, in a way to drive off the only persons who could have prevented its consummation. Half-a-dozen of them, under the style of Independent Democrats, got up a flaming manifesto in such hot haste that it was said to have been dated on Sunday, and put it forth, cock-a-hoop, half-signed, to the utter discomfiture of all who hoped to prevent the bill from passing. They usurped a lead which belonged to others, and gave an odor of abolition to the whole movement.[25]

The reader should notice that the distinction between opposing the Kansas-Nebraska Act because it would inflame sectional conflict and opposing the Kansas-Nebraska Act because it would promote slavery in the West is parallel to the later distinction between opposing imposition of the fraudulent Lecompton Constitution on Kansas because it was not the will of most of the people of Kansas and opposing the Lecompton Constitution because it provided legal protection for slavery. As the appeal made it impossible for northern Whigs to maintain a coalition with moderate southern Whigs, so Lincoln's course in the debates, from the "House Divided" speech to the attack on the Freeport Doctrine, was designed to make it impossible for northern Democrats to maintain a coalition with moderate southern Democrats (an endangered species, anyway).

In both cases the method was the same. Both used conspiracy theories to force moderate northerners into confrontational sectional positions: the appeal argued that the Kansas-Nebraska Act was the fruit of a conspiracy to force slavery into the territories, and the "House Divided" speech argued that Douglas's version of popular sovereignty generally was the fruit of a conspiracy to force slavery back into the free states. Both also placed moderate southerners in an impossible situation by redefining the issues in sectional terms so that the moderate southerners could not make the prudent concessions their northern allies expected of them without appearing to be sectional traitors.

Now Chase and Sumner were both Free Soilers who were put in office by conspiracies with the Democrats against the Whigs, so the destruction of the Whig Party, which was too soft about slavery in their view, was nothing for them to mourn anyway. They may not have been looking for ways to destroy the cohesion of the Whig Party, but they were indifferent to the possibility that the Whig Party would come unglued. Their aim was to radicalize northern opinion about slavery, and if in the process they put the Whig Party in an impossible position, so much the better. They and their allies would have put the Democrats in an impossible situation as well, had they had the power to do so, although it was radicalizing opinion about slavery, not disrupting the Democratic Party, that was their focal intention. Once the southern reaction to the Freeport Doctrine gave Lincoln a similar power in 1858, he did not shrink from using it. But Lincoln did focally intend the destruction of the Democratic Party, as Chase and Sumner did not focally intend the destruction of the Whig Party.

As we will see in more detail in Chapter 7, in the later stages of the debates, Lincoln practically drafted the platform of the Breckinridge faction in 1860; he laid down a sectional dare for them that they could not, without destroying themselves, fail to take up, because he made rejection of the Freeport Doctrine a sectional loyalty issue for southern Democrats. Lincoln sought to put whatever southern supporters Douglas might have had in 1860 in precisely the position Chase and Sumner had put the southern Whigs.

To return from the destruction of the Democratic Party in 1860 to the destruction of the Whig Party in 1854, we must ask, "Was there in 1854 any way to bring forward a territorial government for Kansas and Nebraska that would have had enough southern support to pass Congress but that would not have destroyed the Whig Party?" If Douglas were to have any hope of threading the needle, he would have had to find, before the issue became so sectionally inflamed as to put all hope of compromise beyond reach, a way to bring southern Whigs on board for a bill that did not explicitly call for repeal of the Missouri Compromise line, a bill something like Douglas's January version that Dixon objected to.

That version of the bill put popular sovereignty about the slavery issue in place in what would become Kansas and Nebraska, but did not formally repeal the slavery restrictions from the Missouri Compromise, which would have remained in force until the territorial legislature should get around to repealing them, so that the territorial legislature that might be asked to repeal the slavery restriction would be made up of nonslaveholders. Such a bill would have resembled Douglas's popular sovereignty position in the Mexican Cession, where, Douglas had argued, the existing prohibition of slavery in that region under Mexican law would remain in force until repealed by the territorial legislatures.

Such a bill might have been less inflammatory to northern Whigs. But Dixon had already organized against that version of the bill, arguing that a legislature composed of nonslaveholders would hardly be willing to introduce slavery on its own. Once this issue became a matter of partisan contention between southern Whigs and southern Democrats, it is hard to imagine that southerners of either party would have risked supporting the Kansas-Nebraska Act in Douglas's original form. Indeed, they outdid each other in denouncing that bill as a formula for sectional suicide and in denouncing each other as sectional traitors.

Meanwhile, on the other side of the Mason-Dixon line, it was the pre-Dixon bill, not the Dixon-promoted bill demanding explicit repeal of the Missouri Compromise line, that provoked from Chase, Sumner, Giddings, and Smith the "Appeal of the Independent Democrats," so perhaps Douglas did not have much maneuvering room anyway. Douglas had intended his January 4 version of the Kansas-Nebraska bill to have enough constructive ambiguity to draw support from the North and the South. But each side read the ambiguity in an inflammatory way, with the North seeing only the fact that the territorial legislatures had the power to introduce slavery, and the South seeing only that those legislatures would have to be composed entirely of nonslaveholders. Douglas here, as he was so often, was too clever by half, and wound up sailing into both Scylla and Charybdis.

The debate over the Kansas-Nebraska Act evolved in ways that overtook the original protagonists, the leaders of the Whig and Democratic Parties. Douglas hoped for a bill that was ambiguous enough to draw both moderate and radical southerners as well as moderate northerners. He also hoped the bill would put the South in such a position that, when Kansas entered the Union as a free state, the South would be forced to concede that their views at least had been given a fair chance of success in Kansas and that the victory of the free staters there had been fairly won. Douglas had no intention of beginning a struggle that would destroy the position of moderate Whigs in the South, or of setting off the bloody footrace in Kansas that he did set off. Douglas's original opponents—including Bell and Crittenden for the southern Whigs, and Sam Houston for the southern Democrats—hoped for a debate about the wisdom or folly of admitting new states in view of the effect of doing so on the developing quarrel about slavery. Douglas's concessions to Dixon, and the publication of the "Appeal of the Independent Democrats," guaranteed that the debate would escape the management of its original protagonists and ratchet into an ever-escalating confrontation.

OTHER THEORIES ABOUT THE WHIG COLLAPSE

The destruction of the Whig Party by a loyalty politics attack against southern Whigs mounted by southern Democrats is the center of the traditional account of the collapse of the second party system, which sees the American Party as a kind of interloper, able to take brief advantage of the collapse of the Whigs but unable to establish itself permanently because the slavery issue ultimately trumped the nativism issue.

More recent historians, led by Michael Holt, Ronald Formisano, William Gienapp, Taylor Anbinder, and Eric Silbey, argue that the American Party itself, because of its ability to seem to be above party (and above what we nowadays call "politics as usual"), was able to capitalize upon dissatisfaction with parties per se and to capture the Whig Party's membership, since it shared much of the Whig Party's cultural and class agenda about religious practice, observance of the sabbath, temperance, and other such ethnocultural issues. Indeed, Gienapp has gone so far as to argue that it was the Whig Party's failure to sew up issues such as nativism and temperance that destroyed it, and that antislavery Whigs like Seward were slower to leave the party than the nativists and the Maine-Law men were.[26] The American Party offered a no-party way for people disillusioned with parties to continue to be cultural Whigs.[27]

Whether the Whig Party was killed by the Kansas-Nebraska Act, with the Americans merely serving as a sort of way station for northern Whigs (on their way to Republicanism) and as a place of refuge for southern Whigs (desperately trying to preserve a national party capable of opposing both secession and the Democracy), or whether the Whig Party, weakened by the Kansas-Nebraska Act, was killed by the American Party, which, in its own collapse, left a cleared space for the Republicans to cultivate, is something about which the jury still seems

to be out. What is undisputed, however, is that the party system under-
went a sweeping realignment in the 1850s very unlike the earlier realignment that gave rise to the second party system, that the fates of the
Whig, American, and Republican parties were densely intertwined, and
that the collapse of national party structures was caused by sectional
conflicts and, in turn, helped render those conflicts more intractable by
destroying the national parties whose internal discipline would have
mediated sectional conflicts and made for sectional compromise.[28]

Nativism and Anti-Slavery

In the North, the Americans tended to be hostile to slavery. The anti-
slavery character of the northern Americans is a reflection of the way
the worst kinds of racism and nativism tended in the antebellum era to
repel each other into opposite parties. Indeed, the way anti-slavery
writing portrayed the plantation—as a place of uncontrolled violence,
lascivious forced sex (sometimes involving whips), and in general un-
bridled appetite—owed a great deal to the way nativist propaganda
such as "Maria Monk's" *Awful Disclosures of the Hotel Dieu Nunnery of
Montreal* (1836) depicted monasteries and nunneries.[29] Consider how
the American Party's Anson Burlingame, later a prominent Republican, conflated anti-slavery and hostility to Catholicism in 1854:

> Slavery and Priestcraft . . . have a common purpose: they seek [to an-
> nex] Cuba and Hayti and the Mexican States together, because they
> will be Catholic and Slave. I say they are in alliance by the necessity
> of their nature,—for one denies the right of a man to his body, and the
> other the right of a man to his soul. The one denies his right to think
> for himself, the other the right to act for himself.[30]

The association between nativism and anti-slavery was particularly
strong in Massachusetts, where Know Nothing Party leaders like Henry
Wilson, elected to the Senate in 1855, took advanced anti-slavery positions, and where a largely Irish-American state militia had intervened
during the Anthony Burns crisis to enforce the Fugitive Slave Act,
further enflaming anti-Irish and anti-Catholic feeling.[31] Henry Gard-
ner, the Know Nothing governor of Massachusetts, supported "personal liberty" laws that would have secured to accused fugitive slaves

jury trials and the right to habeas corpus, and Know Nothings in the legislature were able to pass bills that "prohibited state courts from participating in fugitive slave cases, forbade state jails to house runaways, barred all Massachusetts officials from participating in such cases, disqualified from state office any federal official who certified the return of a fugitive slave, and banned from the state courts any Massachusetts lawyer who represented a claimant in a fugitive slave case."[32] They also desegregated the schools. Taylor Anbinder has gone so far as to argue that in the North the American Party was essentially an anti-slavery party, which was able to outcompete the early Republicans because it saw anti-slavery in the context of many issues, whereas the Republicans concerned themselves with only one issue. The least one can say is that because anti-slavery and nativism were in this way contiguous ideologies, the American Party was a natural stopping place for anti-slavery northerners who had given up on the Whig Party and did not yet have a Republican Party to join.

In the South, particularly after the American Party fissured in 1856, the American Party became essentially a refuge for moderate Unionists who would otherwise have been Whigs, and a compromising moderate nationalism characterized that party in Illinois more than hardminded nativism as well. (Indeed, in the South the American Party was not stridently anti-Catholic, and even encouraged Catholics to join.)[33] The last stand of such voters was probably the Constitutional Union Party, which nominated John Bell and Edward Everett for the presidency in 1860.[34] (The Whig Party still had a shadowy existence in New York as late as 1860, where the Whig Committee felt out Edward Bates about accepting the Whig nomination for the presidency that year.)[35] To what extent southern Americans shared the party's nativism is still a subject of dispute; they probably did, however, share other aspects of the party's agenda, to the extent that it inherited the Whig Party's role as expressing the cultural stewardship of the elite.

The American Party's voters in Illinois, whose nativist party had in 1856 nominated the non-nativist Millard Fillmore for president and who, whatever their nativist sympathies, were more invested in a compromising Unionism, were in Douglas's eyes the balance of power in the 1858 contest with Lincoln.[36]

This faction would be better called "southern" Americans, because the northern faction of that party, seceding over the slavery issue, wound up, after a series of truly Byzantine machinations by Massachusetts congressman Nathaniel Banks (who sought the American nomination, planning all the while to withdraw in favor of the Republican candidate, thus bringing the Know Nothings into the Republican fold) nominating Frémont in 1856, with their own candidate for vice president. By 1858 these "northern" Americans had become Republicans.

It is curious that, although these Fillmore voters are better described as rump Whigs than as Know Nothings, Lincoln made almost no play for these voters in the 1858 election, concentrating almost entirely on keeping conservative Republicans from treating Douglas's popular sovereignty position as a practical way to oppose the extension of slavery to the territories. (It is especially surprising, since Mary Lincoln had supported Fillmore, not Frémont, in 1856.)[37] In fact, although Lincoln did go out of his way to dissociate himself from the radicals of his party, the conspiracy tack to which he devoted his campaign, which perhaps kept Republicans from being tempted by Douglas and kept Douglas out of the Republican Party, also drove the Fillmore voters away, as Lincoln's own closest advisors had warned him it would.

Factions in Play between Lincoln and Douglas

To understand why Lincoln did not make a stronger case for the Fillmore voters, one needs to look carefully at how Lincoln and Douglas sought to build political coalitions in 1858. If one analyzes Lincoln's arguments in terms of the partisan faction each is designed to appeal to, one discovers that he sought the votes of only a very limited portion of the electorate.

Lincoln was troubled by the efforts of eastern Republicans like Seward and Greeley to bring Stephen Douglas and his supporters into the Republican Party. (Douglas, aware that a large number of Republicans had been Free Soil Democrats, may well have been trying to rebuild the Democratic Party on a Free Soil basis rather than trying to vault the fence and become a Republican himself.) While his own ambitions may have had something to do with his opposition to this tactic, Lincoln also felt that the ideological compromises needed to woo Douglas and his supporters would destroy the cohesion of the Republican Party as a political organization, both sacrificing arguments that might prove crucial to the party's success later and papering over ideological fissures that might in the medium term render the party unstable in the way the American Party became unstable.

Lincoln could not appeal to the Fillmore voters without making the same fatal concessions he was worried the party might make to woo Douglas and the anti-Lecompton Democrats, and so he was required to sacrifice the support of a faction that might indeed have given him the margin of victory, in order to reject another faction he might have won over but that would have transformed his party in ways he opposed. To put it bluntly: Lincoln could not win without the Fillmore voters, but he could not win the Fillmore voters without opening the party to anti-Lecompton Democrats like Douglas himself, and so, rather than damage the Republican Party by opening it to anti-Lecompton Democrats, he chose to sacrifice the Fillmore voters upon which his own victory depended. These voters were a large constituency, and in 1856 could easily have turned the state for Frémont: they polled 37,444 votes, with Buchanan netting 105,348 and Frémont receiving 96,189.[38]

The final tally of the election reveals that this strategy was costly for Lincoln. Although Lincoln barely outpolled Douglas in popular votes (125,430 to 121,609, with 5,071 votes going to Buchaneer candidates), Douglas took slightly more seats in the legislature (54 to 46), and held eight of the thirteen holdover seats in the state Senate. The northern counties and the counties of Little Egypt provided lopsided tallies (for the Republicans and the Democrats, respectively), as expected. But in the central counties, including Lincoln's own Sangamon, the region where the two parties were both in a position to contest for votes, and where the Fillmore and McLean-Bates voters were concentrated, the Democrats prevailed.[39]

That said, Lincoln was careful not to burn his bridges to the Fillmore voters, which is why he was careful to emphasize what the Fillmore voters would have had in common with conservative Republicans who might have supported McLean or Bates for president: grudging support for the Fugitive Slave Act, and insistence that abolition and racial equality were not on his immediate agenda.[40]

THE BUCHANEERS

Neither Lincoln nor Douglas made any attempt to persuade those whose allegiances were with the southern faction of the Democratic Party. Buchanan's voters were completely lost to both of them. Buchanan's appointees, however, cynically cast their lot with Lincoln, and

Lincoln's operatives aided them locally. Led by John Slidell of Louisiana (who spread ugly rumors concerning the slaves on the plantation Douglas had, to his mortification, inherited from his first wife), and working locally through the father of Lincoln's law partner, William Herndon, Buchanan's machine sought to aid Lincoln against Douglas, whom southern-aligned Democrats thought of as their more formidable opponent.[41] Indeed, Lyman Trumbull himself worked with the "Buchaneers" (or "Danites," after a paramilitary Mormon group), and Republican editors like Joseph Medill and John Wentworth praised them, and helped organize their meetings.[42] The chief Danite organ, the *Illinois State Democrat*, edited by William Herndon's brother, relied upon financial help from Republican circles.[43] And Trumbull secretly told Slidell that he would back Buchanan's efforts to replace federal appointees loyal to Douglas with appointees beholden to Buchanan. In return for this, Buchanan's attorney general, Jeremiah S. Black, agreed to help Lincoln.[44] Lincoln himself, however, preserved plausible deniability about his party's minuet with the Danites. We will examine the cooperation between the Republicans and the Buchaneers in more detail in section 4.6 below.

FILLMORE AMERICANS

Lincoln's failure to woo these voters had serious costs and needs to be explained in detail. The position of former Whigs in the Illinois Republican Party was precarious, since the Republican big guns (Bissell, Trumbull, and Wentworth) were Free Soil Democrats, and bringing Fillmore Whigs into the party might not only have yielded a Republican victory in the Senate campaign, but strengthened the position of former Whigs in the Illinois Republican Party.[45] Most Illinois Republicans seem to have been former Conscience Whigs, but former Conscience Whigs could not win statewide elections, and Free Soil Democrats had better statewide prospects, since before the Kansas-Nebraska Act Illinois had been a strongly Democratic state. But had the Conscience Whigs been able to make a better case for Fillmore Whigs, they might have been able to hold their own better both in statewide elections and within the Republican Party. This thinking seems to underlie Lincoln's campaigning for McLean for the Republican nomination in 1856. But neither in 1856 nor in 1858 were the Republicans able to bring the Fillmore voters into the fold, and in 1858 Lincoln does not seem to have worked as hard for that vote as Douglas did, who persuaded Henry Clay's successor in the Senate, John J. Crittenden of Kentucky, to write a public letter in his behalf arguing that Douglas, although a Democrat, better represented the tradition of Henry Clay Whiggery than Lincoln did.[46]

In 1856 conservative Whigs, in Lincoln's own Sangamon County especially, did not go into the Republican Party but voted out of party nostalgia for Fillmore. And again in 1858 Lincoln failed to bring these Whigs in, who mostly went, following John J. Crittenden's advice and John T. Stuart's advice, to Douglas. In 1860, by contrast, Lincoln did very well among former Fillmore voters.[47]

The 1860 results reveal what the outcome of a different strategy might have been in 1858. Why was Lincoln able in 1860 to reach for the Fillmore voters without also making concessions to anti-Lecompton Democrats, something he could not do in 1858? Probably the reasons have to do with the weakened position of Douglas after the disruption of the Democratic Party during the 1860 party convention in Charleston. After the fissure of the Democratic Party into Douglas and Breckinridge candidacies, Douglas's compromising strategies no longer looked promising. If by 1860 Douglas was every bit as unacceptable to the slave states as Lincoln was, then his greater willingness to compromise would not have given him traction with Fillmore Whigs, because he could not have persuaded the South with his compromise measures anyway, and Fillmore voters whose traditional allegiances had been with Whigs therefore no longer had any reason not to join their former compatriots in the Republican Party. The destruction of the Democratic Party made it possible to draw Fillmore voters into the Republican column without bringing Douglas and his faction with them, because the Fillmore voters were attracted to Douglas only because he represented to them a possible way to ensure sectional peace; once that possibility had evaporated, they no longer had any reason to lean toward Douglas, and an anti-Douglas strategy would no longer alienate them.

ANTI-LECOMPTON DEMOCRATS

Anti-Lecompton Democrats were of course Douglas's core constituency, but Lincoln *could* have made a play for their support, and made no effort to do so. Although they were a very weak faction in Congress, they had considerable strength in the Democratic electorate in the

North (they were probably the majority of Democrats there). They were profoundly alienated from the sources of power in their party, and could have been persuaded to make the switch, as the anti-Nebraska Democrats had been only four years earlier. Why Lincoln did not do this is developed in more detail in section 4.4 below. Lincoln's persuasive efforts do not aim at Democrats of any kind (except for the anti-Nebraska Democrats already in the Republican fold), or at the Americans. Lincoln's arguments in 1858 were aimed entirely at conservative Republicans who might have been tempted, for pragmatic reasons, to embrace popular sovereignty as a practical anti-slavery strategy, arguing that slavery could not prosper in the western territories in any event.

ANTI-NEBRASKA DEMOCRATS

Anti-Nebraska Democrats were (with Conscience Whigs, northern Americans, and Liberty Party men) part of Lincoln's core constituency, but Douglas could argue for their votes by making the claim that his views had in fact secured a free state future for Kansas despite the Kansas-Nebraska Act. The argument might at first seem to be a bit of a stretch, since these voters had after all left the Democratic Party out of disgust with Douglas and with his Kansas-Nebraska Act. But if they had opposed the act because they felt it was the purpose of the act to force slavery into Kansas, the outcome of the struggle could be used to show these voters that the act was always functionally anti-slavery, and that their reading of Douglas's motives had been mistaken. (Certainly Douglas had said enough things about the practical prospects of slavery in the West to give this argument some plausibility, even if those views might have been a surprise to those southerners who had favored Douglas over Buchanan for the 1856 presidential nomination on precisely the grounds that the Kansas-Nebraska Act was a pro-southern measure.) Douglas could reach anti-Nebraska Democrats by showing that popular sovereignty not only had in fact kept slavery out of Kansas but also was a practical way to keep slavery out of the West as a whole.

In his Bloomington speech on July 16, 1858, Douglas had, daringly, made exactly this point, that even with a legislature committed to introducing slavery into Kansas, the will of the people had kept slavery out. Now Douglas, with startling chutzpah, seemed to ignore the fact that the people had done this by fighting a brushfire civil war. But he went on to argue a position, beyond even that staked out by the Freeport Doctrine, that popular hostility can keep slavery out of territories even if the territorial government is not only prevented from abolishing slavery but actively trying to promote it:

> Mr. Lincoln is alarmed for fear that, under the Dred Scott decision, slavery will go into all the Territories of the United States. All I have to say is that, with or without that decision, slavery will go just where the people want it, and not one inch further. You have had experience upon that subject in the case of Kansas. You have been told by the Republican party that, from 1854, when the Kansas-Nebraska bill passed, down to last winter, that slavery was sustained and supported in Kansas by the laws of what they called a "bogus" legislature. And how many slaves were there in the Territory at the end of last winter? Not as many at the end of that period as there were on the day the Kansas-Nebraska bill passed. There was quite a number of slaves in Kansas, taken there under the Missouri Compromise, and in spite of it, before the Kansas-Nebraska bill passed; and now it is asserted that there are not as many there as there were before the passage of the bill, notwithstanding that they had local laws sustaining and encouraging it, enacted, as the Republicans say, by a "bogus" legislature, imposed upon Kansas by an invasion from Missouri. Why has not slavery obtained a foothold in Kansas under these circumstances? Simply because there was a majority of her people opposed to slavery, and every slaveholder knew that if he took his slaves there, the moment that majority got possession of the ballot-boxes, and a fair election was held, that moment slavery would be abolished, and he would lose them. For that reason, such owners as took their slaves there, brought them back to Missouri, fearing that if they remained there they would be emancipated.
>
> Thus you see that under the principle of popular sovereignty, slavery has been kept out of Kansas, notwithstanding the fact that for the first three years they had a legislature in that Territory favorable to it. I tell you, my friends, it is impossible under our institutions to force slavery on an unwilling people.[48]

Douglas had by 1858 lost the best argument he might have made to these voters—that popular sovereignty is a less inflammatory antislavery strategy than nonextension is, since popular sovereignty had

provoked four years of civil war in Kansas that inflamed the very passions Douglas had argued it would put to rest. But even here, Douglas
could have made the case that nonextension was even more inflammatory, since it would have provoked immediate secession by the entire
Deep South. To make this case Douglas would have to show that there
was more than an outside chance that the South would accept the inevitable in Kansas, and that accepting the inevitable there would mean
they would accept it everywhere (since the other territories were even
less promising for slavery than Kansas was). Had southern politics not
been stampeded by loyalty politics, this argument might have had a
chance, but accepting the inevitable had never been a strong suit
among southern politicians, and prudence and patience on either side
of the Mason-Dixon line were in dwindling supply.

For all of the weakness of his positive position, Douglas could still
separate anti-Nebraska Democrats (whom he could hope to persuade)
from anti-Nebraska Whigs (who were lost to him) by playing to racism,
because anti-Nebraska Democrats hated slavery and black people about
equally, and sought to keep slavery out of Kansas in order to make it a
place for poor white people to establish themselves without competition from blacks.[49] This is not to say that the anti-Nebraska Whigs
were not racists too, but their racism was of a piece with their hierarchical thinking about society generally, black as well as white, and for that
reason was not quite so enflamed as the racism of the Democrats. Because the Whig voters, for class reasons, did not face competition from
black labor in the way that the Democratic voters did, they did not have
to hate them with the same intensity, and since for class reasons the
status of the Whig voters in the white community was already assured,
they did not have to use racism to support the claim that all white people
are equal to each other as the Democrats did, a position called "*herrenvolk* democracy" by George Fredrickson (1979).

It was not only racism that separated anti-Nebraska Democrats from
anti-Nebraska Whigs. They had different ways of playing the free labor ideology. Anti-Nebraska Whigs imagined the free labor ideology
as enabling members of the working class to win entry into the professional class, as Lincoln himself did, and as he described in his 1860
speech in New Haven. Anti-Nebraska Whigs saw slavery as preventing
the individual uplift of white workers. Anti-Nebraska Democrats saw
slavery as part of a class conspiracy aimed at their class. Consider, for

instance, a speech Samuel Tilden, a Free Soil Democrat before the war and later the Democrats' 1876 presidential nominee, gave to Democratic members of the New York legislature during the debates over the Wilmot Proviso:

> Where labor is to a considerable extent committed to slaves, to labor becomes a badge of inferiority. The wealthy capitalists who own slaves disdain manual labor; and the whites who are compelled to submit to it are regarded as having fallen below their natural condition in society. They cannot act on terms of equality with the masters for those social objects which in a community of equals educate, improve and refine all its members. In a word society, as it is known in communities of freemen, with its schools and its various forms of voluntary association for common benefit and mutual improvement, can be scarcely said to exist for them or their families.[50]

Douglas's arguments about popular sovereignty were capable of appealing to anti-slavery racists like the anti-Nebraska Democrats.[51] Lincoln's moral case against slavery, by contrast, as powerful an appeal as it was to Conscience Whigs and northern Americans, could not positively appeal to anti-Nebraska Democrats; the best Lincoln could do was to immunize himself against the Democratic style of racial hostility by denying that racial equality was among his aims and by asserting that his opposition to slavery arose from his desire to protect the status of white yeomen more than from tenderness for the condition of the slaves.

Most of Lincoln's racist remarks, from the Peoria Speech through the Emancipation Proclamation, are defensive, intended to immunize him against this specific attack and to hold these particular voters in line. Lincoln had little to fear from the racist politics of pro-slavery factions, since their voters were lost to him anyway. But he did have to fear losing the support of racist anti-Nebraska Democrats, who were a key faction of his party. He had to fear the loss of anti-Nebraska Democrats in 1858 and 1860 much in the same way he had to fear losing the support of racist slaveholders in the border states during the Civil War. Lincoln trimmed his racism to meet the more specific requirements of anti-slavery racists like the anti-Nebraska Democrats. It was not enough merely to (shamefacedly) embrace racism generally; he had to address the particular concerns of racist Free Soilers, their desire to go to

western territories where they would face neither the economic domination of society by slaveholders nor the economic competition of
black labor. It is to this end that, in the Peoria Speech, Lincoln had
argued of Kansas:

> We want them [the territories] for the homes of free white people.
> This they cannot be, to any considerable extent, if slavery shall be
> planted within them. Slave States are places for poor white people to
> remove FROM; not to remove TO. New free States are the places for
> poor people to go to and better their condition. For this use, the na-
> tion needs these territories. (1:331)

Lincoln did mean this argument, and the free staters in Kansas itself were even more serious about it, and included in their Topeka
Constitution a provision prohibiting free black people from emigrating to Kansas. The 1847 constitution of Illinois also forbade the entry
of free blacks unless they posted a thousand-dollar bond (and forbid
them from owning property or serving as witnesses), and so, more
scandalously, did the constitution of 1862.[52] But for Lincoln, as opposed
to the Kansans, the argument that the territories were for whites only,
not even for enslaved blacks, was a subordinate argument, and partly
defensive in character. Lincoln did not foreground the racist argument
in the Peoria speech the way he foregrounded his chief argument, which
has to do with the way slavery corrodes the integrity and influence of
free government and advances the insidious and destructive idea that
people as people do not have an overriding claim to political and moral
equality. Indeed, the argument that slavery must be kept out of the territories in order to protect the interests of white settlers takes a distinct
second place in the Peoria speech to the need to defend the principles of
the Declaration of Independence and to ward off the idea that there is
no guiding principle in politics other than power and self-interest.

This central moral argument, which Lincoln relied upon from the
Peoria speech through the campaigns of 1858, 1859, and 1860, was not
an argument that had power to reach pro-slavery racists like the anti-
Nebraska Democrats. This was why Lincoln made such an effort to
surround it with arguments of a less savory character.

MCLEAN REPUBLICANS

Conservative, former-Whig Republicans, such as those who might be expected to support McLean or Bates for the 1860 Republican nomination for president, could also have been reached with Douglas's popular sovereignty argument, and Douglas made a concerted play for their support. One might include in this category two other related constituencies, the so-called Cotton Whigs, for whom fear of rocking the economic boat trumped whatever hostility they may have had for slavery (the name implies that they included the mill owners in Massachusetts and elsewhere, who of course could not have opposed slavery anyway, since they depended upon it), and the conservative Whigs who would later support the Constitutional Union ticket of John Bell and Edward Everett. Lincoln's arguments against what he calls "Douglas Popular Sovereignty" were mostly aimed at these groups. Indeed, not only in Illinois in 1858 but also in Ohio the next year, where Lincoln campaigned on behalf of the Republican Party, Lincoln treated these conservative former Whigs-turned-Republicans as if they were the only constituency really in play; all of his arguments are aimed at persuading them that popular sovereignty is not a safe strategy for Republicans to adopt, despite its apparent success in Kansas.

Lincoln's choice of this strategy, his decision to keep the Republicans from fusing with anti-Lecompton Democrats (and perhaps bringing Douglas, their leader, into the Republican Party, as Horace Greeley was urging him to do) enabled Douglas to successfully present himself as the legitimate political successor of his lifelong enemy Henry Clay, and to persuade Clay's successor in Kentucky, John J. Crittenden, to write on his behalf for the former Whigs of Illinois. In successfully presenting himself as the heir of Whig political values, against an opponent who had always referred to Henry Clay as his "beau ideal of a statesman" (1:527), Douglas worked his own transformative assault upon the structure of the second party system, seeking to draw the seekers of sectional compromise into one party, and isolating the radicals on both sides in either the Republican Party or the "Danite" faction of the Democratic Party in Illinois still loyal to President Buchanan.

Of course it is fairer to say of both Lincoln and Douglas that they were scrounging for the factional scraps left behind in the ruin of the second party system than that they set out to destroy it. And indeed if any one person was responsible for the destruction of the second party system, that person would be Douglas, for authoring the Kansas-Nebraska Act, not Lincoln.

THE NATIVISM CARD

Douglas's play for the Fillmore voters (and perhaps also his play for the McLean voters, since they were adjacent, even overlapping constituencies) depended upon his choice to see the American Party as a rump Whig Party. Like the Whig Party, the American Party strove to be a national party, with supporters in all parts of the Union, and the Americans sought to use the methods of intraparty politics to moderate sectional tensions over slavery. The Americans sought to include factions on both sides of the slavery issue in their party, so that the only way to rise to leadership in the party was to support compromises on that issue that both sides could live with. Their failure to find such a position— could anybody have found such a position?—destroyed them as a party. But unlike the Republican Party they sought to mount credible campaigns in all sections of the Union. They represented a last chance at national party organization for former Whigs who still gagged at joining the only remaining national party organization, the Democrats. Douglas's aim was to persuade such voters to put aside that historical distaste for Democrats and cast their lot with the only party that was constrained by its internal structure to seek to mediate the slavery conflict.

Why Douglas did not seek to accuse Lincoln of American Party–style nativism in 1858 is something of a question. Lincoln was not a nativist, as he explained in an impassioned passage included in the 1855 letter to Joshua Speed I quoted above:

> I am not a Know-Nothing. That is certain. How could I be? How can anyone who abhors the oppression of negroes, be in favor of degrading classes of white people? Our progress in degeneracy appears to me to be pretty rapid. As a nation, we began by declaring that *"all men are created equal."* We now practically read it "all men are created equal, *except negroes.*" When the Know-Nothings get control, it will read "all men are created equal, except negroes, *and foreigners, and catholics.*" When it comes to this I should prefer emigrating to some country where they make no pretence of loving liberty—to Russia,

> for instance, where despotism can be taken pure, and without the
> base alloy of hypocracy. (1:363)

Lincoln was no nativist, but many of his party were, and Lincoln knew
he could not risk alienating them. One of the peculiar features of
nineteenth-century politics is that nativism and racism were in some
ways opposing ideologies—the nativist party was always the less racist
of the two major parties, and the party that most vehemently embraced
racism usually vehemently rejected nativism. Lincoln knew he could
not lead a party against the extension of slavery without nativist votes.
Indeed, Lincoln out-organized Seward for the presidential nomination
in 1860 by allowing the nativists to believe, mistakenly, that he would
be more sympathetic to them than the outspokenly anti-nativist Seward
was, while at the same time drawing into the party, and into his own
camp, those German Protestants—not German Catholics—whose
anti-slavery convictions would put the Republicans over the top in the
prairies.[53]

Douglas could have wreaked havoc with this arrangement by making the nativism charge against Lincoln. Douglas knew that nativism
had been a major factor in James Shields's defeat in the Senate campaign
in 1855, and nativist charges were an omnipresent undercurrent in the
Republican press in 1858 and in 1860. Indeed, when in 1860 a rumor
arose that Lincoln had entered a Know Nothing lodge, Lincoln was
forced to explain privately to a constituent that although the charge
was false he could not deny it publicly without alienating nativists whose
votes he needed, and that the Democrats had made the charge only in
order to provoke him into denying it.[54] But neither in 1858 nor in 1860
did Douglas press this charge as hard as he might have. Perhaps Douglas did not do so because he too, as I have just said, sought to woo the
remnants of the American Party, although he presented himself through
Crittenden as wooing the remnants of the Whig Party, believing that
the Americans' desire for a moderately Unionist position capable of
compromising the interests of North and South (which Douglas saw as
more crucial to those voters than their nativism anyway) would be able
trump their nativism so long as he did nothing to inflame the nativism
issue. Both politicians needed nativist votes, and Douglas was on record
against nativism, as Lincoln was not, so Douglas had to be especially
cautious about raising the issue of nativism. Charging Lincoln with

nativism might keep former Democrats out of the Republican column, but it also might remind former Americans that Douglas was no nativist, and thus have defeated his purpose of causing their nationalism to trump their nativism. Lincoln neglected these nativist votes in 1858, but relied upon them in 1860. Both Lincoln and Douglas sought to win nativist votes by concentrating upon the slavery issue and downplaying the hostility to Catholics and to the Irish, which were the key features of nineteenth-century nativism.

However much Lincoln may have downplayed hostility to the Irish in public in 1858, and however much he may have deprecated such hostility in private to Speed, he nevertheless practiced it with some deviousness. Suspecting that a large party of Irish-American railroad workers had been shepherded into the region to swell the Democratic tally, Lincoln sought ways to introduce private detectives into their ranks in order to suborn their votes. In his letter of October 20, 1858, to Norman B. Judd, Lincoln, like many politicians, phrases his own adventure in vote fraud as a defense against fraud by the other party:

> I now have a high degree of confidence that we shall succeed, if we are not over-run with fraudulent votes to a greater extent than usual. On alighting from the cars and walking three squares at Naples on Monday, I met about fifteen Celtic gentlemen, with black carpet-sacks in their hands.
>
> I learned that they had crossed over from the Rail-road in Brown county [sic], but where they were going no one could tell. They dropped in about the doggeries, and were still hanging about when I left. At Brown County yesterday I was told that about four hundred of the same sort were to be brought into Schuyler, before the election, to work on some new Railroad; but on reaching here I find Bagby thinks that is not so.
>
> What I most dread is that they will introduce into the doubtful districts numbers of men who are legal voters in all respects except *residence* and who will swear to residence and thus put it beyond our power to exclude them. They can & I fear will swear falsely on that point, because they know it is next to impossible to convict them of Perjury upon it.
>
> Now the great remaining part of the campaign, is finding a way to head this thing off. Can it be done at all?

> I have a bare suggestion. When there is a known body of these vot-
> ers, could not a true man, of the *"detective"* class, be introduced among
> them in disguise, who could, at the nick of time, control their votes?
> Think this over. It would be a great thing, when this trick is attempted
> upon us, to have the saddle come up on the other horse.
>
> I have talked, more fully than I can write, to Mr. Scripps, and he
> will talk to you.
>
> If we can head off the fraudulent votes we shall carry the day. (1:824)[55]

Heckman believes that Lincoln probably intended to bribe these
voters to cast Republican ballots.[56] Lincoln's supporters, if not Lincoln
himself, whipped up a great deal of anti-Catholic feeling during the
1858 campaign. Adele Douglas, Stephen Douglas's second wife, was
Catholic, and their children were raised Catholic, which naturally
made Douglas, in Republican eyes, the focus of a plot to advance the
cause of Papistry worldwide. And wild conspiracy theories involving
Catholics and slaveholders in the 1858 campaign were a staple of the
partisan press.[57] Don Fehrenbacher describes the extent to which anti-
Catholicism was a key feature of Republican organizing strategy in the
1858 Illinois campaign, noting how the *Chicago Democrat* (despite its
name, a Republican paper) had shrieked that "it is the Pope . . . who
says that Abraham Lincoln shall not be United States Senator," and
thundered after the election, "The triumph of Douglas is as much a
triumph over Protestantism as it is over free labor."[58]

Douglas's supporters were able to return the favor with interest.
When, speaking at Meredosia later in October, Lincoln made the
same complaint about the imported Irish-American voters at Naples
that he had made to Judd, the local Democratic paper, the *Jacksonville
Sentinel*, retorted that "Mr. Lincoln entertains a holy horror of all
Irishmen and other adopted citizens who have sufficient self-respect to
believe themselves superior to the negro," adding that the candidate
"would doubtless disfranchise every one of them if he had the power.
His reference to the danger of his being voted down by foreigners was
a cue to his followers . . . that under the pretext of protecting their
rights, they should keep adopted citizens from the polls."[59]

PARTY FRAGMENTS

Both Lincoln and Douglas scrounged among the fragments of the
second party system. But neither intended to cause the collapse of that

system. The fragments of the second party system were up for grabs, and the candidates tried to pull together different collections of factions roughly in the way Table 4.1 describes (some voters would fall under more than one description).

Douglas's conspiratorial account of the origins of the Republican Party correctly argued that tensions remained within the new party between former Whigs and former Democrats. This is why Douglas dwelt on the charge that Trumbull had double-crossed Lincoln for the Senate nomination in 1855. As a conspiracy theorist, Douglas drew an even darker lesson from this story: that the interested men who whipped up popular sentiment against the Kansas-Nebraska Act were so invested in their own individual political advancement that they were not beneath playing what he calls "Yankee tricks" against each other, even at the price of weakening their organization. Without calling in conspiracy theories, it is clear that there was throughout the war era tension within the Republican Party between those who had once been Whig followers of Henry Clay and those who had once been Barnburner, Free Soil followers of Martin Van Buren. Lincoln's cabinet was almost evenly divided between former Whigs like Seward and Bates and former Democrats like Welles, Blair, Stanton, and, arguably, Chase. As Lincoln pointed out, only his own former membership in the Whig Party kept the balance in his cabinet between former Whigs and former Democrats. Indeed, the fault line that divided the mainstream Republicans from the so-called Liberal Republicans in 1872 was frequently the divi-

Table 4.1. Alignment of Party Fragments in 1858

Sought by neither Lincoln nor Douglas	Southern-aligned Democrats
Sought by Douglas alone	Anti-Lecompton Democrats Other northern-aligned Democrats Fillmore "Americans"
Sought by both Lincoln and Douglas	McLean Whigs Anti-Nebraska and Free Soil Democrats
Sought by Lincoln alone	"Conscience" Whigs Anti-Nebraska Whigs Liberty Party voters Frémont "Americans" Pre-1856 Republicans

sion between those who had once been Whigs and those who had once been Democrats.[60]

4.3 From Whig to Republican

Daniel Walker Howe noted in *The Political Culture of the American Whigs* (1979) that it was common for Whigs to analyze political problems by seeing them in terms of animal passions held in restraint by self-discipline, reason, and, most of all, habit.[61] Reason, by which they meant not only rational self-interest but also the ability to reflect upon fundamental moral principles, is the foundation of virtue, but reason alone is insufficient to secure virtuous action. To shape an actual life, reason must enlist feeling in its behalf. More than this, reason must give shape to a host of purely implicit assumptions about the world, intuitions not only about what is right but also about how "people like us" are supposed to behave. Reason establishes a moral habit of being capable of sustaining itself over the long run, so that on a day-to-day basis people are guided not so much directly by reason as by a kind of moral autopilot set by reason. (This is of course what Aristotle meant by habit: an almost automatic pattern of being, or mode of life, shaped ultimately, but not necessarily directly, by reason.) Naturally, the northern Whigs saw themselves as representing the habits of virtue, and the Democrats as representing subjection to animal urges; the Catholics and the slaveholders were, in their view, remarkably similar enemies, representing similar kinds of failures of difficult-to-acquire habits of self control.

Howe's phrase "political culture" itself expresses a Whiggish, and even somewhat Aristotelian, notion of political behavior. The phrase describes something that is more organically whole than a mere congeries of opinions, something that, like the moral personality over the long haul, has a kind of coherence not always entirely revealed by individual acts and not completely reducible to system. Like a *character*, it is an upshot of many instances, but no particular instance gives one a commanding purchase upon it. It is not exactly a world-picture, because it is partly intuitive, and for that matter, partly implicit, never fully articulated even for its adherents. It is also not exactly an *ideology*, by which I mean a structure of intuitions that transcends the agency of those involved within it (while granting them the illusion of freedom).

It is rather a partly reflected-upon structure of intuitions and habits within which (indeed, in the Whiggish view, *only* within which) moral agency is capable of being practically realized.

Although one might also describe a political culture of the nineteenth-century American Democrats, applied to that party the phrase has a slightly different feel, because the key values of that party did not turn upon the inculcation of good habits and the public cultivation of virtues through the stewardship of the custodians of reason. Democratic politics was about expression of popular will, not about cultivation of public virtues, although it too had habits and values and implicit assumptions about the way the world works. One might say about the phrase "political culture" that it describes the Democrats, but embodies the program of the Whigs; "political culture" is a noun to Democrats, a verb to Whigs.

Howe describes different attitudes about thought and about feeling that distinguish Whigs from Democrats: Whigs shaped feelings; Democrats expressed them. Whigs used feeling to illuminate and support and correct thought, Democrats to stampede it. Whigs saw particular exercises of reason only as part of an upshot of habits of reason; Democrats expected an exercise of reason itself to assume immediate sovereignty over action. For example: for Douglas the *Dred Scott* decision was a definitive statement about slavery in the territories, even if it is one he had to find a way to evade and blunt, but for Lincoln it was only part of a larger upshot, and did not, merely of its own power, settle anything more general than the fate of Scott himself.

The Whigs nowadays have a rather bad name for their opposition to universal (white manhood) suffrage, since their insistence upon property qualifications for voting and upon indirect methods of election has often been taken as the consequence of naked class politics. Their class agenda was certainly part of the story, but it was not all of it. Their ideas about suffrage, and about the structure of the political community, grew out of their vision of ideal human behavior. They saw unmediated expressions of popular will in roughly the same way as they saw unmediated compulsions of appetite. Actions even of a majority, even of a unanimous majority, are not works of freedom unless they issue from formal deliberative mechanisms that institutionalize habits of circumspection and reflection. As a person driven by appetites is not free but the slave of the body, so a polity driven by popular will is not free but the slave of whatever urgencies drive King Numbers. For public acts to embody freedom, they must take shape in the context of settled political ways of being and thinking that serve for the public will the same function habit serves for the private one.

The Whiggish cast of mind naturally resembles the conservatism Burke articulated in *Reflections on the Revolution in France* (1790). But there are some important distinctions. The first is that there remains some difference between the decision to restrain popular will within the mechanisms of institutionalized circumspection, on the one hand, and on the other hand, adherence to a traditional regime even in the face of its manifest injustices out of fear that change would likely produce something worse. The Whigs often used Burkean language, and often, like Burke, deprecated overturning the wisdom of history in the name of urgent abstractions; but they also represented a constitutional order that owed at least as much to a broad, transnational vision of the Rights of Man as to a narrower, historically and culturally bounded vision of the Rights of Englishmen. It was people who had been brought up as Whigs, after all, who wielded the language of the Declaration of Independence in the interests of a transformative ideal of freedom, and it was the Democrats who deprecated the idea that the Declaration might declare anything more than that Englishmen on this side of the Atlantic had the same rights as Englishmen on the other side of the Atlantic, to paraphrase Lincoln's derisive reading of Douglas's understanding of Jefferson's ringing words.

A second difference is that it was the Whigs (and not the Democrats, who opposed all of these things) who were most willing to invest themselves in tradition-overturning reforms such as opposition to slavery, property rights for married women, higher education for women, prison reform, humane treatment of the insane, and universal schooling, or even such small matters as the deprecation of physical punishment in school. It is only a thorough immersion in the Whig cast of mind that makes sense of the apparent paradox, examined by Daniel Walker Howe in *The Unitarian Conscience* (1988), of the investment by a culturally conservative economic elite in a wide-ranging program of reform.

That said, the Whigs really did have something of a blind spot about class, and even Whig figures who emerged from the other side of the tracks, such as Lincoln himself, never really understood class as a force in politics. They used the possibility of rising through discipline and

shrewdness out of one's born economic status in such a way as to blunt
the meaning of class in American politics.

The Whig theme of self-control connects the Whigs with a major
strain of nineteenth-century culture, the transformation of religious
thinking, particularly Calvinist religious thinking, by the Second Great
Awakening, which turned American religious culture in an Arminian
direction, emphasizing the role of discipline and habit in working salvation, and reducing emphasis on the innate depravity of the human
race and the limited atonement available only to an elect few. The social movements that arose from this transformation are legion—
temperance, for one, and from temperance came abolition in its midcen-
tury form and feminism as well, not to mention such things as school
reform, prison reform, reform of the treatment of the mentally ill, and
such smaller-scale innovations as Sunday school and kindergarten. The
provenance of some of these reform movements—reform of treatment
of the mentally ill, care of the wounded on the battlefield, even school
reform—was more Unitarian than Calvinist. But the Unitarians too
represented, indeed were perhaps the paradigmatic representatives of,
the Arminian spirit of the age.[62] The theme of self-control was strongly
linked to a different vision of the divine nature: when Horace Bushnell
shaped the modern Sunday school in his 1847 book *Views of Christian
Nurture, and of Subjects Adjacent Thereto,* he sought a form of religious
education in which children were never to imagine themselves at any
time as damned. Paired with his vision of the moral life as unfolding
through disciplined shaping of the feelings was his vision of God not as
harsh and condemning, but as nurturing and forgiving. Much of what
came to be called New Light Calvinism was as alien to the theology of
the canons of Dordt as Unitarianism itself was, which, after all, was likewise of Calvinist provenance.[63]

To what extent Lincoln shared these theological ideas is a subject of
a great deal of contemporary debate. Certainly he shared ideas of self-
discipline and moral nurture with most of his age. Certainly his earliest
theological ideas were freethinking ideas, and whether the ideas of his
"little book on infidelity" that his friends were said to have burned in
the interest of saving his political career were thoroughgoingly skeptical or merely Paineite deist ideas, they were certainly not Calvinist
ones, despite (or maybe because) of the Free Baptist religion of his father. Much has been made of a deepening and darkening of Lincoln's

religious ideas during the Civil War, although whether that involves an attraction to Old Light Calvinism, as White argues (2002), or an attraction to romantic religious thinking such as Herndon was learning from Theodore Parker, as Winger argues (2003), is unclear.[64] However Lincoln's views may have changed, he did not embrace his wife's turn to spiritualism after the death of Willie Lincoln in 1862, and at no point does he ever seem to have seriously entertained the idea of an afterlife.[65] He never seems to have embraced the Second Great Awakening idea of a nurturing or forgiving God either. In the Second Inaugural Address human beings are called upon to forgive each other, and to recognize their mutual imbrication in human fallenness. But the God of the Second Inaugural is still a strenuous judge, a disabuser of the moral pretensions of both sides, and an exacter of harsh punishments.

The theme of self-control illuminates Whig economic thinking as well as its moral and religious thinking. It is a mistake to assume that the Whigs, although a pro-business party led by an economic and cultural elite, took views that are associated with equally pro-business parties from later periods in American history, such as the Republican Party under McKinley or Taft, or the Republican Party of the Reagan and George W. Bush eras. For one thing, the Whigs were not adherents of economic laissez-faire, and were not supporters of minimal government. They were supporters of publicly financed internal improvements such as national roads, canals, railroads, and river and harbor clearing, and they expected the government to shepherd both the economy and the moral life of the people.[66] They were protectionists in the main, although after the so-called Compromise of 1833 were willing to phase out protectionist tariffs as American industries became better able to hold their own against British competition. Laissez-faire in the antebellum period was the hallmark of the Democratic Party, and was then considered an anti-business position, not a pro-business one, since what it opposed was what it took to be government sponsorship for the interests of the economic elite. "Limited government" was also a Democratic, anti-business ideology in the antebellum era, not a Whig, pro-business one, for the same reasons.

Also of crucial importance to note is that antebellum Whig economic thinking did not have the dark underside of social Darwinist brutality that characterizes Republican economic thinking from the 1870s to the present. The vision of the economy as a ruthless struggle for survival, in which the suffering of the losers is a justifiable price for the advancement of the winners, is simply alien to antebellum Whig economic thinking in the United States. The phrase "survival of the fittest" may have originated in economic rather than biological circles, and have had currency in nineteenth-century economic thinking, but it did not have currency among nineteenth-century Whigs. It did have currency, however, among nineteenth-century Republicans in the latter third of the century, and even Progressive-era opponents of the brutalities of capitalism like Theodore Roosevelt and Wood-row Wilson phrased their economic thinking in pseudo-Darwinist language.

When economic Darwinism did make an appearance in antebellum writings in the United States, it was chiefly in the form of a nightmare entertained by opponents of Whig capitalist development; it is only in the post–Civil War era that the brutality of such ideas was taken as bracing rather than horrifying, and it is only in the post–Civil War era that such views, because they give their adherents an unearned claim to superior realism, were adopted by proponents of capitalism rather than critics of it.[67] It was those who, like James Henry Hammond, wished to argue that the northern worker was more oppressed than the southern slave, were the most likely to adopt such a view of capitalism. But they were taking their view of what capitalism was chiefly from Dickens, not from Marx, and their firsthand knowledge of northern capitalism was scanty. A kind of Darwinist understanding of the economic life was also shared by the working-class opponents of capitalism whose political organizations were documented by Sean Wilentz in *Chants Demo-cratic* (1984). These working-class opponents of capitalism sometimes defended slavery, and more often defended the racial inequality upon which slavery depended.

One thing the Whigs did share with their Republican successors was what Eric Foner refers to as the "Free Labor" ideology, the belief that, left to their own devices, workers would, through their own hard work, inevitably improve their standard of living and their class status.[68] This ideology reflects the economic experiences of small entrepreneurs—shopkeepers and the owners of small factories—which was, until the Civil War transformed the American economy, the experience of most of the business class in the United States. Once they came to power, the Republicans transformed the economy, producing large-scale economic enterprises with large-scale effects for good and bad; but nothing in their economic thinking equipped them to understand such enterprises, and they continued to see them in antiquated ways. Even Frederick Douglass's analysis of the economic needs of the freed slaves never gets past the limitations of the free labor ideology, according to his biographer William S. McFeely.[69] Lincoln's economic thinking seems particularly antiquated, given the metamorphosis of the American economy over which he presided.[70]

It is easy to see how the free labor ideology was an anti-slavery ideology, not only because slaves are obviously not free labor, but also because slavery debases the value of free labor. (Anti-slavery racists such as those described by Berwanger and by Nevins were particularly attracted to this idea.) Lincoln, however, did not argue, as, say, Frederick Law Olmsted did in *The Cotton Kingdom* (1861), or, in a different way, as Hinton Rowan Helper did in *The Impending Crisis of the South* (1857), that slavery was an economic drag. Indeed, as Stewart Winger points out, Lincoln everywhere assumed that slavery in his era was profitable, and that economic arguments may wind up favoring slavery.[71] Lincoln's attack on slavery was primarily an attack made on moral grounds, and in his hands even the free labor ideology had a moral, not an economic, flavor.[72]

In Lincoln's speech at the Wisconsin State Fair, given in Milwaukee on September 30, 1859, he contrasted the free labor theory with what he called the "mud-sill" theory. The latter phrase refers to the famous defense of slavery, sometimes called the "Cotton Is King" speech, given by Senator James Henry Hammond of South Carolina in the U.S. Senate on March 4, 1858.

What Lincoln wished to contest, in the Milwaukee speech, was the idea that the free worker's condition is essentially equivalent to that of the slave. That the two were equivalent, and, indeed, that the condition of the northern worker was on balance rather worse than that of the southern slave, was a staple of pro-slavery propaganda.[73] George Fitzhugh, an outlier in the theory of slavery but interesting anyway for the way in which by exaggeration he brings out some of the features that remain unstated in other thinkers, went so far as to dissociate slavery from race and to suggest that it might do northern mill workers a favor to enslave them. (Somehow they did not rise to accept the offer.)[74]

Lincoln began by conceding that labor is the origin of economic value and that the relationship between labor and capital can be a vexed one. He also did not contest the claim that the lot of hired labor is a disempowered one, subject to oppression, although he did not compare the situation of the hired laborer with the situation of the slave. What Lincoln contested was the claim that capital and labor between them exhaust the possibilities; most working Americans, Lincoln argued, work for themselves, and those that hire others frequently work alongside them.[75] Lincoln emphasized this mixed class, among both free proprietors and slaveowners.

Exhibit A of Lincoln's argument here was, of course, Lincoln himself. Lincoln pressed his argument in two directions. First, in a turn of argument much adopted by Republican writers later, he argued that those who fail to rise out of hireling status as he himself did have only themselves to blame for it. Second, he argued that in the United States, education does not grant one exemption from labor:

> The prudent, penniless beginner in the world, labors for wages awhile, saves a surplus with which to buy tools or land, for himself; then labors on his own account another while, and at length hires another new beginner to help him. This, say its advocates, is *free* labor—the just and generous, and prosperous system, which opens the way for all— gives hope to all, and energy, and progress, and improvement of condition to all. If any continue through life in the condition of the hired laborer, it is not the fault of the system, but because of either a dependent nature which prefers it, or improvidence, folly, or singular misfortune. (1:97–98)

Louis Hartz long ago singled out this kind of self-improvement rhetoric as the feature that separated the Whigs from the Federalists, and that to some extent this rhetoric of self-improvement immunized the Whigs from the charges of elitism and aristocracy that had dogged the Federalists.[76] Hartz also noted the limitation of the free labor ideology approach, which is that it can imagine how individuals may free themselves from entrapment in a repressed underclass, and it may moderate the sense that the situation of that underclass is repressed, by treating that situation as temporary (rather like the exploitation of medical interns and residents), but the free labor ideology can at best offer escape to some members of the underclass; it cannot offer liberation to that class.[77] Douglas may have had very retrograde ideas about race. But his party understood class far better than Lincoln's party did.

The habit among the Whigs of seeking to support disciplined and self-reflective habits of agency had other deep cultural consequences as well, beyond the transformation of capitalism by the free labor ideology. The concept of disciplined habits of freedom motivates the characteristic Whig version of democracy as the fruit of a long cultural tradition that inculcated the political habits required for democracy to prosper. Democrats, by contrast, says Howe, saw democracy as the easy and natural inheritance of people as people. This made the Whigs more sympathetic to nativism than the Democrats, but curiously it made them less racist, because, not having a commitment to class equality, they did not need to use race to make all white people equal to each other, and, since equality was never in question anyway, they could depict themselves in patronizing ways as the noblesse oblige guardians of lesser peoples. (The Whigs, for the same reasons, were considerably less hostile to the Native Peoples, opposing the removal of the Cherokees, for instance.)[78]

4.4 Anti-Nebraska and Anti-Lecompton Democrats

Why Lincoln did not make a play for the support of anti-Lecompton Democrats, of whom the most prominent was Douglas himself, is still an open question. Horace Greeley and other eastern Republicans like Henry Wilson had been urging just this.[79] Now the turning point for the future of slavery in Kansas had already been reached earlier in the summer of 1858, when the people of Kansas had by a nine-to-one margin rejected the Lecompton Constitution. They had of course been supported in this by the Republicans in Congress, but the margin of votes that put them over the top was the small group of anti-Lecompton Democrats loyal to Douglas, and Douglas was widely seen in the South, on the strength of this, as a formidable supporter of Free Soil politics. (This is rather a curious reversal of fortune for Douglas, who had previously by the North and the South been taken as a tool of southern interests: nobody seems to have assumed that he *meant* it when he said that he was for letting the people of Kansas decide this issue in their own way.) The anti-Lecompton Democrats were a weak faction in

Congress, but probably had a more formidable constituency among
the voters. It is a fair guess that most northern Democrats were anti-
Lecompton (which is why they voted for Douglas, rather than for Breckinridge, in 1860), and indeed only opposition to the Lecompton Constitution could have kept the Democratic Party at all credible north of the
Mason-Dixon line.

Kansans made their choice about slavery even knowing that the price
of doing so would be that they could not apply again for statehood until
the population of the territory had reached the number required for
a Representative in the House, a gain in population from 35,000 to
93,420.[80] But the question of Kansas was still not a completely moot one,
since Kansas would still (had secession not intervened) have had to be
admitted to the Union by a vote in a Congress in which the South was
still strong, and the support of anti-Lecompton Democrats might still
have been necessary to secure the admission of Kansas.[81]

If one believed that keeping slavery out of the territories would itself
so damage the vitality of slavery that the institution would be crippled,
it might not matter whether the motives of the anti-Lecompton Democrats were moral or merely political and economic, so long as alliance
with them helped keep slavery out of the territory. Lincoln himself
was on record arguing that keeping slavery out of the territories would
fatally compromise it. If anti-Lecompton Democrats had kept slavery
out of Kansas they had already, if for reasons of their own, damaged
slavery every bit as much as Lincoln was capable of doing within the
limits of the Constitution as he understood it, and he could safely have
treated them as allies.

Indeed, as early as 1849, when Calhoun had argued for a bill to ensure
that every new free state admitted to the Union would be balanced by a
new slave state, Douglas had argued that the weight of popular sovereignty would inevitably be brought to bear for freedom:

> I have already had occasion to remark, that at the time of the adop-
> tion of the Constitution, there were twelve slaveholding states, and
> only one free state, and of those twelve, six of them have since abol-
> ished slavery. This fact shows that the cause of freedom has steadily
> and firmly advanced, while slavery has receded in the same ratio. We
> all look forward with confidence to the time when Delaware, Mary-
> land, Virginia, Kentucky, and Missouri, and probably North Carolina

and Tennessee, will adopt a gradual system of emancipation, under the operation of which, those states must, in process of time, become free. In the meantime, we have a vast territory, stretching from the Mississippi to the Pacific, which is rapidly filling up with a hardy, enterprising, and industrious population, large enough to form at least seventeen new free states. . . . Now let me inquire, where are you to find the slave territory with which to balance these seventeen free territories, or even any one of them. . . . Will you annex all Mexico? If you do, at least twenty out of twenty-two will be free states, if the "law of the formation of the earth, the ordinances of Nature, or the Will of God," is to be respected, or if the doctrine shall prevail of allowing the people to do as they please. . . . Then, sir, the proposition of the Senator from South Carolina is entirely impracticable. It is also inadmissible, if practicable. It would revolutionize the fundamental principles of the government. It would destroy the great principle of popular equality, which must necessarily form the basis of all free institutions. It would be a retrograde movement in an age of progress that would astonish the world.[82]

Why, given these possible strategic advantages, did Lincoln choose to frame the campaign in terms of a moral attack upon slavery that seems to have been specifically designed to keep the anti-Lecompton Democrats out of the Republican Party? Possibly the grounds Lincoln himself adduced—that the professed moral indifference to slavery of the anti-Lecompton Democrats, who opposed slavery in the territories because they felt the people of those territories did not want it, not because it was wrong in itself, would in fact have not proven strong enough to resist the temptation to make a fatal compromise with the fire-eaters if the latter really chose to threaten the Union over it—do explain why Lincoln took that position. (But perhaps Lincoln was wrong about the strength of the popular sovereignty position—Douglas after all did not back down about nonextension when the fire-eaters called him on it, not in 1858, not in 1860, and not in 1861.)

But if the fate of slavery not only in Kansas but in the territories as a whole had already been decided, and the fate of slavery itself hangs on the fate of slavery in the territories, as Lincoln himself had argued, then what are Lincoln's arguments about? If keeping slavery out of Kansas and the other territories were the only issue, a coalition with supporters of popular sovereignty would do no harm and might do good. Given the success of the popular sovereignty strategy in the territories, then what does Lincoln's moral case add that Douglas's popular sovereignty case could not have covered? What issue, other than the fate of slavery in the territories, was in play that was decided by the difference between Lincoln's strain of argument and Douglas's strain of argument?

The short answer to this question is that the ultimate focus of Lincoln's argument in the 1858 and 1859 debates was not the fate of slavery in the territories but the slave power conspiracy. Lincoln's fear was that the slave states would use their control of the Supreme Court to effect a judicial revolution that would reimpose slavery in the free states. When he spoke of a "second *Dred Scott* decision" during the 1858 debates, he may have had in mind a case about whether taking a slave to a free state emancipates that slave, a case like *Lemmon v. New York*, which was already working its way through the courts, a case we have examined in section 3.5 above.

If, given that the popular sovereignty case already made by Douglas had practically sufficed to keep slavery out of the territories, the short answer to the question of why Lincoln insisted anyway upon making the moral case is that Douglas's case was not strong enough to meet the threat posed by the slave power conspiracy; the long answer is that only by pressing a moral case against slavery can one hope that what follows the death of slavery—a new birth of freedom—might be shaped by something moral rather than something purely economic.

Here let me make what might be a controversial proposal: moral grounds like Lincoln's, but not popular sovereignty grounds like Douglas's, lend themselves to arguments supporting citizenship rights for all people. Now Lincoln repeatedly and vehemently over the course of the debates denied having any such agenda. The principle for which Douglas argued had already kept slavery out of the only western territory in which it seemed to him and to many others to be viable. If the future of slavery depended upon expansion into the territories, the argument was open for him to make that popular sovereignty had already fatally damaged the prospects for slavery over the long term. But whatever effect Douglas's arguments would have had on the future of slavery, Douglas's arguments could not have secured civil rights for black people, and Lincoln's argument, even though he denied intending it that way, could not be seriously applied without making the establishment of civil rights an issue. Lincoln's choice of strategy, this is to say, gives some color to Douglas's charge that Lincoln's ultimate agenda is not only abolition but also racial equality, despite Lincoln's quite sincere denial that he sought to press either issue.

I do not argue that Lincoln had planned from the beginning to advance the civil rights of black people; I take seriously his own account, in the Hodges letter and elsewhere, that he discovered his intentions rather than entertained them, that he did not shape events, but rather events shaped him. Events intervened in the equilibrium between his racism and his serious if imperfect commitment to human equality. Like those of all people, his vices were entangled with his virtues. But his virtues were more patient than his vices were.

Lincoln was aware of his racism, and prudent enough to invoke it when he needed it for political cover. But he was also always ashamed of it. He knew, however, that you do not change deeply entrenched features of your sensibility merely by deciding they are wrong, because such sudden conversions do not usually create the psychological conditions required to transform one's habit of being.

Throughout the first two years of the Civil War, Lincoln was engaged in a delicate process of manipulation of the people of the border states. He knew he could not press them for more than they were in a position to give, and that if he lost Maryland, Kentucky, and Missouri he would lose the war. He knew he had to revoke the emancipation orders issued by Frémont and Hunter if he wished to have any hope of keeping the loyalty of the border states. But he also kept pressure on the border states to consider their own emancipation plans, and when victory at Antietam gave him the opportunity to give them a nudge, he took that opportunity. Lincoln turned out to have judged that opportunity correctly. Although there was a great deal of immediate hostile reaction to the Emancipation Proclamation, it did not cost him the loyalty of Maryland and the other border states, and in the long run the proclamation itself revolutionized the thinking of the Union as a whole and of the border states in particular. Lincoln chose a time when the border states were ripe to resolve their ambivalences about slavery, and the consequences of his act reveal that latent emancipationism even in the border states was available not far beneath the surface of political appearances, even if most direct gauges of public feeling on

the subject—speeches by local politicians, arguments in local newspapers—argued the contrary. When actually confronted with emancipation, Marylanders turned out to be more ready for it than any of
their public spokesmen had anticipated.

Lincoln understood the ambivalences of the people of the border
states because he partly shared them. But more than that, Lincoln understood the instability and contradictoriness of his own feelings about
race; he knew that however intractable his racism was, it was also nothing to be proud of and was inconsistent with many of the things in
himself (and in his nation) that he most cherished. He knew what he
could ask of himself, and when he could ask it. And he waged the same
kind of persuasive campaign in his own mind that he waged in Maryland. His reason understood his own mind with the same dispassionate
and detached realism with which it understood the politics of the border states, and he waged the same kind of campaign against his own
racism that he waged with the slaveholders of Maryland, with the same
caution, the same patience, and the same inexorableness. His mind was
another Maryland.

4.5 The 1854 Platforms

Douglas's case for the claim that the Republican Party originated in a
radical conspiracy depended largely upon what Douglas believed was
the platform that issued from the Republican state convention in
Springfield in October 1854:

> 1. *Resolved* That we believe this truth to be self-evident, that when
> parties become subversive of the ends for which they are established,
> or incapable of restoring the government to the true principles of the
> constitution, it is the right and duty of the people to dissolve the po-
> litical bands by which they may have been connected therewith, and
> to organize new parties upon such principles and with such views as
> the circumstances and exigencies of the nation may demand.
>
> 2. *Resolved* That the times imperatively demand the reorganization
> of parties, and repudiating all previous party attachments, names
> and predilections, we unite ourselves together in defence of the lib-
> erty and constitution of the country, and will hereafter co-operate as
> the Republican party, pledged to the accomplishment of the follow-

ing purposes: to bring the administration of the government back to the control of first principles; to restore Nebraska and Kansas to the position of free territories; that, as the constitution of the United States, vests in the States, and not in Congress, the power to legislate for the extradition of fugitives from labor, to repeal and entirely abrogate the fugitive slave law; to restrict slavery to those States in which it exists; to prohibit the admission of any more slave States into the Union; to abolish slavery in the District of Columbia; to exclude slavery from all the territories over which the general government has exclusive jurisdiction; and to resist the acquirements of any more territories unless the practice of slavery therein forever shall have been prohibited.

3. *Resolved* That in furtherance of these principles we will use such constitutional and lawful means as shall seem best adapted to their accomplishment, and that we will support no man for office, under the general or State government, who is not positively and fully committed to the support of these principles, and whose personal character and conduct is not a guaranty that he is reliable, and who shall not have abjured old party allegiance and ties. (1:498)

Douglas was mistaken about the provenance of these resolutions, which in fact derived from an 1854 local Republican meeting in Kane County.[83] And Lincoln was not present at the Springfield meeting anyway (although Douglas had spoken with him in Springfield earlier that day), having left town for a meeting in Tazewell County, perhaps so as to avoid the convention. Lincoln, invited by the very men who were organizing the Republican Party, had given a version of the Peoria speech in the Illinois House chamber that afternoon. When Douglas rose to reply, Ichabod Codding rose to announce that what he called the Republican state convention was convening in the Senate chamber immediately. Lincoln did not attend the meeting, but he was reported by the local paper as having been in attendance.[84] Now both the Springfield and Kane County meetings took place not only before Lincoln joined the party but before (in Lincoln's view) the party was truly a statewide organization anyway.[85] (This last might not have mattered for Douglas's case, since his claim was that Lincoln was secretly organizing for the Republicans while still maintaining publicly that he was a Whig in good standing.) Lincoln's response to the challenges these

resolutions represent was evasive at Ottawa (Lincoln did not answer
Douglas's interrogatories about the platform until the second debate,
at Freeport, where he posed a few famous interrogatories of his own),
and when he discovered Douglas's errors about the provenance of the
resolutions, he raised a smokescreen of forgery charges against Douglas and his allies in order not to have to grapple with the main point of
Douglas's attack.

Because Douglas really was mistaken about the provenance of the
platform, he was himself put on the defensive about it. But the nub of
the charge still stands. Theodore Parker made this point in a letter to
Herndon of September 9, 1858, arguing:

> In the Ottawa meeting, to judge from the *Tribune* report, I thought
> Douglas had the best of it. He questioned Mr. Lincoln on the great
> matters of slavery, and put the most radical questions, which go to the
> heart of the question, before the people. Mr. Lincoln did not meet
> the issue. He made a technical evasion: "he had nothing to do with the
> resolutions in question." Suppose he had not, admit they were forged.
> Still, they were the vital questions pertinent to the issue, and Lincoln
> dodged them. That is not the way to fight the battle of freedom.[86]

The issue after all was not whether Lincoln was or was not present at
the meetings where these resolutions were adopted, since similar resolutions were adopted at Republican meetings in many of the northern
counties of Illinois, as Douglas pointed out in the later debates. (At Freeport Douglas quoted very similar language from an 1854 Republican
county convention in Rockford, one county to the east.) Similar resolutions, penned by Owen Lovejoy, had been pressed by the Republican
caucus in the legislature in February 1855, most of whose members
voted for Lincoln in the 1855 senatorial race the very next day.[87]

Exactly where the resolutions were adopted turns out to be a quibble.
The issue was not whether the platform exactly represented Lincoln's
own views (since Douglas was well aware that some of the resolutions
did not); the issue was whether they represented the ideological thrust
of the Republican Party, in which case the provenance of the resolutions themselves was an irrelevant consideration. Indeed, what really
made Douglas's case about the resolutions was not the fact that they
were adopted by a Republican convention, but the fact that they were

lustily cheered by the Republicans in the audience at Ottawa as he read them aloud:

> Now, gentlemen, your Black Republicans have cheered every one of those propositions, and yet I venture to say that you cannot get Mr. Lincoln to come out and say that he is now in favor of each one of them. That these propositions, one and all, constitute the platform of the Black Republican party of this day, I have no doubt; and when you were not aware for what purpose I was reading them, your Black Republicans cheered them as good Black Republican doctrines. My object in reading these resolutions was to put the question to Abraham Lincoln this day, whether he now stands and will stand by each article in that creed, and carry it out. (1:499)

After Lincoln disavowed many of the planks of this supposed platform during the Freeport speech, Douglas took a great deal of delight in reiterating the platform's language to the effect that Republicans would support nobody who did not endorse these planks and promise to act upon them, and indeed went so far as to ask prominent Freeport Republicans, on the stand with Lincoln, whether they still stood by their 1854 resolutions, which they did.[88] Douglas hugely enjoyed baiting the largely Republican crowd at Freeport:

> Well, you think that is a very good platform, do you not? If you do, if you approve it now, and think it is all right, you will not join with those men who say that I libel you by calling these your principles, will you? Now, Mr. Lincoln complains; Mr. Lincoln charges that I did you and him injustice by saying that this was the platform of your party. I am told that Washburne made a speech in Galena last night, in which he abused me awfully for bringing to light this platform, on which he was elected to Congress. He thought that you had forgotten it, as he and Mr. Lincoln desire to. He did not deny but that you had adopted it, and that he had subscribed to and was pledged by it, but he did not think it was fair to call it up and remind the people that it was their platform.
>
> But I am glad to find that you are more honest in your Abolitionism than your leaders, by avowing that it is your platform, and right in your opinion. (1:560–561)

On the basis of the supposed 1854 platform, Douglas propounded six questions for Lincoln, questions that recurred through the rest of the debates.

Douglas's Query about the Fugitive Slave Act

Lincoln in fact did not favor the unconditional repeal of the Fugitive Slave Act of 1850, because, like Douglas, and like Daniel Webster, he felt that it was part of the bargain of the Compromise of 1850. Lincoln had made this point in the Peoria speech in 1854, and he quoted the passage concerning it in his reply at Ottawa, providing further elaboration at Freeport.

The test of the Fugitive Slave Act, as Douglas saw it, was whether opponents of slavery were capable of making a bargain that, on the whole, perhaps advanced their moral case but that included, as a price of that advancement, moral compromises that on their face seemed (and seem) to be damning. Someone who cannot make such a compromise is, in Douglas's view, someone who must ultimately seek unmediated domination of the Republic, since anything less would require in his own views a fatal moral sacrifice.

There is a nuance in the argument here that needs to be stressed, in the interest of fairness to Douglas. To argue that dealmaking must seek durable agreements-to-differ is not to argue that the outcome of issue is ultimately an indifferent one, that the two sides are morally equivalent or are separated only by taste, or lifestyle, or political culture, or economic habit of being, or some other morally neutral way to phrase the conflict. One need not be morally neutral to seek a modus vivendi between parties who are going to have to deal with each other for a future that may go on forever. One need not give up one's convictions to seek a deal, but one does need to give up inflammatory ways of pressing those convictions.

Lincoln's concession on the Fugitive Slave Act enabled him to avoid seeing the choice in the stark terms embraced by the radicals: Lincoln was not among those who preferred morally pure, and possibly violent, conflict to compromising compromises, and he did not see the issue as involving a choice between bloody hands and dirty ones. But he saw the nature of dealmaking in a different way from how Douglas saw it. For Douglas saw compromise as an arrangement between parties who are going to have to deal with each other more or less forever. When Lincoln imagined bargaining with the slave states, he imagined himself as making reasonable concessions to people who must ultimately recognize that history, as well as morality, must finally run against them, although that history may take a very long time to work itself out. Deep down, Douglas seems to have believed that history would run against slavery as well, but, unlike Lincoln, Douglas never sought to make that recognition an explicit part of the bargain, and indeed, always refused to concede what the slaveholders already suspected about him anyway, that he too looked for an end to slavery. This is why, in 1860, the slave state voters treated Douglas as simply a disingenuous version of Lincoln. Lincoln, unlike Douglas, saw the bargains the free states had made with the slave states always in the context of the ultimate destruction of slavery, and he would accept the Fugitive Slave Act, loathsome as it was, not as a kind of living arrangement between the two sections so much as a tactical retreat made as an enabling condition for a sweeping, if far off, strategic advance.

Douglas's aim seems not to have been to characterize Lincoln so much as to characterize his supporters, and his argument seems addressed to a relatively conservative element—anti-Lecompton Democrats, Fillmore Whigs, and Bates or McLean Republicans—who disliked the act but recognized that it was the price of the Compromise of 1850. Douglas knew that Lincoln was more like those people than like the true abolitionists. But Lincoln's supporters may have been different, and what Douglas sought to do here was to ask whether these conservative voters would really feel comfortable in the same camp with these others.

Douglas distinguished three groups, each of whom in a way opposed the Fugitive Slave Act: first, those who opposed the act and sought to subvert it; second, those who opposed the act but submitted to it because it was for the moment the law of the land; and third, those who opposed the act but accepted it as part of a bargain of which they had also accepted the benefit. The first group opposed, did not accept, and would not submit to the Fugitive Slave Act. The second group opposed the act but submitted to it while not accepting it. The third group opposed the act but submitted to it as the law of the land and accepted it as the price of a political compromise it had endorsed. Because Lincoln was himself a member of the third group, Douglas risked losing all three

groups to Lincoln. Douglas wished to argue that if you oppose the act
but think of opposition to the act as politically inflammatory and subversive of a bargain by which all sides are already bound, your allegiance would be better placed with Douglas, most of whose supporters
thought the same way, than with Lincoln, who, whatever his own views,
attracted supporters who were willing to risk the Republic over the
issue and who would feel he owed them something should he be elected.
If Douglas wished to charge that Lincoln and his party sought to subvert the Compromise of 1850, he could hardly have picked a better issue than the widespread Republican hostility to the Fugitive Slave Act,
although to do this he had to maintain the distinction between distaste
for the act and a desire to disobey or repeal it.

Lincoln's response, both in Peoria and in Ottawa, added a nuance
that needs accounting for. In both places Lincoln conceded that, both
as an aspect of the Compromise of 1850 and as a fulfillment of the fugitive slave clause of the federal Constitution, the South had a right to
an effective fugitive slave act, which the 1793 act seems not to have
been. Lincoln had said at Peoria, "I would give them [slaveholders] any
legislation for the reclaiming of their fugitives, which should not, in its
stringency, be more likely to carry a free man into slavery, than our
ordinary criminal laws are to hang an innocent one" (1:316–317). But
saying that is a different thing from endorsing the act actually passed
by Congress in 1850, which after all deprived accused fugitives of most
of the traditional legal protections against unjust detention. At Freeport, Lincoln criticized the 1850 law but also conceded that "inasmuch
as we are not now in an agitation in regard to the alteration or modifi-
cation of that law, I would not be the man to introduce it as a new
subject of agitation upon the general question of slavery" (1:539).

This is a prudent answer, and an accurate reflection of Lincoln's
views. It is also true that Lincoln himself, in 1858 at least, did not seek
to revisit the issue of the Fugitive Slave Act. But it is not true that the
subject was not in agitation in 1858, because it was in continuous agitation during its whole history. Indeed, a powerful legal challenge to
the act was working its way through the courts up to the Supreme
Court, which would finally decide the issue in the case of *Ableman v.
Booth* in 1859.

The constitutionality of the Fugitive Slave Act had long been disputed, and as early as the *Thomas Sims* case in 1851 the argument was

made that the law vests judicial power in commissioners, who are not really judges (and thus the act violates the separation of powers), and that the provision of the law that enabled those commissioners to receive a higher fee if they returned an accused fugitive slave to slavery than if they did not made the commissioner an interested party.[89] In Clark County, Ohio, for instance, a county sheriff attempted to serve a writ of habeas corpus upon a federal marshal and his posse, who were holding four men accused of aiding an escaped slave named Ad White. Violently resisted by the marshal's posse (whose many weapons apparently included a slingshot), the sheriff gathered a posse of his own, and arrested the lot. Because the marshal was held in jail, he could not contest the habeas corpus proceedings of the four rescuers, who were released because of his default, although he too was released on a habeas corpus shortly thereafter.[90] (There was a similar instance of dueling writs in the aftermath of the famous case of Margaret Garner, the subject of Toni Morrison's novel *Beloved*.)[91]

The *Ableman* case turned on the issue of state jurisdiction in fugitive slave cases, exactly what the 1850 act was designed to circumvent. Many states had, in the aftermath of the act, passed personal liberty laws aimed at preventing recapture of fugitive slaves in their jurisdiction, citing the kind of states' rights doctrines that were the usual stock in trade of slaveholders. The *Ableman* case was somewhat more complicated. Stephen Ableman was a federal marshal, who was holding Joshua Glover, an escaped slave, in custody near Racine, Wisconsin. Glover was rescued by a crowd led by Sherman Booth, an abolitionist editor. Booth was tried in federal court but released by the Wisconsin Supreme Court on a writ of habeas corpus on the grounds that the Fugitive Slave Act of 1850 was unconstitutional. Wisconsin's argument was novel, arguing that although the Constitution inhibited the states from freeing fugitive slaves, it did not include the power of recovering them among the enumerated powers of the federal government. The beauty of Wisconsin's case was in its ability to use the traditional elements of slave state legal strategy, state supremacy to the point of nullification, limitation of the federal government to enumerated powers, and so on, against slavery.[92] The South's triumph over its own doctrines of state nullification when the Taney Court overturned Wisconsin's attempt to nullify the Fugitive Slave Act came back to bite it during the struggle over desegregation, where the *Ableman* decision was invoked in the enforcement of the *Brown* decision.[93]

Expedient arguments take strange turns, especially when those who make them can use the threat of violence to back up the claim that their arguments actually not only are consistent but are clear to everyone of common sense.

Lincoln did not see the Fugitive Slave Act as an issue of consequence between himself and Douglas, because in fact their positions were close. Knowing that Lincoln's supporters in the senatorial election, including the unfortunate Thomas Turner, whom Douglas baited from the stand, had, only one day before they nominated Lincoln, pledged to support nobody who was not for the immediate and unqualified repeal of the Fugitive Slave Act, Douglas argued that Lincoln's retreat from radicalism on this issue was disingenuous:

> Mr. Lincoln tells you to-day that he is not pledged to any such doctrine. Either Mr. Lincoln was then committed to those propositions, or Mr. Turner violated his pledges to you when he voted for him. Either Lincoln was pledged to each one of those propositions, or else every Black Republican—[cries of "White, white,"]—representative from this Congressional District violated his pledge of honor to his constituents by voting for him. I ask you which horn of the dilemma will you take? Will you hold Mr. Lincoln up to the platform of his party, or will you accuse every representative you had in the legislature of violating his pledge of honor to his constituents? [VOICES; "we go for Turner," "we go for Lincoln;" "hurrah for Douglas," "hurrah for Turner."] There is no escape for you. Either Mr. Lincoln was committed to those propositions, or your members violated their faith. Take either horn of the dilemma you choose. There is no dodging the question; I want Lincoln's answer. He says he was not pledged to repeal the fugitive slave law, that he does not quite like to do it; he will not introduce a law to repeal it, but thinks there ought to be some law; he does not tell what it ought to be; upon the whole, he is altogether undecided, and don't know what to think or do. That is the substance of his answer upon the repeal of the fugitive slave law. I put the question to him distinctly, whether he indorsed that part of the Black Republican platform which calls for the entire abrogation and repeal of the fugitive slave law. He answers, no! that he does not indorse that; but he does not tell what he is for, or what he will vote for. His answer is, in

fact, no answer at all. Why cannot he speak out and say what he is for and what he will do? (1:568)

Mr. Lincoln had indeed already made his position clear enough, and Mr. Turner was unlikely to abandon him for doing so. But Douglas's point still stuck: it is people of Mr. Turner's views who would be among Lincoln's appointees, and it is their favors to him that Lincoln would have to reckon up, not the favors of people who thought with Lincoln himself about the Fugitive Slave Act, and Lincoln would have to repay those when he began handing out chits and making policy.

Lincoln made sure that this issue did not bedevil him in 1860, warning Chase that an attempt to agitate the issue of the Fugitive Slave Act would explode the party, and indeed the 1860 Republican convention included no plank on the subject in its platform.[94]

Douglas's Query about Admission of New Slave States

The struggle in Kansas naturally prompted Douglas's query about whether the Republicans would allow the admission of any more slave states whatsoever. The question would of course apply not only in Kansas, Nebraska, and the rest of the unorganized territory north of Nebraska from the Louisiana Purchase, and in the rest of the Mexican Cession, but also in the case of Texas (should it choose to exercise the right granted to it at the time of its admission into the Union to be divided into as many as five states), and in the unorganized Indian territory in what is now Oklahoma, which had been reserved for slavery under the Missouri Compromise, and in which the Cherokees and the Choctaws in fact had established a slaveholding regime. The question was not an entirely moot one, because of the Oklahoma problem, and even New Mexico had enacted a slave code to cover the all of two slaves in that territory as late as 1859. There was also the issue of the annexation of Cuba, something dear to Douglas and to the Democrats generally, but that is the subject of another query.

Lincoln answered the query at Freeport, but in an evasive way, arguing that he had made no pledge against the admission of new slave states:

In regard to the other question of whether I am pledged to the admission of any more slave States into the Union, I state to you very frankly

that I would be exceedingly sorry ever to be put in a position of having
to pass upon that question. I should be exceedingly glad to know that
there would never be another slave State admitted into the Union; [ap-
plause]; but I must add, that if slavery shall be kept out of the Territories during the territorial existence of any one given Territory, and
then the people shall, having a fair chance and a clear field, when they
come to adopt the Constitution, do such an extraordinary thing as to
adopt a Slave Constitution, uninfluenced by the actual presence of the
institution among them, I see no alternative, if we own the country,
but to admit them into the Union. [Applause.] (1:540)

As a concession there was less to this than meets the eye, and Douglas was quick to point out the issue. Lincoln would be willing to vote to
admit a new slave state only if it came in under a completely implausible
scenario, if, that is to say, slavery had never entered the region at all
during its existence as a territory. Lincoln could make this concession
because it was consistent with his constitutional views: a free territory
could become a slave state because slavery is a state institution. It would
be as free to adopt slavery as Massachusetts was, and it would be about
as likely to do so. But Douglas really had a different situation in mind.
His question was really this: had the slave states played fair in Kansas
(rather than subverting the process with stolen elections, intimidation,
and violence), and had they legitimately won the footrace for control of
Kansas Territory, would the Republicans have accepted the kind of defeat Douglas was insisting that the southern Democrats accept?

Douglas asked this question, among other reasons, to make clear his
own reasons for asking the slave states to accept their defeat in Kansas.
He wanted to make it clear to the slave states that he had given them
every chance to win Kansas for themselves fairly, and that since he, had
they fairly won the footrace for control of Kansas, would have accepted
a slave state victory, the supporters of slavery too should accept their
defeat there. Locally, he wished this argument to appeal to Whigs and
conservative Republicans, since it offered a non-inflammatory way to
admit new free states. By contrast the Republicans would not have admitted Kansas as a new slave state no matter what the outcome of the
footrace, and they were in a weaker position to demand that the slave
states accept that outcome, since they would not have accepted it had
the shoe been on the other foot.

Despite Lincoln's concession, Douglas on this interrogatory forced him into a position that could not but appear to be a radical one to those nonradical voters who were in play between them. Lincoln could hardly have taken any other position without a fatal sacrifice of principle. But it was a position that had a price anyway. Douglas pressed Lincoln repeatedly in the course of the debates about the evasiveness of his concession, and Lincoln never really addressed that objection.

Douglas's Query about Slavery in the District of Columbia

When Douglas raised the issue of the future of slavery in the District of Columbia, he raised something of a chestnut, since this was the issue over which the gag rule controversy had convulsed Congress in the 1830s and 1840s. It was also an issue about which Lincoln had a public record, having drafted an emancipation bill for the District of Columbia when he served in Congress. Douglas's own answer to this question would not be hard to imagine, since he knew that the white voters of the District would not have favored it, but he did not answer his query himself in the debates.

Lincoln's position was completely in line with his views on this subject up to the beginning of the Civil War:

> I should be exceedingly glad to see slavery abolished in the District of Columbia. [Cries of "Good, good."] I believe that Congress possesses the constitutional power to abolish it. Yet as a member of Congress, I should not with my present views, be in favor of *endeavoring* to abolish slavery in the District of Columbia, unless it would be upon these conditions. First, that the abolition should be gradual. Second, that it should be on a vote of the majority of qualified voters in the District, and third, that compensation should be made to unwilling owners. (1:540)

Lincoln's position on this issue was roughly Clay's. As a matter of principle, he favored emancipation in the District. As a matter of constitutional interpretation, he believed that the federal government had the power to accomplish that emancipation. But as a matter of prudence, he argued that it was too risky to attempt, except upon such terms as were unlikely to succeed.

It is worth noting that the terms Lincoln did offer for emancipation in the District of Columbia depended upon popular sovereignty methods more like those of Douglas than like those of other Republicans, since it depended upon the consent of the white people of the District. The insistence upon gradualness and compensation is consonant not only with his 1849 proposal about the District but also with the emancipation plans he elaborated early in his presidency.

Lincoln's argument here did have one detail that might otherwise have gone unnoticed. Lincoln had argued throughout that he had no intention of interfering with slavery in the states where it existed already. In his argument about slavery in the District of Columbia, as he pointed out in the Quincy speech, he even proposed not to interfere with slavery in the one region of the Union where the federal government did have the power to abolish it (1:740). This concession seems unsavory, but it may have won him some credibility with the moderate voters who are in play between him and Douglas, who also would have liked to see slavery ended, so long as they did not themselves have to do anything difficult to accomplish that end.

Lincoln tied his thinking about this issue to his thinking about the domestic slave trade. The 1854 platform had called for the abolition of the domestic slave trade, but Lincoln replied when queried about it that he not only had made no pledge about it but also had not thought deeply about the issue. He assumed (probably because it was a species of interstate commerce) that the federal government had the kind of power to regulate it that it had over slavery in the District of Columbia, but he had no policy to offer on this question, and Douglas did not raise it further.

Douglas's Query about the Acquisition of New Territories

Because the question of the status of slavery in new territories, from the Louisiana Purchase through the conquest of the Mexican Cession, had always inflamed sectional conflict, one might have expected this issue to have more importance in the debates than it turned out to have. Purchasing or conquering new territory was a special concern of Douglas's, who felt that the United States must continue to expand, or die. It was also an issue that had strong southern support, since the chief region these discussions had in mind was Cuba, which was already a slaveholding society. Cuba had been the object of American ambitions since the Jefferson administration, and in 1854 American diplomats in Europe (among them James Buchanan) had written the secret (although almost immediately leaked) "Ostend Manifesto," proposing to purchase Cuba from Spain for $130 million, and, if Spain demurred, to seize it by force. Influential American politicians, most important among them John Quitman, the governor of Mississippi, had supported Narciso López's filibustering expedition against Cuba in 1850, ostensibly aimed at the liberation of Cuba from Spanish rule, but in fact designed to secure U.S. annexation. López and much of his party were captured and executed after the failure of their second expedition in 1851. Douglas and his party continued to harbor designs upon Cuba, and indeed acquiring Cuba was called for in Douglas's platform in 1860.

Naturally Lincoln and the Republicans took a dim view of these filibustering—really pirating—expeditions, and naturally also Douglas, although not sharing the motivations of Quitman and others, looked upon them with more favor. Curiously, however, Lincoln did as president entertain the plan proposed by Montgomery Blair, his postmaster general, of colonizing freed slaves in Chiriqui (as a more favorable location for such a project than Liberia, and, what is more, one where the freed slaves really would be colonizers as opposed to mere exiles), and as late as the Grant administration, negotiations were undertaken with the Dominican Republic for the same purpose.[95]

4.6 Conspiracies across Party Lines

Lincoln and the Buchaneers

We saw in section 4.2 that the rump pro-Buchanan faction of the Democratic Party in Illinois was hard at work, with a great deal of support from the administration in Washington, organizing cooperation between themselves and the Republicans. Lincoln repeatedly taunted Douglas about Buchaneer opposition in a way that suggests that he had lost sight of what the Buchanan administration actually stood for, and indeed, as Douglas bitterly pointed out in his speech at Bloomington on July 16, Lincoln never bestirred himself to criticize the Lecompton fraud explicitly at all.[96] Nor did Lincoln ever criticize the so-called English Compromise, by which the voters of Kansas were allowed to vote whether to accept or reject the Lecompton Constitution (under the pretext of voting upon whether to accept it without its inflated claim upon federal public lands), with the proviso that if they were to reject the Lecompton Constitution they could not apply for statehood again until their population had nearly tripled. Douglas rejected the English bill because it offered an unfair bribe to the pro-slavery faction, and noted that even William Hayden English himself, the Indiana congressman (and 1880 Democratic nominee for vice president) who had, with misgivings, proposed the compromise, had come around to Douglas's view by the time that the people of Kansas had voted on, and overwhelmingly rejected, the Lecompton Constitution on August 2. But Lincoln commented on the English bill only as a way to divide Douglas's own voters, saying nothing against the bill on its merits.

Throughout the 1858 campaign season Lincoln strategically but unfairly underestimated the gravity of the crisis over the Lecompton Constitution, treating Douglas's break with Buchanan over the issue as a "mere tactical disagreement" between conspirators who still were engaged in the same subversive project. His principal reason for doing this was that he did not want Republican voters to admire Douglas for his role in stopping the Lecompton fraud, and he did not want Republican opinion leaders to draft Douglas and his faction into the party. And, of course, Lincoln had to maintain the fiction about how minimal a break the fight over Lecompton represented if he wished to sustain his wildly implausible theory that Douglas and Buchanan were in a conspiracy to force slavery back into the free states.

Lincoln opened the Alton debate with ironic remarks that can only be read as snide, comparing himself to a woman who finds her husband fighting a bear:

> This is the seventh time Judge Douglas and myself have met in these joint discussions, and he has been gradually improving in regard to his war with the Administration. [Laughter, "That's so."] At Quincy, day before yesterday, he was a little more severe upon the Administration than I had heard him upon any occasion, and I took pains to compliment him for it. I then told him to "Give it to them with all the power he had;" and as some of them were present, I told them I would be very much obliged if they would *give it to him* in about the

same way. [Uproarious laughter and cheers.] I take it he has now vastly improved upon the attack he made then upon the Administration. I flatter myself he has really taken my advice on this subject. All I can say now is to re-commend to him and to them what I then commended—to prosecute the war against one another in the most vigorous manner. I say to them again—"Go it, husband!—Go it, bear!" [Great laughter.] (1:791)

When Douglas complained that the Republican Party is a sectional party (a subject that will be treated in greater detail in section 4.7 below), he argued that Lincoln could not proclaim the platform of his party in all parts of the Union. At Galesburg Lincoln retorted to this argument that ever since Douglas's break with Buchanan his own faction of the party had become sectional as well, and that if the ability to make his case south of the Ohio was the test of sectionality, then Douglas was no less a sectional figure than Lincoln:

I ask his attention also to the fact that by the rule of nationality he is himself fast becoming sectional. I ask his attention to the fact that his speeches would not go as current now south of the Ohio river as they have formerly gone there. I ask his attention to the fact that he felicitates himself to-day that all the Democrats of the free States are agreeing with him, while he omits to tell us that the Democrats of any slave State agree with him. If he has not thought of this, I commend to his consideration the evidence in his own declaration, on this day, of his becoming sectional too. I see it rapidly approaching. Whatever may be the result of this ephemeral contest between Judge Douglas and myself, I see the day rapidly approaching when his pill of sectionalism, which he has been thrusting down the throats of Republicans for years past, will be crowded down his own throat. (1:706)

Lincoln's reply misconstrued the nature of Douglas's attack. Douglas did not argue that the Republicans were a sectional party merely because their arguments did not win electoral victories in the slave states. When Douglas argued that the Republican Party was sectional, he meant that the party exploited sectional divisions for partisan purposes, since it did not need to win any votes in the slave states if its support was firm in the free states, and it sought to consolidate its support in the free states by whipping up a sectional agenda, such as by pressing the slave power conspiracy theory.

Apropos of the sectionalism charge, Lincoln somewhat cattily noted that anyone seeking a party called the "National Democratic Party" would find the Buchaneer organization, not Douglas's wing of the party. Lincoln did not seem to see that the division in the Democratic Party offered him a chance for a cross-party alliance on ideologically adjacent grounds, and even a chance to capture a major faction of the Democratic Party for the Republicans. Douglas, by contrast, was well aware of the possibilities for alliance with factions of the Republican Party, an alliance based, unlike Lincoln's de facto alliance with the Buchaneers, on an ideological congruence.

In his account of the struggle over the Lecompton Constitution in his Bloomington speech, Douglas praised both the role of Kentucky's Whig senator John J. Crittenden (whose later support in the Senate campaign gave Douglas a credible if counterintuitive claim to be the heir of Clay) and the role of the Republicans who supported the Crittenden-Montgomery bill, a bill that would have required submission of the Lecompton Constitution (or any possible constitution) for ratification by the voters of Kansas:

> Besides, I only did what it was in the power of any one man to do. There were others, men of eminent ability, men of wide reputation, renowned all over America, who led the van, and are entitled to the greatest share of the credit. Foremost among them all, as he was head and shoulders above them all, was Kentucky's great and gallant statesman, John J. Crittenden. By his course upon this question he has shown himself a worthy successor of the immortal Clay, and well may Kentucky be proud of him. I will not withhold, either, the meed of praise due the Republican party in Congress for the course which they pursued. In the language of the New York *Tribune*, they came to the Douglas platform, abandoning their own, believing that under the peculiar circumstances they would in that mode best subserve the interests of the country.[97]

What Douglas praised the Republican supporters of the Crittenden-Montgomery bill for was their ideologically aware pragmatism. They compromised their support for congressional prohibition of slavery in the territories, in the interest of securing a ratification vote on the constitution of Kansas, which they knew, as Douglas did, would have an anti-slavery result. This kind of cooperation across party lines made sense to Douglas, because it depended upon finding common ideological ground. Douglas's cooperation with Republicans on the Crittenden-Montgomery bill was in a way not very different from the cooperation of anti-slavery Whigs and anti-Nebraska Democrats that created the Republican Party in the first place, which is of course why Greeley and Seward thought it might indicate that Douglas and the anti-Lecompton Democrats were ripe for the picking by the Republicans.

What Douglas did not understand, because it was a species of expediency politics, not a species of pragmatism, was the cooperation between the Republicans and the Buchaneers. The cooperation with the Buchaneers was a qualitatively different thing from the earlier cooperation with anti-Nebraska Democrats like Trumbull, because it crossed an ideological line, not merely a partisan one. Douglas rebuked it with particular bitterness. At Galesburg, for instance, he complained that Illinois postmasters (federal appointees responsible to the president, and not only the president's agents in local politics but also his eyes and ears) were working for Lincoln, and elsewhere he complained that Lincoln's newspaper editors were promoting the candidacy of the Buchaneer state legislators.[98] Douglas was right to find this cooperation fishy. It is one thing to cooperate with an ideological neighbor against someone whose position you both politically oppose. It is quite another to cooperate with the ideological enemy you are supposed to be fighting with in order to harm the ideological neighbor whose position is not so pure as your own. Douglas saw the cooperation between the Republicans and the Buchaneers as the very definition of a devil's bargain.

If cooperation with the Buchaneers was unprincipled, it was unprincipled in a way that is particularly suited to those who believe they have cornered the market on principle. If you are conscious of your own purity, impure means do not rub off on you. Remember, as an example of this kind of expediency politics, how, during the debate over the Compromise of 1850, after poor Senator Pearce had fallen into the trap (described in section 3.4 above), southern Democrats and northern Whigs had both voted on the Atchison and Yulee Amendments, stripping provisions for a free state government for California from the "omnibus" bill. A free state government for California was something the northern Whigs, as an anti-slavery faction, presumably favored; they voted against it only as a way to sabotage the "omnibus" bill and wreck the possibility of political compromise that that bill represented. To do this, they allied with people whose aim was to make California a slave state. If your aim is to let all of God's will be done, though the Heavens fall, you sometimes, rather than dirtying your hands with those who want to do only part of God's will, find yourself allying yourself with those who want the Heavens to fall.

Now when push came to shove the Buchaneers turned out to be a very weak faction, winning about 2 percent of the vote.[99] But the Republicans' willingness to play ball with them meant more than the Buchaneers' actual electoral threat did. Douglas was more famous as a wheeler-dealer than the Republicans were, particularly since so many of them thought of themselves as being in morals rather than in politics. But this kind of bargain was beyond him. It was incomprehensible to him.

The Elections of Chase and Sumner

One might think at first glance that willingness to cooperate with the Buchaneers proved that the Republicans were not an ideological party. After all, what would seem to be more pragmatic than making a temporary bargain, even a devil's bargain, with one's worst enemy? But, perhaps moved by memories of strategies like the Pearce trap, Douglas saw bargains between Republicans and Buchaneers as examples of the kind of expediency appropriate to fanaticism. There were two recent examples in important senatorial elections of precisely the strategy Lincoln's friends had organized with the Buchaneers, and they were the strategies that brought the two most formidable anti-slavery politicians in the Union into the Senate, Salmon Chase of Ohio and Charles Sumner of Massachusetts.

Chase's election in 1849 was the more complicated, and the more sordid, because the man he dispossessed, Joshua Giddings, was one of the most eloquent anti-slavery politicians in the Union. Chase had run as a Free Soiler, and his small contingent in the state House was the balance of power between the Democrats and the Whigs. The election was preceded by a controversial attempt to gerrymander the legislative districts by the Whig Party, an attempt that blew up in the Whigs' faces when some of the new districts wound up electing Free Soil legislators rather than Whigs. The Democrats had small pluralities in both houses (two seats in the House and one in the Senate), so both parties had to seek deals with the eight Free Soil state representatives and the three Free Soil senators if they hoped to rule.

Most of the Free Soilers in Ohio were former Whigs, and were loath to cooperate with the Democrats.[100] Both the Whigs and the Democrats sought to offer Free Soil the Senate seat in exchange for the (to them more important) control of the legislature. The Whiggish-leaning Free Soilers insisted that Giddings, whom the mainstream Whigs despised, should get the Senate seat. Recognizing that the alliance between Whigs and Free Soilers was at an impasse because of this demand, the Democrats sweetened their offer by agreeing to abolish the state's repressive Black Laws in return for Free Soil support over the apportionment question, Democratic appointments to the State Supreme Court, new Democratic district judges, allowing the Democrats to organize the legislature and the major patronage positions, and Democratic economic legislation attacking the banking system, restructuring taxes, and limiting the work day to ten hours. Chase agreed to the Democrats' economic program and to their political demands, and so peeled away just enough Free Soilers (two) to seal the deal with the Democrats.[101] Bitterness against Chase among Ohio Whigs ran deep, and followed Chase for the rest of his career, even denying him the unified support of the Ohio delegation in the race for the 1860 Republican presidential nomination.[102]

Holt describes similar coalitions between Free Soilers and Democrats over the next couple of years in Indiana, Massachusetts, Connecticut, and Vermont.[103] It was an arrangement like the one that elected Chase that brought Charles Sumner to the Senate in 1851. Sumner, promising support for Democratic economic legislation and support for the gubernatorial candidacy of George S. Boutwell (who would become a Republican in 1855), defeated Whig Robert Winthrop, who had opposed the Fugitive Slave Act (alienating his former mentor, Daniel Webster) and who in most other ways was a credible anti-slavery Whig. In the "Washington" chapter of *The Education of Henry Adams* (1918), Adams tartly refers to the deal that put Chase in the Senate this way:

The men who ran the small Free Soil machine were still modest, though they became famous enough in their own right. Henry Wilson, John B. Alley, Anson Burlingame, and the other managers, negotiated a bargain with the Massachusetts Democrats giving the State to the Democrats and a seat in the Senate to the Free Soilers. With this bargain Mr. Adams and his statesman friends would have nothing to do, for such a coalition was in their eyes much like jockeys selling a race. They did not care to take office as pay for votes sold to pro-slavery Democrats. Theirs was a correct, not to say noble, position; but, as a matter of fact, they took the benefit of the sale, for the coalition chose Charles Sumner as its candidate for the Senate, while George S. Boutwell was made Governor for the Democrats. This was the boy's first lesson in practical politics, and a sharp one; not that he troubled himself with moral doubts, but that he learned the nature of a flagrantly corrupt political bargain in which he was too good to take part, but not too good to take profit.[104]

Douglas paid close attention to the 1849 Ohio election, and, even as a Democrat, was quick to throw Chase's double dealing in his face. Already enraged with Chase over his role in the "Appeal of the Independent Democrats," Douglas said of Chase and Sumner in his March, 3, 1854, speech in the Senate:

> I must be permitted to tell the senator from Ohio that I did not obtain my seat in this body either by a corrupt bargain or a dishonorable coalition! I must be permitted to remind the senator from Massachusetts that I did not enter into any combinations or arrangement by which my character, my principles, and my honor, were set up at public auction or private sale in order to procure a seat in the Senate of the United States! I did not come into the Senate by any such means.[105]

Chase huffily interrupted the speech to defend himself, and got into a slanging match with Weller of California. Then Sumner even more huffily (and disingenuously, since he deprecated making personal attacks even as he traded in them) entered the fray, and Douglas let fly at him, using language that Adams, years later, seems to echo:

> [Senator Sumner] says it is contrary to his principles to engage in personal assaults. If he expects to avail himself of the benefit of such a plea, he should act in accordance with his professed principles, and refrain from assaulting the character and impugning the motives of

better men than himself. Everybody knows that he came here by a co-alition or combination between political parties holding opposite and hostile opinions. But it is not my purpose to go into the morality of the matters involved in his election. The public know the history of that notorious coalition and have formed its judgment upon it. It will not do for the senator to say that he was not a party to it, for he thereby betrays a consciousness of the immorality of the transaction, without acquitting himself of the responsibilities which justly attach to him. As well might the receiver of stolen goods deny any responsibility for the larceny while luxuriating in the proceeds of the crime, as the senator to avoid the consequences resulting from the mode of his election while he clings to the office. I must be permitted to remind him of what he certainly can never forget, that when he arrived here to take his seat for the first time, so firmly were senators impressed with the conviction that he had been elected by dishonorable and corrupt means, there were very few who, for a long time, could deem it consis-tent with personal honor to hold private intercourse with him.[106]

Douglas never used this kind of language about Lincoln. But it is clear that in the cooperation between the Republicans and the Bucha-neers he saw a replay of the politics that brought Sumner and Chase to the Senate. The cooperation between the Republicans and the Bu-chaneers, far from being an instance of pragmatic compromise, seems to be an example of the kind of naked expediency politics that only someone driven by profound fanaticism would allow himself to get away with.

4.7 Sectional and Ideological Parties

The Meaning of Sectionalism

We saw in section 4.6 above that Douglas's charge that the Republi-can Party was a sectional party did not turn merely on the happen-so of where it got most of its votes but on the specifically sectional na-ture of its agenda, especially upon its use of the slave power conspir-acy theory as its central organizing issue. As far back as his March 3, 1854, speech in the Senate on the Kansas-Nebraska Act, Douglas had worried that the divisions between the parties would align themselves

with the divisions between the sections, giving each party's leaders a
motivation for exacerbating sectional hostility as a way to maintain
party discipline, heighten party enthusiasm, and outflank their intraparty competition for leadership positions.

Douglas saw in 1854 that the proponents of the Calhounite joint
property theory about slavery in the territories, on one side, and the
proponents of the Wilmot Proviso and of nonextension, on the other,
depended upon each other, and used each other to scare their own
adherents into line. Douglas anticipated the theory advanced by Holt
and others that the breakdown of the second party system, and the
consequent replacement of pragmatic partisanship by ideological conflict, heightened the sectional divisions that had caused the party system
to break down in the first place.

The Whigs and the Democrats were both intersectional parties, and
the minority factions of each party that were outside of their heart-
lands, the southern Whigs and the northern Democrats, were traditionally exponents of sectional compromise, because neither minority
faction could remain viable if sectional tensions rose too high. Competition between two intersectional parties, when the parties are stronger
in opposing regions, requires party leaders to offer positions that have
some hope of attracting support in their weaker section, on penalty of
defeat by the party better able to appeal across the lines. If I appeal only
to the section where my party is strongest, I may weaken the faction of
my party in the other section, which, if the opposing party has kept its
own regional factions within the fold, might give them the margin of
victory. The point of this constraint is not only that it supports compromise by forcing an appeal to the median voter but also that it requires party leaders to persuasively engage their ideological opponents,
rather than merely preach to their own choirs. In his speech of March
3, 1854, Douglas had complained that only supporters of popular sovereignty bothered to engage differing sectional interests, unlike both the
supporters of nonextension and the supporters of the Calhoun-Davis
position:

> We are willing to stand upon this great principle of self-government
> everywhere; and it is to us a proud reflection that, in this whole dis-
> cussion, no friend of the bill has urged an argument in its favor
> which could not be used with the same propriety in a free State in a

slave State and vice versa. But no enemy of the bill has used an argument which would bear repetition one mile across Mason and Dixon's line.[107]

When Douglas repeated this argument during the Galesburg debate, he used it as a test of the legitimacy of a policy. It is easy to get a wrong idea of the meaning of his argument: his claim is not that a position has to be endorsed by southerners in order to be valid, but that if a position demands, as a precondition of bargaining, something the other side feels it cannot imaginably give without making a fatal sacrifice, then it cannot be treated as a starting point for negotiation, even if that position is morally correct. Douglas's argument was that the foundation of political legitimacy is consent across ideological lines, not fidelity to transcendental principles, and that a party that does not seek to win some measure of agreement from its opponents according to its opponents' own lights is, even if it is morally right in doing so, engaged in subjugation rather than in politics properly so-called:

But now you have a sectional organization, a party which appeals to the Northern section of the Union against the Southern, a party which appeals to Northern passion, Northern pride, Northern ambition, and Northern prejudices, against Southern people, the Southern States, and Southern institutions. The leaders of that party hope that they will be able to unite the Northern States in one great sectional party, and inasmuch as the North is the strongest section, that they will thus be enabled to out vote, conquer, govern, and control the South. Hence you find that they now make speeches advocating principles and measures which cannot be defended in any slaveholding State of this Union. Is there a Republican residing in Galesburg who can travel into Kentucky and carry his principles with him across the Ohio? [No.] What Republican from Massachusetts can visit the Old Dominion without leaving his principles behind him when he crosses Mason and Dixon's line? Permit me to say to you in perfect good humor, but in all sincerity, that no political creed is sound which cannot be proclaimed fearlessly in every State of this Union where the Federal Constitution is the supreme law of the land. ["That's so," and cheers.] (1:693)

Lincoln's reply at Galesburg, as I have said, misconstrued the meaning of Douglas's argument; it did, however, have a fair point to make, although it was not the point Lincoln believed he made:

> The Judge has also detained us awhile in regard to the distinction between his party and our party. His he assumes to be a national party—ours a sectional one. He does this in asking the question whether this country has any interest in the maintenance of the Republican party? He assumes that our party is altogether sectional—that the party to which he adheres is national; and the argument is, that no party can be a rightful party—can be based upon rightful principles—unless it can announce its principles every where. I presume that Judge Douglas could not go into Russia and announce the doctrine of our national Democracy; he could not denounce the doctrine of kings and emperors and monarchies in Russia; and it may be true of this country, that in some places we may not be able to proclaim a doctrine as clearly true as the truth of Democracy, because there is a section so directly opposed to it that they will not tolerate us in doing so. Is it the true test of the soundness of a doctrine, that in some places people won't let you proclaim it? Is that the way to test the truth of any doctrine? Why, I understood that at one time the people of Chicago would not let Judge Douglas preach a certain favorite doctrine of his. I commend to his consideration the question, whether he takes that as a test of the unsoundness of what he wanted to preach. (1:704–705)

Douglas had not, precisely, argued that the ability to be proclaimed in all regions is a test of the truth of a doctrine, if by truth one means the doctrine's validity as a consequence of argument from first principles. Douglas's concern here was mainly a practical concern—he was worried about what will happen to America—not a philosophical one. Although Douglas's concerns here were for the most part practical ones, his arguments did raise a philosophical issue. The fact that a doctrine follows from first principles confers on it logical validity, but not political legitimacy, since the latter requires that all the stakeholders, including those who would lose out under it, be at least willing to tolerate, if not to endorse, the policies that follow from that doctrine.

Minorities sometimes have to submit to doctrines they strongly object to, because the price of entering into a persuasive culture is opening one's self up to persuasion, and the price of entering into a political contest is accepting that one may lose it. But there is always a penalty for demanding that submission, a penalty that is at once practical (the Republic may break up) and philosophical (the Republic has a weakened legitimacy, since no republic can long keep its authority if it gets in the habit of making a particular minority submit repeatedly). A sectional policy may still be a legitimate one, but it has a shaky grasp upon political legitimacy, to the extent that legitimacy depends upon the agreement of those who lose by a policy to accept that loss. The policy of nonextension manifestly did not enjoy such an agreement, and Douglas knew that pressing that policy would result, rightly or wrongly, in secession. (Unfortunately for Douglas, after 1857 the same thing was also true of popular sovereignty.)

Douglas was not a follower of Calhoun's "concurrent majorities" doctrine, which would give a veto to every minority over any issues it felt strongly about. Majority rule was the subject of a lifelong commitment on Douglas's part as a Democrat, and he did not, as Lincoln sometimes did (as for instance in the Lyceum Address) ever feel much temptation to think of majority rule as a form of mob rule. Douglas knew that there are circumstances under which a minority will have to submit to doctrines against which it has strenuous objections— Douglas will argue after the 1860 election season that merely losing an election to people who favor nonextension is no grounds for secession. And of course Douglas knew that the slaveholders in Kansas, however strongly they may have felt about the issue, just plain had no choice but to submit to the abolition of slavery there, however fatal a sacrifice it may have required of them. But Douglas also knew that this kind of submission comes at both a practical and a philosophical price. Minorities sometimes have to submit over issues that seem to require of them a fatal sacrifice, but that submission has to be paid for either by generous concessions in other areas or by facing the consequences that naturally follow once one has forced an opponent to the wall. Imposing a policy that runs against the strongly held (if irrational, even immoral) views of one region, or of a regionally dispersed but distinct minority ("discrete and insular minorities"), will weaken the political legitimacy, even if it strengthens the moral correctness, of the government that does the imposing, since political legitimacy, unlike moral correctness, depends upon principle and consent being in harmony

with each other. Majority rule, even over a deeply contested issue, is
not of itself majority tyranny. But majority rule over a hundred deeply
contested issues with the same minority would seem to be a different
matter. Majority rule in itself is legitimate, but a ruling majority weakens its legitimacy if it presses majority rule too often and too hard.
This is the main point of Douglas's objection to sectional parties.

There is another, and deeper, issue at stake in the charge that the
Republicans are a sectional party. When Douglas claimed that the Republicans were a sectional party, he did not mean that it had no chance
of winning any election in the southern states. He meant that there
were many states in which the Republicans would not receive a single
popular vote. Part of this had to do with the intensity of political opposition to Republican doctrines. But part of this had also to do with
the intense repressiveness of antebellum southern politics, where dissenting views about slavery were not only formally silenced by law but
also silenced by physical violence.[108] This attempt to outlaw criticism of
slavery was abetted, it must be said, by Douglas himself, who not only
continually insisted that critics of slavery treasonably endangered the
Union by expressing their criticism but also, after the Harper's Ferry
raid, argued that important critics of slavery should be made to bear
legal responsibility—Douglas specifically threatened both Lincoln and
Seward with this—for John Brown's acts.[109] Douglas's complicity in the
repression of anti-slavery thought in the South is second only to his
racism among the ugly features of his politics. That an argument has
been successfully repressed, whether by the czar's secret police or by
the southern mobs, is, Lincoln is right to argue, no test of whether the
argument is correct.

Lincoln's reply to the sectional parties question raises a number of
difficult problems. What does it mean for the truth of a doctrine as true
as democracy itself that there are regions where that doctrine cannot be
proclaimed? What does it mean if the region where that doctrine cannot be proclaimed is a region under putatively democratic rule, and
shares a regime with regions where the legitimacy of that doctrine not
only is accepted, but is felt to be foundational?

Within liberal regimes—what Lincoln and Douglas mean by "democracy" is roughly what Rawls means by liberalism—a liberal political culture must make room for many (but not all) nonliberal visions
of life. Purely political liberalism seeks to provide fair terms of coop-

eration among people with many different ideas about how life is to be led, among people with many comprehensive doctrines, to use Rawls's term for a vision of life. It does not seek to impose liberalism in every sphere of life (religion, the economy, sexual mores, and so on); it rejects imposing comprehensive liberalism, this is to say, choosing instead to embrace reasonable pluralism about comprehensive doctrines. A liberal political regime is compatible with many nonliberal visions of the good life, so long as they each, for reasons of their own, can arrive at an overlapping consensus about how best to share a common public world. Indeed, the ability to accommodate reasonable pluralism about visions of the good life, about comprehensive doctrines, is a measure of a liberal regime's liberalism.

A liberal political regime cannot tolerate all comprehensive doctrines. That there are comprehensive doctrines liberal regimes cannot tolerate is not proof that liberal regimes are not tolerant; on the contrary, that limitation is the logical precondition of any tolerant regime. A culture of slaveholding, for instance, cannot claim to be within the reasonable pluralism of comprehensive doctrines a liberal regime must tolerate, both because slaveholding compromises the reciprocity among people which is an essential value of any liberal culture and because slaveholders, in order to defend slavery, must continually find ways to subvert democratic rule. Liberal regimes might have to make lesser-of-two-evils bargains about slavery under some circumstances where they have no other choices. But commitment to reasonable pluralism about comprehensive doctrines does not itself commit one to moral neutrality about slavery.

As a liberal political regime must find space within itself for adherents of many, but not all, nonliberal comprehensive doctrines, so a liberal regime must seek also fair terms of cooperation with many, but not all, kinds of nonliberal regime, the more so since the commitment to seeking fair terms of cooperation is an expression of fundamental liberal values. Liberal regimes can live with many kinds of nonliberal regime, and need not colonize or overthrow them.

Nonliberal regimes come in many flavors, and there are many nonliberal regimes—Rawls calls them "decent hierarchical societies"—with which liberal regimes can work out a fair scheme of cooperation.[110] Within a liberal political order, comprehensive liberalism must, if it wishes to make good on its foundational desire to take part in a

universal scheme of cooperation and tolerance, learn how, without surrender of its key values, to tolerate and to cooperate with many nonliberal comprehensive doctrines with which comprehensive liberalism is
in profound value conflict. Likewise, within a liberal world order, political liberalism must, if it wishes to make good on its foundational desire
take part in a universal scheme of cooperation and tolerance, learn
how, without surrender of its key values, to tolerate and to cooperate
with many decent nonliberal regimes with which political liberalism is
in profound value conflict.

Nevertheless, there are many societies—Rawls calls them outlaw
societies—with which liberal regimes cannot and should not cooperate,
just as there are many comprehensive doctrines (chiefly those that must
repress others in order to prosper) that cannot have a place within a
liberal regime. That outlaw regimes must be excluded casts no discredit
on liberalism's ambition of elaborating, through a law of peoples, a universal scheme of cooperation and tolerance; indeed, the exclusion of
outlaw regimes is not a limitation on the universality of such a scheme
of cooperation but a consequence of that universality.

The line between regimes with which a liberal regime *must* work out
a habit of life and regimes with which it *cannot* work out such a habit
cannot be neatly drawn. But this unhappy fact does not discredit the
foundational desire of liberalism to create such a habit of life, although
it complicates the realization of that desire. The fact that decent hierarchical societies shade into indecent societies is no more an argument
that the two are not different than the existence of twilight is an argument against the difference between night and day. Liberal societies
themselves, after all, shade without clear demarcation into decent hierarchical ones. Perhaps the distinction that matters is not one between
liberal societies and decent hierarchical societies but between decent
hierarchical societies that aspire to liberalism and decent hierarchical
societies that do not.

It is useful to describe, as Rawls tries to do, what a just world order
would look like. But it is also useful, given the constraints of the world
into which we are thrown, to describe the least unjust among the variously unjust worlds we are actually in a position to choose among.
Sometimes the lines between a decent hierarchical society and an outlaw society, the line between a society with which one must cooperate
and a society one must confront, cannot be made the basis of policy

because of the tragic complexities of the world itself. Even the line between unambiguously evil regimes one must confront with force and unambiguously evil regimes one must confront in some other way is often unclear: if it was better to defeat Nazism by armed conflict, it was also better, even if it came at a terrible moral price, to contain and wait out Stalinism. Would I make this distinction if I did not know already that Stalinism ultimately would fail? Perhaps I would, if I had reason to believe that the price of an early confrontation would be the triumph of Stalinism. And the difference in the two cases, between a policy of quasi-cooperative containment with one regime and a policy of confrontation with another, is the consequence of a mere happen-so about the balance of power, not the consequence of the moral difference between the two evil regimes. To understand this is to understand that it was concrete, situated, intuitive practice, not philosophy, that had to decide such cases. It is to understand as well that there were no clean-hands alternatives, and that even the best available course involved moral compromises, whether in the morally twilit wars the West won in Greece and lost in Vietnam, or in the West's morally twilit refusals of war in Czechoslovakia and Hungary. In politics we are always Hawthorne's children, not Emerson's.

The issue between Lincoln and Douglas was not the issue of what the nature is of a just society. It was not the issue of whether a just society can tolerate slavery or must not tolerate slavery. It was not the issue of whether a fair society must, or must not, legislate morals. It was the issue of how a partly just, and partly unjust, society might confront its injustice without destroying itself. It was the issue of whether justice was served better, given the circumstances, by confrontation, or by accommodation; or rather, since both Lincoln and Douglas saw themselves as offering strategies that combined confrontation and accommodation, whether justice was better served by a strategy that gave a privileged position to principle or by a strategy that gave a privileged position to consent, given that no political order can long survive a disjunction of principle and consent. Neither Lincoln's position nor Douglas's sought immediate confrontation with the South over slavery. Douglas correctly saw that Lincoln's position would reduce to confrontation in short order, since he knew, as Lincoln did not, what the convictions of the slaveholders actually were. But Douglas's position too, under conditions that would become abundantly clear by the end of that very summer, also would reduce to a position of confrontation, although it would provide, relative to Lincoln's, a confrontation that was both tardy and on less promising ground.

The difference between immediate confrontation and something short of confrontation is ultimately subject to an educated guess, to a wager, about what the outcome of a contest of force would be; Chamberlain and Daladier made calculations, although mistaken ones, that were not different in kind from those that Truman and Attlee also had to make. There is a scandal in this, but an unavoidable one: it is a wager, an educated wager, but still a wager, which decides not only the prudential question of whether one might win or lose a contest of force but also the moral question of whether it is better to fight or to deal. The ultimate difference between Lincoln and Douglas is not that the one reasoned with moral clarity and the other did not, not that one had a firm sense of the evil of slavery and the other did not, but that one had a better sense of how to make a moral wager than the other did. Lincoln's heroism was his ability to act with self-possession in the face of something incalculable. In pursuing a policy that was ultimately a policy of confrontation, Lincoln made a leap of faith. And in making that leap, both in what he risked and in what he gained, America's Abraham somewhat resembled Kierkegaard's.

When Lincoln compared the South to czarist Russia he did not merely mean that his party would have a hard time building a winning case in either region. He meant that the South had become a region in which it could no longer be taken for granted that the cultural preconditions for liberal government had been satisfied. The implication of this view—that the South was as hostile to truths that are as true as the truth of democracy as Russia was—was, to Douglas, an ominous one, and he was not slow to bring it out: Lincoln meant that the slaveholding states cannot any longer be safely included in the persuasive culture of American democracy, because the repressiveness of their society, driven by the repressiveness of slavery itself, has unfitted them for taking part in the ethos of fair-minded deliberation and dealmaking upon which self-government depends.

In Douglas's view, when Lincoln argues that it may be that in some places we may not be able to proclaim a doctrine as clearly true as the truth of Democracy, because there is a section so directly opposed to it that they will not tolerate us in doing so, he argues also that that section cannot be fully a part of a democratic polity, because conceding the truth of things as true as the truth of democracy is the price of admission to that polity. Lincoln's logic of sectional politics, as Douglas sees it, is this: if one finds one's self bound in a political order with such a region, one cannot trust that region with a say in common affairs, because that region has corrupted the sources of its own freedom; it must be kept in a state of tutelage, for the common safety. But if one does that, then one has also corrupted the sources of one's own freedom, since freedom cannot survive keeping a region in a state of tutelage, since tutelage is different from subjection only in being high-minded.

The phrase "the truth of democracy" is aligned in meaning with the claim in the Declaration of Independence that certain political values arise from self-evident truths. Hannah Arendt pointed out that the sentence is a proclamation, not an observation. Something that is truly self-evident, in the sense of being immediately obvious to everyone, would not require that anyone announce that they hold it so. Holding a truth to be self-evident is a performative, not a constative, linguistic act. That all men are created equal is not a self-evident truth in the way that a tautology is a self-evident truth. It is also not precisely the same thing as declaring that something is a postulate upon which all of his other reasoning will hang. For every system might have its own postulates, but the claim of the Declaration is that what it sees as self-evident is not only true for Jefferson but *ought* to be true for everybody.

Proclaiming the self-evident truths of the Declaration is a way to claim a particular kind of identity, a way to enter a political world in which certain kinds of acts become intelligible and other kinds of political acts become necessary and inevitable. But such an act also transcends the boundaries of particular identities, because what it promises is not merely entry into the political traditions of a particular nation (as, say, proclaiming the Rights of Englishmen does) but entry into a particular vision of the human species. Entering the horizon of that political identity involves not merely membership in a group or a culture, but entering into a vision of the nature and destiny of humanity. From within the horizon of that vision of humanity denying that all men are created equal is as peculiar a thing to do as denying that what I see in front of me right now is my hand.

Now for Lincoln, "As I would not be a slave, so I would not be a master" is a proposition with the same kind of self-evidence Jefferson saw in "All men are created equal." I cannot have agency unless I acknowledge it in others; if I fail to acknowledge it in others, I lose it for myself. If I seek mastery, I become enslaved by it, and debased by it, and spend my life chasing illusions. I give myself to futility. The positive-good slaveholder, like someone who denies the self-evident propositions of the Declaration (as Calhoun in fact did, in his famous 1848 speech during the debate on the admission of Oregon), must ultimately be seen not as a citizen but as a menace.

Because the slaveholding states were becoming regions in which foundational truths, as true as the truth of democracy, could not be taken for granted, they were taking on in Lincoln's view the features of an outlaw regime, a regime that cannot be managed by the normal political machinery of persuasion and negotiation, because with an outlaw regime we can no longer tell what kind of thing would be a commanding appeal to a common value; we can only work out an equilibrium of force. But the slaveholding states were a very peculiar form of outlaw regime, because they were outlaw regimes with many democratic institutions, and, what is more, they were outlaw regimes with which his own regime was so inextricably and fatally bound together in a tangle of mutual dependency and complicity that confrontation with them, even if unavoidable, came with awful risks.

Nonideological and Ideological Parties

At Galesburg Lincoln had a second reply to Douglas's "sectionalism" claim. Douglas had argued that the fact that Lincoln could not proclaim his doctrines in the South was proof that his party was a sectional one (and, furthermore, was proof that those doctrines were not capable of being realized in policy without subverting democracy). Putting the shoe on the other foot, Lincoln jeeringly remarked that Douglas himself could not proclaim some of his own favorite doctrines even in Chicago, never mind in the South, alluding to the occasion in 1854 when Douglas, attempting to defend the Kansas-Nebraska Act to a hostile Chicago audience but unable to get a word in in the hubbub, finally lost his temper, told the audience to go to hell, jammed his hat onto his head, and stalked offstage. Lincoln meant by this only to scout the idea that a political doctrine has to be acceptable everywhere in order to be true, but he also raised a question about the nature of parties and about the nature of party conflict.

The opposition Douglas faced at Chicago was not precisely sectional, although it is true that intensity of opposition to the Kansas-Nebraska Act in Illinois was a function of latitude. The point is that Douglas's position, like all positions, will confront opponents who cannot be reconciled to it. Is a geographically dispersed irreconcilable opposition materially different from a geographically concentrated one? Suppose Douglas had taken a position that Catholics not only opposed, but found to be so threatening that they could not tolerate public advocacy of that position? Suppose he had taken a position that Republicans found so threatening that they could not tolerate public advocacy of that position?[111] Are occasions where a group has no choice but to submit to a doctrine it passionately opposes occasions where democracy gives way to subjection?

I am not thinking here about mere durable opposition to a policy or a durable conflict of factions, but about the claim that two positions are so unalterably opposed to each other that their adherents cannot share power or recognize that the other has the slightest legitimacy. Factions that never expect to see eye to eye can nevertheless share a political culture so long as they can be persuaded to take a "win some, lose some" attitude about their contests with each other. Under most circumstances, a losing faction will concede the legitimacy of a winning faction's victory because that victory only enables the winners to write ordinary law, rather than to so write their views into the higher law as to drive their opposition out of the public square. One of the reasons a losing faction can afford to lose is the prevalence of a political culture in which one side will not do to the other something the other side will be sure to remember when circumstances change and it becomes able to return the favor.

The political culture of the antebellum era had been corrupted by the attempts of defenders of slavery to constitutionalize every issue. From the censorship of the mails and the suppression of the right of petition to the aftermath of the Harper's Ferry raid, defenders of slavery treated their political opponents as not only wrong, but beyond the pale, as advancing positions that were so far outside the boundaries of reasonable disagreement that even to mention them was a violation of the constitutional order. Constitutionalizing each question is not merely a way to raise the stakes, to enlist a truly trumping authority on one's own side. It was, and is, at bottom, an attempt to silence one's opponents completely.

Consent is the gold standard of legitimacy, but since every political contest involves winning and losing, political legitimacy must also involve persuading the losers in political contests to consent to their defeat. This is easiest to do if the losing side knows that it will not be required to make a fatal sacrifice of interest or value, and where even in defeat they are in a position to seek some kind of accommodation to their views from their opponents, who, in granting that kind of accommodation, both gain legitimacy for their own victory and legitimate their opposition. But this is not always possible; there are opposing groups that cannot reconcile, and defeats that are for keeps. Now it is always open to the group that is subject to this kind of defeat to complain that it has been subjected to majority tyranny. And it is always open to the victorious faction to complain that to require it not to pursue its own perhaps passionately held agenda amounts not only to a minority veto but also to minority rule, minority tyranny. The political culture of the antebellum United States did, however, provide ways around both complaints.

The practical culture of politics envisioned by Madison in the tenth *Federalist* provides ways of mediating what appear from close up to be intractable conflicts. The first way, the way embraced by Lincoln in the Peoria speech and never quite abandoned by him even in the "House Divided" speech, was to accommodate the defeated party by stretching its defeat over the long run, so that in the short and medium terms it may take measures to make its defeat less catastrophic, since a continuous, incremental change is less traumatic than a sudden one, and the losing party might accept incrementally what it could not afford to accept were it to take place immediately. The losing faction still has to surrender, but it gets a say in the terms of its surrender, and it gets to salvage at least some of what was at stake for it in the conflict.

A second strategy, which also takes its origin in the vision of politics of the tenth *Federalist*, and which is more characteristic of Douglas than of Lincoln, seeks to mediate disagreement by using the fact that partisans who are divided over one issue are also invested in a host of other issues. Madison had imagined that political agents are enmeshed in a disorderly tangle of interests and allegiances, so that those who oppose each other on one issue have convergent interests on some other, and those who are on the same side on some issue will have to oppose them on other issues. The *Federalist* 10 vision of political life does not seek to secure political justice by enumerating rights (which Madison thought at the time would provide merely a parchment guarantee for those rights anyway), nor does it limit the temptation to majority tyranny by granting specific political minorities power.[112] The *Federalist* 10 vision of political life designs deliberative institutions in such a way as to make the pragmatic interests of the agents in dealmaking converge upon the requirements of a just political order. It is capable of doing this only if certain political conditions prevail, and those preconditions were becoming less and less available as the political crisis of the 1850s deepened.[113]

In *Federalist* 10 politics there are always a wide variety of available positions and contending interest groups. The model here is of course religious toleration: where there are a multitude of sects, no one of which can anticipate having secure domination of the political order, each sect will insist upon religious toleration. Madison himself had made the analogy in his arguments in the Virginia ratifying convention in 1788, where he seems to have followed Voltaire's remarks in the *Lettre Philosophiques* about how England came to enjoy religious freedom.

Political agents in *Federalist* 10 politics have a multitude of interests, and conflicts over one interest do not align with conflicts over other interests. Political logrolling—you can have your treaty, so long as I also get my dam—looks to some people like corruption, but it is one of the ways in which defeated factions can reconcile themselves to their defeat. Or rather, it is a way in which enough of the adherents of a defeated faction can be peeled away from it in order to give legitimacy to the winning faction, since logrolling is a strategy designed to weaken the coherence of factions. Douglas continuously sought to use issues of westward expansion and railroad development—his main issues in any event—to blunt sectional conflict. He was unable to do so, because his means kept enflaming the very conflicts they were designed to put to rest. The logrolling strategy can be successful only so long as some great issue does not reconfigure all of the other issues to transform them into theaters of proxy war. In the 1850s almost every issue, no matter how minor, turned into a quarrel over slavery, so the kinds of politics that normally bridge divisions wound up inscribing them more deeply.

Political interests and values in *Federalist* 10 politics do not have strong internal coherence. A *Federalist* 10 political order can function only so long as it is possible to detach one issue from another. It must be possible for A and B to agree about x but disagree about y. And it must be possible for A and C to disagree about x but agree about y. If, while I am in conflict with you over one issue, I anticipate that I may need your help on some other issue, I would be unwise to trample you completely on the first issue even if I had the power to do so. There is a further assumption here, and that is the assumption that conflicts over value issues have the same heterogeneity that conflicts over interest issues do. This is possible only under the standing assumption—advanced controversially in philosophical circles by Isaiah Berlin but taken for granted I think by working politicians—that we have no reason to believe that our key values sort with each other. We have no reason to assume that our values make a set without internal contradictions. We have every reason to assume that we will always find our values to be in conflict with other values, sometimes with tragic results, and that we will, even in our own minds, never mind in the public square, always be making unstable and temporary trade-offs among them, trade-offs that, in turn, it is futile to see as rigorously principled, since if such rigor were available we would never have had to make the trade-offs to begin with.

The external divisions between factions are not different in kind from the internal divisions within factions. One way to say the same thing is to say that *Federalist* 10 politics are not ideological politics.

I use this term "ideological politics" in two senses. In the weak sense of the word (the sense that is principally at stake, I think, between Lincoln and Douglas) "ideological politics" merely refers to a politics in which parties have a disciplined and consistent policy program in which the elements are all of a piece and to which all of a party's adherents are expected to sign onto.

In the stronger sense the term refers to an often not fully conscious mind-set that organizes the concerns and draws the horizon of intelligibility for those within its ambit. The second kind of conflict requires that a quarrel across a boundary internal to a paradigm be different in kind from a quarrel between paradigms. The assumption of *Federalist* 10 politics is that there are no distinctions between these kinds of quarrels, since its standing assumption is that "our conflict is irrepressible" really only means something like "I feel very strongly over this issue." The assumption of *Federalist* 10 politics is that even under circumstances in which parties claim to be locked in an ideological conflict in the strong sense of that term, each ideological group presumably is not like-minded on every issue, and across these internal divisions one assumes something like persuasive engagement does take place, else all disagreement whatsoever, no matter how trivial, would be an ideological conflict between mutually unintelligible worldviews. The burden of proof would seem to be upon those who describe deep conflicts as ideological in this way to show that in a particular conflict the line between opponents is the external border of conflicting but incommensurable and mutually unintelligible ideologies rather than an internal boundary within a group that holds very great values in common.

In the heat of battle, Lincoln and Seward spoke of the issues as issues of ideological conflict. In Seward's case, his use of this kind of language was almost always the result of hotheaded exaggeration, since his actual political habits were always more conciliatory than the inflammatory language of his speeches would lead one to believe. In Lincoln's case, he usually argued that the free states and the slave states were deeply connected by a common history, by a common moral problem, with its inextricable complicities on both sides, and by a partly tragic destiny never fully understood by either. The sentimental language about the "mystic chords of memory" in his First Inaugural, and the forbearing language about mutual complicity in his Second, suggest that the common traditions, common fate, and common guilt of the North and the South are deeper than any ideological conflict between them. Why else would the Union itself have been an object of value to Lincoln if the North and the South really were dominated by incommensurable habits of thought? But in the "House Divided" speech, and in the 1858 debates, and above all in his reflections in the Ohio debates in 1859 about the effects of Douglas's habits of thought upon the "public mind," Lincoln flirted with the concept of ideological conflict.

Political conflicts in *Federalist* 10 politics are not conflicts about identity. If we see people's views, or their values, as inevitable expressions of their identities, persuasive engagement becomes impossible, because it reduces political arguments to something like "I just don't like your kind!" Such a conflict risks descending into the most intractable and most vicious kind of confrontation, a "war of peoples," in which groups who just plain do not like each other's faces seek to settle scores with each other, as if kinds of people, like deliberative bodies or like individuals, actually had a kind of agency. Persuasion, which is the foundation of truly political life, is possible only if interlocutors can see a change of convictions as possibly expressing a deeper stratum of their identity than maintaining those convictions would express, or as bringing out of the depths of implicitness a development that does better justice to their (always entangled and always partial) sense of themselves than the position they already hold could do.

Political investments in *Federalist* 10 politics are always partial and tentative. Because they emerge as the upshot of a tangle of commitments and interests, each investment must be seen against the background of the other investments they enable or foreclose. Shallow investments may be traded off against other, deeper investments. Only the deepest investments cannot be traded off, but they may require the sacrifice of many other investments in their support, and they place some strain on the network of relationships political engagements establish. The deepest convictions may lead one to break the persuasive network of relationships with other agents, but the price of this is the replacement of negotiation by force.

Political coalitions are always unstable, and that instability supports a stable ethos of dealmaking. Opposing someone today does not preclude allying with him tomorrow, and all parties know that under the right circumstances their allies might just jump ship. The result of this, however, is not a Hobbesian war of all against all but a worldly attempt to invent an order in which the complex dance of agreement and disagreement, cooperation and striving, may go on, because it is safe to disagree and not fatal to lose any particular exchange, because each side must treat its opponents fairly in order to have hope of resorting to them when they need them as friends.

There are important ways in which the political order of the second party system was not a *Federalist* 10 political order. For one thing, Madison did not anticipate the development of stable political parties, although he himself would found a political party within five years of writing the *Federalist*. The idea that an opposition party was a normal feature of political life was not entertained during the period of the first party system; each party viewed the other party as a conspiracy of usurpers aiming to overthrow the legitimate government, whether in the interest of Jacobinical Caesarism or in the interest of Monarchism.[114] As late as the presidency of James Monroe it was assumed that parties were a disease, not a feature, of politics.

In the 1820s under the influence of Martin Van Buren, the Democratic Party became the miscellaneous grab-bag of factions it is today. (Will Rogers once famously remarked: "I don't belong to any organized party. I'm a Democrat.") The party system that Van Buren fostered, and that he defends in his autobiography, had the heterogeneity that Madison had sought to give the legislature in *Federalist* 10, and it was stabilized in some of the same ways. It was important for Van Buren that the major ideological divisions not align themselves with the partisan divisions, since doing that would give party leaders every reason to sharpen conflicts.[115] Heterogeneous parties lead partisan conflict in the direction of political stability by constraining conflict toward the median voter. The party that is best able to compromise among its factions is the party that will prevail.[116]

The destruction of the second party system was set in motion by men whose party allegiances were weak. President Tyler, for instance, whipped up the storm over Texas, which Clay and Van Buren alike knew would open Pandora's box, as a way to organize his reelection after his break with the Whig Party. Calhoun sought for twenty years to break the party system and realign it on a sectional basis. Chase and Sumner, as "Independent Democrats," used an inflammatory style of argument in 1854 they could not have used as Whigs. The destruction of the second party system was caused not only by the emergence of deeply fraught issues about which compromise was difficult but also by the rise of an ideological style of politics that undermined the ability of parties to mediate conflicts. It left in its wake a party that, in Douglas's eyes, had an ideological unity that threatened to turn the ways ordinary partisan politics blunts deep conflicts into another way to sharpen those conflicts.

Now even within Illinois it is an open question whether the Republicans were a truly ideological party, since the party was constructed, as we have seen, out of different fragments of the second party system, each of which had a slightly different sense of what the conflict over slavery was really about. Was it, as anti-Nebraska Democrats often argued, about making sure that the western territories were settled on a white basis, or was it, as anti-slavery Whigs often argued, about making sure that slavery itself was put on the road to final elimination? The party had to make room for cautious opponents of slavery expansion like Bates and for strong-minded opponents of slavery like Chase; it had to include nativists like Banks and liberal Germans like Schurz, and it had to make itself as credible in crypto-southern Jonesboro as in crypto-New England Freeport. Douglas's own attack on the heterogeneity of the Republican Party at different latitudes in Illinois would seem to militate against his view of them as a sectional or ideological party.

Seen from across the Ohio River, however, these factional differences in the Republican Party seemed trivial, seemed distinctions without a real difference. From within, the Republican Party was an ordinary partisan organization, not an ideological one. But the South was prepared for an ideological conflict with the Republicans, not a merely partisan one. And, because of the slave power conspiracy theory, the Republicans were prepared for an ideological conflict with the South; not, perhaps, a power struggle across a barrier of mutual incomprehension, but certainly a struggle with an opponent with whom one's conflicts spanned a host of issues, and with whom one could wage a struggle only in a zero-sum way. The late 1850s was one of the rare occasions in American history when ideological parties—the Republicans and the Breckinridge faction of the Democrats—were possible on a large scale, and it was one of the occasions where each party was doomed to ratchet up the radicalism of the other.

The anomaly of the political crisis of the 1850s was the emergence of stable ideological parties. Conflict between these kinds of parties cannot be managed in the *Federalist* 10 way. Calhoun's theory of "concurrent majorities," expounded in his *Disquisition on Government*, however, gives one insights into the workings of politics under conditions of ideological rather than partisan conflict.[117] This is not to say that Calhoun's theory describes any acceptable theory of justice. It is also not to say that either Lincoln or Douglas felt any attraction to Calhoun's political ideology or to his constitutional inventions. But it is to say that Calhoun's theory registers what happens to republican (lower-case *r*) habits of thought under certain kinds of ideological strain.

A detailed examination of Calhoun's political theory will be part of Chapter 7, since Calhoun's theory provides a telling contrast both with Lincoln's and with Douglas's key political values. But Calhoun's description of what a conflict between a small number of fixed groups is like is uncomfortably close to what the actual political situation became in the 1850s. The only method, says Calhoun, that can prevent the tyranny of the majority is the application of the doctrine of concurrent majorities, in which the legitimacy of rule inheres not in majorities, however large, but in interest communities. Under the doctrine of concurrent majorities, one cannot rule unless one secures the agreement of the majority within each interest community; one must prevail in every sector, and each sector, in effect, has a veto.

Harry Jaffa points out in *A New Birth of Freedom* (2000) that the doctrine of concurrent majorities is tenable only if one assumes that no more than a small number of deeply entrenched interests can claim rights under it. Where the competing interests are few but the lines between them are deep and durable, as in the world Calhoun describes and inhabits—the world of pre–Civil War politics, in which every issue, no matter how trivial, became a theater of proxy war over slavery—one cannot assume, as one could in Madisonian politics, that a worldly economy of horsetrading and dealmaking is not a zero-sum game.

The consequence is that where politics is organized around deeply entrenched conflicts among a small number of interest groups, what one interest has to hold over the others is chiefly its threat of undoing the social order if its desires are not taken account of, a threat one perhaps becomes increasingly tempted to make good on, if only as a way to prove that one is in earnest. In the Madisonian world, by contrast, complex negotiations along many different lines of engagement knit the society as a whole together by giving everyone a positive investment, different from the investments their immediate allies have, in maintaining comity among opponents. In the Calhounian world, each negotiation scribes deeper the division it attempts to manage. For Calhoun, the group was the unit of measure and the unit of value, and the integrity of the group is the chief thing that matters, whereas for Madison groups were heterogeneous and unstable, and the chief thing that matters is the culture of persuasion a political society maintains among the individuals, the unit of measure and of value, who make it up.

There is an obvious external connection between the doctrine of concurrent majorities and the maintenance of racial inequality, in that Calhoun dreamed up that doctrine as a way to defend slaveholding states from critique. But there is an internal connection as well, which one sees when one recognizes that not every group gets to have a veto in Calhoun's state. Put bluntly, slaveholders represent an interest with a concurrent majority veto; slaves do not. And this is not merely a result of the fact that the doctrine was in itself the product of slaveholder special pleading, but inheres in the doctrine of concurrent majorities itself. However one imagines a society, that society will be one in which some minorities have a concurrent veto and some do not.

No social group in a plural society is a natural kind; the boundary lines of each group are crossed, as Madison recognized, by the boundary lines of groups that are organized on some different basis. It is not obvious that one way to divide up the kinds of people trumps every other way to divide them up. And giving primacy to any one way to divide people up necessarily tramples those who, under another division of things, would have been a minority with a concurrent-majority veto. There is no obvious way to distinguish between the external boundaries that demarcate a group with a concurrent-majority veto from the internal boundaries that separate the majority and minority factions within such a group. If, for instance, the slave states should have had a concurrent-majority veto over federal policy on slavery, why shouldn't the Unionist counties of the slaveholding states have had a concurrent-majority veto over the secession of those states? Why assume that poor, nonslaveholding whites are an ignorable minority in a concurrent-majority society organized around the division between free and slave states, rather than a nonignorable minority with a concurrent-majority veto in a society organized around the division between rich and poor? And surely had the dividing line not fallen between slave states and free states but between slaves and masters, the outcome of concurrent majority politics would have been different. But of course the point is that concurrent-majority politics has no reason to treat the division between slave states and free states very differently from the division between slave and master. The concept of group rights would make sense only if we had a clear perception of what the best way to group people is, and that is not something we are likely to have. At the same time we cannot construct a doctrine of concurrent majorities unless we do imagine one way to group people as having trumping claims over every other way, else the argument reduces to the view that every individual has a veto over everything.

What determines whether a minority does or does not have a concurrent veto seems ultimately to be not whether that minority has interests and vulnerabilities, but only whether it has the power to pull the society down around it, Samson-like, if it fails to get its way. The slave states were all too willing to exercise such power, and because of the ruthlessness of repression, the slaves were not in a position to do so, except in the slaveholders' nightmares. But this means that concurrent-majority politics is not an alternative to force but simply a version of it, and indeed, a prelude to more dramatic forms of force, since it depends upon the distinction between those minorities who have a veto and those who do not, and since it gives each group it recognizes a good reason to hold a knife to the throat of the society as a whole.

4.8 Conclusion

Douglas's specific conspiratorial charge, that Lincoln and Trumbull, moved by personal ambition, were revolutionizing the party system by using the slavery issue to inflame sectional conflict, so that they might rise to the head of a new sectional party designed to destroy the tradition of sectional compromise and exercise unchecked power over the Union as a whole, was false. But his analysis of the way a changed attitude toward sectional compromise has led to a transformation of the partisan culture had more than a grain of truth. Douglas's use of the paranoid style, like Lincoln's scarcely more credible use of the same style, ultimately represented his way to frame for himself and his constituents political events that the habits of analysis he had internalized over the course of his political career were inadequate to render. Conspiratorial thinking here, as so often, marked the place where one set of political ideas came under pressure from political events and large-scale changes in political culture, changes that the usual methods of analyzing the behavior of political actors could make sense of.

CHAPTER 5

Douglas's Fanaticism Charge

$\mathscr{H}$OWEVER DOUGLAS MAY HAVE FELT about the abolitionists, or about Chase and Sumner, he knew very well that Lincoln was no fanatic. Douglas's private comments reveal that he had fairly and even generously taken the measure of his opponent. Writing at the opening of the 1858 campaign to John W. Forney (who was himself shortly to join the Republicans), Douglas said of Lincoln, "I shall have my hands full. He is the strong man of his party—full of wit, facts, dates,—and the best stump speaker, with his droll ways and dry jokes, in the West. He is as honest as he is shrewd, and if I beat him, my victory will be hardly won."[1] But his public remarks in the debates seem to describe a different person.

Douglas's charge, however, does not simply reduce to dishonest spin. Like his conspiracy charge, his fanaticism charge reflected something not about Lincoln but about what had been happening in the persuasive culture of the Republic at large. What Douglas feared, both from the Republicans and from the slaveholders, was that they would cause the public square to become dominated by a style of argument that sharpens political conflicts and makes them insoluble by means short of violence. Now Lincoln was not committed to sharpening conflict to the point of violence, and few Republicans, even the most radical, were either. But whatever Lincoln's convictions and commitments, an argumentative style has a momentum of its own, and it can outrun the intentions of those who use it, particularly when it is used against opponents like the slaveholders, who could be counted upon to escalate the conflict in a more than tit-for-tat way.

The persuasiveness of an argument to one's self and allies is all too often a function of the argument's ability to inflame ugly feelings and to enforce factional loyalty. And it is not only arguments in bad causes that have this power. Douglas understood that the ability to maintain a persuasive culture in the face of a deep conflict depended upon the willingness of each side to be talked down from rhetorical high horses. This is why Douglas continually sought to recast the struggle over slavery as a straightforward quarrel over interests, or over moral positions that could be pragmatically compromised in the way interests are, because such quarrels are susceptible to political dealmaking in ways that stark confrontations between absolutes are not. Neither side in the struggle over slavery was willing to recast the quarrel in such a way as to enable dealmaking, because each side assumed, and had reasons to assume, that it could not make concessions without surrendering everything. And, what is more, Douglas's own management of his case was so intemperate, so inflammatory, and so personal that whatever case one could make for his position, he himself was the last person who could plausibly carry the day for that case.

5.1 Hostility to New England

Douglas's jeering description of what Lincoln and Trumbull were supposed to be up to when they confected the Illinois Republican Party compared the party-switching of the former Whigs and Democrats to an involuntary or at least unwitting religious conversion: "Lincoln was to bring into the Abolition camp the old line Whigs, and transfer them over to Giddings, Chase, Ford, Douglass, and Parson Lovejoy, who were ready to receive them and christen them in their new faith" (1:497).

Douglas's figure here seems to derive from southwestern humor, in which evangelists were frequently portrayed as con men, as figures not far removed from horse traders and professional gamblers.[2] But his slighting reference to "Parson" Lovejoy, who will christen his not entirely converted charges into the abolition faith, may have served another agenda. Lovejoy was in fact ordained as a Congregational minister, serving a congregation in Princeton, Illinois, after the murder of his brother Elijah by pro-slavery rioters in 1837. Douglas may well have been playing with anti–New England prejudice in describing the Maine-born Lovejoy this way. He played the same card when he described the Connecticut-born Lyman Trumbull's successful outflanking of Lincoln for the 1855 Republican senatorial nomination as a "Yankee trick" or described Trumbull as leaving Georgia for Illinois once he had "disposed of all his clocks" like the proverbially sharp-dealing Connecticut trader, selling wooden clocks (and wooden nutmegs) to gullible southerners.

Douglas portrayed the champions of abolition as religion-crazed, well-to-do Yankee enthusiasts, incapable of distinguishing between obsessions and convictions, people who, because they are commanded to their positions by God, as they think, are incapable of dealmaking about it (and capable of just about anything else). These Yankees combine in politics the habit of fanaticism with the unscrupulousness of sharp dealers and traveling salesmen, piously seasoning their unscrupulous practices with an inner conviction that they enjoy God's special favor. Douglas treats them as second cousins to the many generations of their fictional co-religionists, from Malvolio to Mr. Bulstrode. It was to emphasize this association that Douglas referred so often to the "abolition church" and treated the Free Soilers as "baptizing" their Whig and Democratic converts into their new faith. Notice that Douglas fused here the insinuation of religious hysteria with contempt for a strong view of the promises of the opening sentences of the Declaration of Independence:

> Mr. Lincoln, following the example and lead of all the little Abolition orators, who go around and lecture in the basements of schools and churches, reads from the Declaration of Independence, that all men were created equal, and then asks how can you deprive a negro of that equality which God and the Declaration of Independence awards to him. He and they maintain that negro equality is guarantied by the laws of God, and that it is asserted in the Declaration of Independence. If they think so, of course they have a right to say so, and so vote. I do not question Mr. Lincoln's conscientious belief that the negro was made his equal, and hence is his brother, [laughter,] but for my own part, I do not regard the negro as my equal, and positively deny that he is my brother or any kin to me whatever. ["Never." "Hit

him again," and cheers.] Lincoln has evidently learned by heart Parson Lovejoy's catechism. [Laughter and applause.] He can repeat it as well as Farnsworth, and he is worthy of a medal from father Giddings and Fred Douglass for his Abolitionism. [Laughter.] He holds that the negro was born his equal and yours, and that he was endowed with equality by the Almighty, and that no human law can deprive him of these rights which were guarantied to him by the Supreme ruler of the Universe. (1:504–505)

In the Jonesboro debate, Douglas seized on the biblical provenance of the "House Divided" metaphor to treat the main argument of the "House Divided" speech as a work of moral hysteria:

Is this sectional warfare to be waged between Northern States and Southern States until they all shall become uniform in their local and domestic institutions merely because Mr. Lincoln says that a house divided against itself cannot stand, and pretends that this scriptural quotation, this language of our Lord and Master, is applicable to the American Union and the American Constitution? Washington and his compeers, in the convention that framed the Constitution, made this government divided into free and slave States. It was composed then of thirteen sovereign and independent States, each having sovereign authority over its local and domestic institutions, and all bound together by the Federal Constitution. Mr. Lincoln likens that bond of the Federal Constitution, joining free and slave States together, to a house divided against itself, and says that it is contrary to the law of God and cannot stand. When did he learn, and by what authority does he proclaim, that this government is contrary to the law of God and cannot stand? (1:596–597)

Douglas here saw the "House Divided" speech as an attack upon the constitutional order itself: the states are different from each other, a house divided (saith the Lord) cannot stand, hence (by divine command) a uniform policy about slavery should be imposed upon them. This is, of course, an implausible attack. After all, Lincoln conceded that the federal government did not have the power to abolish slavery in the slave states without a constitutional amendment the slave states would long be in a position to resist.

If it is implausible to see the "House Divided" speech as an attack upon the constitutional order, it is, however, not implausible to see the "House Divided" speech, as Douglas saw it, as an attack upon the sectional compromises that, in practice, were fundamental to the making and ratification of the Constitution, and that also were the basis of policy in both parties until the 1850s. Lincoln did not understand his position to be a break either with the sectional compromises underlying the Constitution or with the sectional compromises that had shaped policy in later years. But Lincoln's understanding of both sets of compromises, although widely shared then and now, was an idealized one.

Douglas's characterization of the "House Divided" speech was meant to be heard against the background of Garrison's attack upon the Constitution as a covenant with death and an agreement with hell. (Indeed, one of the reasons Douglas wished to hint that Lincoln's convictions have a New England provenance was to tie Lincoln to Garrison.) There is a crucial difference, of course, between Lincoln's view of what compromise with slaveholders meant and Garrison's view. Lincoln after all insisted, from the Peoria speech through the First Inaugural, that he did not reject the tradition of compromise, but sought to restore it to the meaning it had before Douglas distorted it by the Kansas-Nebraska Act. Indeed, nowhere, not even in the "House Divided" speech, did Lincoln propose abrogating any of the compromises made prior to the Kansas-Nebraska Act, including the Fugitive Slave Act. Furthermore, even in the "House Divided" speech, Lincoln was willing to make very extensive practical accommodations with slaveholders who were willing on their part to concede that slavery is wrong and should be put in the way of ultimate extinction. It is hard to imagine Garrison making that kind of practical concession.

There was, as we saw in Chapter 2, less to that concession than meets the eye. In the first place, the kind of slaveholder with whom Lincoln imagined himself compromising, epitomized by the great Virginians of the founding generation, was by 1858 fighting a desperate rearguard action against slaveholders who embraced Calhoun's "positive good" theory of slavery. Proposals of compromise must be addressed to one's actual opponents, not to idealized fictions about them. Douglas's critique might be put this way: with the idealized slaveholder, Lincoln engaged in pragmatic dealmaking and compromise, but with the actual slaveholder, Lincoln's position in the "House Divided" speech was as stringent as Garrison's, since it treated any concession to that kind of slaveholder as ceding the future of the entire Union to slavery.

In the second place, even in the founding generation, as Douglas was well aware, not all slaveholders viewed slavery the way Washington, Jefferson, and Madison did, and the views of those who had the "positive good" view of slavery (or at least of those who did not hope that slavery would somehow vanish in the near future) had a hand in the compromises that made the Constitution and regulated politics before Douglas upset the applecart in 1854. Even from the beginning, American politics, and the American Constitution, accommodated those with a "positive good" view of slavery, although it did not assume that that view was the dominant one among slaveholders. Nothing in the Constitution itself, or in the sectional compromises before 1854, depended in any strong way upon the assumption that slavery was a temporary institution, even if the most articulate and most powerful slaveholders shared that assumption.

Now Lincoln was right that the most prominent slaveholders of the founding generation held views rather like his own. And he was also right, as he would go on to demonstrate in the Cooper Union speech, that many of those Founders embraced the view that the Constitution allowed the federal government to prevent the spread of slavery to the western territories, since a significant number of the authors of the Constitution, including slaveholders, supported the Northwest Ordinance in the Confederation Congress and reaffirmed that support in the First Congress. And Lincoln was right that the Constitution reflected the values of a generation in which those who viewed slavery as an evil but intractable institution predominated over those who viewed slavery as a positive good and that the prevailing view of slavery in the South had changed in the meantime. But he was wrong in claiming that those who viewed slavery as a positive good had no standing in the arguments of the founding generation, and he was wrong to imply that the founding documents did not take their views into account.

At the Constitutional Convention itself, slaveholders from Georgia and South Carolina insisted that slavery be treated as a lasting institution, and those states would not have entered the Union had slavery been treated in the way the Virginians wished it to be treated. The ambivalence of the great Virginians is written into the evasive language about slavery in the Constitution—in its refusal to use the word "slave" directly, in its evasive and loophole-ridden clause about rendition of fugitive slaves, in its (mixed) treatment of the African slave trade. But the three-fifths compromise, with however many qualifications, reflected the views and, what is more, permanently rewarded the interests of people who, unlike the great Virginians, expected slavery to continue into the indefinite future.

The point here is more complex than it at first seems. The three-fifths compromise gave slave states more representation than they would have had had slaves not been counted in determining apportionment, and similar measures in the constitutions of the slave states gave slaveholders extra power in the state legislatures. Abolishing slavery, even if the freed slaves were disenfranchised, would have increased the power of those states in the federal government. But if the experience of the former slave states after the populist revolution is any guide, power would have passed under those circumstances from the former slaveholders to the descendants of nonslaveholding whites. Under slavery, nonslaveholding whites could control the state only if the slaves were not counted at all for apportionment purposes, which would make the slave states much weaker at the national level. Without slavery, if black voters were completely disenfranchised, as happened after the populist revolution, power passed to nonslaveholding whites. The only way former slaveholders could continue to dominate the politics of former slave states was for them to permit some portion of the former slaves to vote and to win their votes by playing on their fear of the more intense racism of the nonslaveholders, giving the former masters a political edge over the nonslaveholders, as happened during the era of Bourbon rule immediately following the end of Reconstruction.[3]

I have taken a somewhat darker view here of the Founders than Don Fehrenbacher did in *The Slaveholding Republic* (2001). Like Fehrenbacher, and for that matter like Salmon Chase, I see the Constitution as expressing ambivalence about slavery. But like Akhil Reed Amar in *America's Constitution: A Biography* (2005) and like Mark Graber in *Dred Scott and the Problem of Constitutional Evil* (2006), I see the Constitution as embodying *compromise* more than it embodies *ambivalence*, and I argue that the Founders left a place at the table for people with "positive good" theories about slavery and did not take ambivalence about slavery as foundational. The Constitution embodied Madison's ambivalence about slavery, but it also accommodated the views of those slaveholders who did not share that ambivalence. Lincoln's reading of the Constitution as ambivalent (as reflecting the prudent concessions to reality of those who hated slavery but recognized that it was a deep-rooted institution that could only be destroyed over time) is more attractive, and has the warrant of the greatest thinkers among the Founders. But Douglas's reading of the Constitution as a compromise (between those who unambiguously favored slavery and those who unambiguously or ambivalently opposed it) may be more accurate. Douglas's view probably also was closer to the mainstream consensus of his era about the Constitution.

Lincoln's thinking, this is to say, was not anticonstitutional in the way Garrison's was. Garrison opposed the ambivalent Constitution (which Lincoln supported) as strenuously as he opposed the compromising Constitution (which Lincoln attacked). But Lincoln's attack upon the compromising Constitution did amount to an attack upon the constitutional order as Douglas, never mind the slaveholders themselves, had reason to understand it. For Douglas to tie Lincoln to Garrison as he sought to do in the passage I quoted above was unfair, this is to say, but it was not entirely wrongheaded.

Douglas repeatedly threw New England at his opponents in order to tie them to Garrison, or to wealthy Massachusetts anti-slavery philanthropists like Amos Lawrence or Samuel G. Howe, and Lincoln's own rhetoric in the "House Divided" speech gave Douglas an opening to do so. Religious, class, and sectional motivations did indeed bind together many New England reformers, whose mind-set Daniel Walker Howe has illuminated in *The Unitarian Conscience* (1988), and Douglas, like many anti-abolitionists, saw anti-slavery as a kind of New England cultural conspiracy.

Behind all of Douglas's charges might be the oldest bugbear of Democratic Party organizing: the Blue-Light, Hartford Convention, New England Federalist, seeking to break up the Union and overthrow the constitutional order in the name of an economic and a moral aristocracy.[4] This view of the nature of hostility to slavery had deep roots. The opposition to the admission of Missouri as a slave state in 1820 was led by Rufus King of New York, one of the last Federalists, and the controversy was widely seen then as an attempt to revive the fortunes of the Federalist Party by stirring up sectional passions. Douglas, like Van Buren, continued to beat the dead horse of possibly resurgent

Federalism long after the Federalist Party expired. Douglas criticized Trumbull, as we have seen in Chapter 4, as an ex-Federalist, and earlier had seen the presidency of William Henry Harrison as the entering wedge of a Federalist restoration. (That James Buchanan was also an ex-Federalist seems to have escaped his notice.) Even his implication that Whig opponents of the Mexican War had treasonable motives seems to echo charges made against New England Federalists during the War of 1812. The Hartford Convention Federalist was a composite specter who had the same kind of afterlife that the 1960s peacenik radical continues to enjoy in the polemics of right-wing talk radio hosts to the present day. Behind the Hartford Convention Federalist is perhaps another bogeyman, the Cromwellian enthusiast, who stamps "God is Love" on the muzzles of his cannons.

Douglas was hardly alone in making equations like this. That New England intellectuals and politicians were the prisoners of enthusiasm—that eighteenth-century term of abuse for those who believe they have swallowed the holy spirit, feathers and all—was a staple of anti-abolitionist polemic. It was common for anti-abolitionist, anti–New England polemics to see the conflict over slavery as a replay of the cultural clashes of the English Civil War, a habit all those southern football teams called "Cavaliers" still attest to. Jefferson Davis, in a speech given in Jackson, Mississippi, on December 26, 1862, put it this way:

> There is indeed a difference between the two peoples. Let no man hug the delusion that there can be renewed association between them. Our enemies are a traditionless and homeless race. From the time of Cromwell to the present moment they have been disturbers of the peace of the world. Gathered together by Cromwell from the bogs and fens of the north of Ireland and England, they commenced by disturbing the peace of their own country; they disturbed Holland, to which they fled; and they disturbed England on their return. They persecuted Catholics in England, and they hung Quakers and witches in America.[5]

To invoke a composite specter of this kind is to imagine a figure who is capable of holding together the disparate strands of a political identity that might otherwise appear to be merely a congeries of positions. There may or may not be a compelling internal logic that ties together all of the convictions that are lumped together in such a figure; they may be tied together in a far from inevitable intuitive *Zusammenhang* such as binds together the tangled strains of thought of actual persons. To invoke a composite specter is to treat one's opponents as having the hard-to-define coherence of persons, even if rather cartoonish persons. One sometimes defines a composite specter because it is easier to hate a kind of person than to hate a grab bag of propositions: those Maine-Law, witch-hunting, sharp-dealing, negro-loving, holy-spirit-swallowing Yankee types are just not like you and me, and we do not want them ruling us.

Part of the power of a composite specter is the way it unites what would seem to be ideological opposites. Anti–New England polemics saw New Englanders as a hybrid of the contemporary cultural right (those ready-to-persecute Calvinist zealots who hung Quakers and witches) and of the contemporary cultural left (those free-loving, spirit-rapping, bloomer-costume-wearing, Fourier-commune-organizing collections of long-haired men and short-haired women). They also tied together the sharp-dealing market sense often attributed to New Englanders or more broadly to Calvinists with their religious zealotry, extending a traditional stereotype about Puritans that goes back at least to Shakespeare. Hostility to a composite specter often transcends coherent ideologies; one might consider, for example, the way twentieth-century anti-Semitism treated the Jewish banker and the Jewish communist as two sides of the same coin.

Baiting New England was in some ways a risky strategy for Douglas, for one thing because the northern third of Illinois, like the northern third of Ohio, was settled by people with roots in New England. This region was also the region that was growing most quickly and therefore the region that would determine the future of the state's politics.[6] Douglas may have simply written off his chances in this region, hoping to cash in instead upon cultural resentment against it. During the Freeport debate, for instance, Douglas provoked the largely Republican audience to cheer for various radical propositions (such as the repeal of the Fugitive Slave Act) that would have been hard to sell farther south, propositions that Lincoln himself had been trying to keep his distance from. Increasingly over the years from 1858 to 1860, Douglas tried to adopt a strategy of triangulation, balancing hostility to opponents of slavery with hostility to southern disunionists. But his own experiences in crafting the Compromise of 1850, which he could only get through Congress by uniting the minority of compromisers with northern factionalists for North-favoring measures and with southern factionalists for South-favoring measures, should have persuaded him of the futility of seeking support only from compromisers.

5.2 The Apodictic Style and Reasonableness

The Apodictic Style

Douglas saw Lincoln's attack upon the "House Divided" as being, like Garrison's attack upon the Constitution, a morally stringent revulsion against morally compromising dealmaking. Such revulsion, in Douglas's view, could be motivated only by an apodictic moral style that always treats dealmaking as a devil's bargain, as something that must violate an absolute value, whether as set forth in the Bible or as set forth in the Declaration of Independence. The language of divine imperative inherent in Lincoln's governing metaphor is inconsistent with the ethos of dealmaking, and Douglas was not wrong to hear intransigence and confrontation in Lincoln's biblical language, however Lincoln may have hedged it, because the very rhetoric of the speech itself raised the question, and is meant to raise the question, of whether pragmatism or moral absolutism had the upper hand in its maker's thinking.

What Douglas's two jeers—the attack on the scriptural reference in the "House Divided" speech and the attack on Lincoln's use of the opening clauses of the Declaration of Independence—have in common is distaste for the apodictic style, which places convictions beyond argument and treats them as articles of faith. Part of Douglas's marked hostility to New Englanders (which he indulged frequently, despite having himself been born in Vermont and Lincoln's having been born in Kentucky) was his hostility to what he assumed to be their taste for a religious habit of argument that frequently became apodictic in style. His distaste for the apodictic style of interpretation of the Declaration will be the subject of Chapter 7, where Lincoln and Douglas argue about what Jefferson meant by the promise that all men are created equal. Douglas had a similar distaste for the apodictic style in legal decisions (although Lincoln accuses him of the opposite when it comes to the *Dred Scott* decision), and designed the Freeport

Doctrine as a countermeasure to that apodictic tendency, as we shall see in Chapter 7.

Douglas's distaste for the apodictic style was distaste for any measure that places a contested view beyond the mediating power of dealmaking. Douglas phrased his critique in terms of hostility to fanaticism. But Douglas was also moved by skepticism about critical rationality itself, since he saw that the ability of critical rationality to generate a trumpingly persuasive argument was a different thing from the ability of practical persuasive engagement to put together a binding deal, and indeed the temptation to indulge in trumpingly persuasive arguments (trumpingly persuasive for *me*, that is—if you do not agree, well, then there is something wrong with you) sometimes forecloses the ability to put together a binding deal. Only the latter, in Douglas's view, could really command political authority in the face of enduring disagreements over crucial issues. Only the latter, in Douglas's view, really does the work of freedom, of binding people to a law they give themselves.

Critical rationality often embraces the apodictic style (particularly when it is using that rationality to run against the grain), in order to force a reconsideration of received opinions from a higher level of abstraction. This embrace of the apodictic style, philosophically attractive as it is, is something that practical politicians have reason to treat warily. The apodictic style is well suited to forcing the opponent to look hard at himself, and perhaps thereby discover that some of his deeply held convictions are wrong. And it is a style that is usually consonant with persuasive engagement, insofar as it treats the opponent as somebody capable of good faith reflection about his views and of transformative action on the basis of that reflection. But under inflamed circumstances what critical rationality sometimes yields, when it avails itself of the apodictic style, are not persuasive resources capable of transforming our opponents' convictions and behavior, but weapons and rallying cries, means of whipping up the enthusiasm of one's own side as an irrepressible conflict comes to a head.

The very rationality of our thinking under inflamed circumstances sometimes blinds us to the ways that our style of thinking can be inflammatory, because our thinking seems (and maybe even is) so obviously right. Under the normal circumstances of persuasive engagement, rationality—the ability to proceed logically from first principles, say—is linked to and bound by reasonableness—the ability to engage and appreciate the claims and needs of those with other points of view. In *Political Liberalism* (1993) the philosopher John Rawls gives us a rough-and-ready sense of the distinction between the two terms by asking us to imagine the circumstances, in a labor negotiation for instance, under which one might say, "Your position is *rational* but completely *unreasonable!*" Although Lincoln and Douglas did not discuss this distinction between the rational and the reasonable, it is fruitful to conceive of their argument as an argument about the nature of the reasonable because doing so makes clear what is at stake between them.

Reasonableness is a key requirement for political authority, because only reasonableness enables one to distinguish an authority based upon deep and widely shared convictions from an authority based on deduction from loaded principles, chosen to serve one's own agenda but backed up by force. Rationality is capable of deriving telling conclusions from within its premises, but rationality remains the prisoner of its own premises. I need not care that other people make a different sense of the world than I do, so long as my way of making that sense continues to make sense to me. The "I have played fairly by the rules as I have been given them" vision of the moral life is thus linked to the rationalization of one group's behavior against some other group that has a different understanding of the world, a different understanding of which my group is not necessarily obliged to take account. Rationality thus has ties to collective conformities, and to a Darwinian conflict among points of view, each guided by consistency to its central premises, and each in a position to enforce that consistency with violence, the position I am calling "deduction plus force." "Rationality" as I mean it here is thus rational in two senses of that word: first, rational in that it promises to give a moral reckoning of its actions in terms of the premises to which it holds itself to account, and second, rational in that the adherents of one set of premises act like "rational maximizers" in their relationships with the adherents of other sets of premises, seeking, so long as they can do so without violating their commitments to their own premises, even opportunist advantages against the adherents of other premises: I need not care about what becomes of your rules so long as I play within the constraints of my own.

Reasonableness provides one, however fleetingly and imperfectly, with an ability to critique one's premises, to give reasons for believing that one's premises are deep, or neutral, or universal, by attending, in a worldly way, to how people of different views engage each other. Reasonableness promises no special access to the absolute. It does not test the depth, or, except incidentally, the universality of those premises. And it is perfectly imaginable that some of the deepest and most widely shared premises of political life might not pass the test of reasonableness. But reasonableness does at least propose a test of premises that is different from simply measuring the intensity of one's own commitment to them. It does not free us entirely from the limitations of our own point of view, of our own premises. But it does promise us the ability to see at least one step beyond our own foregone conclusions. And because reasonableness works by attending to the necessary preconditions of persuasive engagement of any kind, it at least registers some of the necessary features that any set of premises *must* possess, and others that they *must not* possess, in order to play a part in a persuasive culture; it sets boundaries to the kinds of arguments one can employ in the public square.

Rawls's formulation of the "original position," in which we are asked to imagine what parties would do were they placed behind a "veil of ignorance" that prevents them from seeing which of the contending views in play in the actual world is their own, is a thought experiment that makes clear how the good and the fair, the rational and the reasonable, might be harmonized. The thought experiment might be said to give rise to this maxim: if a rule is not loaded, then it is one we would agree to be bound by even if we did not know what our stake and situation would turn out to be.

Roughly speaking, political liberalism requires the harmony of rationality and reasonableness, and in the thought experiment of the original position the behavior of the parties models rationality, and the constraint of the veil of ignorance models reasonableness. If one finds one's self unable to hold one's self to rules chosen from behind the veil of ignorance, one must ask one's self whether one's position can be maintained only by special pleading such as one would never allow one's opponents to get away with. (Describing political obligation this way, as a scruple about one's own convictions rather than as a rule about somebody else's, best captures, I think, the moral force of the test Rawls proposes.)[7]

The boundaries set by reasonableness are not merely pragmatic ones ("If you insist on that, you give color to your opponents' suspicions that you really intend only to drive them to the wall, no matter your professions otherwise"), but moral ones as well, if only indirectly. The moral aspect of reasonableness derives from the fact that the ethical world of the individual is slightly different from the ethical world of the group. In the ethical world of the individual my arguments, and my conscience, are of sufficient power to command me, to direct my will with what seems to be apodictic force. But in the public ethical world reason must win the unforced consent of others, and cannot merely command it. Because of that, reason must resist the temptation to see the opponent as a straw man, a bogey whose wrongness is a precise measure of one's own rightness. Reasonableness may restrain the urgency of rationality, but it has a moral aim as well, because it arises from the recognition that the power we create among ourselves through persuasion depends upon our mutual ability to earn each other's consent, which in turn depends upon the ability to acknowledge each other's freedom and each other's agency.

The classic example of the development of a moral perspective out of a purely pragmatic one is provided by the evolution of religious toleration after the end of the Wars of Religion. Toleration began merely as recognition that neither Protestantism nor Catholicism was in a position to drive the other to the wall. In the United States of the revolutionary era, where many Protestant sects competed with each other, each sect had a practical interest in insisting upon religious toleration, since no sect had reason to feel that it would be in a position to dominate the others, and each sect had reason to feel that it would need toleration from the others. But this purely pragmatic arrangement also, as the authors of the various statutes for religious freedom described it, had a moral element as well, since among the lessons toleration teaches is that faith imposed by force really is not faith at all. When they recognized that compulsion inevitably destroys faith as faith, the Founders also recognized that religious toleration is not a second-best position, adopted only in default of the force to have one's way against all opponents, but a first-best position, since it recognizes a key precondition of faith's own integrity, so that a tolerant Protestant is not merely a Protestant who is not in a position to exterminate all Catholics but a Protestant who serves his Protestantism better than an intolerant one does.

In moments of heightened moral conflict, reasonableness sometimes looks like moral weakness, and one is tempted to give trumping power to rationality. But when that happens, argument no longer seeks persuasive engagement and serves chiefly to bind together, in an explosive compound, the rationality and the angry passions of those on one's own side of the issue.

When Douglas made his arguments against the demand for uniformity of state institutions ("Why should Kansas see things the same way Maine does?"), he wished to see the argument about slavery as if it were a matter of different communities deciding the slavery issue differently. Sometimes he treated the choice as a morally indifferent one, like the choice of whether to raise cattle or cranberries. When he did this his argument was a weak one, and he gave color to the charge that he simply had a blind spot about moral issues. But Douglas sometimes treated what separates slaveholding from free communities as a moral choice instead.[8] The issue, when framed in this way, was whether Illinois can make a moral choice for Kansas. Douglas did not in those versions of the argument see the choice as nonmoral, only as a moral choice that is not to be foreclosed by some other agency. He imagined convictions about slavery as disputable moral convictions, ones that he had decided in one way but could imagine other people deciding in some other way. In making the case as he did, Douglas argued, in effect, that we must imagine each other's distinguishing moral convictions as nonpublic (in that the state cannot write the moral concerns of one group into the higher law and place them beyond the reach of political bargaining), but still as morally charged (in that the state also cannot treat those moral convictions merely as illusions or as arbitrary compulsions). To modern ears, treating the issue of slavery this way takes its moral evil too lightly, especially since the argument about slavery was cast in Douglas's mind as an argument between slaveholding and nonslaveholding white people rather than an argument in which the slaves themselves might be expected to have something to say, but it must be remembered that Douglas's views were not quite as straightforward as he sometimes presented them as being, since he had a strategic agenda in taking the conflict about slavery into some nonmoral arena, as we have seen.

In making his argument about uniformity, Douglas tried to cast Lincoln as somebody whose position is rational, but not reasonable, since Lincoln in his view not only did not concede the necessity of sharing his political world with slaveholders but also was not ready to face up to the consequences—civil war—of his refusing to do so. Indeed, Douglas's fanaticism case essentially sees fanaticism as a matter of exclusive adherence to the rational at the expense of the reasonable. Douglas saw himself as somebody who was responsible to the reasonable, perhaps even more than to the rational, insofar as he was willing to make a very large moral sacrifice to preserve the peace. But this Douglas-inspired view of the argument is mistaken, both as regards Lincoln and as regards Douglas himself, for Lincoln and Douglas differed not in that one owed chief allegiance to the rational and the other to the reasonable, but in holding different ideas about the meaning of the reasonable.

Lincoln and Douglas both entertained, however implicitly, ideas of reasonableness that shaped and constrained their arguments, but their ideas differed in subtle but telling ways. Briefly put, for Lincoln, reasonableness involved explicit principles—core values, one might say—all sides have reason to expect the others to adhere to, and to which they can expect to hold each other. Some of these core values have to do with process: there is no appeal from the ballot to the bullet, for instance. But some of them are material: acceptance of the self-evident truths proclaimed in the Declaration of Independence is a precondition of political comity. It would be fairer to say of this last precondition that it imposes material, not merely procedural, requirements (if you do not accept the truths of the Declaration, you are beyond persuasion), but that these requirements arise from the procedural consequences that follow from rejecting the material core value. If you reject the claims of the Declaration of Independence, I do not know what kind of argument will have traction with you, because you reject a premise that seems foundational to me. Worse, if you reject the Declaration, I do not know what you are *not* capable of, and I have reason to suspect that almost any kind of repression might pass muster with you, either as a social end (you might just be capable of enslaving anybody) or as a means (you might justify repressing my views by force). Furthermore, if you reject the ideal of autonomy that underlies the promises of the Declaration, I have reason to believe that by compromising the agency of others you have compromised your own, and thus are no longer really capable of public freedom. Lincoln's veneration of the principles of the Declaration stands on the dividing line between a substantive requirement (Believe this or be a monster) and a procedural one (You do not get to make a special exception for yourself and your friends).

For Douglas, by contrast, reasonableness involved a live but unstable sense of what, in some particular conflict, specific opponents could or could not be expected to concede. Douglas's position was not unprincipled, but it was unwilling to deploy principle in a way that divided those with whom it is possible to negotiate from those with whom it is not. For Lincoln, to be hesitant to define those explicit principles in whose name you must be willing to draw a line in the sand was to treat all politics as an amoral contest of interests, as a kind of expediency politics. For Douglas, seeking to define principles in this explicit way was always a loaded ambition, a way to attempt to drive one's opponents out of the public square.

Putting it this way enables one to bring up a nuance about what separates Lincoln and Douglas. Both could have imagined deploying the available persuasive resources to wipe out slavery completely, although they disagreed about what kinds of political accommodations for slaveholders would be required in the mean-time. Although Douglas repeatedly proclaimed that he did not see why the Union should not in theory persist forever half slave and half free, and that he did not care what Kansas did about slavery so long as it did what the Kansans, not the Missourians or the Bay Staters, wanted it to do, he nevertheless did imagine, as Lincoln did, that over the very long term slavery would lose out. Douglas did not imagine that slavery must be protected from every eventuality, and he did imagine, and perhaps hope, that it may come to pass that slavery would lose its footing in a thoroughgoing way. But until then, slaveholders were full members of that persuasive culture, and, as full members of that persuasive culture, were entitled to the same kind of dealmaking arrangements other stakeholders were entitled to. Douglas, in short, imagined a place for slaveholders in a liberal political order, although it was a losing place.

For Lincoln, by contrast, "positive good" slaveholders could not quite be full members of a liberal political order, because slavery itself was so fundamentally contrary to liberal values. Other kinds of slaveholder (Jefferson's kind), however, could be members of a liberal political order, since they did not positively defend slavery so much as seek to find practical ways to cope with the existing institution. Lincoln did not imagine the positive good slaveholder as a kind of outlaw, as somebody so outside the bounds of decent society that he must immediately be subjected. Indeed, in Lincoln's view the positive good slaveholder must be approached through the same means one uses to approach other political opponents: persuasion, first of all, and under some circumstances dealmaking, but never the kind of coercion one reserves for one who is so genuinely outside the social order as to represent an immediate mortal threat to it. (Although positive good slaveholders did, in the long term, represent in Lincoln's view a mortal threat, they did not represent an immediate one that required emergency measures to respond to.)

Douglas and Lincoln both saw the positive good slaveholders as being legitimately in a position to demand to be treated only by liberal *means*—they must be persuaded, not forced, and they had the right to the protections the law has already guaranteed them and to the good-faith performance of the political compromises they have been a party to. But Lincoln and Douglas disagreed about whether the slaveholders' *ends* can have a place in a liberal society. Lincoln saw slaveholding as deviant, as something that the society must morally stigmatize for its own safety, even as it confines itself to persuasive means to combat the threat slavery poses. Douglas, by contrast, saw slaveholding as nondeviant, although wrong, as being among the ends it is possible to entertain in a liberal society, but as being also an end he opposes and wishes to defeat in the public square. Both positions look to the ultimate extinction of slavery, and both positions limit themselves to the means available to liberal societies to bring about that extinction, but one position saw slavery as an ordinary opponent to be fairly if sweepingly defeated; the other saw it as a deviant form to be expunged, although with caution and careful attention to the rules. These positions are close, but the distinction between these two versions of the reasonable is a deep and important one, because the reasonable draws the boundary between the world of persuasion and the world of violence. In drawing the boundary of the reasonable more narrowly than Douglas did, Lincoln opened himself to the charge of conceiving the conflict with the slave power in such a way as to make it insoluble by means short of violence, treating politics as a morally decorated contest of force. In drawing the boundary of the reasonable more broadly, Douglas opened himself to the charge of abandoning critical use of the reasonable entirely, and treating politics as entirely a matter of dealmaking about interests, which is to say, also as a morally decorated version of a contest of force.

Acknowledgment, Freedom, and Equality

It would be a mistake to imagine reasonableness as merely a pragmatic concession to human fallibility and variability. Reasonableness is a key feature of moral and political autonomy, because reasonableness is what distinguishes legitimate from illegitimate exercises of force. Reasonableness defines the external boundaries of the public square, since a commitment to reasonableness is a precondition for entering into persuasive relationships with others mediated by such acts as dealmaking, making promises, keeping promises, and holding others to promises. And commitment to reasonableness is a form of recognition of others, which is the precondition of moral and political autonomy. Reasonableness is therefore the basis of an inclusive ideal of citizenship, since anyone who is capable of reasonableness is capable of moral autonomy and thus has a claim to a place in the public square, and those who are already in the public square cannot be said to have autonomy unless they recognize the autonomy of others, and they jeopardize that autonomy every time they fail to do so.

If the vision of moral equality upon which liberal democracy depends is rooted ultimately in a sense of the transcendent value of the human person—when we say that Serb and Croat are equally human we mean something different from what we mean when we say that hawk and chickadee are equally birds—it is reasonableness that gives that vision political meaning by offering persuasive engagement in the public square to everyone with moral autonomy and by making the inclusiveness of the public square, its openness to all with moral autonomy, the price of the exercise of the autonomy of those already within it. Autonomy is tightly linked with offering recognition, and thus politically is the ground of both freedom and equality (two otherwise contradictory values). To specify the conditions under which autonomy and recognition are possible is to specify the ground rules of public reason and thus (as Kant perceived) to establish a public realm in which order and freedom (again, under other circumstances, contradictory values) are harmonized.

When Lincoln said, "As I would not be a slave, so I would not be a master," what he meant was that a slaveholding society, by violating the moral autonomy of those it enslaves, has corrupted its own autonomy. This is a strain of argument that commits those who adopt it to an ideal of political inclusion, and although Lincoln passionately and sincerely denied having any such intention, citizenship for black people was among the entailments of his arguments. Whatever his demurrals, the aims Lincoln did avow—an ultimate end to slavery—were not only necessary preconditions of that citizenship but motivations, however indirectly expressed, for granting it as well; Lincoln's arguments themselves raised the pressure for black citizenship, and ensured that the Republic could not be happy until that citizenship was fully granted. Lincoln's way of framing his hostility to slavery made black citizenship ultimately inevitable whether he faced up to the implication or not and whether it took a week or a century for that ideal of citizenship to be realized.

Douglas's claim for reasonableness, by contrast, applied only to those opponents with whom he was at the moment engaged: if I cannot offer slaveholders a deal they can accept (and they are themselves the judge of that, not me), then ultimately I offer them only the sword, and the political order I represent is driven ultimately by force and chance, not by reflection and choice. Lincoln's understanding of what reasonableness is cannot be maintained in the face of a commitment to racial inequality, and whether Lincoln acknowledged it or not, his idea of reasonableness entailed political equality among people of different races. (My view is that Lincoln both knew and did not know that his views had these entailments, in just the way that Jefferson knew and did not know that the promises of the Declaration committed his nation to abolishing slavery.) Douglas's understanding of what reasonableness is, by contrast, does not entail racial equality, and indeed, because of its commitment to deal with slaveholders where they were and to ask of them only what they were in fact in a position to give without a fatal sacrifice of position, Douglas's version of reasonableness may actually have foreclosed political equality among the races. Requiring the insiders, in their conflicts with each other, to ask from each other only what they are in a position to give puts no pressure on those insiders to offer justice to outsiders.

Both Lincoln and Douglas are partly right about what a commitment to reasonableness entails. In the context of 1850s politics, reasonableness is itself a "house divided," riven by a fatal contradiction.

Lincoln (like Rawls) conceived of the reasonable as providing explicit ground rules for political conflict, common, publicly known principles that all parties, for their own reasons, acknowledge being bound by which serve as necessary preconditions of all political persuasive engagement whatsoever. Parties to a liberal political order need not have the same reasons for subscribing to these ground rules. But they must have moral, not merely pragmatic, reasons for adhering to those rules. Otherwise those rules are merely a reflection of the balance of power between contending parties at the moment they were drawn up, and the parties would have no particular reason to respect those rules should the balance of power change. They must understand these rules in such a way that adhering to them makes them better, not worse, adherents of their most fundamental values. They can adhere to them from within the horizon of their own convictions, for reasons that are consonant with their values (and their reasons might not be shared by the adherents of other doctrines, although the rules those reasons support must be), and they can expect that their interlocutors, for reasons of their own, will be willing to bind themselves to the same rules.

No concept of reasonableness, in Lincoln's view, is consistent with slaveholding as a positive value, and slaveholding itself is not owed reasonable respect, but slaveholders who are entangled in the institution and wish to disenthrall themselves from it are entitled to reasonable concessions, since they did not choose their situation any more than the slaves themselves did.

Douglas, perhaps moved by his understanding of the ways southern politicians had used arguments about the ground rules (in the gag rule debates over petitions about slavery in the District of Columbia, for instance) as ways of exercising will to power over the agenda, was drawn instead to an understanding of the reasonable as something implicit, and never capable of being articulated in clear-cut rules, a live tradition of bargaining, say, held together chiefly by the habit of doing business together and by an intuitive sense of what kinds of demands would or would not be deal breakers or relationship breakers.

Lincoln's understanding of the reasonable was tied to his desire to seek for principled compromise, and Douglas's understanding was tied to his conviction that no settlement deeper than a modus vivendi is ever to be sought about deep disagreements.[9] Lincoln's understanding of the reasonable was aimed at providing a means of coming to consensus about the important issues that would subdue the deepest sources of conflict. Douglas, by contrast, did not require opposing parties to come to consensus and assumed that their differences from each other, even on very deep issues, would continue to be a durable feature of the political landscape. What Lincoln sought was explicit engagement on explicit ground rules, and ultimately what divides the house in the "House Divided" speech was not so much the different status of slavery in different parts of the Union so much as an inability to specify ground rules to which all parties should be held. Because Douglas despaired of seeking this kind of arrangement—remembering that even his most famous compromise, the Compromise of 1850, depended for its success upon being a modus vivendi (since less than a quarter of Congress actually sought compromise), and remembering also that even the Kansas-Nebraska Act could hold together only so long as it preserved some measure of ambiguity about when the people of a territory could exercise their right to choose between legalizing or forbidding slavery—reasonableness did not seem to him to be a function of agreed-upon ground rules, but rather depended upon an unstable congeries of deals always in continuous need of adjustment and reinterpretation. Douglas imagined disagreements so durable that they could not even be mediated by ground rules supported by an overlapping consensus; they could be mediated only by a habit of dealing with each other and an intuitive sense of what kinds of deals are likely to stick.

The best way to understand Douglas's political course, and the best case to make for it, is to take Douglas to understand reasonableness in this way: we can choose to open ourselves to reasonableness, to limit rationality within reasonableness, but we cannot know exactly what reasonableness consists in except as we elaborate it in the dance of demand, offer, and concession we engage in with practical opponents; it is not up to us alone, or up to them alone, to specify what is reasonable. Reasonableness is not a creature of ground rules, but the upshot of a tradition of relationship. It is, for Douglas, only something we can puzzle out together, case by case. Reasonableness involves a knack for knowing the other as someone different from us, and that is something that we can get the hang of only by living our way into it with each other. It is a deliverance of phronetic practice, not the subject of an epistemic rule; it is a fruit of "experience," in the sense of that word we have in mind when we refer to ways of being we have somehow made our own but can never completely explain ("you have to have experience to understand this") and in the sense we have in mind when we refer to experience as the sad wisdom of our own mistakes ("I learned this in the school of experience"). Reasonableness is also, for Douglas, the fruit of imagination, since it requires us to enter into the position of others whose premises not only are not our own but also may seem revolting to us.

Critical rationality is a variety of persuasive engagement only when the rational is made responsible also to the reasonable, and for Douglas that is possible only when the habit of relationship gives us an intuitive sense of what we can ask from each other. No set of rules, in Douglas's view, quite does justice to the concept of the reasonable, and every set of rules is liable to catastrophic misuse. Under strained circumstances we lose the ability to feel out the reasonable, and when that happens our rationality itself turns against us, and rational politics rationally sharpens convictions to the point of shooting. By contrast, dealmaking as a form of persuasive engagement is capable of maintaining itself—for a while at least—under circumstances in which critical rationality is inflammatory, because it has a more flexible, but also less principled, understanding of what reasonableness requires. In Douglas's view, when it is divorced from pragmatic, ad hoc dealmaking, even critical rationality produces a hardening of views that makes it hard to distinguish in its practical effects from fanaticism. This is the gravamen of Douglas's fanaticism charge about Lincoln and the Republicans.

What I have just written makes it sound as though Douglas had laid out an explicit argument about what the nature of the reasonable is. Of course he did no such thing. But his political course, about the Compromise of 1850, the Kansas-Nebraska Act, and the Lecompton Constitution, makes best sense if one understands him to be acting on the basis of intuitions about the reasonable such as those I have attributed to him.

Douglas's aim as a politician was to represent, not to transform, received opinions, to *accommodate* conflicting received opinions to each other when they cannot finally be *harmonized*. Those who aggressively, or subversively, or confrontationally sought to transform received opinion seemed in his eyes to be a kind of insurgent elite, seeking to serve their will to power under the guise of forcing moral improvement upon a reluctant and less enlightened populace. (This is one reason why he kept implicitly comparing abolitionists to temperance advocates and nativists.) In doing this Douglas of course made the traditional

Jacksonian Democratic argument against Whig social engineering. But his thinking on this kind of issue was also consonant with a deeper habit of Douglas's mind, his habit of assuming that in practice we cannot resolve conflict by discovering controlling common values, because even where it might be reasonable to articulate such values, we always play those values in our own way.

But Douglas's critique was not merely a practical one. For the fact that we always play our values in our own way does not only mean that we typically use them to sharpen conflict, it also means that our resort to apodictic arguments about values is almost always contaminated with moral narcissism. We haul God (or Thomas Jefferson, or the Constitution) out of our back pockets whenever we need Him. But He always looks rather like us, and says what we have cued Him to say. If Douglas was suspicious of the ability of high abstraction to slice through the Gordian knot of messy and morally compromising accommodations, it is because for Douglas only the moral restraint required by provisional, ad hoc, modus vivendi dealmaking could serve genuine persuasive engagement, because only modus vivendi dealmaking requires us never to treat our convictions as clubs, and thus only modus vivendi dealmaking enables us to distinguish between moral clarity and moral narcissism.

For Douglas the key task of the politician is dealmaking, and the only legitimate use of values in politics is to advance dealmaking. Values detached from dealmaking were always in Douglas's eyes varieties of hysterical obsession. Douglas is often accused of a kind of moral blindness, and of a kind of muddled and incoherent approach to political conflict that lacks the clarity of principle. But these were not necessarily vices in Douglas's own eyes, for his assumption was that moral clarity almost inevitably leads to crusader politics, and crusader politics, as I have said, almost inevitably kills what it loves. Moral ends, he felt, are better served in a less ardently moral way, not only because one is more likely to secure that end by acting in that way but also because only the dirty-hands moral agent can distinguish between a value he serves in a good-enough way and a haunting obsession that makes a mockery even of his best qualities.

It is after all the things that really do most matter that are most likely to make us act demonically in their service. In most respects critical rationality and persuasive engagement align as values; both seek to prosecute disagreements in terms of agreements, both seek means of moving the reasonable consent of opponents to measures that heal conflict. But the two are opposed to each other in the Lincoln-Douglas debates, where they stand on different slippery slopes, the one down to crusader politics, the other down to expediency politics.

5.3 Appeals to the Divine Will

Douglas liked to imply that behind the enthusiasm of abolitionists was the sting of a bad conscience that the enthusiasts sought to shout down by fanaticism: "The worst Abolitionists I have ever known in Illinois have been men who have sold their slaves in Alabama and Kentucky, and have come here and turned Abolitionists whilst spending the money got for the negroes they sold" (1:630).[10]

In his racist tirade at Charleston, Douglas obliquely compares Lincoln to an African American preacher among others of the same kind:

> Lincoln knows that when we were at Freeport in joint discussion, there was a distinguished colored friend of his there then who was on the stump for him, [shouts of laughter,] and who made a speech there the night before we spoke, and another the night after, a short distance from Freeport, in favor of Lincoln, and in order to show how much interest the colored brethren felt in the success of their brother Abe. (1:666)

Two can play this game, of course, and Lincoln's ridicule of Douglas in the Scott Club speech of 1852 includes a blackface parody of the style of African American preaching almost as acridly racist as anything Douglas attempted in this line. Douglas had (correctly) suggested in a speech at Richmond, Virginia, that when General Scott wrote to the Whig Convention that he accepted its 1852 presidential nomination "with the resolutions attached," Scott meant his endorsement of the Whig platform to be ambiguous. Scott's supporters at the Whig convention had largely opposed the Compromise of 1850, and there had been an ugly fight at the convention over a plank in the platform endorsing the compromise as a final settlement of all the issues about slavery upon which sectional conflict had been raging. Scott meant his letter to be acceptable both to those Whigs who (preferring Fillmore) had opposed him and supported the compromise and to those Whigs who had supported him but opposed the compromise.[11] To defend Scott, Lincoln compared Douglas's literary analysis of that "with" to the kind of rhetorical pirouette he associates with African American preaching. Notice that the passage puts Douglas's presumably pro-slavery audience in blackface as well:

> Try, for yourselves, how Judge Douglas's substitutes for the word "with" will affect this sentence. Let Judge Douglas be brought to understand that he can advance the interest of a locofoco candidate for the presidency by criticising this sentence; and forthwith he will hie away to the African church in Richmond, Virginia, and make a great speech, in which he will find great difficulty in understanding the meaning of the words "walked with God." He will contrast it, greatly to its disadvantage, with the language of that *gallant* and *honest* man, Frank Pierce! He will show that it is, and was designed to be, susceptible of two constructions, one at the North, and another at the South; that at the North the word "with" will be read "NOTWITHSTANDING," "ALTHOUGH HE DEFIES," "ALTHOUGH HE SPITS UPON;" and finally he will thrill, and electrify, and throw into spasms of ecstasy his African church auditors by suggesting that such monstrous duplicity could not have been conceived by Enoch or Moses, but must have been dictated by Gen. Seward!!! (1:279)

The real burden of Douglas's attack was not the theological sound but the theological habit of argument, a habit of argument that was in his mind always contaminated with narcissism and with moral panic. Douglas's behavior in an earlier conflict gives one a sense of what an appeal to transcendence meant to him. In the spring of 1854 Douglas was presented by Senator Edward Everett of Massachusetts with a scroll 250 feet long containing a memorial against the Kansas-Nebraska Act signed by 3,000 New England clergymen.[12] (Curiously, both John Bell of Tennessee and Edward Everett, who between them would lead the Constitutional Union Party in 1860, opposed the Kansas-Nebraska Act. The point here is that the scroll was presented by the moderate Everett, not by the firebrand Sumner.) Douglas's reply, which set off a war of dueling speeches and public letters, was famously intemperate, arguing that if "clergymen had a peculiar right to determine the will of God in relation to legislative action," then "why not simply refer all political questions to them?"[13]

This retort provoked twenty-five Chicago clergymen to object to Douglas's tone:

> We greatly deplore the apparent want of courtesy and reverence towards man and God manifest especially in the speeches of the senators of Illinois and Indiana, and that we regard the whole tone and spirit of that debate, on the part of the opponents of said memorial, as an outrage upon the dignity of the Senate, and upon the claims of the divine name, word, and institutions, to which we owe profound honor and reverence.[14]

In his reply (which characteristically threw gasoline on the fire he ostensibly was attempting to put out) Douglas treated the clergymen's claim to speak for God as itself sacrilegious, far more so than his own intemperance, denouncing the "astounding fact that any body of men, calling themselves clergymen, or by another name, in this age and in this country, would presume to claim that they were authorized by the Almighty, and in his name, to pronounce an authoritative judgment upon a political question pending before the Congress of the United States."[15]

Douglas did not take exception to the clergymen's disagreeing with his views; he conceded that every citizen has the right to do that. Nor did he object to their argument that they were moved to their disagreement by their religious convictions. What he objected to was their claim to speak for God. Now there is a difference between being motivated by religious convictions and claiming to speak for God, and it is worth dwelling on this difference because both Lincoln and Douglas paid attention to it. (When, before he issued the Emancipation Proclamation, clergymen would come to President Lincoln to announce to him that God had told them that he should emancipate the slaves, he would retort, in effect, "Don't you think he would have thought to tell *me* that rather than *you?*"[16]) The difference between the two claims is that the first is a move within a persuasive exchange, and the second is a leap out of the possibility of persuasive exchange, a kind of argument that forecloses persuasive engagement:

Nobody questions your right, no one denies the propriety of your exercising the constitutional right of petitioning government for redress of grievances in your capacity as citizens; nor can there be any well-founded objection to your adding these other words, "as ministers of the Gospel of Jesus Christ," if done only as illustrative of your relations to society and of your profession and occupation in life. This was not the obnoxious feature in the New England protest. The objection urged to that paper was, that the clergymen who had signed it, did not protest in their own names, as clergymen, or citizens, or human beings, or in the name of any human authority or civil right, but they assumed the divine prerogative and spoke to the Senate "in the name of Almighty God!"[17]

Citizens can make theological arguments, but they must make them as citizens, not as prophets, because prophets are not given a kind of veto power over the resolutions of deliberative bodies.[18] Now there are circumstances under which an appeal to the divine will is not a foreclosure of persuasive engagement; when, for instance, it is used to call the interlocutor back to what he himself professes himself to be bound by. ("If you really believe *x*, don't you think that my position, and not yours, is the one that is most consistent with *x?*" or "Remember that we have both professed *y*, which binds me as much as it binds you. Do you really, in your heart of hearts, wish to trample that profession?") One of the characteristics of Dr. Martin Luther King Jr.'s arguments was their attempt to remind his interlocutors of their own best nature, their attempt to call to his interlocutors in the name of common values that mattered to both sides a great deal more than racial segregation did.

Only a nuance, although a very important one, separates persuasive and foreclosing appeals to the absolute, "God has written his argument about this even onto your own heart" from "God has assured me that you have no part of him, and that your position is so wicked that I not only need not but should not give your position the time of day." This latter kind of argument is a temptation to the morally earnest, and it is all the more tempting when the morally earnest do in fact have most of the moral right on their side. Even then, it is a temptation nonetheless, because it opens the door to the kind of contest of force that ought to give even the most morally earnest pause. That said,

there really are positions that are so beyond the pale that they are beyond persuasive engagement, although one makes that claim in specific conflicts only at one's own peril.

Both sides, of course, can pull God out of their back pockets, and
southern orators were no less prone to doing so than northern ones
were. Few situations are more dreary, as Lincoln himself was to remark
in the Second Inaugural, than those in which both sides pray to the
same God, and each invoke His aid against the other. Indeed, if only
our side, and not the other, is a competent judge of God's will, then
what can't we get away with? In the absence of persuasive engagement,
appeals to the absolute are all pretty much alike. There are, as Douglas
went on to argue to the clergymen, no shortage of people around the
world who claim to speak for God:

> I have wandered over distant and extensive portions of the globe dur-
> ing the past year, where the successor of Mahomet proclaimed and
> enforced God's will on earth, according to the principles of inspired
> truth and obligation, as recorded in the Koran; and, by the potency
> of his divinely-appointed institution, held, in the hollow of his hand,
> and suspended upon his breath, the lives, the liberties, and the prop-
> erty of millions of men, women, and children. When within his do-
> minions and surrounded by his bayonets, I had neither the time nor
> the disposition to argue the question of his right to "reprove, rebuke,
> and exhort, with all authority and doctrine," in the name of the Al-
> mighty! But, when I set foot on the shores of my native land, under
> the broad folds of our national flag, and surrounded by the protecting
> genius of our American institutions, I did not feel like recognizing
> any such rightful authority of that divinely-appointed institution, in
> temporal affairs, here, or elsewhere.[19]

For Douglas, the gold standard of political authority is the consent
of the governed. Appeal to the divine will is legitimate as a means of
moving that consent, but it has no force in politics beyond the consent
it is able to win. Douglas did not make the twentieth-century distinction (to my mind sometimes a woolly distinction) between private
convictions (which presumably include religious faith) and public policies. Douglas conceded that religious views may have public bearing.
But they have public bearing so long as they contend in the public

square, as expressions of public reason, not as ways of foreclosing the necessity of seeking consent:

> Our fathers held that the people were the only true source of all political power; but what avails this position, if the constituted authorities established by the people are to be controlled and directed—not by their own judgment, not by the will of their constituents, but by the divinely-constituted power of the clergy? Does it not follow that this great principle, recognized and affirmed in the constitution of the United States and of every State of this Union, is thus virtually annulled, and the representative of the people converted into machines in the hands of an all-controlling priesthood?[20]

Elsewhere Douglas objected to the tendency to treat every political question as a constitutional one, using reasoning similar to his objection against religious dictation. The Constitution was typically invoked by southern politicians to the same kind of end northern ones invoked the divine will to secure: to write their opponents completely out of the public square. Now, as we shall see below, Douglas could fling the Constitution at his opponents as well. But he did so, particularly in his arguments about the *Dred Scott* decision in the debates with Lincoln, in ways that run against the grain of some of his profoundest convictions. His much-maligned Freeport Doctrine, for all its faults, had for Douglas the signal virtue of circumscribing even the *Dred Scott* decision within a political culture of consent, impervious to dictation whether by God or by Chief Justice Taney. The Freeport Doctrine, in 1858, and the "Dividing Line" argument of 1859 (which largely replaced the Freeport Doctrine in his thinking over the next year) made the future of slavery in the territories a matter for the public deliberation of the people of the territories, no matter how powerful the authorities who have attempted to dictate that future for them. Both strategies were failed ones, and ones with deep flaws. But both were at least in accord, as Douglas's main arguments about the *Dred Scott* decision were not, with the most pervasive themes of Douglas's thinking.

The vocation of politics as Douglas conceived of it is a vocation of dealmaking, and that vocation must attribute the slightest shade of provisionalness even to the most deeply held convictions. The apodictic style cannot help but undermine an ethos of dealmaking because it must see every sacrifice made in the interest of accommodation as a fatal one. In interest politics, dealmaking is always possible so long as each party can trade a small interest for a great one, or a great interest for a whole host of small ones, or a great interest now for a chance to secure that interest more certainly later. Douglas assumed that one can make the same kind of prudential bargains about moral issues as well, trading off one moral issue against another in order to secure an outcome that is on balance more morally satisfying than the alternatives.

This kind of argument was famously adopted by Webster in the Seventh of March speech during the debates over the Compromise of 1850: the Fugitive Slave Act is a bad thing, but it is the price of the political domination of the Union by the free states, which is what Webster thought the Compromise of 1850 would secure, by admitting California as a free state. (This last was an argument still endorsed by Lincoln in 1858.) Webster's was an argument that had many disastrous consequences. But not to have made this kind of argument could imaginably have had disastrous consequences as well. One takes a morally strenuous stance, as I said above, out of the conviction that the world is better seen as a place beholden to moral rules, not merely to the will of the stronger. But if one's taking that stance commits one to a contest of force, that moral stance has in fact transported one into a world in which contests of force give it its shape, a world governed, that is to say, by the will of the stronger. Only the effort to preserve some kind of persuasive engagement with the moral opponent keeps alive the hope of a world not governed by force, and that is something very hard to do with completely clean hands. For the sad fact is that it is not decency that determines whether something is within or without the boundaries of the negotiable; that is determined by the kind and amount of force available to both sides should push come to shove.

5.4 Implicitness and Situatedness

Persuasive engagement requires us to assume that we can occasionally be taught something about our own values by our enemies. One way to make sense of this requirement is to treat the values in play in persuasive engagement as having what I have been calling "implicitness," that power of not being fully exhausted by any specific propositional embodiment of them or any explicit account of them, so that our opponents retain the power of revealing something about them whose truth we did not anticipate but could not help but concede. Now the term, of course, is foreign to both Lincoln and Douglas, but brooding upon the meaning of that term makes clear a key theme of Lincoln's thinking in the Gettysburg and Second Inaugural Addresses, the idea that we are bound to a tradition but that our sense of the obligations that tradition imposes *becomes*, so that we keep faith with the Founders not by imitating them but by living our way into consequences of their ideas, consequences they not only knew they were not in a position to fully realize but may indeed have sincerely (but mistakenly) rejected. The story of democracy, in Lincoln's view, is the story of something with a destiny, but it is a destiny never fully understood either by the Founders or by Lincoln himself, never understood fully by the key agents even as they act. What the acts of the present generation mean is something they are not in a position to know; later generations will know the meaning of our acts better than we do, but they too will be enmeshed in a destiny they too will understand scarcely better than we do.

A value has the kind of implicitness we expect of a person: we know in advance that every conception we formulate of that value is inadequate to its concept, that it will always be saturated with entailments and consequences that we cannot anticipate fully and that will continue to surprise and rebuke us as Socrates's daimon rebuked him. We know a concept in the way we know a person: by knowing that we will not know it. We know it by unknowing, by entering into a live relation with it in which we lack knowledge but have knowing and earn acknowledgment.[21] Knowing is never more than phronetic, and always intuitive, or rather, has something of the intensity but also something of the obscurity, of intuition, and the practices that knowing informs are practices into which one can live one's way, into which one can be initiated, but that one can never fully reduce to system. We know people by knowing that there is more to them than our theories about them, and the chief thing we know about them is that their story is not over. So we know our values by knowing that we can never exhaust them with our understanding, and that we never stand in a privileged position as regards them, that they always remain in a position to put us, in some unanticipated way, in the wrong.

Keats's term for this kind of knowledge is "negative capability." He coined that term to explain to himself what he took to be a kind of literary greatness that Shakespeare had and that Coleridge did not. He saw Coleridge's art (wrongly, I think) as entirely invested in an explicit set of doctrines. If one agrees with those doctrines, the works can be edifying, although they serve theses that would have been better served by formal argument. But if one does not agree with those ideas, Keats remarks, the poems put their hands back into their pockets and look blankly back at you. Whatever aesthetic means are at play in such a work is a decoration of an idea, not an assay of it. Shakespeare, by contrast, allowed himself to be in "Mysteries, Uncertainties, Doubts" about the particulars of his convictions, but the result of this is that his art had a kind of inner life that Coleridge's did not have.

I understand the term "negative capability" in the following way. As Keats describes it, it involves, first, a detachment from the strict formulation of key ideas, as a way to recognize that ideas are always a little larger than the things we say about them are. This detachment is a condition of that demanding connoisseurship about one's thinking that Polanyi calls "tacit knowledge." It commits us to the recognition that our ideas have depths one might not get to the bottom of, that whatever one says about them, something will remain unsaid. This detachment from formulations makes available not a messy or flabby impressionism about ideas, but the ability as it were to live with an idea in a kind of intimacy. Negative capability, this is to say, is not a form of impatience with ideas or hostility to ideas, but is instead an insistence on assaying the felt life of an idea by "playing it on the pulse" (to use another of Keats's expressions).

Negative capability is the identifying feature of our knowledge of persons. Romance languages use different words to describe factual knowledge and knowledge of persons (or recognition of persons or acknowledgments of persons); the knowledge of a deep idea, I think, is closer to the latter than to the former. When we know persons, among the things we know is that our knowledge of them is not the whole story. It is not that we lack information about the person—indeed the person we know only a little about is more likely to be summed up (and dismissed) in our minds by virtue of that knowledge than is the person we know a great deal about. It is that what we know about that person raises new possibilities, keeps his or her case open, as it were. It is only those in whom we have no investment, those whom we refuse to acknowledge, that we imagine ourselves as knowing all the way down, as "having their number." Those in whom we have investment are those of whom new knowledge develops new and significant possibilities of freedom. New knowledge leads to new kinds of unknowing, new sorts of implicitness.

Negative capability yields the ability to render and respect the felt life of experience, the felt life of ideas, and the felt life of people. It is an assay of something by a mode of situated knowing that is different from capture in propositions, but different also from unthinking submergence in daily practices. It participates at once in knowing and in unknowing, in the explicitness of the known and in the implicitness of what is never to be fully known. It is in requiring of us a living engagement with something about which we will always be unknowing that negative capability, which shapes for us a sense of the implicitness of persons and of the implicitness of values, ties both persons and values back to a kind of transcendence: "aporia" is a mode of negative capability, the negative capability one employs in the presence of transcendent things.

When I describe a value in this way, I mean to describe it as it is experienced in felt life, as something that has ties to thought, to feeling, to habit, and to intuition, but is not quite any of those things.[22] I do not specifically have Lincoln's or Douglas's theories about what a value is in mind here, although making sense of Lincoln's description of his own experience of moral issues (in such texts as the Hodges letter, or in the Second Inaugural) motivates my thinking on this subject, and constructs like implicitness make sense of some of the entailments of Lincoln's ideas.[23] These constructs have heuristic value locally in making sense of the moral experiences Lincoln articulated in the 1858 and 1859 debates, and in the great speeches of his presidency. And they also provide motivation for the idea that study of particular political conflicts can shed philosophical, not merely practical, light on key political values, that important features of the meaning, not merely the applications, of political values cannot be fully captured by constructions from propositions but must be played on the pulse of actual experience.

When I refer to values as having "implicitness," I mean to refer to them as having implicitness in the public world of discourse and argument. But clearly they also have this feature in private experience, and it is perhaps easier to understand the concept there, since we have all had the experience of following out immensely important but elusive intuitions. I do not have a fully worked out theory of how implicitness in the public world of history and politics differs from implicitness in the private world of duty and feeling, although they are without question somewhat different things, since private obligation, which involves submission to duty, and public obligation, which has a responsibility to persuade others rather than simply to command them, are somewhat different things. But Lincoln does imagine, in a number of classic texts (both Inaugural Addresses, the December 1862 Annual Message to Congress, the Gettysburg Address), that public values *become* in a way consistent with the theme of implicitness, and his remarks on his private working-out of policy, in such texts as the Hodges letter, are consistent with that theme as well, so perhaps not much is risked by understating the difference between public and private implicitness. Lincoln does have a fully worked out theory of what he calls "the public mind," a theory that is in play in the later debates, the 1859 Ohio speeches, and the Cooper Union speech and First Inaugural Address, each of which we will examine below, and Lincoln describes the public mind in ways that the concept of implicitness helps to make sense of.

Discussing the public mind in a speech at a Republican Party banquet in December 1856, Lincoln had argued that the public mind "always has a 'central idea,' from which all its minor thoughts radiate. That 'central idea' in our political public opinion, at the beginning was, and until recently has continued to be, 'the equality of men.' And although it [h]as always submitted patiently to whatever of inequality there seemed to be as matter of actual necessity, its constant working has been a steady progress towards the practical equality of all men."[24]

Values oblige us, but they also remain implicit, and therefore, inexhaustibly, they unfold in ways we cannot render by constructions from first principles, in ways we can neither anticipate nor satisfy nor evade. What we open ourselves to when we enter into persuasive engagement is a rebuke from the implicit space of a concept. Our values, in the words of our opponents, catch us by surprise, despite all our cleverness, in just the way the Socratic daimon trips up Socrates always at that moment when he is most sure that he is on the right track. The Socratic aporia is a translation into the language of argument of the experience of the Socratic daimon, an experience that takes place at the level of the feelings but that drives us to a reconsideration of our thoughts.

That values in persuasive engagement must be conceived of as having implicitness leads us to a second observation about those values, that we always see them in a situated way. I do not mean by using this term to embrace relativism about values, to claim that values are in any strong way culture bound or conventional. In calling values "situated" I mean to imply that they typically do not reveal their consequences through deduction from first principles but by being forced to the surface by historical contingencies.

We never see more than a few steps down the road along which our deepest convictions lead us. But the struggle to realize one entailment of our values faces us with other entailments we might not have recognized in advance, and might in fact have denied had we been put to it. Concepts unfold new layers of consequences, to which prevailing conceptions are always inadequate, and conceptions are always being strained by historical contingencies that force us to reconsider the meaning of commitments we have already made and to revise our conceptions in the light of the concept. The situatedness of values is a consequence of their implicitness, because the implicitness of a value means that our understanding of it is never fully adequate, and that it has entailments we cannot anticipate and that only experience forces us to confront. Because of their implicitness we are never masters of our own values, and contingencies keep forcing us to reconceive them, keep mocking our sense that the story of our values is a finished one.

Conceptions are limitations upon concepts imposed by culture, history, and politics as much as they are realizations of those concepts under specific conditions. But changing contingencies of culture, history, and politics also put pressure upon conceptions and cause them to be reconceived in the light of a fresh grasp upon the concept. To that extent culture, history, and politics not only limit our access to the absolute, which commands us in the form of concepts, but express that absolute's pressure upon conceptions as well: culture and history not only bind us in themselves but also prepare us, however fleetingly, to transcend culture and history as well. Culture is not always the limiting horizon of value. Indeed, sometimes culture itself provides the occasion for insights that lead one, if only a few steps, beyond the limitations of culture.

Think, for instance, of the ways Thomas Jefferson took what seems to be a culturally limited conception—the Rights of Englishmen—

and used it to frame an insight into a universal concept of human rights.[25] Now Americans may be wrong to assume that everyone who seeks freedom is in some way an American, or that everyone who desires freedom desires it in just the way and form Americans do and can easily establish stable institutions to guarantee it. It may not be true that liberal democracy is the ultimate desire of all peoples, and it may not be true that the United States is in a unique position to carry the banner of liberal democracy. (Indeed, it might become open to question just how fully the United States is a liberal democracy at all.) But it would also be a mistake, and a very serious one, to assume that the political values Americans cherish are merely the expression and outgrowth of a peculiar cultural history and are closed to those who do not share that history. The promises of the Declaration were the product of a particular intellectual and political history, the characteristic expression of a particular culture, but they have implications beyond the limits of that culture and are not confined within the horizon of that culture. The unusual way in which American nationality is defined, arising as it does from certain political ideas more than from a common blood or language or history, both makes it hard to draw the boundaries of that nationality and commits the United States to playing a historical role in the world it can barely define, much less enact.

It may perhaps not be so that the grand promises of the Declaration of Independence proclaim the natural and obvious birthright of all people as people—only tautologies are really self-evident, and you only, as Hannah Arendt once pointed out, proclaim that something is self-evident if you expect someone to doubt your argument about it.[26] We saw in section 4.7 above that grave consequences follow if, in some intractable conflict, one cannot agree about what one proclaims in this way to be a self-evident truth. When I proclaim that some truth is self-evident I also proclaim that if you do not think so we are likely to come to blows. The proclamation aims at a universal truth, but it draws a sharp cultural and moral line between those who accept it and those who do not.

It would also be a mistake, however, to interpret the promises of the Declaration as merely the expression of a local political culture, as something more like the "Rights of Englishmen" than like the "Rights of Man," because although it arose from local political circumstances, is the fruit of local political traditions, and is conditioned by the limitations of a local political culture, it is also an insight into a concept that is larger and deeper than that local political culture and that, from its implicitness, unfolds new layers of consequences that continually outrun our ability to shape them into conceptions. (Whether the promises of the Declaration are limited by the cultural horizon of Jefferson's time is of course exactly the issue Douglas and Lincoln will argue about in the last debates, as we shall see in Chapter 7, but it is an issue that had been on Lincoln's mind from the time of the Peoria speech.) Concepts are not propositions, and cannot be fathomed by constructions from first principles; they manifest themselves only by the pressure they put upon conceptions when local political confrontations unanticipatedly force reconsideration of them. Contingencies, such as the quarrel over slavery in the territories, force conceptions to be reevaluated in the light of their concepts; the implicitness of concepts drives conceptions into *becoming*, even as conceptions themselves repeatedly claim for themselves the firmness of strict construction and the stability of *being*.

The concept of a political order, or of a particular law, has the imperative force of a transcendent command, but the obscurity also of an intuition. Concepts without conceptions are blind; conceptions without concepts are morally empty. Now it may be that all terms that carry a strong charge have the same kind of obscurity, and lead to the same kind of insoluble perplexities that always mark essentially contested concepts. What is an "American"? What is a "Jew"? What is a "man"? How do you answer the question, "Are you one of us?" The fact that these concepts are crucial, and charged, and urgent does not make them any less intuitive, does not make them any more capable of being seen in a way with syllogistic clarity. We know that they require to be seen from the inside, to be lived into. We know that along with questions of correctness and incorrectness they also bring along insoluble questions of authenticity and inauthenticity. They demand allegiance, and they bestow identity, while at that same time possession of that identity is never fully secure and allegiance is always contested. Furthermore, even as these concepts are constitutive of a particular identity—they are what makes America a nation, not just a state—they also reach beyond that identity, opening possibilities for the world as a whole, not just for the United States. They inform a habit of life, but also charge that habit of life with a moral calling and an undertone of moral panic. We do not know the meaning of a law's concept when we pledge our allegiance to it; we discover that meaning in the course of working out a decent habit of life illuminated by it. But it is the nature of the concept, because it cannot be known all the way down, to provoke guilt and shame; it will always reveal new ways in which we have always failed it.

One might think that a resort to the concept would be the source of a truly trumping political authority, that if I could successfully enlist it upon my side of a political quarrel, I could use it not only to defeat you but to drive you completely from the public square. But because concepts have implicitness, they almost always play false those who attempt to wield them in this way. We are bound to the concept, but we never control it, we can never claim to have it in our back pockets, and we are never in a position not to be rebuked by it. When I treat it as a weapon, I falsify it somehow, and it usually breaks in my hand. It is important that we put ourselves right with the concept, but no side in a political quarrel can safely claim to have privileged access to the concept. The implicitness of the concept is a standing rebuke to moral narcissism. It calls us to duty, but never assures us that we are in every way, or even in the most important way, among the virtuous. (This is, of course, the central moral lesson of the Second Inaugural Address.)

The concept is always in a position to be the source of a rebuking scruple, and it is never more so than when one is in a position of triumph in a struggle waged in that concept's name. One way to understand this is to see how quickly the idea of the divine, once it is invoked to justify violence, turns into something else. When I draw the sword for God, God turns into something else, into myself with a very loud voice, myself in a demonic frenzy. That is why the voice of the concept is always the voice of a scruple, never the voice of a stampeding imperative, always the voice of the Second Inaugural, never the voice of the Battle Hymn of the Republic.

The conception of equality under classical republicanism (and under the early Republic to the extent that it partook of classical ideals) was the equality of people who could enter the public arena because they were freed from crippling dependencies upon each other. The freedom of the polis depended upon the exploitation of the *oikos*, whose uncompensated labor bought the independence of those who ruled the *oikos*. The conception of republican virtue, so dear to thinkers of the antebellum age, owed much to the classical concept of independence.

Ownership, particularly ownership of land, was an important prerequisite for full citizenship in the early Republic, because ownership was felt to guarantee some measure of independence to the owner. Those who wished to enter the polis need not be radically independent in the sense of having no attachments or interests at all—indeed, they were expected to have both—but they did have to be independent enough to be nobody's creature, to be capable of deciding for themselves whatever might be at issue. What this meant was that membership in the political society was limited to adults (since children are dependent), to males (since in those societies females were dependent in the same ways), to whites (since blacks were by virtue of being slaves ipso facto dependent—although here the presence of a population of free black people complicates things somewhat, and flat-out racism accounts for their exclusion from the res publica as much as the republican notion of citizenship does), and to property owners (since those without property were vulnerable to manipulation by those with property). Notice that the ability to play a role in the res publica has nothing to do with the dignity of human beings simply by virtue of their being human beings. Political rights are quite distinct under this conception from human rights (which under this conception shrink to the dimensions of such things as the right not to be murdered). Political rights under this conception are something that arises not from the moral claims people have on each other, but from the common agreement among the members of a kind of club that certain others are included in that club. Citizenship under republicanism, this is to say, is something more like academic tenure than like a pre-political human right, and the right to be a citizen has no bearing on whatever claim to dignity and worth one has as a human being.

The reader should notice that the movement from a republican ideal of citizenship, in which citizenship neither results from nor results in claims about one's moral status as a human being, to a liberal ideal of citizenship, in which citizenship is an expression of the dignity of being human, is a transformation of conceptions realized under the pressure of the conflict over race and slavery and mediated by civil war. This transformation of conceptions under the pressure of urgent violence ultimately involved a considerable rearrangement of political thought, and we have not yet seen the end of its effects. But the transformation has been so profound that it is sometimes difficult to understand the political ideas of the antebellum generation.

If citizenship is a kind of club, those who are members may enjoy a different status from those who are not, but they do not enjoy a different moral identity. While those who can play a role in public life may more perfectly express what Aristotle would call the *arete* of being human, the characteristic, defining excellences of a human life understood as the life of an animal who is most fully himself when part of a polis, those who do not play this role are not thereby understood as nonhuman. (Aristotle himself, who captured but did not invent this ideal of citizenship, was after all no citizen himself but a *metic*, a resident alien.) Such people may understand those who are excluded from the polis as human in a reduced way (barbarians were not even felt to have the benefits of language), but that exclusion need not be policed by hysteria, since it does not mean anything more than exclusion from particular deliberative arenas. By contrast, once one starts to think of citizenship as the natural birthright of human beings strictly by virtue of their humanness, one must police the boundaries of citizenship by denying, with nervous insistence, that those whom one excludes are human. It is the nervous insistence more than the denial that I wish to emphasize here. It has long been a commonplace among historians of nineteenth-century American politics (and we have already developed some of the logic of this position) that the most strident racists were not the Whigs, who were comfortable with property qualifications for voting rights, who treated racial inequality as just one among many other sorts of inequality, and who were comfortable with inequality as the price of their own leadership and as the occasion for their noblesse oblige, but the Democrats, who had a theoretical commitment to universal manhood suffrage and who therefore could justify racial inequality only by treating it on a basis completely different from that they used to think about other kinds of inequality. Even that increased stridency of racist feeling is a sign of the pressure of the concepts that inform the Declaration of Independence upon the ruling racist conceptions.[27]

Founding a claim to a say in the public square upon moral autonomy rather than upon economic independence necessitated a profound transformation of the political system and of the cultural assumptions that underlay it. Both of these transformations were forged in the crucible of civil war, and given political expression in the three Reconstruction amendments to the Constitution, which, however betrayed and compromised during the eighty years that followed the end of Reconstruction, made promises that the American republic is still struggling to keep but at least understands itself to be bound by.

5.5 Transformation of Conceptions

I understand the ultimate meaning of Hart's distinction between concept and conception to be this: finally we do not entertain our values in the form of propositional imperatives. We sometimes attempt to think them through in the form of such imperatives, but those imperatives are in turn subject to the review of urgencies that arise in the form of hints, hunches, intuitions no less binding for being obscure. The Socratic daimon, that intense form of the creeps that would ambush Socrates at those moments when he was most certain of himself and felt himself to be in possession of the secret of things, is the best example of this kind of intuition, for it says to Socrates that no matter how clever you feel yourself to be, or how ironclad you believe your thinking to be, there is something wrong with it, and you do not know what. The pressure of the concept upon the conception is not the pressure an abstraction exerts over the particulars it is designed to cover; it is the pressure the Socratic daimon exerts over a too-clever train of ratiocination.

The friction between concept and conception is one way to express pragmatism's vexed relationship to principle. And the unpredictable quality of the relationship between concept and conception is one way to express the idea that the law is a living thing, something that *becomes* in a way whose inevitability is only available in retrospect. The fact that implicitness and subjectivity are bound together accounts for the fact that morality is as much the lesson of experience as of ratiocination, for it is the nature of experience as experience to find out a way to live with a value as it unfolds in unanticipated ways, as contingencies force new entailments of a concept to the surface. Moral becoming is not merely changing the rules as circumstances or needs or interests change (as historical relativism might have it) but the living transformation of conceptions under the dual pressure of the concept and of historical contingency.

This transformation of conceptions is the frequent burden of Lincoln's wartime speeches. It is what Lincoln had in mind when he referred to the way the war itself forced him to understand his own intentions in making that war in an ever deeper way, discovering the necessity of a new birth of freedom (in a fresh grasp of the concepts of the Declaration) in the place of the more modest aim of merely restoring the Union. Something like this train of thinking informed the famous last paragraph of Lincoln's December 1862 Annual Message to Congress, where he struggled to understand a destiny to which he was bound but whose moral purpose was only beginning to come clear to him. No course of action will fully suffice to answer the question of the meaning of the war, because it is the nature of such questions, even when seriously addressed, to remain partly open ones. But the question motivates a profound transformation, which is at once a recovery of the concept and a revolutionary rethinking of the conception. "As our case is new, so we must think anew, and act anew" does not merely mean that the practical difficulties of the war require creative, even transgressive solutions earlier generations might not have embraced; more deeply, what it means is, "We must disenthrall ourselves, and then we shall save our country."

The obscure unfolding of the concept, under the bloody pressure of events, is what Lincoln meant by "history," assuming as he always did that that word "history" is meant to describe a story about a realized or unrealized moral destiny. Lincoln often used that word in an almost mystical sense, finding in it a force he would never fully understand but that made him what he was and gave meaning to what he did (or rather, challenged him to live up to its meaning). But he never used that mystical term in the way Stalin used it, as a forgiving judge who will always excuse every brutality. For one thing, Lincoln never was certain, as Stalin was, that he stood in good stead with history, that his acts in history were fully clear to him, that he had understood their meaning, that history was just himself with a louder voice. Lincoln's history is a demanding but skeptical judge, one who never allows you to believe that his verdict about you is certain. And the question of the meaning of history is itself always an open one, because what gives history its order is the unfolding of concepts which, because they will continue to unfold new entailments, are as obscure to us after as before, and leave us, in their light, always slightly inadequate to their continuing challenge. The Republic cannot be happy until it fulfills the concept, but the concept by nature is never completely fulfilled. And the challenge of a historical agent, as Lincoln saw it, is to rise to the challenge presented by the bloody contingencies of history and to gain some transforming insight into their meaning. As Lincoln said, in the peroration to his December 1862 Annual Message:

> Fellow-citizens, *we* cannot escape history. We of this Congress and this administration, will be remembered in spite of ourselves. No personal significance, or insignificance, can spare one or another of us. The fiery trial through which we pass, will light us down, in honor or dishonor, to the latest generation. We *say* we are for the Union. The world will not forget that we say this. We know how to save the Union. The world knows we do know how to save it. We—even *we here*—hold the power, and bear the responsibility. In *giving* freedom to the *slave*, we *assure* freedom to the *free*—honorable alike in what we give, and in what we preserve. We shall nobly save, or meanly lose, the last best, hope of earth. (2:415)

It is because of their implicitness, the situatedness, and their subjectivity that values have, in addition to the external aspect we might call "validity," their ability to pass critical muster as expressions of reasonableness and rationality, an internal aspect we might call "authenticity," their ability to express an allegiance, an identity, even a calling. It is these features of values that distinguish the moral life from merely the set of consequences of moral propositions. These features also render the moral life always problematic, because keeping faith with a concept saturated with implicitness is something we can never securely attest ourselves to have done. This is why the anxious questions that come with affiliation (for instance, "Are you a Christian?") are the kind of things that only the frivolous can honestly answer in the affirmative; the more seriously one gives one's self to such an affiliation, the less certain one can be that one has really kept faith with it.

Two features of this model of the moral life, to the extent that it is Lincoln's model, give color to Douglas's charge of fanaticism in the 1858 debates—first, the fact that values restlessly become, and second, the fact that values never allow us to feel secure in our grasp upon them. Concerning the first of these, restless becoming could in principle lead one anywhere—think of how those who, in the twentieth century, worshipped history as a kind of pseudo-God, and were willing to do anything to align themselves with its flow. It is not far, for such people, from the march of history to the dance of Kali. That concepts provoke continuous transformation in their conceptions naturally unsettles the idea that they can be used as the basis of a disciplined review of policy and law; a conception that becomes can become anything, and it is impossible to expect from it that consistency and rigor we traditionally expect from law. Now Lincoln in fact never used the becoming of conceptions as a way to trump the existing laws in the name of a higher one. In practical policy he remained as much of a legalist as Douglas was, if not more of a legalist; he never, for example, allowed his primary moral hostility to slavery to license him to ignore the Constitution's limitations upon his power to act directly against slavery, as he famously contended in the 1864 Hodges letter. The pressure of the concept was a source of disquiet, and a source of insight, but Lincoln always sought to remedy that disquiet (and always sought to realize that insight) in strictly legal and strictly traditional ways. Only Lincoln's proceduralism kept him from a vision of history like Stalin's, but his language too was often the language of someone swept away by a course of events he can barely understand but embraced with passionate conviction.

Concerning the second feature of this model, the fact that values never allow us to feel secure in our grasp upon them, Lincoln always conceived the anxiety that attends the implicitness of value in a chastening way: if both sides invoke the aid of the same God against the other, one side must be wrong, but both sides may well be intoxicating themselves with moral narcissism, and one would be wise to think twice before asserting that God wholly approves of what one does. But the recognition of the inevitability of bad faith in the face of one's most deeply held values could have had a very different effect, stinging one into a nervous fanaticism driven by moral panic. Arendt's portrait of Robespierre in *On Revolution* (1962) captures the way an ethos of authenticity lends itself to increasingly destructive and increasingly futile attempts to prove its own moral purity to itself, and Lionel Trilling's *Sincerity and Authenticity* (1971) makes a similar argument about radical political thinking in the late 1960s. How many fanatics are driven to violence not by the sternness of their convictions but by a maddening sense that their convictions are inauthentic? Such people kill not because they are believers but because they suspect that they, deep down, may actually believe nothing, may only be playing at belief. They wish to prove to themselves that despite everything they do have beliefs worth killing for, that they would rather, in Nietzsche's phrase, have the void as purpose than be void of purpose. Think how often in our own day suicide bombers—I am thinking especially of Mohammed Atta here—have not been secure insiders to the cause they devote their fanaticism to, but relatively well off but deracinated outsiders who embrace fanaticism as a way to prove to themselves that they are not the alienated creatures all the evidence shows them to be. Without Lincoln's disciplined circumspection, legalism, and skepticism about his own motives, Lincoln's key values could have played out very differently.

One of the crucial differences between phrasing moral conflicts in the language of tensions between concepts and conceptions and phrasing them in the language of conflicts between higher law and positive law is that doing the former preserves the idea that opponents are still morally akin to each other, that each side has a stake in the other's values, in the other's moral autonomy, in the moral claims the other side may be able to press against one's own side. The distinction between concept and conception sounds at first rather like the more familiar distinction between higher law and positive law. But there is a difference: the higher-law idealist assumes that the positive law is irremediably corrupt, a kind of moral poison. And appealing to the higher law is a way to argue that persuasive engagement with political opponents is at an end: you are too corrupt to make a commanding appeal to something I value. The opposition between concept and conception does not work the same way, for it treats the conception as an insight, a limited insight and in some ways a wrongheaded one, into the concept. Indeed it is only through such insights, wrong as they all are in one way or another, that we work out the meaning of the concept. We do not grasp the concept except by seeing it in situated ways, and we have no unsituated access to the concept as an absolute, because we do not know it in a propositional way at all but as a rebuking intuition. Further, the concept has a boundless implicitness, and it perpetually unfolds new entailments that rebuke us with unfulfilled duties at just the point when we are ready to congratulate ourselves. Finally, the concept, as opposed to the higher law, prepares the ground for persuasive engagement, because it expresses premises that both sides can fairly assume the other takes seriously, if differently. Because each side can argue that the other side has already given its allegiance to the concept, and sought authentically to serve it, the appeal to the concept allows each side to appeal to the better nature of the other, arguing that it understands that other's virtues better than they do. The foundation of persuasion is after all something like this: the ability to make a commanding appeal to the opponent's values, to show that the opponent's deep identity is better served by the antagonist's reading than by its own.

Perhaps the best way to make sense of the implicitness of the concept is to recall the curious way Lincoln treated tradition, what I have been calling his "reverse Burkeanism." We are accustomed to thinking about tradition as the embodiment of the insights and folkways of our ancestors, who have lived their way through the world and understand it better than we do, and have bequeathed us, in the form of traditions, habits of being that will serve us in ways better than anything we could cook up for ourselves by reasoning from first principles. Lincoln's traditionalism is very different from Burke's, for what he looks for from the Founders is not so much their knowledge as their anguish. The Jefferson he loves is the one who trembled for his country when he remembered that God is just, and who bound his country to promises that he was not in a position to keep and that his contemporaries may have actively disowned had they reflected upon them. Lincoln wanted his countrymen to remember that promise, and to understand that they can never be happy until they keep it, even as they know that in their own way they will fail that promise as badly as Jefferson did, especially as that promise generates new promises that bind them as deeply. What we honor when we honor the Founders are the promises they could not keep, and we cannot keep either, but that we must keep, and must pass on to trouble our own descendants in ways that have not yet occurred to us.[28]

Lincoln was not a higher-law idealist, and preserved a respect for procedural legitimacy from his earliest public pronouncements on the subject in the Lyceum speech, to his scrupulously and cautiously legal campaign against slavery during the Civil War. Indeed, in the Lyceum speech, it is clear that without procedural legitimacy one cannot distinguish between an enraged love of justice (the mobs that burned McIntosh in St. Louis and hung the gamblers in Vicksburg in the Lyceum speech were moved after all by an enraged love of justice) and that pure love of power that moves the family of the lion, the tribe of the eagle, and the towering genius who disdains a beaten path.[29] It is a claim as old as Plato that the love of power is disempowering, because it leads one to entangle one's self in the metabolism of natural force, and thus commits one to futility. But in the Lyceum speech the angry love of justice has the same power.

Douglas was wrong to think of Lincoln as a higher-law idealist, in just the way that he was wrong about Seward. But there is no question that Lincoln felt the same kind of attraction and repulsion for the figure of towering genius that Milton felt for his Satan. And the kinship—despite the crucial differences—between Lincoln's idealist commitments to the values of the Declaration and those of the higher-law men provides some grounds for the likeness. Douglas's charge points to a side of Lincoln's nature; Lincoln kept that side under firm control, but he felt its power.

5.6 Limits of Persuasive Engagement

The Respectable Opponent

Maintaining persuasive engagement requires opposing interlocutors to invest themselves in several constructs that serve as enabling fictions. Persuasive engagement happens, for instance, between what we may call "respectable opponents." It is impossible to persuade someone if one cannot imagine circumstances under which one might come to believe what that person believes. One cannot engage persuasively with an opponent if there is no way to imagine how decent-enough, intelligent-enough persons could find themselves advancing the convictions that the opponent advances. This does not mean that we have to imagine that our opponent may just be right. But it does mean that we have to imagine that our opponent's stance cannot be wholly accounted for by reflections upon his villainy, his ignorance, his madness, or the disadvantages of his upbringing.

The respectable opponent is an imagined construct; we do not have to know already that our opponent actually is respectable in the way we imagine. Our positing such an opponent is a precondition of *our* access to persuasive engagement, not a condition of allowing *him* to enter into it with us. We posit such an opponent for our reasons—because it is the price of persuasive engagement, and the risks, to us, of rejecting persuasive engagement are high. We cannot know in advance whether our opponent is capable of such engagement until we have already committed ourselves to it.

We imagine our interlocutors in articulate political conflicts as "respectable opponents" in exactly the way, and for exactly the same reasons, that we imagine our interlocutors in private moral conflicts as moral agents. That you are in fact a moral agent is something I cannot positively know. I treat you as one because doing so is a postulate of practical reason: I cannot myself be a moral agent unless I situate myself among other moral agents, whom I must see as ends in themselves, as protagonists in their own moral dramas at least as much as antagonists in mine.

I create an imagined character, and I endow that character with the kind of freedom imagined characters can have.[30] We take a particular rhetorical stance about our knowledge of such characters: we see it as a matter for knowing and acknowledgment rather than for knowledge. The "respectable opponent" plays the role in political engagements that the acknowledged other does in moral ones. We are not moved to invest ourselves in the construct of a respectable opponent by evidence about that opponent. Indeed, there is almost always, in a serious conflict, plenty of plausible evidence that our actual opponent is not and cannot be respectable, and the prophecy that our opponent is such a creature is always a self-fulfilling one. When we take the view that our opponents are always a little larger than our theories about them are, we do so not because we have engaged in a kind of political Turing test that shows them to be so, but because we have made an imaginative leap, for reasons of our own, reasons that have to do with our own access to acknowledgeable agency.

We discover the other's moral freedom in ways not very different from how we discover our own. We do not start from the premise of default unfreedom and then look for some uncaused contingency we treat as evidence of our freedom. We notice instead that we are already embedded in a moral world saturated with duties and reasoned-upon obligations, and we ask what must be true of ourselves for us to already inhabit such a world. Our moral freedom is a postulate that we find necessary to embrace in order to make sense of the moral obligations in which we are already embedded. The other's moral freedom is a postulate motivated by exactly the same things. And the moral freedom of the respectable political opponent, his political agency, is postulated in exactly the same way.

The price of a theological as opposed to a political understanding of a public quarrel is that the concept of the respectable opponent becomes unavailable, and the conflict almost inevitably descends into a contest of force, a contest of force that issues ultimately in futility, because that contest will always be decided by force, not by right, and its outcome is an expression of the metabolism of force rather than of the moral logic of history or whatever other phrase we may wish to use to describe the triumph of force when we do not want to face it for what it is.[31]

If the construct of the "respectable opponent" is the precondition of entering the public square where political freedom happens and where political action is developed through engaged conversation among irreducibly plural human beings, politics must nevertheless not lose sight of the fact that human beings are never completely free, that they are always at the same time bound in chains of causes as much as they are responsible to reasons.[32] Only in visionary moments are the world of causes and the world of reasons, the world of laws of nature and the world of laws of freedom, the world of truth and the world of meaning, transparent to each other, and how the two are to be harmonized under immediate practical circumstances is something that is unlikely to be solved from first principles. People will always be free and bound, and how that freedom and that bondage add up is something we are unlikely ever to understand all the way down.[33]

This irreducible human duality has several consequences. The first is that even if ethics can be purified of thinking of consequences so that its only consideration is about the nature of duty, politics can never be so purified: it cannot ask people to be better than they are capable of being, and it must take account of the fact that human beings, even when they are responding to necessities, never mind to imperatives, are brittle. Political concepts, no matter how deep, will always demand to be realized in practical conceptions, which limit those concepts not only because they are at best phronetic interpretations of those concepts but also because they are accommodated to the limitations of the political cultures in which those conceptions are elaborated.

The second consequence of the irreducible duality of human nature is that people are capable of exercising their freedom in ways that make them for all practical purposes permanently unfree, and that polities can do this as much as individuals can. When Lincoln worries about the corrupting power of slaveholding in a democratic culture, he does not only mean, as Jefferson did, that masters learn habits of domination that are inconsistent with republican mores; he also means that treating other human beings as forever excluded from a culture of deliberation destroys the moral, not merely the psychological, preconditions of one's own freedom. In just the same way that I cannot be free except in a world in which I acknowledge the freedom of others, so members of a polity cannot be free except where they acknowledge the freedom of others. Freedom and equality are sometimes taken as contradictory values, particularly where material equality is concerned. But freedom and moral equality imply each other, and failure to acknowledge equality makes the power one exercises over others something one wields only at the price of one's own freedom. The master is enslaved by mastership, not only because he must enforce acknowledgment from others under conditions that render that acknowledgment empty, as Hegel noticed, but also because mastership itself binds him to a moral order in which force is the only currency, and that is a moral order in which he himself cannot maintain his humanity.

Mastership, in Lincoln's view, is, like addiction, a kind of trap door; to choose it is to freely destroy the possibility of one's own freedom. Mastership is like tyranny: it appears to be an exercise of the agent's power, but it is in fact the suicide of agency. This was, after all, the big lesson of the Lyceum speech: that to commit one's self to power above all, perhaps in the name of a heroically transgressive ideal of action, is to devote one's self to an ultimately humiliating form of futility in which one finds one's self submerged in the workings of natural force, in which one is capable of behavior but not of action.[34]

The slaveholder is a kind of alcoholic, except that he has not only sacrificed his own will to a compulsion but has also sacrificed the agency of any deliberative body in which he has a say to that compulsion as well, for the institution of slavery is so violent, and so politically unstable, that it must draw all of the other institutions of society around it (corrupting them in the process) in order to survive. In seeing slavery this way, Lincoln has in mind not only the primary violence against the slave needed to keep the slave in line, but also the ways in which slaveholders demand and are given a kind of veto power vastly out of proportion to their numbers. By whipping up loyalty politics and holding the knife to the throat of the union somehow about 100,000 slaveholding families were able to project 30 million people into a war that killed 623,000 of them.

The difficulty with viewing slavery as a kind of alcohol in the body politic is that once I treat anyone as somebody who has sacrificed or is sacrificing his agency, I have no choice but to repress him, although I may repress him in the name of what I take his true interests to be (as one represses alcoholics). But if I treat him as someone who has sacrificed his agency, I undermine some of the necessary conditions of my own agency, because I stop seeing myself as engaged in free deliberation with others and see myself as engaged in a kind of test of force, even if I restrict myself to the force of words rather than employing the force of rifles. The master's freedom is corrupted by his inability to see the slave as a political agent like himself. But if the master becomes unfitted for freedom by considering the slave as unfit for freedom, the opponent of slavery risks the same thing once he considers the master as unfit for freedom.

If Lincoln's thinking about the ways in which the public mind of the 1850s is preparing itself to accept the destruction of its own freedom accurately captures the way in which slavery, by foreclosing the political agency of the slave, forecloses the political culture of freedom itself, his thinking on the subject is also subject to temptations that Douglas accurately describes. Lincoln understood that the "respectable opponent" is a vulnerable construct, and that actual political agents are always on the point of making that construct impossible to sustain. But once you have taken the view that your opponents have made that construct impossible to sustain—and this is true even when you are right that they really *have* done so—you have yourself entered a world, not merely recognized that you are already in such a world, but stepped into that world yourself, in which you yourself cannot maintain the persuasive engagement upon which a political culture of freedom depends. If I cannot remain confident that my interlocutor is a respectable opponent, then I must protect myself from him; I need not trample him, and I may seek to act in what I take to be his real interest, but I cannot remain in persuasive engagement with him. And in doing that, I risk my own ability to remain an agent in a free polity.

The Supreme Court justice Peter V. Daniel, the harshest pro-slavery ideologue on the Taney Court, complained at the time of the Wilmot Proviso controversy that the presumption in anti-slavery circles of the moral inferiority of slaveholders rankled him. Daniel wrote to Martin Van Buren:

There is another aspect of this pretension which exhibits it as fraught with dangers far greater than any that can flow from mere calculation of political influence, or of profit arising from a distribution of territory. It is that view of the case which pretends to an insulting exclusiveness or superiority on the one hand, and denounces a degrading inequality or inferiority on the other; which says in effect to the Southern man, Avaunt! you are not my equal, and hence are to be excluded as carrying a moral taint with you. Here is at once the extinction of all fraternity, of all sympathy, of all endurance even; the creation of animosity fierce, implacable, undying. It is the unmitigated outrage which I venture to say, there is no true Southron from the schoolboy to the octogenarian, who is not prepared for any extremity in order to repel it.[35]

Governor Joseph Matthews of Mississippi had argued in his inaugural address in 1848:

We must know whether the compromises of the Constitution are to be respected; whether citizens of the slave states are to be considered as equals with their northern brethren, and whether slavery is regarded as such a crime that they who hold this species of property are unworthy of an association with the inhabitants of the free states.[36]

What exercises both Daniel and Matthews is the moral stigma associated with slaveholding, and their remarks give color to Lincoln's arguments, both in the 1858 debates and in his speeches in the 1859 Ohio campaign, that what the South really wants is for the North to cease to criticize slavery morally. By 1859 the North was no longer even to be allowed to treat slavery as a morally neutral matter of economics, roughly as Douglas was promising to do, and had to be forced to praise it. There is a political edge in both Daniel's and Matthews's remarks as well; they do not think that political equality or persuasive engagement can be maintained between parties who stand on a footing of moral inequality. The issue is not so much wounded narcissism, or even damaged political comity, so much as whether a moral inferior really can take a position in a dealmaking cultural economy.

Lincoln had a reply to this kind of suspicion in the Peoria speech, and that was that he did not think the white inhabitants of the slave states were terribly morally different from the white inhabitants of the free states, and that he was bound to admit that if he were born in the midst of such an institution he would not know what to do with it were all earthly power given to him. (Extending that institution into new regions, of course, was a different matter.) Lincoln's treatment of slaveholders in the Peoria speech is consonant with his treatment of alcoholics in the Temperance address. But it is not consonant with his portrayal of his opponents in the "House Divided" speech, where the suspicion of dark conspiracies on their part suggests at the least that they are not respectable opponents within the ambit of persuasive engagement but sinister manipulators to be thwarted.

Para-Persuasive Engagement

That persuasive engagement requires the construct of the respectable opponent does not mean that persuasive engagement can apply only if the issues at stake are morally trivial or that the issues are already in some way decided on the basis of commanding values to which both sides are already publicly committed. To take that position would be to argue that persuasive engagement can never be brought to bear on any conflict with moral depth. Indeed, opponents whom one seeks to reach through persuasive engagement must include those who embrace positions one finds to be deeply repugnant, else persuasive engagement is futile.

The construct of the "respectable opponent" may not in fact require one to go so far as to stipulate that the issue between us is one about which reasonable persons may disagree. Persuasive engagement with the respectable opponent may only require that one be able to imagine how one might one's self, under different circumstances, have been brought to the same position. And it requires that one imagine the opponent in a nondemonic way, at least to the extent of conceiving that there are appeals to commanding values that one expects the opponent would feel the force of and that there are ways by which the opponent may also make commanding appeals to shared values against one's own side. We need at least to be able to conceive of what kind of thing the opponent would find to be persuasive; else we do not know what persuasive resources to bring to bear upon our conflict with him. We need to imagine how there might be arguments that would have weight with that opponent but that have not yet persuaded him, and we must construct for ourselves a version of our opponent who is at once capable of being brought around and yet also durably in disagreement with us, not merely a stick figure opponent who cannot imaginably make a riposte to us. And we also need to imagine what the opponent's needs are, since we cannot ask the opponent to make a fatal sacrifice that we would not ask of ourselves were we in his place. (At the same time, we are not required to take his view of what his needs are at face value.)

The necessity of imagining the needs of a respectable opponent is especially strong if we are engaged in negotiation—balancing and accommodating positions we do not expect to be able to reconcile, or mediating inevitable contradictory social forces—rather than in persuasion. But something like this construct of the reasonable opponent is in play even as we move further and further from fully fledged persuasion. Metaphorical tests of strength, such as elections, for instance, also depend upon the ability to construct an adversary whose interests can be defeated but must not be trampled upon. Even forms of para-persuasion such as strikes under modern labor rules—in which there is not much violence but in which the possibility of violence is one of the cards each side can play—involve engagement with the imagined more-or-less respectable agency of the other.

Nineteenth-century elections, especially in the South and West, often had an air of impending violence about them. Ballots were not secret, and each side tended to get its own voters roaring drunk and vote them en masse, so as to be able to face down the bullies brought by the other side who would attempt to keep them from the polls. Elections were often accompanied by cockfights and rough-and-tumble wrestling matches between supporters of opposing parties, not to mention attempts by gangs of toughs on each side to hack down the tall symbolic poles—talk about voting as a male affair!—each party would have erected, hickory for the Democrats (for Old Hickory, Andrew Jackson), and ash for the Whigs (for Henry Clay, the Sage of Ashland).[37]

Even war as Clausewitz imagined it—prosecuted by governments, for specified political ends, using a limited repertory of means—has something of this para-persuasive character. The faintest shadow of persuasive engagement only completely disappears in what one calls "a war of peoples,"—I am tempted to use the term "havoc" for such a war—in which contesting peoples just do not like each other's faces.[38]

No kind of war is more intractable than a war of peoples. For one thing, nobody is in a position to end this kind of war. To pick a now somewhat dated example, I know how to end a war with Serbia, but not how to end a war with "the Serbs." For another thing, such a war is prosecuted by actors who do not have normal agency. The government of Serbia has agency, and I know how to gain a promise from it and how to hold it to that promise. But nobody speaks for "the Serbs," yet at the same time every one of "the Croats" feels somehow that every Serb is responsible for what some Serb, acting in the name of "the Serbs," did to some other Croat, perhaps in the distant past, as if there were some kind of moral checkbook in the sky where every bad thing done by Serbs and Croats against each other is reckoned up, a checkbook in which each side mysteriously always has a positive balance.

For reasons that elude me, the morally apodictic style seems to be most available in wars of peoples, perhaps because the most notorious examples of such wars have usually involved religion. And the atrocity with which a war of peoples is prosecuted always seems to rise in proportion to the moral apodicticism each side uses to make its case to itself in that private arena in which it basks in the approval of God and history.

The fact that the sphere of persuasion is surrounded by nesting spheres of para-persuasion in which persuasion increasingly gives way to violence obviously itself plays a role in persuasion, because each party must know where their quarrel will reconvene if they cannot make a bargain where they are. But the same fact also plays a role in transforming conflicts so as to move away from violence toward persuasion, for in each variety of conflict short of people's war the opponents must construct some moral equivalent of "the respectable opponent," and the exercise of imagining that opponent's needs, what he or she cannot be asked to give up, keeps alive the possibility of persuasive engagement even in the midst of force. Only in the case of a war of peoples is persuasive engagement completely foreclosed, because only in the case of a war of peoples is the construct of the respectable opponent completely abandoned.

Even in circumstances where we find it impossible to construct a positive defense of the opponent's position, we must nevertheless be willing to consider the stakes of the quarrel from the opponent's point of view, if only so as to be able to ask of the opponent that course least likely to provoke him to making a last-ditch defense. Otherwise we risk the consequences of encouraging our opponent to believe that anything we might propose to do against him is permitted to us.

Failure of Persuasive Engagement

There are conditions under which persuasive engagement becomes impossible to maintain, and they are each in a way versions of the same thing: the fiction of the respectable opponent cannot be maintained, one can no longer define common appeals that are likely to reach the opponent, the issues between the interlocutors seem to involve metaphysical good or metaphysical evil, ground rules for regulating their engagement seem to have become unavailable, and the sacrifices each side demands of the other have become either morally or practically fatal ones.

Many of the means used to carry out persuasive engagement also corrupt persuasive engagement—appeals to high principle, for instance, often have this character, as do arguments about the ground rules, since in both cases a strong appeal and a foreclosing one are hard to distinguish. Sometimes the interlocutor really is not free to deal. Sometimes the interlocutor really is evil. Sometimes relations between parties really have come to a pass that the only thing they can appeal to is force. It may become clear in retrospect, but in the midst of a conflict it is often impossible to be certain, that the line has actually been irrevocably crossed. Neither philosophy nor politics—nothing except the immediate experience of the quarrel—is much help under circumstances where one is near that line, as all parties were after 1856. The choice of a course of behavior under those circumstances seems to come down to a wager. And it is a wager not only about a practical matter—will this course of action work out for me or not?—but even about a moral one: whether I am standing firm or behaving in a needlessly confrontational way, whether I am showing flexibility or unprincipled cowardice, is often not something that I am, in the midst of it, really in a position to know. Not just the outcomes but even the virtues of the agents are in such situations a wager.

Even in the best case we cannot be certain to avoid conflicts that, even among the most decent opponents, descend to violence, because we have no reason to believe that our deepest values—not just the values that separate the sides of the conflict but also the values both sides have in common—are consistent with each other. We can promise neither that we will come upon an acceptable arrangement to mediate conflicts over values nor that our own values or any set of values rich enough to apply to the circumstances of actual life are not themselves riven by deep contradictions that we will all too often experience as temptations to violence.

One way to describe political obligation is to see it as an obligation to politics itself. Because I cannot will for you, I must persuade you. Because I must persuade you, I must not do anything now that will make it impossible for me to persuade you later, either on this issue or on others. Because I must preserve a persuasive culture between us, I must sometimes concede things that are important to me, but only so long as that persuasive culture matters to me. One of the appealing things about the kind of nonviolent civil disobedience practiced by Gandhi and King is that it enables those who practice it to back away from explicit dealmaking politics when they are at an impasse or when they require morally impossible things, without completely destroying the possibility of a persuasive culture. It is a compelling solution to the problem of the natural tendency of idealism to project political conflicts into a world governed only by the metabolism of force. But it is not, perhaps, a solution that is always politically available.

When I am confronted with a stark contradiction between political and ethical obligation, it is often because the position I oppose strikes me as morally horrifying. Arguing for the priority of ethical over political obligation, I may argue that some positions are so beyond the pale of reasonable disagreement that I do not owe those who take those positions the respect that is the precondition of all moral cultures of bargaining and persuasion, and in fact I would be morally soiled if I were to offer such persons that respect. It does not take much stretching of the imagination to come up with such a beyond-the-pale position; the story of the last hundred years is the story of the murderous consequences of several such positions. But once I take the view that my opponent's position is beyond the pale of reasonable disagreement—a view I sometimes take, I am sorry to say, as a way to prove my own earnestness to myself or as a way to advance my own standing among those on my own side of the conflict at hand—I can only see my issue with my opponent as a conflict of force, and I must be prepared for the consequences.

Among those consequences may be defeat. That is an honorable, clean-hands outcome, perhaps, but it is also an outcome that arguably may leave the world in a worse state than I might have left it in by using other means, even those that soil the hands. This is why that maxim "Let God's Will be done, though the world perish" is usually cited in derision.

An even worse consequence of a contest of force with an enemy whom I think is beyond the moral pale might be a victory that transforms me in the winning into something I would rather not have become. This was the great fear of Union-loyal Democrats during the Civil War. Perhaps the most thoughtful of these Democrats was Herman Melville, who like many Union-loyal Democrats was hostile to slavery but also afraid that the war measures the Lincoln administration would be forced to adopt—not necessarily only out of an ambitious and repressive desire for power (although Melville feared this too) but also on account of the inexorable logic of force itself in a huge and hugely violent war—would forever subvert free government.

Democrats would point to the suppression of newspapers, the suspension of habeas corpus, the expulsion of the population of the Missouri-Kansas border area from their homes, the police apparatus that was deployed against dissenters (including the secret tabs that were kept on members of Melville's own family after the New York City Draft Riots), and the persecution of hapless idiots like President Pierce and General Stone (whose defeat at Ball's Bluff was widely attributed to treason, a suspicion that prompted the formation of the sinister Committee on the Conduct of the War, which eagerly looked for evidence of treason by other prominent Democrats, including General McClellan). When one compares these attacks upon civil liberties to those that have occurred in other civil wars, these attacks do not look like a systematic attempt to subvert free government. Mark Neely has recently argued that these abuses do not for the most part reflect merciless partisanship, although they are more profound than the abuses war has brought into play during later wars.[39] But the paranoid suspicions Democrats and Republicans entertained about each other were not entirely without foundation, especially given the tendency of paranoids in confrontation to confirm each other's worst nightmares, as Kingman Brewster once remarked.[40]

The general lesson, however, is this: even if I am driven by absolute ethical commitments, once I descend into a contest of force, my choice of what to be is limited. One good measure of how deeply we hold a moral principle may indeed be how immoral we are willing to be in its defense. If our enemies are so far beyond the pale of reasonable disagreement that they can only be seen as a kind of demonic force (as indeed many of the great movements of the last hundred years do in fact demand to be seen), then almost anything is permissible to prevent their triumph. It is hard not to be drawn into a kind of death spiral by that argument, because in the world that argument projects, scruples look like weakness of will or shallowness of commitment, and it is one's very virtues that most motivate acts that sober retrospects may find to be causes for shame and that cast discredit even upon good causes.

But even if I am no idealist, even if I never for a moment imagine myself to be the sword of God, once I am in conflict with a demonic power, I will be strongly tempted, and perhaps even driven by the iron logic of the conflict itself (what Clausewitz calls *wechselwirkung*), to demonic means. For an appalling evil demands, even from those who tend to see politics as for the most part a pragmatic arrangement among people with different but ordinary interests, an urgent moral response that can easily become tipped over into a kind of moral panic. Because it is the tendency of moral urgency to ratchet up the level of force that must be brought to bear in a conflict, it is the acts of morally serious people in the service of what most matters to them that most motivates the corrosive and unfair suspicion that history really is only a sphere of force and that moral motives are fairy tales cooked up by the winners. Because moral urgency has a way of transforming conflicts over ideas into tests of force, it also has a way of catapulting the decent pragmatist, no less than the idealist, into the very world that ideals are least able to survive in with his moral identity intact.[41]

In the at least partly amoral world in which we live, absolute moral commitments are subject to a dual irony. On one hand, because a severe morality must see its opponents as beyond the pale of persuasion and bargaining, that severe morality places one on a slippery slope to a world governed only by contests of force, a world in which only the strong, and not the good, can prosper. (In a nutshell, this is the strongest argument Douglas has against Lincoln.) The moral dogmatist, in ironic consequence of the willingness to draw lines in the sand that is the measure of his ideals, inevitably places himself in the same situation as the moral nihilist, who gleefully subjects himself to the devastating metabolism of force.

On the other hand, those who wish to keep open a space of engagement in which something other than force might decide the important questions also stand on a slippery slope to a world in which everything is negotiable and nothing cannot be bargained away. If we must, even at a price, create with our enemies a space of persuasion and bargaining in which each of us, however horrible we are, has the respect due to agency, then a truly committed enemy can always drive us to the wall by raising the price of engagement with him. (In a nutshell, this is the strongest argument Lincoln has against Douglas.)

It is not only malevolent and vicious figures who wind up talking themselves into positions that are beyond the pale; in an overheated political world, many kinds of people can be stampeded. But in concrete conflicts, whether they take such positions because they have been stampeded into doing so or whether they genuinely are as bad as our dark suspicions about them lead us to believe, we can risk treating our enemies as beyond the pale only if we have the force to have our way with them. No matter how horrible their convictions or acts may be, so long as we are not ready to kill or be killed, to risk everything in an absolute contest of force with no holds barred, we are still in the arena of persuasion and bargaining. It is not philosophy but force that draws the outer limits of persuasive arenas. And yet it is only philosophy that offers any alternative to force, and it is only philosophy that enables us to imagine a political world that is not in every way already bound to futility.

That it is willingness to resort to force that determines where the limits of what politics is capable of mediating are to be drawn seems embarrassing—as if politics were merely an attempt to make ad hoc sense of experiences that finally retain their character of randomness and inscrutability, and as if that ad hoc sense must finally rest on rationalization rather than reason. That *this* question but not *that* question is capable of a political resolution is a function not of the question itself but rather of just how ready we are to spring at each other's throats about it. Force determines what remains within politics to the extent that political opponents must be so willing to use force that they must take each other seriously but not so committed to force that they lose their terror not only about what will happen to them if they lose but also about what they will become if they win.

It is always tempting to put Douglas in Neville Chamberlain's class, as someone who attempted to make a deal with the devil to hold off war, and failed even at that. Surely it would have been both morally and pragmatically better to face the irrepressible conflict in a more head-on way? Yes, surely, now that I know how the struggle that view invites came out. But in forty-five years of struggle with Stalin and his heirs, whose acts were arguably in the same class as Hitler's, the West was not prepared to take so high a tone, because it knew what the outcome of a war with Stalin and his heirs would have been: in the best case a victory bought at the price of the destruction of the world.

In fact, the comparison, so often implied, is not really germane. Lincoln did not really follow a Churchillian policy of confrontation. And Douglas also did not follow a Chamberlain-like policy of appeasement. Both sought policies of containment, although only Lincoln made that policy a fully explicit one. Both resembled George F. Kennan more than either resembled Churchill or Chamberlain.

Political thought can manage but not resolve the contradiction between its view of human beings as moral agents and its view of human beings as objects of destiny and causality, its view of humans as capable of action and its view of humans only as exhibiting behavior. It must see human beings in an unstable middle state: they hold convictions and act on them, but are at the same time subject to folly and capable of fitful violations of morality that do not always destroy their moral identities, and they are subject also in some ways to destiny, capable of sacrificing entirely their capacity for freedom. The distinctive feature of practical reason—and the thing that distinguishes political agency from the cunning of the *homo economicus*—is that it makes an ethical account of itself and seeks to be held to that account. It wishes to be held to something other than strategic posturings for an ulterior end. But it is always in danger not only of mistaking one for the other but also of becoming insensitive to the difference. Politics seeks to discover in the phenomenal world the fittest condition for the realization of noumenal claims, but noumenal claims will always be unstable in a phenomenal world.

The failure of politics is force. The outer regions of politics increasingly take on the color of force. And force itself, and no rationality from within politics, no principle deeper than politics on which all contestants feel themselves bound to agree, draws the line outside of which politics cannot mediate a conflict. If it is force itself, and no rationality from within politics, that draws the limits to politics, then the fact that we are in a position to engage in politics at all is a lucky accident—a feature of destiny, not a feature of moral agency. At the same time, to concede that the possibility of politics is entirely the product of a lucky contingency is to undermine the seriousness of politics as a moral vocation. This is why it is hard to provide a consistent view of politics that is able to do justice to the dual responsibility politics has to the noumenal and to the phenomenal, to the teleological and to the causal.

Resort to the argument that one's opponent is beyond the moral pale has high prestige—it both certifies the moral credentials of those who make it and places the opponent in a very unenviable position. The prestige of that kind of argument is high enough that reasonable people are tempted to employ it whenever they are in a spot. But the argument also raises the stakes in such a way as to render conflicts that may be perfectly tractable by ordinary political means into stark confrontations between nonnegotiable positions. One uses such language best when one has to rally one's own side to a test of force that seems inevitable. But it is best to be sure that that test of force really is inevitable first, and the rhetorical prestige of that style of argument specifically clouds one's judgment about which conflicts are tractable and which are not. Indeed, the inevitability of a conflict of force is not in any obvious way always a function of the moral distance between opponents: it is simply not true that every abomination requires a war to eliminate it. The inevitability of a conflict is more often a function of the investments and resources both sides bring to the quarrel and a local history of conflict that unfolds in such a way as to discredit the normal procedures and institutions of persuasion and bargaining.

The problem here is that politics draws not only its problems but its principles from the world of contingency. It is because we live in a world liable to force and subject to force-drawn contingencies that we invent politics and hope for anything from it. And politics must reckon with force where it finds it, and cannot merely read it out of existence (like the mathematician who proved that the fire in his house was impossible). If the hope that politics embodies were a completely rational one to entertain, the fact that force draws the limits to politics would be a scandal. If this hope were a completely irrational one, however, the fact that politics so often descends to force would be no tragedy, since nothing that is a mere fact of nature can be a tragedy.

It is the work of politics to reclaim what it can of the public world from force. For politics to do this it must take a cold look at the public world, not conceding all of it to force, as if force were ultimately the only reality, but equally not asking more of principled argument and compromise (its two main instruments) than they can offer. If politics concedes the world to force, it becomes a counsel of despair. If politics pretends to envision a world without force, it immediately loses its role as the restrainer of force and becomes, blinded by its utopianism, an unwitting apologist for force. Politics can have no strength unless it sees clearly its weakness, for its strength is a clear sense of how ugly the consequences of its failure would be, and have been, and are.

CHAPTER 6

Douglas's Racial Equality Charge

*D*OUGLAS'S CHARGE THAT THE FOUNDERS of the Republican Party aimed to create an abolitionist party is false, although hostility to slavery was one of the new party's key convictions. Nor was the Republican Party in general, or Lincoln in particular, committed to racial equality, as Douglas charged of both. While confining slavery to the states where it already existed was intended to compromise its vitality, to "put it in the course of ultimate extinction," to cite Lincoln's oft-repeated phrase, this free soil policy posed no immediate threat to slavery, since the end of slavery envisioned under that policy may have been, as Lincoln remarked, as much as a hundred years off.[1]

That said, Lincoln managed his own case against the extension of slavery in such a way as to give color to the charge that, whether in acknowledged ways or not, racial equality would eventually be on the agenda. Despite repeated denials that he favored racial equality, Lincoln consistently chose the arguments that would lay the groundwork for racial equality later, and rejected arguments that would have supported preventing the spread of slavery into the territories but that would have ruled racial equality out. Making the case in moral rather than in political terms, as Lincoln, at a political price, insisted upon doing, would inevitably raise the question of the entailments of those moral commitments.

6.1 Lincoln's Nonextension Position and Anti-slavery

The 1837 Protest

Lincoln's basic position, which was never far from that adopted by the Republican Party during the prewar years, had been made clear during his time as a state representative, when, with Dan Stone, he submitted his March 1837 Protest on Slavery, in which he argued that Stone and Lincoln

> believe that the institution of slavery is founded on both injustice and bad policy; but that the promulgation of abolition doctrines tends to rather increase than to abate its evils.
>
> They believe that the Congress of the United States has no power, under the constitution, to interfere with the institution of slavery in the different States.
>
> They believe that the Congress of the United States has the power, under the constitution, to abolish slavery in the District of Columbia; but that that power ought not to be exercised unless at the request of the people of said District. (1:18)

The statement appears at first to be more ambiguous than it is, since on its face it has a "pox on both houses" way of condemning slavery and abolitionism in the same breath and even its proposal to end slavery in the District of Columbia is hedged about with impossible conditions.[2] At a time of hostility to abolition so profound that members of the Illinois legislature itself (including Usher Linder, to whose denunciation of abolitionism Lincoln and Stone were replying) would be whipping up the anti-abolitionist mobs that would murder the abolitionist editor Elijah Lovejoy in Alton that November, the denunciation of abolition was a rhetorically necessary preamble to any statement against slavery, a kind of protective coloration, as if Lincoln might have said, "Now I'm not an Abolitionist but . . ."[3] Stone and Lincoln were, after all, protesting anti-abolition measures, not anti-slavery measures, when they submitted their protest. More important than the hedging is the fact that in the face of all this the protest stuck to its guns about slavery as a moral evil and, what is more, that it stuck to its guns about the power of the Congress to abolish slavery in the District of

Columbia. The latter was a particularly fraught issue during the years of the gag rule that prevented Congress from even acknowledging that it had received petitions on the subject (southern representatives treated even consigning such petitions to an unconsidered death in committee as a kind of incitement to slave insurrection).[4] The protest announced that the authors may have had no plans to overturn slavery at the moment but that they intended to keep an eye out for circumstances that might enable them to do more. Lincoln and Stone were among only six legislators to oppose the anti-abolitionist resolution. Douglas was also in the legislature then, and voted for it.[5]

The Speed Letter

In the 1855 letter to his once-close friend Joshua Speed in which Lincoln tried to decide whether he was still a Whig, Lincoln provided some elaborating detail about his views of slavery.[6] Speed, like many Kentuckians, both owned slaves and professed dislike for slavery. Lincoln took Speed to task for only lukewarmly opposing the depredations of the pro-slavery Border Ruffians in Kansas that year. Speed had argued that although he would be happier were Kansas to enter the Union as a free state, if the current uproar in Kansas were to wind up making Kansas turn in a pro-slavery direction, he would support the dissolution of the Union rather than agree to allow opponents of slavery prevent its admission as a slave state. Speed wished the Border Ruffians to be hung but, Lincoln rather tartly remarked, would vote in the next election for their "exact type and representative." Lincoln felt that Speed rather underestimated the warmth of his feelings on the subject:

> I confess I hate to see the poor creatures hunted down, and caught, and carried back to their stripes, and unrewarded toils; but I bite my lip and keep quiet. In 1841 you and I had together a tedious low-water trip, on a Steam Boat from Louisville to St. Louis. You may remember, as I well do, that from Louisville to the mouth of the Ohio there were, on board, ten or a dozen slaves, shackled together with irons. That sight was a continual torment to me; and I see something like it every time I touch the Ohio, or any other slave-border. It is hardly fair for you to assume, that I have no interest in a thing which has, and continually exercises, the power of making me miserable. You

ought rather to appreciate how much the great body of the Northern people do crucify their feelings, in order to maintain their loyalty to the constitution and the Union. (1:360–361)

Lincoln's memory of this event in the 1855 letter is not entirely consonant with his account of it in a September 1841 letter to Mary Speed, Joshua's sister. There he remarked that the slaves, some of them being separated from their wives and children, and all of them bound in chains and headed for a place where slavery was harsher than in Kentucky, bore their misfortune with a cheerfulness that took him aback:

By the way, a fine example was presented on board the boat for contemplating the effect of *condition* upon human happiness. A gentleman had purchased twelve negroes in different parts of Kentucky and was taking them to a farm in the South. They were chained six and six together. A small iron clevis was around the left wrist of each, and this fastened to the main chain by a shorter one at a convenient distance from, the others; so that the negroes were strung together precisely like so many fish upon a trot-line. In this condition they were being separated forever from the scenes of their childhood, their friends, their fathers and mothers, and brothers and sisters, and many of them, from their wives and children, and going into perpetual slavery where the lash of the master is proverbially more ruthless and unrelenting than any other where; and yet amid all these distressing circumstances, as we would think them, they were the most cheerful and apparently happy creatures on board. One, whose offence for which he had been sold was an over-fondness for his wife, played the fiddle almost continually; and the others danced, sung, cracked jokes, and played various games with cards from day to day. How true it is that "God tempers the wind to the shorn lamb," or in other words, that He renders the worst of human conditions tolerable, while He permits the best, to be nothing better than tolerable. (1:74–75)

It would be a mistake, however, to use this passage to cast doubt on the sincerity of the convictions in the later letter to Speed.[7] Events often have many layers, and what they really mean is sometimes not available until a much later retrospect. Indeed, the fact that Lincoln reverted at all to the incident fourteen years later argues that it must in some sense have meant to him even in 1841 what he said in 1855 it meant to him, even if, like many people, he did not acknowledge as much at the time.[8] The deepest meanings of experience are often not available until later reflection; at the time of the actual experience their meanings are obscured by rationalization, mixed motives, and other conflicting agendas. It is quite plausible that only in a long retrospect did Lincoln puzzle out what the 1841 experience really meant to him; indeed, it is characteristic of experiences that have an implicit dimension that they do not make their meanings available at short range.

The Durley Letter

In 1845, Lincoln wrote to his friends Williamson and Madison Durley, twitting them for their support for the Liberty Party. Lincoln praised them for their attempt to bring about a local fusion of the Whig and Liberty tickets, but he could not resist noting that the Liberty Party's refusal to support the Whig anti-slavery slaveholder Henry Clay in New York in 1844 had given that state's electoral vote to the Democrats, elected Polk, and brought about the annexation of Texas, which both the Whigs and the Liberty men had opposed. Polk's election also wound up leading to war with Mexico, to the conquest of the Mexican Cession, to the exacerbation of the slavery question concerning the territories, and to a whole host of other evils. Polk's election was a parting of the ways in American history, and had a few thousand Liberty men swallowed their distaste for Clay as a slaveholder, it is imaginable that American history would have taken a very different course. In the Durley letter the Liberty men's inability to engage the views of an anti-slavery slaveholder like Clay, whose position, while morally ambiguous, was still, relative to the position of Polk and the Democrats, rather more than merely the lesser of two evils, seemed to Lincoln a paradigmatic example of suicidal adherence to principle:

> If the whig abolitionists of New York had voted with us last fall, Mr. Clay would now be president, whig principles in the ascendent, and Texas not annexed; whereas by the division, all that either had at stake in the contest, was lost. And, indeed, it was extremely probable, beforehand, that such would be the result. As I always understood, the Liberty-men deprecated the annexation of Texas extremely; and,

this being so, why they should refuse to so cast their votes as to prevent it, even to me, seemed wonderful. What was their process of reasoning, I can only judge from what a single one of them told me. It was this: "We are not to do *evil* that *good* may come." This general, proposition is doubtless correct; but did it apply? If by your votes you could have prevented the *extention*, &c. of slavery, would it not have been *good* and not *evil* so to have used your votes, even though it involved the casting of them for a slaveholder? By the *fruit* the tree is to be known. An *evil* tree can not bring forth *good* fruit. If the fruit of electing Mr. Clay would have been to prevent the extension of slavery, could the act of electing have been *evil*? (1:111–112)

The moral purity, and in Lincoln's view the moral narcissism, of the Liberty men put them in a class with the angry temperance crusaders he had attacked in his Temperance address of 1842. In their furious self-righteousness, the old-style temperance crusaders' very moral earnestness drove the alcoholics they should have sought to redeem away from them, as if the purity of their temperance convictions mattered more to them than putting those convictions to work.

Lincoln was not as vehement on the subject of extension of slavery in the Durley letter as he became at the time of the Wilmot Proviso debates (and particularly after the Kansas-Nebraska Act), arguing here, somewhat naively, that taking a slave to Texas removed a slave from somewhere else and so did not in fact increase the power of slavery. Having made that demurral, however, he took a position that became his trademark after 1854:

I hold it to be a paramount duty of us in the free states, due to the Union of the states, and perhaps to liberty itself (paradox though it may seem) to let the slavery of the other states alone; while, on the other hand, I hold it to be equally clear, that we should never knowingly lend ourselves directly or indirectly, to prevent that slavery from dying a natural death—to find new places for it to live in, when it can no longer exist in the old. (1:111–112)

The Bailey *and* Matson *Cases*

These convictions did not, however, prevent Lincoln in 1847 from taking the case of Robert Matson, a Kentucky slaveholder who had brought one of his female slaves to work in Illinois for two years, after which she sued for freedom.[9] Lincoln's argument in the *Matson* case ran somewhat against his argument in his only other famous slavery case, *Bailey v. Cromwell* of 1841, in which he had successfully argued that the state must presume that black people within its jurisdiction are free until proven otherwise and that a slave is made free when transported into free Illinois. Neither the opposing counsel nor the judge in the *Matson* case cited the *Bailey* case, which is curious because the judge's final opinion followed the *Bailey* case's reasoning, and it would have been particularly devastating to have cited Matson's attorney against Matson's case. But the opposing counsels, Orlando B. Ficklin and Charles Constable, Ficklin reported later, took pleasure in making Lincoln squirm by quoting John Philpot Curran's defense of Rowan, which itself seems to allude to the precedent of the *Somerset* case:

> I speak in the spirit of the British law, which makes liberty commensurate with and inseparable from British soil; which proclaims even to the stranger and sojourner the moment he sets foot upon British earth, that the ground upon which he treads is holy and consecrated by the genius of universal emancipation, no matter in what language his doom may have been pronounced; no matter what complexion incompatible with freedom an Indian or African sun may have burned upon him, no matter in what disastrous battle his liberty may have been cloven down; no matter with what solemnities he may have been devoted upon the altar of slavery; the first moment he touches the sacred soil of Britain the altar and the gods sink together in the dust his soul walks abroad in her own majesty; his body swells beyond the measure of his chains that burst from round him and he stands regenerated and disenthralled by the irresistible genius of universal emancipation.[10]

The *Matson* case resembles the *Dred Scott* case, not only in its details (turning as it did upon the question of whether residence in a free state emancipated a slave who had been brought there) but also in the personal entanglements of the principals. Jane Bryant, Matson's slave, had been brought to Illinois in order to accompany her husband, Anthony Bryant, a free black man who worked a farm owned by Matson. Anthony Bryant had become free as a consequence of long residence in Illinois, but apparently he still believed he was a slave of Matson's, since nobody had told him otherwise and he had never been given free papers. Once in Illinois, Jane Bryant fell out with Mary Corbin, Matson's mistress and housekeeper (with whom Matson lived "in more or less respectable sin"),[11] and Mary threatened to have her lover sell Jane. Anthony Bryant, his wife, and their four children sought shelter with the abolitionists Gideon M. Ashmore and Dr. Hiram Rutherford. Matson hired Usher Linder, a longtime Illinois political figure (and, the reader will remember, one of the people who whipped up the mob in Alton to murder Elijah Lovejoy) to use Illinois's notorious Black Laws, which forbade free blacks from living in the state and provided for the sale into slavery of any black who did not have free papers ready to hand, to compel Ashmore and Rutherford, who were also charged with "enticement" of fugitive slaves, to deliver Jane Bryant and the four children up to Matson.[12] Linder hired Lincoln, who happened to be in Charleston, as co-counsel. Ashmore and Rutherford concurrently brought a habeas corpus case on Jane Bryant's behalf. Their attorney, Orlando B. Ficklin, also approached Lincoln about being co-counsel in the case, but Lincoln was already committed to Linder.

Lincoln lost, but did not "throw," the *Matson* case. The Court took the view that an extended residence in a free state (as opposed to a brief sojourn) had the effect of emancipating slaves brought to those states. Lincoln, who represented his client ably and vigorously, had conceded that if Bryant had been brought to Illinois to live she would have been freed by the Northwest Ordinance (and for that matter by the Illinois Constitution). He argued instead that her two-year stay in Coles County—a county named for the governor, and protégé of Jefferson, who more than anyone else was responsible for keeping slavery out of Illinois—amounted to an extended visit rather than a residence. Now Matson had indeed made, as Lincoln pointed out, efforts to make his transportation of slaves in and out of Illinois take on the aspect of so-journing rather than of residence—he would be sure to move them back to Bourbon County, Kentucky, every fall after harvest time, and would arrange to swear before witnesses that he was only bringing his slaves in temporarily each spring when he brought them back in—but clearly the judge saw through the pretense.

When Lincoln lost the case, Matson left the state without, accord-ing to David Herbert Donald, paying his legal fees.[13] Donald argues that the case means that Lincoln's primary loyalty was to law, which

makes his conduct of this case consonant with his loyalty to the Constitution as an anti-slavery politician later, and consonant with his
claim in the 1864 Hodges letter that he did not put his primary abstract hostility to slavery above his loyalty to the Union in issuing the
Emancipation Proclamation. Well, perhaps. Anton-Hermann Chroust
argues, persuasively I think, that Lincoln's ambition to take a big
"case," particularly one in which he was brought in at the last minute
by a somewhat bigger legal shot, outweighed whatever feeling he had
about slavery. The most one can say about this case is that Lincoln's
views of his moral position as an attorney were different from those
about his moral position as a citizen or as a politician; that is of course
true of all attorneys, and indeed representing unsavory clients in weak
cases is sometimes taken to be a kind of moral duty among attorneys.

Lincoln's Hostility to Racial Equality

As we have seen, Lincoln had denied any aim of producing political or
social equality for black and white as early as the Peoria speech, and he
repeated the language from the Peoria speech in the Ottawa debate.
He used rather stronger language in the Charleston debate, which is
worth quoting in extenso:

> While I was at the hotel to-day, an elderly gentleman called upon me
> to know whether I was really in favor of producing a perfect equality
> between the negroes and white people. [Great Laughter.] While I
> had not proposed to myself on this occasion to say much on that sub-
> ject, yet as the question was asked me I thought I would occupy per-
> haps five minutes in saying something in regard to it. I will say then
> that I am not, nor ever have been, in favor of bringing about in any
> way the social and political equality of the white and black races,
> [applause]—that I am not nor ever have been in favor of making vot-
> ers or jurors of negroes, nor of qualifying them to hold office, nor to
> intermarry with white people; and I will say in addition to this that
> there is a physical difference between the white and black races
> which I believe will forever forbid the two races living together on
> terms of social and political equality. And inasmuch as they cannot
> so live, while they do remain together there must be the position of
> superior and inferior, and I as much as any other man am in favor of

having the superior position assigned to the white race. I say upon this occasion I do not perceive that because the white man is to have the superior position the negro should be denied every thing. I do not understand that because I do not want a negro woman for a slave I must necessarily want her for a wife. [Cheers and laughter.] My understanding is that I can just let her alone. I am now in my fiftieth year, and I certainly never have had a black woman for either a slave or a wife. So it seems to me quite possible for us to get along without making either slaves or wives of negroes. I will add to this that I have never seen, to my knowledge, a man, woman or child who was in favor of producing a perfect equality, social and political, between negroes and white men. I recollect of but one distinguished instance that I ever heard of so frequently as to be entirely satisfied of its correctness— and that is the case of Judge Douglas's old friend Col. Richard M. Johnson. [Laughter.] I will also add to the remarks I have made (for I am not going to enter at large upon this subject,) that I have never had the least apprehension that I or my friends would marry negroes if there was no law to keep them from it, [laughter] but as Judge Douglas and his friends seem to be in great apprehension that they might, if there were no law to keep them from it, [roars of laughter] I give him the most solemn pledge that I will to the very last stand by the law of this State, which forbids the marrying of white people with negroes. [Continued laughter and applause.] (1:636–637)

Now as far as actual policy goes, this is not very different from the remarks in the Peoria speech. What is missing here is the grudging quality of Lincoln's own racism; in the Peoria speech he had treated his racial feelings as nothing to be proud of, as an instance of a deeply set revulsion that could not be changed overnight by will and that would therefore have to be reckoned with, if only in the way that other deeply set bad habits have to be reckoned with. The tone here is different, and the mean playfulness of Lincoln's tone here sets up the brief role-reversal I discuss in section 6.2 below, in which Douglas, noticing the difference between the Peoria and Charleston speeches, took Lincoln to task for his racism.[14]

Even in the Charleston debate, it is worth noting that Lincoln did not precisely say that black people are in fact inferior, only that if one group is going to be in charge he would just as soon it be his own group, and his views reflect the natural partiality of one group for its own rather than a fully fledged theory about the natural hierarchy of the races. That said, what stands in the way of social equality in the Charleston speech was not, as in the Peoria speech (or even in the startlingly crude and tactless remarks he made in 1862 to a group of African American clergymen about colonization, remarks he made while the Emancipation Proclamation was sitting in his desk, awaiting the battlefield victory that would make it possible to be issued), a bad history charged with complicated and hard-to-live-down resentments, but a crude physical difference and a simple physical revulsion.

Probably the reason the Charleston speech resorted to this repellent shorthand was that the real focus of the passage was on the sexual rather than on the political aspect of the question. Douglas had played the sexual card in the Freeport debate, and Lincoln had to find a way to blunt Douglas's charge. He did this by reducing the charge to a claim about his own sexual desires: "I do not understand that because I do not want a negro woman for a slave I must necessarily want her for a wife." The effect of this was to turn the charge around, to say, in effect, "If you take such an obsessive interest in this question, it must be something about the state of your own sexual tastes that leads you to take it." He treated sexual desire across racial lines as so perverse that only someone in the grip of that perversion would be interested enough in it to seek to outlaw it. That is a rhetorical trick, of course, not an argument. And the price of the trick is Lincoln's support for anti-intermarriage laws. Anti-intermarriage laws seem to be drawn from a different deck from the laws concerning limitations of rights to vote or hold office, since these latter involve limitations that apply to other groups (such as women or, in most states, unnaturalized aliens), and do not have their foundation, as anti-intermarriage laws by nature must, in brute physical revulsion.

Even at Charleston Lincoln did not anticipate denying blacks the right to own property, to testify, to sue, to make contracts, and so forth; he denied political rights, but not civil rights of a nonpolitical kind. (By "political" here I mean "concerning access to public deliberative bodies," whether as officeholders, voters, or jurors, using the narrow definition of that term that prevailed in the nineteenth century rather than the broader one that prevails now.) But the right to marry is a nonpolitical civil right, like those Lincoln allowed to black people,

not a political right like those he denied them. There is a consistent, if
ugly, way to grant private civil rights and to withhold public political
ones, but there is not a consistent way to grant some private civil rights
and to withhold others. Lincoln's argument was distorted and inconsistent, because he found it politically necessary to cater to an ugly but
intractable sexual and racial prejudice, and would sacrifice consistency
to that necessity.

Lincoln's mention of Martin Van Buren's vice president, Richard
Mentor Johnson of Kentucky, is interesting for what it did not say.
Lincoln could have had a trumping reply to the sexual charge, but he
did not use it, although it is an obvious one that must have occurred
to everyone in the audience: if you really feel horror about interracial
sexual relations, then do not put female slaves in the power of their
masters. That kind of charge had long been a staple of anti-slavery
propaganda (most memorably in Weld's *American Slavery as It Is*
[1839]), and arguments about the sexual escapades of one of the most
famous of political masters, Thomas Jefferson, had been made by his
political opponents (led by James Callender), even during the struggles of the first party system.

One may counter that in the public mind the exploitation of black
women by white men was a different matter from sexual relations between black men and white women. One can grant that difference,
without granting at the same time that the former was not also a fraught
issue; exploitation of enslaved black women could not have played such a
role in anti-slavery literature if it were not an issue to more than only
abolitionists. If the exploitation of enslaved black women by white masters were not a fraught issue for white people, it would not have brought
forth the paroxysms of enraged and implausible denial that such charges
always provoked from defenders of slavery. Sexual relations between
black men and white women may have been the stuff of nightmares to
white people north and south. But the repeated charge that white masters exploited black women also deeply rankled even southerners like
James Henry Hammond, who knew from his own case that those
charges were true. Mary Chesnut may have resented the implication
that plantations were a kind of harem (her comparison), but she also
knew of, and was scandalized by, many cases where the master's young
servants bore undeniable resemblances to him. Indeed, what provoked
Preston Brooks to beat Charles Sumner unconscious on the Senate

floor in May 1856 after the latter delivered his "Crime against Kansas" speech was Sumner's oblique implication (a very oblique implication, it seems to me) that Brooks's uncle, Senator Andrew Butler of South Carolina, had taken a slave mistress.

For Lincoln to have made the sexual argument would have been inflammatory, but it would have been pretty much in the mainstream of anti-slavery opinion, and would in fact have merely repeated what was a commonplace about slavery even outside abolitionist circles. But Lincoln's example, Richard Mentor Johnson, was not exactly a master who sexually exploited his female slaves. Johnson lived openly with his father's slave Julia Chinn (until her death from cholera in 1833), whom he treated publicly as his wife in all but name, and by whom he had two children, whom he educated, attempted to introduce into society, and saw into marriage with white men, upon whom Johnson settled some property. Johnson proved a political liability to Van Buren in the South, where opponents portrayed Johnson, implausibly, as a living example of the practical consequences of abolition (to quote the U.S. Senate's Web page about him). Now Johnson was no friend of abolition, and his story is a tangled and complicated one that perhaps even William Faulkner could not make sense of, but Johnson's story is not the story of sexually aggressive mastership either. Lincoln told this story *in place of* the predatory master story, perhaps only to show that if white men really do take black women for wives, it was a Democratic politician, not any Republican or abolitionist, who showed them the way.

Lincoln could have gone considerably further, and in his speech on the *Dred Scott* decision back on June 26, 1857, he had approached the issue more directly:

> But Judge Douglas is especially horrified at the thought of the mixing blood by the white and black races: agreed for once—a thousand times agreed. There are white men enough to marry all the white women, and black men enough to marry all the black women; and so let them be married. On this point we fully agree with the Judge; and when he shall show that his policy is better adapted to prevent amalgamation than ours we shall drop ours, and adopt his. Let us see. In 1850 there were in the United States, 405,751, mulattoes. Very few of these are the offspring of whites and *free* blacks; nearly all have sprung from black *slaves* and white masters. (1:400–401)

If Lincoln telegraphed a punch, then pulled the punch, on the racial/ sexual charge, he also never quite allowed himself to go all the way in making concessions to racist feeling. In the debates, whenever Lincoln made a racist remark, he then qualified it somewhat: "I say upon this occasion I do not perceive that because the white man is to have the superior position the negro should be denied every thing" (1:636). This remark was unelaborated at Charleston, but developed in detail at Ottawa:

> I hold that, notwithstanding all this, there is no reason in the world why the negro is not entitled to all the natural rights enumerated in the Declaration of Independence, the right to life, liberty, and the pursuit of happiness. [Loud cheers.] I hold that he is as much entitled to these as the white man. I agree with Judge Douglas he is not my equal in many respects—certainly not in color, perhaps not in moral or intellectual endowment. But in the right to eat the bread, without the leave of anybody else, which his own hand earns, *he is my equal and the equal of Judge Douglas, and the equal of every living man.* [Great applause.] (1:512)

In practical terms, what Lincoln envisioned here in the nation as a whole was not much different from what Douglas envisioned for Illinois: black people will not have citizenship rights, but will not be slaves. Lincoln was rather more explicit than Douglas was in claiming that he saw black people as enjoying most of the same private rights white people do—although even Douglas never said that black people should not own property, make contracts, inherit, testify in court, and so on. It would be interesting to know what Douglas thought about access to public education for black people, but it also must be remembered that at that time outside of the Northeast public education was not always a given for white people either. We do know that during the war Lincoln came to favor access to public education for black people, because, as he wrote General Banks, who then led the army in Louisiana, if Louisiana, having freed its slaves, is to "adopt some practical system by which the two races could gradually live themselves out of their old relation to each other, and both come out better prepared for the new," then "education for young blacks should be included in the plan."[15] But we do not know whether Lincoln thought this way in 1858.

Like much else about the post-slavery future, Lincoln simply seems to have put off thinking about it. Too much thought about what the post-slavery future would require would have endangered the anti-slavery movement anyway.

There is a large difference between the music of Lincoln's statement and the music of Douglas's, which implies an underlying difference in stance as well. Lincoln bluntly used the language of the Declaration of Independence, indeed emphasized it rhetorically. His aim here was to argue that the rights of black people are not merely humane concessions by white people, as Douglas would have it, but something black people have a claim to by virtue of the promises of the Declaration. Indeed, Lincoln's use of the rhetoric of the Declaration set up the later argument he and Douglas had about whether the Founders, or Thomas Jefferson, really meant those promises to apply to everyone. What is more, the sweep of Lincoln's rhetorical gesture here, as Douglas was well aware, could not help covering a great deal more than the comparatively piddling rights Lincoln was willing to enumerate for black people. The emphatic tone of the last sentence is the measure of a kind of moral pressure that would carry Lincoln far beyond the small-bore uses for which he was at the moment employing it. Lincoln denied this, perhaps sincerely (within the tangle of motivations that all intentions reduce to upon analysis), but Douglas noticed the implications of Lincoln's argument, and he was right to do so. If the intensity of Lincoln's turn of phrase here was not designed to prepare the public mind for a post-slavery future, it was at the very least designed to prepare his own.

Lincoln's Compensated Emancipation Plans

Gradual, compensated emancipation plans, usually accompanied by voluntary colonization, were a feature of Lincoln's thinking about slavery from early on. His program, and his rationale for it, was essentially complete in the 1852 eulogy for Clay, which is treated in greater detail below, and even included a defense against the charge that colonization is merely a form of what we now call ethnic cleansing. He developed his thinking at length in the Peoria speech, as we saw in Chapter 2.

Even the compensated emancipation plans that Lincoln himself proposed, such as the plan he developed during his term in Congress for emancipation in the District of Columbia, or his wartime plan for the loyal slave states of Delaware, Maryland, Kentucky, and Missouri, envisioned only a gradual end to slavery. The 1849 bill for the District of Columbia, for instance, proposed immediate freedom only for children born after 1850, and apprenticeship for those children in the households of their mothers' masters until they reached adulthood; existing adult slaves would have been freed only at the discretion of masters who chose to accept compensation for emancipating them.[16] The bill also provided that no new slaves would be brought into the District, and that no current slave in the District could be sold out of it; the latter feature was designed to prevent masters from selling their young slaves before they came of age to be freed by the act, an ugly aspect of *post-nati* emancipation in the northern states. Finally, the bill required that emancipation be contingent upon the outcome of a referendum among the voters of the District. Of this last requirement, Wendell Phillips remarked that Lincoln "should be, perhaps, in favor of gradual abolition, when the slave-holders of the district asked for it! Of course he would. I doubt there is a man throughout the whole South who would not go so far as that."[17]

The draft of an emancipation bill that Lincoln drew up in November 1861 for the Delaware legislature, but that was never introduced there, did not propose to end slavery completely until 1893, although it would free all those born after the passage of the act (subject to apprenticeship during childhood), and all other slaves upon reaching the age of thirty-five, with the state (not the masters) receiving compensation from the federal government for the slaves. A gradual elimination of slavery, brought about by nonextension, was also a feature of the Peoria speech, as we saw in Chapter 2. Compensation was a feature of the emancipation proposals Lincoln presented for the loyal slave states even after the Emancipation Proclamation. Gradualism, compensation, and colonization were consistent features of Lincoln's thinking about emancipation throughout the prewar period. But all of these were proposals he thought of as more or less wishful; the policy he was willing to fight for, because he thought it might have a chance of coming into force, was nonextension.

The Eulogy for Henry Clay

Lincoln developed his early thinking about colonization in the eulogy for Henry Clay he delivered at Springfield on July 6, 1852. His first reference to colonization in the speech was an oblique one. Describing Clay's role in resolving the Missouri crisis, Lincoln quoted extensively from Jefferson's "Fire Bell in the Night" letter to John Holmes of April 22, 1820. Jefferson in that letter had lamented that the Missouri crisis had divided the union at a geographical line. Such a line, Jefferson had written, "co-inciding with a marked principle, moral and political, once conceived, and held up to the angry passions of men, will never be obliterated; and every irritation will mark it deeper and deeper." Jefferson heard in the conflict over slavery the "knell of the union," and even the resolution of the Missouri crisis had yielded, in Jefferson's view, "a reprieve only, not a final sentence."

Faced with the Missouri crisis, Jefferson professed (with a fatal qualification) that he would be willing to incur all of the economic losses the end of slavery would require without complaint, but only if the freed slaves could be expatriated so as to no longer be a source of political conflict in the Union. When Jefferson compared his situation to that of a man with "a wolf by the ears," he was referring not, as he is usually taken to be, to the difficulty of ending slavery itself, but to the difficulty of carrying out expatriation of former slaves. He assumed that it would be impossible for former slaves and former masters to share a republic with each other, and he was daunted by the difficulties of separating them from each other. The crux, this is to say, for Jefferson, was not emancipation but expatriation, and it was not so much the fear of the economic costs of emancipation as the fear of an integrated society, which drove him to the brink of endorsing ethnic cleansing:

> The cession of that kind of property, for so it is misnamed, is a bagatelle which would not cost me a second thought, if, in that way, a general emancipation, and *expatriation* could be effected; and, gradually, and with due sacrifices I think it might be. But as it is, we have the wolf by the ears and we can neither hold him, nor safely let him go. Justice is in one scale, and self-preservation in the other. (cited in 1:267)

It is important to pick up some of the nuances and ambivalences in the passage Lincoln quoted, because they cast light on Lincoln's own ambivalences about colonization. Jefferson treated the economic cost of emancipation as no more than a bagatelle, but he did this perhaps only to emphasize the gravity of the problem of how master and slave might live together after emancipation. Somewhat wishfully, Jefferson went on to say that *imaginably*, with gradualness and "due sacrifices" a colonization policy *might* come into force. The nearly hysterical thrust of the argument was: we must preserve slavery even though we despise it because we cannot manage colonization and we cannot live with our former slaves. Colonization was intended even by Jefferson here as a kind of magic spell to ward off racial panic, but even as he intoned the spell he knew that it would be ineffective, and he intoned it only so that he did not have to avow more directly what he in fact had just avowed indirectly: that slavery must continue because he could not think of a good way to end it.[18]

Lincoln's own extended treatment of colonization in the 1854 Peoria speech (to recap) had this same off-center, off-kilter quality as Jefferson's treatment in the "Fire Bell in the Night" letter. The immediate context of the discussion of colonization in the Peoria speech had been his acknowledgment that the southern people are no more responsible for the introduction of slavery than the northern people are, and that the institution is so deeply entrenched that it is hard to get rid of: "I surely will not blame them for not doing what I should not know how to do myself. If all earthly power were given me, I should not know what to do, as to the existing institution" (1:316). Lincoln then developed three possible courses: emancipation with colonization, emancipation without colonization but with the free slaves remaining as a subject class, and emancipation with political and social equality. All three solutions seemed to Lincoln in the Peoria speech to have fatal problems. Colonization has fatal practical problems (the colonists, Lincoln says, would most likely starve in Liberia). Of keeping the freed slaves as underlings, Lincoln remarked, "Is it quite certain that this betters their condition?" (1:316). (As far as he, personally, was concerned, Lincoln adds, this condition is still better than slavery, but not so obviously much better that Lincoln would feel free to denounce the other side for thinking differently.) Of the alternative of freeing the slaves and making them the political and social equals of their former masters, Lincoln said, as we have seen, that "My own feelings will not admit of this; and if mine would, we well know that those of the great mass of white people will not" (1:316). Lincoln conceded that that feeling is wrong, that it does not "[accord] with justice and sound judgment," but at the same time he also conceded, "A universal feeling, whether well or ill-founded, can not be safely disregarded" (1:316).

Lincoln mentioned colonization in the Peoria speech, this is to say, mostly to claim that it was an unworkable notion and that, because all of the other available alternatives were also unworkable, he did not feel he had the right to make a morally stringent denunciation of slaveholders, however much he faulted them for not thinking harder about other possibilities: "It does seem to me that systems of gradual emancipation might be adopted; but for their tardiness in this, I will not undertake to judge our brethren of the south" (1:316). Lincoln's demonstration of the difficulty faced by all of the alternative methods of emancipation was meant to show that he did not intend to score a morally easy point at slaveholder expense. And Lincoln, in turn, ruled out a frontal attack on slavery itself in the Peoria speech, because he wished to focus on what seemed to him to be the main point, the separate but related issue of whether slavery should be allowed to go into the Kansas and Nebraska Territories, an issue in which the future of slavery was at stake but that did not involve a direct attack upon slaveholders.

Like Jefferson in the "Fire Bell in the Night" letter, Lincoln's thinking about colonization in the Peoria speech was meant simply as a demonstration of how intractable the problem of ending slavery was. But there was, of course, a crucial difference: Jefferson's letter smells throughout of panicked flurry, alternating between defensiveness and hysteria. Lincoln's speech, by contrast, was, for all the limitations of its thinking, soberly and sadly fair-minded. Jefferson's letter was meant to foreclose his own emancipationist habit of thinking. Lincoln's concessions were meant to chasten his temptation to judge his slaveholding opponents but also to keep an eye out, in the midst of his acknowledgment of the difficulty of the problem, for a way to end slavery after all, in spite of all the difficulties.

Having brushed on Jefferson's response to the Missouri crisis, Lincoln did not develop the theme of colonization at this point in the elegy for Clay, but focused instead upon how Clay managed to pass the Missouri compromises. Each side in Congress in the Missouri crisis felt that the survival of the Union was at stake in the question. Neither side wished to destroy the Union. But the political logic of the conflict hardened their positions, and did so even against their better judgment. The quarrel, this is to say, had its own logic and its own force, apart from the intentions of those engaged in the quarrel, because it put those who wished for compromise in impossible political positions. Each side

knew it must cut a deal. Each side wished to cut a deal. But the unfolding of the conflict kept foreclosing any deal:

> All felt that the rejection of Missouri, was equivalent to a dissolution
> of the Union: because those states which already had, what Missouri
> was rejected for refusing to relinquish, would go with Missouri. All
> deprecated and deplored this, but none saw how to avert it. For the
> judgment of the Members to be convinced of the necessity of yield-
> ing, was not the whole difficulty; each had a constituency to meet,
> and to answer to. (1:268)

Lincoln's point here was complex. He did not only mean (although
he did mean) that the members of Congress lacked the courage to pay
the political price of supporting compromise. He also meant that, as
representatives, they were not completely free to support compromise
measures that they knew their constituents opposed. The problem was
the traditional problem of representative democracy, whether the representative is meant to represent the will of the constituency or is instead chosen by the constituency to use his or her own best prudential
judgment, even in the face of the will of the people. Lincoln's language
about a conflict having a logic that overpowers even the intentions of
those engaged in the conflict anticipated the argument he made in the
early paragraphs of the Second Inaugural Address, when he recapped
the failed efforts to produce a political compromise during the secession winter of 1860–1861: "Both parties deprecated war; but one of
them would make war rather than let the nation survive; and the other
would accept war rather than let it perish. And the war came."

Clay solved the problem by dividing the compromise measures, so
that nobody would have to vote for something his constituents opposed, with the minority of people who actually had a license to compromise providing the balance of power for each side of the compromise. This provided practical cover for those who favored compromise
but represented districts that opposed it. Lincoln did not mention that
this was precisely the strategy Stephen Douglas had used to pass the
compromise measures of 1850.

Lincoln's treatment of Clay's role in the nullification crisis, and in
the Compromise of 1850, was abbreviated. But Lincoln wished to make
it as clear as possible that Clay was very deeply an anti-slavery politi-

cian, although a slaveholder, and indeed in Lincoln's account he comes off rather better than Jefferson does:

> The very earliest, and one of the latest public efforts of his life, separated by a period of more than fifty years, were both made in favor of gradual emancipation of the slaves in Kentucky. He did not perceive, that on a question of human right, the negroes were to be excepted from the human race. And yet Mr. Clay was the owner of slaves. Cast into life where slavery was already widely spread and deeply seated, he did not perceive, as I think no wise man has perceived, how it could be at *once* eradicated, without producing a greater evil, even to the cause of human liberty itself. (1:268–269)

Jefferson prevented slavery from invading the Old Northwest, but Clay by contrast repeatedly sought to end it in his own state. Jefferson was kept from pressing for emancipation by fear of living with his former slaves, Clay by fear of unleashing a civil war that might put an end to free government. Like Lincoln himself, Clay was described as seeking to act effectively against slavery while resisting pressure from slaveholders, on one side, and from reckless opponents of slavery on the other (Lincoln all but named Garrison). Notice how even here, as in the 1835 protest, Lincoln had to begin with a defensive claim that neither he nor Clay was one of those abolitionist types who would burn the Constitution or (what abolitionist ever actually threatened this?) the Bible:

> His feeling and his judgment, therefore, ever led him to oppose both extremes of opinion on the subject. Those who would shiver into fragments the Union of these States; tear to tatters its now venerated constitution; and even burn the last copy of the Bible, rather than slavery should continue a single hour, together with all their more halting sympathizers, have received, and are receiving their just execration; and the name, and opinions, and influence of Mr. Clay, are fully, and, as I trust, effectually and enduringly, arrayed against them. But I would also, if I could, array his name, opinions, and influence against the opposite extreme—against a few, but an increasing number of men, who, for the sake of perpetuating slavery, are beginning to assail and to ridicule the white man's charter of freedom—the declaration that "all men are created free and equal." (1:269)

If the abolitionists burn the Constitution, the defenders of slavery burn the Declaration. Clay's task, like Lincoln's, was to harmonize the contradictions between the Republic's two founding documents, to find a way, without breaking the Constitution, to bring the promises of the Declaration into effect.

Lincoln in the Clay eulogy, as in the debates, argued that what was at stake in the slavery issue was the meaning of the Declaration. Against Douglas in the debates, Lincoln argued that the promise of equality applied to black and white alike. Against Calhoun, who was the real target of this passage, Lincoln in the Clay eulogy defended the idea that political equality has any meaning at all. (The distinction between Douglas's views and Calhoun's is developed in greater detail in Chapter 7.) This passage is an early instance of Lincoln's claim that the future of freedom was at stake in the struggle over slavery, and that those who defend slavery in itself must attack the Declaration of Independence, because slavery and liberty cannot coexist forever.

Lincoln pointed with alarm to the spread of the attack upon the promise of equality, citing Calhoun's classic attack upon it in his speech about the admission of Oregon (which we will also discuss in more detail in Chapter 7) and recent messages by other South Carolina politicians. That South Carolinians believe such things was not shocking to Lincoln, since "we look for, and are not much shocked by, political eccentricities and heresies in South Carolina." But Lincoln was shocked by the jeering use of the same arguments by a "very distinguished and influential clergyman of Virginia," a state whose citizens should have known better, since that state produced Jefferson and Washington. And he was also shocked by the quotation of that clergyman "with apparent approbation" in a St. Louis newspaper, since St. Louis, unlike Charleston, was the largely anti-slavery major city of one of the most marginally enslaved states.[19] Here are the clergyman's words:

> I am fully aware that there is a text in some Bibles that is not in mine. Professional abolitionists have made more use of it, than of any passage in the Bible. It came, however, as I trace it, from Saint Voltaire, and was baptized by Thomas Jefferson, and since almost universally regarded as canonical authority *"All men are born free and equal."*
>
> This is a genuine coin in the political currency of our generation. I am sorry to see that I have never seen two men of whom it is true.

But I must admit I never saw the Siamese twins, and therefore will not dogmatically say that no man ever saw a proof of this sage aphorism. (2:269–270)

Lincoln himself could only shake his head at finding such sentiments entertained by anyone not from South Carolina. As a demonstration of the idea that the future of all political freedom everywhere was at stake in the struggle against slavery, and as a defense of his sense of the meaning of the promises of the Declaration, Lincoln quoted at length the speech Clay gave before the American Colonization Society in 1827 (a speech he also quoted repeatedly during the debates with Douglas, as if Douglas himself were, like Calhoun, an opponent of democracy, rather than an example of democracy run amok in a riot of ugly but popular will). To the charge that the activities of the American Colonization Society had encouraged anti-slavery feeling and agitation, Clay replied that it was not the society but the entire course of history that had turned public feeling against slavery, and that the same worldwide moral revolution that freed the Latin American republics from Spain was also working the freedom of the American slaves. To stop that liberation, not only the course of history but the deepest facts of human nature would have to be changed, and the moral lights all around would have to be blown out:

It is not this society [the American Colonization Society] which has produced the great moral revolution which the age exhibits. What would they, who thus reproach us, have done? If they would repress all tendencies towards liberty, and ultimate emancipation, they must do more than put down the benevolent efforts of this society. They must go back to the era of our liberty and independence, and muzzle the cannon which thunders its annual joyous return. They must renew the slave trade with all its train of atrocities. They must suppress the workings of British philanthropy, seeking to meliorate the condition of the unfortunate West Indian slave. They must arrest the career of South American deliverance from thraldom. They must blow out the moral lights around us, and extinguish that greatest torch of all which America presents to a benighted world—pointing the way to their rights, their liberties, and their happiness. And when they have achieved all those purposes their work will be yet incomplete.

They must penetrate the human soul, and eradicate the light of reason, and the love of liberty. Then, and not till then, when universal
darkness and despair prevail, can you perpetuate slavery, and repress
all sympathy, and all humane, and benevolent efforts among free
men, in behalf of the unhappy portion of our race doomed to bondage. (1:270–271)

In another address to the American Colonization Society on December 17, 1829, Clay had taken even stronger grounds:

And may we not indulge the hope, that in a period of time, not sur-
passing in duration, that of our own Colonial and National existence,
we shall behold a confederation of Republican States on the western
shores of Africa, like our own, with their Congress and annual Legislatures thundering forth in behalf of the rights of man, and making
tyrants tremble on their thrones?[20]

Clay had no doubt, this is to say, that the values of the Declaration of
Independence not only called for the end of slavery but also called for
citizenship rights for blacks. He supported colonization not because he
argued for the inferiority of black people, or because he argued that
they were incapable of governing themselves in a democratic society
(an argument vehemently and repeatedly made by Douglas), but because the racism of white people was simply too intractable. What was
behind colonizationism for Clay was not fear of black people but fear of
white people. Lincoln's point in the eulogy for Clay is not only that the
Declaration and the Defense of Slavery must kill each other, but also
that in Clay's mind, as (in some moods) in Lincoln's, colonization was a
firmly anti-slavery and antiracist doctrine, not merely a form of ethnic
cleansing. Clay's account of colonization, this is to say, was strongly different from Jefferson's, and less tinged by racism and racial panic. Indeed, there is less racial panic in Lincoln's account of Clay's colonizationism than in his account of his own:

He considered it no demerit in the society, that it tended to relieve
slave-holders from the troublesome presence of the free negroes; but
this was far from being its whole merit in his estimation. In the same
speech from which I have quoted he says: "There is a moral fitness in

the idea of returning to Africa her children, whose ancestors have been torn from her by the ruthless hand of fraud and violence. Transplanted in a foreign land, they will carry back to their native soil the rich fruits of religion, civilization, law and liberty. May it not be one of the great designs of the Ruler of the universe, (whose ways are often inscrutable by short-sighted mortals,) thus to transform an original crime, into a signal blessing to that most unfortunate portion of the globe?" This suggestion of the possible ultimate redemption of the African race and African continent, was made twenty-five years ago. Every succeeding year has added strength to the hope of its realization. May it indeed be realized! Pharaoh's country was cursed with plagues, and his hosts were drowned in the Red Sea for striving to retain a captive people who had already served them more than four hundred years. May like disasters never befall us! If as the friends of colonization hope, the present and coming generations of our countrymen shall by any means, succeed in freeing our land from the dangerous presence of slavery; and, at the same time, in restoring a captive people to their long-lost father-land, with bright prospects for the future; and this too, so gradually, that neither races nor individuals shall have suffered by the change, it will indeed be a glorious consummation. (1:271)

Where Lincoln had enthusiasm for colonization, he had enthusiasm for it as an anti-slavery strategy, and as a means of "restoring a captive people to their long-lost father-land." Where (as is more typical) he embraced colonization grudgingly, he embraced it either as a concession to the persistence of white racism, and black resentment of it, since those things would make a common political culture hard to maintain, or he embraced it strategically, simply as a way to have a ready answer to the politically devastating question of what his plans were for the former slaves; but Lincoln never embraced colonization in order to eliminate black economic competition with the labor of whites, or in order to eliminate the contaminating presence of black people from the country governed by the "white man's charter of freedom."

Lincoln himself became a "director" of the American Colonization Society in January 1857.[21]

The Twilight of Colonization

Lincoln's thinking about colonization could not have been entirely merely a strategic misdirection, because he continued to entertain what seem to be harebrained schemes about colonization well after he had issued the Emancipation Proclamation. But there was also something halfhearted and unthought through about all these schemes, which suggests that Lincoln's commitment to them was shallow. In his Annual Message of December 3, 1861, for instance, Lincoln proposed that loyal slave states could give their slaves to the federal government in lieu of direct taxes, and that these freed slaves, together with those slaves from the Confederacy who came into Union hands under the operation of the first Confiscation Act, should be colonized "at some place, or places, in a climate congenial to them" (2:292). It is unclear from Lincoln's vague phrase ("steps should be taken") whether he has in mind voluntary or involuntary colonization of these classes of former slaves, but he added that inclusion, on a voluntary basis, of free colored people, should also be considered, noting that the United States may have to acquire additional territory in order to make colonization happen. Lincoln never endorsed involuntary colonization, and, once the war began, never treated colonization as a necessary precondition of emancipation but as a palliative, to lull the concerns of white people—including his own concerns—about what a post-emancipation society would be like.[22]

In April 1862, in his message announcing his signing of the bill abolishing slavery in the District of Columbia, Lincoln included a brief plug for colonization (2:316). Three months later, Lincoln alluded, in passing, to the idea of acquiring land for colonization in South America, in the midst of the plea he made on July 12, 1862, to the representatives of the border states to accept a plan for compensated emancipation before military necessity and the "friction and abrasion" of war foreclose the option by breaking down slavery even in the absence of formal emancipation (2:341). (Notice that the support of colonization here is conditional: if you accept compensated emancipation, then I will offer colonization, but if, through stubbornness or dithering, you allow the friction and abrasion of war to end slavery, then colonization, like compensation, will be off the table.) Then, on August 14, 1862, Lincoln gave a peevish lecture on the subject of colonization on the Chiriqui region of Panama to a delegation of African American clergymen who visited him (2:350–357). He complained that intelligent free blacks who might do well enough in the United States nevertheless owe it to those who might not prosper in a free United States to help them get a footing elsewhere. And he argued that the region he had in mind had some natural resources (control of transit across the isthmus between the Atlantic and Pacific, and abundant, although as it turned out purely imaginary, coal mines), that the local population was less hostile to blacks than white Americans were, and (surely this is a fantasy) that the political leadership in Central America was unanimously in favor of the colonization plan. The Preliminary Emancipation Proclamation itself included a passing mention of colonization. Each of these three statements could conceivably have served purposes of strategic disguise, but it would be hard to treat these statements as entirely strategic. Pulling the wool over the eyes of racist white people was certainly in Lincoln's mind. But fooling himself was also in his mind. As he both did and did not see through his own racism, so he both did and did not see through the stratagem of colonization, lulling his own racism to sleep in the way he lulled other people's.[23]

Lincoln's realism about his own racism, his recognition that it would pose formidable barriers to full citizenship for black people, and that the racism of white people and the resentment of black people might make for a volatile combination, underlay his endorsement of colonization at those moments when he seemed to take it most seriously. As Lincoln was to say in his Address on Colonization to a Committee of Colored Men of August 1862 (while he was awaiting the opportunity to issue the Emancipation Proclamation):

> Your race are suffering, in my judgment, the greatest wrong inflicted on any people. But even when you cease to be slaves, you are yet far removed from being placed on an equality with the white race. You are cut off from many of the advantages which the other race enjoy. The aspiration of men is to enjoy equality with the best when free, but on this broad continent, not a single man of your race is made the equal of a single man of ours. Go where you are treated the best, and the ban is still upon you. (2:353)

To the extent that he took colonization seriously, Lincoln saw colonization, this is to say, as an escape from racism, not as a means of purifying the United States to lily-whiteness.[24] Lincoln was aware, however, even from his first full development of this theme in the 1854 Peoria speech, that colonization, even if it were acceptable to the former slaves—Lincoln's plans, unlike some others, were always voluntary plans—was a logistical and for that matter a cultural impossibility. (Even the Blair brothers, recognizing that the freed slaves could no longer seriously be considered Africans and would go to Liberia only as the settlers of an unpromising colony, thought to settle the former slaves in some location—usually the Mosquito Coast of Nicaragua—where they would be thought of as Americans and would implement an American colonial agenda. This fantasy died hard; as late as the Grant administration, serious efforts were undertaken to purchase the Dominican Republic as a homeland for freed American slaves.)[25]

Given the very qualified endorsement of colonization in the Peoria speech, and his frank recognition of its likely impossibility in the same speech, perhaps the fairest thing to say about Lincoln's embrace of colonization is that it usually served a rhetorical rather than a policy purpose, and even where he took it more seriously as policy, he never fully thought through the policy. The concept of colonization gave him a ready answer to questions about the future relations of white and black in the United States, or rather, a rhetorically successful way to postpone the question, recognizing that any of the practical and decent answers to that question would have been disastrous to give and would have foreclosed his ability to do anything at all. Colonization, this is to say, was mostly, but not entirely, strategic cover for Lincoln, not policy, although strategic cover can become policy under the right kind of pressure, and if Lincoln's remarks to the Committee of Colored Men are any indication, he might have been willing to press even more strongly for voluntary colonization had any remotely plausible plan for doing so presented itself and had the would-be colonists had the slightest enthusiasm for the plan. But even here, under the tone of somewhat impatient pique that characterizes this address, one senses Lincoln's recognition that the colonization expedient was ultimately not a very promising one. (That recognition might indeed account for the uncharacteristically snappish tone of the remarks.)

By the time of Lincoln's December 1, 1862, Annual Message, it is clear that although Lincoln was still pursuing colonization plans with Liberia and Haiti, the preparations were desultory, and Lincoln's own enthusiasm for the project, while not completely deflated, had considerably fallen: although he included a proposed constitutional amendment enabling Congress to appropriate money for colonization purposes in the speech, he also noted that most of the other countries where Lincoln had contemplated planting colonies had declined to receive or protect the colonists or to grant them the rights of freemen were they to emigrate there, and the would-be colonists themselves, given the choice of Liberia or Haiti, "do not seem so willing to migrate to those countries, as to some others, nor so willing as I think their interest demands" (2:395). Indeed, explaining his proposed constitutional amendment, Lincoln went out of his way to make it clear that he did not have in mind involuntary emigration, and he sought only to further the aims of those who already wished to emigrate.[26]

In the same Annual Message, Lincoln also went out of his way to criticize the idea that the presence of black laborers injures white free labor in any way, either by competition or by some kind of degrading contamination:

It is insisted that their presence would injure and displace white labor and white laborers. If there ever could be a proper time for mere catch arguments, that time surely is not now. In times like the present men should utter nothing for which they would not willingly be responsible through time and in eternity. Is it true, then, that colored people can displace any more white labor by being free than by remaining slaves? If they stay in their old places, they jostle no white laborers; if they leave their old places, they leave them open to white laborers. Logically, there is neither more nor less of it. Emancipation, even without deportation, would probably enhance the wages of white labor, and very surely would not reduce them. Thus the customary amount of labor would still have to be performed—the freed people would surely not do more than their old proportion of it, and very probably for a time would do less, leaving an increased part to white laborers, bringing their labor into greater demand, and consequently enhancing the wages of it. With deportation, even to a limited extent, enhanced wages to white labor is mathematically certain. Labor is like any other commodity in the market—increase the demand for it and you increase the price of it. Reduce the supply of black labor by colonizing the black laborer out of the country, and by precisely so much you increase the demand for and wages of white labor.

But it is dreaded that the freed people will swarm forth and cover the whole land. Are they not already in the land? Will liberation make them any more numerous? Equally distributed among the whites of the whole country, and there would be but one colored to seven whites. Could the one in any way greatly disturb the seven? There are many communities now having more than one free colored person to seven whites and this without any apparent consciousness of evil from it. The District of Columbia and the States of Maryland and Delaware are all in this condition. The District has more than one free colored to six whites, and yet in its frequent petitions to Congress I believe it has never presented the presence of free colored persons as one of its grievances. But why should emancipation South send the free people North? People of any color seldom run unless there be something to run from. Heretofore colored people to some extent have fled North from bondage, and now, perhaps, from both bondage and destitution. But if gradual emancipation and deportation be adopted, they will have neither to flee from. Their old masters will give them wages at least until new laborers can be procured, and the freedmen in turn will gladly give their labor for the wages till new homes can be found for them in congenial climes and with people of their own blood and race. This proposition can be trusted on the mutual interests involved. And in any event, can not the North decide for itself whether to receive them? (1:412–413)

There is a great deal of ugliness in this passage—the argument that deportation of black labor would raise white wages (although the passage argues that forgetting about deportation would probably not lower white wages and may wind up raising them too); the idea that the states of the North, like Illinois throughout the antebellum period, might simply refuse entry to free blacks; and the assumption that freed slaves will still in some way be economically dependent upon their former masters. But it is hard to say where the center of gravity of this passage is, since it insisted also that black labor was no real threat to white labor, that a mass exodus of blacks to the North was unlikely, and would probably not have ill effects even if it did occur, since at worst it would make other states resemble Maryland and Delaware, which were not exactly backward or depressed states. The passage advocated colonization—deportation—but it also provided telling arguments against deportation, arguments that indeed undermined the strongest case colonizationists could make for it, the argument about the security of white labor, and the argument about mass emigration of black people to the North. If the passage's advocacy of colonization was not in fact duplicitous, it at the very least reflected even more mixed feelings than Lincoln's canonical expression of mixed feelings about colonization in the Peoria speech. Lincoln played both sides of the street in these two paragraphs. The best way to see them is to remember that in context they are addressed to skeptics hostile to the Emancipation Proclamation, whom Lincoln attempted, in a number of contradictory ways, to talk down off their high horses. If that was the purpose—the strategic purpose—of all this ugliness, then the best thing to remember about this passage is that the dirty work it did was intended keep down the objections and make possible the great peroration of this speech, the peroration that ends:

> Fellow-citizens, we can not escape history. We of this Congress and this Administration will be remembered in spite of ourselves. No personal significance or insignificance can spare one or another of us. The fiery trial through which we pass will light us down in honor or dishonor to the latest generation. We say we are for the Union. The world will not forget that we say this. We know how to save the Union. The world knows we do know how to save it. We, even we here, hold the power and bear the responsibility. In giving freedom to the slave we assure freedom to the free—honorable alike in what we give and what we preserve. We shall nobly save or meanly lose the last best hope of earth. Other means may succeed; this could not fail. The way is plain, peaceful, generous, just—a way which if followed the world will forever applaud and God must forever bless. (2:415)

When the final Emancipation Proclamation was issued on New Year's Day, Lincoln silently dropped the language about colonization that had been in the preliminary version.

There was a coda to the colonization story in the strange, failed attempt of the speculator Bernard Kock to set up a colony for American freed slaves on the Ile á Vache, off Haiti. He persuaded Lincoln to give (halfhearted) financial support to the venture, which immediately went off the rails, and Lincoln finally had to dispatch a transport on February 1, 1864, to rescue the 453 miserable colonists.[27]

Nonextension as a Political Strategy

Concerning the anti-slavery position Lincoln took in 1858, Richard Hofstadter famously argued in *The American Political Tradition* (1948) that the free soil, nonextension position enabled Lincoln to claim for himself the moral prestige of earnest hostility to slavery without his having to pay the political price of adopting openly abolitionist convictions.[28] This policy also appeared to promise to the political nation (which is to say to the white citizens) a painless solution to the slavery problem, since the emancipation it proposed was so gradual that it might take place without economic or social disruptions. Indeed, since Lincoln's thinking on this subject until a very late date included compensation for masters, and support for voluntary emigration of the freed slaves either to Liberia or to Central America, it could fairly be argued (were not both of these provisions the creatures of wishful thinking) that the Republican platform demanded very little sacrifice from slaveholders, from shippers and weavers of cotton, or from racist nonslaveholders, since the first two would be shielded from economic disruption and the last would be shielded from economic competition (and cultural contact) with black people. Martin Duberman described nonextension as a policy that "promised in time to do everything and for the present risked nothing."[29] Whether or not in the final analysis Lincoln was committed to the pipe dreams of compensated emancipation and colonization, the end of slavery as the Republicans envisioned it would have taken place in that long run that nobody survives to see, much like the withering away of the state under Communism.

The Republicans' core constituency was people who disliked slavery but feared the consequences of abolition. The nonextension strategy provided such people with an economically and politically safe way to put their hostility to slavery into practice. In addition, the Republicans sought to persuade those hostile to slavery that they were in earnest while persuading slaveholders that they did not represent an immediate and sweeping threat to their way of life. This last aspect of their strategy must in the final analysis be judged to be a failure. The constitutional hedging and the promise of compensation and colonization persuaded the most serious opponents of slavery (and some of the current generation of historians) that the Republicans were temporizers and hypocrites. But these same things did not persuade the slaveholders that the Republicans were no threat to them, for they understood that the reliance upon compensation and colonization offered no realistic prospect of insulating them from social change. They also understood that the Republicans' primary hostility to slavery, however qualified, would necessarily threaten their position in the politics of the Republic, since if such convictions came to be the views of a majority committed to acting upon them, the slaveholders could no longer dominate the political system by extorting political concessions from northern politicians, as had been their habit since the 1820s. Not only would a Republican-dominated electorate be immune to the slaveholder blackmail that had characterized the political compromises of the forty years preceding the Civil War (because they could come to power only under circumstances in which they would not need any support at all from the slave states), but the victorious Republicans would also fill the South with federal employees who, however much they might restrain themselves in the actual prosecution of policy, would nevertheless be a continuous standing rebuke to the legitimacy of slavery.[30]

The Republican strategy, this is to say, had the opposite of its intended effect, threatening those it meant to mollify and disappointing those it intended to rally. But perhaps that was all to the good, since a more forthrightly anti-slavery party would never have come into a position to have any practical effect upon slavery, and the panicked reaction of the slaveholders itself was among the exigencies that made it possible for Republican hostility to slavery to have, ultimately, a practical effect.

6.2 Douglas on Abolition and Black Citizenship

Douglas's own racism needs to be characterized in detail, since, as George Fredrickson taught long ago, not all racism in the antebellum era was of a piece, and the northern Democratic racism of Douglas, for all its virulence, was slightly distinct both from the racism of the southern slaveholders and from the (more closely related) racism of southern nonslaveholders.[31] Douglas's racism was in many ways stereotypical of his class, party, and faction. But there are a few ways, ways not fully acknowledged perhaps even by Douglas himself, in which his racism slightly differs from what he first projects.

Douglas's use of racist appeals was particularly aggressive, and charging that his opponents were secret abolitionists was a habit with him as far back as the 1840 election campaign. Douglas's racism in the 1858 campaign was florid, but also a bit repetitive, and built around utterly traditional themes. Lincoln, says Douglas, opposed the *Dred Scott* decision, for instance, only because it stood in the way of citizenship rights for black people. The Republicans were always the "Black Republicans" up in Freeport, although Douglas conceded that their principles bleached out as they went farther south, becoming a "decent mulatto" in Sangamon County, in the middle of the state, and "almost white" down in Little Egypt.[32] Indeed not only the color of the party but the color of the party's *spokesmen* paled as one moved south, since up in Stephenson County the spokesman was Frederick Douglass, and down in Little Egypt the spokesman was Lyman Trumbull. But Douglas was not alone in slinging this kind of language—Lincoln himself had referred to Pierce as a "political mulatto" for attempting to appeal to both Free Soilers and secessionists.

In an especially noisome sally at the state fair in Centralia during September, Douglas "was particularly severe on the unfortunate odor of the black man [and] asked if his audience wished to eat with, ride with, go to church with, travel with, and in other ways bring Congo odor into their nostrils."[33] Douglas also was not above playing the sex card about race (the word "miscegenation" will be coined by his party for the 1864 presidential campaign), although he did it indirectly. In the Freeport debate, knowing that he was speaking to an anti-slavery audience in the northern tier of counties, he baited his audience about their presumed taste for racial equality, hinting also at a touch of interracial sexual freedom:

> The last time I came here to make a speech, while talking from the stand to you, people of Freeport, as I am doing to-day, I saw a carriage and a magnificent one it was, drive up and take a position on the outside of the crowd; a beautiful young lady was sitting on the box seat, whilst Fred. Douglass and her mother reclined inside, and the owner of the carriage acted as driver. [Laughter, cheers, cries of

right, what have you to say against it, &c.] I saw this in your own town. ["What of it."] All I have to say of it is this, that if you, Black Republicans, think that the negro ought to be on a social equality with your wives and daughters, and ride in a carriage with your wife, whilst you drive the team, you have a perfect right to do so. (1:556)

Douglas ground a class axe here as well as a racial one: abolition, and racial equality (and sexual relations between black men and married white women whose husbands connive at it), was the kind of thing only those who were rich enough to grow a conscience would do. Good plain folk do not do such things. The idea that racial equality is not only a fashion statement for the elite but also a way the elite use to keep lower-class white people in their place was a common theme of what Fredrickson calls *herrenvolk* democracy. That granting rights to black people was part of a conspiracy against the rights of poor whites was an idea not confined to the likes of Twain's Pap Finn. Andrew Johnson and his followers believed the same, although what Johnson feared was not a political combination between former slave and abolitionist but a political combination between former slave and former master.[34] Similar sentiments underlay the final disenfranchisement of black voters, and the imposition of formal racial segregation, by the insurgent Populists in the 1890s. For that matter, similar sentiments are common enough today.

Douglas's use of this class rhetoric had a taunting quality in Freeport—he was hoping to get a rise out of his audience there, which he could put to good use elsewhere. When he replayed this incident in the Charleston debate, a touch of hysteria crept into his tone:

In the northern part of the State I found Lincoln's ally, in the person of FRED. DOUGLASS, THE NEGRO, preaching abolition doctrines, while Lincoln was discussing the same principles down here, and Trumbull, a little farther down, was advocating the election of members to the legislature who would act in concert with Lincoln's and Fred. Douglass' friends. (1:666)

Frederick Douglass seems to have been a talismanic bugbear for anti-abolitionists. The Free Soil leader George W. Julian remarked in his memoirs that it was a standing charge among his opponents "that I carried in my pocket a lock of the hair of Frederick Douglass, to regale my senses with its aroma when I grew faint."[35]

Douglas also sought to play to the class fear of poor whites about competition with blacks for work, land, and political power:

> Do you desire to strike out of our State Constitution that clause which keeps slaves and free negroes out of the State, and allow the free negroes to flow in, ["never,"] and cover your prairies with black settlements? Do you desire to turn this beautiful State into a free negro colony, ["no, no,"] in order that when Missouri abolishes slavery she can send one hundred thousand emancipated slaves into Illinois, to become citizens and voters, on equality with yourselves? ["Never," "no."] (1:504)

Concretely, this position is not very different from the free state position in Kansas, since the free staters, like Douglas, wanted neither slavery nor black people in their state. (It is worth noting that Douglas said "when" rather than "if" Missouri abolishes slavery. Douglas believed, despite the power of pro-slavery politicians like Senator David Atchison, that slavery in Missouri would fail.) Nor was it very different from Lincoln's own position in 1858. But although the words were the same, the music was different. Lincoln always described his racism grudgingly, as a concession made to strong and long-established structures of feeling, which, irrational and wrong as they may be, cannot lightly be opposed. Douglas, by contrast, took a schoolyard bully's pleasure in baiting race.

That said, there are a few and-yets and howevers even about Douglas's racism. When Lincoln said of Douglas in the Peoria speech that he had "no very lively conviction that the Negro is a human; and consequently has no idea that there can be any moral question in legislating about him" (1:346), Douglas took offense. Douglas had said in Memphis in 1858, and repeatedly in Illinois that year (although not in the debates with Lincoln) that "in all contests between the negro and the white man, he was for the white man, but that in all questions between the negro and the crocodile he was for the negro."[36] Campaigning in Cincinnati in September 1859, Lincoln interpreted this figure aggressively. First, about the conflict between the white man and the negro:

The first inference seems to be that if you do not enslave the negro you are wronging the white man in some way or other, and that whoever is opposed to the negro being enslaved is in some way or other against the white man. Is not that a falsehood? If there was a necessary conflict between white man and the negro, I should be for the white man as much as Judge Douglas; but I say there is no such necessary conflict. I say that there is room enough for us all to be free, [loud manifestations of applause,] and that it not only does not wrong the white man that the negro should be free, but it positively wrongs the mass of the white men that the negro should be enslaved; that the mass of white men are really injured by the effect of slave labor in the vicinity of the fields of their own labor. [Applause.] (2:68)

Notice that Lincoln began, as he so often did, by making what looks to be a concession but is in fact merely a way to focus attention upon the actual nub of conflict ("If there was a necessary conflict between white man and the negro, I should be for the white man as much as Judge Douglas"). His key aim was to turn the class attack frequently leveled by Douglas in the opposite direction. Douglas had treated hostility to slavery as if it were something brandished by the well off against the less well off. Douglas's reasoning employed class war, but the class war it invoked was a cultural, not an economic, one: that effete corps of impudent snobs is not like us, and they just do not share our values. Lincoln's counterattack was more straightforwardly economic, and employed the rhetoric of the free labor ideology: slavery is one of the ways the master class uses to degrade the position of free white labor. There is a further nuance to be noticed in the way Lincoln deployed this argument. The argument could easily, and consistently, have been employed not against *slave* labor but against *black* labor. But Lincoln did not do this, arguing that there is no necessary economic conflict between black and white. The reason he made this argument is that the economic damage is done not by the competition for jobs and wages between white and black, but by the specially subjected position slave labor occupies.

Lincoln's response to the second part of Douglas's figure (during the "second round" of debates between Lincoln and Douglas in Ohio in 1859) was more pointed:

But what, at last, is this proposition? I believe it is a sort of proposition in proportion, which may be stated thus: As the negro is to the white man, so is the crocodile to the negro, and as the negro may rightfully treat the crocodile as a beast or reptile, so the white man may rightfully treat the negro as a beast or a reptile. (2:68)

Lincoln's interpretation is clever, but also a trifle unfair, because it treated the passage as arguing what Douglas was in fact trying to deny, that he believed the negro is not fully human. Lincoln was able to do this by exploiting an ambiguity that Douglas had in fact intended: Douglas had wished to affirm that he was a racist, but to deny that he was *that* kind of racist. Douglas's intention was to distinguish between his own racism and that of, say, Josiah C. Nott and George R. Gliddon, whose 1854 book *Types of Mankind* argued for a strongly biological understanding of race and argued that the differences among the races amounted to (or nearly amounted to) differences among species (a theory known as "polygenesis").[37] Douglas wanted his supporters to know that he was, like them, a racist. But he also did not want to adopt a racism so thoroughgoing that it imagined black people as nonhuman beasts of burden. Douglas had in fact complained in 1858 that Buchanan and his administration had "reduced Negroes to the status of mules."[38] Douglas was no deep thinker, and for that reason one should not seek in him a fully blown theory of race supported by all of the apparatus of nineteenth-century pseudo-science, such as that upheld by Louis Agassiz; but even without the biological claptrap, Douglas sought here to distinguish himself from people like Buchanan, who, Douglas argued, really did, unlike himself, see black people as beasts of burden. Lincoln took the defensive qualification ("I'm a racist too") as if it were the assertion, and ignored what Douglas was actually trying to assert ("I'm not *that* kind of racist").

What Lincoln sought to exploit was the incoherence of Douglas's position: Douglas wished to affirm that blacks are human but do not have a share in the basic human rights to life, liberty, and the pursuit of happiness. But they do have *some* kind of moral claim on white people, in virtue of their being human; hence treating them as beasts of burden or as farm equipment is wrong. Yet that claim did not rise in Douglas's mind to a claim that they should not be made into slaves. Douglas will go so far as to say that Illinoisans are right in not wanting to have slaves but not so right that they should deny Kentuckians the ability to have them if they so wish. As Douglas argued in the Bloomington speech, just before the debates began:

> Will you ever submit to a warfare waged by the Southern States to establish slavery in Illinois? What man in Illinois would not lose the last drop of his heart's blood before he would submit to the institution of slavery being forced upon us by the other States, against our will? And if that be true of us, what Southern man would not shed the last drop of his heart's blood to prevent Illinois or any other Northern State, from interfering to abolish slavery in his State?[39]

Lincoln was correct that there is something incoherent about Douglas's "freedom of choice" position about slavery: if Douglas wanted to affirm that slavery is wrong for him, he had to give reasons why it is not also wrong for everybody else. (Lincoln spent considerable energy in 1859 and 1860 trying to argue that Douglas treated slavery either as right or as something morally indifferent, which was in Lincoln's eyes equivalent to treating it as something right. It would be fairer to say that Douglas treated it as something wrong but could not allow himself to treat as wrong in other than a provisional way.)

But the contradictions in which Douglas was entangled were not very different from those in which Lincoln was himself entangled. Lincoln wished to affirm that black people do have a share in human rights enumerated by Jefferson, at least to the extent of not being made slaves of, but have only a limited share in civil rights (to own property, to make contracts, to sue, to serve as a witness, but not to marry across racial lines) and none at all in political rights (to vote, to serve on juries, and to hold office). Before the Revolutionary era, it would not have been assumed that those varieties of rights were tightly connected, that possessing one gives one a claim on the others.[40] After the Civil War it became commonplace to assume that human rights somehow include civil and political rights, that membership in the political society is not like membership in a club, something one has or lacks merely in virtue of the agreement of those who are already members to admit one to membership (as, say, Taney had argued in the *Dred Scott* decision), but rather something that all human beings, merely in virtue of their being human beings, have a kind of claim on. Douglas's position was at least consistent with the traditional distinction among human rights (the right not to be killed or enslaved), civil rights, and political rights. But Lincoln's position was not consistent with that distinction, since even as he denied seeking political rights for black people he used moral arguments that link civil and political rights in a single concept of the moral value of persons as persons, arguments that, unlike Douglas's purely political ones, could not be made consistently without extending both civil and political rights to blacks.

What Douglas actually thought of slavery is a question, because, as Lincoln did with his thought about nativism, he confined his views to his private correspondence and conversation. On January 22, 1854, the day of the appearance of the Chase-Sumner-Giddings "Appeal of the Independent Democrats" in the *National Era* (which had earlier published *Uncle Tom's Cabin*), Douglas vented his anger at the attacks on him in that document to the son of his friend Murray McConnel. The authors had accused Douglas of setting in motion via the Kansas-Nebraska Act "an atrocious plot to exclude from a vast unoccupied region immigrants from the Old World, and free laborers from our own States, and convert it into a dreary region of despotism, inhabited by masters and slaves."[41] Fuming to McConnel, Douglas said, "I am not pro-slavery. I think it a curse beyond computation, to white and black. [But the only power that could destroy slavery] is the sword, and if the sword is once drawn no one can see the end."[42] Like Lincoln, Douglas felt that the Constitution prohibited him from acting directly against slavery. Unlike Lincoln, he (wishfully) felt that slavery might disappear on its own by the mere course of time:

> I know I am politically right in keeping within the pale of the Constitution. I believe I am right as to the moral effect, and I know I am right as a party leader anxious to help in keeping his party true to the whole country. . . . No man loves his country better than I. I know she is not faultless. I see as clearly as they that she is afflicted with a dangerous tumor. But I believe she will slough it off in time, and I am not willing to risk the life of the patient by the illegal and unscientific surgery they demand.[43]

Douglas had gone on to tell McConnel that he had been reluctant to repeal the Missouri Compromise line (as we know, because Senator

Dixon had to push him to do it) but also felt that on balance the repeal might hurt slavery more than it would help it, since without that provision slavery would not be able to "crouch behind a line which Freedom is cut off from crossing."[44]

Douglas's public remarks about slavery are more guarded. When in 1848 Senator Henry Foote of Mississippi threatened Senator John P. Hale of New Hampshire, saying he hoped the latter would "grace one of the tallest trees of the forest, with a rope around his neck," Douglas rose to rebuke him.[45] Douglas went on to rebuke the "positive good" theory of slavery, arguing that his support for popular sovereignty on the slavery issue was merely a kind of toleration for something he in fact felt distaste for:

> In the North it is not expected that we should take the position that slavery is a positive good—a positive blessing. If we did assume such a position, it would be a very pertinent inquiry, why do you not adopt this institution? We have moulded our institutions at the North as we have thought proper; and now we say to you of the South, if slavery be a blessing, it is your blessing; if it be a curse, it is your curse; enjoy it—on you rests all the responsibility![46]

Douglas's position was complicated, because he actually had inherited slaves from his first wife's estate. His father-in-law in Mississippi, in the will that gave those slaves to his wife, had reminded her "that her husband does not desire to own this kind of property and most of our collateral connection already have more of that kind of property than is of advantage to them."[47] Douglas wanted, in a desultory way, to end his connection with slavery, but manumission was forbidden by local law, emigration to Liberia was opposed by the slaves who would be doing the emigrating, and Douglas never seems to have considered bringing them north. On the whole, he tried to keep the management of his slaves at arm's length, and paid just enough attention to the conditions of his slaves to keep from being the subject of scandal. Douglas's opponents in any event naturally seized on his ownership of slaves as the real reason he proposed the Kansas-Nebraska Act, and pro-Buchanan organizers such as John Slidell of Louisiana spread rumors about conditions among Douglas's slaves during the 1858 campaign.

Even about race, Douglas sometimes backs away from racist claims he could easily make. For instance, during the Ottawa debate, he

interrupted one of his more virulent tirades against Lincoln's presumed advocacy of racial equality with this:

> I do not hold that because the negro is our inferior that therefore he
> ought to be a slave. By no means can such a conclusion be drawn from
> what I have said. On the contrary, I hold that humanity and christian-
> ity both require that the negro shall have and enjoy every right, every
> privilege, and every immunity consistent with the safety of the society,
> in which he lives. [That's so.] On that point, I presume, there can be
> no diversity of opinion. You and I are bound to extend to our inferior
> and dependent being[s] every right, every privilege, every facility and
> immunity consistent with the public good. The question then arises
> what rights and privileges are consistent with the public good. This is
> a question which each State and each Territory must decide for itself—
> Illinois has decided it for herself. We have provided that the negro
> shall not be a slave, and we have also provided that he shall not be a
> citizen, but protect him in his civil rights, in his life, his person and his
> property, only depriving him of all political rights whatsoever, and
> refusing to put him on an equality with the white man. (1:505)

Douglas made almost identically worded claims several times in the
debates, sometimes providing examples of states that have taken different courses, not only about slavery, but also about citizenship rights
for black people, noting for instance that in Maine blacks could vote
and have all of the other rights of citizens, and that in New York they
could vote so long as they could meet a high property requirement.
Douglas did not disavow racism in this passage; as in the crocodile passage his argument was that he was a racist but not *that* kind of racist.
Douglas's description of Illinois's rejection of slavery has a note of pride,
which again marks Douglas as wishing to take a position of somewhat
qualified racism:

> We have settled the slavery question as far as we are concerned; we
> have prohibited it in Illinois forever, and in doing so, I think we have
> done wisely, and there is no man in the State who would be more
> strenuous in his opposition to the introduction of slavery than I
> would; [cheers] but when we settled it for ourselves, we exhausted all
> our power over that subject. We have done our whole duty, and can
> do no more. (1:506)

Douglas went on to deny that Illinois took this step for moral reasons, arguing that despite the Northwest Ordinance there was a limited amount of slavery that the early state governments not only tolerated but connived in, and that in addition, the early state governments also invented varieties of "apprenticeship" (a ninety-nine-year indenture, which applied to the children of the indentured servant until they reached age thirty and which included such things as whipping), which differed only in small ways from actual slavery. When Edward Coles, whose influence ended slavery in Illinois, wrote a letter claiming that Douglas was wrong about slavery existing in Illinois, Douglas wrote to my mind a devastating reply demonstrating the persistence of slavery de facto in Illinois, both in defiance of the law and with the law's complicity.[48] Douglas was both right and wrong about this. It is true that slavery existed in Illinois despite the Northwest Ordinance, since those who held slaves in the region prior to the adoption of the ordinance, chiefly French-speaking residents of Kaskaskia, kept their slaves afterward. And Illinois courts chose until 1845 to interpret the Northwest Ordinance as prohibiting the entry of new slaves into Illinois but also as leaving not only the existing slaves but also their descendants in slavery, a pro-slavery interpretation of the ordinance that was rejected even by courts in Missouri and Kentucky.[49] And Coles himself was very hard put to defeat an 1824 attempt to reintroduce slavery in Illinois. (The vote on the question was 4,972 in favor, 6,640 opposed.)[50] But it is also true that it was the Northwest Ordinance that prevented slavery from having the vitality in Illinois that it had in Missouri, as Fehrenbacher argues on many occasions. Illinois's black codes were more stringent than those of any other northern state; its provisions for transit of slaveholders unmolested across Illinois were, as Paul Finkelman shows, the most generous of any northern State save New Jersey; and in many ways it deserved the reputation it has among recent historians of being the most racist of the free states. On the whole, Douglas was closer to the truth about Illinois than Lincoln was.

Douglas made this argument about slavery in Illinois for an interesting reason. His explicit rationale was to argue that dictation from Washington never ended slavery anywhere, that slavery was always ended when the people of particular regions decided to reject it, and that popular sovereignty, not the Northwest Ordinance, drove slavery out of Illinois as it did out of Kansas. Douglas also wished to argue, against Lincoln, that the fate of slavery in a territory is not decided by the first settlers who arrive and create the state's political machinery. The first settlers of Illinois were slaveholders, but Illinois did not become a slave state.[51]

But Douglas had another motive, and that was to chasten a kind of moral pride in anti-slavery circles: our hands were dirtied too, he implied, and even when we got rid of slavery we did so because we could not make it pay, so we have no reason to imagine ourselves as riding a moral high horse. As Douglas had wryly noted in 1848, "We tried slavery once in Illinois. . . . It did not suit our circumstances or habits, and we turned philanthropic and abolished it."[52] These sentiments are closer to Lincoln's in the Second Inaugural than anything Lincoln himself says in the 1858 debates is. This qualification, this is to say, did not contradict Douglas's approval of the end of slavery in Illinois so much as fend off the temptation to moral narcissism about it.

One of the more curious moments in the debates occurred at Galesburg, where Douglas turned the tables and accused Lincoln of racism. Lincoln had at Charleston, as we have seen, famously denied that he had any commitment at all to racial equality, using rather blunter language than he had used about the same subject at Freeport. This got Douglas's back up:

> If the negro was made his equal and mine, if that equality was established by Divine law, and was the negro's inalienable right, how came he to say at Charleston to the Kentuckians residing in that section of our State, that the negro was physically inferior to the white man, belonged to an inferior race, and he was for keeping him always in that inferior condition? (1:722)

Now of course Douglas's main point was that Lincoln argued differently in Charleston in the middle of the state from how he argued in Freeport, up near the Wisconsin border. That part of the charge is false, since it is not hard to reconcile the apparent contradictions. Douglas pressed his case, however, in an unexpected direction. Noticing the distinction between the two arguments, one might have assumed that Douglas would have argued that the racial appeal to white solidarity at Charleston was disingenuous, and that Lincoln was always really an amalgamationist under the skin. Instead, Douglas twitted Lincoln for his racism, implying that if *Douglas* thought the promises of the Declaration applied to black people, he would feel duty-bound to support social and political equality between the races. Douglas could safely do this, because he did not read the Declaration in that way in the first place. But it is peculiar to charge someone with hypocrisy for believing the same thing you do, particularly if you have been investing a great deal of rhetorical effort to make the opposite point. It licenses one to wonder whether Douglas's racism was shakier than he had proclaimed it to be.[53]

In his Bloomington speech of July 16, 1858, Douglas had reached out to free soil voters by arguing that popular sovereignty was a better strategy for ending slavery than nonextension was, because nonextension would get the slaveholders' backs up and postpone emancipation in those marginal slave states that might otherwise have wavered. Douglas further argued that the federal prohibition of slavery was designed to fail, because its chief purpose was to enflame sectional hostilities that the Republicans and the fire-eaters alike could use to maintain the ideological discipline of their organizations.

Douglas could not quite take this tack in the debates themselves, because there he was trying to bait race, to argue that Lincoln was covertly pushing social and political equality among the races. Lincoln could not, of course, have been covertly pushing for racial equality if he was not really even serious about emancipation. But at Bloomington it was precisely the issue of Lincoln's seriousness about emancipation that Douglas was trying to raise; Douglas at Bloomington made as effective a pitch as he ever made for the support of those moderate Republicans of McLean's or Bates's stripe that were in play between him and Lincoln in 1858:

> Who among you expects to live, or have his children live, until slavery shall be established in Illinois or abolished in South Carolina? Who expects to see that occur during the lifetime of ourselves or our children?
>
> There is but one possible way in which slavery can be abolished, and that is by leaving a State, according to the principle of the Kansas-Nebraska bill, perfectly free to form and regulate its institutions in its own way. That was the principle upon which this republic was founded, and it is under the operation of that principle that we have been able to preserve the Union thus far. Under its operations, slavery

disappeared from New Hampshire, from Rhode Island, from Connecticut, from New York, from New Jersey, from Pennsylvania, from
six of the twelve original slaveholding States; and this gradual system
of emancipation went on quietly, peacefully, and steadily, so long as
we in the free States minded our own business and left our neighbors alone. But the moment the Abolition societies were organized
throughout the North, preaching a violent crusade against slavery in
the Southern States, this combination necessarily caused a counter-
combination in the South, and a sectional line was drawn which was
a barrier to any further emancipation.

Bear in mind that emancipation has not taken place in any one
State since the Free Soil party was organized as a political party in
this country. Emancipation went on gradually in State after State so
long as the free States were content with managing their own affairs
and leaving the South perfectly free to do as they pleased; but the
moment the North said, We are powerful enough to control you of
the South; the moment the North proclaimed itself the determined
master of the South; that moment the South combined to resist the
attack, and thus sectional parties were formed, and gradual emancipation ceased in all the Northern slaveholding States. And yet Mr.
Lincoln, in view of these historical facts, proposes to keep up this
sectional agitation; band all the Northern States together in one political party; elect a president by Northern votes alone; and then, of
course, make a cabinet composed of Northern men, and administer
the government by Northern men only, denying all the Southern
States of this Union any participation in the administration of affairs
whatsoever.[54]

Toward the end of the 1858 debates, Douglas made a very strange
argument that is hard to square with his florid racism. He argued
that Lincoln's plan to confine slavery to the states where it already
existed was a plan to confine black people to those regions as well, and
that that plan hardly served the interests of black people, and indeed
would result in their starving to death, leaving a republic at once free
of slavery and of black people. The idea that Lincoln's nonextension
plan would result in a kind of famine-induced ethnic cleansing of
black people from the South is, to say the least, far-fetched. But what
is strangest in the passage is that Douglas treats anti-slavery racism—a

doctrine more characteristic of his supporters than of Lincoln's—with repugnance:

> He first tells you that he would prohibit slavery everywhere in the ter-ritories. He would thus confine slavery within its present limits. When he thus gets it confined, and surrounded, so that it cannot spread, the natural laws of increase will go on until the negroes will be so plenty that they cannot live on the soil. He will hem them in until starvation seizes them, and by starving them to death, he will put slavery in the course of ultimate extinction. If he is not going to interfere with slavery in the States, but intends to interfere and prohibit it in the territories, and thus smother slavery out, it naturally follows, that he can extinguish it only by extinguishing the negro race, for his policy would drive them to starvation. This is the humane and Christian remedy that he proposes for the great crime of slavery. (1:753)

The starvation charge may not be plausible, but the critique is not entirely wild. (Indeed, David Zarefsky points out that this is one of the few points about which Douglas makes a moral charge to which Lincoln is unable to reply.)[55] In the first place, Douglas saw through Lincoln's temporizing strategy—radical in ends, but moderate in means—calling it deceptive to the extent that it postponed thought about the future status of former slaves. Second, he saw that in the absence of civil rights, Lincoln's strategy was a bantustan strategy, not just for slavery, but for black people.

William Freehling points out in the first volume of *The Road to Dis-union* (1990) that the possibility of being cooped up forever with their slaves was a recurring nightmare for white people in the Deep South, one of the reasons they favored expansion of slavery into the territories and one of the reasons they sometimes offered "diffusionist" argu-ments in favor of that expansion. They were well aware that the slave states of the lower North had freed themselves of slavery and of black people by exporting their slave populations farther south. They feared that the states of the upper South sought to do the same. Certainly many Virginians entertained precisely such fantasies.[56] Exactly what Douglas was up to by playing on that fear is uncertain, since Illinoisans did not share that fear, and indeed Douglas slanted the argument to em-phasize not the racist fears of slaveholders that they might themselves be

quarantined in a kind of bantustan but the fear that doing so might
lead to the extermination by starvation of the black race. An argument
this odd must be sincere.

Traditionally, and plausibly, scholars have defended most of Lincoln's
racist utterances as strategic. But there is the barest possibility that
Douglas's racism was strategic as well. That said, there is still a substantial difference between deploying racism defensively, as Lincoln did, and
enlisting racism as a weapon, as Douglas did.

6.3 From Nonextension to Emancipation

The story of the evolution in office of Lincoln's policy, and Republican policy, against slavery has often been told, although it continues to
be a subject of considerable debate. My view, a view articulated by
LaWanda Cox in *Lincoln and Black Freedom* (1981) and given recent
development by Allen C. Guelzo in *Lincoln's Emancipation Proclamation:
The End of Slavery in America* (2004), is that Lincoln's anti-slavery convictions were deep and genuine, but constrained by his understanding
of the limitations imposed upon him by the Constitution, and that at
every step he sought to attack slavery only in ways he knew he would
never have to retreat from.[57] Emancipation and citizenship rights for
black people were consistent, although not perhaps inevitable, developments of themes Lincoln embraced in the 1850s, even in cases where
he then explicitly denied entertaining any ambitions to advance either
emancipation or racial equality. Lincoln sincerely denied that he had
the power, absent some unlikely series of events, to end slavery, and he
sincerely denied having any investment in political or social equality
for black people. But he was also already deeply committed to certain
values that demanded both things.

Anti-slavery and Bracketing in the Hodges Letter

In a letter of April 4, 1864, to Kentucky editor Albert G. Hodges, Lincoln gave a retrospective account of the thinking that led him to issue
the Emancipation Proclamation.[58] Lincoln began by noting that hostility to slavery had been a central conviction of his for as long as he
could remember, but he also noted that as president he could not merely
write his convictions into the law. Indeed, he almost treated acting

officially upon his own moral intuitions as if it would be an act of moral narcissism, supposing that in order to have moral legitimacy any act he proposed against slavery must respect the deliberative mechanisms provided for by the Constitution, must acquit itself in a public world guided by public rules. The argument here was of a piece with his earlier distinction between nonextension as an indirect and perhaps morally compromised, but formally legal, attack upon slavery on the one hand and abolition as a direct and moral, but extralegal, attack upon slavery on the other. It is also of a piece with the argument he had made in the Greeley letter of 1862 that his primary motive in fighting the Civil War was to restore the Union, not to end slavery, and that he only sought to end slavery once it became clear that doing so was necessary for restoring the Union:

> I am naturally anti-slavery. If slavery is not wrong, nothing is wrong. I can not remember when I did not so think, and feel. And yet I have never understood that the Presidency conferred upon me an unrestricted right to act officially upon this judgment and feeling. It was in the oath I took that I would, to the best of my ability, preserve, protect, and defend the Constitution of the United States. I could not take the office without taking the oath. Nor was it my view that I might take an oath to get power, and break the oath in using the power. I understood, too, that in ordinary civil administration this oath even forbade me to practically indulge my primary abstract judgment on the moral question of slavery. I had publicly declared this many times, and in many ways. And I aver that, to this day, I have done no official act in mere deference to my abstract judgment and feeling on slavery. (1:585)

There is a nuance in this passage that is worth examining. When Lincoln stepped back from treating his primary moral convictions as absolutely and immediately binding, he saw himself as backing away from a view that would claim "Let God's Will be done though the Heavens fall." Moral aims must be realized through institutions, Lincoln contended as early as the Lyceum speech, because without institutions moral politics reduces to a contest of force among enthusiasts, and only the machinery of public deliberation enables us to separate conviction from obsession, reasoned consent from deduction backed up by force (or force backed up by rationalization). Indeed, the license to act from primary moral imperatives without engagement with public institutions, however flawed, invites all partisans to enter into a violent struggle in which there is no assurance that those who actually are morally right will win, since the outcome of such conflicts is determined by the one who brings to bear the most violence, not the most reason.

Loyalty to institutions is ultimately adherence to an ideal of persuasive engagement across lines of political and moral difference, and what motivates it is not a belief that institutions are more important than morality but that only the persuasive engagement that institutions mediate can keep moral conflicts from transforming themselves into naked contests of force in which morality serves only as a way to brandish weapons or to muster passions. Without persuasive engagement we can never tell our convictions from our passions, our moral conflicts from morally rationalized struggles over power.

Now one of Lincoln's most telling arguments against Douglas in the later stages of the 1858 debates and in the speeches he gave in 1859 in Chicago, Columbus, and Cincinnati was that Douglas, who was moved by a loyalty to political process not ultimately very different from Lincoln's own, was forced by that loyalty to pretend that slavery was a matter of moral indifference. Restraining his moral attack on slavery in this way, even in the name of protecting institutions without which freedom cannot be practically realized, Lincoln argued, deprived Douglas of the argumentative resources he would need in order to avoid being driven to the wall by the slaveholders, who might have argued, "If you don't say that slavery is absolutely wrong, then why shouldn't you allow me to have slaves? Because of your feelings? Because of your preference? Well, if you don't like slavery, then don't own slaves. But don't expect your sentimentality on that issue to be binding on me!" A moral recusal of Douglas's kind also encourages the people more generally to harden themselves to the moral affront of slavery, which makes the triumph of the slaveholders even more likely: "If it's only a *preference*, not a moral imperative, that you bring to bear against slavery, then why quarrel about it, particularly if the other side is willing to resort to shooting about it and you aren't?"

Why was Lincoln himself not vulnerable in the Hodges letter, and, more pointedly, in the rebukes he gave to Generals Frémont and Hunter (who had attempted military emancipation), to the charges he had made against Douglas in 1858 and 1859? Certainly, impatient anti-slavery speakers like Wendell Phillips, who called Lincoln "The Slave-Hound of Illinois" for his support of the 1850 Fugitive Slave Act, did not think there was much distinction between Lincoln's views here and Douglas's views earlier. From Phillips's point of view Lincoln had chosen law over justice, dealmaking pragmatism over right, institutions over their meaning, letter over spirit.[59]

Now of course Lincoln did not back away from his central political promise, to prevent the extension of slavery into the territories, and over the "secession winter" of 1860–1861 he resisted considerable pressure to compromise on this issue, some of it coming from Republicans. And he never pretended, as Douglas did, to moral neutrality about slavery. But even though it was clear to everybody that what threatened the Union was the politics of slavery, he insisted until 1862 that hostility to slavery would not play a role in his efforts to restore the Union, and he "bracketed" his hostility to slavery somewhat in the way Douglas had done earlier.

"Bracketing" here is a term of art coined by Edmund Husserl to describe how, in order to examine the quality of experiences, one must put to one side questions about whether statements about those experiences actually describe some external reality; it is "bracketing" that distinguishes phenomenology, the philosophical discipline most associated with Husserl and his followers (which let us call "the theory of experience"), from epistemology, the theory of knowledge.[60]

The use of the term "bracketing" in discussions of the quarrel between Lincoln and Douglas originated with a famous criticism of Rawlsian political liberalism by Michael Sandel.[61] A key feature of John Rawls's thinking about how to mediate conflicts, first over economic issues and interest issues in *A Theory of Justice* (1971) and then over moral, religious, and cultural issues in *Political Liberalism* (1993) and *The Law of Peoples* (1999), is the recourse to a thought experiment in which one imagines hypothetical persons examining possible societies from behind a "veil of ignorance" that prevents them from knowing their own position in that society.[62] These hypothetical persons are deliberately thinly conceived so as not to load their choices in a preconcerted direction. A just society is a society one would choose to enter after examining it from the "original position," behind the veil of ignorance. Only a just society is one into which you would be willing to parachute from nowhere, since only in a just society would it be safe to land in any of the positions it offers. The motivating insight behind this thought experiment is this: any arrangement you could only defend if you knew in advance how it would work out for you could not possibly be a fair one.

Slaveholders argued a great deal, Lincoln remarked, about how benevolent an institution slavery was for the slaves; but they never seemed to line up to become slaves themselves. And they always seemed to know, when they constructed defenses of slavery, not only that they would themselves be free in the society they were describing but that they would have to give up something that mattered to them if they were to choose a free society rather than a slave society. As Lincoln remarked in an 1858 note on the pro-slavery theology of one Rev. Frederick A. Ross, the author of *Slavery Ordained by God:*

> The sum of pro-slavery theology seems to be this: "Slavery is not universally *right,* nor yet universally *wrong;* it is better from *some* people to be slaves; and, in such cases, it is the Will of God that they be such."
>
> Certainly there is no contending against the Will of God; but still there is some difficulty in ascertaining, and applying it, to particular cases. For instance we will suppose the Rev. Dr. Ross has a slave named Sambo, and the question is "Is it the Will of God that Sambo shall remain a slave, or be set free?" The Almighty gives no audable answer to the question, and his revelation—the Bible—gives none—or, at most, none but such as admits of a squabble, as to it's meaning. No one thinks of asking Sambo's opinion on it. So, at last, it comes to this, that *Dr. Ross* is to decide the question. And while he considers it, he sits in the shade, with gloves on his hands, and subsists on the bread that Sambo is earning in the burning sun. If he decides that God Wills Sambo to continue a slave, he thereby retains his own comfortable position; but if he decides that God will's Sambo to be free, he thereby has to walk out of the shade, throw off his gloves, and delve for his own bread. Will Dr. Ross be actuated by that perfect impartiality, which has ever been considered most favorable to correct decisions?
>
> But, slavery is good for some people!!! As a *good* thing, slavery is strikingly peculiar, in this, that it is the only good thing which no man ever seeks the good of, *for himself.*
>
> Nonsense! Wolves devouring lambs, not because it is good for their own greedy maws, but because it is good for the lambs!!! (1:685–686)

All defenses of slavery depend upon the defender's knowledge that he or she will not be a slave. If there is anything that cannot be defended from the original position, slavery is among those things.

Against this kind of argument, Michael Sandel (1982) argues that the Rawlsian thought experiment of imagining the behavior of parties in the original position requires one to act as though actual persons do not have identities, passions, convictions, or values, that real human beings, this is to say, are something like the *homo economicus*, concerned with nothing beyond satisfying their most basic needs. The Rawlsian experiment, Sandel argues, requires one to treat very important features of the human personality, such as people's values or religious beliefs, as if they were somewhat unreal, or at least as if they did not have the foundational quality in people's moral lives that are often attributed to such things. In the Rawlsian conception, the persons behind the veil of ignorance know everything about the society they look at except which persons in it will be themselves. Rawls understands very well that real people have all of the features Rawls denies the parties in the original position, and the parties understand this as well, to the extent of knowing that they are choosing a society whose members will have all of these features, although which particular ones they will have is something they are not allowed to know. What the experiment is designed to do is not to separate what is real and what is unreal in human nature but to reduce the temptation to self-dealing that knowledge of one's own specific passions, convictions, values, and interests would create.

The parties in the original position are not, however, to be seen as versions of real people. For not only does the veil of ignorance deny them knowledge of all of the givens of their experience (race, class, religion, history, and so on), but they also are unlike people in that they are *only* rational maximizers, concerned with doing the best for themselves, without either moral motivations or an interest in the welfare of others. But we are not to conclude from this that Rawls, like some economists, believes that things like moral motivations are slightly unreal; Rawls designs the parties this way because he has assigned the role of those other aspects of human nature to the veil of ignorance itself. As we saw in section 5.2 above, people are both rational (concerned with themselves) and reasonable (concerned with making a fair deal with others), both interested and capable of practical reason, both driven by causes (or purely strategic agency, which is a version of the same thing) and responsible to laws of freedom given by reason. Rawls, to clarify the nature of the process, teases these aspects of human nature apart, assigning one to the parties and the other to the veil of ignorance. Although the parties lack many of the given aspects of real people and do not have religions, theories of the good, or allegiances to country or family or group, nevertheless they know that the people who will belong to the society they design from behind the veil will have such things. The parties have to design a society in which people have many different and passionate and conflicting investments, but the parties do not know in advance which of those investments will be theirs.

The veil of ignorance constrains the parties procedurally to a kind of fairness. If, when two children divide a cake between them, one cuts the cake but the other chooses which piece to take, the one cutting the cake will divide the cake in a way that is not only fair "by definition" (as if to say that wherever he or she cuts the cake it makes for a fair division in that the proper procedures have been followed) but also fair in that it corresponds in some way to already common intuitions about fairness, in that the portions are bound to be as equal as the child can make them.[63] So, for instance, Rawls argues that parties behind the veil of ignorance would not establish a society in which some people suffer terribly in order that others (the majority, perhaps) can prosper, because they would not allow a situation to develop in which they might come out on the losing end of that bargain. Rawls provided a sturdy general theory in *A Theory of Justice* (1971) of how societies should distribute the goods they have to offer among their members.

In his 1993 *Political Liberalism*, Rawls extended this theory to govern conflicts over ways of life—"comprehensive doctrines," which are entire ways of being, such as religions, ideologies, moral schemes, and so on—by arguing that justice requires a similar negotiation over these issues: an arrangement among religious groups, for instance, is fair only if the parties could imagine themselves choosing it from behind the veil of ignorance. Rawls has in mind here how religious toleration did in fact develop in the United States: as Tocqueville famously argued, because there were a multitude of sects flourishing in the United States, they each, for their own reasons, chose to favor a policy of religious toleration, because the followers of no sect could feel certain of dominating the developing republic. So far so good. But a truly stable political liberalism, Rawls argues, required a further step: each sect needed not only to make this pragmatic recognition that it was constrained to develop a habit of life with adherents of other sects but also to find ways of persuading itself, from within the horizon of its own values, that this arrangement is a good thing in itself, that one is a better Catholic, for instance, for engaging in relationships of reciprocity and fairness with Protestants than one would be if one could exterminate them and establish one's own version of the kingdom of Christ.

Sandel (1982) argued, against this theory, that the requirement of placing the parties in the "original position," behind the veil of ignorance, amounted to a demand that they "bracket" their values, treating those values as being somehow not fully serious, as not being matters of life-or-death urgency upon which the moral fate of the world hangs. He compared this position to the position of Douglas in the Lincoln-Douglas debates, arguing that Douglas, who declared to the public world that he did not care whether slavery was voted up or down in Kansas, so long as what Kansas did was what the people of Kansas wanted, was in effect doing what would be required from the Rawlsian original position. Douglas offered a kind of procedural fairness, but to offer that he had to blind himself to substantive unfairness, treating the conflict over slavery itself as requiring the kind of irrational "value judgment" (to use Weber's pejorative term for such things) whose correctness cannot be decided one way or the other by argument. One cannot step behind the veil of ignorance, Sandel maintains, without treating very great convictions as if they were merely sentimental preferences. Sandel, this is to say, by arguing that Douglas brackets his moral convictions and Lincoln does not, replays the Lincoln-Douglas debates with Rawls as Douglas and himself as Lincoln.

Sandel has a second objection that strikes me as more telling. Like Kant, Sandel argues, Rawls treats only those aspects of convictions that are *chosen*, that are expressions of practical reason, as worthy of the respect of reasonable people. But in fact, Sandel goes on, many of the deepest aspects of identity are *given* rather than chosen, and treating what is given, what we are born into rather than what we choose for ourselves from our own reason, as if it were merely superstition or hysterical conformity, is bound to produce an account of human identity that is false to what is most human about it. This is a version of the attack Hegel makes upon Kantian morality in *The Philosophy of Right*

(1821). Hegel argues that there is something inhuman about a moral world inhabited only by reasoning machines, in which the human stain but also the human warmth and the never completely explicit wisdom of experience embodied in custom, in what Hegel calls *sittlichkeit*, is seen as something to be ashamed of rather than as something whose meaning one must seek to grasp.[64]

Rawls's first line of defense is that nobody could choose a slaveholding society from the original position, since nobody in that position would risk winding up a slave, so the issue of whether one would have to bracket one's moral criticism of slavery in the original position cannot arise, since the original position is one from which it is impossible to defend slavery in the first place. But suppose we are asked to use the original position in a second-order way, to regulate conflicts among adherents of different comprehensive doctrines separated by strongly held moral convictions, between slave and free societies? Certain as I am that slaveholding could not be an option in the first kind of use of the original position, am I as certain that it could not have a position in the second kind of use? Could slaveholders and nonslaveholders have a decent republic in common between them, or is any scheme of cooperation in which slaveholders might have a place to be rejected, and if so, is the alternative a contest of force between them? Can slaveholding societies be at peace with nonslaveholding societies, or can they only agree to an armistice? And if I am certain that even in this second-order way slaveholding is beyond the bounds of reasonable argument from the original position, then might not *all* serious moral conflicts raise the same kind of issue that slavery does? If it is always possible to rule a moral opponent out of the arena of the original position, if moral opponents must always see each other as outside the bounds of "reasonable pluralism" about comprehensive doctrines, then does the Rawlsian thought experiment really offer ways from adherents of different moral views, different comprehensive doctrines, to work out fair terms of cooperation with each other, or does it, like so much else, reduce to a way to mobilize those whose convictions one shares against those whose convictions one opposes?

The issue is how to distinguish those conflicts the Rawlsian thought experiment is capable of mediating from those it is not. If one draws the boundaries too broadly, then Sandel's critique becomes justified. But if one draws it too narrowly, then the idea of the original position does not in fact provide a way to mediate moral conflicts between adherents of comprehensive doctrines, since any position one might wish to stigmatize can always be ruled out of bounds. The issue would seem to put Rawlsian liberalism in a cleft stick: either it must embrace amoral value-neutrality or it must enforce a dogmatic morality with a parade of broad-mindedness.

A second possible reply to Sandel's critique is that the Lincoln-Douglas debates do not provide a test case for political liberalism because the nineteenth-century United States, because it was a slaveholding society, was ipso facto not a liberal society. This might be a winning argument but it is not an illuminating one, because liberalism can always be defended in the way Communism was, by denying that any existing society ever tried to put its values into practice. Nineteenth-century America was, to say the least, an extremely imperfect liberal society, but it was also as close to a liberal society as history had offered up to its own time. And both Lincoln and Douglas were trying to come to grips with the slavery issue in ways that owe something to the intellectual traditions of liberalism.

Another, slightly different way to make this point would be to argue that slavery is by nature so heinous that it does not lend itself to the dealmaking style of political liberalism, any more than genocide does. This argument is undoubtedly right, but it also is not very illuminating, since it is an argument one can safely make only if one has already won the civil war it seems to invite one to enter. If dealmaking politics is possible only among decent people with decent aims, why engage in dealmaking over really serious issues at all?

What one looks for is some reasonably liberal way to proceed under circumstances in which liberalism matters but does not rule, which was certainly the state of affairs in the United States in the 1850s. One looks to such means to make bad democrats into better ones, and to talk those over whom liberalism has some appeal off of nonliberal high horses. In most of the actual conflicts of this era, liberal and anti-liberal values were intertwined, on both sides of the issues, in ways that make the argument that the opponent is so part-and-parcel demonic that one cannot deal with him at all an unattractive one. Even were the opponent demonic—and what real human being is not under some circumstances demonic?—giving one no alternative but a contest of force seems like the counsel of despair, not only because it treats everything short of force as a kind of bad faith but also because it makes it nearly impossible to reestablish persuasive engagement with one's opponents after one has beaten them, assuming that one does in fact beat them and assuming that one is not transformed in a dark way by the conflict. If political liberalism cannot manage the conflicts of people who are not only imperfect but even in their deeper aspects occasionally demonic, as all people are, then it has nothing to say about actual fallen humanity. The test of liberalism is how it manages actual conflicts between people as they are, and that is why history, as much as philosophy, casts light on the meaning of liberalism.[65]

It is not true that liberalism requires one to bracket all of one's moral convictions. Indeed, Rawls (1993) argues that adherents of different comprehensive doctrines can bring their moral claims into the public square, even when those are the claims that divide them from their opponents and even when those claims arise from deep-seated aspects of the comprehensive doctrine rather than from convictions shared by all members of the liberal political order. Political liberalism does not require people not to have convictions. It merely requires them not to treat their convictions as freeing them from the necessity of engaging their opponents. I may, for instance, be moved to vote or to campaign in particular ways by my religious convictions, so long as I do not do so in a way that forecloses fair dealmaking. I may get my co-religionists to outvote you about some issue that strikes me, but not you, as morally central. But I may not use the fact that I believe God is with me to license my executing you if you do not agree; the distinction is between persuasive resort to the powers of one's comprehensive doctrine and use of the state machinery of violence for repression licensed by that doctrine. But within the persuasive culture of liberalism there is no requirement that people treat their values as anything other than as values. This is why Rawls, in his reply to Sandel in *Political Liberalism* (1993), sees Lincoln's position in the 1858 debates as being within the orbit of liberalism. Sandel sees Douglas as arguing a "liberal" position, and he sees Lincoln as arguing a "communalist" or "republican" position—in the political-philosophical sense, not in the partisan sense. Rawls by contrast sees Lincoln as arguing from a liberal position, since liberals can resort to arguments from their comprehensive doctrines so long as they do not do so as a way to destroy the public square, and he sees Douglas, by contrast, as an unprincipled fixer, not engaged in liberal politics under any definition.

If it is not true that liberalism always requires one to bracket one's convictions, it is also not true that bracketing one's convictions is always the sign of an amoral pragmatism. Every opponent, even a partially demonic one, is occasionally capable of making a claim against one whose justice one is bound to concede. And every person with a claim of principle is bound (and does not sacrifice that claim of principle by doing so) to imagine how the world might look to those with whom he or she is in conflict. For one thing, that is the only means through which one might gain access to those deeper levels of conviction that might be used to persuade the opponent. For another thing, only by doing so can one gain an appreciation of the persuasive resources—other values, a shared history ("the better angels of our nature"), and so forth—that might be brought to bear in the conflict at hand. Only by engaging in the kind of imaginative exercise that bracketing makes possible (and which Lincoln engaged in in the Peoria speech) is one enabled to distinguish between those things the opponent can and cannot give up without a fatal sacrifice of principle or interest.

Does making the concession Lincoln made in the Peoria speech make it impossible for Lincoln to oppose the extension of slavery? Do those concessions place emancipation out of his imaginative reach forever? Hardly. We do not ask of bracketing that it completely free us from our preconceptions and from the limitations of our own needs and point of view and ideology. We only ask that it enable us to see six inches from our own noses, and once we have gone those six inches, the next six inches become a little clearer. Far from being a sacrifice of principle, bracketing is the price of that persuasive engagement that distinguishes between principle and obsession. Bracketing is not what distinguishes the amoral from the moral; it is what distinguishes persuasive engagement from narcissist fanaticism.

Even this vision of liberalism, the one that underlies Rawls's views of Lincoln, seems to me an idealized solution to the political problems that bring us to liberalism, because all politics takes place in the shadow of the violence that will prevail if politics comes to grief, and the recognition that even the most threadbare modus vivendi offers possibilities that confrontation usually forecloses makes me hesitate to draw the boundary between conflicts that liberal habits can address and conflicts they cannot address any too clearly. The rhetorical thrill of pronouncing that one's opponents are so depraved that they need not be bargained with is too deep, too intoxicating, and too rewarding not to be regarded with extreme suspicion. What one looks for is not a way to show that one no longer needs to resort to liberal methods of persuasion and dealmaking—the world is always giving everyone too many ways to do just that—but a way to proceed with liberal instincts in a world in which liberalism's success is a long shot. Usually the most politics can offer is a good reason for two opponents to postpone killing each other for today; if there is any hope for liberalism, it arises not from a philosophical sense of the things liberals can and cannot bargain about, but from a concrete, here-and-now sense of what means are or are not available to bring particular nonliberals to the table and to draw out better liberalism from particular bad ones.

The distinction that matters is not between morally stringent Lincoln and morally lax Douglas, or between morally stringent Phillips and morally lax Lincoln. Nor is it the distinction between bracketing moral convictions and being driven by them. Both Lincoln and Douglas occasionally bracketed their convictions. All political agents do this, and they have to do this if they are to preserve any hope of not killing each other this very afternoon. The distinction is not between bracketing and not bracketing, but between styles of bracketing that each offer different terrible risks. Neither Lincoln nor Douglas solved the problem. Douglas's attempted solution would be better described as seeking a modus vivendi than as seeking a liberal solution, because for practical, not philosophical, reasons, he despaired of finding anything else in the short run. Douglas's approach failed not only because of its internal weaknesses, which Lincoln relentlessly pointed out, chief among them its inability to define a position that would justify one's own side in holding its ground against really determined but unprincipled resistance, but also because the fire-eaters, who had the upper hand among the slaveholders, were simply not interested in a modus vivendi solution in the first place and really did seek the kind of political domination of the Republic that we usually ridicule under the name of the "slave power conspiracy."

Douglas felt, in my view, that he could not preserve persuasive engagement with his opponents if he presented explicitly moral arguments against them, because he thought those arguments would have inflammatory effects. He was forced, as I argued above, to present a position he partly held for moral reasons as if it were entirely the product of a purely economic calculus. He had, in other words, to pretend that his moral motives were only economic ones, which turned out to be a fatal error.

Lincoln did not present his moral motives as anything other than moral, but he too chose in the interest of persuasive engagement to hold those moral motives at arm's length. But this is to say that obedience to the Constitution did for Lincoln roughly what moral recusal did for Douglas. Unlike Douglas, Lincoln could present moral hostility to slavery as moral; but he always had to do so while keeping it firmly in check. Lincoln, who unlike Douglas genuinely did seek what Rawls defines as a politically liberal solution, and not a mere modus vivendi, failed because in the final analysis he did not understand the nature of his opponents, and persisted in believing that the Jeffersonian vision of slavery—hostile to it, if more than cautious in dealing with it—would ultimately defeat the Calhounian vision in the South if given the chance. Lincoln, like Douglas, made a worldly calculation of what he thought his opponents would be in a position to concede— Douglas, that the slaveholders would accept defeat in the territories if they were allowed a run for their money there, Lincoln that the slaveholders would accept nonextension if it were phrased in such a way as to postpone any direct threat to slavery to the indefinite future and if it were coupled with a pledge to respect the widely held sense that the Constitution prohibited federal abolition of slavery in the states. Both Lincoln and Douglas went rather further in making these concessions than most modern readers might wish they did. Both were mistaken about whether the slaveholders would in fact be willing to concede what Lincoln or Douglas felt it would be reasonable for them to concede. Lincoln's and Douglas's positions and methods are much closer to each other than either is to the positions dichotomously ascribed to them, whether by Sandel or by Rawls, because what separates them is a nuance in the way they bracket their moral convictions.

There are obvious vices to clinging to the ideal of persuasive engagement as the descent to violence gains speed. Certainly history offers many examples of figures who did just that. And certainly there is no telling in advance just at what point the line between when it is better to deal and when it is better to fight has been crossed, because it is the particulars of history, the kind and intensity of violence at both sides' disposal and their willingness to use it, that tells us this, and nothing about what the two sides are arguing over. We are all wise about such things in retrospect. We should hesitate to claim that we would have clearly known what to do had we not known how it all came out. Indeed, not analysis but hunches, maybe even riverboat gambles, seem to be all one has to go on as one approaches the line between dealing and violence, even though the price of a wrong guess is very high. But the fact that the stakes of a choice are high does not make the evidence upon which that choice is to be made any clearer.

There is a virtue in reluctance to give up persuasive engagement even in the face of strong pressure to do so, and that is that doing so makes it possible that even in the world of violence one can keep an eye to the restoration of persuasive engagement once the violence is over. The temptation of a certain kind of moral strenuousness is not merely that it makes violence easy but also that it changes the nature of violence, yielding not just war, which is in some ways always still rule-bound, but havoc, in which all things are permitted and in which the permission is granted by the very depth of the moral commitment that drives the havoc. If anything restrains us in war from descending from war to havoc, it is a sense that we will ultimately have to restore persuasive engagement with those who are now our enemies. Otherwise, and particularly when one is struggling with a genuinely demonic enemy, the temptation to become like that enemy is a large one. Something every biographer of Lincoln notes is his ability even in the midst of a hugely violent war, the bloodiest conflict, except for the contemporary Tai-Ping rebellion, between Borodino and the Marne, to keep before him the common humanity he shared with his enemies. It is a hard trick to fight a bloody war with an enemy you know you must sooner or later stop hating. And few leaders—I cannot come up with any, after long thinking about this—have managed that so well as Lincoln did.

Bracketing one's hostility to slavery and acting practically against it anyway do sometimes go together—was it seriously possible to believe, even among those who stoutly insisted that they would fight for the Union but not for the end of slavery, that it was anything but slavery that was putting the Union in danger? Who could not have known, however much they refused to acknowledge it, that even a war waged only for Union could not help but inflict fatal damage on slavery, whether as a matter of conscious policy or not? But a similar argument is true of Douglas's popular sovereignty position too: Douglas insisted that he did not care whether slavery was voted up or voted down in

Kansas. But suppose Douglas believed, as he did, that slavery could not prosper in the West, squatter sovereignty or not. Isn't even squatter sovereignty, in that case, like "defense of the Union," an accidentally on purpose weapon against slavery? The argument that Douglas's squatter sovereignty strategy (in its 1858, if not its 1854, version, although a case can be made for both) is morally indifferent to slavery applies just as strongly to Lincoln's "defense of the Union" strategy in 1861 and 1862. And if Lincoln's strategy can be defended as despite everything an oblique but effective weapon against slavery, that too is true of squatter sovereignty, at least as Douglas understood it.

Lincoln continued, within the limits imposed upon him by the Constitution, to seek practical ways to press his case against slavery. What is more, Lincoln was aware that each small movement against slavery opened possibilities for further acts against slavery. However hostile Douglas may have been inwardly to slavery, he never imagined that there would almost inevitably come a time when the Republic would be free of it, and Lincoln, by contrast, always acted on the assumption not only that such a time would come, but that small acts would continue to open the possibilities of larger ones. The Emancipation Proclamation, limited as it was, for instance, opened the possibility of recruiting black soldiers into the Union army, which in turn not only opened the possibility of the Thirteenth Amendment but also, although Lincoln himself hedged about this, raised the question of civil and political rights for black people in an irresistible form. Lincoln knew, for instance, that the exigencies of war would enable him to argue that military necessity required him to act against slavery. As Lincoln argued in the Hodges letter, even if his understanding of the Constitution forbade him from acting immediately against slavery, he could act against slavery if the survival of the Republic that Constitution governed required it: "I did understand however, that my oath to preserve the constitution to the best of my ability, imposed upon me the duty of preserving, by every indispensable means, that government—that nation—of which that constitution was the organic law" (2:585).

Defense of the Union in the Greeley Letter

The Hodges letter's argument about the defense of the Union requiring the destruction of slavery is meant to echo what had at the time seemed a demurral from emancipation, the letter Lincoln wrote to Horace Greeley on August 22, 1862, in response to Greeley's editorial "The Prayer of Twenty Millions," which had called for vigorous prosecution of the Second Confiscation Act. Even in the Greeley letter, Lincoln's most famous defense of the idea that his aim was to defend the Union, not to attack slavery, Lincoln's argument had an indirect point Greeley might not have noticed.[66] While the Army of the Potomac was still in disarray after Second Bull Run and while the Emancipation Proclamation waited in Lincoln's desk for an occasion to be released, Lincoln wrote:

> I would save the Union. I would save it the shortest way under the Constitution. The sooner the national authority can be restored; the nearer the Union will be "the Union as it was." If there be those who would not save the Union, unless they could at the same time *save* slavery, I do not agree with them. If there be those who would not save the Union unless they could at the same time *destroy* slavery, I do not agree with them. My paramount object in this struggle *is* to save the Union, and is *not* either to save or to destroy slavery. If I could save the Union without freeing *any* slave I would do it and if I could save it by freeing *all* the slaves I would do it; and if I could save it by freeing some and leaving others alone I would also do that. What I do about slavery, and the colored race, I do because I believe it helps to save the Union; and what I forbear, I forbear because I do *not* believe it would help to save the Union. I shall do *less* whenever I shall believe what I am doing hurts the cause, and I shall do *more* whenever I shall believe doing more will help the cause. (2:358)

The quotation was susceptible to two readings. First, of course, was its explicit claim that the restoration of the Union was not only Lincoln's central war aim but his only war aim. But the passage also supported a second, contrary meaning: if ending slavery were what was required to save the Union, slavery would be ended. And Lincoln knew, as Greeley could not have known, just how soon he would put the death of slavery in motion. Underneath the explicit disavowal of an intention to end slavery was a presentation of the conditions under which he would act against it.

Lincoln had to act against slavery with a certain amount of indirection. Moncure Daniel Conway, the Virginia abolitionist and theologian, captured some of it in his memoirs. Paying a visit to the White House with the younger William Ellery Channing in January 1862, Conway pressed Lincoln about issuing a plan for compensated emancipation. Lincoln conceded that there was increasing feeling in favor of emancipation, but that the issue was controversial enough that it could be advanced only in disguise:

> "I think the country grows in this direction daily, and I am not without hope that something of the desire of you and your friends may be accomplished. Perhaps it may be in the way suggested by a thirsty soul in Maine who found he could only get liquor from a druggist; as his robust appearance forbade the plea of sickness, he called for a soda, and whispered, 'Couldn't you put a drop o' the creeter into it unbeknownst to yourself?'" Turning to me the President said, "In working in the antislavery movement you may naturally come in contact with a great many people who agree with you, and possibly may overestimate the number in the country who hold such views. But the position in which I am placed brings me into some knowledge of opinions in all parts of the country and of many different kinds of people; and it appears to me that the great masses of this country care comparatively little about the negro, and are anxious only for military successes."[67]

It is a mistake to read even the primacy of restoring the Union as somehow antithetical to opposition to slavery, as if restoring the Union were a kind of diversion from the serious business. Even if the Union might have been restored without the destruction of slavery, slavery could not have been destroyed without the restoration of the Union, since without the Union the slave states could have done whatever they wished about slavery. Restoration of the Union was a necessary but not sufficient precondition for the destruction of slavery.

At the same time, the defense of the Union was not merely a *pretext* for action against slavery, and Lincoln had to wait until it became clear that he was not acting only from a pretext, else risk having his act disastrously overturned by the Supreme Court, still presided over by Roger Taney. The Greeley letter was a promise, although a highly qualified one, of action, even as it was made to appear as if it were a defense of inaction. But the action was not inevitable, because it depended upon things not under Lincoln's control—not just the outcome of Lee's

Maryland campaign, but whether the cause of the defense of the Union really did require emancipation. Under different circumstances—say, had Maryland been as close to secession in September 1862 as it had been in March 1861—the Greeley letter would have been seen only as a defense of Lincoln's failure to act more directly against slavery. The complexity of the tone is related to the complexity of the act, because Lincoln both willed and did not will the death of slavery. He could not act from a plan to destroy slavery, even from an accidentally on purpose plan clothed in a pretext. But he wished it to be destroyed (unbeknownst to himself, like the druggist in the joke). And by August 1862 he knew it would be destroyed.

Lincoln was quite serious when, in the Hodges letter, he confessed not to have guided events but to have been guided by them. For the end of slavery was at the same time his deepest act and not his act at all, and he both controlled events and was controlled by them in a way that even a theologian would find difficult to unravel. He did not plan for the military necessities to unfold as they did, and had they not done so (had the Confederacy collapsed at First Bull Run, say), he could not have acted and would have been constrained to act consistently with his promises in the 1858 and 1860 campaigns. But the course that actually did unfold was also, however obscurely, present in the penumbra of Lincoln's action; he did not imagine that his speeches in Illinois would make him president and that he would lead the Union through a war that would bring about the death of slavery. But he knew that opposition to slavery was as consistent with what was deepest about him as mere nonextensionism was and that events might unfold to give expression to things at this deeper level of motivation.

Military Necessity in the Browning Letter

In the Hodges letter, Lincoln explained that he held back from using the military necessity argument until he felt that it would be clear that it was no mere rationalization, turning back earlier attempts by General Frémont, Secretary Cameron, and General Hunter to call for military emancipation. Lincoln's rebuke of Frémont was particularly sharp, since he treated rationalizing attempts to claim military necessity as the hallmark of caesars. In a letter of September 22, 1861, to his old friend Orville Browning, then the junior senator from Illinois, Lincoln defended his revocation of Frémont's order. Arguing that the condition of the slaves must ultimately be set "by lawmakers, and not by military proclamations," Lincoln had tartly added:

> The proclamation in the point in question, is simply "dictatorship." It assumes that the general may do *anything* he pleases—confiscate the lands and free the slaves of *loyal* people, as well as of disloyal ones. And going the whole figure I have no doubt would be more popular with some thoughtless people, than that which has been done! But I cannot assume this reckless position; nor allow others to assume it on my responsibility. You speak of it as being the only means of *saving* the government. On the contrary it is itself the surrender of the government. Can it be pretended that it is any longer the government of the U.S.—any government of Constitution and laws,—wherein a General, or a President, may make permanent rules of property by proclamation? (2:268–270)

Now Lincoln would indeed go on to "permanent rules of property by proclamation" less than a year after writing this, but he did not make such a proclamation merely because he wanted to or because it was consonant with his values, but because military necessity required it.[68] In the autumn of 1861 the military necessities all pointed away from emancipation by proclamation. Frémont's order, Lincoln was aware, might have driven the border states into the arms of the Confederacy. Indeed, Lincoln had been receiving warnings about the effect of Frémont's proclamation from many sources in Missouri, Maryland, and Kentucky (not least from Joshua Speed).[69] "I think to lose Kentucky," Lincoln explained to Browning, "is nearly the same as to lose the whole game. Kentucky gone, we can not hold Missouri, nor, as I think, Maryland. These all against us, and the job on our hands is too large for us. We would as well consent to separation at once, including the surrender of this capitol."[70]

Grave as these pragmatic considerations were, however, Lincoln wanted to make sure that Browning understood that it was the legal issue, not the practical one, that moved him to overturn Frémont's proclamation, and that he had chosen to do so even before reports from Kentucky and the other loyal slave states had begun to filter in. Without a strong argument that military necessity required emancipation, to free the slaves by fiat, even on the basis of strong moral arguments, would have been a violation of the Constitution and would have compromised the rule of law. Emancipation by proclamation in 1861 would have been, not only practically, but also legally, the destruction of the Union Lincoln had sworn to save. Even as he was writing to Browning, however, Lincoln was aware that time would come when the argument of military necessity would become capable of deciding the question, an argument that would change both the practical and the legal meaning of emancipation by proclamation, and Lincoln pressed the loyal slave states to abolish slavery on their own as a way to prepare the ground for that step.

Lincoln's proclamation on May 19, 1862, revoking General Hunter's emancipation order (which order sought, from Hunter's tiny liberated enclave at Port Royal, to free all of the slaves of South Carolina, Georgia, and Florida) made clear that a main issue was the fact that Hunter had issued the order completely on his own hook. "No commanding general shall do such a thing, upon *my* responsibility, without consulting me," Lincoln had fumed to Chase. At the same moment, however, he also made clear in the language of the revocation that he himself, as commander in chief, might choose to issue such a proclamation if "it shall have become a necessity indispensable to the maintenance of the government" (2:318).

In the revocation order itself, Lincoln also alluded to recent federal legislation promising federal aid to any slave state that chose to adopt compensated emancipation. Lincoln's language took on an uncharacteristically pleading tone:

> The resolution, in the language above quoted, was adopted by large majorities in both branches of Congress, and now stands an authentic, definite, and solemn proposal of the nation to the States and people most immediately interested in the subject matter. To the people of those states I now earnestly appeal. I do not argue. I beseech you to make the arguments for yourselves. You can not if you would, be blind to the signs of the times. I beg of you a calm and enlarged consideration of them, ranging, if it may be, far above personal and partizan politics. This proposal makes common cause for a common object, casting no reproaches upon any. It acts not the pharisee. The change it contemplates would come gently as the dews of heaven, not

rending or wrecking anything. Will you not embrace it? So much good has not been done, by one effort, in all past time, as, in the providence of God, it is now your high previlege to do. May the vast future not have to lament that you have neglected it. (2:319)

This was not the language of someone with doubts about his anti-slavery convictions. It was not the language of someone who revoked Hunter's emancipation order in order to rescue slavery, or even in order to reassure the leaders of the loyal slave states that their own possession of slaves was secure, as he had assured those same people at the time of his revocation of Frémont's order. It was the language of someone who, despite the pleading tone, wanted the political leaders of the loyal slave states, not just of the seceding states, to understand that slavery had already been stricken a mortal blow by the war itself, and the revocation proclamation warned them to make provisions so that the end of slavery, inevitable anyway, might come to them on their own terms. In fact, Lincoln seems, partly on the basis of these fruitless negotiations with the loyal slave states, to have decided to emancipate the slaves in the seceding states only about ten days after revoking Hunter's order.[71]

Lincoln describes in the Hodges letter how the question of slavery in the border states and the question of slavery in the Confederacy were linked in his mind:

When, in March, and May, and July 1862 I made earnest, and successive appeals to the border states to favor compensated emancipation, I believed the indispensable necessity for military emancipation, and arming the blacks would come, unless averted by that measure. They declined the proposition; and I was, in my best judgment, driven to the alternative of either surrendering the Union, and with it, the Constitution, or of laying strong hand upon the colored element. I chose the latter. (2:586)

Indeed, even as Lincoln revoked his subordinates' attempts at military emancipation, the two Confiscation Acts were laying the legal groundwork for emancipation and, more, preparing the public mind to accept its inevitability. Lincoln was making clear to the representatives of the border slave states that the time when he might use the doctrine of military necessity to end slavery was approaching, and that the mere "friction and abrasion of war" would inevitably inflict fatal damage upon slavery in those states in any event, so that it would be wiser for them to adopt an emancipation plan of their own right away, so as to have some control over a process that was going to take place in any event.[72] The border state congressmen and the Democrats more generally continued to reject voluntary emancipation plans through the summer of 1862. But events would unfold in a way that enabled Lincoln to test whether their constituents really would make good the threats their representatives continued to breathe.

At the time he committed himself Lincoln had, at best, evidence that emancipation was not the obviously suicidal move it would have been six months previously. He did not, however, have persuasive evidence that emancipation would most likely play out his way. It could never have been completely clear to Lincoln, even at the moment of issuing the Emancipation Proclamation, whether emancipation would nerve the arm of the Union to its task or shatter the Union, because there was strong evidence both ways. Nor even could it have been entirely clear to Lincoln that issuing the proclamation would forestall intervention by Britain or France. The leaders of those countries could have treated emancipation as a desperate ploy designed to stir up a slave insurrection, an outcome that they may have felt called upon to forestall. Or on the other hand they may, as happened in Britain, have been foreclosed from intervening by the strong endorsement of emancipation by their own industrial working class. But that the weavers of Manchester would take this view at all was as uncertain as whether the government would have been swayed by their views, since it was, as Lincoln afterward pointed out in his grateful letter to the Manchester workers, exactly those working people who would most have borne the brunt of the destruction of the Confederacy's cotton economy. The British government, which only days after the proclamation was still publicly predicting a Confederate victory and still privately exploring with France the possibility of joint intervention, afterward conveniently chose to behave as though the proclamation itself, not the support of the workers, had foreclosed intervention.[73] It is hard to make the case that Lincoln issued the Emancipation Proclamation only for prudential or interest reasons, because there were strong calculations of interest tending in opposite directions, both in the United States and abroad, so that issuing the Emancipation Proclamation was, in the final analysis, something of a riverboat gamble, although a gamble guided by a shrewd player's intuition about the strength of his hand. The conflicting commentaries over the last twenty years have only deepened the mystery of why Lincoln acted against slavery when he did, and for what reasons.

Emancipation and the Loyalty of the Border States

Lincoln limited the scope of the Emancipation Proclamation (excepting the loyal slave states and regions of the seceded states already under federal control) in the ways required by the claim of military necessity. Had he chosen to use the claim of military necessity to abolish slavery in the loyal border states, the Supreme Court may have chosen to overturn the proclamation as a whole, arguing that since the claim of military necessity did not plausibly apply to the cases of the border states, the rationale for the proclamation as a whole was a pretext, not a reason. The proclamation had to be a half-measure, but it staked out a position there could be no abandoning, and, precisely because it was a half-measure, it motivated a sturdier and more sweeping solution. Having built the case for emancipation, having drawn former slaves into the army, and, further, having discovered what could not have been obvious in 1861, that the proclamation did not devastate the cause of the Union in the border states, Lincoln was enabled to press for a permanent and clear constitutional settlement through the adoption of the Thirteenth Amendment.

If the shaky loyalty of the border states had something to do with Lincoln's delay in issuing the Emancipation Proclamation, his impatience with the border states also had something to do with his commitment to issuing it. After a frustrating meeting with border state representatives at the White House on July 12, 1862, in which he encouraged them to adopt a scheme of gradual, compensated emancipation before "the institution in your states will be extinguished by mere friction and abrasion," (2:340–342) Lincoln crossed the Rubicon in his own mind. The next day, as he rode in a carriage with Secretaries Seward and Welles on their way to the funeral of Secretary Stanton's infant son, he announced (according to Welles's diary) that after several weeks of thought he had resolved to emancipate the slaves in the seceded states, a

policy he said had been "forced upon him by the rebels." He explained
to Welles that emancipation "was a military necessity absolutely essential to the salvation of the Union, that we must free the slaves or be
ourselves subdued." Such an act would, at the least, weaken the power
of the Confederacy, since it used its slaves to do such things as dig
entrenchments or move supplies, jobs that otherwise would have to be
performed by white soldiers. He further noted that the border states
would do nothing, left to themselves, and could be persuaded to free
their slaves only if the slaves were freed in the Confederacy first.[74]

Lincoln had determined to make the proclamation months before
he formally issued it, but he was persuaded by Seward to postpone doing so until after a military victory (which, on balance, the battle of
Antietam was), so that it would not seem to be a desperation strategy,
or a hopeless gesture ("like the Pope's bull against the comet," as Lincoln remarked in his reply to an emancipation memorial presented to
him by Chicago clergymen only a few weeks before issuing the proclamation that was already in his desk).

Three things came together to make the Emancipation Proclamation politically possible: a convincing argument that emancipation was
required by military necessity, a battlefield victory to make the proclamation not seem to be a desperate improvisation, and evidence that
the border states would not be driven to secession by the act. The
battle of Antietam settled both of the last two matters, first by being in
a way a Union victory but also, more importantly, by demonstrating
the people of Maryland would not rise up in support of the Confederacy (as the Confederates, remembering how Union troops had had to
fight their way through Baltimore to the defense of Washington only a
year before, had reason to believe they might). Barbara Frietchie as
much as George McClellan made possible the Emancipation Proclamation. But it had been waiting its occasion a long time before that,
and Lincoln may have been considering the possibility as early as the
attack on Fort Sumter itself.

6.4 From Emancipation to Citizenship

Military Necessity in the Conkling Letter

Lincoln could have framed the argument that military necessity required emancipation in several ways. He did not argue that emancipa-

tion would strike at the root cause of the war and thus remove its necessity. Nor did Lincoln make the somewhat harsher argument that
emancipation would weaken the Confederacy by attacking its vital economic institutions. Nor did he make the harshest argument of all, that
emancipation would provoke a slave insurrection that would cripple the
enemy's resistance (as the British had attempted to do, both during the
Revolution and during the War of 1812). The possibility of a large-scale
slave insurrection was something Lincoln in fact was repulsed by, and
which he was relieved did not occur. Nor did Lincoln argue even that
emancipation would strengthen the Union's position abroad by foreclosing possible interventions by Britain and France. The key military
necessity Lincoln built his case for emancipation upon was the need for
manpower; slavery was ended, Lincoln explained in the Hodges letter,
to make possible the recruitment of black soldiers for the Union army.[75]

If Lincoln framed the argument for military necessity in the Hodges
and Conkling letters on the basis of the need to recruit black soldiers,
he was considerably more ambivalent about this prospect—and more
worried about whether the Democrats and the border states would accept it—at the time of the proclamation itself. The thinking in the
Hodges letter may have been retrospective. But it was clinching.[76]

The value of framing emancipation this way, and the reason this
particular military necessity was given prominence over every other,
was not merely that emancipation did in fact provide needed manpower (a rationale that even Roger Taney could not claim was only a
pretext) but also that framing emancipation this way would make clear
that there could be no going back once emancipation occurred, and
furthermore that the fact of military service would give substance to
demands for a freer political order once the war was over. Of all the arguments about military necessity Lincoln might have chosen, he chose
the one that most opened the way for black citizenship later. And this in
the face of repeated denials, both before and after, that such a thing was
in his thoughts.

As Lincoln tartly wrote to James C. Conkling on August 26, 1863:

> I thought that in your struggle for the Union, to whatever extent the
> negroes should cease helping the enemy, to that extent it weakened
> the enemy in his resistance to you. Do you think differently? I
> thought that whatever negroes can be got to do as soldiers, leaves just
> so much less for white soldiers to do, in saving the Union. Does it

appear otherwise to you? But negroes, like other people, act upon motives. Why should they do any thing for us, if we will do nothing for them? If they stake their lives for us, they must be prompted by the strongest motive—even the promise of freedom. And the promise being made, must be kept. (2:498)

The edge in this passage needs some accounting for, because it is after all taken from a letter written in reply to an invitation to address a mass meeting in support of the Union in Illinois. Now Lincoln was certainly not in this letter speaking directly to Conkling, a close family friend from Springfield who had been one of his electors in 1860, and who indeed had criticized Lincoln in 1861 for his tentativeness in attacking slavery.[77] And he was also not speaking directly to the attendees at the Union meeting, who after all were gathering to support, not to criticize, the Emancipation Proclamation. (Indeed, they intended their meeting as a rebuke to anti-emancipation rallies being convened by the Democrats.) Lincoln spoke past Conkling, and past the attendees of his rally, directing his comments at Union-loyal but anti-emancipation Democrats. Lincoln addressed such people, who may have been skeptical of emancipation but who were sincere supporters of the Union, as if their very racism were grounds for suspicion of their Unionism. Unionists who opposed emancipation were no different from Copperheads, Lincoln argued, because, like Copperheads, they valued slavery more than they valued Union, and rather than attack slavery would deny the Union what it needed to survive.

Lincoln in the Conkling letter pointedly contrasted black soldiers with halfhearted white Unionists who did not risk themselves in this cause and whose "malignant hearts" and "deceitful speeches" class them with the allies of the Confederacy. It is hard to see in this contrast anything other than an oblique promise of black suffrage. There was no direct promise of suffrage in this passage, of course; but one cannot ask people to die for the sanctity of the ballot while intending to withhold the ballot from them, particularly if it is indeed the ballot, not merely the Union, that is foremost in one's own rhetoric:

It will then have been proved that, among free men, there can be no successful appeal from the ballot to the bullet; and that they who take such appeal are sure to lose their case, and pay the cost. And then, there will be some black men who can remember that, with silent tongue, and clenched teeth, and steady eye, and well-poised bayonet, they have helped mankind on to this great consummation; while, I fear, there will be some white ones, unable to forget that, with malignant heart, and deceitful speech, they have strove to hinder it. (2:499)

Notice that in this passage it was the ballot, the fact that the ballot is the final court of political appeal, that even the black soldiers were fighting for, not just emancipation.[78] The last sentence is particularly stinging in the context of the letter, because it explicitly reduced patriotic but anti-emancipation Unionists to disloyal Copperheads. The two were of course quite different—opposing emancipation and supporting secession are not the same thing—and these Unionists would have been quite right to take exception to the aspersion on their loyalty that that last sentence not-too-obliquely cast. These racist Unionists also—and it is hard to doubt that Lincoln was specifically twitting their racism here, specifically rubbing them on a sore place—might well also have taken exception to being compared unfavorably to black people: your racism makes you a bad citizen, and black people who lay their lives on the line for the Union and the sanctity of the ballot are better citizens than white people who oppose emancipation. The two insults were closely related, and both ultimately made what was in Lincoln's mind the same point: first, that those who would deny the Union something completely necessary to its survival cannot really be its friends, and, second, that when it comes to recognizing people's service to the Republic, black soldiers have earned a right to public respect, which is to say, to citizenship, that anti-emancipation Unionists have forfeited. Those who would oppose that citizenship, the passage implies, are no less Copperheads than those who opposed emancipation. Indeed, the black soldiers have already done what most distinguishes the citizen from the mere consumer, from what in classical times was called an "idiot," in that, unlike the halfhearted Unionists, they have put the Republic ahead of getting and spending, ahead of me and mine. The white racist Unionists were loyal only to their race, but the black soldiers were loyal to the res publica.[79]

The key to the connection between citizenship and military service, however, seems to be something that happened to armies all over the developed world in the latter half of the nineteenth century. Eighteenth-century armies were recruited by impressment, which is the closest thing white people have experienced (except for those taken by the Barbary Pirates) to capture by slave traders. John Keegan argues that eighteenth-century soldiers were like slaves in other ways as well in that they wore their master's livery (bright uniforms), were subjected to extremely harsh discipline (harsher even than nineteenth-century military discipline), fought in gangs (in order to make the very inaccurate musket a useful weapon), and were in most ways treated like rabble. ("Will Napoleon be afraid of your army?" the Duke of Wellington was asked. "He had better be," he is said to have replied; "they certainly scare me!")

What changed the status of soldiers, Keegan argues, was the draft, the necessity of which seemed to run in parallel with the development of the rifle, which put sophisticated deadly force in the hands of ordinary men, required of them discipline and self-control rather than mere submission, and brought, in Keegan's phrase, a measure of liberty, equality, and fraternity to military life.

The case is somewhat more complicated in the Civil War–era United States, because both sides, although armed with muzzle-loading rifles, never fully understood the lethality of the weapon, their officers being for the most part barely trained civilians who learned soldiering out of *Hardee's Tactics*, and, with suicidal results, continued to employ the massed tactics of fighting with muskets almost to the end of the war. But attributing all this political force to riflery tactics may be an overstatement anyway. Conscription, and for that matter the ways in which popular democracies have to wage war if they wage it at all, can account for all of the effects Keegan described.

The impressed soldier was a slave of the state, the draftee a citizen doing a citizen's duty, like a member of a jury. Conscription differed from impressment in being rulebound, in depending upon lists and registrations roughly the way voting does, and in being regulated, not merely licensed, by law. And if conscription obligates the conscripted, it also binds the state in obligations. Keegan demonstrates that universal suffrage followed upon the heels of conscription in all of the major European states in the last half of the nineteenth century. Conscription, even more than volunteer militia service, is the foundation of the modern idea of citizenship.[80]

Military Necessity in the Randall Interview

In a dark period during the summer of 1864, when the stalemates in both the Virginia and Georgia theaters had persuaded Lincoln that he would lose the 1864 election to the Democratic nominee, George Mc-Clellan, he had an extended conversation with Alexander W. Randall and Joseph T. Mills about his conduct of the war, and the probable consequences of McClellan's victory. He knew that McClellan was no Copperhead, and that he would be "in favor of crushing out the rebellion." But he was also sure that McClellan's desire to undo the Emancipation Proclamation and to seek to restore the "union as it was" could never succeed. First, Lincoln knew that the seceded states would not accept reabsorption into the Union. The argument embraced by many Democrats in 1864, although probably not seriously by McClellan himself, that the Confederate states could be talked into reunion if the Union agreed to tolerate slavery, was never anything but fantasy.[81] Second, Lincoln knew that without the between 100,000 and 200,000 black soldiers whom emancipation had provided for the Union army, the odds of military defeat of the Confederacy would be lengthened. McClellan believed that embracing the cause of emancipation had weakened the commitment of white soldiers to Union victory. But dismissing all those black soldiers would likely have damaged the war effort far more. And of course breaking the promise of emancipation would itself have disastrous practical effects. As Lincoln told Randall and Mills at the White House on August 19:

> Abandon all the posts now possessed by black men surrender all these advantages to the enemy, & we would be compelled to abandon the war in 3 weeks. We have to hold territory. Where are the war democrats to do it? The field was open to them to have enlisted & put down this rebellion by force of arms, by concilliation, long before the present policy was inaugurated. There have been men who have proposed to me to return to slavery the black warriors of Port Hudson & Olustee to their masters to conciliate the South. I should be damned in time & in eternity for so doing. The world shall know that I will keep my faith to friends & enemies, come what will. My enemies say I am now carrying on this war for the sole purpose of abolition. It is & will be carried on so long as I am President for the sole purpose of

restoring the Union. But no human power can subdue this rebellion
without using the Emancipation lever as I have done. Freedom has
given us the control of 200 000 able bodied men, born & raised on
southern soil. It will give us more yet. Just so much it has subtracted
from the strength of our enemies, & instead of alienating the south
from us, there are evidences of a fraternal feeling growing up between our own & rebel soldiers. My enemies condemn my emancipation policy. Let them prove by the history of this war, that we can
restore the Union without it.[82]

Lincoln made several points in this passage that are worth separating.
The first was the obvious moral point that you cannot withdraw a promise of emancipation, particularly when the emancipated have risked their
lives in the service of the Republic on the basis of your promise.[83] The
second was the obvious practical point, that the War Democrats would
be hard put to replace the between 100,000 and 200,000 soldiers emancipation had brought into the Union army. But the main point was a
point about the meaning of the war. Lincoln did not see restoration of
the Union and abolition of slavery as separate aims. He had not replaced
a war for Union with a war for abolition. He still saw himself as acting,
as he had promised to act in the Greeley letter, only in such a way as to
save the Union, and to do nothing except what advances the cause of
restoration of the Union. But he had come to see that the restoration of
the Union required emancipation, that without emancipation there
could be no Union. Lincoln's statement here was in fact rather stronger
than the one he made in the Greeley letter. One way to read that letter,
indeed, the way Greeley must have taken it, since he did not know that
the Emancipation Proclamation was waiting in Lincoln's desk as he
wrote the letter, is that without the Union there can be no emancipation
and that the goal of emancipation must be subordinated to the goal of
Union, and, if necessary, sacrificed to it. In fact, what Lincoln meant by
the Greeley letter, but did not wish Greeley to understand until after the
fact, was that emancipation had become a means of saving the Union
and that therefore emancipation would follow imminently upon a prudent occasion of announcing it. The Randall interview shows this problem from the other end of the telescope. Lincoln did not argue that
without Union there could be no emancipation. He argued that without
emancipation there could be no Union. Emancipation and Union were

not contradictory goals. They were not separate goals. They were not linked goals. They were the same thing.

Nonextension, Emancipation, and Racial Equality

The question of what kind of future Lincoln imagined for the freed slaves in the restored Union is a separate one from the question of when and how Lincoln began to think about emancipation. Although one cannot really promise emancipation until one has some idea about what life after emancipation will be like, Lincoln had used the fantasy of colonization to postpone thinking this question through, which is perhaps fortunate because the problem of post-emancipation life was so daunting and so fraught that looking too closely at it might have politically foreclosed emancipation itself. As we have seen, Lincoln was, until late in the Civil War, skeptical about whether the former slaves and their former masters would be able to work out a habit of life with each other. But once colonization had been taken off the table, it was incumbent upon him to figure out a way for them to do so, and this forced him, in a very tentative way, to rethink the question of political and social equality.

One starting point may have been the idea that the ex-slaves would continue to do gang work, as under slavery, but for wages, as they did in many post-slavery economies (although only briefly in the United States).[84] Where Lincoln did speak of gang labor for wages, as in his December 1862 Annual Message to Congress, he clearly had in mind only a temporary solution. Lincoln did not seem to have imagined debt peonage, as in Mexico, or even the sharecropper system that eventually came into place in the South. More consonant with Lincoln's free labor ideology would be a future as small farmers, small proprietors, and independent laborers. Even in 1858 Lincoln was imagining black people as having the same position and stake in a free labor economy that white people had. Presumably, although Lincoln said nothing in detail about this, black people could have some of the more basic citizenship rights, such as the ability to own property (which slaves themselves often had), the ability to transmit, bequeath, or inherit property, the right to marry, the ability to hold professional licenses, the ability to make and enforce contracts, the ability to sue and be sued, and the ability to give testimony, since all of these would seem to inhere in the free labor ideology of the Republican Party. In the Ottawa speech and elsewhere, no sooner did Lincoln get through disavowing racial equality, and remarking that black people and white people are obviously not equal in some things (although color was the only such thing he always explicitly cited, which may be a bit of a joke), than he went on, as we have seen, to argue that in some important respects, such as the right to "eat the bread, without the leave of anybody else, which his own hand earns, [*the black man*] *is my equal and the equal of Judge Douglas, and the equal of every living man.*" This passage rather clearly implies that Lincoln meant for the blacks to enjoy all of the fruits of the free labor ideology, which means all of the things I have been listing as "private civil rights," even if they are not listed in full. The more properly political aspects of citizenship, such as the ability to serve on juries, to vote, and to run for office, are things Lincoln did not yet imagine in 1858, and he specifically disavowed the intention of giving black people the vote (although, as Douglas noted, they already had that right in Maine and, if they met relatively high property qualifications, in New York as well).[85]

Lincoln was well aware, as he wrote in 1863 to Nathaniel Banks, the military governor of Louisiana, that it would be necessary for the loyal state government he charged Banks with setting up to "adopt some practical system by which two races could gradually live themselves out of their old relation to each other, and both come out better prepared for the new," and he proposed a scheme of public education for the long run and a (rather shoddy) system for contracted gang-labor for the short run.[86] Lincoln never got further than the proposal, in his April 11, 1865, speech on Reconstruction, of giving the ballot to the Union army veterans and the "very intelligent" among the freed male slaves. (This was the speech that persuaded John Wilkes Booth that Lincoln intended "nigger citizenship," and that his assassination was a matter of urgent and immediate necessity. Booth's original plan was to kidnap Lincoln and deliver him to the Confederacy, a plan made moot by the surrender at Appomattox. Hearing this speech seems to have breathed new life into his plans and to have changed his objective.)

Lincoln had been considering that proposal for limited black suffrage for at least a year. He had written on March 13, 1864, to Michael Hahn, the newly elected governor of Louisiana under the "10 percent" plan:

I congratulate you on having fixed your name in history as the first-free-state Governor of Louisiana. Now you are about to have a Convention which, among other things, will probably define the elective franchise. I barely suggest for your private consideration, whether some of the colored people may not be let in—as, for instance, the very intelligent, and especially those who have fought gallantly in our ranks. They would probably help, in some trying time to come, to keep the jewel of liberty within the family of freedom. But this is only a suggestion, not to the public, but to you alone. (2:579)[87]

The sentence about keeping the jewel of liberty within the family of freedom demonstrates that Lincoln had a practical motive for advancing black suffrage as well: black suffrage would make it more difficult for the former slaveholders to reinstall all of the repressive political machinery they had employed, not only against slaves but also against nonslaveholders. The sentence is evidence that Lincoln was worried that after the war the former slaveholders, having forgotten nothing, forgiven nothing, and learned nothing, would come back into power and resume their repressive ways, as indeed they did once the victorious Union tired of enforcing civil rights.[88]

Lincoln's proposal to Hahn, repeated in the Reconstruction speech, was a very limited one. But Lincoln also was very well aware that giving the ballot to African Americans who served in the Union army would create pressure for black suffrage more generally. It is a fair, but not a clinching, argument to see that position as inevitably creating a situation where a broader franchise would have to result. We simply do not know how Lincoln's thinking would have developed further, or whether it would have developed further at all, had he not been murdered four days after making this speech.

Even the hedging in the Reconstruction speech, however, offers rather more than first meets the eye. Lincoln addressed the objection that the constitution for Louisiana that the loyalists had proposed did not provide for black suffrage, for instance, by arguing that the interests of those who wished for that wider suffrage would have been better served by accepting the Constitution before them, with all its faults, than by rejecting it and running the risk that starting over again would yield a less satisfactory result. This argument did not commit Lincoln to supporting black suffrage, but it was also the kind of argument that someone seriously opposed to black suffrage would not have made, since its key premise was that the existing plan would make a wider suffrage ultimately more likely. When he praised the constitution, it is hard not to hear a promise underneath all the hedging:

> Some twelve thousand voters in the heretofore slave-state of Louisi-ana have sworn allegiance to the Union, assumed to be the rightful political power of the State, held elections, organized a State govern-ment, adopted a free-state constitution, giving the benefit of public schools equally to black and white, and empowering the Legislature to confer the elective franchise upon the colored man. Their Legis-lature has already voted to ratify the constitutional amendment re-cently passed by Congress, abolishing slavery throughout the nation. (2:700)

Indeed, the chief rhetorical burden of his argument was that accept-ing the rather limited constitution Louisiana had proposed would ad-vance rather than set back the cause of black suffrage, and that reject-ing it was more likely to risk the progress that had already been made than to advance it:

> Now, if we reject, and spurn them, we do our utmost to disorganize and disperse them. We in effect say to the white men "You are worth-less, or worse—we will neither help you, nor be helped by you." To the blacks we say "This cup of liberty which these, your old masters, hold to your lips, we will dash from you, and leave you to the chances of gathering the spilled and scattered contents in some vague and undefined when, where, and how." If this course, discouraging and paralyzing both white and black, has any tendency to bring Louisiana into proper practical relations with the Union, I have, so far, been un-able to perceive it. If, on the contrary, we recognize, and sustain the new government of Louisiana the converse of all this is made true. We encourage the hearts, and nerve the arms of the twelve thousand to adhere to their work, and argue for it, and proselyte for it, and fight for it, and feed it, and grow it, and ripen it to a complete success. The colored man too, in seeing all united for him, is inspired with vigi-lance, and energy, and daring, to the same end. Grant that he desires the elective franchise, will he not attain it sooner by saving the al-

ready advanced steps toward it, than by running backward over them? Concede that the new government of Louisiana is only to what it should be as the egg is to the fowl, we shall sooner have the fowl by hatching the egg than by smashing it? (2:700)

What the change of Lincoln's views on the subject of black citizenship between, say, the Peoria speech and the Reconstruction speech illustrates is not just the maturing of Lincoln's views, although all people's views were transformed under the pressure of war. For despite the explicit denials and hedging, Lincoln's final views were in a way implicit in his earlier ones, and in coming out in favor of black suffrage after years of explicit denial of a commitment to such a thing, he was still not completely reversing field, since the commitment had precedents as deep as the denials did. Louisiana's constitution was not an open-suffrage constitution, but it would make such a constitution possible, Lincoln argued, and a more forthright approach would in Lincoln's view have been more likely not only to have failed but to have foreclosed further progress. Lincoln's views on racial equality, like the Louisiana constitution, are charged with implicitness. Implicitness and reverse Burkeanism have often been features of historians' thinking about Lincoln—it is usually treated as a sense of Lincoln's ability to grow and change under the pressure of events, although historians differ about whether what they see is development, in LaWanda Cox's view, or William Lee Miller's, or David Carwardine's, or merely successful improvisation, as in David Herbert Donald's views. The reason these themes figure so largely in thinking about Lincoln is that they figure largely in Lincoln's own thinking, whether about Jefferson and his Declaration or about America itself.[89]

Nonextension, Emancipation, and the Slave Power Conspiracy

As deep as their primary hostility to slavery (but also logically dependent upon it) was the Republicans' fear that the political interests of slaveholders would inevitably corrupt the politics of the Union as a whole. Some of the particulars of the slave power conspiracy theory, as we saw in Chapter 3, are fanciful, but the idea that slaveholding has a corrosive effect upon liberal political institutions need not depend upon conspiracy-theory fantasies, since the ugly measures required by the defense of slavery were patent and obvious in any event. Indeed, secession itself is the greatest argument that the slave power theory was correct, since the seceding states' inability to abide by the result of a fair election they had fairly lost is trumping evidence of the rule-or-ruin mentality that seems to have driven southern politics during the descent to war.

Examples of the ways the defense of slavery demanded measures that corrupt popular government include slaveholder insistence upon the famous three-fifths compromise of the federal Constitution, which granted slaveholding states for apportionment purposes three fifths of a vote for every slave in their limits, a vote that would of course be cast by the masters. Similar provisions applied within slaveholding states, so that, for example, the nonslaveholding western counties of Virginia were underrepresented, and effectively disenfranchised, by the slaveholding eastern counties. A fairly apportioned Virginia House of Burgesses would without question have passed a *post nati* emancipation bill at the time of the Virginia anti-slavery debates of 1832.[90] The majority of the white population of Virginia in 1861 had overwhelmingly rejected secession during the secession winter of 1860–1861, and Virginia voted to secede only after the bombardment of Fort Sumter panicked the political elite into withdrawing Virginia from the Union. Although the final secession decision in Virginia was formally ratified by a large majority vote of 125,250 to 20,373—from a total free population of 1,105,453—given the disenfranchisement of poor, nonslaveholding voters, especially in the western counties, it is far from certain that a majority of the free population of Virginia actually favored secession. Indeed, the election returns from 1860 indicate some weakness in secession sentiment in the South generally. The majority in eight of the fifteen slave states voted for either Bell or Douglas in 1860, and in the slave states as a whole Douglas and Bell combined won 705,000 votes to Breckinridge's 570,000. In the first group of seceding states, Bell and Douglas still had 48 percent of the vote.[91]

Lincoln said in his July 4, 1861, message to Congress:

It may well be questioned whether there is, to-day, a majority of the legally qualified voters of any State, except perhaps South Carolina, in favor of disunion. There is much reason to believe that the Union men are the majority in many, if not in every other one, of the so-called seceded States. The contrary has not been demonstrated in any one of them. It is ventured to affirm this, even of Virginia and Tennessee; for the result of an election, held in military camps, where the bayonets are all on one side of the question voted upon, can scarcely be considered as demonstrating popular sentiment. At such an election, all that large class who are, at once, *for the Union*, and *against* coercion, would be coerced to vote against the Union. (2:258)

Lincoln also felt he had evidence, as he said in a letter he wrote to Cuthbert Bullitt on July 28, 1862, that the majority population even of Louisiana probably opposed secession but were too cautious or too servile to resist the state's elite. It is clear from the second volume of William W. Freehling's *The Road to Disunion* (2007) that secession in every state was the work of a determined minority. Alabama's governor, for instance, seized the federal fortifications in his state before secession had even occurred, to present the doubters there with a fait accompli.

The victory of the secessionists reflected the essential failure of democracy in the slave states. Hostility to popular rule, in the North and the South, often took the form of a tender regard for the rights of property, but in the South the property in question was inevitably property in slaves, the protection of which required subversion of popular rule within the states, in the Republic as a whole, and in the territories.

Beyond the special political power given to slaveholders, slavery distorted how political competition took place, locking southern politics into a death spiral in which each party had to race the other to the bottom in order to outdo the other in their professions of loyalty to their section and its peculiar institution, and each party had to struggle to invent new ways to force the free states into making humiliating concessions. How else to explain the ferocity with which southern politicians imposed insane imperatives such as support for the Lecompton Constitution, or for a federal slave code, or for reviving the African slave trade, unless they are seen as attempting to outbid other southerners in a loyalty-politics bidding war (looking for the opportunity to brand their opponents as Yankee-lovers), or testing to see how much they could wring out of the nervous politicians of the free states? Take, for example, the Fugitive Slave Act itself, which was designed to address a problem that posed no serious economic threat to slavery. If one

considers only those escaping slaves who made a successful break for
the free states or Canada, there were apparently, out of about four million slaves, a maximum of about 10,000 fugitives.[92] During the eleven
years of its operation, the enforcers of the Fugitive Slave Act returned
only about 300 persons to slavery.[93] Because the original problem and
the concrete practical effect of the law were so minimal, the Fugitive
Slave Act seems, according to Fehrenbacher, largely to have been designed as a symbolic insult, intended to rub their complicity with slavery
in the faces of northern politicians. The most repulsive features of the
act, insisted upon with what Fehrenbacher describes as "unrelieved abra-
siveness" by its southern supporters, all seem to have been specifically
designed to humiliate the free states and to force their submission.[94]

The Fugitive Slave Act was not only designed to compel the free
states; it was also designed to blackmail the slave states of the upper
South. When during the Senate debates over the Compromise of 1850
Maryland Whig Thomas Pratt offered an amendment to the Fugitive
Slave Act providing that the federal government would compensate
slaveholders in cases in which northern communities successfully resisted the return of their slaves, senators from the Deep South united
to defeat Pratt's amendment. William Freehling provides two expla-
nations for this course of action. In the first place, what mattered to
the Deep South was that the North submit to the act, not that the
master not lose the value of his slave. The senators from the Deep
South resisted a face-saving compromise because the point was precisely to cost the North face. But Freehling also argues for another,
even more interesting explanation. The senators from the Deep South
suspected that the slaveholders from the border South would use this
provision to provide cover for emancipating their own slaves, and the
rejection of Pratt's amendment was intended to make sure that in a political conflict over slavery the border South would not question its
loyalty to the Deep South.[95] Indeed, since the Fugitive Slave Act was
of more importance to the border South—where most of what fugitive
slaves there were came from—than to the Deep South, the timing of
the different bills that went into the compromise, Michael Holt has
argued, was designed to ensure that the border South would get its
Fugitive Slave Act only if it stood with the Deep South on issues such
as the boundary of Texas, and the organization of territorial governments for New Mexico and Utah Territories, as Mississippi senator

Henry Stuart Foote frankly admitted in a speech to the Senate in December 1851.[96] The repressive loyalty politics to which defense of slavery committed slaveholders played out, this is to say, not only in the way the slave states applied coercive pressure to the free states, particularly in the great debates over the Compromise of 1850 and the Kansas-Nebraska Act of 1854, but also in the tensions between the upper and lower South and in the tensions between slaveholding and nonslaveholding regions of the slave states.

Beyond even the concrete distortions of the political process imposed by slavery is the more general sense that slavery required an elaborate and vicious machinery of social and cultural repression to insulate itself from criticisms that might undermine its legitimacy. This repressive agenda underlies many formal acts of Congress pushed by the slave states over the thirty years preceding the Civil War, such as the censorship of the mails to prevent abolition literature from passing into the slave states, the gag rule concerning petitions about ending slavery in the District of Columbia (under which such petitions were not only tabled but also rejected unheard, since even tabling them was treated as a kind of incitement to slave insurrection), and the censure of Congressman Giddings. But the repressive agenda of the slaveholders was also served by physical intimidation in the Capitol itself, such as for example the assault upon Senator Charles Sumner by Congressman Preston Brooks of South Carolina, the threat by Senator Henry Stuart Foote of Mississippi to lynch Senator John P. Hale of Vermont if he ever came into his power (for which Foote was given the sobriquet "Hangman Foote"), the brawl started by South Carolina's Laurence Keitt's attack upon Pennsylvania's Galusha Grow during the House debates on the Lecompton Constitution, and finally, the brawl started by Virginia's Roger Pryor's attack upon Owen Lovejoy. These last two outbreaks—talk about schoolyard puerility!—were occasioned by the northern congressman's daring to actually stand in some part of the House chamber claimed by southerners. After the Pryor brawl, in which pistols were cocked in southern pockets, many congressmen came to work armed. Strangest of all of the slaveholder attempts to have their way in Congress by violence was the December 1859 suggestion by South Carolina congressman William Porcher Miles, during the long struggle over whether the Republicans would be able to elect John Sherman of Ohio as Speaker of the House, that he and his colleagues, with the help of a regiment of South Carolina militia, should forcibly seize the U.S. Capitol. South Carolina governor William Gist promised the troops if push came to shove, although he also cautioned Miles not to make his move unless it was absolutely necessary.[97]

More sinister than these outbreaks in Congress, because more widespread, were the blunter forms of cultural repression in the antebellum South, many of which had to do with collective defense of slavery, such as the murder of Elijah Lovejoy, and the incidents described in Clement Eaton's *The Freedom-of-Thought Struggle in the Old South* (1964), or, more recently and graphically, in David Grimsted's *American Mobbing, 1828–1861: Toward Civil War* (1998).

Repressive political violence also had a particular partisan edge, since, as Daniel Walker Howe argued in *The Political Culture of the American Whigs* (1979), political violence during the years of the second party system was typically something inflicted by Democrats on Whigs, but it is hard sometimes to separate the slavery aspect of these incidents from the more strictly partisan aspects. There was for instance considerable political violence, particularly in Baltimore and Philadelphia, between the Democratic and American Parties, each backed up by their own private armies of thugs, both at the polls and over such issues as the reading of the Bible in the public schools. But anti-anti-slavery violence had a uniquely repressive force, as David Grimsted has recently argued, because it not only silenced its objects but imposed a kind of censorship upon others (how often one reads in the writings of former slaveholders the mixed feelings about slavery they did not express when it might have mattered). Nativist mobs never successfully silenced their political opponents completely, but anti-anti-slavery mobs often did, silencing not the abolitionists themselves perhaps (Garrison really meant it when he said, "I WILL BE HEARD") so much as those who disliked slavery in a lukewarm way.

The question of citizenship for the former slaves was inevitably tied up with how slavery itself had corrupted the meaning of citizenship and repressed popular rule throughout the early Republic. If one of the aims of the Union during the Civil War became the "new birth of Freedom" Lincoln called for in the Gettysburg Address, that new birth would require an end to the repressive practices that characterized the slaveholding regimes. But those practices could not be ended without raising the question of black citizenship. And it was that citizenship, after all, that Lincoln had in mind when he spoke of a new birth of freedom in the first place.

6.5 Racism and Freedom

One way to put the slave power conspiracy theory is this: "Slavery is incompatible with freedom, not merely in itself, but also because the exigencies of slavery require slaveholders to trample democratic politics in order to protect it." But the relationship between slavery and freedom is more complicated than that, since the development of freedom would not have been possible without slavery, and how Americans thought about freedom was strongly rooted in their experience of mastery, even as, with a kind of Hegelian logic, they began to turn against the slavery that had made their freedom possible.

Polis, Oikos, *and* Herrenvolk *Democracy*

The slaveholders' best political thinkers were well aware, despite the Revolutionary generation's widely held sense that slavery and republican government were incompatible, that the freedom of their political community was in fact obtained by the enslavement of those who were excluded from it, and indeed they believed that wherever freedom is found it has been obtained by means of subjection and exclusion. Edmund S. Morgan showed in *American Slavery, American Freedom* (1975) that American-style African chattel slavery emerged in colonial Virginia as part of a complex political bargain between the landowning elite and a poorer class who originated either as (white) indentured servants or as yeoman farmers working the marginal lands that were available to them after the elite had laid claim to the most productive fields. The economic order of the elite depended upon subjection, and the poor whites had experienced subjection at the hands of the landowning elite. After Bacon's Rebellion in 1676 the elite class understood that the poor whites were so restive under their domination that the political order had become unstable. Bacon's Rebellion forced the elite to extend some political rights to the poor whites, but doing this threatened the economic order of the colony, since you cannot safely share political rights with those you must keep under heel in other ways. The introduction of African slavery freed the slaveholders from

economic dependence upon a class whom they otherwise had to master but to whom they could no longer deny a say in the affairs of the
colony. African slavery allowed the elite to secure their position by
exploiting another, politically safer population (safer because excluded
from political life both by perpetual slavery and by racial difference).
And the introduction of African slavery also freed the poor whites by
making them marginal players in the economy of the colony; they
knew all too well that only the enslavement of the Africans had rescued them from an analogous fate, and that such political rights as the
elite gave them were paid for by the exclusion of enslaved Africans
from all of the rights of citizenship. Political rights for poor whites
were made possible by the emergence of a slave economy in which the
great landowners did not depend upon the labor of the poor whites
and the poor whites were no longer subjected by their own crushing
dependencies upon the landowners. For both groups African slavery
was the price of their own freedom from each other.

Morgan's analysis of the situation in colonial Virginia provides a
model for Orlando Patterson's argument about the relationship between freedom and slavery generally. In *Freedom in the Making of Western Culture* (1991) Patterson sees slavery as frequently emerging as the
price of a deal between elite and nonelite classes, in which the provision of political rights for the nonelite is tied to the ability of the elite
to hold slaves. Under these circumstances the elite can grant the nonelite political rights, since they do not need their labor, and the nonelite
can grant the elite the right to hold slaves, because they are aware that
otherwise they would themselves be subjected by the elite.

Southern political thinkers frequently insisted that freedom generally
was only possible among citizens who did not stand in relationships of
dependency and necessity toward each other, and that therefore some
other portion of society, some portion excluded from political rights,
must bear the burden of the necessities without which no society can
function. Freedom is always, to paraphrase the stinging argument of
Senator James Henry Hammond's famous "Cotton Is King" speech of
1858, built upon a mud-sill of subjection, of which chattel slavery is only
one conspicuous example.

Freedom on this view is always the exclusive property of those who
are granted entry into the world of the polis, the world in which free
persons engage each other in persuasive deliberations about public

acts, a world characterized by the formal equality of its members and by their investment in free relationships of agreement and disagreement mediated by rhetoric in which the disavowal of force between them makes possible the generation of public power and public will. Those who are granted entry into the polis are enabled to do so by the imprisonment of others into the world of the *oikos*, the world of the household, a world characterized by an economy of obedience and subjection to the will of the head of the household, a world devoted not to developing the fame of public action but to the satisfaction of physical necessity, what Hannah Arendt calls "the metabolism of nature." The world of the polis is a world of freedom, equality, argument, public-mindedness, world-historical action, honor, and fame. The world of the *oikos* is a world of bondage, inequality, need, intimacy, shame, futility, and obliteration from history.[98]

What distinguished the American South among all of these visions of "classical" republican inequality was that the division between *oikos* and polis was not just the division between the hierarchical and authoritarian world of the household and the political world of free deliberation among formally equal citizens but also the division between bond and free, black and white.[99]

The connection between racism and democracy played out in two slightly different ways. For the masters, slavery freed them to enter into relations of equality with each other by freeing them from necessity, from the metabolism of nature. Because they were not dependent, and because mastery is what made them so, they were in a position to enter the public arena; their ideal of civic virtue was the consequence of an unholy bargain between republicanism and slavery.[100]

The racialization of slavery had a different effect upon white non-slaveholders. In the first place, the very history of slavery's introduction licensed the use of racial difference as a way to politically neutralize class difference. Only racism, and, better still, racism and slavery bound together, made all white people equal. And what better way for the white person who perhaps doubted that other whites really did consider him to be their equal than to insist loudly upon the shared privilege of whiteness? Since the claim to equality among white people depended upon the inequality of black people, the more serious the commitment to class equality, in the nineteenth century, the more serious also the commitment to racial inequality.[101] Indeed, those who

made programmatic claims to class equality were rather more likely to
embrace red-hot negrophobia than those who did not, since racial inequality need not be specially marked if it were merely one among
many forms of inequality, but it could be defended by egalitarians only
on the grounds that those it excluded were marked out by nature for
special contempt. Those at home with hierarchy, as the elite were,
need not imagine those on the lower levels of that hierarchy as nonhuman, but those who have a theoretical commitment to equality, as the
Jacksonians did, could only exclude black people from that equality by
having, as Lincoln says that Douglas did, "no very vivid impression
that the Negro is a human" (1:346).

The special relationship between racism and an angry demand for
equality among white people is the origin of that ideology George
Fredrickson calls "*herrenvolk* democracy."[102] The triumph of popular
democracy in the years of Jackson's presidency was indissolubly connected with the rise of the slave power, and the hardening of racial attitudes toward blacks and toward Native Americans over the same
years. In the Jackson era, greater democracy always also meant more
intense racism and more effective subjugation of the racial other; Jacksonian democracy was *herrenvolk* democracy, and the more serious its
democratic class agenda, the angrier its racism became.[103] Enflamed
racism was one of the ways in which the poor white extorted recognition from the elite white. Behind it is the outraged suspicion, never
fully shouted down, that the elite white deep down rather preferred
the blacks, so that whipping up talk of white supremacy on the part of
the poor white had the effect of suggesting the very fact it was designed
to repress, that his status was not much different from the black's status, indeed, from the slave's status.[104] This is why the white nonslaveholder was always paradoxically ready to claim that the slaveholder was
not really quite as committed to white supremacy as he himself was.
During the Reconstruction era, for instance, it was common for *herrenvolk* democrat nonslaveholder politicians, especially those from the
hilly regions of the South, where the people were often ardent racists
but also ardent Unionists, to argue that the freedmen would become
the political tools of their former masters; indeed, they frequently
hated the former slaves as the emblems of the elite white class's power.
Few went further in this regard than President Andrew Johnson, except perhaps Hinton Rowan Helper, the onetime anti-slavery author

of *The Impending Crisis of the South* (1857), whose florid racist tirades made him possibly the postwar era's most rabid negrophobe.[105] The conviction not only that racism was the chief guarantor of white equality (and the suspicion that the elite whites were not completely persuaded of white equality) had profound effects in postwar politics generally, destabilizing the political alliances necessary to sustain Reconstruction—between the Freedmen and the Unionists, most especially—and leading to the disenfranchisement of the black voter (and the imposition of formal racial segregation) not by the Bourbon governments that arose at the end of Reconstruction (which indeed depended upon the votes of such black people who retained the ballot to outpoll the upcountry voters), but by the insurgent Populists in the 1890s.[106]

Hammond's "Mud-Sill" Speech

The statement of the relationship among subjection, racism, and republican government that was most on the public mind during the Lincoln-Douglas debates was James Henry Hammond's "Mud-Sill" speech (often called the "Cotton Is King" speech) delivered in the Senate on March 4, 1858.[107]

Hammond began the speech with an attack on popular sovereignty as Douglas had framed it during the Kansas debates. This attack seemed to turn on an argument about what precisely constituted the will of the people of Kansas, and just who was in a position to ascertain what that will was; only toward the end of the speech did Hammond reject the idea that government should closely reflect popular will at all, and only at the end did he describe the dependence of freedom upon slavery, but his main concepts lurked in unacknowledged forms even in his opening arguments.

Hammond's technical argument was that only the Lecompton Convention was in a position to represent the will of the people of Kansas about their form of government. Only a convention is formally accredited to do so because a convention is the highest political body—higher than a legislature elected under the constitution the convention designs; higher than a territorial legislature responsible to the federal government; and, because it is a deliberative body, higher even than the expression of the people's sentiments by plebiscite.

Now there were obvious problems with this position that would have occurred to every hearer of Hammond's speech. For example, the election that sent the delegates to the convention was, as we have seen, a flagrantly illegitimate one that was not only marked by the usual pro-slavery frauds that characterized almost every election in Kansas during the territorial period but was also boycotted—against the advice of the newly appointed territorial governor, Robert Walker—by the anti-slavery settlers, who were arguably not only the majority, but the vast majority, of the people of Kansas. Hammond had several available retorts to these charges. The first was that only those who vote have a right to a say, and that in refusing to vote the free staters had ceded the constitutional convention to the Border Ruffians, an argument that might have had more weight had outrageously fraudulent elections dominated by intimidation not been the universal experience of elections in Kansas Territory.

Hammond's second retort was simply to charge the free staters with electoral frauds of the same kind:

> I hear, on the other side of the Chamber, a great deal said about "gigantic and stupendous frauds;" and the Senator from New York [Senator Seward], yesterday, in portraying the character of his party and the opposite one, laid the whole of those frauds upon the pro-slavery party. To listen to him, you would have supposed that the regiments of immigrants recruited in the purlieus of the great cities of the North, and sent out, armed and equipped with Sharpe's rifles and bowie knives and revolvers, to conquer freedom for Kansas, stood by, meek saints, innocent as doves, and harmless as lambs brought up to the sacrifice. General Lane's lambs! They remind one of the famous "lambs" of Colonel Kirk, to whom they have a strong family resemblance. I presume that there were frauds; and that if there were frauds, they were equally great on all sides; and that any investigation into them on this floor, or by a commission, would end in nothing but disgrace to the United States.[108]

Finally, even granting that the elections to the Lecompton Convention were marked by fraud, Congress had no authority, Hammond argued, to look into the legitimacy of the territorial convention, since Congress had only the power to "acknowledge" or "recognize" the sovereignty of the people of the incoming state, a sovereignty Congress had no power to ask critical questions about, not being sovereign itself (since even Congress was, in Hammond's view, a creature of the states, which had the only true sovereignty). Congress could ascertain whether the proposed constitution was formally a republican one, but it could not investigate whether the sentiments of the people of the territory were really behind it.[109] Congress could not insist that the constitution be ratified by a popular vote, since in fact the constitutions of many states, including Illinois, had not been so ratified at the time of their admission as states.[110]

Defending the legitimacy of the elections for the Lecompton Convention did not solve all of Hammond's problems, for a new territorial legislature had just been elected, this time with free-state voters casting ballots, and the new legislature was, needless to say, hostile to the Lecompton Constitution, and soon began also to repeal the repressive laws against free staters that its predecessor had enacted. Hammond responded by minimizing the authority of such a legislature, treating it as having no relationship to the will of the people of Kansas and as being merely the creature of the federal government: "The Territorial Legislature is a mere provisional government; a petty corporation, appointed and paid by the Congress of the United States, without a particle of sovereign power."[111]

More daring still was the way Hammond orchestrated an indirect assault on the idea of majority rule:

> But when that convention assembles to form a constitution, it assembles in the highest known capacity of a people, and has no superior in this Government but a State sovereignty; or rather the State sovereignties of all the States alone can do anything with the act of that convention. Then if that convention was lawful, if there is no objection to the convention itself, there can be no objection to the action of the convention; and there is no power on earth that has a right to inquire, outside of its acts, whether the convention represented the will of people Kansas or not, for a convention of the people is, according to the theory of our Government, for all the purposes for which the people elected it, THE PEOPLE, bona fide, being the only way in which all the people can assemble and act together.[112]

What this meant was that it was irrelevant whether the convention in fact reflected the opinion of the people of the territory, because the convention was itself what one means when one refers to "the people of the territory." Congress could ask of the work of a convention not whether it represented the people of the territory, but only whether the constitution it provided offers a republican form of government. It was not the business of Congress to question whether the constitution of Kansas invested power in a minority any more than it was the business of Congress to question the legitimacy of the existing constitution of South Carolina (which, in fact, did vest power in a minority) or the constitution of Rhode Island (whose minority regime, challenged during the "Dorr War" by a popularly elected but extralegal government, was upheld by Congress, and by the Supreme Court, where the position of the minority regime was defended by Daniel Webster himself). The sole proviso was that the calling of the convention must preserve the barest formal legality, which of course even the Lecompton Convention did.

Hammond's argument did not turn, however, entirely on the merely formal legality of the Lecompton Convention, but on a generalized skepticism about any reliance upon truly popular will:

> If what I have said be correct, then the will of the people of Kansas is to be found in the action of her constitutional convention. It is immaterial whether it is the will of a majority of the people of Kansas now, or not. The convention was, or might have been, elected by a majority of the people of Kansas. A convention, elected in April, may well frame a constitution that would not be agreeable to a majority of the people of a new State, rapidly filling up, in the succeeding January; and if Legislatures are to be allowed to put to vote the acts of a convention, and have them annulled by a subsequent influx of immigrants, there is no finality.[113]

The argument at first looks as though the problem was that popular will is changeable and nothing a popularly elected legislature can entertain has the stability to count as a fully formed intention about the people's form of government, relative to the decisions of a deliberative body specifically created to design that form of government. Legislatures can make ordinary law, but they cannot make constitutions.[114] This argument might have been more plausible had the Lecompton Constitution allowed for amendment of its most controversial provisions, most especially its slavery provisions in Article VII. At least in that way if the people in January really did disagree with the views of their counterparts of the previous April, they might be in a position to do something about it. But Hammond's argument was not that the popular will was so changeable and evanescent a thing that it could not be used to judge constitutions in a stable or reliable way; the argument was that the popular will is so changeable that it is not in the final analysis even real. If a slaveholding elite can manage, even for a few days, to seize control of a constitution-making body, it can so write that constitution to place their interests permanently beyond popular will, even permanently beyond the power of constitutional amendment, and no power on earth, not the people of that territory, not the people of that state after admission, and not Congress, can undo what they do, save by revolution. What Hammond meant by "THE PEOPLE" was always only the elite perpetrators of a successful putsch. That a constitution is a minority constitution was not in Hammond's eyes ultimately a vice at all:

> If this was a minority constitution I do not know that that would be an objection to it. Constitutions are made for minorities. Perhaps minorities ought to have the right to make constitutions, for they are administered by majorities. The Constitution of this Government was made by a minority, and as late as 1840 a minority had it in their hands, and could have altered or abolished it; for, in 1840, six out of the twenty-six States of the Union held the numerical majority.[115]

For a moment, Hammond sounds as though he was about to introduce the Calhounian concept of "concurrent majorities." It is the primary purpose of constitutions to hobble majorities in case they might take it into their heads to dispossess minorities. Since constitutions will (except in South Carolina) be administered by majorities, they must be designed by minorities with an eye to disempowering those majorities, lest the most significant minority, those without much property, seek to help themselves to the possessions of a propertied minority. As Hammond pointed out, the anti-democratic protection of property was hardly something the South had a monopoly upon. Hammond's ultimate target, however, in his attack upon Douglas's concept of popular sovereignty for Kansas, was rule by the people, except under very limited circumstances:

In all countries and in all time, it is well understood that the numerical majority of the people could, if they chose, exercise the sovereignty of the country; but for want of intelligence, and for want of leaders, they have never yet been able successfully to combine and form a stable, popular government. They have often attempted it, but it has always turned out, instead of a popular sovereignty, a *populace* sovereignty; and demagogues, placing themselves upon the movement, have invariably led them into military despotism.[116]

If the first half of the speech was directed against Douglas, and argues that popular rule and freedom are opposite things, the second half was directed against Seward, and argued that only slavery made freedom possible. Hammond responded to the challenge with the cold, understated tone of one who is provoking a duel:

As I am disposed to see this question settled as soon as possible, and am perfectly willing to have a final and conclusive settlement now, after what the Senator from New York has said, I think it not improper that I should attempt to bring the North and South face to face, and see what resources each of us might have in the contingency of separate organizations.[117]

The resources in question for the South's part were for the most part familiar geographical and economical ones—a mild climate, a long coastline, a great river, a large export of a valuable staple whose world cultivation the South dominated, and large economic resources which could tide the South over in times of economic crisis (such as the recent crash of 1857).

The most important source of southern strength, however, was not, according to Hammond, the wealth that slavery gave its economy, but the stability that slavery gave its social system. As Hammond put it in the most famous passage of his speech:

In all social systems there must be a class to do the menial duties, to perform the drudgery of life. That is, a class requiring but a low order of intellect and but little skill. Its requisites are vigor, docility, fidelity. Such a class you must have, or you would not have that other class which leads progress, civilization, and refinement. It constitutes the very mud-sill of society and of political government; and you might as well attempt to build a house in the air, as to build either the one or the other, except on this mud-sill. Fortunately for the South, she found a race adapted to that purpose to her hand. A race inferior to her own, but eminently qualified in temper, in vigor, in docility, in capacity to stand the climate, to answer all her purposes. We use them for our purpose, and call them slaves.[118]

The difference between the slave states and the free states was not that the latter did not have slavery but that the latter did not call the slavery they practiced by its right name:

The Senator from New York said yesterday that the whole world had abolished slavery. Aye, the *name*, but not the *thing*; all the powers of the earth cannot abolish that. God only can do it when he repeals the *fiat*, "the poor ye always have with you;" for the man who lives by daily labor, and scarcely lives at that, and who has to put out his labor in the market, and take the best he can get for it; in short, your whole hireling class of manual laborers and "operatives," as you call them, are essentially slaves.[119]

The difference was not that in the North labor was free, but that in the North oppressed labor was part of the political community, and should the laborers wake to that fact, trouble must necessarily follow, because political stability demands that labor and dependency be confined to the *oikos* and excluded from the polis. The power of racism was that it confirmed the separation of *oikos* and polis by demarcating the difference between them on the body. Without that demarcation, the injustice of the separation of subjector and subjected would be obvious to everybody, and the natural resentment would destabilize the society. Now of course Hammond's assumption was that the injustice of slavery was not as obvious to the slave as the injustice of capitalist exploitation was to the industrial worker, and that was at best a debatable assumption. It is especially worthy of note that what Hammond says was most to be feared was not armed revolution but mere electoral defeat by the ballot-bearing underclass:

We do not think that whites should be slaves either by law or necessity. Our slaves are black, of another and inferior race. The status in which we have placed them is an elevation. They are elevated from the condition in which God first created them, by being made our slaves. None of that race on the whole face of the globe can be compared with the slaves of the South. They are happy, content, unaspiring, and utterly incapable, from intellectual weakness, ever to give us any trouble by their aspirations. Yours are white, of your own race; you are brothers of one blood. They are your equals in natural endowment of intellect, and they feel galled by their degradation. Our slaves do not vote. We give them no political power. Yours do vote, and being the majority, they are the depositaries of all your political power. If they knew the tremendous secret, that the ballot-box is stronger than "an army with banners," and could combine, where would you be? Your society would be reconstructed, your government overthrown, your property divided, not as they have mistakenly attempted to initiate such proceedings by meeting in parks, with arms in their hands, but by the quiet process of the ballot-box. You have been making war upon us to our very hearthstones. How would you like for us to send lecturers and agitators North, to teach these people this, to aid in combining, and to lead them![120]

Hammond went on to predict a kind of apocalypse for the North. Strangely, it was not to be a class-conflict apocalypse so much as a religious-conflict one, although given the large numbers of Irish immigrants in the working class the two may have come in Hammond's mind to the same thing. Nevertheless, the anti-Catholic edge to Hammond's predictions is startling, considering that urban Catholic Democrats were the most reliable northern allies of the slave power. Perhaps only a South Carolina politician could have been so isolated from the actual political currents of the North as to be unable to distinguish his allies from his enemies. Hammond also, curiously, anticipated the Turner thesis, arguing that only the availability of cheap land in the West freed the North from having to face its intractable economic conflicts, and that that cheap land must eventually run out:

Have you heard that the ghosts of Mendoza and Torquemada are stalking in the streets of your great cities? That the inquisition is at band? There is afloat a fearful rumor that there have been consultations for Vigilance Committees. You know what that means.

Transient and temporary causes have thus far been your preservation. The great West has been open to your surplus population,

and your hordes of semi-barbarian immigrants, who are crowding
in year by year. They make a great movement, and you call it progress. Whither? It is progress; but it is progress towards Vigilance
Committees.[121]

If Hammond's argument here proved anything, it proved rather too
much. For if the point of race-based slavery was to insulate the white
community from social conflict, if racism really had the effect of making the rich white and the poor white equal, then the poor white had a
claim to equal representation in the public square. But Hammond could
no more concede majority rule to poor southern whites than he could
concede majority rule to the white people of Kansas, because doing so
would ultimately risk slavery.

Hammond could not resolve the contradiction within all visions of
herrenvolk democracy. The elite invoked *herrenvolk* democracy to secure
their rule: blacks were excluded as the price of the freedom of whites.
The exclusion of blacks secured the freedom of the poor white because
it freed the rich white from the necessity of subjecting the poor white.
But at the same time the rich white demanded a special status in the
Republic, using arguments about the rule of the elite and the necessity
of protecting property from expropriation by the poor that were not all
that different from the arguments he had used to exclude the blacks
from the polis in the first place. The unresolved question was whether
the poor white was part of the polis or part of the *oikos*. The black was
unambiguously part of the *oikos*. The poor white seemed to straddle the
division: he was not subjected like the members of the *oikos*, but he was
not enfranchised like the members of the polis either. Slavery was the
price of freedom for the elite, and *herrenvolk* democracy promised the
poor white entrance into that elite. But the poor white could not really
enter that elite, because he still had interests that threatened the elite,
because he had interests that threatened slavery.

Even after the end of slavery, the rich white could not really share
power with the poor white, but he could keep him at bay temporarily
by claiming to better represent the common interests of white people
against black people. Only by keeping racism at a boil could he keep
down the poor white's suspicion that he thought of the poor white and
the black in similar terms, and the poor white, in turn, could extort recognition from the rich white by demanding ever-uglier demonstrations
of racial solidarity. But without the domination of state institutions

written into the slaveholding constitutions, the rich white could not forever resist ceding power to the poor white, which is how, after the populist revolution, the populist demagogues, overturning the former slaveholders' claim to speak for all whites by outdoing the former slaveholders' racism, seized control of the state governments throughout the South and put both the former slaves and their former masters under heel. The Bourbon aristocrat and the populist *herrenvolk* Democrat both had reasons for whipping up racism, although they did so for opposite reasons, each seeking to use it to destroy the other.

The Douglas and Seward halves of Hammond's speech represented different moments in the history of the relationship between slavery and freedom. Against Seward, Hammond argued that only slavery provided the economic basis, the mud-sill, upon which a free polity could be erected for those whom the uncompensated labor of those in the mud-sill class freed from dependency. Against Douglas, Hammond argued that popular rule must be chained, lest it destroy the public order, by which he meant lest it threaten slavery. Both parts of the speech shared the elitist republicanism characteristic of pro-slavery thinking generally, and South Carolina thinking specifically. But they looked in opposite directions—one, looking back to the ordeal of colonial Virginia, and, beyond that, to the slaveholding democracy of Athens, saw slavery for the many as the precondition of freedom for the few; the other, looking at the present in Kansas and into the post-Jacksonian world in general, saw freedom in general as a threat to slavery and to the stability of a slave society. Hammond's speech touched both sides of the story, unintentionally capturing just how it was that slavery transformed itself from being the precondition of freedom to being its enemy.

Stephens's "Corner-Stone" Speech

When Alexander Stephens gave his "Corner-Stone" speech in Savannah on March 21, 1861, it was clear that it was precisely democracy as Jefferson understood it that the new Confederacy, which Stephens had reluctantly joined, and of which he had just been elected vice president, was to transcend and leave behind.[122] Stephens was remarkably frank in conceding that it was slavery, not states' rights or the tariff or any of the other proxy issues, that finally broke the Union apart, and that the chief superiority of the Confederate constitution over the federal one was its explicit endorsement of slavery and racial inequality:

> The new constitution has put at rest, forever, all the agitating questions relating to our peculiar institution—African slavery as it exists amongst us—the proper status of the negro in our form of civilization. This was the immediate cause of the late rupture and present revolution. Jefferson in his forecast, had anticipated this, as the "rock upon which the old Union would split." He was right. What was conjecture with him, is now a realized fact. But whether he fully comprehended the great truth upon which that rock stood and stands, may be doubted. The prevailing ideas entertained by him and most of the leading statesmen at the time of the formation of the old constitution, were that the enslavement of the African was in violation of the laws of nature; that it was wrong in principle, socially, morally, and politically. It was an evil they knew not well how to deal with, but the general opinion of the men of that day was that, somehow or other in the order of Providence, the institution would be evanescent and pass away. This idea, though not incorporated in the constitution, was the prevailing idea at that time. The constitution, it is true, secured every essential guarantee to the institution while it should last, and hence no argument can be justly urged against the constitutional guarantees thus secured, because of the common sentiment of the day. Those ideas, however, were fundamentally wrong. They rested upon the assumption of the equality of races. This was an error. It was a sandy foundation, and the government built upon it fell when the "storm came and the wind blew."[123]

Even more startling than his frank embrace of racial inequality was his concession that Jefferson's ideals, as Jefferson himself understood them, would have committed the Union ultimately to emancipation. However much the origins of freedom may have depended upon slavery, for Jefferson slavery was not only unjust but a kind of atavism, something he expected the Republic to outgrow. But in attacking the Jeffersonian promise of freedom, Stephens did not, as Hammond did, merely return to a pre-Enlightenment vision of republican society. He believed he was embracing a racist future, not returning to a racist past, and he grounded his racism not in tradition but in what he believed to be science. Indeed, he thought of the racism of the Confederacy as a kind of new departure in politics, a new kind of regime:

> Our new government is founded upon exactly the opposite idea; its foundations are laid, its corner-stone rests upon the great truth, that the negro is not equal to the white man; that slavery—subordination to the superior race—is his natural and normal condition. [Applause.]
>
>   This, our new government, is the first, in the history of the world, based upon this great physical, philosophical, and moral truth. This truth has been slow in the process of its development, like all other truths in the various departments of science. It has been so even amongst us. Many who hear me, perhaps, can recollect well, that this truth was not generally admitted, even within their day. The errors of the past generation still clung to many as late as twenty years ago.[124]

Stephens's Confederacy, this is to say, is in his view not a traditional society but a modern one, not a manifestation of conservative loyalty to old and tried, if ugly, ways of being, but a breaking through of sentimental illusions into a harsh but accurate understanding of the world, not a retreat from liberal democracy but a transcendence of it:

> As I have stated, the truth of this principle may be slow in development, as all truths are and ever have been, in the various branches of science. It was so with the principles announced by Galileo—it was so with Adam Smith and his principles of political economy. It was so with Harvey, and his theory of the circulation of the blood. It is stated that not a single one of the medical profession, living at the time of the announcement of the truths made by him, admitted them. Now, they are universally acknowledged. May we not, therefore, look with confidence to the ultimate universal acknowledgment of the truths upon which our system rests?[125]

Stephens in fact went out of his way to distinguish the Confederacy from traditional hierarchical societies, arguing that traditional hierarchical societies, unlike the Confederacy, are unjust because their inequalities are not founded in nature:

> It is the first government ever instituted upon the principles in strict conformity to nature, and the ordination of Providence, in furnishing

the materials of human society. Many governments have been founded upon the principle of the subordination and serfdom of certain classes of the same race; such were and are in violation of the laws of nature. Our system commits no such violation of nature's laws. With us, all of the white race, however high or low, rich or poor, are equal in the eye of the law. Not so with the negro. Subordination is his place. He, by nature, or by the curse against Canaan, is fitted for that condition which he occupies in our system. The architect, in the construction of buildings, lays the foundation with the proper material—the granite; then comes the brick or the marble. The substratum of our society is made of the material fitted by nature for it, and by experience we know that it is best, not only for the superior, but for the inferior race, that it should be so.[126]

For all their daring, none of the apologists of slavery ever was able to produce a fully consistent defense of it. Those who defended a racialized order of slavery were never able to account for the presence of free blacks, who were a significant population in the border slave states, and existed in significant concentrations even in such slave-state economic and cultural centers as Charleston and New Orleans; nor could such pro-slavery thinkers ever fully convince the masters of their own doctrines, except when the masters were themselves in the act of facing down their critics. (Else why, despite agitating the subject before secession, did the seceding Confederacy write a prohibition against reopening the African slave trade into its constitution?) Furthermore, as both Clay and Lincoln pointed out, those who defended a racialized version of slavery always used arguments that would have justified making the most capable and intelligent blacks into masters and making the least capable and intelligent whites into slaves, perhaps into slaves of those black masters.[127] Those who on the other hand defended a nonracialized version of slavery, contrasting the capitalist division of worker and owner with the slaveholding division of "patron" and "servant," "warrantor" and "warrantee," could not explain to nonslaveholding whites why they did not intend to enslave them.

Irrepressible Conflicts

Lincoln, it is worth noting, was, like Clay, always skeptical of the racial rationale for slavery. During the campaign with Douglas, in a speech given September 11, 1858, at Edwardsville, Lincoln quoted a telling passage from an 1849 letter Clay had written advocating voluntary emancipation in Kentucky:

> I know there are those who draw an argument in favor of slavery from the alleged intellectual inferiority of the black race. Whether this argument is founded in fact or not, I will not now stop to inquire, but merely say that if it proves anything at all, it proves too much. It proves that among the white races of the world any one might properly be enslaved by any other which had made greater advances in civilization. And, if this rule applies to nations there is no reason why it should not apply to individuals; and it might easily be proved that the wisest man in the world could rightfully reduce all other men and women to bondage. (1:582–583)

The conflict over slavery reached the point of war because both sides ultimately came to the view that their opposition to each other was both irreconcilable and inescapable. The truth of the slave power conspiracy theory is that, as William Freehling has so eloquently pointed out, even *herrenvolk* democracy could not render the absolute sway mastership required compatible with the survival of free society, because the masters could never fully trust that nonmasters, northern or southern, really would give them unforced loyalty, and so they could not dominate their slaves without dominating the people of the free states and the nonslaveholders of the slave states. And conversely, even the loudest proclamations of loyalty to *herrenvolk* democracy never quite sufficed to prove to the nonslaveholders of the slave states that the masters did not secretly despise them. The nonslaveholders, in the North and in the South, were not altogether wrong to fear that the slaveholders entertained the desire to "reduce all other men to bondage."

On the other side, the idea of freedom itself had changed, so that even though slavery had been the nurse of freedom, freedom and slavery could no longer coexist. Lincoln had captured the change in a fragment he dashed off, for unknown reasons, in 1858: "As I would not be a slave, so I would not be a master. This expresses my idea of democracy. Whatever differs from this, to the extent of the difference, is no democracy" (1:484).

Few passages can render so succinctly and pointedly the difference between a republican (small *r*) sensibility, at home with inequality to the point of treating it as the precondition of republican freedom, and a democratic (small *d*) sensibility, turning as it does on a Kantian refusal to treat human beings only as means and a Kantian acknowledgment of all persons as ends in themselves. Lincoln's interpretation of Jefferson's "All men are created equal" in the Peoria speech has an equally Kantian tang: "No man is good enough to govern another man, *without that other's consent*. I say this is the leading principle—the sheet anchor of American republicanism" (1:328).

These passages explain why slavery and freedom came to seem contradictory. But they do not explain why that contradiction had to escalate to the point that one or the other had to be destroyed. It is the power of the political necessities of slavery that explains, on the southern side, why slaveholders had to demand ever-more-profound forms of submission from nonslaveholders. It is the slave power thesis that explains, on the northern side, why slavery was not only wrong but a threat: slavery had to suppress dissent in order to survive. But beyond the concrete evidence of a movement by slaveholders to suppress free government, it is the moral logic of Kantian reciprocity itself that explains why Lincoln felt that free government's survival was at stake in the conflict over slavery, because even tolerating slavery does things to free societies that risk their survival as free societies.

Replying on April 6, 1859, to an invitation from Henry L. Pierce and others to address a festival in Boston in honor of the birth of Jefferson, Lincoln had remarked on the power of allegiance to Jefferson's promises in the Declaration of Independence to prevent the reappearance of tyranny. Lincoln said this in the face of his feeling that the temptation of tyranny was still a strong one, and that only a firm rededication to Jefferson's promises was capable of preventing a reappearance of tyranny that was not only otherwise inevitable but also already far advanced:

> All honor to Jefferson—to the man who, in the concrete pressure of a struggle for national independence by a single people, had the coolness, forecast, and capacity to introduce into a merely revolutionary document, an abstract truth, applicable to all men and all times, and so to embalm it there, that to-day, and in all coming days, it shall be a rebuke and a stumbling-block to the very harbingers of re-appearing tyranny and oppression. (1:19)

The arguments deployed by the defenders of slavery are arguments, Lincoln maintained, whose use themselves portends the destruction of freedom generally. Worse yet, they are arguments that mere rational persuasion was becoming less and less capable of prevailing against, since increasingly the defenders of slavery denied premises so basic that they left Lincoln with no clear idea of how the defenders of slavery might be reached by argument. But if those who advance pro-slavery views are not crushed, democracy itself must fail:

> One would start with great confidence that he could convince any sane child that the simpler propositions of Euclid are true; but, nevertheless, he would fail, utterly, with one who should deny the definitions and axioms. The principles of Jefferson are the definitions and axioms of free society. And yet they are denied, and evaded, with no small show of success. One dashingly calls them "glittering generalities"; another bluntly calls them "self evident lies"; and still others insidiously argue that they apply only to "superior races."
>
> These expressions, differing in form, are identical in object and effect—the supplanting the principles of free government, and restoring those of classification, caste, and legitimacy. They would delight a convocation of crowned heads, plotting against the people. They are the van-guard—the miners, and sappers—of returning despotism. We must repulse them, or they will subjugate us. (2:19)

An escalating confrontation over slavery could not be avoided, because slaveholders could not maintain slavery without repressing the dissent of nonslaveholders, and democrats could not accommodate the tyranny of slavery without losing their democracy. Lincoln's formulation in the Pierce letter adopts the grim, Emersonian language of "compensation," but its sense of how the quest for absolute power, for mastership, leads only to futility, has its roots in Lincoln's thinking as far back as the Lyceum speech: "This is a world of compensations; and he who would be no slave, must consent to have no slave. Those who deny freedom to others, deserve it not for themselves; and, under a just God, can not long retain it" (2:19).

If it was freedom (of a sort) that the slaveholders thought slavery would secure, it was also freedom, the freedom of all nonslaveholders, that slavery threatened, and each, slavery and freedom, rightly saw each other as a mortal threat. It was freedom as well that ensured that when the conflict over slavery escalated, it would escalate into bloody violence on a hyperbolic scale unknown in the West between Waterloo and the Marne. Every other slaveholding society in the New World except Haiti ended slavery without civil war. The difference between the United States and the British West Indies, or Cuba, or Brazil, was not that slavery was more heinous and brutal in the United States than in those places, but that in the United States the slaveholders had a share of the political say, and not only were in a position to prevent slavery from ending by any means short of war but also were in a position to foreclose, by using loyalty politics to enflame even the smallest compromises, those half-measures that might have made emancipation easier. It was democracy that made war over slavery in the United States inevitable. And it was democracy that ensured that when war did come, it would be a total war, the first one in history.[128]

History, Complicity, and God in the Hodges Letter

Lincoln denied that he aimed to attack slavery directly, but he also at the same time argued that slavery and freedom could not both survive. Whatever his own intentions or program, he understood that history had a logic that transcended his intentions and that would always remain partly obscure to him. Over the course of the war, he came to understand that even his intentions had a meaning and a purpose that he himself had only partly understood, that emancipation had revealed itself to be in the space of implicit entailments of nonextension, in the shadows of his own willing. What is more, racial equality was also in that implicit space, even under denial, even if it was acknowledged only in hindsight, in the way some crucial act, always both intended and denied, acknowledged and unacknowledged, seen and unseen, lurks in and gives meaning to our agency. In ways that Douglas could not have seen, and that Lincoln, with perfect sincerity, could reject, Douglas's charge that Lincoln intended to emancipate the slaves and to bring about political and social equality among the races was true, but true in a way that brings out all the shadowy recesses of terms like "will," "intention," and "acknowledgment." It is this, the implicitness of his own intentions, their obscurity even to him, that Lincoln had in mind when he said in the Hodges letter that "I claim not to have controlled events, but confess plainly that events have controlled me."

The conclusion of the Hodges letter is even more startling. Lincoln modestly denied that he planned the course of events that culminated in emancipation.[129] But he did not mean to describe his act as a mere improvisation, for he portrayed it in the language he had used in his famous Meditation on the Divine Will, language to which he would recur in the Second Inaugural Address:[130]

> Now, at the end of three years struggle the nation's condition is not what either party, or any man devised, or expected. God alone can claim it. Whither it tending seems plain. If God now wills the removal of a great wrong, and wills also that we of the North as well as you of the South, shall pay fairly for our complicity in that wrong, impartial history will find therein new cause to attest and revere the justice and goodness of God. (1:586)

This at first sounds like an argument about providence. But usually when one makes an argument about providence the argument is intended as a not-very-oblique boast about one's own wisdom, as indeed usually when one invokes God the God one invokes turns out to be a version of one's self, except with a much louder voice.

As in the Second Inaugural Address, Lincoln wished in the Hodges letter to make clear that he did not see the Mason-Dixon line as the frontier between good and evil. As in the Peoria speech, Lincoln conceded in the Hodges letter that those in the South right then did not invent slavery, were not completely free to abolish it, and were not responsible for the accident of birth that placed them where they found themselves, any more than nonslaveholders deserved the moral good fortune of being born where they were born, or indeed any more than the slaves themselves deserved their accident of birth. What is more, Lincoln argued here, the fact that the people of the northern states did not physically own slaves did not free them from complicity in slavery. As in the Second Inaugural, and as in the Meditation on the Divine Will, Lincoln did not imagine the Civil War as a contest between a good Union and an evil Confederacy, but as a kind of trial given to both North and South because of their mutual imbrication in slavery. Indeed, in the Hodges letter when Lincoln referred to "you of the South," he was not in fact referring to the Confederacy at all, but to Union-loyal slaveholding Kentuckians like Hodges, Dixon, and Bramlette themselves, and to the readers of Hodges's newspaper.

"The recognition of complicity is the beginning of innocence," Robert Penn Warren said near the end of his own epic about slavery, *Brother to Dragons* (1953). Moral agency begins when one divests one's self of the illusion of moral purity, something that it is very hard to do without also being paralyzed by the sense of one's own impurity. If war is to bring a new birth of freedom, it can do so only in the context of a forbearing and un-self-righteous settlement between former enemies who have at least a chastening recognition of complicity in common with each other. But a forbearing and un-self-righteous settlement is not necessarily an easy one, since each side forgives the other chiefly by recognizing their mutual involvement in a huge crime for which they must jointly atone.

Arguments about providence usually congratulate those who make them for their insight into God's design. Lincoln's argument here, however, was that his policy on slavery had turned out in a way he did not anticipate and did not plan, and the emphasis here was not that God does have a plan, but that no human knows precisely what that plan is, and that those who say otherwise are kidding themselves. Neither party—the Union or the Confederacy—devised the end of slavery, because the Confederacy sought to preserve slavery, and the Union, whatever it may have felt about slavery, was unwilling to take any step that might have jeopardized the restoration of the Union until hard experience forced them to take that risk, for the Union's sake. The Union's illusion about the purpose of the war was at much in play in the Hodges letter's vision of moral complicity as the North's economic stake in slavery was. Indeed the illusion that the Union could have been restored without the destruction of slavery, the illusion that God seems to have been rebuking by continuing the war, was not only the North's illusion, but Lincoln's illusion as well.

This last charge, that the prolongation of the war was God's rebuke of the free states, and of Lincoln himself, for embracing the illusion that the Union could be restored without the destruction of slavery, needs more specifying. It might at first be read as maintaining that the Union and Lincoln himself were simply wrong about the meaning of the war, thinking of it as a war for union when it was in fact a war for emancipation. But the idea that it was a war for emancipation was not simply a revelation that came to Lincoln, and to the Union, from nowhere. Obscurely both always knew but did not acknowledge (in fact explicitly denied) that slavery, not mere secession, was the issue. All knew, as Lincoln argued later, in the Second Inaugural, that slavery was "somehow, the cause of the war." The obliqueness of the phrasing captures the experience, how the agents both know and do not know, acknowledge and do not acknowledge, the meaning of their conflict. Their error was not their ignorance, but their failure to acknowledge something they obscurely but certainly knew yet lacked the courage or the honesty to own up to.

And it was that, not just error and not just racism but what Aristotle calls *acrasia*, persistence in something one knows better than to do, that is the crux of Lincoln's rebuke of the Republic, and God's rebuke of him: both knew better, but did not allow themselves to recognize it, in just the way that we all usually do in fact know better when we do something that ought to run deeply against the grain of our own convictions. The Union knew and did not know that it could have no peace until slavery was destroyed, and even as it set the death of slavery in motion it earnestly and repeatedly denied being on the course it had in fact long been embarked upon already. So also Lincoln in the 1858 debates and after both knew and did not know that there could be no stable solution to the slavery problem short of citizenship for the former slaves. Lincoln persisted in proposing halfway solutions up to the final days of his life. And he clung to the fantasy of voluntary colonization, sometimes only for rhetorical purposes (so as not to have to give answers about what the shape of postwar society might be that it would have been fatal to give), but sometimes also as a way of not facing up to the meaning of the war even inwardly. Sometimes the fantasy of voluntary colonization was used to throw sand in the eyes of the voters. But sometimes Lincoln used it to deceive himself. Even in his first presentations of the idea of colonization he saw clearly enough that the idea was a confection of wishful thinking. But he also kept proposing it, kept pressing it. Like "the Union as it was" (a tag phrase used by many who favored modest Union war aims), voluntary colonization was something Lincoln at once saw through and did not see through, and black citizenship, like emancipation, was something he both willed and did not will, embraced and did not acknowledge.

America both meant and did not mean to deliver what Jefferson promised (and what Lincoln kept referring to throughout the debates with Douglas), the promise of moral equality. Lincoln himself both knew and did not know the same thing: like Jefferson, he too promised equality. And under pressure from Douglas, he too denied ever making that promise. Douglas was right that black citizenship and social and political equality among the races were the ultimate meaning of the "House Divided" speech. Lincoln denied this because to acknowledge it would have been suicidal and would have put it out of reach. But he also denied it because he himself could not acknowledge it, until the pressure of violence, like the promise of being hung in the morning, clarified his mind.

Neither side expected the outcome of the war, because it turned on events that could not have been predicted, such as the military victory at Antietam, the strengthening of the Unionist political position in the border states, and, what is more, the transformation of views all over the Union on the slavery question itself. The Union's aims, and its moral personality, were revolutionized under the pressure of violence, in ways that could not have been predicted (and might even have been rejected as possibilities) at the beginning of the war. When Lincoln spoke of God's claiming the outcome of the struggle on slavery, what he meant by "God" here seems to be the inner logic of violence as an agent of implicitness and becoming, which transforms the moral personalities of human beings in unpredictable but in retrospect comprehensible ways.

Even Lincoln's guess in the Hodges letter about God's intention was a veiled one, since what he knew is matched with what he not only did not know but could not know. To claim that the hand of God has shaped events is not to claim that events are intelligible but rather that they have a depth that intelligence will never be able to plumb. God in the Hodges letter is not only unknowable but always in a state of restless becoming whose direction no human is clever enough to foresee; God's course makes sense, but only in retrospect, and the retrospective knowledge is never enough to ground prospective designs, because that course always turns out to subvert or overturn human expectations and desires. The divine will is not unknowable, but it is knowable only with a later knowledge, and even then only provisionally, because it is charged with both endless implicitness and endless becoming. Like all matters that become and develop from implicitness, it can be interpreted, but not predicted.

The unknowability of the divine will is not only a standing rebuke to human cleverness and human plans but also a standing rebuke to the moral personality. The one most important consequence of God's unknowability is that nobody is in a position to claim to have a hold on the good so secure as to license using the good as a weapon against their enemies. Crucial as it is to seek to do the right, it is also crucial never to succumb to the illusion that one can claim moral purity. Lincoln rebuke of the North referred most of all to the North's own complicity in slavery, its economic dependence upon it, its political supineness, its willingness to let racism and laziness cloud its perception of its own acts. But he also wished to rebuke the vanity of imagining that one speaks for God, and, more important still, the vanity of imagining that one ever has a secure hold on the good. Our moral acts, like our motives, are always mixed, and their meaning is never available to us when we make them. Not only is the practical outcome of our acts a kind of wager, but how precisely the good and evil in our own motives, and even in our acts, work out in the long run is also a wager. God knows, but we cannot, the meaning of our acts. God knows, but we cannot, whether our acts are even on balance good acts. Because the divine is always shrouded in implicitness, and indeed because our own motives are also shrouded in implicitness, their meaning is not available to us at the moment of action.

America's Abraham is to this extent then rather like Kierkegaard's Abraham, who in *Fear and Trembling* (1843) had to prepare to sacrifice his son in the face of what would seem to be a paralyzing doubt about the justice of the act, since the act was immoral on its face. Kierkegaard's Abraham, his "knight of faith," made a dramatic, but also a desperate, leap of faith, in the face of the absurd. Lincoln by contrast always acted cautiously, deliberately, waiting until it was clear to him that whatever act he did could not be reversed. But he too could not know the meaning of his own acts when he did them. He could not know what the object of the war was when he began to fight it. He could not know, of course, whether his own sacrifice of many American sons would have a good effect. Indeed, in taking unavoidable risks that might have led to the triumph of slavery (had emancipation provoked the secession of the border states), Lincoln could not even be sure whether what he was doing was morally right, if outcomes matter at all when it comes to evaluating acts morally. Pushing for racial equality, emancipating the slaves, even fighting a war to restore the Union and proposing a forbearing settlement to follow victory were all in their own ways leaps of faith.

CHAPTER 7

The Dred Scott *Case*

*L*INCOLN AND DOUGLAS EACH STROVE to use the *Dred Scott* decision against the other. In different ways, Chief Justice Taney's opinion put pressure upon the politics of both of them, and each sought to evade its force while foreclosing the attempt of the other to do the same.

The methods they adopted to respond to the decision differed as the threat to them differed. Douglas could claim to support the decision since he supported its holding that the federal government could not prohibit slavery in the territories (a holding that ruled the central policy of the Republican Party out of constitutional bounds). And he supported those parts of Taney's opinion that affirmed white supremacy in terms even more naked than Douglas's own. But Taney had also specifically attacked popular sovereignty, Douglas's own central policy, arguing that the territorial legislatures, being creatures of Congress, had no more power to prohibit slavery than Congress had. Douglas could evade the thrust of this charge by arguing that it was not what the Court as a whole had decided, and in point of fact there really was reason to doubt whether the aspects of the opinion most threatening to Douglas really were the opinion of the Court. But he also had to prepare a position in case that part of Taney's opinion were to be affirmed by the Court as a whole later.

Lincoln, by contrast, had to respond to a decision that was part and parcel hostile and that contradicted his vision of the meaning of politics in wholesale ways. And he had to do this without, on one hand, presenting an anarchist challenge to the constitutional order, such as sometimes proceeds from a critique of that order from the point of view of a divine alternative law, and also without, on the other hand, engaging in the kind of regal high-handedness he and his party had criticized when President Jackson engaged in it over the constitutionality of the Bank of the United States and over the removal of the Cherokees. He had, this is to say, to avoid replacing law with theology, and he had also to avoid replacing law with politics.[1]

The methods Lincoln and Douglas used to respond to the threat the *Dred Scott* decision posed differed as their key political values differed. Lincoln characteristically sought a deeper layer of controlling principle, and sought to define that principle in a way that avoided the pitfalls of higher-law idealism. By reimagining how moral conflict represents itself in law, Lincoln produced one of the deepest meditations about the authority of law and the meaning of legal decisions in the American canon. Douglas, also characteristically, sought to return the issue, which the Court had sought to place beyond politics, to the political world, where conflicts over that issue could be mediated by dealmaking, negotiation, and agreement to differ. He responded to Justice Taney's fiat that territorial legislatures could not legally prohibit slavery with the so-called Freeport Doctrine, the argument that notwithstanding the Court's ruling, the territorial legislatures could evade the force of that prohibition and still prevent slavery in practice either by hostile regulation or merely by failing to provide the special police codes slavery needed in order to prosper. As happened with almost every attempt Douglas made to mediate moral conflicts through political dealmaking, Douglas's efforts wound up inflaming the conflict he was trying to settle, and the controversy over Douglas's Freeport Doctrine wound up destroying the Democratic Party, the last remaining truly national institution in the Republic.

The methods Lincoln and Douglas used to foreclose each other's responses were also characteristic. Douglas, with his usual ugliness, sought to portray Lincoln's resistance to the decision as being no more than an expression of a sentimental attachment to racial equality.[2] And he continued, in the face of persuasive evidence to the contrary, to assert that Lincoln was moved by a kind of fanatical absolutism foreign to his nature (but perhaps held by the most resolute among his supporters), as if evidence of any deep moral commitment at all were evidence of a politics-destroying moral obsession.

Lincoln's methods were more subtle. It used to be argued that Lincoln somehow tricked Douglas into making the fatal misstep of embracing the Freeport Doctrine. In so doing, the argument ran, Lincoln prepared the ground for his own victory over Douglas in 1860. But Douglas required no prompting from Lincoln to articulate the Freeport Doctrine, which he been making for years, and which influential southerners such as James Orr of South Carolina and Jefferson Davis of Mississippi also made. Arguments about the Freeport Doctrine wound up destroying the Democratic Party not because the doctrine was itself inflammatory, but because Douglas's opposition to the Lecompton Constitution had changed what the Freeport Doctrine meant in southern eyes.

That said, Lincoln's attacks upon the Freeport Doctrine resembled those mounted by the South more than they resembled those mounted by Republicans, and if he did not trap Douglas into inventing the Freeport Doctrine, he certainly did try to shape the southern Democratic response to it. Lincoln could have stressed, in Republican fashion, that the Freeport Doctrine was likely to fail to prevent slavery from taking root. He could also have argued that Douglas's policy left open the devastating riposte—insisting upon a federal slave code for the territories—that the slaveholders in fact wound up arraying against it. Instead, Lincoln himself made the slaveholders' riposte, as if attempting to box them into making it themselves. Rather than predicting the practical failure of the Freeport Doctrine, Lincoln pushed the claim—a claim he was in a way daring southern radicals to make as well—that the *Dred Scott* decision positively mandated Congress to elaborate a federal slave code. That argument is a stretch, as was Lincoln's contention that he was less obligated by that decision to provide a federal slave code for the territories than Douglas was, since he opposed the *Dred Scott* decision in the first place, as if to disagree with an opinion made one not bound by it. But his aims were more partisan than philosophical: Lincoln was seeking to make sure that the southern Democrats who had pledged themselves to Douglas's destruction could not turn back, and that southern moderates who were looking to Douglas to save their party as a national organization would be driven from their position by southern loyalty politics. Lincoln did not make his claim to advance his own presidential ambitions—Don Fehrenbacher showed long ago that all of the once widely cited evidence about this is unreliable—but to argue to Illinois voters that Douglas could not at the same time prevent slavery from being imposed upon Kansas and rein in the increasingly furious sectional conflict over slavery.[3] That said, even if Lincoln had no presidential ambitions in 1858, a line of attack that would have destroyed Douglas's prospects for 1860 would still have had attractions for him.

7.1 Legal Background of the Case

The Somerset *Case*

When the Supreme Court ruled that the slave Dred Scott was not emancipated by having lived both in the free state of Illinois and in the free territory of Wisconsin, the Court ran against the grain of eighty-five years of legal precedents tending in the opposite direction. The deepest precedent, Mansfield's decision in the case of *Somerset v. Stewart* in 1772, had held that bringing a slave from the West Indies, where slavery was legal, to Britain proper, where there was no law about slavery, caused British law to recognize Somerset as a free man.

Mansfield's decision reflects an interesting reading of the tradition of natural law as Britain had received it from Grotius, Vattel, and others.[4] When we use the term "natural law," we usually mean to refer to a source of moral authority deeper than the positive law, which can be appealed to in cases where the positive law conflicts with deep and commonly honored intuitions about justice. It is sometimes formally equivalent to what we sometimes call "higher law" or "divine law." Now not every vision of natural law derives from dictation by the divine, but even those that derive from the moral order of nature (in the modern era as problematic a notion as the notion of the divine will) carry with them well-recognized risks of anarchic moral narcissism. A slightly less general version of higher-law thought, deriving not from the order of nature itself but from widely held if implicit assumptions about the nature of the moral life, assumptions sometimes rooted in history and tradition, is not fraught with the same dangers, but cannot transcend the limitations of a merely customary morality in the way that deeper visions of the higher law can, sometimes justly, claim to do.

Mansfield's decision reflects a completely different idea of what natural law is. He sees it not as a higher law but as a default law, the law
that holds, on the basis of common reason, where there is not positive
law to the contrary. Slavery, according to Mansfield, was immoral, and
thus could not be justified by natural law. But that itself did not make
slavery illegal. It did, however, limit the rights of slaveholders to situations in which specific provisions had been made for them in positive
law, and deprived them of the ability to resort to natural-law arguments about property rights, since natural law did not recognize slaves
as property at all. Somerset's owner could not claim property rights in
him because English positive and common law did not include such
rights, and, since they could not be derived from natural law either,
the owner was forced to grant Somerset his freedom once he brought
him to England:

> The state of slavery is of such a nature, that it is incapable of being
> introduced by courts of justice upon mere reasoning or inferences
> from any principles, natural or political; it *must* take its rise from *posi-*
> *tive* law; the origin of it can in no country or age be traced back to any
> other source: immemorial usage preserves the memory of positive
> law long after all traces of the occasion, reason, authority, and time of
> its introduction are lost; and in a case so odious as the condition of
> slaves, must be taken strictly.[5]

Mansfield's reasoning underlies some of the Constitution's hedged
thinking about slavery. The fugitive slave clause from Article IV, section 2, for instance, reads this way: "No Person held to Service or
Labour in one State, under the Laws thereof, escaping into another,
shall, in Consequence of any Law or Regulation therein, be discharged
from such Service or Labour, But shall be delivered up on Claim of the
Party to whom such Service or Labour may be due." Noticing the evasive locution the authors used in place of "slave" ("persons held to service, in one State, under the Laws thereof," language that would seem
to apply to indentured servants and apprentices as much as to slaves),
Lincoln argued correctly that such language reflects their squeamish-
ness about slavery, their reluctance to recognize slavery in the Constitution in so many words, and their wishful conviction that slavery
might ultimately disappear. There is also a slight Mansfieldian touch

to the language of this clause: persons are "held to Service or Labour" under the laws of one state, which is to say that the laws that make people slaves are state laws, not federal ones, and not natural ones either. The fugitive slave clause thus arises from arguments about comity among states, not from arguments that slavery is a federal institution, and not from arguments to the effect that slavery is a natural-law kind of property, deserving of protections beyond those offered by the positive laws of the slave states.[6] Even the language about "the Party to whom such Service or Labour may be due" involves a Mansfieldian hedge, as if the master does not own the slave, only the slave's labor. Speaking to northerners, even Jefferson Davis made this kind of hedge (see section 7.4 below). Now it was of course a meaningless hedge. But only restiveness provokes meaningless hedges; like hypocrisy such hedges are taxes vice has to pay to virtue.

Mansfield's reasoning also underlies the Liberty Party's arguments about slavery in the District of Columbia and the Republican Party's arguments about slavery in the territories. More generally, Mansfieldian reasoning underlies the common Republican maxim, most famously put forward by Chase, that "slavery is local, but freedom is national." It is precisely this Mansfieldian understanding of the legal limitations upon the right of property in slaves that Lincoln feels is at stake in what, in the "House Divided" speech, he describes as a push to nationalize slavery. And the Calhoun-Davis joint property theory about slavery in the territories was also aimed against Mansfield's doctrine.

The argument that slavery is entirely a creature of local positive law and cannot be justified by natural law had curious developments during the Civil War. When General David Hunter proclaimed on May 9, 1862, that all of the slaves in the Department of the South, very little of which was actually under his control, were from that moment forever free, he based his argument on an understanding of the law of war that recognizably descends from the *Somerset* decision.

Emancipation had often been used—by the British both during the Revolution and during the War of 1812, for instance—as a weapon of war. Since the law of war justifies putting the enemy's property beyond his use, as well as putting it at one's own disposal if one can get control of it, it could justify both taking the enemy's slaves for one's own use (whether as slaves or as soldiers) and depriving the enemy of the benefit of the slaves' labor (by freeing them). The law of war here does not obligate one to free one's own slaves, however: France and Spain, at war with each other, offered emancipation to each other's slaves, but made no such offer to their own.

But Hunter's argument was rather more than just that emancipation would be a useful weapon of war. Hunter argued that it is the nature of war to abrogate any variety of positive law that might have obtained between the combatants, replacing it with the law of war. Now the "law of war" is an old concept, going back to Grotius, and it refers not to anything passed upon by a lawmaking body but to a set of rules commonly available to the light of reason when it contemplates the necessities of war. The "law of war," this is to say, has the same origin in widely held common premises and experiences that "natural law" has for thinkers in Grotius's tradition. Because the law of war is derived from the same sources as the law of nature, like the law of nature it cannot recognize slavery, since slavery cannot be a creature of natural law, only of positive law. Therefore, the existence of war itself by its nature frees any slave in the regions at war. As Hunter's proclamation has it:

> The three States of Georgia, Florida and South Carolina, comprising the Military Department of the South, having deliberately declared themselves no longer under the protection of the United States of America and having taken up arms against the said United States, it becomes a military necessity to declare them under martial law. This was accordingly done on the 25th day of April, 1862. Slavery and martial law in a free country are altogether incompatible; the persons in these three States—Georgia, Florida and South Carolina—heretofore held as slaves are therefore declared forever free.[7]

Hunter's legal understanding was cloudy. For one thing, as Francis Lieber pointed out at the time, martial law and the law of war are not quite the same thing, and as Lincoln tartly pointed out, drawing the conclusion that slavery could be ended by calling upon the law of war was something for the president to do, not for a mere major general. Lincoln's letter to Hunter not only denied Hunter the power to emancipate the slaves of the South, it also reserved that power to the president, and hinted that his use of that power was more than a remote possibility. (His earlier rebuke of Frémont's emancipation order in

Missouri, written when the secession of Kentucky was an imminent threat, contained no such hint.)

That said, Hunter's reasoning bore similarities to ideas Lieber himself would develop in writing General Order 100, the "Lieber Code" on the rules of war, which was signed by Lincoln on April 24, 1863, and which forms the basis for the modern Geneva Convention. Lieber's use of the natural-law basis of the law of war to attack slavery was somewhat less sweeping than Hunter's, but significant nevertheless. Because slavery could not be justified by natural law, only by positive law, and because enemies are bound not by positive law but only by the law of war, which treats all persons as equals, any slave who came under Union control immediately became not only practically speaking but legally speaking free. Lieber also argued that because the law of war must treat all people as equal by nature, all prisoners of war must be treated equally, and no nation can, under the law of war, single out any group among its prisoners—black Union prisoners of war in the Confederacy, specifically, but also Jewish prisoners of war during World War II—for specially harsh treatment.

Lieber's understanding of the law of war also profoundly changed the meaning of being defeated by the United States. When the United States took the Mexican Cession by the treaty of Guadalupe Hidalgo, followers of Calhoun, arguing that "the Constitution follows the flag," and that the Constitution provides enough in the way of positive law to carry slavery into every new territory as the default state, sought to reimpose slavery upon regions that under Mexican rule had been free. The Lieber Code made that interpretation impossible.[8]

Mansfield's views about slavery were widely accepted even in the slave states during the early Republic. The Kentucky Court of Appeals in 1820, in the case of *Rankin v. Lydia*, had argued that "slavery cannot be founded in common law or law of nature and exists by positive law alone. Outside of positive law there is no slavery."[9] Lydia had traveled with her owners from Kentucky to Indiana, and was compelled by her owner's widow to return to Kentucky upon the owner's death. The idea that Lydia would revert to being a slave upon her return gave offense to Benjamin Mills, the Kentucky jurist who wrote the opinion. Alluding to Mansfield's maxim that "the air of England is too pure to be breathed by slaves," he exclaimed, "Is it to be seriously contended that so soon as he transported her to the Kentucky shore, the noxious atmosphere of this state, without any express law for the purpose, clamped upon her newly forged chains of slavery, after the old ones were destroyed!"[10]

When in the *Matson* case in 1847 Lincoln sought to return Matson's slave Jane Bryant to captivity in Kentucky, Bryant's attorney, who won the case, threw not only the reasoning but the language of the *Somerset* case and its successors at him.[11]

Even Mississippi, in 1818, had, in *Decker v. Hopkins*, issued a ringing defense of the Northwest Ordinance, disposing of Decker's claim that the ordinance deprived him of his property by pointing out that Decker, as a citizen and moreover as a Virginian, had a say in the adoption of the ordinance and thus could not claim to have been expropriated by it. The decision argued, in Mansfield's style, that slavery exists only "through municipal regulations," the default ruling being *"in favorem vitae et libertatis."*[12]

At the same time Mansfield's reasoning could take odd turns in proslavery hands. Judge Ruffin's decision in the notorious case of *State v. Mann* (13 N.C. 263 [1829]) used some of Mansfield's arguments. It is precisely, Ruffin argued, because slavery is immoral that the violence masters can legally inflict must be unlimited. The slave cannot be induced to obey (as, say, children can be induced to obey) by the claim that the master has the slave's ultimate interest in mind, because in fact the master does not have the slave's interest in mind. Because slavery is immoral, but legal, Ruffin argued, using immoral means to protect it is legal if the masters believe those means are really necessary; therefore the state cannot tell a master how brutally he may beat his slaves, but must leave it completely to the master's discretion, else, the master's power not being absolute, slavery would dissolve.

In the years preceding the *Dred Scott* case, two kinds of qualification of the Mansfield doctrine worked their way into the law. The first involved the distinction between true residence (domicile) and "sojourning," which is to say, transit by slaves through free states, or suitably brief residence by slaves in free states.[13] The second involved the closely related issue of "reattachment," which is to say, the issue of whether return to a slave state of someone freed by domicile in a free state caused that person's status to revert to slavery.

Lemuel Shaw of Massachusetts, known principally nowadays as the judge who felt it his duty to enforce the Fugitive Slave Act of 1850 against his moral scruples about it (thus becoming the model for Captain Vere in his son-in-law Herman Melville's short novel *Billy Budd*), vehemently argued for the freedom of slaves even in transient passage through Massachusetts, in the case of *Commonwealth v. Aves* (1836).[14] Shaw's Mansfieldian language is very strong:

> Though by the laws of a foreign state . . . a person may acquire a property in a slave, such acquisition, being contrary to natural right, and effected by the local law, is dependent upon such local law for its existence and efficacy, and being contrary to the fundamental laws of this state, such general right of property cannot be exercised or recognized here.[15]

In the aftermath of the first wave of emancipation acts, the free states nevertheless felt obliged to grant slaveholders the right of transit through their states, and the right to travel or sojourn briefly there as well. Beginning in Pennsylvania, which first limited "sojourning" to six months and then dispensed with it altogether, the right of masters to sojourn with their slaves in the free states or to pass fleetingly through them began to be rejected. *Commonwealth v. Aves* swept aside a tradition of "comity," by which one state traditionally deferred to the laws of another state as far as its citizens in transit were concerned. Shaw's rejection of comity argued that if Massachusetts were to grant comity to sojourning masters, in the name of protecting their slave property, then "the law of slavery must extend to every place where such slaves may be carried." This conclusion amounted to Shaw to a reductio ad absurdum (although as we have just seen this is precisely the argument Lincoln expected the slaveholders to make in their attack upon emancipation in the free states), and, sensibly arguing that comity can "apply only to those commodities which are everywhere, and by all nations treated and deemed subject of property," concluded that considerations of interstate comity did not require Massachusetts to recognize property in slaves of sojourning masters.[16]

Shaw's decision essentially meant that Massachusetts did not have to help a Louisiana mistress recover her slave who had fled her control during her stay in Massachusetts. But it did not free anyone if that slave were unfortunate enough to be compelled back to Louisiana. (It also did not free any slave who had escaped from Louisiana to Massachusetts, since such cases were covered by the Constitution's fugitive slave clause.) But Shaw's arguments put an end to sojourning or transit with slaves in Massachusetts, and in the two decades prior to the Civil War, most of the North—except New Jersey, Indiana, and Illinois— followed the example of *Aves*.[17]

New York passed a law in 1841 freeing slaves who entered the state even in transit to other states, treating sojourning and domicile equivalently.[18] New York's Supreme Court upheld its law about sojourning in the *Lemmon* case in 1860, but rules about sojourning, visiting, and transient passage through free states with slaves were never drawn by the Supreme Court, so we will never know whether the Taney Court would have overturned New York's law about sojourning with slaves, much less whether it would have used the pretext of the *Lemmon* case to confect a "second *Dred Scott* decision" legalizing slavery in the free states.

The developing anti-slavery jurisprudence about sojourning in the North paralleled a hardening of stance about reattachment in the South. Some slave states during the early Republic—Kentucky, as we have just seen—for a while took the view that slavery did not reattach upon the return to the slave state of a former slave freed by domicile in a free state. Louisiana slaves were freed even by sojourning in free states as late as 1846, when a state law on the subject came into force.[19]

In the British world, reattachment became the rule in Lord Stowell's ruling in the *Slave Grace* case of 1827 (only a few years before all of the British law of slavery became moot). In the United States, the question of reattachment after sojourning involved a conflict between the laws of the free state (which, unlike England in the *Somerset* case, sometimes had positive laws against slavery, not merely a default assumption against it) and the laws of the slave state, which sometimes imposed reattachment in all cases, sometimes imposed reattachment only in cases of sojourning, and sometimes freed slaves even in cases of sojourning. Reattachment was the issue in the case of *Rankin v. Lydia* cited above. Paul Finkelman shows that rejection of reattachment, argued in the manner of the *Rankin* case, was the rule in much of the South before 1830, and in Kentucky, Missouri, and Louisiana for some time after. Only after 1840, as the northern states tightened rules about "sojourning," did the southern states begin to insist upon reattachment.[20] Indeed, for some years, while Illinois and Indiana were extending themselves to defend the comity rights of masters in transit to their slaves, some of those masters' home states would free slaves merely on evidence of their temporary residence in free states.[21]

The Quock Walker Cases

In the wake of the Revolution, somewhat stronger grounds were taken against slavery in the 1781–1783 *Quock Walker* cases, which ended slavery in Massachusetts. Walker's case involved a conflict between his current master, Nathaniel Jennison, who had married the widow of his former master, James Caldwell, and the former master's younger brothers, Seth and John Caldwell, who sought Walker's freedom, which in fact their brother had promised Walker before his death.

Chief Justice William Cushing's charge to the jury in the case argued along the lines set out by the *Somerset* case, maintaining that although the Massachusetts Constitution of 1780 did not explicitly outlaw slavery (and indeed a *post nati* emancipation bill had failed in the General Court only a few years prior to the adoption of the new constitution), it did not legalize it either, and positive law had in fact never firmly declared in favor of slavery in Massachusetts. But Cushing also pressed one degree further, arguing that John Adams's language in the preamble to the Massachusetts constitution (in force to this day) was inconsistent with slavery:

> These sentiments [that are favorable to the natural rights of mankind] led the framers of our constitution of government—by which the people of this commonwealth have solemnly bound themselves to each other—to declare—that all men are born free and equal; and that every subject is entitled to liberty, and to have it guarded by the laws as well as his life and property. In short, without resorting to implication in constructing the constitution, slavery is in my judgment as effectively abolished as it can be by the granting of rights and privileges wholly incompatible and repugnant to its existence. The court are therefore fully of the opinion that perpetual servitude can no longer be tolerated in our government, and that liberty can only be forfeited by some criminal conduct or relinquished by personal consent or contract.[22]

The road opened by this case was largely not followed, although prominent Virginians of the post-Revolutionary age like George Wythe and St. George Tucker were tempted by it, and the latter turned away from this line of reasoning with profound regret, afraid of the social effects of sudden judicial lawmaking, but seeking wherever they felt they had room to decide close cases in favor of freedom. Although judges backed away from *Quock Walker* over the antebellum years, the arguments made in Cushing's opinion continued to have a rhetorical afterlife, with the abolitionists Alvan Stewart and Lysander Spooner (and their follower, Frederick Douglass) arguing that even the U.S. Constitution is founded upon anti-slavery principles that contradict and overrule its pro-slavery provisions.[23] Probably the most important courtroom defender of fugitive slaves, Salmon Chase, stoutly if unsuccessfully made both kinds of argument, using natural law in Mansfield's default-status way in the *Matilda* case in 1837, and in Cushing's higher-law way in the *Jones v. van Zandt* case in 1847.

Prigg *and* Strader

Two later Supreme Court decisions, *Prigg v. Pennsylvania* (U.S. 539 [1842]) and *Strader v. Graham* (51 U.S. 82 [1851]), illustrate the changing climate about slavery in the middle third of the nineteenth century.

The *Prigg* decision, which struck down Pennsylvania's personal liberty law (a law designed to protect fugitive slaves, or for that matter free blacks, from kidnapping) seems at first to be a gift to slaveholders.[24] The circumstances of the case were ugly enough. The Pennsylvania law in question forbade anyone from removing any negro or mulatto from the state "by force, fraud or false pretense" for the purpose of keeping him or her as a slave. The law had been on the books since 1826, but similar laws in Pennsylvania had been in force since 1788.

Margaret Morgan had been a slave in Maryland, but her owner John Ashmore had given her practical if not formally legal freedom, and she lived on her own in Maryland before moving to Pennsylvania with Ashmore's consent. She and her free husband, James Morgan, had several children in Maryland, and several more in Pennsylvania, where they lived openly for at least four years. After Ashmore's death, his heirs decided to seize Margaret and her children, including those who had been born in freedom in Pennsylvania. Like *Quock Walker* and *Dred Scott*, this case turns on the complicated relations between different generations of slaveholder, and all three cases indicate something of the instability of slave life, since death has a way of conveying slaves from more-or-less generous masters to greedy and brutal ones.

Now Pennsylvania was required by the fugitive slave clause in the federal Constitution not to prohibit the recapture of fugitive slaves (although that clause did not provide a formal means of recapture), and by the 1793 fugitive slave law Pennsylvania was also required to allow masters to recapture their slaves provided that they received certificates from judges in the state proving that those whom they claimed ownership of really were fugitive slaves. Pennsylvania had formal mechanisms for the legal recapture of fugitive slaves, but its 1826 personal liberty law required Ashmore's heirs to consult with authorities in Pennsylvania before laying hands upon Margaret Morgan and her children. When the Pennsylvania authorities, with very good reason, looked askance at their claims, especially their claims on Margaret's children born in freedom in Pennsylvania, Ashmore's heirs chose simply to grab the entire lot, employing one Edward Prigg for the purpose, selling them all once they arrived in Maryland.[25] Pennsylvania understandably viewed this attempt to circumvent the due process rights of its putative citizens as kidnapping, and, having at length persuaded Maryland to extradite Prigg, indicted and convicted him.[26] It was this conviction that Justice Story's opinion overturned.

Now the irony of this is that Story was in most ways an anti-slavery judge, and his son thought of Story's decision in *Prigg* as harming slavery more than helping it. Don Fehrenbacher parses the decision this way. First, Story took the ground that although (in Mansfield fashion) slavery was a creature of state rather than federal law, interstate comity required the federal government to guarantee obedience to the fugitive slave clause in the Constitution and to enforce the 1793 fugitive slave law. Second, since the fugitive slave clause was "self-executing," a master did not need the support of any state institution to recapture his slave, and could recapture a slave by any private means at his disposal (such as by employing Prigg and his thugs) without consulting anyone in the free state about his plans. A consequence of this was that the burden of proof was not on the master to prove that someone he intended to seize is his slave, but on the person being seized to prove that he is not a slave. *Prigg* deprived black people living in the free states of the presumption that they were free. Third, Story argued that despite what to most people look like violations of the Fourth and

Fifth Amendments, the 1793 Fugitive Slave Act was constitutional, and in consequence free blacks were not entitled to the constitutional protections granted to whites. Story took these steps because he believed, mistakenly, that the fugitive slave clause in the Constitution was a sticking point during the Philadelphia Convention, and that the document could not have been ratified without it.

What Story was particularly exercised about was the possibility that each state would regulate the rendition of fugitive slaves in its own way, and that some states would make the process so difficult that masters would give up. Story was afraid that states might continue to see the recovery of fugitive slaves as something still politically in play, rather than as an issue settled once and for all (and with a hammer) by the Court. Story's fear was precisely of the kind of solution—let the local jurisdictions regulate it to death—Douglas would adopt to meet the possibility that the Court would rule that territorial governments could not abolish slavery; what Story attacked was the Fugitive Slave Act equivalent of the Freeport Doctrine. Because allowing the states to devise their own means for ensuring that free blacks are not kidnapped into slavery opens to door to God Knows What, the states must be denied any role in the matter whatsoever. The issue was, Story thought, too inflammatory to be mediated in the messy way politics usually mediates conflicts, and therefore the conflict as a whole must be foreclosed by the higher law.[27]

All of these rulings look like rather large concessions to the slave power. But the fourth holding of the *Prigg* decision, that recapture of fugitive slaves was a federal responsibility, went in two directions, since if the states could not prohibit or for that matter regulate rendition of fugitive slaves, they were also under no obligation to aid it either.[28] Indeed, states could prohibit their citizens from cooperating with masters who were seeking to recover their slaves, although they could not prohibit those masters from recovering them themselves. What the decision guaranteed was that masters seeking to recapture fugitive slaves would not have to face possibly unsympathetic state judges, and could choose to face possibly more sympathetic federal ones. Since there was not any such federal machinery in place in 1842 to assist these masters, however, masters who sought to recapture fugitive slaves did not have institutional means and regular procedures at their disposal and had to take their chances as kidnappers.[29]

If Story thought he had the last word with this final provision, he was sadly mistaken, for it was specifically to meet the threat that Story had planted in the *Prigg* decision that Senator Mason designed the Fugitive Slave Act of 1850, which appointed federal commissioners to replace the federal judges who might have been a little more sympathetic to the rights of accused fugitive slaves than commissioners whose whole job consisted of rendition of fugitive slaves. The act also established hearings at which those accused slaves could not testify, and paid the commissioners more if they ruled that the accused was a slave than if they ruled that he or she was not. Robert Burt points out that there is a formal equivalence between the South's insistence in 1850 upon a federal Fugitive Slave Act, to provide federal machinery for the recapture of fugitive slaves in order to forestall state attempts to control the process which might give an opening to unfriendly regulation, and its insistence in 1859 and 1860 upon a federal slave code for the territories, to provide federal machinery for regulating slavery in the territories in order to forestall territorial attempts to prohibit slavery indirectly by unfriendly legislation.[30]

Strader v. Graham (1851) did not arise out of circumstances quite so dire as *Prigg* did, but it was another ruling that makes clear just how deeply the tide was turning against freedom in the Court. The facts of the case were as follows: Dr. Graham's three Kentucky slaves, George, Henry, and Reuben, were professional musicians, whom Graham permitted occasionally to travel from Harrodsburg to Louisville to practice with a bandleader named Williams, and to Indiana and Ohio with Williams to perform at balls and public entertainments, after which they would return promptly to Kentucky. In 1841, all three slaves boarded the steamboat *Pike*, sailed to Cincinnati, and escaped to Canada. Apparently searching for a deep pocket to recompense him for the loss of his slaves, Graham sued Jacob Strader and James Gorman, the owners of the *Pike*, and John Armstrong, its captain. Armstrong's defense was that the three travelers had often traveled on his boat as if free, and he assumed they were. Furthermore, he argued, by virtue of their having traveled to Ohio and to Indiana, they actually were free, according to the 1787 Northwest Ordinance. The Kentucky courts ruled in favor of Graham, and Strader and his co-defendants appealed to the Supreme Court.

The Court ruled that it did not have jurisdiction over the case, because whether sojourning in a free state, effected emancipation of

Kentucky slaves was something for Kentucky, and nobody else, to decide. Note that *Strader* was not precisely a reattachment case. George, Henry, and Reuben were in Canada, and their fate was not at issue. The issue was whether Kentucky, for legal purposes, could treat them as slaves, and whether therefore Strader and the others had to pay Graham for their role in the escape. The reattachment issue enters the case only indirectly: if, having visited Indiana and Ohio, George, Henry, and Reuben were still free when they returned to Kentucky, then they were free when they boarded Strader's steamboat, and Graham could not recover their value from Strader.

The case raised two slightly different issues of comity. The first question was whether Kentucky owed any deference to Ohio and Indiana's prohibition of slavery. The answer to this was no, unless Kentucky itself chose to do so. Ohio and Indiana did not have specific laws about sojourning, as New York did, so the comity issues raised by an actual law emancipating sojourning slaves was not an issue in *Strader*. The only issue was whether the prohibition of slavery in Ohio and Indiana themselves permanently freed slaves who set foot in those two states as far as Kentucky was concerned if Kentucky felt that it did not. If Kentucky chose to overturn its own precedent in favor of the slaves, its ruling in *Rankin v. Lydia*, the Supreme Court ruled that that was Kentucky's business and not the Court's.

The second question was whether Kentucky owed any deference to the federal government's—actually, the Confederation Congress's—prohibition of slavery in the Old Northwest. Again the answer was no, because the ordinance was no longer in force (since Ohio and Indiana were by that time states). Taney's opinion argued even further, that the federal government could not tell Kentucky how to decide the issue of reattachment, even were it to involve a federal territory—Wisconsin Territory, say—where a federal prohibition against slavery was still in force. This last point, however, was extrajudicial. Taney here, as everywhere, looked as hard as he could for reasons to expand slaveholder power, but his extension of his *Strader* argument to allow the slave states to thumb their noses at the federal government seems to have put him on legal thin ice.

Although the *Strader* case was not in so many words an endorsement of reattachment, it did indicate an increasing tendency to give national, not merely local, recognition to slavery. And Kentucky's position also indicated that the state of the debate had changed there as

well, since Kentucky had formerly rejected reattachment. It is curious
that the distinction between domicile and sojourning did not come up
in the opinions, since during their musical travels Graham's slaves
were clearly not residents of Ohio or Indiana. Perhaps the issue of reattachment and, even more, the chance to prevent the federal government from intervening in comity cases in favor of freedom, mattered
so much to Chief Justice Taney that he let all the other issues slide.

In the "House Divided" speech, Lincoln had characterized one of
the main points of the *Dred Scott* decision as holding that "whether the
holding a negro in actual slavery in a free State makes him free, as
against the holder, the United States courts will not decide, but will
leave to be decided by the courts of any slave State the negro may be
forced into by the master" (1:429–430). This is a pretty accurate description of the meaning of the *Prigg* and *Strader* decisions.

7.2 The *Dred Scott* Case in Court

Not much is known of Dred Scott's biography, and much of it is in dispute. He was probably born in Virginia in 1799, and came to St. Louis
in 1830 as the slave of Peter Blow. Either immediately before or immediately after Peter Blow's death he became the property of Dr. John
Emerson, a mediocre and quarrelsome assistant surgeon in the U.S.
Army, traveling with Emerson for two years to Fort Armstrong in Illinois, and twice for a year or so to Fort Snelling, in what is now Minnesota (but was then Wisconsin Territory). Scott married his wife
Harriet while at Fort Snelling. They had four children, two of whom
survived to adulthood, one of them indisputably born in free territory.
The Scotts also accompanied Emerson to Fort Jesup in Louisiana (traveling unaccompanied down the Mississippi) but were left with Emerson's wife in St. Louis while Emerson served in Florida during the
Seminole wars. Upon Emerson's death at the age of forty, ownership
of the Scotts passed to his widow, Eliza Irene Emerson. In St. Louis,
either in the intervals of Dr. Emerson's tumultuous military career or
while left behind with Irene, Scott renewed his acquaintance with the
Blow family, especially with the son Taylor Blow, who, although later a
Confederate sympathizer, was attached enough personally to Scott to
provide the financial support for his later suit for freedom, bought and
freed Scott after the final failure of his case, supported him in old age,
and saw to his burial.[31]

When the Scotts brought their cases in April 1846, the matter would not have seemed to pose challenges. Don Fehrenbacher points out that the Missouri Supreme Court had regularly granted freedom to slaves whose masters had taken them to free states or territories and returned with them. Missouri, that is, not only recognized domicile in the free states as emancipating slaves taken to them, but also rejected reattachment of slavery to emancipated slaves who were returned to Missouri. (This means, of course, that the *Strader* case would have offered Mrs. Emerson no relief.) In fact, as Fehrenbacher again has shown, Missouri had decided to reject reattachment in the 1836 case of *Rachel v. Walker*, a case bearing uncanny similarities to the Scotts' own, since Rachel, like Dred Scott, had been taken in slavery to Fort Snelling by her master. To Walker's plea that he was required to go to Fort Snelling by the government, Judge Matthias McGirk snapped, "No authority of law or the government compelled him to keep the plaintiff there as a slave." Indeed, the issue seemed so obvious to McGirk that he was angered by having to hear case after case concerning slaves freed by domicile in free states, peevishly remarking, "It seems that the ingenuity of counsel and the interest of those disposed to deal in slave property, will never admit anything to be settled in regard to this question."[32]

As it happened, the Scotts lost their first case on a technicality. They proved that they had resided in a free state and in a free territory, that Peter Blow had sold Dred Scott to Dr. Emerson, and that Scott had been hired out since Emerson's death. But they neglected to prove that Mrs. Emerson was their actual owner. They appealed to the Missouri Supreme Court, where the Scotts won a right to a new trial in state court. The new trial in state court, presided over by the original judge in their first suit, took place on January 12, 1850, and the Scotts won their suits.

The political climate had changed in Missouri while the Scotts were pressing their case, and when Mrs. Emerson appealed the case to the Missouri Supreme Court, she found herself in a different legal world. For one thing, pro-slavery ideologues persuaded the state legislature to formally endorse the Calhoun-Davis view of slavery in the territories, and machinations between pro-slavery Democrats and Whigs forced Andrew Jackson's long-serving friend Thomas Hart Benton, who had had moderate views on slavery questions, out of the Senate. The justices of the Missouri Supreme Court were looking for a way to

make a pro-slavery statement, partly as a way to drive another stake
through Benton's heart, partly as a way to demonstrate to moderate
elements in St. Louis that a new era had begun.

The *Strader* case had just been decided, and it gave the Missouri Supreme Court the license to argue that if they decided that Dred Scott
was a slave, neither the federal government nor Illinois had anything to
say about it. Now *Strader* was not directly relevant to the Scott case,
because in fact Missouri law *had* favored the Scotts, and *Strader* did not
involve a suit for freedom anyway. But it told the Missouri Supreme
Court that if they wanted to reinterpret Missouri's law and precedents
in a radical way, the federal courts would not stop them.

Curiously, the Missouri decision, written by Justice William Scott,
did not make the (very marginally) plausible case that Dred Scott had
only been sojourning in Illinois and in Wisconsin Territory. It rested
its entire argument on the claim that Missouri did not have to respect
the views of these other jurisdictions. In fact, it did rather more than
just ignore the distinction between domicile and sojourning: it argued
that Mrs. Emerson retained her property rights in Dred Scott and his
family no matter how long they resided in the free states. It would seem
that Judge Scott was edging toward arguing that no free state had the
power to free any slave, the argument Lincoln feared from the "second
Dred Scott decision." But perhaps the issue would have been different
had the Scotts not come back to Missouri and given the Missouri court
the opening, such as it was, for playing the *Strader* card. After the *Dred
Scott* case went to the Supreme Court, the issue of domicile versus sojourning becomes more complex. If Judge Scott had elided the distinction, at least Justice Nelson, probably Justices Catron, Grier, and Daniel, and possibly even Justice Campbell felt that Dred Scott's residence
in Illinois was a case of sojourning, not residence, and felt that the distinction might have made a difference had it made a difference to Missouri. Yet after the case, Missouri judges themselves began, on the authority of *Dred Scott*, to elide the distinction between domicile and
sojourning, taking the line sketched in by Judge Scott and adopted by
Taney but probably not adopted by the majority of the Court.

Judge Scott made clear that he had in mind to show those other jurisdictions a thing or two, particularly aiming at those ancestors of the
now-abolitionists who forced slavery upon the unwilling South in the
first place:

Times are not now as they were when the former decisions on this subject were made. Since then not only individuals but States have been possessed with a dark and fell spirit in relation to slavery, whose gratification is sought in the pursuit of measures, whose inevitable consequences must be the overthrow and destruction of our government. Under such circumstances it does not behoove the State of Missouri to show the least countenance to any measure which might gratify this spirit. . . . Although we may, for our own sakes, regret that the avarice and hard-heartedness of the progenitors of those who are now so sensitive on the subject, ever introduced the institution among us, yet we will not go to them to learn law, morality or religion on the subject.[33]

At this point the relationships among the principals become confusing. After eighteen months of inaction, the case was moved to the U.S. Circuit Court for Missouri, with a new lead attorney on Scott's side, Roswell Field, and a new defendant, Irene Emerson's brother, John F. A. Sanford. Whether Mrs. Emerson had conveyed Scott to her brother or whether he was acting as her agent or as the executor of her husband's will is unclear, and the unclarity has provoked generations of conspiracy theories on both the pro-slavery and anti-slavery sides, none of them completely persuasive. Sanford's status is muddied by the fact that once the case was over it was Mrs. Emerson (by this time Mrs. Chaffee, since she had married a Republican congressman from Massachusetts in the meantime), not Sanford's executor, who sold Scott to Taylor Blow.

Judge Robert Wells, who first heard the case in April 1854, in the U.S. Circuit Court for Missouri, first disposed of Sanford's claim that Scott, as a descendant of African slaves, could not be a citizen of Missouri and therefore could not sue. Notice that the argument was that Scott could not sue because he was a descendant of slaves, not because he was a slave (the latter point being, after all, what the trial was supposed to decide). The idea here was that no blacks could have access to the federal courts.[34] Considering the use that Chief Justice Taney made of this same argument, it is interesting that Judge Wells brushed it aside, arguing that he did not have to accept that Scott was a citizen in the full sense of the word, with all of the privileges and immunities of citizens in the several states, only that if he were a free black he would be, in Fehrenbacher's words, enough of a citizen for the case to go forward.[35] One unintended consequence of Wells's ruling was that it seemed to open the courts of the free states to fugitive slaves, who, being "citizens enough" to have their cases heard in those courts, could thereby get around the hasty summary proceedings before commissioners established by the Fugitive Slave Act of 1850. Wells of course had no intention of opening this door, and one of the reasons Taney took such an extreme line about the citizenship of free blacks when the case came to the U.S. Supreme Court was to close the door Wells had unintentionally opened. On the merits of the case itself, Wells ruled, in *Strader* fashion, that if the Missouri Supreme Court felt that Scott was a slave, the federal circuit court was foreclosed from second-guessing them.

The circuit court case seems to have been designed by both sides for appeal to the Supreme Court, and both sides brought powerful advocates to that forum. Sanford (whose name the Court misspelled as "Sandford") was by this time in an insane asylum, so it is not entirely clear whose bidding his attorneys were doing. But by this time the case had taken on its own momentum, and clearly both sides were bringing it to the Supreme Court no longer with the possession or liberation of Dred Scott himself in mind, but with a view to making a general statement about the status of slavery. Sanford was represented by Reverdy Johnson, the former senator from Taney's home state of Maryland, and the attorney general under President Taylor, and by Henry S. Geyer, whom pro-slavery advocates in Missouri had put in the Senate in Thomas Hart Benton's place. Scott was represented by George T. Curtis, the brother of Justice Benjamin Curtis, and by Montgomery Blair of Missouri, a supporter of Benton, the scion of an old Jacksonian family, and more recently a supporter of Free Soil. Blair would go on to become Lincoln's postmaster general.

Blair's brief defended Judge Wells's ruling about Scott's right to sue, and further argued, against Wells's ruling, that the federal court had a right to second-guess the Missouri Supreme Court about issues of slavery and interstate comity. Blair did not anticipate the attack upon the Missouri Compromise restriction that would play a central role in Geyer and Johnson's defense and in Taney's view of the case. Argument before the Court began on February 11, 1856, with reargument after the November election. Blair argued before the Court essentially that Wells had been right to see free blacks as having at least a diluted form of citizenship, since they could own property and be sued, and the Articles of Confederation had understood "all free inhabitants" of the states to be owed the privileges and immunities of citizens of the other states, a formulation broad enough to include free blacks. Geyer argued that freed blacks could not be citizens, because they were neither born citizens nor formally naturalized as citizens, since emancipation gave them emancipation itself but nothing else. Geyer also made the distinction, an important one in Taney's later argument, between state and federal citizenship, arguing that a state cannot make other states take its own views of who is a citizen of the United States simply by granting them citizenship rights within its own limits.

On the actual merits of the case, Blair concentrated on attacking the use of the *Strader* case to argue that slavery reattached to Scott upon his return to Missouri, arguing, first, that in *Strader* the Court had merely refused to take jurisdiction in the Kentucky case rather than ruling that Kentucky was within its rights in asserting reattachment, and, second, that the precedents in Missouri were against reattachment anyway even if the *Strader* precedent applied.

Blair seems to have believed that rejection of *Strader* would work in Scott's favor both as regarded his residence in Illinois and as regarded his residence in Wisconsin Territory. (Judge Scott, after all, had made the same argument on the other side in both cases back in the Missouri Supreme Court.) But Geyer and Johnson only made the *Strader* argument concerning Illinois, arguing instead about the Wisconsin Territory aspect of the case that the slavery restriction provision of the Missouri Compromise was unconstitutional, and that therefore Scott was not freed by his residence at Fort Snelling. Geyer and Johnson made these arguments about the Missouri Compromise only during the reargument of the case after the 1856 election; in the original argument about the case, before the 1856 election, they based their case entirely upon *Strader*. The constitutionality of the Missouri Compromise was, Fehrenbacher points out, a new issue in the case, not raised in any of the state court cases, in the federal circuit court, or even in the first round of argument before the Supreme Court. President Buchanan treated the outcome of the 1856 election as if it were an endorsement of the position the Court took about the Missouri Compromise. But in fact the subject was not mentioned before the Court until after the election, and indeed the subject was touchy enough that had it been mentioned in the original arguments, the outcome of the 1856 election may well have been different.[36]

Since we are accustomed to reading this case backward, reading from its major holdings, its attack upon the possibility of black citizenship and its attack upon the federal and territorial power to restrict the expansion of slavery, we tend to see these two issues as shadowing the case from the beginning. Certainly Taney and his faction were looking for an occasion to hurl a thunderbolt at the Missouri Compromise, and used the occasion of this case to throw it. But Geyer and Johnson may have had different reasons for raising the Missouri Compromise issue. So long as Geyer and Johnson based their case chiefly on *Strader*, as Blair expected them to do, and as Justice Nelson's preliminary majority opinion (later his concurrent opinion) did, the case had a weakness. *Strader* has been received as bearing upon interstate comity: Kentucky does not have to treat someone freed in Ohio as if they were free in Kentucky as well, should that person be found in Kentucky, and someone freed in Illinois comes under Missouri law when he enters Missouri, leaving it up to Missouri to decide whether he is free in Missouri or not. But to use *Strader* to argue that Missouri need not recognize freedom granted in a federal territory by the Missouri Compromise is not to argue about state comity but to argue that the states do not have to respect federal law, which would seem to be a rather different issue than those that were in play in *Strader*. Now in his opinion in *Strader* Taney had indeed argued that states do not have to respect federal law on this issue, but his argument in that case was dictum and thus could not really be relied upon for precedent. Geyer and Johnson were rushing to plug a hole in their tactical case that Blair and Judge Scott had not noticed. This effort to plug the hole in *Strader* gave Taney the pretext he needed to launch the sweeping attack on the Missouri Compromise that made his opinion famous.

The historical record on the constitutionality of the Missouri Compromise, and on the constitutionality of federal prohibition of slavery in the territories more generally, as Lincoln would exhaustively show in the Cooper Union speech, was firmly on Dred Scott's side, since many of the Founders who wrote the language concerning territories in the Constitution had sat in the Confederation Congress when it passed the Northwest Ordinance and some still sat in the U.S. Congress at the time of the Missouri Compromise. It hardly mattered, however, that the precedents were on Scott's side, because the opposite view, that the language concerning territories in the Constitution referred only to unorganized territory belonging to the United States and that the territories were the joint property of the states severally, not of the people as a whole, had come to be the reigning orthodoxy in the South and with northern politicians who sought to curry favor there, and the Court was looking for an opportunity to impose this doctrine upon the nation by writing it into the higher law. Neither side raised the issue of whether territorial governments could abolish slavery; it was simply not at issue in this case, and Taney's argument on the subject can be attributed only to his own ambition to have the Court on record on this issue.

We know that during the Court's deliberations on the case in February 1857, Justice Nelson sought to write a limited decision on the basis of *Strader* that would return Scott to slavery but duck all three of the issues that made the case famous, the issue of black citizenship, the issue of the constitutionality of the slavery restriction provision of the Missouri Compromise, and the issue of whether territorial governments could prohibit slavery. Historians used to believe—because Justice Catron said so later—that the majority was forced to make the more radical decision it rendered by word that Justices McLean and Curtis planned to issue forceful dissents to Justice Nelson's ruling. Most no longer believe this claim, and the move from a limited to a sweeping decision seems to have been Taney's idea, although Justice Wayne was employed to engineer the switch of the assignment of the majority opinion from Nelson to Taney. Since Justices Wayne, Taney, and Campbell were probably planning to write separate concurrences that would have dealt with the Missouri Compromise restriction, shifting the authorship of the majority decision from Nelson to Taney probably reflected the ability of the radical justices to seize the agenda from the (relatively speaking) moderates Grier, Nelson, and (possibly) Catron.

What was actually decided in the case is a complicated question, because not only were multiple decisions submitted, but some of the justices left where they agreed with Taney's opinion implicit, and some of the elements of the case are intricately tied with each other. There were four major issues in Taney's opinion:

1. Can the Court go behind Judge Wells's decision to hear the case in the first place? Now Judge Wells had decided to hear the case on the grounds that even if free blacks are not citizens of the United States

in the full sense of that word, they are nevertheless close enough to citizens to have a right to a day in court. The issue here was not whether that ruling was correct but whether Judge Wells even had a right to make it. This "plea in abatement" argued not only that black people are not citizens but also that federal courts cannot even entertain questions about whether they might be.

2. Can black people be citizens of the United States? (In other words, not only was Judge Wells within his rights in ruling on the question, but did he rule on it correctly?)

3. Was the slavery restriction provision of the Missouri Compromise constitutional, and, if so, was Scott freed by his residence in Wisconsin Territory notwithstanding his return to Missouri?

4. Was Scott freed by residence in Illinois notwithstanding his return to Missouri?

Now what the Court majority felt about the first two issues has been a subject of debate ever after because not all of the justices rendered their opinions explicitly one way or the other. Taney, Wayne, Daniel, and Curtis explicitly said that the plea in abatement was before the Court, and Catron and McLean denied it. Nelson and Grier would have preferred to avoid this issue, but probably bowed to Taney about it. Campbell apparently felt otherwise, but then struck his dissent on this issue in draft. From all this it is safe to conclude that seven of the nine justices acquiesced in Taney's decision on this point that the plea in abatement was before the court, and that Wells's decision to hear the case at all could be second-guessed.

On the question of whether a black person can be a citizen, the issues are murkier. Taney, Wayne, and Daniel denied in their opinions that blacks, free or slave, can be citizens of the United States, and McLean and Curtis affirmed that they could. Campbell, Catron, and Grier also held that Scott was not a citizen, and therefore the case had to be dismissed, but in these cases the reason was that Scott was a slave, not that he was black. That would seem to be rather a different matter, but since all of them behaved afterward as if Taney spoke for them, perhaps it was not as much of a difference to them as it seems to be to us. (It also would seem, though, that the fact that he was a slave was something that needed proving, and had to be decided on the merits, not on jurisdictional grounds.)

On the issues that had been in play in the Missouri cases, the views of the majority are less murky, with all seven of the majority weighing in to the effect that Scott's return to Missouri re-enslaved him, regardless of the law on the subject in Illinois, and six of the seven (Nelson being the exception) arguing that the Missouri Compromise was unconstitutional.

A controversy has raged for over a century about whether, six of the majority having rejected the suit on jurisdictional grounds, it was proper for them to go on to register opinions on the merits of the other issues in the case, such as the Missouri Compromise. Nothing prevents a judge from using jurisdictional and substantive arguments to the same end. Besides, as both Fehrenbacher and Graber have argued, since the entire country was looking to the Court to decide the issue of the Missouri Compromise restriction, and it had been raised in the case during reargument, they were not really in a position to duck the issue. The jurisdictional and substantive cases in a way depended upon each other and could not be decided separately. For at least three justices the question would involve both: if Scott is a slave, then the Court has no jurisdiction, but the Court cannot decide whether it has jurisdiction until it has decided whether Scott is a slave.

The jurisdictional issue amounted to a way to raise the stakes in such a way as to silence opposition. It is analogous to the way pro-slavery advocates in Congress sought to "constitutionalize" every question in such a way as to silence debate. Accepting jurisdiction would be a way to open the case that would have given some color to the idea that the Court could think about which way it could go. Refusing jurisdiction, particularly if it secures the pro-slavery outcome anyway, not only wins the case but closes the door on reconsideration if similar cases come up. The idea here is that if the Court even deliberates about the master class's authority, it has already begun to erode it fatally. The jurisdictional issue has a "Don't get started with me" aspect that seeks to foreclose trains of thought that may lead to negotiation and wearing away of authority.

Robert Burt, in *The Constitution in Conflict* (1992), sees a similar logic at work in cases such as the Cherokee Removal cases, in which conflicts are seen as deeply and inevitably subjugative, and in which any attempt to mediate such conflicts by judicial reasoning or by political dealmaking leads only to chaos. Underlying this view is the common

Jackson-era assumption, not so bluntly or unambivalently adopted by the Founders, that the relationship between black and white, and the relationship between red and white, is one of unremitting hostility that only unquestioned and unitary force can keep from descending into annihilating war.[37]

The arguments about citizenship in *Dred Scott* and, even more, the arguments about jurisdiction were intended in a foreclosing way. Like Judge Ruffin in *State v. Mann*, the Court refused to allow the right of the master to be brought into discussion in the courts of justice, since every slave must be made sensible that there is no appeal from his master. But it was not only the slave who had to be deprived of the hope of appeal. The South in general and Chief Justice Taney in particular seem to have seen their conflict with the North in much the same way they viewed their conflict with blacks, as one in which they must either completely subjugate the other or be obliterated by them. It is not for nothing that the advocates of the slave power conspiracy theory thought of the master class as seeking to treat free whites roughly as they treated their slaves.

Judicial supremacy arose in the middle years of the nineteenth century, Robert Burt argues, as a subjugative way to foreclose conflicts between races, and as a subjugative way to foreclose conflicts among whites over race and slavery.[38] After the war the same means was used by the Court as a subjugative way to foreclose conflict over class. It is important to remember this about the origin of the concept of judicial supremacy; otherwise one is likely to swallow the view that judicial supremacy is a necessary consequence of respect for the rule of law—it is not—or that it is the only effective means of securing the principles of right from the vagaries of public passion—which it also is not.

Taney's historical argument about whether blacks are or can be citizens was shaky, to say the least. And it was also the feature of his opinion to which he devoted the most effort and made the most insistent if not the most persuasive arguments. Taney confected the idea that under the Articles of Confederation there was no citizenship in the United States—that citizens of the different states did not owe each other recognition as citizens of a common country—and argued, mistakenly, that free blacks had no citizenship rights in any of the states under the articles. He did this to argue that free blacks were not part of the political community that ratified the Constitution. To make this case, he somewhat overestimated the racism of the Revolutionary era, so that it appears even more loathsome than the racism of his own era. To quote his much-cited passage about the racial state of affairs at the time of the Constitution:

> They [black people, slave and free] had for more than a century before been regarded as beings of an inferior order, and altogether unfit to associate with the white race, either in social or political relations; and so far inferior, that they had no rights which the white man was bound to respect; and that the negro might justly and lawfully be reduced to slavery for his benefit. He was bought and sold, and treated as an ordinary article of merchandise and traffic, whenever a profit could be made by it. This opinion was at that time fixed and universal in the civilized portion of the white race.[39]

To dispute Taney's claim is not to deny that racism was a profound feature of the Founders' thinking. But it is to deny that the evidences of racism are also evidences that the Founders thought of free blacks as incapable of citizenship. Indeed, the fact that a group does not enjoy equality does not of itself mean that they have no rights at all, and most of Taney's evidence about the legal disabilities of free black people in the colonial era, under the confederation, and in the early years of the Constitution proves nothing at all.

Some of the evidence Taney cited, the three-fifths clause, for instance, did prove that the Constitution was intended to provide political protection for slavery. But it proved nothing about whether free blacks had citizenship rights, because free blacks were apportioned by that very clause on a one-to-one basis, not, like slaves, on a three-fifths basis or, like Native Americans, on a zero-fifths basis. To pick another example, Taney noted that when the Confederation Congress set the quota of state militias requisitioned by the Congress, they set that quota to be in proportion only to the *white* inhabitants of the states. This did prove that the states had racist ideas about putting guns in the hands of blacks. But it also proved that when they meant to refer only to whites they did so, and they did not do so in their language about citizenship rights, which referred only to "free inhabitants," a term that on its face would seem to include free blacks.[40] Again, the naturalization laws Taney cited may have extended naturalization only to white, not to nonwhite, foreigners, but that proved (as Fehrenbacher has argued) only that they did not want more black citizens, not that free blacks already in the country were not citizens. Taney's argument went so far, Fehrenbacher insists, as to deny free blacks the status not only of citizens but also that of persons, since Taney denied them the protection of the Fifth Amendment, which protects persons, not just citizens.[41]

Now the reason why Taney wanted to insist, against the evidence, that no black persons had citizenship rights under the confederation, that the Constitution not only protected slavery but also treated even free blacks like domestic animals, and even that blacks were not included in the preamble to the Declaration of Independence was that he wished to argue that if they were not part of the political community that ratified the Constitution, and did not become formally naturalized in the way immigrants are naturalized, and had not been made citizens by constitutional amendment, the fact that they have since that time been given citizenship rights in some states (such as the right to vote in Maine and, with high property qualifications, the right to vote in New York as well) did not require the other states to give citizens of those states all the privileges and immunities of citizens, notwithstanding the language in Article IV, section 2 of the Constitution that citizens of any state must enjoy the same privileges and immunities in all of the other states. Taney argued, but produced no convincing evidence, that although Congress can make laws naturalizing just about anyone else, only a constitutional amendment can naturalize American blacks. This argument was just silly, and only an implicit threat of force or secession could make anyone take it seriously.

Taney's attack on the Missouri Compromise restriction was shoddy as well. Some of it had become pro-slavery dogma—that the language in the Constitution granting the federal government power over the territories did not refer to the territories exactly, but only to unorganized land owned by the federal government. Taney did this argument one better, by arguing that the territories clause really only referred to unorganized land actually owned by the federal government in 1789. And, by counterintuitively deriving the power to govern the territories not from the territories clause of the Constitution but from the power to create new states, Taney did his best to write the Calhoun-Davis joint sovereignty thesis, that the territories are the joint property of the states, not the property of the American people, into the Constitution. And he argued, by taking exactly the Fifth Amendment grounds that Lincoln feared from the hypothetical "second *Dred Scott* decision," that Congress not only lacks the power to abolish slavery in the territories but also has a positive, constitutionally mandated duty to protect it. Taney extended his argument about the federal government to the territorial governments as well, maintaining that Congress cannot confer on any local government a power it cannot itself exercise.

If the attack on the Missouri Compromise restriction (and for that matter the attack on the idea that free blacks could ever be citizens) was aimed at the Republicans, this last was clearly designed to be an attack upon Douglas, an attempt to read southern interests into the higher law. It should be noted, first, that the claim is logically faulty: if the federal government could not confer any power it could not exercise, as Douglas would point out in 1859, it could not establish new states. And of course the more important premise about the federal government's power over slavery in the territories is false as well. But the key thing to remember in this passage is that it refers to issues that were simply not at stake in the *Dred Scott* case, since Scott was never in any territory whose legislature had abolished slavery, and the issue had not been raised, one way or the other, either by Scott's lawyers or by Sanford's. Taney was merely using his position as Chief Justice to cast an anathema, charged with unearned authority by virtue of his post, at his political enemies. The citizenship aspects of the decision were decided wrongly, but they were before the Court. The attack on the Missouri Compromise was wrong, but the Missouri question was before the Court. But this issue was not before the Court, and Douglas was right to regard it later as not really part of the holding of the Court in the case.

Probably there was no conspiracy involved in the Court's attack on the Missouri Compromise restriction. Geyer and Johnson made the argument during the case, and the Court, for bad reasons perhaps, accepted their argument. But there just may have been conspiracy involved in the attack on popular sovereignty, since it was the Court's ruling on popular sovereignty that President Buchanan said in his inaugural that he would cheerfully submit to when the Court got around to issuing the *Dred Scott* decision, and arguments about popular sovereignty came in nowhere in the case except in Taney's own written final opinion.

7.3 Lincoln's Response

What Opposition Means

Given the role that the *Dred Scott* decision would play in the slave power conspiracy theory Lincoln developed in the "House Divided" speech and in the senatorial debates later, the surprise is that Lincoln's first views of that decision showed no traces of the paranoid style, and in his most extended treatment of that decision, his Springfield speech of June 26, 1857, on the *Dred Scott* decision, the slave power conspiracy theory played no role at all.

Lincoln was careful not to adopt either of the two main Republican lines of attack on the decision. He did not treat the decision as the fruit of a conspiracy between Buchanan and Taney—not yet, anyway—and he did not argue that the Court, having argued that the federal circuit court in Missouri had no jurisdiction over the case, was foreclosed from examining the case on its merits. He did not, this is to say, treat the attack upon the Missouri Compromise restriction as dictum. But he also did not treat the attack on the popular sovereignty position as dictum either, although it probably was.

Lincoln also did not adopt the common anti-slavery ways of countering the decision. He proposed no popular acts of resistance, he did not propose nullifying the decision through the acts of the other branches or the state legislatures, and he did not propose attacking the Court's power by changing the number of justices. He not only submitted to the decision as regards Dred Scott himself but also conceded that the case would govern other persons in Scott's position. But he did not concede that he would have to treat the decision as prescribing a political rule for his future course. In other words, he did not feel that as a legislator he was obligated to support further laws that would seem to have been called for in Chief Justice Taney's opinion, or to pass other laws that would be consistent with that opinion. And he felt that he could still support laws that would challenge the decision at the margins, testing its limits and providing occasions for the Court to rethink its views. Lincoln also proposed pushing the gradual change in the Court's point of view that would follow from political control over the confirmation of new justices over the long term: a Republican Senate could put in motion the reversal of the decision one justice at a time, in a process that might have taken decades to complete.

Lincoln's concrete analysis of the *Dred Scott* decision in the June 26 speech was searching. He began by characterizing the mode of his opposition to the decision. When Stephen Douglas responded to Lincoln's attacks upon the *Dred Scott* decision, he often assumed that such attacks could arise only from the claim that one has in one's own conscience an authority higher than the Court to declare the meaning of the Constitution.[42] Douglas thought of this kind of claim as a version of burning the Constitution as a covenant with death and an agreement with hell. This playing of a moral trump, Douglas argued, poses the problem all playing of moral trumps poses, that ascetic idealism which in the name of a higher law destroys the machinery of justice in order to serve an idea of justice. But Lincoln's attack did not take this course. And Lincoln's argument arose from a vision of the nature of authority and principle in a democracy different from those that depend upon the distinction between positive law and higher law, between human law and God's law, or between politics and law.

Lincoln was very careful to seek a deeper layer of controlling principle that did not run the risks of higher-law idealism. To argue that a Supreme Court decision is a mistake, Lincoln argued, is not to overthrow the rule of law, to set up an alternative private court, in one's own moral intuition, or an alternative public court, in excited public feeling, to take the place of the actual institution. Nor is to deny that a single Supreme Court decision settles a constitutional issue sweepingly and permanently an attack upon the constitutional order or upon the independence of the judiciary. It is simply a way to recognize that the Court is not a very small, very indirectly elected legislature, with absolute power over all issues, capable of being second-guessed by nobody. The Court plays a part, a very strong part but nevertheless a part, in a persuasive conversation among the branches and with the people. It is only the upshot of that conversation, not any one decision of the Court (which even in the best of cases will face what Alexander Bickel, in *The Least Dangerous Branch* [1962)], famously called "the countermajoritarian difficulty"), that ultimately settles the meaning of the Constitution.

In the Quincy debate, Lincoln distinguished between accepting the *Dred Scott* decision and adopting it as a political rule. The idea is that Lincoln did not propose to defy the Court in that case, or in any following similar case. But he did propose to treat the question it had attempted to close as one that is still open, subject to further legal testing, capable of being eroded around the edges by political challenges, until finally *Dred Scott* loses its legitimacy:

> We oppose the Dred Scott decision in a certain way, upon which I ought perhaps to address you a few words. We do not propose that when Dred Scott has been decided to be a slave by the court, we, as a mob, will decide him to be free. We do not propose that, when any other one, or one thousand, shall be decided by that court to be slaves, we will in any violent way disturb the rights of property thus settled, but we nevertheless do oppose that decision as a political rule, which shall be binding on the voter to vote for nobody who thinks it wrong, which shall be binding on the members of Congress or the President to favor no measure that does not actually concur with the principles of that decision. We do not propose to be bound by it as a political rule in that way, because we think it lays the foundation not merely of enlarging and spreading out what we consider an evil, but it lays the foundation for spreading that evil into the States themselves. We propose so resisting it as to have it reversed if we can, and a new judicial rule established upon this subject. (1:740–741)

Douglas's riposte to this was to argue that when one takes an oath to support the Constitution, one recognizes that the Supreme Court is the authoritative interpreter of the Constitution, and to refuse to conform one's political course to its decisions, to refuse to act as if what it has decided is not only right but obvious, is to attack the Constitution itself and to make one's oath to that Constitution a kind of lie. This view, Alexander Bickel points out, is good *Marbury v. Madison*, but it is not good U.S. Constitution; those are, after all, slightly different things.[43]

The issue, of course, was whether the *Dred Scott* decision fully settled the question. Criticism of the decision might have been a different matter, might in fact have run more risk of becoming an attack upon the constitutional order, had the decision been unanimous, had it been free of partisan bias, had it been in accord with legal public expectation and general public practice, and had been based on assumed historical facts that were really true. But none of these things, of course, was the case in *Dred Scott*. Since the decision lacked all of those features, Lincoln remarked with dry understatement, "it is not resistance, it is not factious, it is not even disrespectful, to treat it as not having yet quite established a settled doctrine for the country" (1:393). Despite all these problems the decision could yet, in Lincoln's view, have become "a settled doctrine for the country," if it were it to be "affirmed and re-affirmed through a course of years" (1:393). But Lincoln assumed that it would be possible to exploit the weaknesses of *Dred Scott* to ensure that it could not be so reaffirmed, and he set himself to deprive the decision of legitimacy over the long run.

Now Lincoln's language was not explicitly the language of legal evolution, but the language of legal reconsideration: he imagined that upon reflection a later Court would correct the Taney Court's mistake in *Dred Scott* and restore what Lincoln took to be the more egalitarian legal order prior to that decision. The Court did not have to treat *Dred Scott* as a precedent binding upon it forever, because precedent is the upshot of a legal culture, and no one case suffices to define that upshot, so that outrider precedents are eventually worn away and eventually the law, in Mansfield's widely quoted phrase, "works itself pure."[44]

Lincoln's sense of that upshot was idealized: if Taney's understanding of American legal culture was rather more racist than its actual history, Lincoln's was rather less, since it depended upon the unkept promises of the opening sentences of the Declaration of Independence. What Lincoln sought to restore was a legal order that did not actually exist but that had been promised, and what he described as a restoration really is better seen as an evolution. The method Lincoln imagined—continuous refinement upon reflection—is an evolutionary method, and the correction, since it restores a legal order that, like the promises of the Declaration, did not in fact ever actually have institutional or political realization, looks more like an evolution than a reconsideration.

To imagine precedent as an upshot, this is to say, rather than as a rigorous network of postulates and theorems, is inevitably already to imagine legal culture as evolving, however conservatively one may imagine that upshot. One might put Lincoln's argument this way: reconsideration will restore the legal *concept* of the constitutional order, from which *conceptions* had begun to diverge, even though that concept has not yet been cashed out in conceptions and may not ever be cashed out fully. The ultimate outcome of a process of continuous refinement and reconsideration of conceptions would be convergence in the long run upon the concept. What is to be restored is not a set of concrete legal conceptions, which in recent days had been tending in Taney's direction, not in Lincoln's, but an underlying aspiration for moral equality which underlies the American legal order even though it is constantly betrayed by that order. Lincoln's thinking elides the distinction between restoration and evolution, since it seeks the restoration of a *concept*, which itself is something that by nature can be realized only by evolution.[45]

Lincoln's thought here about the gradual change of a legal climate of opinion has implications about the sources of a legal decision's authority, and about the kind of access to principle generally possible in a good-enough democracy.[46] A legal decision's authority seems to be won not by its ties back to its precedents but by its ties forward to the consent it wins from later judges and later cases. Lincoln's view of judicial authority here resembles what I have called his "reverse Burkeanism," in which the meaning of the Founders' commitments is not to be sought in their documents and laws in an unmediated way, but in the future in which those commitments unfold consequences they could not have anticipated. (This is of course also Lincoln's own analysis in the Gettysburg Address of the meaning of the Civil War: only if there is a "new birth of freedom" after the war can it truly be called a Union victory.) Reverse Burkeanism asserts that a decision's meaning, although an interpretation of a prior concept, is a function of that decision's ability to work its way down into the fabric of legal decisions until it becomes an assumption so fundamental that it almost no longer needs articulation. To keep faith with the Founders is to keep faith with the things that made them ashamed, and to reinterpret their conceptions, their concrete workings out of a legal idea in a here and now, in the light of a fresh grasp upon their underlying concept. Reverse Burkeanism assumes that the Founders were, no less than we ourselves are, entangled in the contradiction between their concepts, the deepest values they sought to serve, and their conceptions, the concrete workings out of those values under particular political and cultural circumstances.[47] To keep faith with the Founders is to recognize that they too understood that their conceptions were imperfect realizations of their concepts.

This view of law as a "living growth" is not precisely that articulated by Oliver Wendell Holmes Jr. in *The Common Law* (1881), because what shapes the growth of law in Holmes is a kind of Darwinism. Nor is it quite the same as the more traditional view that precedents deepen as later cases accumulate that rely upon them, so that overturning the precedent becomes gradually more costly (although still possible if other legal arguments prove the necessity of paying that cost). The idea here is that legal reasoning has its own internal, phronetic logic dictated by its form of life.[48]

When Lincoln imagined law as evolving, he did not compromise its authority as law; rather, he imagined it (as Aristotle imagined all things that have to do with human flourishing) as something capable of only phronetic certainty. Phronetic certainty, as I argued in section 5.2 above, is bound up with the implicitness of values, which in turn is bound up with the idea of law as a reflection of the public mind, by which, through its unfolding, a people caught up in ways of being that are partly conventional and socially constructed and partly rooted in things beyond convention and social construction feel their way among conceptions of the just in the direction of a concept of justice that is never fully exhausted by constructions from first principles and never fully disclosed even to its adherents.

Lincoln's reverse Burkeanism, and his concept of the public mind, together with his vision of the ultimate sources of authority as implicit values inhabiting the sphere of tacit knowledge, insulated his view of the remedy for *Dred Scott* from the most telling charge Douglas had to make against it. Douglas repeatedly argued that seeking to overthrow the *Dred Scott* decision by appointing only judges unsympathetic to it would undermine the distinction between law and politics. Judges are supposed to make their decisions by thinking like judges, not by following the instructions of the party that appointed them, and if they are thinking like judges, that means they must be free to examine the question all the way around, rather than foreclosing thought from the beginning and engaging only in rationalization of convictions they already hold dogmatically.

Now one might reply to this charge of seeking to elide the distinction between law and politics by pointing out that this is exactly how the *Dred Scott* decision was made in the first place, and one might also reply that the distinction between law and politics is finally unreal, that law, like war, is politics carried on by other means. Lincoln did make the first of these arguments. President Jackson and for that matter

Senator Douglas himself had blurred the boundary between law and politics, ignoring decisions that stood in their way and manipulating the courts into giving them permission for things they had already decided to do. But Lincoln was foreclosed from the second argument by his own reformist conception of law. Eliding the distinction between law and politics can never serve a reformist purpose, because skepticism about justice can never actually serve any practical purpose other than confirming the power of those who already have power, since it fatally compromises any appeal those who do not have power might be able to make against what power wants. Where relativism amounts to circumspection, it can serve justice by prompting second thoughts, but wherever relativism amounts to skepticism, it can only serve tyranny. Lincoln knew that he had to find a way to effect the reversal of *Dred Scott* without giving color to the charge of having put politics in place of law, because his own moral allegiances demanded that law serve justice, not politics.

What Lincoln imagined in his attack upon *Dred Scott* was not merely a gradual shift in the membership of the Court, but a gradual shift in the convictions of the public mind, a shift that would reflect itself in the climate of legal opinion in which the Court operates. For this reason he cannot fairly be charged with seeking to overrule *Dred Scott* by partisan dictation. He imagined that future justices would have to win out in a persuasive exchange over the long run, and he believed that the principles of *Dred Scott*, if they were to triumph, would also have to win out in such a persuasive exchange, which in the long run he believed they could not possibly do.

One might reply to this that a shift in the climate of legal opinion of the kind Lincoln described still amounts to partisan dictation, except that by adding a great deal of time to the equation, the sources of the shift become obscured by the mists of years, so that what appears to be an evolution in the public mind's point of view is merely the outcome of an extended process of political manipulation. It is impossible to completely rule out this argument. On the other hand, it is also unlikely that one can prevail over the very long haul without making some commanding appeal to the public mind's deepest sources of conviction. Even the legal culture of the United States is ultimately ruled by We the People, and if one inclines to the view that the convictions of the public mind are always and inevitably the consequences of manipulation rather than of thinking, then one might as well appoint Platonic Guardians (after making sure that they are members of one's own party) and give up the pretense of democracy entirely.

For the southern Democrats in particular, the decision of the Court could, on the mere onetime ipse dixit of the Court, establish a durable and compelling sense of what the Constitution means, so that the only course would be submission, not only in the case under consideration, and not only in all similar cases that might arise under its purview, but also in the political acts of the Congress and in the campaign behavior of politicians. Congress could not pass laws that would raise the issues of the case again, prompting the Court to refine, rethink, or even repeal its views (in the classic manner of separation of powers) without posing an anarchic threat to the constitutional order. Politicians could not campaign against the decision without being mad enthusiasts seeking to impose their own convictions by force. Now no court decision in fact takes on this kind of authority, but since the Supreme Court had never actually declared a congressional statute invalid before the *Dred Scott* case, perhaps the question was seen to be more open then than we see it now. But the claim that being able to capture a transient bare majority on the Court would also enable one to embed one's platform into the Constitution for all time to come is a claim that can in practice only undermine the moral authority of the Court, and for that matter, undermine the moral authority of the law.

Lincoln's vision of the authority of a legal decision also sheds light on Lincoln's sense of what it is that embodies principle in the dance of principle and consent that makes for political legitimacy. Principle is not dictated by the heavens. But it is not exactly mere custom either. It seems to embody itself in a publicly held body of assumptions and values about which reason sometimes critically reflects, but which it also sometimes feels the force of in implicit ways, or even as habits of being so deeply ingrained that they are hard to articulate at all. It is these working assumptions of a democratic political culture, some of which seem to be the necessary preconditions of all democratic political culture, and some of which seem to be essentially the traditions of this one, that Lincoln calls "the public mind." It is something not quite so abstract as "the Rights of Man," and not so concrete as "the Rights of Englishmen." It depends upon cultural preconditions for realization, but it is also not entirely a creature of social construction.

It is important to remember, when one discusses the dance of principle and consent, that in a democratic culture a ruling principle is not dictated from some source exterior to the democracy—it is not declared by God or his book or his church. Ruling principle in democracies arises from both explicit and implicit sources internal to democratic living, on the one hand from an analysis of the meaning of democracy and of the necessary preconditions of any theory of self-rule, and on the other hand from an intuitive sense of the moral demands of democratic political culture. Democratic polities cannot survive without principle and cannot afford to be neutral in all questions of principle. But they must see those principles from within the horizon of democratic commitments if they are to be bound by them.[49] Principles arise in democracies, in Jaffa's elegant phrase, "from within the democratic ethos as perfections of that ethos."[50] Lincoln's argument was that the defense of slavery requires sacrifices of principle that must ultimately be fatal to democracy, and therefore a principled confrontation over slavery could not be avoided.

Lincoln's view is that the survival of democracy depends upon some things—certain structures of feeling, for instance—that cannot be captured by the formalism of rules about fairness, and cannot be made the subject of state compulsion either. To pick an example closer to our own time, consider feelings about race during the desegregation era. It is within the power of the government to prohibit racial discrimination in the public world. It can prohibit states from preventing black people from voting. It can even extend its regulation into the economic world, to the extent that (since 1937 anyway) much of the economic world has been seen to be part of the public world, not the private one. So, to reconsider a case I examined above, the law can prohibit white restaurant owners from refusing to serve black people. But it cannot prohibit their ugly feelings, and would not succeed in doing so even were it to try. And were these feelings to get the upper hand among the people over the long term, were they to express themselves nakedly rather than in the coded language of "crime," "welfare dependency," and "voter fraud," equality in our republic would be again in danger and our republic would be incapable of using the law to save itself.

These structures of feeling are unexamined, not propositional in form, and charged with all the pathos and panic of identity and loyalty. We know them intuitively, as we know our first language, rather than explicitly, as, until we master it, we might know a second language. Because we know them intuitively, the boundary between what is merely conventional, or a cultural property of our people, and what has roots deep in human nature or in the absolute requirements of democracy itself, is necessarily an unclear one. We have only indirect access to them, and we cannot quite reason away even gross errors that arise from within the public mind, although occasionally we can help ourselves outgrow them. The public mind is a creature of history, not a creature of philosophy, but it casts light on, illuminates the meaning of, takes the pulse of philosophical questions. Only a kind of negative capability puts one in touch with the public mind. At the same time, because it is as much something given as something chosen (although it can over the long run be shaped, in the way that habits are shaped), it sets a limit to the power of critical reason, which can bend the public mind but not transform it at once. And because it is as much something given as something chosen, the power of the public mind is as often a heteronomous power as an autonomous one, in the way that all appeals to kin and kind are sources of heteronomy just as much as they are sources of identity.

This view of the sources of principle in a democratic society has several consequences. The first is that it is to be expected that argument will continue about the meaning of these principles, and how they apply to particular cases, and that argument of this kind is not proof that no principle is involved or that appeals to principle are never telling, only that they are bound to a history that shapes and constrains them even if it does not necessarily imprison them. It means that each side owes the other the respect that follows from the ideal of persuasive engagement, and cannot compel except under conditions where the right to compel is won by persuasive engagement. One's own reading of a principle must win its authority by persuasion and reasonable assent, or by shaping a modus vivendi if assent cannot be won.

The second consequence is that however absolute one's command of principle, one is still bound to practice the art of the possible when it comes to the means of realizing that principle. Alexander Bickel put it this way:

> The teaching of [Lincoln's] life is that principled government by the consent of the governed often means the definition of principled

goals, and the practice of the art of the possible in striving to attain them. The hard fact of an existing evil institution such as slavery and the hard practical difficulties that stood in the way of its sudden abolition justified myriad compromises short of abandoning the goal. The goal itself—the principle—made sense only as an absolute, and as such it was to be maintained. As such it had its vast educational value, as such it exerted its crucial influence on the tendency of prudential policy. But expedient compromises remained necessary also, chiefly because a radically principled solution would collide with widespread prejudices, which no government resting on consent could disregard, any more than it could sacrifice its goals to them.[51]

The idea here is that a decision has to earn legitimacy by being affirmed as the upshot and basis of a long series of opinions in cases that unfold from the original one. The argument resembles Madison's argument in *Federalist* 37 that it is pointless to seek in the will of the author the meaning of a law or a constitutional clause, because (quoting Madison) "All new laws, though penned with the greatest technical skill, and passed on the fullest and most mature deliberation, are considered as more or less obscure and equivocal, until their meaning can be liquidated and ascertained by a series of particular discussions and adjudications."[52] The meaning of a law, and the legitimacy of an interpretation, cannot be secured by reaching back to a founding act of will but only by reaching forward to a legal habit shaped by that law and given meaning by the ongoing process of a life that exfoliates its implications. The test is neither the strict constructionist test of the (unknowable) will of the Founders or of a crisp but in practice impossible comparison of the language of the statute and the language of the Constitution nor the legal positivist test of whether a decision predicts the decisions of future judges, but the reverse-Burkean test of whether it gives form to a habit of life articulated in its name and by its means, working its way down into a position among the implicit assumptions a legal culture has grown to rely upon.

Lincoln's Response to Douglas's Attack

Having defined what is and is not at issue for him in the question of judicial review, Lincoln picks up the argument he expects from Douglas, citing Douglas's own words:

The courts are the tribunals prescribed by the Constitution and created by the authority of the people to determine, expound and enforce the law. Hence, whoever resists the final decision of the highest judicial tribunal, aims a deadly blow to our whole Republican system of government—a blow, which if successful would place all our rights and liberties at the mercy of passion, anarchy and violence. (1:393)

Douglas's argument is telling against certain kinds of higher-law argument, but it does not reach Lincoln because Lincoln did not in fact make the argument Douglas attributed to him. Rather than arguing that Douglas's attack did not in fact apply to the position Lincoln had taken, however, Lincoln pointed out that Douglas's political father, Andrew Jackson, had attacked the Supreme Court in roughly the same ways that Douglas would later accuse Lincoln of doing. Jackson had ignored the Court's ruling on the constitutionality of the Bank of the United States when he exercised his own veto against it, saying:

If the opinion of the Supreme court covered the whole ground of this act, it ought not to control the co-ordinate authorities of this Government. The Congress, the executive and the court, must each for itself be guided by its own opinion of the Constitution. Each public officer, who takes an oath to support the Constitution, swears that he will support it as he understands it, and not as it is understood by others. (1:394)

We might call this the "So's your old man!" argument: Jackson did it too, so what is Douglas complaining about? The parallel is not very exact, for the Court's ruling that the bank was constitutional did not require President Jackson not to veto the act renewing its charter. Something does not have to be unconstitutional to be vetoed, and it does not much matter whether he vetoed the bill because he thought it was unconstitutional or because he did not like the shape of Henry Clay's ears. Even if the case were a better fit, the argument is not all that telling, because if it were wrong for Jackson to overslaugh the Court, then it was still wrong for Lincoln.

In the 1858 debates Lincoln used a stronger and more pointed example. In the Ottawa debate Lincoln compares Douglas's behavior in an 1841 Illinois case about alien voting to his own about *Dred Scott:*

And I remind him of another piece of history on the question of
respect for judicial decisions, and it is a piece of Illinois history,
belonging to a time when the large party to which Judge Douglas
belonged, were displeased with a decision of the Supreme Court of
Illinois, because they had decided that a Governor could not remove a Secretary of State. You will find the whole story in Ford's
History of Illinois, and I know that Judge Douglas will not deny that
he was then in favor of overslaughing that decision by the mode of
adding five new Judges, so as to vote down the four old ones. Not
only so, but *it ended in the Judge's sitting down on that very bench as
one of the five new Judges to break down the four old ones.* [Cheers and
laughter.] It was in this way precisely that he got his title of Judge.
Now, when the Judge tells me that men appointed conditionally
to sit as members of a court, will have to be catechised beforehand upon some subject, I say, "You know, Judge; you have tried it."
[Laughter.] When he says a court of this kind will lose the confidence of all men, will be prostituted and disgraced by such a proceeding, I say, "You know best, Judge; you have been through the
mill." (1:526)

Lincoln referred to two simultaneous, intertwined cases which, although they involved different issues, played out in linked ways. Lincoln mentions only one part of the case, the case about whether the
governor could remove the secretary of state. But the case could not be
separated from the second case, which involved whether unnaturalized aliens could vote in state elections.

The latter case bears a number of interesting similarities to the *Dred
Scott* case. Unnaturalized aliens could vote in state elections in Illinois
in the 1830s so long as they met the state's rather minimal residency
requirements.[53] Whig judges, of course, looked askance at this, and
sought, motivated partly by the traditional Whig hostility to a wide
franchise but also partly by anti-Catholic nativism, to purge the voter
rolls, provoking the Democratic legislature to pack the Court in their
own favor. Anti-Catholic nativism was a powerful force in the prewar
era, and for complicated reasons nativism and racism tended to repel
each other into opposite parties. The Whigs challenged the election
law in 1839, and the case was decided in their favor by Judge Daniel
Stone, whom the reader may remember as the other Whig state legis-

lator who filed a protest against slavery in the Illinois legislature with Lincoln in 1837.

When the case was appealed to the state supreme court, Douglas represented the Democrats, along with his friend Murray McConnel, whom the reader will recognize as the father of the source of testimony concerning Douglas's hostility to slavery. Douglas's argument was that the states controlled the franchise, even if naturalization was a federal responsibility, thus making the kind of distinction between state and national citizenship that would be at issue in *Dred Scott* later. Aware that the Whig-dominated court was likely to rule against him, Douglas discovered an error in the charge that enabled him to retry the case after the 1840 election, which the Democrats won, with the help of all those votes Douglas had saved by his trick.

Douglas was simultaneously engaged in a case, where he was opposed by Lincoln, to determine whether the Democratic government could sack the long-serving Whig secretary of state, Alexander P. Field, and replace him with John McClernand, a Democrat, or whether Field's appointment amounted to life tenure. The outcome of this confusing case somehow was that Douglas was himself appointed secretary of state.

While the alien voter case was still pending, the Democrats proposed a bill reorganizing the court, essentially packing it with their own partisans, adding five new judges to the state supreme court, and, having them each ride circuit, eliminating the position of circuit court judge. (In the Democrats' defense, this bill was not completely an innovation; it restored the status quo of six years earlier.) Before this blatant power grab could take effect, the Whig supreme court tried to appease the Democrats by adopting an ambiguous ruling on the alien voter case, a move that discouraged their Whig supporters without in fact appeasing the Democrats. Douglas managed the new court bill and, in the end, was appointed to one of the seats, along with Sidney Breese, later the Buchanan Democrat candidate for governor in 1858, and Thomas Ford, whose history of Illinois Lincoln cited.[54]

The interest of the 1841 court-packing case is the way in which it echoes the *Dred Scott* case with the parties reversed, turning as *Dred Scott* did on arguments about the distinction between state and national citizenship, and seeking to exclude a stigmatized and feared population from the public square.

Whatever its value as a retort, Lincoln's reference to the 1841 alien voting case raises more questions than it answers. The substance of Douglas's charge, after all, was that judges should not be merely taking partisan dictation, that whatever justice is it cannot simply be the platform of one's own party. That Douglas had himself done this does not defend Lincoln against the charge of doing the same thing. Nor is the defense that all legal decisions are motivated by partisan considerations and factional power a useful one, even if it is an accurate description, because Lincoln's aims are reformist aims, and that argument subverts reformist aims. Now Douglas might have defended himself from this kind of charge with the argument that in a democracy the people rule, and the more directly they rule the better, and that judges had better remember that fact. But that argument is not available to Lincoln, because it would run against the grain of Lincoln's thinking from the Lyceum speech on, where unmediated popular rule is seen as imprisonment by popular passions, especially ugly ones.

Now it is impossible to ask judges not to have political convictions, and those who insist most firmly that they should not have them (or that they themselves do not have them) are usually the ones who are most eager to impose their party's platforms on the sly. But it is possible to ask a judge to make a rule by thinking like a judge, and to argue that to do this the judge must give himself or herself to habits of thought different from those that prevailed in a prior life as a political figure. (For one thing, we expect a judge to recognize when the opposing party has a case.) The line between politics and law may not be a bright one, but in a rough-and-ready way nobody denies sometimes being able to recognize a "political" decision, even one made by a judge of one's own party.

The Declaration and Black Citizenship

Considerations about the public mind as a seat of the concepts that underlie the conceptions of political and legal practice formed the basis of Lincoln's response to the *Dred Scott* decision. They also shaped his interpretation of the Declaration of Independence, the promises of whose preamble were, in Lincoln's mind, what was really at stake in the case. Following the dissenting opinions of Justices McLean and Curtis, Lincoln in the *Dred Scott* speech examined the decision's distortions of historical fact and legal precedent. Chief Justice Taney, as we have already seen, had argued that no black people, whether free or slave (although Taney does not seem to have understood that there were free black people anywhere in the Union then) could have been a part of the political community that designed for itself the Constitution, ignoring, as Lincoln pointed out, that in five of the original thirteen states, one of them North Carolina, free blacks were voters, "and, in proportion to their numbers, had the same part in making the Constitutions that the white people had" (1:395).

Lincoln also criticized Taney's assertion that the Founders' racial thinking was uglier than the racism of his own day, noting for instance that free blacks had over the previous half century lost the franchise in states where they once enjoyed it, that manumission had increasingly become illegal, that state constitutions had been rewritten so as to preclude emancipation by the state legislature. Lincoln might also have pointed out (but did not point out) that free state constitutions increasingly prohibited free blacks from entering the state, as the constitution of Illinois did when Lincoln gave his *Dred Scott* speech, and as the Topeka Constitution, written by insurgent opponents of slavery in Kansas Territory only the previous year, also did.

Worst of all, Lincoln argued, the grand promises of the Declaration of Independence had over the intervening years become increasingly either revised out of existence or sneered at as obvious nonsense. This last struck Lincoln most powerfully—since the Peoria speech it was the threat to the values of the Declaration that most got him stirred up, even when his opponents were not explicitly seeking to undermine those values. The attack upon the Declaration was to Lincoln the strongest possible evidence not only of the deterioration of the feeling of a common human project shared across races but also of the deterioration of the political culture necessary for freedom. The darkening prospects for blacks were to Lincoln also the darkening prospects for democracy. It should be remembered that Lincoln's most famous passage on the worsening situation of African Americans was introduced by him as a commentary on the decay of the public mind's investment in the Declaration of Independence:

> In those days, our Declaration of Independence was held sacred by all, and thought to include all; but now, to aid in making the bondage

of the negro universal and eternal, it is assailed, and sneered at, and construed, and hawked at, and torn, till, if its framers could rise from their graves, they could not at all recognize it. All the powers of earth seem rapidly combining against him. Mammon is after him; ambition follows, and philosophy follows, and the Theology of the day is fast joining the cry. They have him in his prison house; they have searched his person, and left no prying instrument with him. One after another they have closed the heavy iron doors upon him, and now they have him, as it were, bolted in with a lock of a hundred keys, which can never be unlocked without the concurrent of every key; the keys in the hands of a hundred different men, and they scattered to a hundred different and distant places; and they stand musing as to what invention, in all the dominions of mind and matter, can be produced to make the impossibility of his escape more complete than it is. (1:396)

Lincoln in the *Dred Scott* speech defined the meaning of the promises of the Declaration in very memorable but also very precise language that is worth quoting at length:

Chief Justice Taney, in his opinion in the Dred Scott case, admits that the language of the Declaration is broad enough to include the whole human family, but he and Judge Douglas argue that the authors of that instrument did not intend to include negroes, by the fact that they did not at once, actually place them on an equality with the whites. Now this grave argument comes to just nothing at all, by the other fact, that they did not at once, *or ever afterwards,* actually place all white people on an equality with one or another. And this is the staple argument of both the Chief Justice and the Senator, for doing this obvious violence to the plain unmistakable language of the Declaration. I think the authors of that notable instrument intended to include *all* men, but they did not intend to declare all men equal *in all respects.* They did not mean to say all were equal in color, size, intellect, moral developments, or social capacity. They defined with tolerable distinctness, in what respects they did consider all men created equal—equal in "certain inalienable rights, among which are life, liberty, and the pursuit of happiness." This they said, and this meant. They did not mean to assert the obvious untruth, that all were then actually enjoying that equality, nor yet, that they were about to confer it immediately upon them. In fact they had no power to confer such a boon. They meant simply to declare the *right*, so that the *enforcement* of it might follow as fast as circumstances should permit. They meant to set up a standard maxim for free society, which should be familiar to all, and revered by all; constantly looked to, constantly labored for, and even though never perfectly attained, constantly approximated, and thereby constantly spreading and deepening its influence, and augmenting the happiness and value of life to all people of all colors everywhere. The assertion that "all men are created equal" was of no practical use in effecting our separation from Great Britain; and it was placed in the Declaration, not for that, but for future use. Its authors meant it to be, thank God, it is now proving itself, a stumbling block to those who in after times might seek to turn a free people back into the hateful paths of despotism. They knew the proneness of prosperity to breed tyrants, and they meant when such should re-appear in this fair land and commence their vocation they should find left for them at least one hard nut to crack. (1:398–399)

Lincoln began here by noticing where his opponents made their case. Taney and Douglas argued that the fact that the Founders did little to put equality of human rights for white and black into action proves that they did not mean to promise it. Douglas's argument was not only that if the Declaration means what it appears to mean, then Jefferson and the others were all hypocrites. But Douglas did cite all the evidence used by skeptics about Jefferson's meaning to this day: that he did not free his slaves, that many other signers were slaveholders, that all thirteen colonies at the time of the Declaration were slaveholding colonies, that if they had understood Jefferson's ultimate intention to be freedom for the slave that Georgia and South Carolina, at the least, would never have signed the Declaration. (Indeed, one might add that without slavery the English settlement in the New World would have been a failure, and that every aspect of the American experiment was made possible by and is rooted in slavery.) In many ways, Douglas sounds like recent revisionist historians on the same subject. And Lincoln's historical counterargument—Jefferson's exclamation in *Notes on the State of Virginia* that he trembled for his country when he reflects that God is just, which Lincoln cited at Galesburg—relies on the same kinds of argument contemporary defenders of Jefferson use.

That the Founders did not actually make blacks equal to whites did not in Lincoln's view prove that blacks were not included in the promises of the Declaration, because the Founders did not make all whites equal to each other either. Lincoln carefully distinguished among the species of equality in order to define what it was that the Founders promised. Moral equality does not mean equality in the accidents of the human condition—trivially, it does not mean equality in color or size; somewhat less trivially, it does not mean equality in intellect, moral development, or social capacity. People are different in all these things, and therefore under any set of political conditions they will not all prosper equally. But these differences do not make any difference in the moral claims they owe and are owed by others. Notice also that Lincoln here did not distinguish between individual differences and differences among groups. Individual differences do not diminish the claims each exacts and owes, and collective differences, if indeed they exist at all, do not do so either.

Lincoln conceded that even concerning the kind of equality that did matter to the Founders, equal possession of certain inalienable rights, among which are life, liberty, and the pursuit of happiness, it is clearly not the case that all actually enjoyed them at the time of the Founding, or did so in 1857, or, I might add, do so even now. They meant the doctrine of moral equality to constitute a promise that, however impossible it may be of fulfillment in the short run, would continue to exert pressure upon the public conscience until it found itself in a position to fulfill that promise. The power that promise exerts is an indirect one. Lincoln's language here about a "standard maxim for free society" is something that works by influencing the habits of thought and the structures of feeling of the society upon which it works. It is meant to reinforce a not fully conscious predisposition in favor of equal freedom. When Lincoln described the power of the meaning of the Declaration as something "which should be familiar to all, and revered by all; constantly looked to, constantly labored for, and even though never perfectly attained, constantly approximated, and thereby constantly spreading and deepening its influence, and augmenting the happiness and value of life to all people of all colors everywhere," he was describing the same kind of half-conscious structure of thought and feeling he referred to as a "political religion" back in the Lyceum speech, and which in the 1858 debates he would call the "public mind." Here, as in the Lyceum speech, these half-conscious, half-instinctive tendencies of the public mind are intended to turn the people away from the tyranny to which human beings, by their nature, continue to be intermittently attracted. The political religion of the nation, its public mind, is a never-exhausted source of becoming, arising from beneath the stratum of conscious thought where thought and feeling interpenetrate each other, reflecting the pressure of an impossible to fully articulate, impossible to fully realize concept upon an imperfect world of conceptions.

Hart's distinction between concept and conception would of course have been unavailable to Lincoln. But embracing that distinction in a heuristic spirit clarifies Lincoln's public addresses and his public acts, and draws out their intellectual unity. Further, doing so helps make sense of that tension between means and ends, and the tension between the practical requirements of political institutions and the values those institutions are intended to serve, to which all institutions, imperfectly laboring under the constraints imposed by their concrete histories, by the half-understood urgencies in which they are always entangled, and by the fallibility of actual historical agents, are subject.

Employing Hart's distinction in this perhaps idiosyncratic way also enables one to call upon Lincoln's aid in engaging both sides of the long-standing philosophical quarrel between legal realism and natural law. This course has the attraction of recognizing that each side has telling, even devastating arguments. The legal realists and their more modern successors are right that laws are creatures of culture and history, and are marked as much with the social contradictions and forms of special pleading of their era as they are with the majesty of justice. But the advocates of natural law are right that law is as much a critique of its society as an expression of it, and that the realist view risks seeing not only law but justice itself not as an imperative but as a convention, as if slavery were vulnerable to criticism only in societies where nobody holds slaves anyway. Embracing the distinction between concept and conception, this is to say, enables one to mark also the distinction between tragic pragmatism and relativism.

To the legal realist, the notion of the concept will always appear to be a brooding omnipresence smuggled into the back door of legal thinking after being thrown out of the front: it will still look like a platonic abstraction, however shrouded in implicitness. But implicitness is not really just another word for mystification: Lincoln really did mean it when he said, in his 1864 letter to Kentucky editor A. C. Hodges, that he did not guide events, they guided him. Lincoln meant it in the Second Inaugural when he argued that however much he sought to do the right as he understood it, neither he nor anyone else really understood the meaning of their acts when they did them. Nobody has untroubled access to the concept, and nobody appears very pure in its light. It is recognizing the implicitness of the concept that stands in our way when we attempt, as we usually do with our values, to brandish them in our opponents' faces and drive them from the public square. It is the implicitness of the concept that demands of us recognition of our own complicities and requires us to keep alive a forbearing and un-self-righteous state of mind even in the midst of a titanically violent conflict.

To the natural lawyer, the notion of a legal conception will always look like a version of Jerome Frank's claim that a legal decision is determined by what the judge had for breakfast. But Lincoln knew what it was to be lost in a bad history one cannot find a way out of for all one's seeking. And that is an experience one can have only if one feels the force of something beyond one's conceptions. Even in the entanglements of an unmastered past, one sometimes hears the call of a better way of being.

Douglas's argument at Jonesboro about the meaning of the promises of the Declaration describes the racism of the signers of the Declaration very bluntly. At Alton, Douglas engaged in a thought experiment about what the effect would have been had Lincoln's interpretation of the Declaration been the order of the day. Noting that at the time of the Constitutional Convention twelve of the thirteen states were slave states, Douglas argued that had Lincoln insisted that "a house divided against itself cannot stand" at that time, the twelve slave states might well have imposed a uniformly pro-slavery policy upon the entire Republic. Only a popular sovereignty policy is capable of ending slavery, Douglas argued, because only popular sovereignty makes room for the kind of reflection and reconsideration that have to happen before a major social change is possible:

How has the South lost her power as the majority section in this Union, and how have the free States gained it, except under the operation of that principle which declares the right of the people of each State and each Territory to form and regulate their domestic institutions in their own way? It was under that principle that slavery was abolished in New Hampshire, Rhode Island, Connecticut, New York, New Jersey, and Pennsylvania; it was under that principle that one half of the slaveholding States became free; it was under that principle that the number of free States increased until from being one out of twelve States, we have grown to be the majority of States of the whole Union, with the power to control the House of Representatives and Senate, and the power, consequently, to elect a President by Northern votes without the aid of a Southern State. (1:777–778)

Douglas argued that the free states were able to become free without destroying the Union because their treatment of emancipation as an issue of local self-government (like slavery itself) enabled them to carry out emancipation without posing an ontological threat to slavery elsewhere. Emancipation was successful because the emancipators did not frame it in a way that forced the issue sectionally, and they failed to emancipate more slave states once it became a sectional issue. As a political analysis, this is probably faulty, but it is worth pointing out that as an argument it is designed to serve the interest of the free states, not the interest of the slave states.

But Douglas's argument was not only a historical one about what Jefferson meant and what the consequences of a more straightforwardly anti-slavery policy among the Founders would have been; it was also an argument about what political acts in general are capable of meaning. His argument was that the meaning of a political act is to be sought in (and limited by) the immediate circumstances into which it is an intervention and in the aims of the agent in making that intervention. Nowadays in literary criticism we call that "historicizing interpretation," and in legal interpretation we call that "originalism." And Douglas's understanding of the very limited meaning of the Declaration is also one that has an afterlife in the scholarship of the intervening years, which has often sought to portray the Declaration as an ordinary political document aimed, for instance, at securing French support for American independence, rather than a transcendental setting forth of principles.

Douglas was so eager to see the Declaration only in its local terms that he rewrote its language about the Rights of Man into language about the Rights of Englishmen. Doing this thins out an idea of moral equality rooted ultimately in a sense of the transcendent value of the human person and replaces it with a set of conventional practices and moral or political habits characteristic of some particular people or culture. Douglas said of the authors of the Declaration that "they were speaking of British subjects on this continent being equal to British subjects born and residing in Great Britain," which suggests to Lincoln that Douglas would have the preamble of the Declaration read something like: "We hold these truths to be self-evident[:] that all British subjects who were on this continent eighty-one years ago, were created equal to all British subjects born and *then* residing in Great Britain" (1:400).

Now it was characteristic of Douglas to be skeptical of apodictic proclamations of any sort. Indeed, throughout the debates, he treated Lincoln's use of the sweeping language of the Declaration, with its apodictic force, in precisely the same way he treated Lincoln's biblical citation in the "House Divided" speech. All apodictic citations were in Douglas's mind evidences of fanaticism, because it is the nature of apodictic statements to foreclose the give-and-take of dealmaking that was in Douglas's view the sole guarantor of assent. To make an apodictic claim was always in Douglas's mind a way to announce that one's differences were too deep to settle; that one cites high principle is always a sign that one is about to draw a weapon.

Douglas's seizing upon the apodictic language of the *Dred Scott* decision as a kind of "Thus Saith the Lord" (because most of it supported his own political position) was in a way out of character, out of synch with his earlier Jacksonian reasoning about the meaning of legal decisions in the Bank case, and out of synch with his own later reasoning about the Freeport Doctrine. The meaning of any act for Douglas is the meaning it reveals in the back-and-forth of concrete political acts under concrete circumstances, and any other meaning an act may have is just so much hot air. But it is clear to us if not to Douglas that in restating the Declaration he not only cheapens it but makes it seem ridiculous.

There was no political price for Douglas to pay for arguing that the Declaration of Independence was not intended to refer to blacks, since after all racism rather helped than hurt him. But in narrowing the focus of the Declaration of Independence to the Rights of Englishmen, in treating it as arguing that by "equal" all Jefferson meant is that British citizens here in 1776 had a claim on the same customary procedures and habitual political practices from the British government that British citizens in Britain did, Douglas lost something that mattered a great deal to him as a Democrat in both the partisan and philosophical senses of that word. It was not merely that such a view seems to exclude the immigrant populations that Douglas depended upon (although Lincoln did point this out). It is that such a view cost him the ability to appeal to what brought those immigrant groups to America in the first place. These immigrant populations have in the Declaration a stake that arises precisely from the fact that it has a universal appeal of the kind Douglas had been at pains to deny. It was not merely that the immigrants have a right to enjoy the same freedoms the native-born enjoy, although it was that as well; it is that the immigrants themselves were partly drawn here by the moral promise of the Declaration, by the promise of a share in polis life in a society that will test an ideal of freedom in which the whole rest of the world has an investment. Douglas's constituents are not only people who sought to make better money and live more comfortable lives in America. They are also people who sought the common moral project of America. This was the promise of Jackson as much as the promise of Clay, and it was a promise Douglas himself repeatedly made in his own speeches.

At Freeport, for instance, Douglas objected to the "House Divided" speech because in his view it threatened the stability of the Union. But he objected to the threat to the Union partly because of the promise the Union makes to the world:

> I will pursue no course of conduct that will give just cause for the dissolution of the Union. The hope of the friends of freedom throughout the world rests upon the perpetuity of this Union. The downtrodden and oppressed people who are suffering under European despotism all look with hope and anxiety to the American Union as the only resting place and permanent home of freedom and self-government. (1:570–571)

Partly, this was spread-eagle bluster, something Douglas and all of Young America could belt out by heart on cue. But it was also more than that. It was in fact the promise of equality that accounted even in Douglas's mind for the magnetic force of that document and the nation it founded. But somehow in Douglas's hands that equality was only equality among nationalities and classes, not equality among races. It is the fact that he really in some sense did believe in equality that makes his beliefs hard to figure; indeed, it makes the beliefs of most of the northern Democrats of his era hard to figure, since that belief seems to have sharpened rather than to have subverted their racism, to have led them to the brink of arguing that black people are not quite human. The democratization of American culture in the Jacksonian era did sharpen its racism, in one of the bitter ironies of the antebellum era. The increasing hysteria with which more than nominal democrats like Douglas had to embrace *herrenvolk* democracy might be a measure of the strain of maintaining the contradiction.

Lincoln understood that the traditions embodied in the Declaration stood in America in the place that blood, soil, language, and history stood in other countries: the federal Constitution made the United States a state, but the Declaration of Independence made it a nation, a people. As Lincoln said during the 1858 campaign in a speech in Chicago:

> We have besides these men—descended by blood from our ancestors—among us perhaps half our people who are not descendants at all of these men, they are men who have come from Europe—German, Irish, French and Scandinavian—men that have come from Europe themselves, or whose ancestors have come hither and settled here, finding themselves our equals in all things. If they look back through this history to see their connection with those days by blood, they find they have none, they cannot carry themselves back into that glorious epoch and make themselves feel that they are part of us, but when they look through that old Declaration of Independence they find that those old men say that "We hold these truths to be self-evident, that all men are created equal," and then they feel that that moral sentiment taught in that day evidences their relation to those men, that it is the father of all moral principle in them, and that they have a right to claim it as though they were blood of the blood, and

flesh of the flesh of the men who wrote that Declaration, and so they are. That is the electric cord in that Declaration that links the hearts of patriotic and liberty-loving men together, that will link those patriotic hearts as long as the love of freedom exists in the minds of men throughout the world. (1:456)

Lincoln also understood that if one acknowledged that rights enumerated in the Declaration did not apply to one kind of human, it would be all too easy to use the Declaration to deny those rights to other kinds of human, with the result that nobody would be safe. As Lincoln elaborated in the Chicago speech:

Now I ask you in all soberness, if all these things, if indulged in, if ratified, if confirmed and endorsed, if taught to our children, and repeated to them, do not tend to rub out the sentiment of liberty in the country, and to transform this Government into a government of some other form. Those arguments that are made, that the inferior race are to be treated with as much allowance as they are capable of enjoying; that as much is to be done for them as their condition will allow. What are these arguments? They are the arguments that kings have made for enslaving the people in all ages of the world. You will find that all the arguments in favor of kingcraft were of this class; they always bestrode the necks of the people, not that they wanted to do it, but because the people were better off for being ridden. That is their argument, and this argument of the Judge is the same old serpent that says you work and I eat, you toil and I will enjoy the fruits of it. Turn in whatever way you will—whether it come from the mouth of a King, an excuse for enslaving the people of his country, or from the mouth of men of one race as a reason for enslaving the men of another race, it is all the same old serpent, and I hold if that course of argumentation that is made for the purpose of convincing the public mind that we should not care about this, should be granted, it does not stop with the negro. I should like to know if taking this old Declaration of Independence, which declares that all men are equal upon principle and making exceptions to it where will it stop. If one man says it does not mean a negro, why not another say it does not mean some other man? If that declaration is not the truth, let us get the Statute book, in which we find it and tear it out! (1:457)

Revisionism about the Declaration, Lincoln argued, corrupts the civil religion, corrupts those resources of unexamined feeling without which democracy cannot maintain itself. Lincoln notices that those arguments have a seductive if false inner logic, in that they do not directly appeal to the dark side of human nature, its love of dominating others, so much as enlist its apparent virtues in the service of that dark side. Whites are supposed to enslave blacks in order to civilize and protect them. This is not much different from the moral logic of kingship, in which the king's power is seen as a function of his better knowledge of what is in the people's interest. The straightforward will to power would announce itself with such baldness that people might feel revulsion against it. But this form of tyranny, tyranny cloaked in benevolent concern, is far more seductive, and can be used to put nationalities and classes under the thumb of power no less than it can be used to put races under the thumb of power.

At Alton, Lincoln developed a theory about the origin of the attack upon the Declaration, arguing that before the *Dred Scott* decision was rendered, nobody thought that "all men are created equal" did not include black men. Indeed, the attack Lincoln describes was invented, he says, specifically to defend *Dred Scott*, and, more particularly, to overturn the presumption against slavery held in Lincoln's view by the Founders, to prepare the public mind to accept at least the permanent existence of slavery, and possibly its renationalization.

Lincoln here distinguished between the attempt by Taney and Douglas to undermine the Declaration of Independence by claiming that it applied only to white men and the attempt by Calhoun and Pettit to deny it outright, to treat its self-evident truths as "glittering generalities" or "self-evident lies." Lincoln treated Douglas's position as the more sinister, perhaps because it did not announce itself in so many words as hostile to democratic values and culture in the way that Calhoun's declaration did. There was also one really crucial difference: Calhoun and his friends adopted inequality with their eyes open, understanding what it meant, never blushing at the implications of what they were advocating. By contrast, the friends of Douglas and Taney, and perhaps those gentlemen themselves, seem to be "borne along by an irresistible current—whither, they know not?" The difference between Calhoun and Douglas, this is to say, is that Calhoun may have had a dark aim, but his aim was within the focus of his acts, which sought to produce the effect whatever his making the argument would have. If the Republic, following Calhoun's guidance, arrived at a bad place, that place would at least have been the place toward which Calhoun was driving it. But the same cannot precisely be said of Douglas, who not only nominally but sincerely was an advocate of democratic equality but whose racism subverted the ethos of democratic equality and turned the Republic in the direction of hierarchy and tyranny despite itself.

Douglas had not formed the intention of replacing the Republic with a tyranny. But he had adopted arguments that encourage tyrannical habits of thought. Republics must fend off habits of thought whose triumph would destroy their ability to remain republics. But these habits of thought that would corrode the public habits necessary for a republic to survive are also within the horizon of things republics have programmatically agreed to tolerate. Does this mean that under circumstances that may rise in history republics must resort to violent repression in order to defend the habit of mind a republic needs? Doing this risks the republican habit itself, and Lincoln draws back from that. But the secessionists took choice in the matter out of Lincoln's hands. In the Second Inaugural Address Lincoln will describe how the bloody course of events undeceived both sides about the aim and meaning of their actions in the prewar era. Both sides were mistaken about what the war was about, and only violence itself taught them, a violence that wagered the public mind and the future of democracy itself. Nobody could have known beforehand whether that war would have destroyed the public mind in fire or merely burned it clean. And once it was over, the Republic, in about a decade, almost completely forgot the lesson.

Calhoun's Attack on the Declaration

The threat that slavery might soon be nationalized by a "second *Dred Scott* decision" was a remote one. But the threat that the key values of the Declaration of Independence might fall from the public mind was real, a threat whose depth becomes clear when one examines closely the work of the men who wrote against it.

Lincoln did not invent the idea that the Declaration of Independence was under threat from the slaveholders. Indeed, as early as the debates over the Missouri Compromise, southern ideologues had behaved as if any allusion to the language of the Declaration was a not very veiled attempt at stirring up a slave insurrection. For instance, during the Missouri debates, Timothy Fuller of Massachusetts (the father of Margaret Fuller) argued that the Constitution's requirement that new states must adopt a republican form of government itself required slavery to be prohibited in new states (an argument that would surface later during Reconstruction). When Fuller cited the Declaration of Independence to articulate the meaning of the phrase "a republican form of government," southern congressmen responded with enraged denunciation, pointing out "the probability that there might be slaves in the gallery listening to the debate." Fuller demurred, arguing that he could not "believe that the reading of our Declaration of Independence or a discussion of republican principles on any occasion, can endanger the rights, or merit the disapprobation, of any portion of the Union."[55]

Calhoun's most extended attack on the Declaration came in his speech on the status of Oregon on June 27, 1848, and that attack is further developed in his posthumously published *Disquisition on Government* (1851). Lincoln would still have been in Congress when the Oregon speech was delivered. Lincoln must have been profoundly shocked by it, since he obliquely referred to the Oregon speech repeatedly between the Peoria speech and his own election as president. Even the opening sentence of the Gettysburg Address (whose description of the new nation as something dedicated to the proposition that all men are created equal seems aimed first of all at Democratic skepticism about emancipation as an aim of the war) also has to be understood as a kind of final riposte to Calhoun's Oregon speech: equality is not merely a private enthusiasm that Jefferson, in Calhoun's view, smuggled into the Declaration, but the central value of American political life. Calhoun, not Douglas, was Lincoln's deepest and most intransigent opponent, and it was with Calhoun that the issue was joined whether the United States is to be a liberal society, offering civil rights and possibly even political rights to all persons by virtue of their being human, or a merely republican society, offering procedural equality only to a handful of elite players.

To examine the great defenses of southern politics, Calhoun's Oregon speech, Hammond's Mud-Sill speech, and Stephens's Corner-Stone speech is to be faced with the question of whether the tragedy of the South is an episode in the history of liberalism or the consequence of a betrayal of liberal values. Surely many ordinary southerners did not share Calhoun's thoroughgoing republican elitism. But Calhoun, Hammond, and Stephens were opinion leaders, whose vanguardism presented in exaggerated form possibilities latent in the thinking of less daring spirits. Ordinary southerners, in whose views an elitist republicanism dominated by slaveholders was qualified and broadened by a *herrenvolk* democracy that promised some say in the course of affairs to white nonslaveholders, may have seen their thinking as a form (a deviant form) of the American political tradition, in the way that David Ericson (2000) has described. But opinion leaders like Calhoun should be seen as Louis Hartz saw them long ago, as representing a challenge, even an ontological threat, to a liberal political order.

The circumstances under which Calhoun gave this speech were sketched in Chapter 2. Residents of Oregon Territory had organized a de facto territorial government using the laws of Iowa Territory as a template, and had petitioned Congress for recognition. Their petition included the language of the Northwest Ordinance, applying its prohibition of slavery to Oregon Territory. Calhoun's speech was aimed at objects far more general than the organization of a territory where few gave slavery much chance anyway. He sought to provide, first of all, a detailed account of his joint sovereignty thesis about the territories, his claim that since the territories are the joint property of the states that application of the Northwest Ordinance's language would deprive the slaveholding states of their equal stake in the territories. He also sought to reargue earlier cases about slavery in the territories, attacking the constitutionality of the Missouri Compromise restriction and of the Northwest Ordinance itself. None of these aims would seem to require Calhoun to attack the Declaration of Independence, and indeed it is hard to imagine how such an attack would not in fact damage the immediate cause, by arousing defenders of the Declaration, in the South as well as in the North. Calhoun in this speech was laying down a marker, staking out a philosophical position that he did not expect would have an immediate effect but that might, in a long retrospect, be seen as the beginning of a fundamental change in American thinking about its republic.

The debate must be seen against Calhoun's general treatment of political conflict as conflict between groups who each seek chiefly to drive the others from the field and monopolize all of the resources of the country and groups who see each conflict as an occasion to enrich themselves at the expense of their antagonists. This is the stark vision of politics Calhoun develops in more detail in his *Disquisition on Government*.[56] Calhoun's view of political conflict is notably harsher than Madison's, since, unlike Calhoun, Madison felt that political agents had interests but were not the prisoners of them, had values that were not merely rationalizations, and were enmeshed in a complex and shifting network of other agents with whom they expected sometimes to agree and sometimes to disagree, rather than being enmeshed, as Calhoun saw them, in a zero-sum conflict among two or three more or less permanent groups who sought chiefly to put each other under the thumb. Calhoun's particular analysis of sectional conflict followed from this view of politics: hostility to slavery, like the protective tariff, was simply a means by which the northern states sought to expropriate the wealth of the southern ones, and any principled argument about slavery was only so much rationalization.

Even the conflict over strict and broad construction of the Constitution, Calhoun argued, is essentially only a contest of force, and can only be maintained that way, although perhaps by force of numbers rather than of arms. As Calhoun had put it in the *Disquisition on Government*:

> The party in favor of the restrictions would be overpowered. At first, they might command some respect, and do something to stay the march of encroachment; but they would, in the progress of the contest, be regarded as mere abstractionists; and, indeed, deservedly, if they should indulge the folly of supposing that the party in possession of the ballot box and the physical force of the country, could be successfully resisted by an appeal to reason, truth, justice, or the obligations imposed by the constitution. For when these, of themselves, shall exert sufficient influence to stay the hand of power, then government will be no longer necessary to protect society, nor constitutions needed to prevent government from abusing its powers. The end of the contest would be the subversion of the constitution, either by the undermining process of construction—where its meaning would admit of possible doubt—or by substituting in practice what is called party-usage, in place of its provisions—or, finally, when no other contrivance would subserve the purpose, by openly and boldly setting them aside. By the one or the other, the restrictions would

ultimately be annulled, and the government be converted into one of unlimited powers.[57]

It is not for nothing that Richard Hofstadter, thinking of Calhoun's vision of economic conflict, called him the "Marx of the Master Class."[58] Notice here Calhoun's vision of steadily escalating class conflict, in which the more advanced the society becomes, the more turbulent and repressed its lower classes become, and the greater the proportion of the society that falls into those lower classes. We usually think of economic and culturally backward societies as the ones that are most vulnerable to mob tyranny. But for Calhoun it is the most advanced, most progressive, most modern societies that are most at risk from their have-nots:

> For, as the community becomes populous, wealthy, refined, and highly civilized, the difference between the rich and the poor will become more strongly marked; and the number of the ignorant and dependent greater in proportion to the rest of the community. With the increase of this difference, the tendency to conflict between them will become stronger; and, as the poor and dependent become more numerous in proportion, there will be, in governments of the numerical majority, no want of leaders among the wealthy and ambitious, to excite and direct them in their efforts to obtain the control.[59]

Without the class analysis, Calhoun's argument in the *Disquisition* so far looks merely like Whiggish orthodoxy—only those who have the cultural preconditions for maintaining freedom can be trusted with a say in the affairs of the res publica. With that class analysis, however, Calhoun's argument seems to confirm the *herrenvolk* democrat's worst nightmare about the master class, that the master class seeks to put him, no less than the slave, under the heel of domination. It follows from this view of liberty, as something only those who are freed by wealth from need are capable of, that liberty is a reward a republic bestows upon its economic winners, not a right it must make available to all in order to be a republic:

> It follows, from what has been stated, that it is a great and dangerous error to suppose that all people are equally entitled to liberty. It is a

reward to be earned, not a blessing to be gratuitously lavished on all alike—a reward reserved for the intelligent, the patriotic, the virtuous and deserving—and not a boon to be bestowed on a people too ignorant, degraded and vicious, to be capable either of appreciating or of enjoying it.[60]

It is because liberty is a reward to those who have, by economic independence, earned entry into the polis, rather than a right owed all persons as persons, that the promises of the Declaration are, in Calhoun's view, dangerous and puerile nonsense:

These great and dangerous errors have their origin in the prevalent opinion that all men are born free and equal—than which nothing can be more unfounded and false. It rests upon the assumption of a fact, which is contrary to universal observation, in whatever light it may be regarded. It is, indeed, difficult to explain how an opinion so destitute of all sound reason, ever could have been so extensively entertained, unless we regard it as being confounded with another, which has some semblance of truth—but which, when properly understood, is not less false and dangerous. I refer to the assertion, that all men are equal in the state of nature; meaning, by a state of nature, a state of individuality, supposed to have existed prior to the social and political state; and in which men lived apart and independent of each other. If such a state ever did exist, all men would have been, indeed, free and equal in it; that is, free to do as they pleased, and exempt from the authority or control of others—as, by supposition, it existed anterior to society and government. But such a state is purely hypothetical. It never did, nor can exist; as it is inconsistent with the preservation and perpetuation of the race. It is, therefore, a great misnomer to call it *the state of nature*. Instead of being the natural state of man, it is, of all conceivable states, the most opposed to his nature—most repugnant to his feelings, and most incompatible with his wants. His natural state is, the social and political—the one for which his Creator made him, and the only one in which he can preserve and perfect his race. As, then, there never was such a state as the, so called, state of nature, and never can be, it follows, that men, instead of being born in it, are born in the social and political state; and of course, instead of being born free and equal, are born subject, not only to parental authority, but to the laws and institutions of the country where born, and under whose protection they draw their first breath.[61]

Two different propositions are under attack here: first, the idea that all men are born free and equal, and second, that the idea of the state of nature has any meaning. About equality, Calhoun argued that the idea that all men are equal is "contrary to universal observation, in whatever light it may be regarded." By this he meant that one never really finds equality of attributes among human beings, whether those attributes are of a merely natural kind, such as strength or intelligence, or of a moral kind, such as self-restraint or virtue, or of a social kind, since there is subordination in every system known to the human race, beginning, as Calhoun points out in the Oregon speech, with Eve's subordination to Adam. Calhoun here misconstrues what the term really means; humans are not equal in any of the accidents of human being, they are equal in the way people are supposed to be equal before the law, where accidents of birth and circumstance do not outweigh a fair application of the law. It is this kind of equality that distinguishes between the rule of law and the rule of force, since this kind of equality has as its principal consequence impartiality of rule, a rejection of special pleading, special favors, and special disabilities. It is the kind of equality Saint Paul had in mind when he argued that Jew and Greek are equal in Christ.

Calhoun's error about the meaning of equality seems so obvious that it is hard to understand, so hard to understand, in fact, that Harry Jaffa pointedly wondered whether Calhoun made this claim in jest. But there is a reason why Calhoun considered only objective equality and never thought about moral equality, and that is because it did not occur to Calhoun that people as people really do have moral claims upon each other that the political world is bound to respect, because their claims upon each other are only disguised forms of their quest for power over each other. Lincoln often complained of Douglas that he substituted economic and political reasoning for moral reasoning, and that the consequence of his views is an understanding of the world in which power is real but moral claims are not. This was not quite true of Douglas, I have argued, because his moral recusal was essentially strategic, a reflection of his belief that explicit moral reasoning in the public world is self-defeating and inflammatory. Calhoun's vision of political life was closer to Darwin, and to Hobbes, than to Douglas; the difference between them is the difference between a strategic moral recusal and a genuine denial that human beings have transcendental moral claims upon each other.

Calhoun also, in rather loaded ways, under-reads the concept of the state of nature as if it described some actual historical state of affairs. He had a great deal of nineteenth-century company in this misreading, but it is still a misreading. The idea of the state of nature was not a hypothesis about how human beings ever were but part of a thought experiment designed to separate those aspects of political thought that arise from practical reason from those aspects that arise from tradition. The motivation of the experiment was to discover what kinds of obligations it would be reasonable to expect that people would impose upon themselves if they were to construct a society from reflection and choice, giving as much rein to reflection and choice as they could reasonably imagine. The idea of the state of nature provided a way to think about the consequences of the idea that freedom is obedience to a law one gives to one's self through reason. The equality imagined in the state of nature is the kind of moral equality that is a necessary feature of the experiment of asking what the light of reason declares about the sources of binding agreements among people. In other words, the idea of equality and the idea that obligation is a deliverance of practical reason, a law one gives to one's self on the basis of reflection, imply each other. Equality follows from imagining agency at the center of political life, since agency is possible only under circumstances under which one acknowledges others, which in turn is possible only under circumstances of moral equality. The power of the concept of the "state of nature" does not in any way depend upon it having ever been a state in which humans actually lived.

Calhoun rejected both the concept of the state of nature and the concept of foundational equality because his conception of identity was founded not in the concept of agency but in social construction. Men are not born free agents, but already subordinated parts of an already existing network of relationships, and their identity is not shaped by agency and reason, but by tutelage, by being subject to parents, to laws, and to institutions. Calhoun's critique here shares some features with Hegel's critique of Kantian ethics; Hegel likewise saw that human beings are always enmeshed in a social world, and that key features of their moral identities are given, not chosen; they are the products of what Hegel calls *sittlichkeit*, our rootedness in a social order that precedes us and shapes us unconsciously, not of practical reason. And Calhoun's vision also shares some features with Aristotle's politics as well, not only his belief in natural hierarchies but also his belief that human beings are ineluctably social and inevitably arrange themselves in a social order. But Aristotle's social world, like his natural world, is a moral order in which to find one's place is also to discover one's characteristic excellence, one's end of being, one's arête, not a Hobbesian world of struggle for mastery. And when Hegel sought to place human life in a densely realized network of custom and tradition, the idea was to give human complexity and human warmth to moral thought, not to subject it to a stark if bracing dose of natural compulsion, and certainly not to undermine the idea that the human being, as a human being, is a creature of natural worth.

One might be inclined to take what Calhoun says in the *Disquisition* with a grain of salt, since it was not published in his own lifetime. But what Calhoun said on the same subjects on the Senate floor in his Oregon speech was at once more pointed and more inflammatory.

Calhoun argued in the Oregon speech that the Union is in grave danger, and only the adoption of the joint sovereignty thesis about the territories can save it, arguing that a future historian, inquiring about the self-destruction of the United States, might place the root cause at the very beginning, in the adoption of the Northwest Ordinance in 1787. Then, with barely a pause of breath, he pressed deeper, into an analysis of the ultimate philosophical errors that he believed must finally bring the American republic down, and thus into arguments that are far deeper than those required to deal with the political problem (the Oregon question) which provoked his speech:[62]

> If he should possess a philosophical turn of mind, and be disposed to look to more remote and recondite causes, he will trace it to a proposition which originated in a hypothetical truism, but which, as now expressed and now understood, is the most false and dangerous of all political errors. The proposition to which I allude, has become an axiom in the minds of a vast majority on both sides of the Atlantic, and is repeated daily from tongue to tongue, as an established and

incontrovertible truth; it is, that "all men are born free and equal." I
am not afraid to attack error, however deeply it may be intrenched,
or however widely extended, whenever it becomes my duty to do so,
as I believe it to be on this subject and occasion.

Taking the proposition literally (it is in that sense it is understood), there is not a word of truth in it. It begins with "all men are
born," which is utterly untrue. Men are not born. Infants are born.
They grow to be men. And concludes with asserting that they are
born "free and equal," which is not less false. They are not born free.
While infants they are incapable of freedom, being destitute alike of
the capacity of thinking and acting, without which there can be no
freedom. Besides, they are necessarily born subject to their parents,
and remain so among all people, savage and civilized, until the development of their intellect and physical capacity enables them to take
care of themselves. They grow to all the freedom of which the condition in which they were born permits, by growing to be men. Nor is
it less false that they are born "equal." They are not so in any sense in
which it can be regarded; and thus, as I have asserted, there is not a
word of truth in the whole proposition, as expressed and generally
understood.[63]

The natural state of the human being, Calhoun went on to argue, is
not the individual state, but the social state, and, what is more, the
political state, since nowhere is man not under government. Like
Aristotle, Calhoun believed that man is a polis animal, an animal that
comes to its fullest development only in a political world, and whose
identity is inescapably an identity in relation, enmeshed in the complex
relationships of domination and subordination that are an inevitable
feature of polis life. All freedom is civic freedom, freedom exercised as
a function of a privileged role in a social and political order, and thus is
imaginable only within the hierarchy that produces that order. There
is no freedom without hierarchy, because freedom is the creature of
hierarchy. The individual has no claim to equality, and has no claim to
freedom beyond that which is appropriate to the role he or she is fitted
for in the public order:

Instead, then, of all men having the same right to liberty and equality,
as is claimed by those who hold that they are all born free and equal,

liberty is the noble and highest reward bestowed on mental and moral development, combined with favorable circumstances. Instead, then, of liberty and equality being born with man; instead of all men and all classes and descriptions being equally entitled to them, they are high prizes to be won, and are in their most perfect state, not only the highest reward that can be bestowed on our race, but the most difficult to be won—and when won, the most difficult to be preserved.[64]

The paragraph in which that last passage appears is in fact ambiguous, since it begins by discussing the kinds of societies in which freedom is possible at all but ends by speaking about those groups within a society who have greater and lesser capacities for freedom. The conflation is deceptive, and the deception is central to the persuasiveness of Calhoun's argument. Explaining the geographical or cultural preconditions under which societies can enjoy greater freedom—societies under strain can less afford freedom—is rather a different thing than justifying different degrees of freedom within one society. What makes the distinction more pointed is Calhoun's assumption that an advanced society, one in which the elite are the most sophisticated and the most capable of public freedom, is also an increasingly hierarchical one, since the price of the advancement of that elite is the subjection of those who do the heavy lifting. If a society becomes capable of freedom, it becomes capable of freedom only for some. And the price of the availability of that freedom for some is increased subjection of the others. Indeed the society that is most advanced and enlightened, the society in which its elite is most culturally capable of freedom, will also be the most hierarchical society, the society that has the most to fear from the increasing number of the ignorant and dependent, who become a greater proportion of the community as a whole. A society that forgets this lesson, a society that attempts to offer freedom to the whole, inevitably descends into anarchy:

They have been made vastly more so by the dangerous error I have attempted to expose, that all men are born free and equal, as if those high qualities belonged to man without effort to acquire them, and to all equally alike, regardless of their intellectual and moral condition. The attempt to carry into practice this, the most dangerous of all political error, and to bestow on all, without regard to their fitness either to acquire or maintain liberty, that unbounded and individual liberty supposed to belong to man in the hypothetical and misnamed state of nature, has done more to retard the cause of liberty and civilization, and is doing more at present, than all other causes combined. While it is powerful to pull down governments, it is still more powerful to prevent their construction on proper principles. It is the leading cause among those which have placed Europe in its present anarchical condition, and which mainly stands in the way of reconstructing good governments in the place of those which have been overthrown, threatening thereby the quarter of the globe most advanced in progress and civilization with hopeless anarchy, to be followed by military despotism. Nor are we exempt from its disorganizing effect. We now begin to experience the danger of admitting so great an error to have a place in the declaration of our independence. For a long time it lay dormant; but in the process of time it began to germinate, and produce its poisonous fruits.[65]

Calhoun meant this last grim prediction of a French Revolution, American-style, to be aimed at the adherents of racial equality. He singles out Jefferson as the man responsible for the coming catastrophe, seeing his role in that catastrophe in the same role other conservative thinkers gave Rousseau in the French Revolution, as the well-meaning but woolly unleasher of notions that must ultimately bring the entire society down around him. But none of Calhoun's arguments really distinguish between a racial underclass and an economic one, and those last sentences can just as easily (more easily, perhaps) be read as a sally against Jacksonian Democracy as a sally against Free Soil. Despite the perfunctory embrace of *herrenvolk* democracy in the Oregon speech, Calhoun sees racial inequality and class inequality in the same ways, and arguments about the former are all too easy to turn into arguments for the latter.

One is tempted to argue—because Lincoln himself does argue— that there is a slippery slope that connects Douglas's view of the Declaration of Independence (that it did promise equality, that it was right to do so, but that it made no such promise to black people) to Calhoun's view (that the Declaration should not have promised equality because the concept is nonsense, and it should not have promised freedom because freedom is limited to those with the means to enjoy it, means they can control only by denying them to others). But Douglas could never have taken the view of the Declaration of Independence that Calhoun took, and it is impossible to imagine a course of events that might lead Douglas to adopt Calhoun's view. Douglas was a sincere believer in equality, so long as that equality was equality among white people of different classes, or white people of different religions, or white people of different national origins. And he was a virulent and flamboyant racist, who believed that racial inequality was a guarantor of equality among white people. He could not make arguments such as Calhoun's about freedom being the reward for superior breeding, because those arguments are the arguments his opponents make to disenfranchise the Irish, the Catholics, and the poor, his chief constituencies. Douglas embodies one of the central paradoxes of the Jacksonian Democrat, the inner connection between class equality and racism, a connection which, in that era, tends to mean that the more deeply one is committed to class, religious, or ethnic equality, the more deeply one is committed to racism.

What Calhoun's attack upon the Declaration reveals is not the kind of thing Douglas might come to were he to let himself, but the inner incoherence of the *herrenvolk* democracy that is his deepest political motivation. Ultimately, Douglas's view of the Declaration makes very little sense. But he could maintain that view because it was the epidemic illusion of his time. Calhoun's attack upon the Declaration reveals the rock upon which Douglas's views must founder, so that he would have to spring one way or the other. Lincoln is right that if Douglas's case writes racial equality out of the Declaration of Independence, Douglas makes it easier for others to do something Douglas could never imagine doing, writing class equality out of it too, because as Calhoun's argument reveals, the fate of the white worker and of the black slave are linked, however much the former may despise the latter, however much the former may believe that his color protects him from the fate of the latter. Unlike Douglas's views, Calhoun's views, once one strips away a few items of insincere decorative window-dressing aimed to appease the white worker, have a powerful consistency. They have the powerful if dark consistency one sometimes finds in the speeches of Milton's Satan.

7.4 Douglas's Response

Freeport before Freeport

What we now call the "Freeport Doctrine" was not new to Douglas when he articulated it at Freeport on August 27, 1858. He had given its substance in a speech at Springfield more than a year before, on June 12, 1857. If, Douglas had said at Springfield, slaveholders had the right to take slaves to the territories, and if the territories could not forbid them outright from doing so, nevertheless

> it necessarily remains a barren and a worthless right, unless sustained, protected and enforced by appropriate police regulations and local legislation, prescribing adequate remedies for its violation. These regulations and remedies must necessarily depend entirely upon the will and wishes of the people of the Territory, as they can only be prescribed by the local Legislatures. Hence the great principle of popular sovereignty and self-government is sustained and firmly established by the authority of this [*Dred Scott*] decision.[66]

The reader should notice the irony of Douglas's language: what will be called the "Freeport Doctrine" is "firmly established" by the authority of the *Dred Scott* decision, even though its aim and effect would be to subvert one of the points most cherished by the chief justice in his majority opinion. Few politicians have, relative to Douglas, so earned a reputation for *chutzpah*. Douglas knew that the attack upon popular sovereignty in Taney's opinion was dictum, and so could be brushed aside. But even so, it is a stretch to say that the *Dred Scott* decision, apparently not because it says anything positive on the subject but because the negative things it says are not authoritative, "firmly establishes" popular sovereignty.

Even before Taney's opinion made its claim against the power of territorial legislatures to prohibit slavery, Douglas had made substantially the Freeport argument in 1856 on the Senate floor, in a debate with Trumbull.[67] In the Springfield speech and in the 1858 debates, Douglas argued that what we now call the Freeport Doctrine was consistent with the *Dred Scott* decision. In the debate with Trumbull the aim was slightly different.

As we saw in Chapter 2, there had long been among Democrats an ambiguity about when the people of the territories could exercise the right of popular sovereignty about slavery, with Douglas and his supporters arguing that the territorial legislatures could rule on this issue, and with Douglas's southern opponents arguing that this decision could be made only by the constitutional convention that wrote the constitution under which the territory would seek admission to the Union as a state. (Lincoln had noted this ambiguity as far back as the Peoria speech.)

During the debate with Trumbull, Douglas had engaged in a double strategy, and the two aims of the strategy were in tension with each other. On one hand, in 1856, Douglas sought to kick the issue of resolving the ambiguity about when popular sovereignty applies upstairs, to the courts. He did this, Fehrenbacher argues, because his political survival depended upon maintaining ambiguity about the position, something that passing the buck to the Court could do, so long as the Court either did not render an opinion at all or rendered ambiguous ones.

The second part of the strategy in the debate with Trumbull was to defang the opinion in advance in case it did not come down in Douglas's way. It is the fact that he sought to defang the opinion before it was even written that most shows that the strategy of referring the question of popular sovereignty to the Court was meant to be a delaying strategy to preserve ambiguity. If Douglas really thought the issue was the Court's to call, he would not have been looking for ways to subvert the decision—all the while insisting that his strategy was consistent with that decision—before it was even made.

The immediate rhetorical aim in the debate with Trumbull was to take an apparently pro-southern line: the ambiguity in popular sovereignty is a matter for the Court, not for Senator Trumbull, and by trying to make it a political question rather than a judicial one, Senator Trumbull was somehow undermining the rule of law in the name of politics. But it had an anti-southern edge too, unnoticed at the time, which came into focus only when Douglas used the same arguments to show that his version of popular sovereignty would, for practical reasons, and for legal ones, prevail whatever Congress decided, and whatever the Court decided. The arguments were aimed at a political enemy (Trumbull) to preserve the ambiguity Douglas needed to keep a difficult political friend (southern Democrats) at his side. But they also anticipated the circumstances under which those political friends would themselves become enemies, and made provision for dealing with them. And they anticipated the predicament of another set of difficult political friends (restive northern Democrats, worried about southern domination of their party), by pointing out that practical difficulties stood in the way of the South's actually imposing slavery upon the territories against the will of their people (the people of the territories will retain the means to defend their position) and by proposing what seemed to him to be an effective strategy in case the South actually did try to impose slavery.

In trying to keep northern and southern Democrats on the same page, Douglas employed an ambiguous tone, a tone that includes reassurance (as if to say, "Surely the southern Democrats know they can't really get away with imposing slavery in the territories against local popular will, so you need not worry that they might do such a thing") but hints at an iron fist in the velvet glove ("and here is what you can do if the southern Democrats really are so foolish as to give imposing slavery against the popular will a try"). The explicit aim of the strategy, as regards the different Democratic factions, is one of accommodation, but it provides the means of confrontation should accommodation fail. Which strategy—accommodation or confrontation—is the dominant, and which the undertone, depends upon whether you read this passage looking back, to the struggle with Trumbull, or forward, to the struggle with Buchanan. But it is susceptible of being read both ways.

Both in the debate with Trumbull and in the Springfield speech, Douglas had kept it ambiguous whether the Freeport Doctrine was a political strategy or a legal one. As a political strategy, the Freeport Doctrine depended upon the idea that the legislature will always find ways to contest legal decisions with which it disagrees. But that is only a truism, of course, and does not answer the question of whether the legislature can practically defeat the legal decision, or only challenge it at the margins. As a legal strategy, the Freeport Doctrine was designed to provide a constitutional response to the habit on both sides of the political crisis of the 1850s of constitutionalizing every quarrel. Douglas always claimed that the Freeport Doctrine was consistent with the *Dred Scott* decision, and since he was probably right that the Court did not in fact rule on the question of the right of the territories to decide the slavery question, he was probably also right about that. He was on shakier ground (but not completely untenable ground) when he wished to argue that the Freeport Doctrine would pass constitutional muster even if, in some later decision, the Court were to decide the question of territorial power over slavery in a pro-slavery way. His argument was essentially this: the Court can rule a law unconstitutional, but it cannot write the law in the first place, since it is a court, not a legislature. If a territorial legislature does not wish to write a slave code, a court cannot write one for it. That is what Douglas meant when he said, "These regulations and remedies must necessarily depend entirely upon the will and wishes of the people of the Territory, as they can only be prescribed by the local Legislatures."

Now there is a reply to this (and Lincoln made it), which is that courts will protect property (by ruling in the owner's favor) even where legislatures refuse to do so. (This was also Jefferson Davis's reply to the Freeport Doctrine, once he renounced that doctrine himself.) But Douglas had a reply to that, too: legislatures often fatally undermine the standing of some kinds property in favor of others, and the courts have not rushed to prevent them, so the courts have no obligation to provide the economic and police legislation slavery requires, any more than they are obliged to provide the economic and liability protection, and the eminent domain power, railroads require in order to be practical.

There is also a practical argument that Douglas did not make, and that is that it is possible to exhaust a position by requiring it to defend itself in court repeatedly or by throwing so many practical difficulties in the way of its complete enforcement by the courts that it becomes unenforceable. With all of the advantages slaveholders were given by the Fugitive Slave Act of 1850, popular resistance, as we saw in the statistics cited above, had largely but not wholly defeated the Fugitive Slave Act by the outbreak of the Civil War. (One of the ironies of the conflict over the Fugitive Slave Act is that each side had reason to believe that it had been not only defeated but also humiliated by the other. The Fugitive Slave Act stoked up the resentments of both sides.) Douglas of course could never have made this argument in public even had he embraced it. But Lincoln did compare what Douglas had in mind in the Freeport Doctrine with the popular resistance to the Fugitive Slave Act. He did not refer to the resistance to the act in the streets, as for instance in the case of Anthony Burns, but to legal harassment of attempts to enforce the act, such as what underlay the Wisconsin personal liberty law that was challenged in the case of *Ableman v. Booth,* saying, in effect, "How can you criticize resistance to the Fugitive Slave Act as mob rule by legislatures when you yourself are proposing something similar?" Lincoln's reply has an edge of anger in it, because he himself had counseled submission to the Fugitive Slave Act, as part of the bargain of the Compromise of 1850, and thus Wisconsin's behavior put him in a false position. Expedients such as the Freeport Doctrine would make such bargains as the Compromise of 1850 impossible, because it would always be available for hostile local authorities to subvert them.

The Freeport argument was, as Fehrenbacher pointed out, not received harshly in southern circles when Douglas first made it in 1856. Indeed, the Freeport Doctrine was received as anti-southern only after Douglas chose to oppose the Lecompton Constitution, and probably it would be better to say not that the Freeport Doctrine undermined Douglas's support in the South but that after the Lecompton struggle Douglas's embrace of the Freeport Doctrine discredited it in southern eyes.

Prominent southerners like James. L. Orr of South Carolina and Jefferson Davis, both of whom Douglas quoted during the debates, had made arguments resembling the Freeport Doctrine. Orr had argued, during congressional debates over Kansas in 1856, that slavery could not be forced on a people who did not want it (Douglas cited him during the Galesburg debate).

At the Quincy debate, Douglas cited a raft of southerners making the same claim, including not only Speaker Orr and Senator Davis but also Aleck Stephens of Georgia and Sam Smith of Tennessee. In a later letter to the San Francisco *National,* Douglas noted that Georgia's Howell Cobb, a member of Buchanan's cabinet and by 1859 a rabid critic of the Freeport Doctrine, had himself advocated that doctrine in speeches in 1856.

At the final debate at Alton, Douglas cited a speech given that very summer by Jefferson Davis on September 11, 1858 (after Douglas's argument to the same effect at Freeport), in Bangor, Maine:

If the inhabitants of any Territory should refuse to enact such laws and police regulations as would give security to their property or to his, it would be rendered more or less valueless in proportion to the difficulties of holding it without such protection. In the case of property in the labor of man, or what is usually called slave property, the insecurity would be so great that the owner could not ordinarily retain it. Therefore, though the right would remain, the remedy being withheld, it would follow that the owner would be practically debarred, by the circumstances of the case, from taking slave property into a Territory where the sense of the inhabitants was opposed to its introduction. So much for the oft-repeated fallacy of forcing slavery upon any community. (1:787)

Now there is a shade of difference between what Orr and Davis meant and what Douglas meant. Davis and Orr were not making a policy, but merely recognizing a political reality, and their aim was not to provide a way for the territories to keep slavery out in the face of a hostile court decision, but to reassure the people of the free states that the popular sovereignty policy could not conspiratorially force slavery into the territories against the will of their people. Their statements were in the indicative mode, not in the optative. Davis later said that he was issuing a warning about what free state settlers might do, not recommending a policy to them. But this is an implausible reinterpretation of his remarks, because he meant his comments to be reassuring to the audience in Maine to which he delivered them. Did the reassurance Davis and Orr offered to the North really mean anything if the territorial legislatures could not put what they described into action? If they meant their arguments about the Freeport Doctrine to be reassuring to the North, they could only have meant that the territories had a right to apply that doctrine.

Davis immediately got into trouble in the South after his Bangor speech, and had to beat a not completely logical retreat. No, he backtracked, he did not recommend to free-state territorial legislatures that they refuse to enact slave codes, he merely pointed out how threatening the possibility that they might do so was to the South. No, he did not mean to leave slaveholders in the territories without the protection of slave codes, and yes, the territories owed the slaveholders the protections due to all property. Davis argued that for the moment, however, there was no need for Congress to leap in and impose a federal slave code, since he expected that the courts would sufficiently protect slave property in the territories if the territorial legislatures would not, and Congress need step in only if the courts failed their duty.[68] What Davis was trying to do here, having been called out over his earlier attempt to reassure the people of Maine, was to avoid making an inflammatory and party-destroying demand for a federal slave code right away, but he did so under conditions that would render making exactly that demand an inevitability, since northern Democrats were likely to take as much exception to a Court-imposed slave code for the territories as to a federally imposed one, and a Court-imposed code would be on shaky constitutional ground anyway.

Lincoln's Freeport Questions

At the Ottawa debate, Douglas had put to Lincoln a number of questions, all of them arising from what he mistakenly thought was a Republican state platform adopted in Lincoln's presence, and all of them tending to put Lincoln in the position of either endorsing that platform's radicalism, and alienating mid-state former Whigs, or of rejecting it, and angering his supporters in the northern counties. Lincoln did not answer those questions at all at Ottawa, but did answer them in the opening passages of his Freeport speech, choosing to give in Stephenson County, one of the most radically anti-slavery counties in the state, a set of very moderate answers.

In return, Lincoln proposed four questions of his own, questions that were not based on any particular document of Douglas's and questions that Douglas, with a hint of peevishness, said that he had answered on several occasions before. The four questions were the following:

Question 1. If the people of Kansas shall, by means entirely unobjectionable in all other respects, adopt a State Constitution, and ask admission into the Union under it, before they have the requisite number of inhabitants according to the English bill—some ninety-three thousand—will you vote to admit them? [Applause.]

Q. 2. Can the people of a United States Territory, in any lawful way, against the wish of any citizen of the United States, exclude slavery from its limits prior to the formation of a State Constitution? [Renewed applause.]

Q. 3. If the Supreme Court of the United States shall decide that States cannot exclude slavery from their limits, are you in favor of acquiescing in, adopting and following such decision as a rule of political action? [Loud applause.]

Q. 4. Are you in favor of acquiring additional territory, in disregard of how such acquisition may affect the nation on the slavery question? [Cries of "Good, good."] (1:541–542)

The second question is of course the famous one, because it elicited a crisp statement of what later came to be known as the Freeport Doctrine. Let us dispose briefly of the other inquiries before attending to it, since they set the context for the second question.

The first question essentially asked whether Douglas felt bound by the terms of the English Compromise. Perhaps the point of the question was to make it harder for Douglas to mend fences with Buchanan's supporters, by eliciting a further denunciation of the English Compromise. Or perhaps it was simply to trip him up, since Douglas had originally proposed—before the Lecompton Constitution was dreamed up—waiting for any constitution until the population of Kansas had enough inhabitants for a congressional district. Douglas's answer was suitably blunt: he would have preferred to have waited until Kansas had enough population for a congressional district in the first place, but since the pro-slavery side had decided that Kansas had enough population to make a slave state, it must also have enough population to make a free state. He noted also that English himself had come to his view of the matter.

The third question essentially concerned the "second *Dred Scott* decision" that Lincoln's conspiracy theories turned upon: if the Supreme Court were to upend the emancipation laws of the entire North, would that be all right with you? Douglas rejected the question, as we have seen, as turning upon an impossible hypothetical, and concluded that its only motivation was to cast an imputation upon the motives of the Supreme Court. Merely asking the question was a way to cast an imputation on Douglas, even in the expectation of a firm denial from him.

The nub of the question was the phrase about "following such decision as a rule of political action." Douglas had argued about the *Dred Scott* case that the Supreme Court is the final and ultimate interpreter

of the Constitution, and therefore that Lincoln was bound to treat the
decision "as a rule of political action." Having argued this, Lincoln
claimed, Douglas was also morally required to treat the Court's ruling
in the hypothetical case as a rule of political action.

Lincoln actually made a rather stronger assertion, but one with less
logic behind it: Douglas would be not only morally but also legally and
constitutionally required to acquiesce in a "second *Dred Scott* decision," adopting and following such decision as a rule of political action,
passing any laws that such a decision would seem to call for, and treating any criticism of that decision as an attack upon the Constitution.
To this, Douglas answered that he was not required to say whether he
would submit to a hypothetical judgment of the Court if that hypothetical is implausible. Consider, for instance, how one might answer the
question, "If the Supreme Court of the United States shall decide that
the Fourteenth Amendment is no longer binding, are you in favor of
acquiescing in, adopting and following such a decision as a rule of political action?"

In his attack on the Freeport Doctrine at the Jonesboro debate in
Little Egypt, Lincoln made much the same argument: if the Supreme
Court were to rule that territorial legislatures could not forbid slavery,
would you not only submit to that ruling but treat it as a guide to your
future political conduct? Douglas gave a very pointed answer to this
during the Quincy debate:

> Down at Jonesboro, [Lincoln] went on to argue that if it be the law
> that a man has a right to take his slaves into territory of the United
> States under the Constitution, that then a member of Congress was
> perjured if he did not vote for a slave code. I ask him whether the
> decision of the Supreme Court is not binding upon him as well as on
> me? If so, and he holds that he would be perjured if he did not vote
> for a slave code under it, I ask him whether, if elected to Congress, he
> will so vote? I have a right to his answer, and I will tell you why. He
> put that question to me down in Egypt, and did it with an air of tri-
> umph. This was about the form of it: "In the event of a slaveholding
> citizen of one of the Territories should need and demand a slave code
> to protect his slaves, will you vote for it?" I answered him that a fun-
> damental article in the Democratic creed, as put forth in the Nebraska
> bill and the Cincinnati platform, was non-intervention by Congress

with slavery in the States and Territories, and hence, that I would not vote in Congress for any code of laws, either for or against slavery in any Territory. I will leave the people perfectly free to decide that question for themselves. (1:757–758)

The fourth question had more practical point, since it took its meaning from recent pro-slavery colonial adventures by American or American-supported filibusters in Cuba and in Nicaragua. And it was also meant to call to the minds of cautious Whigs the recklessness of the Democrats about the Texas question and about the conquest of the Mexican Cession. Douglas, as the representative politician of Young America, favored expansion in whatever direction it was possible, and favored ignoring whatever effect it might have upon the slavery question. Since Lincoln knew that the 1858 election would turn on Douglas's ability to bring former Whigs over to his side, Lincoln may well have sought to remind them of how they had traditionally opposed the acquisition or conquest of new territories, on precisely the ground that doing so might enflame conflict over slavery.

Douglas's answer to the second Freeport question reflected his impatience. He had made the argument in 1857, and in fact had made similar arguments as far back as 1850, and he had repeated it in his speeches in Bloomington and Springfield that very summer:

The next question propounded to me by Mr. Lincoln is, can the people of a Territory in any lawful way, against the wishes of any citizen of the United States, exclude slavery from their limits prior to the formation of a State Constitution? I answer emphatically, as Mr. Lincoln has heard me answer a hundred times from every stump in Illinois, that in my opinion the people of a Territory can, by lawful means, exclude slavery from their limits prior to the formation of a State Constitution. Mr. Lincoln knew that I had answered that question over and over again. He heard me argue the Nebraska bill on that principle all over the State in 1854, in 1855, and in 1856, and he has no excuse for pretending to be in doubt as to my position on that question. It matters not what way the Supreme Court may hereafter decide as to the abstract question whether slavery may or may not go into a Territory under the Constitution, the people have the lawful means to introduce it or exclude it as they please, for the reason that

slavery cannot exist a day or an hour anywhere, unless it is supported
by local police regulations. ["Right, right."] Those police regulations
can only be established by the local legislature, and if the people are
opposed to slavery they will elect representatives to that body who
will by unfriendly legislation effectually prevent the introduction of
it into their midst. If, on the contrary, they are for it, their legislation
will favor its extension. Hence, no matter what the decision of the
Supreme Court may be on that abstract question, still the right of
the people to make a slave Territory or a free Territory is perfect and
complete under the Nebraska bill. I hope Mr. Lincoln deems my
answer satisfactory on that point. (1:551–552)

Lincoln was not surprised by Douglas's answer, and indeed had predicted it. He did not think that Douglas would hesitate before giving
an answer that would alienate southern supporters, because he knew
that Douglas's attack upon the Lecompton Constitution had destroyed
that support already, and that Douglas's main concern was shoring up
the Democratic Party in the north. Lincoln wrote as much to Henry
Asbury on July 31, 1858:

He cares nothing for the South—he knows he is already dead there.
He only leans Southward now to keep the Buchanan party from
growing in Illinois. You shall have hard work to get him directly to
the point whether a territorial Legislature has or has not the power
to exclude slavery. But if you succeed in bringing him to it, though he
will be compelled to say it possesses no such power; he will instantly
take ground that slavery can not actually exist in the territories, unless the people desire it, and so give it protective territorial legislation. If this offends the South he will let it offend them; as at all
events he means to hold on to his chances in Illinois. (1:483)[69]

Douglas's argument has never been treated with much sympathy by
historians, even those friendly to him. Douglas did not say so here in
so many words, but it is clear in his other responses to this question
over the course of the debates that he did not think Taney's remark on
the powers of the territorial government over slavery carried the weight
of the Court behind it. The Freeport Doctrine, it must be remembered, was a fallback position, not the main line of defense for popular

sovereignty in the territories, even though it has traditionally been treated otherwise.[70]

Douglas argued this point very bluntly in a letter to the San Francisco *National* of August 16, 1859:

> The Court did *not* declare that "neither Congress or a Territorial Legislature possessed the power either to establish or exclude slavery from a Territory, and that it was a power which exclusively belonged to the States."
>
> The Court did *not* declare "that the people of a Territory can exercise this power for the first time when they come to form a Constitution."
>
> The Court did *not* declare "that the right of the people of any State to carry their slaves into a common Territory of the United States, and hold them there during its existence as such, was guaranteed by the Constitution of the United States."
>
> The Court did NOT declare "that it [holding slave property in federal territories] was a right which could neither be subverted nor evaded, either by non-action, by direct or indirect Congressional legislation, or by any law passed by a Territorial Legislature."[71]

It is also important to see the Freeport Doctrine in the context of Douglas's traditional reluctance to constitutionalize political issues. Compare for instance his view of popular sovereignty as a prudential way to mediate the conflict over slavery in the territories with Cass's view of popular sovereignty as a constitutionally mandated doctrine that foreclosed all of the other alternative doctrines.

The distinction may seem subtle, but something important hangs on it. Here, as everywhere else, to constitutionalize a struggle is to foreclose mutual accommodation by negotiation and to announce an ambition to dominate one's political opponent, to drive the opponent from the public square. To make a policy argument, by contrast, is to concede that there is enough play in the Constitution that negotiation among opponents is possible. The best way to interpret the Freeport Doctrine is not to argue that it proposes a constitutional contradiction (here is a constitutional way that the constitution can be subverted) but that it proposes that even if the *Dred Scott* decision had ruled what Taney said it did, that did not leave the people of the territories with no response, and they still had some cards to play, some ways to keep the issue alive in hopes of working out a better deal about it than Taney was willing to offer them. It is a move, not a solution. But as a move, it is a move within the rules. It is not an argument that any Court decision may be subverted, it is an argument that no constitutional argument can successfully put slavery beyond the reach of politics, beyond the reach of popular will when that popular will opposes slavery.

Douglas characteristically dismissed abstract questions, just as he dismissed apodictic pronouncements, dwelling as he always did upon the concrete give-and-take of actual political situations. Did the Freeport Doctrine only mean that local governments can always find ways to obstruct Court rulings they find disagreeable? Did it amount to nullification, as Lincoln repeatedly argued over the course of the debates? The charge is not completely false, but it misses the meaning of Douglas's argument. In some ways Douglas's position was not far different from Lincoln's: Douglas meant that any court decision has to win its authority in retrospect by persuading the people to whom it is supposed to apply, and that it cannot prevail unless those people are willing to let it. If a Supreme Court decision is to be resisted by refusing to treat it as a political rule, it is hard to find a better example of such a refusal than the Freeport Doctrine provided. The principal difference was that in Lincoln's case what he sought was an evolution of the underlying political culture so that ultimately, reasoning from a common underlying and not fully articulated layer of convictions, all sides come to a meeting of minds about issues of principle, whereas Douglas, characteristically despairing of the meeting of minds, sought through pulling and hauling to bring all sides to a modus vivendi in the here-and-now, and for the here-and-now, with the future having to take care of itself.

Douglas did not argue that the territories could simply defy the Court and pass their own prohibition of slavery. Nor did he argue that the territories could, as South Carolina sought to do during the nullification crisis, interpose their own authority against the federal government or against the Court over a constitutional question in which their views conflict with the Court's. Douglas did not propose that the territories have a higher authority than the central government (as Calhoun did about the states), or that they have a deeper and independent sovereignty. Douglas did argue, both here and in his 1859 article in *Harper's* magazine about the dividing line between federal and local authority in the territories, that territories have a right to rule on local matters.[72] But he did not argue that the territories are in effect independent countries and that the United States is an alliance, rather than a nation, as the nullifiers sought to do.

What he did argue was that the Court cannot simply foreclose a political question by fiat, and that the other branches are always left with room for rejoinders which, even if they do not at the moment enable the overthrow of the decision, also keep the ruling in play as something not completely settled. His thinking, this is to say, was not that far different from Lincoln's own, with the difference that what Douglas proposed was something that could be done in the here-and-now rather than in the bye-and-bye of future appointments, and that it turned on the explicit play of forces in articulate conflict rather than on the developments among the implicit sources of conviction.

One might treat all resistance to the Court's decision as essentially subversive of the authority of law. The Freeport Doctrine looks analogous, on this view, to all the means by which the South defeated the Fifteenth Amendment between the end of Reconstruction and the Voting Rights act, by inventing impossible literacy tests that applied only to blacks, for example.

But there is one difference. Douglas seized the argument the slaveholders were most invested in—slaves are property and should be regulated as property—and used it to his own advantage. The literacy requirements adopted by the southern states were transparently examples of special pleading, got up in an ad hoc way to trip up the Constitution. But both the positive resistance strategy—hostile legislation—and the negative one—refusal to pass the required police legislation—resemble very closely the kinds of economic legislation states had been adopting for years and thus would not have had that ad hoc quality. States effectively broke the power of banks, for instance, by refusing to allow them to establish branches. Later on, states that wished to encourage free-range cattle ranching adopted laws that required farmers to fence cattle *out*, and did not penalize ranchers for damage their cattle might have done to farms they entered. By contrast, in the eastern states, owners of cattle were liable for the damage their cattle did, and the law required cattle to be fenced *in*, not out. Mining states, Nevada in particular, gave mining interests scarcely believable powers over landowners whose rights might have interfered with the mineral interests' projects, on the grounds that mining would be economically unfeasible without those laws. But nobody has ever argued that Nevada was legally, even constitutionally, required to pass such laws by the mere fact that it is legal to operate a mine there. If, as slaveholders kept insisting, slaves were to be treated as property, then they could be subject to all of the kinds of regulation that property had always been subject to from local jurisdictions, and a territory could no more be required to pass burdensome police legislation and to establish an expensive police infrastructure in the interest of slavery than it could be required to grant mining interests the extraordinary powers Nevada wound up granting them.

The negative version of the Freeport Doctrine (refusal to pass police and economic legislation) and the positive version (directly hostile legislation short of emancipation) have slightly different meanings that it is worth teasing apart. The negative version of the case turned on whether the state is required to make the investments to make every business enterprise possible. Clearly the state is no more required to make slavery profitable than it is required to provide the easy credit needed for constructing office buildings or laying railroads. The state can do these things if it wishes—and in the railroad case, the state wished to do it quite a bit. But if private investors have the right to build a railroad, and if they cannot do so without easy credit from the state, the constitutional mandate to protect property rights does not require the state to provide easy credit.

The positive version of the Freeport Doctrine—the use of hostile legislation—was susceptible of several kinds of development, only a few of them promising. The problem turned on the question of whether the territorial governments could put legal pressure on something the law nevertheless permitted. My argument is that they could apply pressure, but only so much, and only some kinds of legal pressure. Douglas's own example at Jonesboro was the Maine Law, a law prohibiting the sale of alcohol:

> My doctrine is, that even taking Mr. Lincoln's view that the decision recognizes the right of a man to carry his slaves into the territories of the United States, if he pleases, yet after he gets there he needs affirmative law to make that right of any value. The same doctrine not

only applies to slave property, but all other kinds of property. Chief Justice Taney places it upon the ground that slave property is on an equal footing with other property. Suppose one of your merchants should move to Kansas and open a liquor store; he has a right to take groceries and liquors there, but the mode of selling them, and the circumstances under which they shall be sold, and all the remedies must be prescribed by local legislation, and if that is unfriendly it will drive him out just as effectually as if there was a constitutional provision against the sale of liquor. (1:634)

This is plausible, but only so long as slaves are considered only property. Increasingly, however, slaves were beginning to be treated as a kind of super-property, having protections stronger than those we normally think of as applying to property, protections that transcend every aspect of government oversight and control, because they embodied not only the individual property rights of the owners but the collective property rights of the slave states. Slaves became a kind of super-property, because they were not only the possession of their owners but an emblem of the equality of the states, so that forbidding slaveowners from entering Kansas was somehow tantamount to treating South Carolina as a second-class party in the federal Union.

Even as ordinary property, some kinds of regulation are within bounds and some kinds are out of bounds. Governments can legally harass some kinds of legally legitimate property and some kinds of legally legitimate practices. (Consider, for instance, what contemporary governments do about smoking.) And governments can formally frown on things they cannot formally forbid. (Consider, for instance, the way the contemporary government frowns upon ugly public manifestations of race hatred.) But it cannot do so capriciously. The question about the Freeport Doctrine is whether the hostile legislation Douglas imagines is reasonable enough not to seem capricious, in which case it might not work, or whether it is strong enough to amount to a back-door prohibition, in which case it would most likely not pass legal muster.

This requirement might seem to put Douglas in a cleft stick— nothing strong enough to work would be legal, and nothing legal would be strong enough to work. But this assumes that his ambition was to make slavery illegal with one swipe. His case was stronger if his ambitions were more modest. In the first place, laws as strong as the fence-out legislation in the cattle states, or the mining laws of the mineral states, might well be strong enough to give the coup de grâce to an institution that already labored under disadvantages, as slavery did in any of the existing territories in 1858. In the second place, the intention of hostile legislation may well not be to score an immediate and sweeping victory, but to provide for a continuing series of probes and tests of the Supreme Court's position, such as might erode the authority of the decision around the edges, and possibly, in the longest run, deprive it of the public consensus it needs to prevail over time. A more credible case for the Freeport Doctrine can be made if it is viewed not as a solution but as a response. This defense is tenable only so long as one resists the temptation to translate political quarrels into legal terms, and the parallel temptation to translate legal quarrels into constitutional terms. And it is tenable only so far as the strategy is used only in limited ways, and only so far is it does not provoke a crushing response from the pro-slavery side (as it wound up doing). If this is what Douglas's intention in the Freeport Doctrine was, what Douglas did was, under cover of agreeing with the *Dred Scott* decision, to refuse to take it as a political rule governing his future action. This involves some prevarication on Douglas's part, but as a strategy it is not all that far from Lincoln's.

Lincoln's Attack on the Freeport Doctrine

Lincoln's attack upon the Freeport Doctrine was fierce, and indeed was characterized by a sharpness of tone that was unusual for him. At Jonesboro, Lincoln began by arguing that the history of slavery showed that it had been able to plant itself in new regions without protective police legislation, and therefore that the Freeport strategy would most likely fail. After all, Dred Scott himself was a slave held in a territory where there were no police regulations about slavery, because slavery itself was illegal in Wisconsin Territory when Scott lived there.

This argument was factually correct. But it had two weaknesses. The first was that the presence of a small number of enslaved personal servants like Dred Scott in a territory was not quite the same thing as a fully developed and fully modernized slave economy there. The Freeport Doctrine was aimed at hindering the development of a slave economy, not at preventing the entry of a few slaves into a territory.

The second weakness was that the historical counterexamples of other territories where a developing slave economy prospered although the necessary police legislation did not yet exist were all cases where slavery had economic advantages it did not have in Kansas, Nebraska, Utah, or New Mexico. Slavery could survive in east Texas because it was economically robust there, and lack of legal protections would not cause slaveholders to hesitate before going there. Douglas never believed that slavery had these kinds of advantages in Kansas, Nebraska, Utah, or New Mexico. Where slavery for a host of reasons was expected to be weak, a legal nudge like the Freeport Doctrine might suffice to persuade prospective slaveholding settlers to bring their slaves to a more promising place, like Texas.[73]

Lincoln went on to argue that since "it is a maxim held by the courts, that there is no wrong without its remedy; and the courts have a remedy for whatever is acknowledged and treated as a wrong," the federal courts would therefore intervene if the territorial legislatures failed to provide the protection for property in slaves that the Constitution guaranteed. The Court might either itself impose a slave code upon a recalcitrant territory or require Congress to impose a federal slave code. This was essentially the position Jefferson Davis would take in his attempt to stop one inch short of directly calling for Congress to enact a federal slave code.[74] By stating the case in this blunt, no-exceptions way, Lincoln essentially made Davis's case for him.

Lincoln followed with an argument that Douglas himself had used against Lincoln: the oath of office he will take includes a duty to protect the Constitution, but attempting to overslaugh a Supreme Court decision is subversive of that oath:

What do you understand by supporting the Constitution of a State or of the United States? Is it not to give such constitutional helps to the rights established by that Constitution as may be practically needed? Can you, if you swear to support the Constitution, and believe that the Constitution establishes a right, clear your oath, without giving it support? Do you support the Constitution if, knowing or believing there is a right established under it which needs specific legislation, you withhold that legislation? Do you not violate and disregard your oath? (1:619)

Both of Lincoln's arguments, the argument about the judiciary's duty
to respond to the Freeport Doctrine and the argument about Douglas's
subversion of his own constitutional obligations by proposing it, misconstrued Douglas's intentions. What the Freeport Doctrine forbade
was not the holding of slaves, but the establishment of a developed slave
economy. It did not withhold the normal protections of property—it
did not say, for instance, that anyone might be permitted to seize and
free slaves without consequence, or that nobody could take legal action
to recover his or her slaves, or that nobody could establish or defend a
title to their slaves.

Douglas might have given other examples of Freeport-style hostile
legislation that stigmatized slavery but stopped just short of expropriation—legislation holding that slaves cannot be sold, or that the
children of slaves become free adults, or that slaves cannot be inherited, for example. At least the first of these would have been within constitutional bounds, since Congress had imposed it upon the District of
Columbia in 1850, even if such a move might have been seen as taking
from the slaveholders some of the property rights they held in their
slaves. And the second course was how the North abolished slavery
without taking any actual slave, although such laws did, arguably, lay
hold of the owner's interest in the slave's offspring. But Douglas's chief
example of hostile legislation was much more modest: the refusal to
provide special policing legislation and special policing institutions
(such as patrollers or public disciplinary procedures). The example was
important, because it made clear that Douglas did not have in mind
withholding the ordinary protections of property, but withholding the
special economic preconditions for successful exploitation of that
property.

Since Douglas had always argued—perhaps disingenuously—that
the slavery question was really only an issue of what kind of economic
development a state or territory chose to support, he argued that it
was as legitimate for a territory to favor free agriculture over slave
agriculture as it was for a territory to favor an agricultural future over
a future devoted to industry and trade, or a ranching economy over
a farming economy. In elaborating the Freeport Doctrine, Douglas
gave an anti-slavery turn to an argument—slaves are property, slavery is an economic matter—that was usually found in the pro-slavery
repertoire.

Lincoln's argument fudged the distinction between what the state permits and what the state promotes. The state (or territory) may not have the right to forbid someone from attempting a kind of development the state has not chosen to promote. But it is under no obligation to provide the preconditions for making that development a success, particularly if the people of the state favor another course that is incompatible with the one that the developer projects.

Lincoln's argument also fudged the distinction between what the state permits and what it approves of; his argument was that whatever the state permits it also approves of, and the state is therefore bound to provide all the means to assure the success of what it permits, no matter how onerous those means are. But states often frown on things they do not or cannot forbid, and they do so not only over economic questions but also over moral ones.

Lincoln's arguments against the Freeport Doctrine are also arguments against all of his own anti-slavery policies. Lincoln was highly invested in the idea that the Founders permitted slavery because they could not think of a satisfactory practical way to remove it; they felt obligated to protect the rights and interests of those invested in the existing institution, but they also wished to be sure that slavery would be put in a position where its ultimate extinction would be inevitable. That position was subject to every vulnerability Lincoln attributed to the Freeport Doctrine, if the state is obligated, as Lincoln says, to promote the interests of those who hold whatever property it legally recognizes.

If Lincoln's argument overturned the Freeport Doctrine, it also overturned everything that had been done since the time of the Founders against slavery, including the *post nati* emancipation laws of the free states, the closing of the international slave trade, and the closing of the slave trade in the District of Columbia.

What was worst about Lincoln's argument here was not just that it was wrong, but that it played with fire. What Lincoln sketched in as an argument against Douglas was essentially the argument for the "second *Dred Scott* decision" we saw in Chapter 3: if the Constitution recognizes slaves as property, then it guarantees slaveholders not only all the protections due to property but also all the means they need in order to make successful economic use of that property. Now Lincoln gave himself an out, since he denied the major premise of that argument (it is not true that the Constitution recognizes property in slaves). But he did not make that quite crystal clear in the passage we have just seen, and in fact he seemed to be sketching in a southern line of attack upon Douglas, as if daring the southerners *not* to take this position. The way Lincoln made this argument, this is to say, seems to foreclose the escape from its strictures he had prepared for himself.

Even where Lincoln did leave himself an out, his position was extremely vulnerable. Whether the Constitution gave property in slaves the kind of protection it gave to other kinds of property was a disputed point in the 1850s, and in the context of courts increasingly prepared to take the view that the Constitution did provide that protection, Lincoln's argument against the Freeport Doctrine had the paradoxical effect of shoring up the slaveholder position, since only what was in context a very debatable and vulnerable premise separated his view from theirs. Indeed, throughout the debates on the Freeport Doctrine, Lincoln used against Douglas arguments that, with only a few shifts in the background music, supporters of Breckinridge would use against Lincoln, and the secessionists would use later to break up the Union.

It is true that the greatest Founders were ambivalent about slavery, and that the authors of the Constitution did their best to keep explicit recognition of slavery out of its language. But the Constitution also makes many devil's bargains about slavery, and if it does not clearly provide slavery with property protection, it does not clearly refuse it either. Just how far the Constitution treats slaves as property is in fact unclear, since it does so in some ways and does not do so in others.

If Lincoln's ability to avoid being subject to the logic of the "second *Dred Scott* decision" depended upon the claim that the Constitution does not recognize slaves as property, his position was on shaky ground, since the Constitution can be plausibly seen either way and it can never be conclusively shown to take either position firmly. If Lincoln could evade the logic of the "second *Dred Scott* decision" by denying that slaves are in all senses of that word property, so also could Douglas, because the popular sovereignty position itself argued that the territories, like the states, have a say about how to treat that kind of property. Further, the Freeport Doctrine argued that even if slaves are property, slavery could be hedged in by the means states or territories use to regulate other kinds of property they must tolerate but do not have to privilege.

Lincoln's argument also fudged the distinction between what one is *morally* bound to do, by the requirement of applying principles consistently, and what one is *legally* or *constitutionally* bound to do. The argument against Douglas is strongest when it is seen as an argument about moral consistency: how can you consistently offer slavery protection with the right hand and take it away with the left? But by making the argument turn on the oath to obey and protect the Constitution, Lincoln changed the nature of his argument. The conditional form of the argument (if you believe *x*, then you must also support *y*) can only apply to moral arguments about consistent policy. But constitutional arguments are not made in that conditional way: either the Constitution does or does not treat slaves as a specially protected kind of property. If it does, then both Lincoln and Douglas are bound to protect it. The argument does not turn on whether they *believe* the Constitution provides that protection, only upon whether it does in fact do so. And if it does not in fact do so, then Douglas was as free to oppose the imposition of slavery upon the territories by using the Freeport Doctrine as Lincoln was by changing the makeup of the Court.

Douglas noticed this flaw in Lincoln's argument, and replied that Lincoln somehow believed that the Constitution imposed different requirements upon Democrats from those it imposed upon Republicans. Because Lincoln phrased his argument not as turning on what Douglas was morally obligated, by his interpretation of the *Dred Scott* decision, to support, but on what Douglas was constitutionally obligated to provide by virtue of his oath to support the Constitution, Lincoln in effect handed the South a weapon to use against Douglas, a weapon they would also use against Lincoln. Lincoln's position was not an argument, but a dare:

> Lastly I would ask—is not Congress, itself, under obligation to give legislative support to any right that is established under the United States Constitution? I repeat the question—is not Congress, itself, bound to give legislative support to any right that is established in the United States Constitution? (1:619–620)

Lincoln made a pointed comparison between resistance by the state legislatures to the Fugitive Slave Act and resistance to the protection of slavery by territorial legislatures:

> Let me ask you why many of us who are opposed to slavery upon principle, give our acquiescence to a Fugitive Slave law? Why do we hold ourselves under obligations to pass such a law, and abide by it when it is passed? Because the Constitution makes provision that the owners of slaves shall have the right to reclaim them. It gives the right to reclaim slaves, and that right is, as Judge Douglas says, a barren right, unless there is legislation that will enforce it. (1:620)

Lincoln's reasoning from the fugitive slave provision of the Constitution to the actual Fugitive Slave Act of 1850 is faulty. That the Constitution requires states to render up fugitive slaves does not require Congress to pass the particular fugitive slave law, with all of its repulsive features, that it did pass in 1850. In fact, since that provision of the Constitution was self-executing, it did not in fact require any fugitive slave law out of Congress at all, including the weaker Fugitive Slave Act of 1793.[75] The fugitive slave clause may have imposed upon Congress a moral obligation to make the rendition of fugitive slaves work. But it did not impose a constitutional requirement for them to pass either of the two fugitive slave laws it did pass. Furthermore, the Fugitive Slave Act of 1850 was not passed because the Constitution required it; it was passed as part of a system of bargains, something offered in exchange for the admission of California as a free state. The Fugitive Slave Act was not the fulfillment of a constitutional mandate, but part of a political deal. It deserved the respect other unsavory political bargains deserve—you agreed to it, so you have to live with it—but not more.

There was another case Lincoln did not make but that would have been stronger. Attempts by states to complicate the rendition of fugitive slaves under the 1793 law, attempts that seem similar in strategy to those Douglas proposed in the Freeport Doctrine, had provoked the 1850 law as a response. And attempts, such as Wisconsin's personal liberty law, to nullify the 1850 law by hostile state legislation were in the process of provoking still more sweeping responses from the slaveholders. The risk of the Freeport Doctrine was that it might provoke the South to insist upon a federal slave code for the territories. But Lincoln did not point this out as a risk. Instead, he did everything he could to make sure that pro-slavery politicians would in fact push for such a code:

> At the end of what I have said here I propose to give the Judge my fifth interrogatory which he may take and answer at his leisure. My fifth interrogatory is this: If the slaveholding citizens of a United States Territory should need and demand Congressional legislation for the protection of their slave property in such territory, would you, as a member of Congress, vote for or against such legislation? (1:621)

Douglas did answer this question directly, and indeed went to the wall to oppose a federal slave code, whether one imposed by Congress or by the courts. Lincoln of course did not have to answer this question, since he denied its premise, that property in slaves is protected under the Constitution. But there is another question he did not answer, the question of what he would do were the courts in fact to impose slave codes upon the territories. Were that to have happened, Lincoln would have had either to support a Freeport-like strategy or to have submitted. Lincoln's argument against the Freeport Doctrine foreclosed any practical defense on his part against imposition of a federal slave code imposed by the courts; he would have been reduced to impotently disagreeing with the decision, since it would have foreclosed the kinds of political resistance he had proposed to the *Dred Scott* decision more generally, and the specific kind of political resistance Douglas proposed in the Freeport Doctrine.

Lincoln did not have to make this argument to discredit the Freeport Doctrine, and the argument did not derive from the anti-slavery principles Lincoln espoused. It was not an argument that expresses a critique of slavery (except indirectly, in that it put pressure on a weakly anti-slavery position in order to advantage a stronger one not in play in the immediate context). Nor did he have to make the argument in this form, with its implication that a federal slave code for the territories is a constitutional necessity. He could, for instance, have pointed out that pro-slavery interests would respond to the Freeport Doctrine by demanding a federal slave code and federal police legislation, as they responded to the challenge made by the free states' interpretation of the *Prigg* decision with the Fugitive Slave Act. He made *this* argument, and he made it this way, to make sure that the southern Democrats would make the same argument. His aim was not to point out the weakness of the Freeport Doctrine as an anti-slavery strategy. His aim was to destroy the Democratic Party as the last national political organization. Lincoln most likely was not seeking to make himself president with this argument. But he certainly was seeking not only to prevent Douglas from becoming president but also to destroy any chance of sectional reconciliation within his party.

Lincoln knew very well that Douglas had argued that the language from Taney's opinion under consideration here was not part of what the Court as a whole had ruled. But he treated that argument as merely an example of interpretive sleight of hand:

> I am aware that in some of the speeches Judge Douglas has made, he has spoken as if he did not know or think that the Supreme Court had decided that a territorial Legislature cannot exclude slavery. Precisely what the Judge would say upon the subject—whether he would say definitely that he does not understand they have so decided, or whether he would say he does understand that the Court have so decided, I do not know; but I know that in his speech at Springfield he spoke of it as a thing they had not decided yet; and in his answer to me at Freeport, he spoke of it so far again as I can comprehend it, as a thing that had not yet been decided. Now I hold that if the Judge does entertain that view I think he is not mistaken in so far as it can be said that the Court has not decided anything save the mere question of jurisdiction. I know the legal arguments that can be made— that after a court has decided that it cannot take jurisdiction of a case, it then has decided all that is before it, and that is the end of it. A plausible argument can be made in favor of that proposition, but I know that Judge Douglas has said in one of his speeches that the court went forward *like honest men as they were* and decided all the points in the case. If any points are really extrajudicially decided because not necessarily before them, then this one as to the power of the Territorial Legislature to exclude slavery is one of them, as also the one that the Missouri Compromise was null and void. They are both extra-judicial or neither is according as the Court held that they had no jurisdiction in the case between the parties, because of want of capacity of one party to maintain a suit in that Court. (1:621–622)

Lincoln here elided an important distinction. Republicans had argued that the whole decision, except the parts about the plea in abatement and the part about black citizenship (the parts about the question of whether the Court could hear Scott's case at all, since he was black), was extrajudicial; they argued, this is to say, that having decided that Scott could not sue in federal court because he was not a citizen, the Court could not go on to examine the issue Scott had sued about, whether he was made free by residence in Illinois and in Wisconsin Territory, or the issue Sanford's counsel raised upon reargument, whether the Missouri Compromise restriction was unconstitutional. But that was not the case Douglas made: Douglas's case was that it is not clear that this particular aspect of the decision (not the whole decision), the aspect concerned with the power of territorial legislatures over slavery, was really the opinion of the whole Court rather than only of Taney himself, since Taney's opinion here raised points neither side had argued in the case, and, what is more, turned on issues that were not at stake in the case, since Scott had lived in a free territory made free by the Missouri Compromise restriction, not in a free territory whose territorial legislature had prohibited slavery.

When Lincoln turned to his own views about whether slavery could be prohibited in the territories, he phrased the question as being about his moral obligation to consistency. Consistency did not require him to protect property in slaves in the territories because he did not believe the Constitution promised such protection. But when he turned to Douglas, Lincoln's argument was as much about Douglas's absolute constitutional obligation as it was about his moral inconsistency. The way Lincoln phrased the argument during the final debate at Alton was in fact ambiguous about whether Douglas's moral inconsistency or his evasion of a constitutional obligation was the real issue. But the hyperbolic language Lincoln used at Alton suggested where he intended the emphasis:

> Can he withhold the legislation which his neighbor needs for the enjoyment of a right which is fixed in his favor in the Constitution of the United States which he has sworn to support? Can he withhold it without violating his oath? And more especially, can he pass unfriendly legislation to violate his oath? Why, this is a *monstrous* sort of talk about the Constitution of the United States! *There has never been as outlandish or lawless a doctrine from the mouth of any respectable*

man on earth. I do not believe it is a Constitutional right to hold slaves in a Territory of the United States. I believe the decision was improperly made and I go for reversing it. Judge Douglas is furious against those who go for reversing a decision. But he is for legislating it out of all force while the law itself stands. *I repeat that there has never been so monstrous a doctrine uttered from the mouth of a respectable man.* (1:812–813)

Lincoln is rightly known as an orator who avoided bombast. But the hyperbole of this passage is the sign not only of partisan excitement but also of a slippery argument.

Lincoln concluded his Alton speech with an ironic sally:

I defy any man to make an argument that will justify unfriendly legislation to deprive a slaveholder of his right to hold his slave in a Territory, that will not equally, in all its length, breadth and thickness, furnish an argument for nullifying the Fugitive Slave law. Why, there is not such an Abolitionist in the nation as Douglas, after all. [Loud and enthusiastic applause.] (1:813–814)

The remark in the last line that "there is not such an Abolitionist in the nation as Douglas, after all" was in context only a flash of wit, and that is how Douglas took it in his own reply. But the underlying comparison between the Freeport Doctrine and the personal liberty laws was a deep one. The analogy depended upon the (false) assumption that passing the Fugitive Slave Act was a constitutional obligation, not merely a political one. The opportunity to compare Douglas's Freeport Doctrine with the Wisconsin personal liberty law at that moment being challenged in the case of *Ableman v. Booth* was delicious, especially since in the *Ableman* case itself Wisconsin had lifted arguments about state sovereignty and nullification straight from Calhoun's playbook. But the comparison was a dangerous one for Lincoln, for it raised a question, which Douglas did in fact ask but which Lincoln never answered, which is what *Lincoln* would do were the Supreme Court actually to write Taney's view about the lack of power of territorial legislatures over slavery into the higher law.

Lincoln's *Dred Scott* speech had sketched in a line of defense against the *Dred Scott* decision's claims about the citizenship rights of free blacks, and he had sketched in a line of defense against that same decision's claims about the constitutionality of the Missouri Compromise restriction. He proposed to submit to the decision without taking it as a political rule (a privilege he denied to Douglas), hoping that in the long run a shift in the public mind and a shift in the personnel of the Court would lead to the overthrow of that decision. That was a strategy he could afford to take about the citizenship question and about the Missouri Compromise restriction question, because he himself proposed only addressing the citizenship question in the longest run (because it would be politically suicidal for him to do otherwise), and the question about the Missouri Compromise restriction was a moot one anyway, since that provision had been repealed by Congress in 1854 when it passed the Kansas-Nebraska Act. Waiting for the longest run in those instances required no fatal sacrifice on Lincoln's part.

But the territorial question was a different kind of issue. Suppose Taney's views were to be affirmed by the entire Court. (Lincoln believed that they had already been so affirmed.) Suppose that Kansas tested that decision by refusing to pass a police code for slavery. Suppose that act (or rather, failure to act) were challenged in court, and the Supreme Court were to rule that Kansas must provide such a code. (Or, alternatively, suppose it were to rule that Congress must provide such a code.) Now, there are problems with this hypothetical ruling, chief among them that it has the Court acting like a legislature rather than like a court, writing laws rather than interpreting them, ruling about them, or enforcing them. But that is an objection only Douglas could raise, because Lincoln, like Jefferson Davis, had argued that the federal courts have exactly this power, and indeed had argued that the courts would not only be *likely* to exercise it against uses of the Freeport Doctrine, but would be *obligated* to. Such a ruling would place Lincoln's pledge to submit to the Court in contradiction to his pledge not to take the Court's ruling as a political guide. He would have to either directly defy the Court, as Douglas had unfairly accused him of doing already, or allow it to impose slave police codes on the territories by demanding such a code either from the territorial legislatures or from Congress.

Lincoln's strategy of waiting for the winds to change and give him the ability to change the decision over the long run would be unavailing in this case, because unlike the citizenship or Missouri Compromise aspects of the *Dred Scott* decision, the effects of a decision about the territorial legislatures would be felt immediately, and would have irrevocable effects. And the slaveholders would be able to make, citing Lincoln's own words with devastating effect, exactly the argument against Lincoln about this hypothetical situation that Lincoln had made against Douglas in his arguments against the Freeport Doctrine.

Douglas often charged that the Republicans in Illinois were in political collusion with the Buchaneers, with the pro-slavery national Democrats who still supported Buchanan. Nothing in Lincoln's speeches makes this case so much as the strategy he adopted against the Freeport Doctrine.

7.5 Conclusion

Fraught Supreme Court cases like *Dred Scott* require one to remind one's self that the distinction between principle and consent does not map precisely onto the distinction between the judicial and legislative branches. The finality of the Supreme Court's views is a function of the institutional arrangements among the branches, not a function of any assumption that the Court somehow stands closer to the higher law. All institutions within their own boundaries operate on the basis of consent among the stakeholders, and no institution has privileged access to principle. But all institutions are also bound to their own traditions, folkways, and habits of thinking, some of which embody the experience of attempting to work out insights about principles. No institution embodies principle, but principle matters in the persuasive engagements through which institutions come to take action, and institutions have different ways of deploying principle in a persuasive conversation among their stakeholders.

Principle embodies itself, this is to say, not in institutions, but, as Madison proposed, in the structure of interaction of institutions, and in the background of convictions and assumptions that give shape to moral thinking and to the moral arguments participants in institutions use in their engagements with each other. It is the effect of the *Dred Scott* decision upon these background convictions that Lincoln chiefly feared, and it was from the legal consequences of a transformed legal culture, not from the actual, pending *Lemmon* decision, that Lincoln feared a "second *Dred Scott* decision."

What ultimately mattered most about the *Dred Scott* decision to Lincoln was not its attack upon the Missouri Compromise restriction, or even its attack upon popular sovereignty, but its claim that blacks do not have (and, in the popular reception of the decision, should not be given) any citizenship rights, even the right to defend themselves in court, a claim that in Lincoln's view undermined the culture of freedom as much for whites as for blacks. The issue between Lincoln and Douglas was in Lincoln's mind an issue between those who committed themselves to views that corrupt democracy and those who rejected such views.

The survival of democracy depends upon the prevalence of views democracy cannot impose but must nurture. Chief among these views is the belief that there is something so fundamentally wrong about one person enslaving another that those who do not see the issue in this way are not fully to be trusted as keepers of a democracy. Lincoln is particularly at pains to point out that those who wish to remain morally neutral about slavery have already compromised the democracy of which they are citizens no less than those who positively defend slavery. He treats those Democrats who feel that slavery might not be quite right but who will not take a public step to stigmatize it as a wrong—he of course has in mind Douglas's supporters, but his language cites what he had written to Speed back in 1855 on the subject—as lacking in honesty, lacking in courage, or so stampeded by party loyalty as to put it beyond either honesty or courage.[76] At Alton he made that case this way:

> On the other hand, I have said there is a sentiment which treats it [slavery] as *not* being wrong. That is the Democratic sentiment of this day. I do not mean to say that every man who stands within that range positively asserts that it is right. That class will include all who positively assert that it is right, and all who like Judge Douglas treat it as indifferent and do not say it is either right or wrong. These two classes of men fall within the general class of those who do not look upon it as a wrong. And if there be among you any body who supposes that he, as a Democrat can consider himself "as much opposed to slavery as anybody," I would like to reason with him. You never treat it as a wrong. What other thing that you consider as a wrong, do you deal with as you deal with that? Perhaps you *say* it is wrong, *but your leader never does, and you quarrel with any body who says it is*

wrong. Although you pretend to say so yourself you can find no fit place to deal with it as a wrong. You must not say any thing about it in the free States, *because it is not here.* You must not say any thing about it in the slave States, *because it is there.* You must not say any thing about it in the pulpit, because that is religion and has nothing to do with it. You must not say any thing about it in politics, *because that will disturb the security of "my place."* [Shouts of laughter and cheers.] There is no place to talk about it as being a wrong, although you say yourself it is a wrong. But finally you will screw yourself up to the belief that if the people of the slave States should adopt a system of gradual emancipation on the slavery question, you would be in favor of it. You would be in favor of it. You say that is getting it in the right place, and you would be glad to see it succeed. But you are deceiving yourself. You all know that Frank Blair and Gratz Brown, down there in St. Louis, undertook to introduce that system in Missouri. They fought as valiantly as they could for the system of gradual emancipation which you pretend you would be glad to see succeed. Now I will bring you to the test. After a hard fight they were beaten, and when the news came over here you threw up your hats and *hurraed for Democracy.* (1:809)

Lincoln's strongest point in the whole debates is his claim that when one recuses one's self from moral judgment in the name of keeping the peace, one makes moral sacrifices whose depth one does not understand when one makes them. But Lincoln does not say that the price of escape from complicity in wrong may well be a confrontation in which wrong will triumph:

The Democratic policy in regard to that institution will not tolerate the merest breath, the slightest hint, of the least degree of wrong about it. Try it by some of Judge Douglas's arguments. He says he "don't care whether it is voted up or voted down" in the Territories. I do not care myself in dealing with that expression, whether it is intended to be expressive of his individual sentiments on the subject, or only of the national policy he desires to have established. It is alike valuable for my purpose. Any man can say that who does not see any thing wrong in slavery, but no man can logically say it who does see a wrong in it; because no man can logically say he don't care whether a wrong is voted up or voted down. He may say he don't care whether an indifferent thing is voted up or down, but he must logically have a choice between a right thing and a wrong thing. He contends that whatever community wants slaves has a right to have them. So they have if it is not a wrong. But if it is a wrong, he cannot say people have a right to do wrong. He says that upon the score of equality, slaves should be allowed to go in a new Territory, like other property. This is strictly logical if there is no difference between it and other property. If it and other property are equal, his argument is entirely logical. But if you insist that one is wrong and the other right, there is no use to institute a comparison between right and wrong. (1:809–810)

What was risked, Lincoln argued at Alton, by the attempt to evade moral confrontation with slavery was not only complicity with evil, although that was indeed risked. What was risked was also that the means that strategy legitimized against blacks would be means that might become legitimized against other groups, since that strategy legitimized all kinds of hierarchy, that of class and money as well as that of race, and all hierarchy is, in Lincoln's understanding, a version of the old argument of the divine right of kings:

That is the real issue. That is the issue that will continue in this country when these poor tongues of Judge Douglas and myself shall be silent. It is the eternal struggle between these two principles— right and wrong—throughout the world. They are the two principles that have stood face to face from the beginning of time; and will ever continue to struggle. The one is the common right of humanity and the other the divine right of kings. It is the same principle in whatever shape it develops itself. It is the same spirit that says, "You work and toil and earn bread, and I'll eat it." No matter in what shape it comes, whether from the mouth of a king who seeks to bestride the people of his own nation and live by the fruit of their labor, or from one race of men as an apology for enslaving another race, it is the same tyrannical principle. (1:810–811)

Douglas and his supporters probably would not have recognized themselves as adherents of the divine right of kings, or of any morally equivalent position. They also certainly did not see themselves, as

Calhoun and his supporters did, as opponents of the promises of the Declaration of Independence.

Their conviction, or better, their assumption, that the promises of the Declaration did not apply to blacks, was aligned with the political lines of force of their era, in which increased class equality almost always meant decreased racial equality. Their assumption that equality was promised to the poor white but not to the black, enslaved or free, was probably the working assumption of most Democrats of their age, and perhaps of most whites generally, and from it derives the paradox of the Jacksonian era, that the democratization of the franchise and of the public world led to a vicious intensification of racial hatred and racial repression.

But the structure of the Democrats' assumptions was incoherent, as *herrenvolk* democracy was itself incoherent, and the power of that structure was as a set of unexamined working assumptions, as *doxa*, not as a body of examined convictions. It was used at the same time by the poor white to extort recognition from the rich white, and by the rich white to redirect the poor white's resentment from the rich white to the black. Because extorted recognition is not recognition, and because the redirection was easily seen through, *herrenvolk* democracy never quite delivered the social peace it promised. It is natural that the passion invested in some article of *doxa* rises in proportion to its incoherence, since nothing quite has the power hysteria has of transforming a naked contradiction into a mystical coincidence of opposites.

If Douglas was right that what he argued about race and the Declaration was in fact what most whites of his time and earlier believed, as he probably was, Lincoln was also right that that conviction could not be held in a stable or examined way, and that in some deep unlit recess of the public mind the people could nevertheless continue to smell the obscure stink of bad faith that would have to hang about a state of affairs in which the loudest yelps for liberty were being made by the drivers of negroes. But if the contradiction of a more than nominally democratic society nevertheless continuing not only to embrace race-based slavery but also to expand it is the mark of an inner incoherence that sooner or later must break out in chaos, so the contradiction of Lincoln's own *doxa*, that blacks as a group could be offered some forms of civil equality and denied others, and that civil equality and social equality could be rigorously separated, also was a mark of an inner incoherence ripe for collapse.

Lincoln's hope was that for all the passion whites of his era had invested in racial slavery, somehow, somewhere, most people dimly knew better. Our hope about Lincoln is the same, that somehow he knew that the half-measures he kept proposing throughout the 1850s were inadequate, however necessary they were as preconditions, and however politically unavailable better positions would have been at that time. But that is the hope one always has about democracies, too, that somehow deep down they know better than to stick with the vices they seem most completely imprisoned by, and that somehow, some way, they will find a way to work themselves free.

The central theme of Lincoln's attack on the *Dred Scott* decision was his attack upon its racism, not upon its immediate political aims, because it was the racism of the decision that most corroded the habits of thought that democracies cannot survive losing. Lincoln understood the instability of the *herrenvolk* democracy embraced by the Democrats: those who forge shackles are destined ultimately to wear them. The Democrats had wanted to believe that racism was not only consistent with political equality but also a precondition of it, since it made the poor white the political equal of the rich white. Lincoln understood that when the black is sacrificed, the poor white stands next in line. It was a lesson the next generation, after the destruction of slavery, was to experience, although not to learn, in the wake of the betrayal of the promises of Reconstruction, when the same legal philosophy that underwrote *Plessy* also underwrote *Lochner.*

CHAPTER 8

Aftershocks of the Debates

$\mathcal{A}$LTHOUGH AT LEAST a plurality of voters probably favored Lincoln, Douglas managed to win enough seats in the legislature to eke out a narrow reelection to the Senate in 1858. Douglas had an edge in the legislature to begin with, because some of the votes were cast by Democratic holdovers, whose districts may have turned Republican but whose seats were not at risk. In addition, the census of 1850, upon which the apportionment of election districts was based, was old enough to favor Douglas, although the districts were not outrageously gerrymandered by nineteenth-century standards. In the final tally Douglas had fifty-four votes in the legislature to Lincoln's forty-six.[1]

If, as a rough indication of the popular strength of the parties in Illinois, one averages the vote for the two statewide offices at stake in the 1858 election (the state treasurer and the state superintendent of public instruction), the Republicans won a plurality of votes, 125,212 to 121,810 for the Douglas Democrats, but their edge was slightly less than the 2 percent of votes that went for the Buchanan Democrats.[2] Allen Guelzo has recently suggested more accurate ways of estimating the voter support for the Senate candidates, casting up the results in the state representative districts. His estimates give Lincoln a considerably larger edge in popular ballots than the traditional accounts do, giving the Republican candidates 190,468 votes, the Douglas Democratic candidates 166,374 votes, and the Buchaneer candidates 9,951. The results are even more lopsided in the open Senate districts. None of this prevented Democratic press in Illinois from celebrating Douglas's re-election as if it were epoch-making, braying such hyperbole as "DOUGLAS SUSTAINED! LINCOLN'S COMB IS CUT!"[3]

Despite retaining his seat against a formidable challenger, Douglas's prospects for the presidency had been mortally wounded. Douglas's chances in the North depended upon his finding a credibly independent position for the northern Democrats, one that could separate them from the Lecompton fraud and free them from the charge of craven submission to the slave power. Douglas's chances in the South depended upon his ability to appeal to moderate southerners by showing that he offered a policy that had enough plausibility in the North and in the South to preserve the Democratic Party as a national organization and to promise some modus vivendi within which southern and northern moderates could operate. Southern moderates understood that their section could not dominate the Union except through the Democratic Party, and the Democratic Party could not win if it insisted upon forcing northern Democrats to the wall.

Because he had won the support of John J. Crittenden, who was as close to being Henry Clay's successor as an upper South moderate as it was possible to be, he had reason to believe that his case at least in the border states was a promising one. Crittenden's support, and the alienating effect of Lincoln's own inflammatory conspiracy arguments in the "House Divided" speech and in the debates, had won Douglas enough support among the conservative ex-Whigs who had voted for Fillmore in 1856 to give him a strong showing in the middle counties of Illinois, where the Senate election was decided, and showed that he retained the possibility of winning similar voters on both sides of the Ohio.[4] In addition, the indirect endorsement given to Douglas by eastern Republicans like Horace Greeley, William Seward, and Henry Wilson had raised hopes in Douglas's camp that he might lead a moderate free soil coalition in 1860 that would be able to prevent the spread of slavery to the western territories without provoking secession by the slave states. Holding a coalition of northern Democrats, cautious Republicans, and border South ex-Whigs together seems in retrospect like trying to ride three horses at the same time, since attempts to appeal to the free soil convictions of moderate Republicans

would alienate southern ex-Whigs. But Douglas's position might not
have been so desperate had he been able to persuade each side to seek
only policies they could realistically imagine the other side agreeing
to, policies that he could argue represented the best outcome for each
side, given the opposition of the other.

Although this grand strategy did return Douglas to the Senate, the
campaign had exhausted his ability to employ a similar strategy at the
national level. Implausible as Lincoln's conspiracy charges in the campaign against Douglas were, Lincoln nevertheless made it clear that
Douglas was not a safe candidate about whom to build a free soil coalition, particularly if Lincoln could show that the possibility of compromise attracted Douglas more than the success of free soil in the territories did. Douglas could only make a case for the moderate Free Soilers
at the expense of his appeal to border South ex-Whigs. To each side he
had to offer ambiguities, while trying, with winks and nods, to show
each side that his sympathies were really with them. To undermine this
strategy, all Lincoln had to do on one side, or the southern Democrats
on the other, was to make the case that Douglas's sympathies for their
own side were uncertain, which was easy to do, because in fact they
were uncertain.

Lincoln's arguments about the effect of Douglas's professed public
indifference about the slavery issue perhaps made his case that Douglas could not be a Free Soil candidate more plausibly than his conspiracy charges did, but probably merely waging a hard-fought campaign
against Douglas, in which Douglas engaged in predictably vituperative
tactics, was enough to deprive Douglas of the conservative, Bates- or-
McLean-leaning Republicans he sought to persuade. To persuade the
ex-Whig supporters of Fillmore to support him, Douglas had further
to show them that he remained credible as a national candidate, that he
offered a policy that could win a large enough minority of the southern vote to offer the possibility of sectional accommodation. The responses of southern Democrats to his candidacy, and the continuing
hostility of the Buchanan administration, foreclosed this possibility as
well, since Douglas could hardly achieve sectional accommodation if
his name became anathema in the South.

Douglas had sought to persuade southern Democrats that their only
hope of retaining the presidency in 1860 was to nominate a candidate
who could win enough northern votes to carry those marginally Demo-

cratic states (Pennsylvania, New Jersey, Illinois, and Indiana) that had given Buchanan his skin-of-the-teeth victory in 1856, something that no Buchaneer or pro-southern candidate could possibly do after the Lecompton debacle. But this strategy could succeed only if there were still southern Democrats prudent enough to realize that their influence in the federal government depended upon their keeping some large fraction of northern Democrats on their side. Increasingly, however, southern Democrats began to value sectional loyalty more than the unity of the Democratic Party, even when that unity was the precondition of their influence in the national councils. Indeed, as they posed ever-more-stringent tests of sectional loyalty for each other, the idea of making prudent concessions to retain national relevance became less and less important to them, since the idea of remaining a part of that nation became less important.

By the beginning of 1859 Douglas found himself losing a two-front battle, struggling to shore up the Democratic Party in the North and struggling against increasingly intransigent, even suicidal, opposition in the South. In December 1858 southern opposition succeeded in removing Douglas from the chairmanship of the Committee on Territories in the Senate. And demands in southern circles for a federal slave code, and even for the resumption of the African slave trade, rose to such a pitch that even Douglas's speeches began to suggest that southern politicians were engaged in a conspiracy to nationalize slavery. In the late summer and autumn of 1859, Lincoln and Douglas both gave a series of speeches in Ohio, in support of friendly candidates for governor. Lincoln's speeches were consistently better honed, more sharply phrased, more fairly and more tellingly argued than his speeches had been in the 1858 Illinois campaign. And Douglas's speeches, flailing wildly in all directions but gamely taking on all comers, reflected the increasing desperation of his position.

If Douglas's prospects for the presidency in 1860 were mortally weakened by the course of the 1858 debates, partly because they put him in an impossible political position and partly because they revealed ironies in liberal politics itself that neither Lincoln nor Douglas could solve, it is possible that the committed step in the descent to war took place not at the time of the Democratic convention in 1860 or at the time of John Brown's raid in 1859, but at the time of the Lincoln-Douglas debates in 1858. Politically speaking, after 1858 the destruction of the Democratic Party became inevitable, which ensured the election of a Republican president, which in turn ensured secession and war, whatever that Republican president did or said. And philosophically speaking, the debates revealed that persuasive engagement with the South hung by only the slenderest thread (a thread the South was doing its level best to cut), and that precious little space remained between the Scylla of a principled politics that hastens the descent to war and the Charybdis of spineless compromises that hollow out the value of peace.

8.1 Southern Responses to the Freeport Doctrine

Until Douglas set forth the Freeport Doctrine on August 27, 1858, its argument had been a respectable one in southern circles, being articulated by no less than Jefferson Davis in a speech in Maine at roughly the same time, as we have seen. Douglas's embrace of the same policy put Davis in a spot, and he had to walk back his statement by implausibly reinterpreting what he really meant. At least as striking as Davis's retraction was the debate in southern circles about whether his retraction was stringent enough.

Davis had meant to argue that since slavery could not maintain itself in the face of hostile local law the slave states (northern conspiracy theories notwithstanding) could not force slavery into territories where the people living did not want it to go. Challenged about his embrace of the Freeport Doctrine, Davis, as we have seen, changed front and argued that what he had really intended to do was to point out the need for further protection for slavery in the territories in the event a territorial legislature did not do its duty about slavery. Then he resorted to a quibble. Davis had to defuse some of the pressure on the southern Democrats to respond to Douglas's doctrine, especially since embittered ex-Whigs were using the opportunity to finally play against the Democrats the sectional loyalty card that the Democrats had played so devastatingly against them earlier. But at the same time Davis realized that to press immediately for a federal slave code might destroy the Democratic Party, upon which the South's power in the Union depended. Therefore, he sought to pass the hot potato to the judiciary. A federal slave code, Davis declared, would become necessary only if the courts, faced with recalcitrance from a territorial legislature, failed to declare that the territorial legislatures could not withhold the special protection for property in slaves that slavery required in order to prosper.

Davis's argument was intended, William Freehling argues, as a desperate improvisation, designed to draw the sting of the Freeport Doctrine, and to discredit Douglas, without demanding congressional debate about an inflammatory new law.[5] In other words, it was not a call for judicial intervention in the *Dred Scott* mode of ruling one's opposition completely out of the public square, but a call for judicial intervention in the Clayton Compromise mode of buying time to muddle through while the courts mulled over a question that the political branches had punted to them.[6]

Davis's local rival, Mississippi senator Albert Gallatin Brown, sought to up the ante, and to question Davis's sectional loyalty, by pushing for debate on a federal slave code for the territories immediately. Brown demanded, first of all, that the enabling acts for new territories require the legislatures to pass slave codes, and second, that a federal slave code be devised in case a territorial legislature defaults on its responsibilities.

Next to this nakedly confrontational demand, Davis's strategy looks like moderation, like compromise. Brown was unable to persuade his southern colleagues to go along with him. But this apparent retreat from bare-knuckled confrontation was a very ambiguous one, because even the more moderate version of the demand championed by Davis posed a condition northern Democrats were unlikely to stand for, and the result could only be to discredit Davis's compromising strategy and to drive even the compromisers into the extremist camp. In Davis's victory over Brown, a compromising strategy seems to have won out over a confrontational one, but since the compromise depended upon an unreasonable premise, that the North would accept judicial imposition of a federal slave code for the territories rather than fight out the question of whether Congress should impose such a code, the effect was to entrap even the cooler heads into adopting a confrontational strategy. Once the North proved unable to meet the conditions of compromise these comparatively cooler heads had set, the compromisers would be driven to take a hard line in order to retain their credibility as loyal sons of the South.[7]

The hard-liners were well aware of the flimsiness of the compromise offered by Davis. They transformed how that compromise was received, so that rather than being an expedient way to postpone a disastrous confrontation over a federal fugitive slave law, it became a test of whether the North was capable of conciliation with the South. At the Democratic convention in Charleston in April 1860, the radicals, using their reading of the Davis version as a fulcrum, were able to lever the moderates away not only from Douglas but also from the northern Democrats more generally. After the walkout of eight southern delegations, desperate Buchaneer northerners, such as Benjamin Butler of Massachusetts, attempted to conciliate the South by requiring the nominee at Charleston to receive a two-thirds vote of the convention (including the departed southerners in that number), exactly the strategy the South had used in 1844 to deny the nomination to Martin Van Buren, another doughface northerner who, like Douglas, had reached his turning point. Presumably Butler's strategy was designed not to deliver the party to the radicals, but to force out Douglas in favor of some dark horse the northern and southern factions could agree on, as in 1844 they had agreed upon James K. Polk. (Many of the seceders, apparently, were also hoping for this strategy, and expected to return to the convention once Douglas was disposed of. But this was forestalled by the Douglas delegates' successful motion to adjourn the convention and to reconvene in Baltimore on June 18.)[8] But the party was irreparably broken, and even reconvening the rump convention under different rules at Baltimore later did nothing to heal the breach.[9]

8.2 Douglas's "Dividing Line" Doctrine

Douglas published an extended and considered reply to the arguments of his southern opponents in *Harper's* magazine in September 1859.[10] He prepared the article with extensive historical research, assisted by the historian George Bancroft.[11] It is fair to say that most of the historical arguments, Bancroft's research notwithstanding, were special pleading. But as an intervention in contemporary politics, the article tells a different story.

Douglas opened with a surprisingly fair-minded statement of Republican policy:

> The political organization which was formed in 1854, and has assumed the name of the Republican Party, is based on the theory that African

slavery, as it exists in this country, is an evil of such magnitude—social, moral, and political—as to justify and require the exertion of the entire power and influence of the Federal Government to the full extent that the Constitution, according to their interpretation, will permit for its ultimate extinction.[12]

Douglas made an important qualification in this passage: Douglas conceded that the aim of the Republican Party was only the "ultimate extinction" of slavery, which meant that Republican policy did not represent an immediate threat to slaveholders. He immediately qualified that concession, however, by quoting from Lincoln's "House Divided" speech and from Seward's "Irrepressible Conflict" speech, in both cases making the point that the speeches proposed an immediate all-or-nothing choice, in which either slavery will be nationalized or it will be abolished. Douglas's argument here was that the high stakes, the all-or-nothing quality of the decision, and the imminence of the turning point both speeches imagined meant that the concession that only the ultimate extinction of slavery is in prospect meant less than it first appeared to mean, because for both Lincoln and Seward the fate of the Union would be settled in a sweeping and irrevocable way almost immediately, however long it took for the ultimate outcome to be realized.

The principal target of the article, however, was not the Republican position, but the Buchaneer position. Douglas presented it in two alternative versions, distinguishing Brown's hard-line position and Davis's more cautious one. To Douglas, as to most northerners, the distinction ultimately made no difference. But the way Douglas attacked the Davis position makes something clear about his own understanding of the status of slavery. It is nonsense, Douglas argued, to ask the judiciary to invent a law, because the job of the judiciary is to enforce and interpret law, not to invent it, and in the absence of the very territorial laws the territorial legislature has refused to pass, there is no law to be enforced. Now if the judiciary in question is a territorial judiciary, this argument is trivially true. But Douglas made the same case for the federal judiciary as well, because there is no national law about slavery other than the Fugitive Slave Act; slavery is a state institution.

To make this case Douglas had to reject the idea that natural-law arguments about the right to property apply to slave property. The way Douglas attacked the Davis view means that Douglas understood

slavery along *Somerset*-like lines, holding that slavery requires positive local law to exist and that the default state, in the absence of
positive law to the contrary, is freedom. The opposing position is possible only if the obligation to protect property in slaves is somehow
pre-political, higher than and prior to all law in the way that natural
rights are. Douglas, like Lincoln, this is to say, did not concede that the
right of masters to their slaves is "distinctly and expressly affirmed in
the constitution."

Douglas used *Somerset*-like language in his Columbus speech on
September 7, 1859:

> Now, by the express provisions of that clause of the Constitution, a
> slave is a person held to service or labor in one State under the laws
> thereof—not under the Constitution of the United States—not un-
> der the laws of the United States—not by virtue of any federal au-
> thority, but in a State under the laws thereof. What becomes of this
> newly discovered doctrine that slavery exists everywhere by virtue of
> the Constitution of the United States? It is denied by the Constitu-
> tion itself. Every child who has ever read the instrument knows that
> slavery is the creature of the local law, exists only where the local law
> sanctions and establishes it, and exists only in a State under the laws
> thereof; and inasmuch as a Territory is a State within the meaning of
> that clause of the Constitution, slavery may exist in a Territory the
> same as in a State, under the laws thereof. Hence, if the people of a
> Territory desire slavery, all they have to do is to pass laws sanction-
> ing and protecting it. If they do not want slavery, all they have to do
> is to withhold all legislation and all protection. Thus you find that
> the people of the Territories, as well as of the States, have the right to
> regulate that question for themselves.[13]

Brown's version, the argument that it is the "imperative duty" of
the federal government to supply a federal slave code in the face of
territorial refusal to provide one, turns on a slightly different understanding of the nature of the compulsion to protect property in slaves
in the territories. If territorial slave codes really can be legitimately
imposed by the courts, then slavery is pre-political, a creature of the
higher law, and the master's right to the slave transcends anything the
political branches might do either by action or by pointed inaction to

the contrary. If, however, it is up to the federal government to impose a slave code, then whatever obligation the federal government might be understood to have to the slaveholders is a sterile obligation until the government actually fulfills it. A law is not binding just because some people strongly believe that the government should impose such a law; it is binding only if the government actually does so, since in the absence of the actual law all one really has is one side's sense that it has a very strong argument, something that is open to the other side to have as well. Here the compulsion behind imposing a federal slave code for the territories does not arise from the higher law, but from ordinary politics, with arguments about "imperative duty" providing some of the means by which persuasion in the ordinary political arena is carried out.

The distinction between what the federal government is morally obliged to do (or rather, what some parties believe it is morally obliged to do) and what it is legally compelled to do is a porous one, raising all of the traditional problems of the higher law. Moral obligations rise to legal compulsions only under the pressure of the higher law, but in the absence of consensus about what those moral obligations are (and the issue arises in the first place precisely because of the absence of that consensus), a higher-law compulsion often enough reduces to "what I will kill you over if you really stand in my way about it." It is not for nothing that Douglas was always ill at ease with this apodictic, line-in-the-sand style of argument, even though he resorted to it, chiefly when he was driven into a corner by his opposition's resorting to it. Like the drive to treat one's own view of every political issue as something mandated by the Constitution, this style of argument is motivated not by the desire to persuade one's opponents, but by the desire to drive them entirely out of the public square.

Taney had argued that (in Douglas's paraphrase) "a Territory is the mere creature of Congress; that the creature can not be clothed with any powers not possessed by the creator; and that Congress, not possessing the power to legislate in respect to African slavery in the Territories, can not delegate to a Territorial Legislature any power which it does not itself possess."[14] Douglas had an ingenious reply to this in the "Dividing Line" article. Douglas began by making a distinction between powers the federal government can exercise but cannot delegate (only the federal government can declare war or regulate commerce with foreign nations) and powers the federal government can delegate but cannot exercise (it can create federal tribunals inferior to the Supreme Court, but it cannot be one). The power to abolish slavery, like other powers given to the states, is one of those powers the federal government can delegate (because it can create new states, which will have the power to abolish slavery) but not exercise. The fact that the federal government cannot exercise power over slavery is therefore not proof that the territories cannot either. If territories have the power to make decisions about other varieties of property (they can prohibit alcohol, for instance), then they must also have the power to make decisions about property in slaves.

What makes this argument formidable is that it arises from grounds not very different from those Taney himself had taken. Taney, like Calhoun before him, derived the federal authority to create temporary governments for the territories not from the territories clause but from the clause empowering the federal government to admit new states into the Union. But the power to admit new states is of course as good an example of the federal government delegating powers it cannot itself exercise as one could come up with, and if one wishes to deny to the territories the power of abolishing slavery within their limits, one has to have a better reason for doing so than merely that the federal government itself cannot abolish slavery there.

Southerners traditionally went to two different places to find that better reason. First, they argued that the territories were joint property of the states and that prohibiting slavery there amounted to prejudicing the institutions of the territory in favor of some partners and against those of others. This argument has somewhat less telling force if the decision against slavery is made by the people of the territory rather than by Congress, since in that case the federal government itself actually has done nothing prejudicial to the interests of the slave states in the territories. Second, southerners argued that the right to property is higher than and prior to all government and that property in slaves is not different in this respect from all other forms of property. Lincoln met the challenge of this argument by denying that to the Founders property in slaves really was just another kind of property. Douglas, by contrast, conceded that slaves were treated like other property, but only where there was local positive law on the subject. And even so, it still fell to the local authorities, and only to them, to set the conditions that determine whether that property could be profitably exploited or not.

One might at first think that Douglas simply elided the distinction between a territory and a state. The traditional reply to Douglas's argument is that territories are only states *in embryo* and thus cannot be given quite the free rein that actual states have. But Douglas did not in fact argue that territories are no different from states, and he conceded that territories were not ready to play the role on the national stage (having representation in Congress, for instance, or electoral votes) that states have. But since territories are inhabited by groups of citizens, he saw no reason why, even if territories are not ready to play a role in shaping the policy of the nation, they should be deprived of a say in local affairs of crucial importance to them. If they have enough authority and enough autonomy, for instance, to decide rules of inheritance for themselves, Douglas argued, then there is no reason why they should not also have authority and autonomy enough to make up their own minds about slavery. It is one thing to deny a territory a say in whether a treaty with a foreign power will be ratified. It is another to force slavery down the unwilling throats of its citizens.

In his speech at Wooster, Ohio, on September 16, 1859, Douglas added to this the straightforward (and probably true) claim that Taney's dictum about the territorial legislatures' lack of power over slavery was not actually among the holdings of the Court in the *Dred Scott* case anyway. He made the further argument that in recognizing slaves as property, the Court had not made a Fifth Amendment case to the effect that the right of a master to his slave property trumps the territory's interest in having its own say about slavery, but had asserted only that the Fugitive Slave Act applies to the territories in the same way that it applies to the states. This last point, it is fair to say, was an aggressive reinterpretation of Taney's remarks, one Taney would certainly find to be a forced one, to say the least.

Douglas's reading of the *Dred Scott* decision sometimes relies not only on aggressive misreading but also on plain subterfuge, for he transposes lines and drops phrases to bend the language of the decision to fit his interpretation.[15]

Douglas surrounded this essentially legal argument with a rather weak historical argument to the effect that it was local autonomy of

exactly the kind he argued for in the territories that motivated the colonists in the early stages of the struggle with Britain that led to American Independence. Now there is something delicious about throwing
what are essentially states' rights arguments in the faces of the slave
power. But it is hardly the case that the principal motive for independence from Britain was states' rights (or rather "colonies' rights") or
local autonomy.

The main attraction of this line of argument, for Douglas, was that
his principal evidence concerned Virginia's repeated attempts to limit
the slave trade, attempts that were frustrated by Britain, which acted
in the interest of the slave traders. Curiously, Douglas did not cite the
impassioned paragraph about the slave trade that Thomas Jefferson
intended to include in the Declaration of Independence, perhaps because the paragraph in fact was deleted. But surely no reader of Douglas's article could have missed the fact that the key instance of imperial
tyranny he cited was the Crown's attempt to force the slave trade upon
its unwilling colony. And such readers also could not help but notice
that frequently—Virginia kept trying to end or restrict the slave trade
for the three quarters of a century before the Revolution—the means
Virginia chose, special taxes and charges, were exactly the kind of
thing that Douglas had meant by "unfriendly legislation" when he set
out the Freeport Doctrine. The irony is all the more sharp when one
considers that the political class of that very polity was at that moment
not only attempting to force slavery upon an unwilling Kansas but also
beginning to lobby for the reopening of the African slave trade itself.

The pointedness of the examples outweighs the fact that the article's
theory of the motives of the Revolution was wrong, and of doubtful
relevance in clarifying the relationship between the territories and the
federal government anyway. The article's "Dividing Line" theory of
the relationship between the territories and the federal government is
historically false. But Douglas's examples have a rhetorical force independent of the general historical claim they are invoked to support,
because the examples are a standing rebuke to the pretensions of the
slave power.

It is hard to miss the analogy Douglas proposes between the South's
joint property theory about the territories and the imperial view, or to
miss the analogy between the situation of Kansas in 1859 and that of
Virginia in 1772:

The people of Virginia at that day did not appreciate the force of the argument used by the British merchants, who were engaged in the African slave trade, and which was afterward indorsed, at least by implication, by the King and his Ministers; that the Colonies were the common property of the Empire—acquired by the common blood and treasure—and therefore all British subjects had the right to carry their slaves into the Colonies and hold them in defiance of the local law and in contempt of the wishes and safety of the Colonies.[16]

Douglas also endeavored to show that the *Dred Scott* decision did not forbid territorial legislatures from outlawing slavery, arguing rather unconvincingly that what Taney had in mind when he argued that what Congress could not do, and could not delegate, were forbidden powers such as denying the right to trial by jury, which were forbidden to the states as much as to Congress and to the territorial legislatures. But here the argument took an interesting turn. Douglas argued that if Taney's dictum *did* refer to anything other than these obviously forbidden powers, then Seward and Lincoln were correct in arguing that the *Dred Scott* decision must ultimately result in forcing slavery back into the free states:

If this sweeping prohibition—this just but inexorable restriction upon the powers of government—Federal, State, and Territorial—shall ever be held to include the slavery question, thus negativing the right of the people of the States and Territories, as well as the Federal Government, to control it by law (and it will be observed that in the opinion of the Court "the citizens of a Territory, so far as these rights are concerned, are on the same footing with the citizens of the States"), then, indeed, will the doctrine become firmly established that the principles of law applicable to African slavery are uniform throughout the dominion of the United States, and that there "is an irrepressible conflict between opposing and enduring forces, which means that the United States must and will, sooner or later, become either entirely a slaveholding nation or entirely a free labor nation."[17]

What is striking here is how Douglas appropriated the arguments Lincoln had made against him in the "House Divided" speech, and turned them for use against Buchanan. Now there is some of Douglas's usual sleight of hand in this: he treated what Taney actually meant as if it were just a misinterpretation of the chief justice's text by Buchanan and his followers. One wonders who could have been fooled by this. It is also worth noting that what Lincoln had presented as a conspiracy charge, Douglas presented as a reductio ad absurdum: Buchanan's interpretation of the *Dred Scott* decision cannot be right, because if territories cannot deprive slaveholders of their slave property, then the states cannot do so either, and the Republic will have to become either all slaveholding or all free. Since the conclusion, slavery becoming national, seemed to Douglas to be absurd, the premise, that territorial legislatures cannot prohibit slavery, must be false.

Douglas's argument needs to be parsed carefully. He cannot actually have believed that the idea of slavery becoming national was really unthinkable, because he himself had accused the administration's organ, the *Washington Union* (and, although he denied this implication, through the *Union* the administration itself) of entertaining precisely the ambition to nationalize slavery. And of course he had himself been fending off exactly the same charge from Lincoln all through the summer of 1858. The key step is the connection between the rejection of territorial power over slavery and the nationalization of slavery: if you reject territorial power over slavery, then you must also support a federal slave code, and you cannot support a federal slave code without nationalizing slavery, but, since nationalizing slavery is absurd, rejection of territorial power over slavery must also be absurd. What Douglas proposed here was not so much an argument as a threat: if you, President Buchanan, reject popular sovereignty in the territories over slavery, you will persuade me that you really do have in mind to nationalize slavery, and I may not join the Republicans, who also reject popular sovereignty in the territories over slavery, but I will make common cause with them and will argue that their reading of your motives is correct.

Douglas inched up to the very kinds of argument and evidence that the Republicans had been using. Indeed, he seemed to be paraphrasing Lincoln from the Alton debate:

> If the proposition be true, that the Constitution establishes slavery in the Territories beyond the power of the people legally to control it, another result, no less startling, and from which there is no es-

cape, must inevitably follow. The Constitution is uniform "everywhere within the dominions of the United States"—is the same in Pennsylvania as in Kansas—and if it be true, as stated by the President in a special Message to Congress, "that slavery exists in Kansas by virtue of the Constitution of the United States," and that "Kansas is therefore at this moment as much a slave State as Georgia or South Carolina," why does it not exist in Pennsylvania by virtue of the same Constitution?[18]

Perhaps most startling of all is the way in which Douglas seized upon the phrase "subject only to the Constitution of the United States." This, it must be remembered, was Douglas's *own* phrase from the Kansas-Nebraska Act, and Lincoln had in the "House Divided" speech argued that it was evidence that the scheme to nationalize slavery had been in Douglas's mind from before the beginning of the debates over the Kansas-Nebraska Act. Of course the first thing that might have occurred to skeptics about the slave power conspiracy theory is that there is still quite some distance between forbidding a territory to abolish slavery and requiring the free states to reestablish it. It was to bridge this gap that Lincoln built his conspiratorial interpretation of the "subject to the Constitution" phrase. Douglas used the same interpretation for the same purpose, as if he were not himself the author of that phrase:

> The question recurs then, if the Constitution does establish slavery in Kansas or any other Territory beyond the power of the people to control it by law, how can the conclusion be resisted that slavery is established in like manner and by the same authority in all the States of the Union? And if it be the imperative duty of Congress to provide by law for the protection of slave property in the Territories upon the ground that "slavery exists in Kansas" (and consequently in every other Territory), "by virtue of the Constitution of the United States," why is it not also the duty of Congress, for the same reason, to provide similar protection to slave property in all the States of the Union, when the Legislatures fail to furnish such protection?[19]

Douglas proceeded to attack a key element of the slaveholder argument, the proposition that property in slaves is property like any other. Douglas could have adopted Lincoln's strategy, quoting the

indirect and evasive language of the Constitution about slavery to
show that slavery was not "distinctly and expressly affirmed in the Constitution." Douglas instead argued that if it were true that the Constitution does not distinguish between property in slaves and other kinds of
property, it is true mostly because the Constitution leaves laws concerning property up to the states. But the Constitution does provide special
recognition to slavery in one particular, in its fugitive slave clause. However, this recognition, Douglas argues, amounts to less than it might
seem, because although the euphemistic language about "persons held
to service or labor in one State under the laws thereof" would in
Douglas's eyes fool nobody, that language itself concedes that slavery
is only a state matter, "*under the laws thereof*—not under the Constitution of the United States, nor by the laws thereof, nor by virtue of any
Federal authority whatsoever, but under the laws of the particular
State where such service or labor may be due" (106). More than treating slavery as a matter of state concern, the fugitive slave clause also
specifies that the only federal duty concerning slavery is to assert that
states have the duty to return fugitive slaves who come to them from
other states.

Douglas's interpretation of the fugitive slave clause turned a familiar
pro-slavery argument upon its head. Northerners had often been talked
into accepting unsavory things—the fugitive slave clause itself, for instance, particularly in the ruthless and brutal way it was interpreted in
Prigg v. Pennsylvania—by the argument that had the authors of the
Constitution not conceded those things, they could never have persuaded Georgia and South Carolina to ratify the Constitution. Douglas
argued that the free states (well, the one free state at that time, Massachusetts, but in fact many of the other states of the North, although
nominally slave states in 1787, expected to abolish slavery soon) would
not have ratified the Constitution had it been their understanding that
that document would force slavery upon them.

Further, even if the Constitution had specified a federal duty to protect slavery, Douglas argued, the slave states would have been wary
about it, because a federal government that had the power to protect
slavery would also (like a federal government with the power to invest
in internal improvements or to impose a protective tariff) have the power
to do slavery harm: "under pretense of protection and regulation, . . .
under the influence of the strong and increasing anti-slavery sentiment

which prevailed at that period, [it] might destroy the institution, and divest those rights of property in slaves which were sacred under the laws and constitutions of their respective States so long as the Federal Government had no power to interfere with the subject."[20]

The reader will notice that Douglas's argument here is a version of the argument I proposed in Chapter 7 to the effect that if the Supreme Court were, in a hypothetical decision in the *Lemmon* case, to decide that slavery is a federal rather than a state matter, then that victory for the slave power might ultimately be dearly bought, since it would hand opponents of slavery a weapon.

Douglas concluded his article with a detailed recounting of the debates over the popular sovereignty provisions during the deliberations over the Compromise of 1850 and over the Kansas-Nebraska Act. Now it had long been maintained that there was ambiguity in the language of the Compromise of 1850 about when the territories were to decide the fate of slavery, whether they could do so during the territorial stage or only at the point of admission to the Union as states. But Douglas cited relatively unambiguous language from Henry Clay and from Lewis Cass that makes it clear that they understood popular sovereignty the way he does, as something the territorial legislatures could legally exercise.

Douglas also argued that the legislative history of the Compromise of 1850 makes clear that the ambiguity about when the territories are to decide the slavery question for themselves is a later confection. The Committee of Thirteen, which Clay was persuaded against his better judgment by Henry Foote to appoint to tie all of the compromise bills together in one package, had originally reported language forbidding the territorial legislatures from writing any laws about slavery at all, whether for or against, to which Davis and Chase had proposed further amendments forbidding the territories from outlawing slavery or from permitting it. (Chase's entry was the infamous "Chase Amendment" discussed in Chapter 3.) Ultimately all of this language was struck from the bill, and the territorial legislatures were given power over "all rightful subjects of legislation consistent with the Constitution of the United States," a power that, Douglas noted, made no exception of the subject of slavery.

Douglas was probably right that his is the most plausible interpretation of the bill, particularly since language supporting the joint property theory about slavery in the territories was explicitly struck from the bill. Indeed, in the summer of 1858, anti-Douglas supporters of slavery referred to this very thing, the act of striking this language in 1850, in an effort to prove that Douglas had been a covert Free Soiler all along, as we saw in Chapter 3.

Douglas, finally, recapped the arguments over the same issues during the debates over the Kansas-Nebraska Act. Again, the most plausible interpretation of the language Douglas cites is his own:

> From these provisions it is apparent that the Compromise Measures of 1850 affirm and rest upon the following propositions:
>
> "First.—That all questions pertaining to slavery in the Territories, and in the new States to be formed therefrom, are to be left to the decision of the people residing therein, by their appropriate representatives to be chosen by them for that purpose.
>
> "Second.—That all cases involving title to slaves and questions of personal freedom, are referred to the adjudication of the local tribunals, with the right of appeal to the Supreme Court of the United States.
>
> "Third.—That the provision of the Constitution of the United States in respect to fugitives from service, is to be carried into faithful execution in all the organized Territories, the same as in the States. The substitute for the bill which your Committee have prepared, and which is commended to the favorable action of the Senate, proposes to carry these propositions and principles into practical operation, in the precise language of the Compromise Measures of 1850."[21]

Two comments are necessary about this language from the Kansas-Nebraska Act. First, what the first paragraph refers to as the "appropriate representatives [of the people of a territory] to be chosen by them for that purpose" would seem broad enough to include both the territorial legislature and the territorial constitutional convention, allowing the legislature to prohibit slavery and allowing the convention to write that prohibition into the constitution of the state at the time it applies for admission to the Union. The Buchaneer interpretation of this language, that it referred only to the constitutional convention and forbade the territorial legislatures from deciding "questions pertaining to slavery," can be maintained only by torturing the meaning of the phrase "appropriate representatives" so as to mean only the delegates to the constitutional convention. This reading is very strained, but the slave power and the Buchanan administration lacked only a few votes of making that interpretation into the rule. And it is possible that some southern representatives explained their votes for the Kansas-Nebraska Act to their constituents by resorting to the same interpretation, so a case can be made that their view too is part of the meaning of the act, although it still seems to be, to say the least, a rather far-fetched case.

Second, although the second paragraph has long been received as punting the question of the constitutional status of the territorial legislature's control over slavery to the Supreme Court (as demanding, in other words, what Taney provided in his dictum in the *Dred Scott* decision), at first blush what the paragraph seems to mean is that the territorial courts shall have the same kind of power over cases involving slavery and freedom that state courts have, and that parties to those cases will have recourse to the same kinds of appeal to higher courts that parties to state cases do.

The chief aim of Douglas's "Dividing Line" article was to maintain that the Freeport Doctrine was only a fallback position, and that historical precedents going back to before the Revolution supported the idea that territorial legislatures should have power over slavery. Douglas partly intended this argument for use against the Republicans. But the main thrust of the article is clearly against the joint property theory of Calhoun and Davis. To the supporters of the joint property theory Douglas also threw down a gauntlet: if they successfully drive the doctrine of popular sovereignty out of the public square, they give color even in Douglas's eyes to the worst charges made against them by the Republicans, that they seek to nationalize slavery. Douglas knew that the defenders of slavery could not control the political arena without winning the support of some significant fraction of the northern Democratic Party. His argument, and his threat, is aimed at persuading a significant fraction of the southern Democracy that pressing the joint sovereignty theory would lose them the sympathy of northern Democrats, and bring about the collapse of the Democratic Party, with disastrous consequences for the slaveholders if the slaveholders sought any future within the Union. Douglas hoped to make southern Democrats think twice before adopting a suicidal strategy. But the southern Democrats he was attempting to awaken were already being crushed to atoms by the pressures of loyalty politics in the South that were only bound to increase.

8.3 The Pamphlet War with Jeremiah Black

The Buchanan administration's response to the "Dividing Line" article came almost immediately, in the form of an article in the *Washington Constitution*, the administration organ, on September 10, 1859.[22] The article was published anonymously, although nobody doubted that the author was Jeremiah S. Black, Buchanan's attorney general.

Black began by denying that the Buchanan administration had ever claimed, as Douglas said it did, that the Constitution establishes slavery in the territories. But he went on to assert nearly the same thing by arguing that natural law holds that the status of a slave as a slave remains with him when he is transported from a slave state to a territory. It is a different question, said Black, when that slave is transported to a free state, where there is positive law against slavery; but there can be no positive law against slavery either from the federal government or from the territorial legislature, so therefore a slave taken into a territory remains a slave. The effect of Black's argument is that slavery is national, and freedom is local. Notice how breezily he swept away the *Somerset* precedent without even so much as mentioning it:

> It is an axiomatic principle of public law that a right of property, a private relation, condition, or status, lawfully existing in one State or country, is not changed by the mere removal of the parties to another country, unless the law of that other country be in direct conflict with it. For instance: A marriage legally solemnized in France is binding in America; children born in Germany are legitimate here if they are legitimate there; and a merchant who buys goods in New York according to the laws of that State may carry them to Illinois and hold them there under his contract. It is precisely so with the status of a negro carried from one part of the United States to another; the question of his freedom or servitude depends on the law of the place where he came from, and depends on that alone, if there be no conflicting law at the place to which he goes or is taken. The federal Constitution, therefore, recognizes slavery as a legal condition wherever the local governments have chosen to let it stand unabol-

ished, and regards it as illegal wherever the laws of the place have forbidden it. A slave being property in Virginia, remains property; and his master has all the rights of a Virginia master wherever he may go, so that he go not to any place where the local law comes in conflict with his right. It will not be pretended that the Constitution itself furnishes to the Territories a conflicting law. It contains no provision that can be tortured into any semblance of a prohibition.[23]

Black's argument, which uses the logic of transit and sojourning cases, gives some color to the fear Lincoln had expressed in the 1858 debates that these kinds of Fifth Amendment arguments about property could lead to the nationalization of slavery. And it is precisely this broadening of focus from a mere concern with slaves in transit to a full-blown slave economy that was to be feared from the *Lemmon* case, which likewise turned on its face only on a question of transit with slaves.

Black never quite went that far, since he never attacked the power of the free states to pass laws abolishing slavery, and indeed built his whole case on the right of the states to do what they pleased about slavery. But the property logic of Black's article must have seemed, to Douglas as much as to Republican exponents of the slave power conspiracy theory, to demand the extension. Black does not seem to have had in mind such an extension, and the arguments he made about the states' powers demonstrate that he would have opposed it. But his arguments about state power and his arguments about property rights were at odds with each other, and it is not beyond imagination to see how some later generation might have resolved that contradiction.

Further, Black argued, the question of whether the territorial government can abolish slavery has already been answered by the Supreme Court, and therefore Douglas's opposition to Taney's dictum amounts to a Garrison-style assault upon the Constitution as a covenant with death and an agreement with hell. Echoing an argument that Lincoln himself had made, Black argued that Douglas could not, were he to be elected to the presidency, honestly swear to support the Constitution if he supported the Freeport Doctrine as a way to subvert the *Dred Scott* decision:

In former times, a question of Constitutional law once decided by the Supreme Court was regarded as settled by all, except that little

band of ribald infidels, who meet periodically at Boston to blaspheme
the religion and plot rebellion against the laws of the country. The
leaders of the so-called Republican party have lately been treading
close on the heels of their abolition brethren; but it is devoutly to be
hoped that Mr. Douglas has no intention to follow their example. In
case he is elected President, he must see the laws faithfully executed.
Does he think he can keep that oath by fighting the Judiciary?[24]

Black also interpreted the meaning of the Kansas-Nebraska Act with
legerdemain. If, he argued, there is no slavery except where the local
law establishes it explicitly, if, that is to say, the default state is freedom,
then the Kansas-Nebraska Act would have been a snare for the slave
states, since until the territorial legislature writes laws to the contrary,
it would be illegal for slaveholders to go to the territory, and the legislature that decides the fate of slavery in the territories would have to be
made up entirely of nonslaveholders, exactly as if the Missouri Compromise restriction had remained in effect. Southern Democrats, says
Black, would never have voted for this law if they had thought that this
was what it meant, and they do not in fact think this is what it meant.
(Douglas made pretty clear in his "Dividing Line" article, however,
that that is indeed what *he* thought his own language meant.)

Like Buchanan, Black denied territorial legislatures control over
slavery because territories are not states. Like Buchanan, he conceded
the right of state constitutional conventions to make up their own minds
over slavery. Like Buchanan, he was willing to treat the Lecompton
Convention's constitution as the legitimate expression of the people's
will in Kansas, and opposed Douglas's demand for a popular ratification vote on the Lecompton Constitution as a whole. Like Buchanan,
he accepted the Lecompton Convention's loaded ratification vote about
only the slavery clauses of the Lecompton Constitution, in which either outcome would have ensured that Kansas would become a slave
state, as all the popular ratification the Lecompton Constitution would
need to have in order to count as an expression of the will of the people
of Kansas about slavery. But also like Buchanan, Black later allowed
Kansas to become a state under the anti-slavery Wyandotte Constitution in the closing days of the Buchanan administration, when the
secession of the Deep South had removed the most serious obstacles.
Whether Black would have insisted upon the recognition of the

Wyandotte Constitution had the Deep South's representatives tried to block it, however, is an open question.

Black treated Douglas's insistence that the territorial legislature has power over the future of slavery as if it were a species of enthusiasm, rather like abolitionism. And he picked up the threat that Douglas had laid down in the "Dividing Line" article. When Douglas argued that insistence upon the joint sovereignty theory would give color to the Republicans' slave power conspiracy theory, hinting that it would make him too find that theory plausible, Black took him as hinting that his real sympathies were with Seward and Lincoln, and not with the majority of his own party.

Black made merry with Douglas's distinction between powers the federal government can exercise but not delegate and powers the federal government can delegate but not exercise, but he completely misrepresented the argument, perhaps because he did not care to figure out what Douglas meant by it. Black imagined that Douglas meant that *anything* forbidden to the federal government, such as making ex post facto laws, or laws impairing the obligation of contracts, would be permitted to territorial governments.

More seriously, Black conceded that there are some powers the federal government bestows but does not exercise because they are judicial or executive powers, but he went on to argue that territorial power over slavery is not such a power, because it is not a violation of the separation of powers, such as pretending that Congress has judicial powers, but a forbidden power, like hanging a man without trial, because abolishing slavery involves taking people's property without compensation. Here Black proved too much, because if it is forbidden to a territorial legislature to abolish slavery because that is a taking of private property without compensation, it is equally forbidden to a state government. Without intending to, Black here as elsewhere gives color to the most outlandish suspicions entertained by the Republicans.

Black concluded his article by citing a series of cases in which Douglas did not hold the doings of territorial legislatures in the high reverence he professed in the "Dividing Line" article. Most of the examples seem to be loaded, and will not stand detailed examination. For instance, Black cited a speech Douglas gave in New Orleans in which he praised the *Dred Scott* decision (but Black did not note that Douglas did not treat Taney's dictum about territorial governments as one of

the holdings of that decision). He quoted Douglas's attacks upon the
Topeka government (which was not a territorial legislature, but a state
legislature in waiting) and his attack on the Lecompton legislature's
plan to submit the Lecompton Constitution directly to Congress
without any popular ratification (an act of a territorial legislature, to be
sure, but one subversive of popular sovereignty). Black cited Douglas's
opinion, given during the 1857 "Mormon War" between the Mormon
settlers in Utah and the federal government about control over the
territorial adminstration, that the organic act establishing the Utah
territorial government should be repealed (an attack on a territorial
government—Lincoln made this argument against Douglas as well—
but a territorial government at the point of war with the United States).
Black proposed a theory about what ties Douglas's changes of front
together: "These views of his, inconsistent as they are with one another,
always *happen* to accord with the interests of the Opposition, always give
to the enemies of the Constitution a certain amount of 'aid and com-
fort,' and always add a little to the rancorous and malignant hatred with
which the abolitionists regard the Government of their own country."[25]
When during the Alton debate Lincoln, apropos of the Freeport Doctrine, observed, "Why, there is not such an Abolitionist in the nation as
Douglas, after all," he was making a sharp-edged joke. But Black apparently intended the same charge in all seriousness.

Douglas replied in detail to Black's article in his speech at Wooster,
Ohio, on September 16, and in a series of increasingly vituperative and
repetitive pamphlets. In both he denied attacking the Supreme Court
over the *Dred Scott* decision, which he could fairly do inasmuch as he
had aggressively interpreted that decision to suit his own views rather
than attacking it outright. And he denied that allowing the territorial
legislatures to outlaw slavery amounts to confiscation of private property. He went on to note that if the act of a territorial legislature to
outlaw slavery amounts to a forbidden seizure of private property, then
the same thing is true of the emancipation acts of all of the free states
too (as Lincoln had been arguing about the same subject).

Douglas had, over the first few months of 1859, been cautious about
pressing the Freeport Doctrine and about clarifying his position about
the powers of territorial legislatures. Southern Democrats who still
cherished realistic ideas about what it would take for them to continue
to dominate the national agenda—the support of a major northern

figure—had been looking for a way to support Douglas, and his argument, that they could not have their way nationally without the support of his faction, which would never allow slavery to be forced upon the territories, was more than plausible. Conservative Republicans and ex-Whigs cautiously looked to popular sovereignty in the territories, particularly if supported also by elections for territorial governors and judges (so that pro-slavery officials could not be forced upon the territories by the federal government), as a strategy to secure the territories for freedom without endangering the Union.[26] Douglas had hoped that his "Dividing Line" article would persuade the former to stick with him, even if popular sovereignty were still a bitter pill for them. And as regards the latter, he had hoped also that the article might—without himself becoming a Republican—peel away enough in the way of conservative Republican votes to rebuild the fortunes of the Democratic Party in the North. Although his arguments did, surprisingly, win the endorsement of Reverdy Johnson, who had argued the pro-slavery side of the *Dred Scott* case, thus winning at least some traction for his claim that his interpretation of the decision was more accurate than Buchanan's, the controversy over his "Dividing Line" article persuaded none of his enemies in the South, and damaged the position of his friends.[27] By the time the pamphlet war with Black had concluded, Douglas's hold on southern moderates had weakened; their loyalty probably depended not upon Douglas making a case for his views, but upon his maintaining a discreet silence, something his Buchaneer opponents would not have let him keep up for long and something that was not in his nature anyway. Meanwhile, Lincoln's campaign in Ohio, following each of Douglas's engagements by a few days, was destroying Douglas's position with Republican moderates.

8.4 The 1859 Ohio "Lincoln-Douglas Debates"

Lincoln's Columbus Speech

The Ohio Republican Party invited Lincoln to speak because the Democrats had invited Douglas. The cause of the Democrats was nearly hopeless in Ohio, so the state party leaders had nothing to lose, and perhaps something to gain, by choosing Douglas over the national party leadership. That said, Buchanan's supporters were nonplussed, and Douglas's supporters worried that he might widen the breach with the national party. What they wanted him to do was to reach out to the former Whigs and to conservative Republicans, as he had in Illinois. They did not want him to engage his intraparty opposition, with whom they were still trying to keep on good terms. Lincoln was the natural person to reply to Douglas, and the texts of their debates the previous year had been reprinted in newspapers all over the country. (Indeed, the first book publication of the Lincoln-Douglas debates was prepared under the auspices of Ohio Republicans, which is why it included Lincoln's Ohio speeches as well as the Illinois debate texts.)

The Republicans who invited Lincoln to Ohio, like those who would invite him to New York to give the Cooper Union speech the next year, perhaps had a local agenda in mind as well. As Lincoln's New York hosts intended their invitation to Lincoln to be a way to put a thumb in the eye of Seward, so his Ohio hosts seem to have intended their invitation of Lincoln as a rebuke to Chase. The anti-slavery Republicans of Ohio were made of far sterner stuff than their Illinois counterparts, and they were led by the once-rivals Joshua Giddings and Salmon Chase. But as in Illinois, anti-slavery convictions in Ohio generally grew weaker (except once one reached the area around Oberlin) as one moved south from the Western Reserve, a cultural province of New England, to Hamilton County in the Ohio Valley, where there were strong cultural and economic ties to Kentucky and where the opponents to the Democrats were simply called the Opposition Party, not the Republican Party, in deference to the followers of the not-quite-dead American Party, who were still a force in that region.

Lincoln had followed events in Ohio with apprehension. Lincoln in Illinois had always been cautious about challenging the Fugitive Slave Act, for several reasons: because he felt a fugitive slave act of one kind or another had been promised in the Constitution, and because direct resistance to the Fugitive Slave Act risked making the Republicans appear to be anarchists, seeking to break laws they did not have the political power to change. Ohio Republicans, inspired by the Oberlin-Wellington fugitive slave rescue in September 1858, had added a denunciation of the Fugitive Slave Act to their state platform at their convention, an act that moved Lincoln, worried about the effect this plank might have on the prospects for the party nationally, to write directly to Chase on June 9 to complain about it. On July 6 Lincoln wrote to Schuyler Colfax, arguing that Ohio's "tilting against the Fugitive Slave law" (Lincoln's verb implies that the act is quixotic) would "utterly overwhelm us in Illinois with the charge of enmity to the constitution itself" (2:25–26).

When the federal authorities arrested the Oberlin rescuers, the state authorities arrested the federal marshal, and Ohio and the United States issued dueling habeas corpus petitions calling for the release of the rescuers and of the marshal who arrested them. Only two of the rescuers ultimately were convicted, and after they received light sentences, they appealed to the Ohio Supreme Court on the grounds that the Fugitive Slave Act was unconstitutional. By a single vote the Ohio court declined the invitation to confront the federal government. The deciding justice, Chief Justice Joseph Swan, although an opponent of slavery and indeed one of the founders of the Republican Party in Ohio, ruled that it was not in an Ohio court's power to decide whether or not a federal law was constitutional. Justice Swan's renomination was rejected at the state convention. The rejection of Swan, whose position, after all, was Lincoln's own, galled Lincoln almost as much as the fugitive slave plank did, and he wrote to Samuel Galloway, an Ohio friend, to complain about it. Douglas made hay at his Cincinnati speech on September 8 about the Swan case, since the removal of Judge Swan seemed to be motivated by something akin to nullification:

> Now, my friends, what safety or security is there for a citizen who is not willing to abide by the law and the constituted authorities. The only alternative is mob law and violence. You have had a specimen of that upon the Fugitive Slave Law. A political party has arisen which declares that their consciences will not permit them to obey and execute any law which they disapprove of. Did you ever find a lawbreaker who approved the law that imposed penalty upon him? Whenever you allow a man to interpose his conscience against the law of the land, your law is subverted and all constitutional authority is destroyed.[28]

Lincoln's task in the Ohio campaign was, as it had been in Illinois, to argue that popular sovereignty was not a safe strategy for Republicans, even if it had played out against slavery in Kansas. In Illinois he had begun to make this case by pressing a fanciful conspiracy charge against Douglas, but by the time of the Alton debate his strategy had

shifted to rely upon the argument that the failure of the popular sovereignty argument to make a moral case directly against slavery would
have a corroding effect upon the public mind, weakening its opposition to the revival of the African slave trade or to the adoption of a
federal slave code for the territories.

Since Douglas in point of fact had been campaigning against the
federal slave code, and since the alarm about the revival of the African
slave trade had been largely raised by Douglas himself, who reported
seeing newly landed slaves in Vicksburg and in Memphis in 1859, both
charges against Douglas are on their faces unfair ones.[29] But "public
mind" arguments often turn on cases where people lay the groundwork for consequences that are against their intentions. For instance,
Black had argued that territories could not abolish slavery because
they were not states, and abolition of slavery, with its consequent seizure of what he took to be private property, was something only states
could do. Black, this is to say, would not have conceded that his argument attacking emancipation laws in the territories was laying the
groundwork for an attack upon the emancipation laws of the free states.
But the private property argument he made against abolition in the
territories would be hard to confine only to the territories once its full
force was appreciated, and Douglas was right to argue that Black was
indeed, despite himself, clearing the way for the nationalization of
slavery. Similarly, Douglas's argument in 1854 that the popular sovereignty provisions of the Compromise of 1850 had changed the rules,
and made possible a policy that was at least uniform for all the territories rather than a patchwork policy in which each territory had a different rule depending upon who was in the political ascendency when
the territory's enabling act was written, was a public mind argument of
the same kind, holding that even those who in the 1850 debates had supported popular sovereignty only for Utah and New Mexico, and never
dreamed of applying the same rule to Kansas and Nebraska (and would
have opposed the 1850 measure had they thought it might be so applied),
played a part in the evolution of the Kansas-Nebraska Act.

Public mind arguments are versions of what I have been calling arguments from implicitness, in that they depend upon the notion that
an idea has an inner life to which even those who act upon their basis
are not always completely privy. Now both of Douglas's arguments,
and Lincoln's as well, could be dismissed as mere slippery slope arguments. But the fact that criticism of the "glittering generalities" of the

Declaration of Independence had spread beyond the confines of South Carolina eccentrics to become a widely held conviction all over the South shows that Lincoln had a point. Douglas did not share this view of the Declaration, but the view he did hold, that its promises apply only to whites, stands in the same relationship toward the Calhounite critique of the Declaration that Black's states' rights critique of popular sovereignty does to the nationalization of slavery. Both were instances of how the implications of ideas could overrun the intentions of those who articulated them.

Lincoln had first developed these public mind arguments in the Peoria speech, and returned to them in the later stages of the 1858 debates. But he made the argument more acutely and persuasively in the Ohio campaign, because he cleared away the conspiracy theory he had embraced in the "House Divided" speech. Lincoln gave a succinct statement of the new form of his argument in a speech in Chicago on March 1, 1859:

> The Republican principle, the profound central truth that slavery is wrong and ought to be dealt with as a wrong, though we are always to remember the fact of its actual existence amongst us and faithfully observe all the constitutional guarantees—the unalterable principle never for a moment to be lost sight of that it is a wrong and ought to be dealt with as such, cannot advance at all upon Judge Douglas' ground—that there is a portion of the country in which slavery must always exist; that he does not care whether it is voted up or voted down, as it is simply a question of dollars and cents. Whenever, in any compromise or arrangement or combination that may promise some temporary advantage, we are led upon that ground, then and there the great living principle upon which we have organized as a party is surrendered. The proposition now in our minds that this thing is wrong being once driven out and surrendered, then the institution of slavery necessarily becomes national. (2:15)

At Chicago, Lincoln had provided an example of how such a surrender would work:

> You all remember that at the last session of Congress there was a measure introduced in the Senate by Mr. Crittenden, which proposed that the pro-slavery Lecompton constitution should be left to

a vote to be taken in Kansas, and if it and slavery were adopted Kansas should be at once admitted as a slave State. That same measure was introduced into the House by Mr. Montgomery, and therefore got the name of the Crittenden-Montgomery bill; and in the House of Representatives the Republicans all voted for it under the peculiar circumstances in which they found themselves placed. You may remember also that the New York *Tribune*, which was so much in favor of our electing Judge Douglas to the Senate of the United States, has not yet got through the task of defending the Republican party, after that one vote in the House of Representatives, from the charge of having gone over to the doctrine of popular sovereignty. Now, just how long would the New York *Tribune* have been in getting rid of the charge that the Republicans had abandoned their principles, if we had taken up Judge Douglas, adopted all his doctrines and elected him to the Senate, when the single vote upon that one point so confused and embarrassed the position of the Republicans that it has kept the *Tribune* one entire year arguing against the effect of it? (2:14–15)

This is a very peculiar interpretation of the Crittenden-Montgomery bill, which was hardly, as Lincoln described it here, a way to put the Lecompton Constitution into effect, and was in fact received not only by Douglas but by the congressional Republicans as a very effective way to put the Lecompton fraud down. Without the alliance around the Crittenden-Montgomery bill, it is more than conceivable that administration pressure would have peeled away enough of Douglas's supporters to impose the Lecompton Constitution over his opposition.

Lincoln was in most circumstances a pragmatic politician. In denouncing the Crittenden-Montgomery bill as a surrender of principle, Lincoln found himself in the unusual position of being among those who demand that God's will be done though the heavens fall. Perhaps he was swayed by hostility to Crittenden, whose support in 1858 put Douglas over the top with former Whigs in Illinois, and by hostility to Greeley, who had suggested that a Douglas victory in Illinois might not be so bad an outcome. But perhaps Lincoln also could not distinguish between making common cause with Douglas on this and other particular issues, on one hand, and surrendering the leadership of the Republican Party to Douglas or abandoning its primary hostility to slavery, on the other. Surely the Republicans in Congress were wise to support the Crittenden-Montgomery bill, especially since failure to do so would have opened them to the charge (made also against them at the time of the Toombs bill) of simply seeking to keep the conflict alive for political advantage.[30] And, no matter what Lincoln said here, surely the general public were still pretty certain that the Republicans had not all suddenly been transformed into anti-Lecompton Democrats by cutting a deal with them over the Crittenden-Montgomery bill.

Historians of James G. Randall's generation saw the failure to make this distinction between *working with* Douglas and *surrendering to* Douglas as a sign of a destructive purism on Lincoln's part, as a way to rule out every strategy other than naked confrontation. But there is some difference between accepting pragmatic arrangements among imperfect allies in Congress and supporting that imperfect ally for president when better alternatives are available and electable. In office, Lincoln was perfectly willing to deal with Douglas, and, after his death, with his supporters. But that does not mean that he had to wish that Douglas were in the Oval Office rather than himself.

In Columbus on September 16, pressing the case that the *Dred Scott* decision prepares the way for the nationalization of slavery, Lincoln backed away from an explicit conspiracy theory, and conceded that the nationalization of slavery may not even have been in Chief Justice Taney's focal attention:

> That decision lays down principles, which, if pushed to their logical conclusion—I say, pushed to their logical conclusion—would decide that the constitutions of the Free States, forbidding slavery, are themselves unconstitutional. Mark me, I do not say the judge said this, and let no man say that I affirm the judge used these words; but I only say it is my opinion that what they did say, if pressed to its logical conclusion, will inevitably result thus. (2:35)

Lincoln did not imagine here that the nationalization of slavery was imminent, or that the African slave trade would soon be revived, or even that a federal slave code was in the offing. But all of those things would be easier, he argued, if Douglas's version of popular sovereignty prevailed, because his version of popular sovereignty was a species of moral indifference.

Lincoln assumed that Douglas adopted this moral neutrality about slavery because he thought that the slavery question was a trivial one. When Douglas claimed that "I don't care" whether slavery is voted up or voted down in Kansas, he meant, in Lincoln's view, not that slavery was an issue that, however important, was not his to decide for the people of Kansas because the decision should belong to them, but that slavery was an issue too minor for Douglas to care about.

Much of the Columbus speech was an attack upon Douglas's "Dividing Line" article, which Lincoln often referred to as his "copyright essay," because Douglas had taken the unusual step of copyrighting it, which prevented other periodicals from reprinting it. Lincoln argued, incorrectly, that the dividing line to which Douglas referred divides small matters from great ones, leaving only the former to the judgment of the states and the territories:

> According to his Popular Sovereignty, the general government may give to the territories governors, judges, marshals, secretaries, and all the other chief men to govern them, but they must not touch upon this other question. Why? The question of who shall be governor of a territory for a year or two, and pass away, without his track being left upon the soil, or an act which he did for good or for evil being left behind, is a question of vast national magnitude. It is so much opposed in its nature to locality, that the nation itself must decide it; while this other matter of planting slavery upon a soil—a thing which once planted cannot be eradicated by the succeeding millions who have as much right there as the first comers or if eradicated, not without infinite difficulty and a long struggle—he considers the power to prohibit it, as one of those little, local, trivial things that the nation ought not to say a word about; that it affects nobody save the few men who are there. (2:40–41)

In his restatement of Douglas's "don't care" position, Lincoln misconstrued Douglas's argument, as Harry Jaffa pointed out long ago. Lincoln assumed that Douglas argued that what is local is trivial, and can be left to state or territorial governments because it is not a weighty enough matter for the federal government to bother with. In fact Douglas's distinction was not between the minor and the major, but between what is inward-looking, and thus of local concern, however important, and what is outward-looking (such as foreign policy, or national policies such as the tariff). The territory is given responsibility over slavery in its own bailiwick not because it is a trivial matter, but because the people of the territory have the most stake in it one way or another, and therefore it is too important an issue to have somebody else decide it for them. To show that the territory itself has the most at stake in the slavery question, however, is not to show that the federal government has no stake in it as well, for clearly the outcome would change the balance of power in the federal government no matter what it was. But to capitalize upon this argument, the Republicans would have had to make a version of the joint property argument that they had long opposed.

Douglas also did not assume, exactly, that slavery is a matter of moral indifference. It is a matter of moral importance about which people violently disagree. Douglas's argument was not that the issue is so small that it can be left to the territorial government, but that it is a decision of such importance to the territory that only the territory itself should make it.

Douglas pressed this same point at Wooster on September 16 a little further, perhaps beyond the breaking point, arguing that how to interpret moral issues is entirely and only the business of those who are in a position to choose about them. Douglas presses beyond his main point, which is that people have moral agency only where they choose for themselves, which is defensible, to the idea that right and wrong themselves are completely open to choice and mean only what they are socially constructed to mean, which is not:

> It is no answer to this argument to say that slavery is an evil or a crime, and therefore the people should not be permitted to ruin themselves for inflicting such a curse upon them. It is the right of every people to judge for themselves whether it be an evil or not. It is their right to judge whether it be a crime. It is the right of every community to judge for themselves the character and nature of every institution it is proposed to adopt. Virginia has judged that question for herself, and decided in favor of slavery. You have judged it for yourselves and decided it against slavery. You each have the right to arrive at the conclusion to which you have come, and neither has any right to interfere with the other. So it is with the Territories.[31]

This flirtation with uncritical moral relativism wound up provoking a slanging match with a member of the audience:

> The doctrine of the Republicans is that you are free because you cannot help it. [Laughter and applause.] That you are free because Congress passed an act saying that you should be free. I thought that you were all free because you chose to be free. I thought that you prohibited slavery because you did not want it; but now we are told by the Republicans, "Oh, no; Ohio would be a slave State now but for the Ordinance of 1787, and would always have been a slave State but for that Ordinance." So in Illinois and Indiana and all of the Northwestern States, the people were so depraved that they would have had slavery if Congress had not interfered—this is the Republican doctrine. On the other hand I hold that Ohio derives her freedom from the glorious action of her own citizens, and Ohio will remain free just so long as her own citizens are true to the doctrine of popular sovereignty. [Cheers.] Whenever you become so depraved and degenerate that Congress can force either freedom or slavery on you, you do not deserve to be free any longer.
>
> [A voice, "Is slavery a Christian institution?"] I do not know of any tribunal on earth that can decide the question of the morality of slavery or any other institution. ["Good," and cheers.] I deal with slavery as a political question involving questions of public policy. I deal with slavery under the Constitution, and that is all I have to do with it. Allow me to tell you that when the Constitution was being framed, a party arose in the Convention demanding the instant prohibition of the African slave trade upon moral and religious grounds. [A voice, "That does not answer my question."]
>
> My dear sir, I take my own time to answer the question, and you ought to be very thankful that I did not rebuke your impertinence in interrupting me. [Cries of "Good," and applause.] The Convention which framed the Constitution decided that the slave trade might continue until the year 1808, from and after which time it was, and would be, abolished. Thus the moral and religious ground is waived under the Constitution, leaving each State to have it as long as it pleases and abolish it when it pleases. Now, sir, if the people of Ohio declare slavery to be a moral and religious evil, they have a right to decide this question for themselves; and if the people of Kentucky

believe that slavery is not a moral and religious evil, they have a right so to decide and so to construe it. You have no right to interfere with Kentucky, nor has Kentucky a right to interfere with you. ["Good."] And permit me to say that both States, having decided that question to suit themselves, let me warn you, judge not Kentucky, lest you be judged yourselves![32]

Douglas had a point here, although not the entire point, and it is not the point he at first appears to be making. The interlocutor took Douglas, when he said "I deal with slavery under the Constitution, and that is all I have to do with it," to argue that politics and morality are entirely separate worlds, and that morality is a private business that has no place in the public square. This defense of moral relativism would seem to be the point of his citation of Jesus's admonition to judge not, lest you be judged, an admonition quoted for a very different purpose in Lincoln's Second Inaugural. But there is another argument in the passage that is somewhat different from the cravenly relativist argument with which Douglas ended the exchange. His example about postponing the prohibition of the African slave trade, for instance, does not turn on moral relativism. What Douglas argued was that when at the Constitutional Convention those who favored an immediate end of the slave trade agreed to postpone doing so until 1808, they realized they could bring their moral convictions to the public square, but they could have their way there only to the extent they could persuade their opponents to go along with them, and that absent that kind of consent across ideological lines, they could not claim to have their way merely because they were morally right. Douglas's position here does not demand that he take a morally neutral stance about slavery any more than Lincoln's arguments about the Fugitive Slave Act demand the same from him. Both made arguments about the kinds of prudent compromises one has to make in order to give public effect to one's moral ideas. The issue between Lincoln and Douglas was not the difference between moral and amoral politics, but the difference between one set of prudential compromises about moral issues and another set. Lincoln used morally absolutist arguments against Douglas (either slavery is right or it is wrong, and therefore the Union must ultimately become either all slaveholding or all free), but those arguments do not render what his actual difference with Douglas was, because Lincoln was no

moral absolutist either, and on the Fugitive Slave Act and a host of other
issues made moral compromises different in degree but not in kind
from those made by Douglas. The issue was not that moral absolutism
is better than compromise, but that Douglas had made compromises
that gave away more than he had to. Further, the issue was also what
effect Douglas's compromises would have on his bargaining position
when he came to face further conflicts over the same issue.

The explicit version of the public mind argument that Lincoln made
in the Ohio campaign has to be wrong: it is hard to imagine that the
people of the free states would have tolerated a forced reintroduction
of slavery no matter how strenuously some Supreme Court even worse
than the Taney Court might have insisted upon it. But it is quite imaginable that following Douglas's route would cause one to sacrifice so
many of the argumentative resources at the disposal of the free states
that they would lose many marginal conflicts over slavery (over transit
and sojourning, for instance), and perhaps some big ones as well (over
slavery in New Mexico, for instance, about which Douglas's position,
and for that matter Lincoln's too, in 1861, was already beginning to
collapse).

To take the decision out of the hands of the people because it is too
important really is, in a way, to compromise their moral agency. At the
same time, to leave it entirely up to them would seem to imply that
what is right and wrong is strictly a social construction, with no meaning outside of the society within which it is constructed. Surely Douglas does not mean to imply that slavery is wrong only in societies that
do not have it anyway. What abominable practice could relativism of
this kind not be invoked to defend? Yet just as surely the opposite
view—this is what my reason has told me is morally necessary, and if
you do not see it the same way, we will have to come to blows if we really mean what we have to say—is fraught with problems as well. The
reason this question is an interesting one, the reason it is an unanswerable one, is that it teases apart two aspects of collective moral agency
that cannot stand being separated: what is moral is moral because it is
a deliverance of practical reason, but it has moral force because one
freely gives one's self to obey the laws reflection enables one to discover. But because I cannot will for other people, I must persuade
them if I am to have a moral effect upon them, and if I do not persuade
them, and resort to compulsion, we are no longer in the world of giv-

ing reasons but are instead in the world of force, a world dominated not by the one who has the most compelling arguments, but by the one who has the most powerful weapons. We cannot just choose our morals—or if we do, we are engaged in something other than morals—but we do not just deduce them for the world (and back up our view of things with rifles) either.[33]

Having made this moral critique of popular sovereignty, Lincoln went on to bring up a subtle political argument concerning the period before a territorial legislature is organized. Douglas had answered the objection that popular sovereignty gave the first handful of settlers the power to dictate the future to the many more people who would come into the territory later by arguing that popular sovereignty about slavery was to be put in place when popular sovereignty about anything else was, in other words, when a territorial legislature is organized by the enabling act. But there was still the question of what becomes of slaves brought into the territory before it reached the threshold of popular sovereignty. Lincoln's point that if there is no law at all on the subject before that time, then slavery may well be established de facto by the first settlers, who would have already so grafted slavery into the politics and culture of the territory that it would be extremely difficult to remove.

Now there are two possible answers to this. The first is that since slavery requires (in Douglas's view) positive local law to become legal, the default state of the unorganized territory is freedom. Douglas implied this often, as we have seen, but rarely said it in so many words, because doing so would have licensed the conclusion by slaveholders that the whole concept of popular sovereignty had been loaded against them from the beginning. And slavery had sometimes—as for instance in the Old Southwest—established itself without the benefit of law anyway, as Lincoln had pointed out as early as the Peoria speech.

The second answer is that before the enabling act, the territory is not legally open to white settlement anyway, and the first settlers would have to be illegal squatters. The term "squatter sovereignty" itself, indeed, had been coined by Calhoun in the 1840s to describe the state of affairs in Oregon before the enabling act by Congress establishing the territory. Calhoun meant that the spontaneous government set up by Oregon settlers before the enabling act allowed them to go there, a government that had cobbled together anti-slavery territorial laws on the basis of the laws of Iowa Territory and asked Congress to recognize them, was extralegal and thus not deserving of respect by Congress.

At Columbus, Lincoln took a new tack, asking who determines when a territory is ready for an enabling act. Douglas's answer was simple enough: Congress does. But if it is Congress that makes the decision, Lincoln argued, then Congress can in practical terms also load the dice for or against slavery, by postponing writing an enabling act until enough extralegal settlers are already in place to make sure that the tide will run in the direction Congress wishes:

> That is what all those who are for slavery want. They do not want Congress to prohibit slavery from coming into the new territories, and they don't want Popular Sovereignty to hinder it; and as Congress is to say when they are ready to be organized, all that the south has to do is to get Congress to hold off. Let Congress hold off until they are ready to be admitted as a State, and the south has all it wants in taking slavery into and planting it in all the territories that we now have, or hereafter may have. (2:44)

Lincoln only slightly changed the tack he had taken against the Freeport Doctrine in the Ohio debates. As in the Illinois debates, he argued that if something is legal in a territory, then it must be supported by the territorial legislature, else it amounts to the absurdity that *a thing may be lawfully driven away from where it has a lawful right to be* (2:51). He argued that Douglas had himself changed front in the face of the criticism his doctrine had received, no longer talking about excluding slavery in so many words so much as "controlling it as other property," leaving it to the reader to draw the implication that that "control" includes keeping that kind of property out of the territory entirely. Lincoln interpreted "controlling slave property as other property" to mean, properly speaking, only controlling it "in such a way that it would be the most valuable as property, and make it bear its just proportion in the way of burdens as property." He further argued that any "control" by the legislature that would not further the interests of slavery would unhesitatingly be ruled unconstitutional by the Supreme Court:

> Now, as to this indirect mode by "unfriendly legislation," all lawyers here will readily understand that such a proposition cannot be tolerated for a moment, because a legislature cannot indirectly do that

which it cannot accomplish directly. Then I say any legislation to control this property, as property, for its benefit as property, would be hailed by this Dred Scott Supreme Court, and fully sustained; but any legislation driving slave property out, or destroying it as property, directly or indirectly, will most assuredly, by that court, be held unconstitutional. (2:52)

This argument was wrong, and it arises out of a misconception about how the Freeport Doctrine was supposed to work that we discussed in Chapter 7. Douglas had replied to Lincoln's argument in advance in his own speech at Columbus on September 7. Douglas noted that the territorial legislature of Kansas, now controlled by the free staters, had already begun writing the kind of "unfriendly legislation" Douglas had been describing, and he expected that the Republicans would hardly oppose their efforts, which, of course, they did not. The legislature had repealed some of the most repellent acts its earlier incarnation had put in place, such as its law making denial that Kansas was a slave territory a felony offense, its law making assisting in the escape of a fugitive slave a capital crime, its attempt to prohibit any Free Soiler from sitting on a jury in any case involving slavery, and its law suppressing anti-slavery newspapers. At the same time, the legislature of New Mexico,[34] up to that time in free soil hands, passed a slave code to cover the handful of slaves in the territory, exercising the same authority on behalf of slavery that the Kansas legislature had exercised against it:

> The people of New Mexico, which Territory was organized in 1850, refused for many years to sanction or protect slavery, but about twelve months ago the legislature passed a law establishing a slave code for the Territory and protecting the institution in their midst. On the other hand, in the Territory of Kansas, which was organized in 1854, the first legislature that assembled passed a slave code and established slavery in the Territory, and that act remained on the statute books until the 9th day of February, 1858, when they passed another act in the following words:
>
> > *Be it enacted* That an act entitled "An Act to punish offences against slave property," which took effect on the 15th of September, 1855, be and the same is hereby repealed.

By that unfriendly legislation on the part of Kansas in repealing all laws providing for the protection of slave property, all laws punishing crimes against slave property, and all laws conferring jurisdiction upon the Courts to try men for offences against that kind of property, slavery has been and is excluded from the Territory; and by the slave code established in New Mexico about the time it was repealed in Kansas, slavery exists in the former Territory.[35]

Lincoln also at Columbus repeated the argument that Douglas's popular sovereignty position would have the effect of reviving the African slave trade:

The Judge says that the people of the territories have the right, by his principle, to have slaves, if they want them. Then I say that the people of Georgia have the right to buy slaves in Africa, if they want them, and I defy any man on earth to show any distinction between the two things—to show that the one is either more wicked or more unlawful; to show, on original principles, that one is better or worse than the other, or to show by the constitution, that one differs a whit from the other. (2:54)

This is the familiar argument concerning the public mind. Douglas had responded to it by claiming that the prohibition of the African slave trade was one of the compromises of the Constitution and was therefore constitutionally forbidden. As Lincoln went on to point out, Douglas was wrong about this—the compromise was to forbid the prohibition of the African slave trade until 1808, and to permit, but not require, prohibition after that date. The compromise had the force of prohibiting the African slave trade only because it was the general assumption at the time that the trade was wicked and would have to be stopped. But it was also the standing assumption of that era that slavery was wicked and would have ultimately to be abolished. Lincoln's argument about the decay of opposition to the African slave trade (which was only beginning to happen, and then only among the most radical southern elements) is plausible chiefly because his generation had watched the same thing happen to opposition to slavery itself.

Finally, Lincoln directly addressed Free Soil Democrats who thought of Douglas as providing a safe way to oppose the spread of slavery to the territories:

It is to be a part and parcel of this same idea, to say to men who want to adhere to the Democratic party, who have always belonged to that party, and are only looking about for some excuse to stick to it, but nevertheless hate slavery, that Douglas' Popular Sovereignty is as good a way as any to oppose slavery. They allow themselves to be persuaded easily in accordance with their previous dispositions, into this belief, that it is about as good a way of opposing slavery as any, and we can do that without straining our old party ties or breaking up old political associations. We can do so without being called negro worshippers. We can do that without being subjected to the jibes and sneers that are so readily thrown out in place of argument where no argument can be found; so let us stick to this Popular Sovereignty—this insidious Popular Sovereignty. Now let me call your attention to one thing that has really happened, which shows this gradual and steady debauching of public opinion, this course of preparation for the revival of the slave trade, for the territorial slave code, and the new Dred Scott decision that is to carry slavery into the free States. Did you ever five years ago, hear of anybody in the world saying that the negro had no share in the Declaration of National Independence; that it did not mean negroes at all; and when "all men" were spoken of negroes were not included?

I am satisfied that five years ago that proposition was not put upon paper by any living being anywhere. I have been unable at any time to find a man in an audience who would declare that he had ever known any body saying so five years ago. But last year there was not a Douglas popular sovereign in Illinois who did not say it. Is there one in Ohio but declares his firm belief that the Declaration of Independence did not mean negroes at all? I do not know how this is; I have not been here much; but I presume you are very much alike everywhere. Then I suppose that all now express the belief that the Declaration of Independence never did mean negroes. I call upon one of them to say that he said it five years ago. (2:56–57)

Notice that here, as always, it is the decay of the broadest interpretation of the Declaration of Independence that is the strongest evidence that the public mind has been debauched. The surprising turn in this passage is that Lincoln assumed that even Democrats would concede that the idea that the promises of the Declaration were extended only to white men was a new one. The assumption seems rather daring, since, given the racism of the era, Douglas's view would seem to be a more likely approximation of what most white people (and certainly what most Democrats) felt. Perhaps the truth of the matter is that all parties knew what the promises meant, but that there is a difference between knowing something and acknowledging it, and that these promises were understood in the grudging and halfhearted and rationalized way we always understand promises we are not strong enough to keep. This rather muddled attitude toward those promises, however, would seem to be something even the Republicans were not free of. But the audience in Columbus cheered Lincoln's remarks here, and clearly felt that Lincoln had scored a palpable hit in them. This clearly means that these moderate, mid-state Republicans, not just radicals from the Western Reserve, took it for granted that the promises of the Declaration applied to black and white alike. It also means that they assumed that even the Democrats had meant the same thing, and had been changing their tune.

The force of Lincoln's rebuke here was not aimed at pro-slavery Democrats, whose racism could safely be taken for granted, but at Free Soil Democrats, who were looking for some way to accommodate their hostility to slavery to their racism. It is the weakness and muddledness of the morally best among Douglas's supporters, as much as the deviousness and lust for power of slaveholders, that is debauching the public mind and preparing, in Clay's old phrase, to blow out the moral lights around us:

> Now, if you are opposed to slavery honestly, as much as anybody I ask you to note that fact, and the like of which is to follow, to be plastered on, layer after layer, until very soon you are prepared to deal with the negro everywhere as with the brute. If public sentiment has not been debauched already to this point, a new turn of the screw in that direction is all that is wanting; and this is constantly being done by the teachers of this insidious popular sovereignty. You need but one or two turns further until your minds, now ripening under these teachings will be ready for all these things, and you will receive and support, or submit to, the slave trade; revived with all its horrors; a slave code enforced in our territories, and a new Dred Scott decision to bring slavery up into the very heart of the free North. This, I must say, is but carrying out those words prophetically spoken by Mr. Clay

many, many years ago. I believe more than thirty years when he told an audience that if they would repress all tendencies to liberty and ultimate emancipation, they must go back to the era of our independence and muzzle the cannon which thundered its annual joyous return on the Fourth of July; they must blow out the moral lights around us; they must penetrate the human soul and eradicate the love of liberty; but until they did these things, and others eloquently enumerated by him, they could not repress all tendencies to ultimate emancipation. (2:58)

Lincoln's Cincinnati Speech

The Cincinnati speech was not simply a reprise of the speech Lincoln had given at Columbus the previous day, but a sophisticated attempt to pry apart the different elements of the coalition Douglas had been attempting to put together. The speech has three broad sections: a section ostensibly addressed to Kentuckians but in fact addressed to conservative Republicans tempted by Douglas, arguing that Douglas is the best ally the slaveholders could realistically hope for; a section replying to Douglas's argument that it was really popular sovereignty, not the Northwest Ordinance, that kept slavery out of the Old Northwest; and a section actually addressed to southerners outlining what to expect in the event of a Republican victory in 1860. This last section is especially interesting, because it is the first public occasion since the Peoria speech in which Lincoln attempted to persuasively engage actual slaveholders rather than spectral powers behind Douglas.

The ironic ostensible advice to Kentuckians, that their opposition to Douglas is self-defeating because only Douglas can win them enough support in the North to enable them to have their way in Congress (and that for Douglas to compromise over the issues over which southern politicians were criticizing him, such as over popular sovereignty, would cost him the northern support he would need to do the South's bidding) is actually the advice Douglas himself might have given. But Lincoln gave it, of course, to tell northerners that Douglas was not in fact with them and would not protect their interests.

Lincoln's ironies no sooner reached this point than he addressed southerners directly. Lincoln did not consider how the slaveholders would hear his speeches during the Illinois campaign. He had, of course, even in the "House Divided" speech, offered many concessions to what seemed to be southern interests. But these concessions were hobbled by his characterization of the slave power's aims, methods, and point of view as alike fraught with secret malignity. The concessions offered in the "House Divided" speech seem aimed more at northern ex-Whigs, at Fillmore voters or at Bates voters, than at slaveholders. They were designed to assure them that Lincoln was not a fire-breathing enthusiast, ready to trample the Constitution in the name of the higher law. But they were not concessions that were likely to impress actual slaveholders.

In the Cincinnati speech, however, as in the Peoria speech, Lincoln went out of his way to disclaim an enraged moral superiority over southerners. These conciliatory acknowledgments of moral kinship across political lines are more in Lincoln's grain, over the long run, than the hectoring conspiracy-mongering he engaged in in 1858. He even went on to make a surprisingly good-humored joke about the charge of seeking sexual amalgamation of the races, noting that he could hardly hate the South, having taken a southern wife:

> We mean to remember that you are as good as we; that there is no difference between us other than the difference of circumstances. We mean to recognize and bear in mind always that you have as good hearts in your bosoms as other people, or as we claim to have, and treat you accordingly. We mean to marry your girls when we have a chance—the white ones I mean—[laughter] and I have the honor to inform you that I once did have a chance in that way. [A voice, "Good for you," and applause.] (2:76–77)

Lincoln also for the first time in the Cincinnati speech took public notice of the secessionist threat. His response was jocular, with a hint of toughness under it. As John Channing Briggs says of the Cooper Union speech, Lincoln holds out an olive branch while wearing a sword.[36] It is clear in the Cincinnati speech that he took secession to be an empty threat, and the point of his treatment of it seems not so much to be aimed at arguing to southerners against secession as arguing to northerners that they need not fear it, because it is an unrealistic alternative:

> I often hear it intimated that you mean to divide the Union whenever a Republican, or anything like it, is elected President of the United

States. [A voice, "That is so."] "That is so," one of them says. I wonder if he is a Kentuckian? [A voice, "He is a Douglas man."] Well,
then, I want to know what you are going to do with your half of it?
[Applause and laughter.] Are you going to split the Ohio down through,
and push your half off a piece? Or are you going to keep it right
alongside of us outrageous fellows? Or are you going to build up a
wall some way between your country and ours, by which that moveable property of yours can't come over here any more, to the danger
of your losing it? Do you think you can better yourselves on that subject, by leaving us here under no obligation whatever to return those
specimens of your moveable property that come hither? You have
divided the Union because we would not do right with you as you
think, upon that subject; when we cease to be under obligations to do
anything for you, how much better off do you think you will be: will
you make war upon us and kill us all? Why, gentlemen, I think you
are as gallant and as brave men as live; that you can fight as bravely in
a good cause, man for man, as any other people living; that you have
shown yourselves capable of this upon various occasions; but, man
for man, you are not better than we are, and there are not so many of
you as there are of us. [Loud cheering.] You will never make of a
hand at whipping us. If we were fewer in numbers than you, I think
that you could whip us; if we were equal it would likely be a drawn
battle; but being inferior in numbers, you will make nothing by
attempting to master us. (2:77)

Lincoln also developed how he understood the economic conflict
between the North and the South, articulating the "free labor" theory
he would develop in more detail in his speeches at Hartford and New
Haven in 1860. Defenders of slavery often made their case by comparing the exploitation of slaves to the exploitation of factory workers. At
Cincinnati, as at Hartford and New Haven, Lincoln did not make the
obvious riposte that factory workers are not driven to work with whips
and are not routinely sexually exploited by the factory owners. Indeed,
he did not even contest the rather benign characterization of slavery
the slaveholders put forward, in which when slaves get old they have
"kind masters to take care of them." Instead, he merely argued that
their characterization of free labor was mistaken. In the first place,
most people in the free states work for themselves, and in the second
place, most people who work for others, Lincoln maintained, do so

only for a while, ultimately setting up on their own and hiring other
people in their turn. Securing economic autonomy, Lincoln went on
to argue, is one of the purposes of government, and improving the
whole community by the exercise of that autonomy is the best realization of a democratic policy. But the success of that policy requires that
no one group of people think of themselves as entitled to exploit other
groups of people. Free labor, this is to say, depends not only upon freedom, but also upon equality.

It is the dynamism of free labor, Lincoln claims, that drives westward expansion, but that expansion requires that the territories remain
places fit for free laborers to go to, which in turn requires that they
prohibit slavery. Here again Lincoln could make a much harsher case
than he does make about the way the presence of slave labor warps and
stunts the development of free economies. Instead, he merely asks those
numerous southern-born Ohioans in his audience, who came north of
the river to get away from slavery (just as Thomas Lincoln did), whether
or not they would prefer their own westward-bound sons to face the
very things they left Kentucky to get away from:

> My good friends, let me ask you a question—you who have come
> from Virginia or Kentucky, to get rid of this thing of slavery—let me
> ask you what headway would you have made in getting rid of it, if by
> popular sovereignty you find slavery on that soil which you looked
> for to be free when you get there? You would not have made much
> headway if you had found slavery already here, if you had to sit down
> to your labor by the side of the unpaid workman.
>
> I say, then, that it is due to yourselves as voters, as owners of the
> new territories, that you shall keep those territories free, in the best
> condition for all such of your gallant sons as may choose to go there.
> (2:86)

Lincoln also took issue with Douglas's claim that it was popular sovereignty, not the Northwest Ordinance, that kept slavery out of the
Old Northwest. Lincoln agreed that keeping slavery out was the will
of the people of Ohio at the time they formed their state constitution,
but they were able to do so only because they were "unembarrassed by
the actual presence of the institution" among them, which, had there
been slavery, would have caused difficulties that "most probably, would

have induced you to tolerate a slave constitution instead of a free one, as indeed these very difficulties have constrained every people on this continent who have adopted slavery" (2:78). Lincoln here had in mind the failure of promising recent attempts to end slavery in Kentucky and Missouri. But he also had in mind what a near thing the introduction of slavery had been in the Old Northwest despite the Northwest Ordinance, since Indiana had petitioned Congress to introduce slavery during its territorial period, and only the steadfastness of Congress, including many slaveholder congressmen, had kept slavery out. Illinois, Lincoln noted (as Douglas had also done), had had French slaveholders for at least a hundred years when the ordinance was adopted, and its territorial government not only made no effort to free those slaves but also made unsuccessful attempts to introduce more. Only the pressure of the ordinance kept Illinois from following the example of Missouri, which likewise inherited a small number of slaves from early French settlers, but in which slavery flourished because no federal law kept it out.

Lincoln's argument here was not simply that it was not popular sovereignty that kept slavery out of the Old Northwest and crippled it where it already existed, but that freedom itself is a different thing from what Douglas understood it to be. Freedom, in Lincoln's view, is fragile, and depends upon being nurtured by conditions that freedom itself is not always able to set. Once slavery is introduced, it entrains around it the politics, economics, and culture of the society in which it finds itself, becoming almost impossible to eradicate. Once slavery is established, the people do not really have the freedom to rid themselves of it, and indeed are subject to further rounds of compulsion in the interest of slavery, dragging them ever more deeply into subservience to slavery. The choice of introducing slavery is never made in a completely free way anyway—either there are some slaves already in the region, or a group of slaveholders bring their slaves with them and force the territory to make a choice which, once made, they cannot take back, so that either way a small but empowered group dictates conditions for everyone. Only the compulsion of the federal government prevented a minority of slaveholders from foreclosing not only the possibility of every territory becoming a free state but also from foreclosing popular rule more generally. In Douglas's view of freedom, Lincoln argued, the people of the territories have only the kind of freedom people in the Hobbesian state of nature have, the freedom to be driven by compulsions they are never fully in a position to understand. In *The Social Contract*, Rousseau speculated, in a much derided phrase, that people have to be forced to be free. The prohibition of slavery by the power of the federal government is perhaps a good example of what Rousseau meant about forcing people to be free, since only that prohibition prevents the self-enslavement of the territories by slavery, chosen for the territory as a whole by a handful of slaveholders, who freely choose to destroy the conditions of their own freedom.

8.5 The Cooper Union Speech

Lincoln's speech at the Cooper Union in New York City was a work of scholarship over which Lincoln had labored for several months. In it he provided a careful, detailed, and fairly reasoned account of how the thirty-nine men who wrote the federal Constitution voted on issues involving slavery in the territories, whether before writing the Constitution, as members of the Confederation Congress, or afterward, as members of the federal Congress.[37] Rather unlike Douglas's effort in his "Dividing Line" article, Lincoln presented his evidence with scrupulous accuracy, and never drew conclusions from it that were beyond what the evidence warranted, although he did starkly limit the kind of evidence that could be applied to decide the question before him in ways that influenced but probably did not determine the outcome. The entire speech, which was Lincoln's first speech delivered from a written text rather than notes, was his most carefully crafted work so far, and few political papers before or since quite match it for discipline and intellectual rigor.[38]

The speech has three broad sections: a thorough refutation of the arguments concerning the power of the federal government over slavery in the territories made by Douglas in his "Dividing Line" article, an address to the southern people laying out his disagreements with them and responding to some of their charges against the Republican Party, and some words of advice to fellow Republicans.

If one were to know the "Dividing Line" article chiefly through Lincoln's refutation of it in the Cooper Union speech, one might assume that Douglas's principal rhetorical target was the Republican policy of preventing slavery from spreading to the territories. In fact, although

Douglas does direct a few sallies at the Republicans, for the most part Douglas directed his fire against the Calhounite joint property position, as we have seen. One might also believe that Douglas's popular sovereignty position stood or fell entirely on the claim that it is mandated by the Constitution, and on the related claim that the joint property and nonextension positions are constitutionally forbidden.

Now Douglas did make those claims, and those claims are not only wrong, but nonsense. In fact, as we have seen, he made an even more risky claim, that his understanding of popular sovereignty over slavery had roots in the pre-Revolutionary era, and indeed, that the War for Independence was partly waged in the name of his own doctrine. Stated this baldly, this last claim seems absurd, even astounding. But that argument was in the actual article merely the pretext for a stinging historical analogy: that the Virginia Burgesses, in attempting to limit slavery many times between 1699 and 1772, had behaved rather like the anti-slavery legislature of Kansas Territory in 1858, and that the Buchanan administration, in attempting to impose slavery upon Kansas in the name of its joint property doctrine, had behaved rather like the Crown, which was moved by imperial doctrines not far different from the joint property doctrine. As a broad theory of the meaning of the Revolution or of the dictates of the Constitution, the "Dividing Line" article is a failure. As small-arms fire directed against the Buchanan administration, and, behind the administration, at a southern political doctrine reaching back through Davis to Calhoun, the article makes a better case for itself.

Even without Lincoln's careful refutation, any schoolboy could take apart Douglas's historical case, as Damon Wells argued long ago. But despite his professions to the contrary, Douglas was not actually moved to the popular sovereignty position by his sense that it was constitutionally mandated or demanded by the makers of the Revolution, but by his sense that popular sovereignty was a prudent compromise policy by which the free states could offer some sort of fair play to the slave states without completely surrendering the territories to the slave states (and indeed, given Douglas's arguments concerning the geography and sociology of slavery, without even seriously risking losing the territories to the slave states). Douglas was moved, this is to say, by the desire to articulate a reasonable compromise that would slightly advantage his section without risking the stability either of the Union or of the Democratic Party, a position that promised to the slave states a defeat that would not completely drive them from the political arena.

When Douglas made constitutional arguments, he made them defensively, because Calhoun and the other proponents of the joint property position had made their arguments in constitutional terms from the beginning. All Douglas really needed to do was to prove that his popular sovereignty position was constitutionally *permitted;* he did not have to prove that it was constitutionally *mandated,* and that the alternative positions were unconstitutional. If he lost the argument that his position was constitutionally mandated, he still, so long as he could maintain that his position was constitutionally permitted, could propose his version of popular sovereignty in the territories as a reasonable solution to the problem of slavery there. But losing the constitutional arguments had other risks, even if doing so did not completely logically discredit his position. If Douglas lost the constitutional argument because he made that argument sloppily, and even dishonestly, as he did, he would lose also some of the persuasive credibility he needed to make headway on cases where his arguments were stronger.

Lincoln delighted in repeatedly turning a key phrase of Douglas's against him, his claim that "our fathers, who framed the Government under which we live, understood this question just as well, and even better, than we do now" (2:111). It is worth noting, as Briggs points out, that Lincoln and Douglas had slightly different understandings of what the phrase "our fathers" refers to. For Lincoln in this speech the term referred only to the thirty-nine men who signed the Constitution. Douglas had in mind all those of the Revolutionary generation who opposed the Crown's attempt to impose its will on the colonies, whether about taxation or about slavery. Douglas's case was completely impossible if one understands "our fathers" to be the thirty-nine. But it had a great deal more plausibility if one understands the term more broadly.[39]

Lincoln's historical case began before the Constitutional Convention, and proceeded all the way to the Missouri Compromise debates, during which the last of the thirty-nine authors of the Constitution still served in Congress. Four of the thirty-nine had served in the Confederation Congress in 1784, when it first considered outlawing slavery in the Northwestern Territory. Three of these men voted for prohibiting slavery there, showing that they did not think it was forbidden by the Articles of Confederation for them to do so; one voted against it, but there is no evidence that proves that he did so because he thought the Articles of Confederation prohibited the act. Two more of the thirty-nine were serving in the Confederation Congress as they deliberated on the Northwest Ordinance, serving concurrently in the Constitutional Convention; both of them voted to prohibit slavery in the Northwest Territory. Although the Constitution has no explicit language about who will control the status of slavery in the territories, the First Congress, in 1789, unanimously prohibited slavery in the Northwest Territory. This bill was authored by one of the thirty-nine, and sixteen of the thirty-nine, many of them southerners, served in that Congress. And one more of the thirty-nine, President George Washington, signed it into law.

Even where early Congresses did not vote to forbid slavery in the territories (as for instance when territories were organized for what is now Tennessee, Mississippi, and Alabama, regions where slavery had already taken root and where the states who ceded the territory to the federal government, North Carolina and Georgia, had made a promise not to abolish slavery there a condition of the cession), Congress exercised a kind of control over slavery inconsistent with the "Dividing Line" article's view of them, in 1798 forbidding anyone from bringing newly imported slaves into Mississippi (the international slave trade still being legal then). Lincoln argues that the three of the thirty-nine who were in Congress then voted for this provision, and none registered constitutional objections to it.

When after the Louisiana Purchase a territorial government was organized for Louisiana, Congress again chose to tolerate preexisting slavery, but again forbade slaves from being imported into Louisiana from abroad, forbade any slave from being taken there who had been brought to the United States after 1798, and forbade any slaves from being brought there except by the owner, for his own use. Here again two of the thirty-nine were present, both may have supported it (individual votes were not recorded), and neither raised constitutional objections.

In 1820 one of the principal opponents of admitting Missouri as a slave state was one of the thirty-nine, Rufus King, who also voted against the later compromise. Another of the thirty-nine, Charles Pinckney, consistently voted in favor of slavery in Missouri, and also opposed the compromise, but Lincoln finds no evidence that his reasons were constitutional ones.

All told, twenty-three of the thirty-nine registered opinions about slavery in the territories, and of those, twenty-one favored restricting it, and the two who felt otherwise are not known to have raised constitutional objections to slavery restriction. Some of the sixteen who were not in a position to vote on these measures—Benjamin Franklin, Alexander Hamilton, and Gouverneur Morris—were known supporters of abolition, so it is not safe to assume that the sixteen as a group felt differently from the twenty-three who were on record. The case might have been slightly weaker had it considered what members of the thirty-nine who were not in Congress might have said about these issues (we know that Madison felt that the Missouri Compromise was probably, but not certainly, constitutional, and we know that Jefferson, while not one of the thirty-nine but clearly a Founder of consequence, had, to say the least, mixed feelings about abolishing slavery in Missouri). But probably the outcome would not have been materially different even if reckoned in this way.[40]

Lincoln went on to make a subtle argument against Taney's proslavery interpretation of the Fifth Amendment in the *Dred Scott* decision. Taney had argued that the Fifth Amendment's prohibition against depriving persons of their property without due process of law means that the state can only take property from people it has convicted of crimes.[41] Taney's attack on the Missouri Compromise restriction depended upon this reading of the Fifth Amendment, as did the responses from southern circles to the Freeport Doctrine. But the authors of the Fifth Amendment, Lincoln argues, could not have intended it to prevent the prohibition of slavery in the territories, because sixteen of the thirty-nine signatories to the federal Constitution were in Congress when the Fifth Amendment was passed, and one of them, George Washington, was president. None of them raised this kind of issue; none of them dreamed that it might conflict with the Northwest Ordinance, which the First Congress had reconfirmed.

The same argument applies to the use of the Tenth Amendment by Calhoun's followers in denying the federal government power over slavery in the territories: if the members of the thirty-nine who were members of the First Congress approved the language of the amendment to the effect that powers not specifically assigned to the federal government were reserved to the states or to the people, and yet still re-passed the Northwest Ordinance, they must have felt that the territories clause (or perhaps the general welfare clause) did indeed give Congress power over slavery in the territories.

Now there is an answer to this argument, but it is one that was unavailable to the defenders of slavery. The answer is that lawmakers often make precedents they are not in a position to follow out. Lincoln ridiculed this idea:

> Is it not a little presumptuous in any one at this day to affirm that the two things which that Congress deliberately framed, and carried to maturity at the same time, are absolutely inconsistent with each other? And does not such affirmation become impudently absurd when coupled with the other affirmation from the same mouth, that those who did the two things, alleged to be inconsistent, understood whether they really were inconsistent better than we—better than he who affirms that they are inconsistent? (2:118)

Lincoln's ridicule notwithstanding, this inconsistency is not far different from what he charges Jefferson and the other Founders with, which is to say, affirming that all men are created equal and continuing to hold slaves. But the difference is that the men of the Revolutionary generation were in fact well aware of this inconsistency between free government and slaveholding, and meant it to be a sore point until it was resolved. Certainly it was felt to be so by Franklin, and Hamilton, and Morris, not to mention Jefferson himself and for that matter George Washington. And all of these men were aware of the purely practical difficulties that stood in the way of resolving that inconsistency. One can hardly make this same kind of case about the idea that the Fifth Amendment protects slavery in the territories. And the defenders of slavery anyway were committed to the idea of "strict construction" (on their own rather deviant theories of what that construction was), and thus could hardly embrace a doctrine that requires some notion of implicitness.

Lincoln conceded that to argue that the Founders did not embrace a doctrine like Douglas's "Dividing Line" doctrine did not of itself mean that that doctrine was wrong. But it did mean that Douglas in putting forth that doctrine could not clothe himself in the authority of the Founders. If he wished to advance that doctrine, he must treat it as a new one, and must concede, as Lincoln puts it, that there is no evidence

that any of the thirty-nine ever embraced such an idea. As Lincoln
went on to say, he defies "any one to show that any living man in the
whole world ever did, prior to the beginning of the present century,
(and I might say prior to the beginning of the last half of the present
century,) declare that, in his understanding, any proper division of local from federal authority, or any part of the Constitution, forbade the
Federal Government to control as to slavery in the federal territories"
(2:118–119).[42]

It is the Free Soil position about the territories, Lincoln argued, that
is the conservative position, if by conservative one means in keeping
with the views of the Founders of the government. Lincoln makes this
point in firm but not precisely confrontational language, in a passage
he felt strongly enough to italicize on publication:

> Let all who believe that "our fathers, who framed the Government under
> which we live, understood this question just as well, and even better, than
> we do now," speak as they spoke, and act as they acted upon it. This is all
> Republicans ask—all Republicans desire—in relation to slavery. As those
> fathers marked it, so let it be again marked, as an evil not to be extended,
> but to be tolerated and protected only because of and so far as its actual pres-
> ence among us makes that toleration and protection a necessity. Let all the
> guaranties those fathers gave it, be, not grudgingly, but fully and fairly
> maintained. (2:120)

The second section of the speech turns on the meaning of the commitments Lincoln made at the end of his refutation of Douglas. Harold Holzer has rightly pointed out that one should not be misled by the
reasonable tone of the passage to conclude that the speaker's anti-
slavery convictions were soft. For one thing, Lincoln was very blunt
about the fact that most southern ears were completely closed to argument, and that loyalty politics had set preconditions about what could
be argued that in effect silenced the voice of reasonable argument and
foreclosed persuasive engagement. Knowing that they were unlikely
to listen to him, Lincoln nevertheless said what he would have said to
them if they would have listened. He assumed that they are not by nature demonic, that "in the general qualities of reason and justice you
are not inferior to any other people." But he noted also that loyalty
politics has enforced a destructive intellectual conformity upon them:

You will grant a hearing to pirates or murderers, but nothing like it to "Black Republicans." In all your contentions with one another, each of you deems an unconditional condemnation of "Black Republicanism" as the first thing to be attended to. Indeed, such condemnation of us seems to be an indispensable prerequisite—license, so to speak—among you to be admitted or permitted to speak at all. (2:120)

There are two ways to interpret the act of saying to people who would not listen to you what you *would* have said if they did. The first is that one is actually speaking over their heads to other people who *are* listening—in this case to moderate northerners who might be afraid that the Republicans will take too radical a position. Clearly Lincoln did have something to say to such people. But his address to southerners here was not merely rhetorical. Everybody who has ever been locked in a cycle of reciprocated vituperation understands that sometimes one listens a little better to the other side than one allows one's own side to see. This is particularly important to remember when, even as one embraces one's own side's doctrines, one also fears one's own side's partisans, because of their insistence on policing one's orthodoxy, their readiness to brand the slightest flexibility as the sign of treason, and their eagerness to out-hard-line each other in the internal competition for leadership. Reciprocated vituperation is wearying, and it locks one into a kind of unreality. If Lincoln did expect that some southerners, despite themselves, would listen to him, it is because he hoped to reach those who were restive under the conformity pressures of southern politics.

John Channing Briggs points out how much less confrontational the Cooper Union speech is than the "House Divided" speech. The "House Divided" speech was starkly deductive, the Cooper Union speech meticulously inductive. The "House Divided" speech struck a note of urgency and crisis, the Cooper Union speech an emotionally restrained tone of reasoned argument. The "House Divided" speech turned on the threat to the values of the Declaration of Independence, the Cooper Union speech on the assumption by the South and the North alike at the time of the Revolution that slavery was an evil, if intractable, institution.[43]

There is always a point to constructing an imagined reasonable opponent, even if that opponent is a little different from the one one actually faces. Putting aside the benefit of demonstrating to third parties that one is capable of fairly weighing the strengths and weaknesses of one's own position, there is a benefit in showing even the most committed opponent that one is at least reasonable, if only in showing someone on that side who might be interested in carrying out the same exercise where to begin. Even if the exercise does not uncover persuasive common ground it at least makes it harder for the hottest heads on the other side to persuade whoever is restive among their followers that you really are a demonic opponent with whom it is a waste of time to persuasively engage. There is still, after all, a difference between an intractable conflict with a reasonable opponent and a death-struggle with a demonic one. And that difference persists even if the struggle escalates to violence.

Lincoln proceeded to answer some of the specific charges southerners had made against the Republicans. The first charge, that they are a sectional party, Lincoln had handled differently in the Illinois debates. Here, as in the Illinois debates, he argued that the happenstance that the Republicans do not get votes in the South is not of itself proof that they are a sectional party, because the test of whether a party is sectional is whether its principles are loaded against a section, which, since all they proposed to do was to restore the views of slavery in the territories held by George Washington and a host of other southerners, the principles of the Republicans were certainly not. Washington, indeed, Lincoln noted, had written to Lafayette in praise of the Northwest Ordinance, and told him that he looked forward to the day when all of the states of the Union would be free of slavery. In Illinois, Lincoln had argued, rather more boldly, that Republican principles may not be able to go south for the same reason that they may not be able to go to Russia, because the South, like Russia, no longer met the cultural preconditions for being a democratic culture. Lincoln did not take that tack here, arguing instead, probably on the basis of the modest efforts of Cassius M. Clay in Kentucky and John Minor Botts in Virginia to create Republican organizations in their states, that in 1860 it will not be true that the Republicans will get no votes in the South.

Against the charge that the Republicans are "revolutionary, destructive, or something of the sort" (the phrasing carries the tang of Lincoln's impatience with this charge), Lincoln noted that his position was, as he had just shown, the position of the Founders, southern as much as northern, and that the "conservatives" in the sectional conflict are the Republicans, not the southern Democrats. Against the charge that it was only the Republicans, or only anti-slavery northerners, who had driven the conflict over slavery, Lincoln replied that since the innovations about slavery—that it is a positive good, that it must be protected in the territories, and so on—have been the work of southerners, blame for the escalating conflict can hardly be laid entirely at the door of the North, as Democrats from Van Buren to Douglas had been trying to do.

Lincoln reserved his closest reasoning for his argument against the claim that the Republicans stir up slave insurrections, and in particular against the claim that the Republicans bear responsibility for John Brown's Harper's Ferry raid, which had taken place only four months previously. Lincoln began with the obvious fact that none of the participants in the raid seem to have been Republicans. And he noted that the Republican promise not to seek to use federal law to abolish slavery in the states itself refutes the charge that Republicans somehow whipped up John Brown's raid or represented any immediate threat to the slaveholders. Indeed, if anything gave the slaves of the South the idea that the Republicans might support a slave insurrection, Lincoln said, it was nothing said or done by Republicans but the kind of denunciations of Republicans that masters had been unburdening themselves of in their slaves' hearing. And Lincoln noted, despite the wave of hysterical accusations against northern traveling salesmen and the like in the wake of John Brown's raid, that slave insurrections were in fact no more common in 1859 than they had ever been, and, furthermore, whether because of the love the masters claimed their slaves had for them or because of the practical difficulties, it is hard to imagine that a serious insurrection conspiracy could have been put into action anyway without one of the conspirators divulging it, perhaps "to save the life of a favorite master or mistress." Lincoln rather bluntly mentions, however, that slaveholding was still a risky business, but saying that is rather different than anticipating a widespread slave revolt:

> Occasional poisonings from the kitchen, and open or stealthy assassinations in the field, and local revolts extending to a score or so, will continue to occur as the natural results of slavery; but no general insurrection of slaves, as I think, can happen in this country for a

long time. Whoever much fears, or much hopes for such an event, will be alike disappointed. (2:124)

Neither of Lincoln's arguments could have sounded quite as reassuring to southern ears as he intended them to sound. It is true, for instance, that none of the Harper's Ferry raiders were Republicans, if by that term one means Republican officeholders. And certainly their politics were rather more radically anti-slavery than the Republicans' politics were. But if by "Republican" one means "supported Frémont in 1856," probably some of the "Secret Six" who funded the Harper's Ferry raid (possibly without clear knowledge of what Brown planned to do) would count as Republicans.

Probably more damaging, as far as the prospects for the Union were concerned, were those numerous Republicans who, moved by the eloquence of Brown's letters from prison, came to sympathize with him over the course of his trial, listened to sermons that deprecated his acts but defended his ideals, or rang bells in his honor on the day of his execution.[44] Yes, no Republican attacked Harper's Ferry. But many Republicans, even those who deplored the raid, had a more than grudging admiration for Brown as the kind of idealist who gave deeds to words. Once southerners heard that, it would only be human for them to draw the worst possible conclusions, even if those too were oversimplifications. Lincoln did not address the estranging effects of what happened on both sides of the Mason-Dixon line in the weeks after John Brown's raid. It is hard, for that matter, to imagine how he could have done so successfully anyway. Even had he denounced Brown in far more fulsome language than he did—his treatment is in fact remarkably cool in tone—it could easily have been written off as "something he just had to say, whether he really believed it or not." Once one gets into a persuasive economy of reciprocated vituperation, even conciliatory gestures seem to be only "what he has to say."

The observation that "occasional poisonings from the field" are much more to be expected than full-scale insurrections, while true, could scarcely have been very comforting either, because the idea that their loving slaves could lovingly cut their masters' throats in bed was much closer to the bone, as far as southern nightmares were concerned, than the idea that the slaves were about to prepare a new Santo Domingo. William Freehling captures very well how southern suspicions of the genuineness of northern horror at John Brown's raid mirror their suspicions of the genuineness of the love of their own slaves, and their suspicions of the genuineness of the loyalty to the South, however loudly proclaimed, of southern nonslaveholders or border state slaveholders.[45] During the crisis over the speakership of the House in early 1859, for instance, Congressman Laurence Keitt, who had earlier been one of the men who prevented bystanders from intervening to break up Congressman Brooks's assault on Charles Sumner, learned that his brother in Florida had been killed by one of his slaves.[46] The southern diarist Mary Chesnut reported frequently surveying the faces of her slaves, trying to see whether they were thinking about doing her some ill, and when she commented upon John Brown's raid, it was always in the context of providing encouragement to stealthy single murders, not in the context of setting in motion large-scale insurrections. Lincoln's language on this subject, particularly in its bluntness and in its coldness, could not have been very reassuring.

That said, Lincoln was probably right when he argued that Brown's raid made poor enough tactical sense that it is unlikely that many serious Republicans would have signed onto it anyway:

> John Brown's effort was peculiar. It was not a slave insurrection. It was an attempt by white men to get up a revolt among slaves, in which the slaves refused to participate. In fact, it was so absurd that the slaves, with all their ignorance, saw plainly enough it could not succeed. That affair, in its philosophy, corresponds with the many attempts, related in history, at the assassination of kings and emperors. An enthusiast broods over the oppression of a people till he fancies himself commissioned by Heaven to liberate them. He ventures the attempt, which ends in little else than his own execution. Orsini's attempt on Louis Napoleon, and John Brown's attempt at Harper's Ferry were, in their philosophy, precisely the same. The eagerness to cast blame on old England in the one case, and on New England in the other, does not disprove the sameness of the two things. (2:125)

Lincoln correctly argued that the only thing that really would reconcile the South to the North would be if the latter were to cease to criticize slavery at all. It is this, he implied, that underlies the constitutional arguments that the South has been presenting through its

interpretation of the *Dred Scott* decision and underlies its current political program. The constitutional questions, Lincoln argued, do not
seem to be, in fact, so clear and obvious as to justify secession if one
does not have one's way about them. For instance, although Chief Justice Taney had affirmed that the right of property in a slave is *"distinctly* and *expressly* affirmed"* in the Constitution, the language of that
document about slavery is shamefacedly indirect, and the concessions
made to slavery there are grudging ones. In addition to Taney's historical mistakes, the decision itself was reached in such a way as to compromise its authority:

> Perhaps you will say the Supreme Court has decided the disputed
> Constitutional question in your favor. Not quite so. But waiving
> the lawyer's distinction between dictum and decision, the Court
> have decided the question for you in a sort of way. The Court have
> substantially said, it is your Constitutional right to take slaves into
> the federal territories, and to hold them there as property. When I
> say the decision was made in a sort of way, I mean it was made in a
> divided Court, by a bare majority of the Judges, and they not quite
> agreeing with one another in the reasons for making it; that it is so
> made as that its avowed supporters disagree with one another about
> its meaning, and that it was mainly based upon a mistaken state-
> ment of fact—the statement in the opinion that "the right of prop-
> erty in a slave is distinctly and expressly affirmed in the Constitu-
> tion." (2:127)

Ultimately, Lincoln saw that he faced a rule-or-ruin mentality that
would not accept a fairly elected Republican president under any circumstances. This intransigence gave him little persuasive room to
maneuver, and all he really could do was to point out that they have
placed themselves beyond the reach of reason. Lincoln's sarcasm was
clear-eyed and firm, but it reflected a rhetorical situation that he had
begun to see as futile:

> But you will not abide the election of a Republican President! In that
> supposed event, you say, you will destroy the Union; and then, you
> say, the great crime of having destroyed it will be upon us! That is
> cool. A highwayman holds a pistol to my ear, and mutters through

his teeth, "Stand and deliver, or I shall kill you, and then you will be a murderer." (2:127)

It is with this increasing sense of the futility of persuasively engaging the South that Lincoln turned in the last section of the speech to address his fellow Republicans. He began by promising to retain his temperate tone and recommending it to the rest of his party: *"Even though much provoked, let us do nothing through passion and ill temper. Even though the southern people will not so much as listen to us, let us calmly consider their demands, and yield to them if, in our deliberate view of our duty, we possibly can"* (2:128).

The slaveholders' position about slavery in the territories is intractable, Lincoln argued, because it is logically coherent, following rigorously from their premises about slavery and property. Because the slaveholders' position is coherent, it cannot be resolved by compromise, since coherent positions stand or fall in an all-or-nothing way. Therefore the only plausible policy for Republicans is forbearance in the face of intractable conflict, a policy that can postpone but not evade war if the conflict is over something crucial:[47]

> If slavery is right, all words, acts, laws, and constitutions against it, are themselves wrong, and should be silenced, and swept away. If it is right, we cannot justly object to its nationality—its universality; if it is wrong, they cannot justly insist upon its extensions—its enlargement. All they ask, we could readily grant, if we thought slavery right; all we ask, they could as readily grant, if they thought it wrong. Their thinking it right, and our thinking it wrong, is the precise fact upon which depends the whole controversy. Thinking it right, as they do, they are not to blame for desiring its full recognition, as being right; but, thinking it wrong, as we do, can we yield to them? (2:129)

Lincoln was clear that the only thing that could have bought sectional peace was the one thing the Republicans could not offer without a fatal sacrifice. Giving in on the territorial issues would not have itself satisfied the South; rigorously suppressing imagined insurrections would not have satisfied the South; even actually leaving the South alone would not have satisfied the South. The only thing that would have satisfied the South was to concede that slavery is morally right, which no Republican, and for that matter no Douglasite Democrat, could have conceded:

> These natural, and apparently adequate means all failing, what will convince them? This, and this only: cease to call slavery *wrong*, and join them in calling it *right*. And this must be done thoroughly—done in *acts* as well as in *words*. Silence will not be tolerated—we must place ourselves avowedly with them. Senator Douglas's new sedition law must be enacted and enforced, suppressing all declarations that slavery is wrong, whether made in politics, in presses, in pulpits, or in private. We must arrest and return their fugitive slaves with greedy pleasure. We must pull down our Free State constitutions. The whole atmosphere must be disinfected from all taint of opposition to slavery, before they will cease to believe that all their troubles proceed from us. (2:128–129)

Now the South had not, in so many words, exactly demanded that every northern voice unite in praise of slavery, as Lincoln went on to concede. But Lincoln was aware that this demand was the upshot of a series of acts by southern radicals going back to the censoring of the mails and the gag rule in Congress of the 1830s. Although his southern opponents would, if asked, have said that all they wanted was for the North to leave them alone, to let slavery continue in the states where it already existed, the fact that making and keeping this concession had no effect on the demand for concessions meant that there was some urgent but unarticulated demand beneath the explicit ones. Their belief that slavery is right, in Lincoln's view, compelled them to force an agreement that it is right from everyone else.

Michael Gilmore has pointed out that this demand amounts to a form of mind control.[48] Succeeding at this kind of mind control involves scarcely imaginable kinds of coercion, particularly since if you stigmatize an idea with a not very subtly implied threat of force, you tend to make that idea stronger rather than weaker, and thus have to use even stronger threats, even more naked varieties of force. Nothing is more likely to grave an idea deeper in your mind than my telling you, on pain of death, that you must not think it.

Like most perpetually escalating demands, this mind-control demand was a futile one. For one thing, even if every northern politician were to have made this morally fatal sacrifice and to declare that slavery was a positive good, nevertheless, since what was demanded of them was that they change their *feelings* about slavery, nothing they could have done would have sufficed to lay to rest the suspicion that that profession of feeling was not genuine. No amount of hard-line behavior by southern nonslaveholders persuaded the slaveholders that the nonslaveholders did not secretly wish to threaten them. No amount of successful loyalty politics coercion by politicians of the Deep South sufficed to erase their suspicion that the politicians of the border and middle South were not really with them (and indeed the "positive good" view of slavery still had to contest with older views about slavery in the border South right up to the moment of secession). Why should a similar attempt to silence northern politicians have shown any more promise of success?

As with the demand that the North prove that it did not secretly have sympathies for John Brown, so this demand turns on something that becomes more doubtful the more strenuously one asserts it. How does one answer demands like "Prove that you love me" or "Prove that you are not a self-hating Jew" or "Prove that you love your country"? Every answer one might make to the demand provokes the remark, "Well, that's something you'd *have* to say whatever the real story is, and the fact that you've said it only compounds my doubts about you."

William Freehling argues that this nervous, even hysterical, demand for intellectual conformity must always continue to futilely escalate because the critic of slavery it attempts to shout down is not the external critic, the northerner, but the internal one, the slaveholder caught in the contradictions of slaveholding—the attempt to hold in one mind "Surely my slaves love me" and "My slaves scare me to death." Certainly no surrender the external critic could make would suffice to silence the internal critic, since the internal critic, in unacknowledged ways, tends to escalate his criticism to match the repression directed at him step for step. This is why reasonable, compromise-seeking northerners increasingly found themselves with no traction in the South, and why, more and more, moderately anti-slavery southerners could not voice their moral repugnance about slavery without the threat of violence.

Lincoln's description of the demand captured the relationship between the demand's futility and the inevitability with which it escalated. It was not merely that the slaveholders thought that slavery was right and the Republicans thought it was wrong; it was that the rightness of slavery was in the slaveholder's mind the center of his wounded narcissism, enflamed because it had become something upon which his identity was staked, unhealable because wounded narcissism is unhealable. The slaveholders had not directly demanded the overthrow of the constitutions of the free states. But they could not keep themselves from making this demand ultimately:

> Those Constitutions declare the wrong of slavery, with more solemn emphasis, than do all other sayings against it; and when all these other sayings shall have been silenced, the overthrow of these Constitutions will be demanded, and nothing be left to resist the demand. It is nothing to the contrary, that they do not demand the whole of this just now. Demanding what they do, and for the reason they do, they can voluntarily stop nowhere short of this consummation. Holding, as they do, that slavery is morally right, and socially elevating, they cannot cease to demand a full national recognition of it, as a legal right, and a social blessing. (2:129)

Lincoln did take a firm line about slavery in the Cooper Union speech. He did so because he was aware that the South had backed itself into a persuasive corner, where even complete surrender by the North would not be quite enough. The upshot of the last part of the speech was: if this is what the South wants, and why it wants it, then persuasive engagement with the South is at an end, because it urgently desires what the North cannot give without a fatal sacrifice, and it has locked itself into a cycle of ever-escalating demands. Now among individuals it is sometimes possible to escape a death-spiral of this sort—sometimes you overhear yourself and think, "Am I really the kind of jerk I seem to sound like?" But it is hard to imagine a collective doing this, particularly when even the most irrational and extreme demands have become the basis for a loyalty politics competition among its leaders.

Douglas's concessions were just as incapable of appeasing the South as Lincoln's were, which is not to say that Douglas did not try. Lincoln referred here glancingly to "Douglas's new sedition law." Lincoln must have had in mind a measure, discussed in Michael Gilmore's article cited above, that sought to pin responsibility for the Harper's Ferry raid on the Republican leadership and to define what they did as criminal sedition. Henry Wilson, in the second volume of his *History of the*

Rise and Fall of the Slave Power in America (1872), mentions a January 1860 resolution by Douglas "for the suppression and punishment of conspiracies or combinations in one State against another." Wilson says of Douglas's speech about his resolution:

> The speech of Mr. Douglas in support of his resolution was particularly marked, though exhibiting far more of the partisan than of the patriot, more of the advocate, intent on making out his case, than of the statesman enunciating the great principles of political truth. He quoted Mr. Lincoln's expression of belief that "this government cannot endure permanently half slave and half free," and Mr. Seward's utterance concerning the "irrepressible conflict between opposing and enduring forces," as a "fair exposition" of Republican doctrines and policy; and he gave utterance to the insinuation that the causes which produced the Harper's Ferry invasion were then "in active operation."[49]

It is not completely clear from Wilson's account that the intent of Douglas's bill was to throw Lincoln and Seward in jail. But Lincoln does seem to have taken the threat seriously in his paragraph about "Douglas's new sedition law," and of course if what Douglas said about Lincoln's and Seward's speeches (the same passages he quoted throughout the Ohio campaign and in his "Dividing Line" article) being the causes that produced the Harper's Ferry invasion meant also that Douglas saw them as evidence of a "conspiracy or combination in one State against another," then Douglas's bill did amount to a threat to try the whole Republican Party for sedition. This threat is what Lincoln had in mind in the last paragraph of the Cooper Union speech when he encouraged his fellow Republicans not to be frightened from their duty "by menaces of destruction to the Government nor of dungeons to ourselves."

In the debate in Congress on Douglas's bill, the speeches that followed by Fessenden, for the Republicans, and Hunter, for the southern Democrats, seem to treat Douglas's remarks more as a cheap shot than as a legal threat, because they did not take up the legal gauntlet Douglas seemed to have laid down, only the political one, as if what Douglas had said was "Harper's Ferry is the kind of thing that comes of your loose talk," not "Your speeches are evidence that you were engaged in a conspiracy against Virginia."[50] God only knows what use the South

could have made of this bill had it become law, whatever Douglas
intended by it. They had already criminalized anti-slavery speech in
Kansas in 1855, and it is not at all unlikely they would have tried to do so
nationally. But since Douglas could never have mustered the votes in a
Congress with a Republican majority in the House to make his bill law
in any event, even as a legal threat Douglas's bill amounted to a cheap
shot, perhaps another failed attempt to show the South that he was not
its enemy. The advanced elements of the slave power continued to hate
Douglas as intensely as they hated Lincoln, sedition bill or no sedition
bill, so even if he was planning to sell his soul by putting forward his
sedition bill, the Devil was not in the market to buy it anyway.

Lincoln's concluding argument in the Cooper Union speech was an
exhortation to Republicans to stand firm about morally condemning
slavery in the face of threats either of disunion or of imprisonment.
His argument took the form of an excluded middle:

> Let us be diverted by none of those sophistical contrivances where-
> with we are so industriously plied and belabored—contrivances such
> as groping for some middle ground between the right and the wrong,
> vain as the search for a man who should be neither a living man nor
> a dead man—such as a policy of "don't care" on a question about which
> all true men do care. (2:130)

As a philosophical argument, there is an answer to this, and that is
that the simple alternatives of right and wrong do not in fact exhaust
the possibilities, and, as stated, the argument poses a false dichotomy. It
is possible to imagine that there are morally serious issues that are not
morally neutral but about which the people are in such profound, even
violent disagreement that no state should seek to settle if it wishes to
reflect the consent of the governed. A great many of the hardest issues
in politics, issues upon which turn things like the state of one's immortal soul or the salvation of the world, are issues of this kind, and if such
issues can be faced down at all it can only be by threading Scylla and
Charybdis, by agreeing to disagree without disowning one's moral stake
in one's own position or one's hope to have one's own way about it in
the end, which is a hard art, but not always an impossible one.

As a political argument, however, Lincoln's demand was not only
powerful but perfectly fair. If, as Lincoln argued, what the South re-

ally insisted upon was to impose moral approbation of slavery upon the entire Union, Douglas's position was no more promising as a strategy of reconciliation than Lincoln's was, since it offered only an agreement to disagree, not the moral approbation the South had bound itself to demand. But if a strategy of restraint like Douglas's was also bound to fail, and if the slaveholders were determined to drive the nonslaveholders to the wall anyway, the only credible position was one of firm moral denunciation of slavery. This was also ultimately, given the state the South has worked itself into, a strategy of confrontation, in which persuasion of the other side has been despaired of. It was not, however, a strategy of aggression, although it was a strategy that despaired of gaining an argumentative purchase on the opponent. Its main hope was that someone on the other side would wake up before pulling both sides into the abyss. To take this tack, even if it leads only to confrontation, was not to propose that might makes right. It was to propose, indeed, that right makes might. But except to the extent that consciousness of having the right nerves people to face a confrontation they cannot avoid, it is wishful thinking to believe that right in any other way actually makes might.

8.6 The First Inaugural Address

To modern readers the First Inaugural is a cautious and temperate speech, one that offers every reasonable reassurance to the South while not sacrificing the aims the Republicans had just won the right at the polls to make policy about. Northern Republicans read the speech that way. At least one important northern Democrat—Stephen Douglas—read it that way too, and made sure that his fulsome but not completely accurate sense of it was reported in the papers. But the seceding states took it as a declaration of war, and the soon-to-secede states of the middle South were not impressed by it either. Why is it that what struck Stephen Douglas as a generous renunciation of crusader politics struck the Deep South and middle South as a philippic?

Historians for the most part have not given Lincoln very much praise for his role during the secession crisis. From Henry Adams through Allan Nevins and David Potter, Lincoln has been portrayed as isolated in Springfield, and without a realistic sense of the depth of the crisis. Lincoln, in the traditional view, seems to have underestimated secession, seeing it as a bluff to extort concessions such as the extension of the Missouri Compromise line to the Pacific or an amendment forbidding the abolition of slavery (the latter of which Lincoln was willing to grant). Historians have also been critical of Lincoln's aloofness, even hostility, to the different attempts—the Crittenden Compromise, pushed by Crittenden, Douglas, Stephens, and even, briefly, by Seward, or the "Washington Peace Conference" organized by former President Tyler— to craft yet another sectional compromise.

This view of Lincoln during the secession crisis has recently been powerfully contested by Harold Holzer in *Lincoln President-Elect: Abraham Lincoln and the Great Secession Winter* (2008) and by William H. Freehling in the second volume of *The Road to Disunion* (2007).[51]

Freehling portrays secession in the Deep South essentially as the work of an aggressive minority that outmaneuvered the majority in public, and then, before their legislatures or conventions had even had a chance to deliberate about it, conspiratorially pushed their states past the point of no return. This view at first seems to suggest that there was room for Lincoln to rally the majority who at least began the post-election season with qualms about secession. But the way the loyalty politics debate was turning in the South wound up putting the unionists in an increasingly untenable position, and they kept requiring, as a condition of remaining in the Union, things that it is hard to imagine that Lincoln could have conceded.

Crittenden, for instance, in order to keep the middle South from seceding, proposed including in his compromise measures an amendment extending the 36° 30′ line to the Pacific. In an attempt to lure back the already seceded states, Crittenden reluctantly added language that included in that amendment territories to be acquired later— presumably he had Cuba in mind—allowing slavery to expand southward. Lincoln could not have accepted either proposal, since either would have forced him not only to concede that there was some region of the United States where slavery would always be permitted but also to surrender the great living principle upon which his party was organized, the idea that slavery is wrong.

But even this concession, which Crittenden (who had opposed the Lecompton Constitution) made with extreme reluctance, did not impress the other southern members of the committee that had been appointed to consider his proposals. They insisted that slavery must be protected in *all* territories (north and south of the Missouri Compromise line), and pushed other proposals such as an amendment forbidding presidential appointments without majority votes from the senators from both sections, an amendment requiring majority votes from representatives of both sections in both houses on all matters concerning slavery, or an amendment requiring there to be two presidents, one northern and one southern, each with a veto.[52]

Crittenden wound up proposing six amendments: (1) extending the Missouri Compromise line to the Pacific, with a mandated slave code for territories south of that line during the territorial period (but the territory could enter the Union as a free state if it so desired); (2) prohibiting Congress from abolishing slavery in federal installations; (3) prohibiting Congress from abolishing slavery in the District of Columbia, so long as it existed in either Maryland or Virginia; (4) prohibiting Congress from interfering with the interstate slave trade; (5) mandating compensation for the owners of escaped slaves rescued in the free states; and (6) prohibiting amendments to the previous six amendments. Crittenden also proposed to modify the Fugitive Slave Act as follows: (1) to affirm the law's constitutionality; (2) to require repeal of the "personal liberty laws" some free states had passed to obstruct the fugitive slave law; (3) to pay fugitive slave commissioners the same amount whether they decided that an alleged fugitive slave was actually free or a slave; and (4) to more effectively suppress the African slave trade.

The Washington Peace Conference ultimately submitted its recommendations to Congress on February 25, 1861. Its version of the Thirteenth Amendment included extending the Missouri Compromise line, a prohibition of acquiring new territory except after separate majority votes from the free and the slave states, a prohibition against Congress abolishing slavery in the slave states, a new fugitive slave law, and a ban on the international slave trade. These proposals attracted very little southern support, and went down to defeat in the Senate by a vote of 28 to 7.[53]

If these kinds of things were what the nominal Unionists were demanding, it is hard to imagine that anything Lincoln could have plausibly offered, including his own amendment prohibiting the abolition of slavery, could have persuaded the Deep South to return to the Union, and even these rather large concessions would have been of little use in stopping the tide of disunion anyway, since the Deep South brushed aside the Crittenden compromisers even more brusquely than Lincoln did. Furthermore, any attempt to resist the secession of the Deep South would, as events ultimately showed, provoke the secession of the middle South. In the final analysis, what drove the South to secession was no concrete policy proposal advanced by Lincoln, none of which posed any immediate realistic threat to slavery, but the mere fact that the Republican Party had elected a president at all, and had been able to do so over the South's veto. What the South objected to about Lincoln had little to do with what he promised and everything to do with who he was.

It is therefore very unlikely in any event that any deal Lincoln could have offered would have talked the Deep South out of seceding, since it was Lincoln's election itself that they objected to. Secessionist forces were already seizing federal installations before their secession conventions had even met, with the idea of presenting those who might hesitate with a fait accompli.

Is there a case that a more moderate course might have prevented at least the middle South from seceding? It is hard to imagine how such a scenario might have played out. Lincoln would have been forced to confront the Deep South anyway, and once he did this the upper South would most likely have stampeded into secession by the confrontation, just as it came to pass in reality. A supine course during the secession winter would, I think, not have have moved the Deep South to rescind secession, nor would it have prevented the secession of the middle South. On the other hand, it was not prescience about the futility of compromise that led Lincoln to take a hard line during the secession winter, but inability to grasp that secession was not a bluff. Lincoln took the right course for wrong reasons.

Lincoln had had a draft of his First Inaugural set in type for circulation among select friends and advisors before he left Springfield for his journey to Washington, and he received extensive commentary on his draft, most especially from Seward, but also from Carl Schurz, from Orville Browning, and even, according to Holzer, from Stephen Douglas.[54] The draft set by Springfield printer William Bailhache differed in many particulars from the final version. For one thing, it spoke not only of holding the harbor forts still in Union possession (Fort Sumter in South Carolina and Fort Pickens in Florida), but of reclaiming those that had already fallen to the state troops of the seceding South. (Lincoln softened this language in the final version on Browning's advice.)[55] It included a passage, dropped in the final version, in which Lincoln argued, as he had in several private letters from Springfield during the secession winter, that he was not at liberty to compromise about the platform upon which he had been elected, and that as an elected president he had a right to rule.[56] It also lacked the famous concluding paragraph, which built upon late suggestions by Seward, and so concluded not with the famous invocation of "the better angels of our nature," but with the ominous question "Shall it be peace, or a sword?"[57]

Lincoln's correspondence and remarks during the secession winter reflected some of the uncertainties of his position. On November 20, 1860, a little more than two weeks after his election, Lincoln inserted two paragraphs into a speech given by Lyman Trumbull:

> I regard it as extremely fortunate for the peace of the whole country, that this point, upon which the Republicans have been so long, and so persistently misrepresented, is now to be brought to a practical test, and placed beyond the possibility of doubt. Disunionists *per se*, are now in hot haste to get out of the Union, precisely because they perceive they can not, much longer, maintain apprehension among the Southern people that their homes, and firesides, and lives, are to be endangered by the action of the Federal Government. With such *"Now, or never"* is the maxim.
>
> I am rather glad of this military preparation in the South. It will enable the people the more easily to suppress any uprisings there, which their misrepresentations of purposes may have encouraged. (2:187)

There are two arguments in this passage: (1) that since it should be obvious that the Republicans really represent no threat to slavery in the slave states, Lincoln's election will provide an occasion to separate those who have legitimate concerns with slavery from those who are disunionists per se, and (2) that the mobilization of all of the southern state militias will prove to be useful in suppressing any secessionist insurrections. Both arguments manifest either a desperate attempt to whistle through the graveyard or a scarcely believable level of wishful thinking. Trumbull, understanding this, omitted the last point when he gave his speech.[58]

Writing on December 15, 1860, to John A. Gilmer of North Carolina, whom he had been considering for a post in his cabinet, and who had written to Lincoln asking him make the concessions Gilmer felt might keep the South in the Union, Lincoln declared, with considerable asperity:

> Is it desired that I shall shift the ground upon which I have been elected? I can not do it. You need only acquaint yourself with that ground, and press it on the attention of the South. It is all in print and easy of access. May I be pardoned if I ask whether even you have ever attempted to procure the reading of the Republican platform, or my speeches, by the Southern people? If not, what reason have I to expect that any additional production of mine would meet a better fate? It would make me appear as if I repented for the crime of having been elected, and was anxious to apologize and beg forgiveness. (2:190–191)

Lincoln did conciliate Gilmer by noting that he had no thought of recommending the abolition of slavery in the District of Columbia, or of ending the interstate slave trade. He promised also to end the practice in certain free states of resisting the Fugitive Slave Act by passing personal liberty laws, an issue of particular importance in Wisconsin, whose challenge to the Fugitive Slave Act was working its way up through the courts, although he somewhat disingenuously added that he "could hardly be justified, as a citizen of Illinois, or as President of the United States, to recommend the repeal of a statute of Vermont, or South Carolina."

Gilmer had also raised the question of whether Lincoln would appoint Republican northerners to patronage posts in the South. This was, as William Freehling has shown, a particularly sensitive issue in the South, where such appointees might be thought of as an abolitionist fifth column.[59] (The issue was even more fraught in Virginia and Kentucky, where there was already a home-grown, if tiny, contingent of southern Republicans.) Lincoln understood this issue very well, and promised Gilmer that "where there are few or no Republicans, I do not expect to inquire for the politics of the appointee or whether he does or not own slaves. I intend in that matter to accommodate the people in the several localities, if they themselves will allow me to accommodate them. In one word, I never have been, am not now, and probably never shall be, in a mood of harassing the people, either North or South" (2:191).

Lincoln's tone in addressing the key concession he refused to make to Gilmer is interesting, because he at the same time firmly insisted upon the sternness of his commitment to nonextension and minimized the force of that insistence. In the Ohio debates and in the Cooper Union speech, Lincoln had avowed that making a moral critique of slavery was a matter of the highest moment, and failure to make that critique, even in the name of confining slavery, would so debauch the public mind as to make the triumph of slavery inevitable. Writing to Gilmer, he treated the moral conflict over slavery as something that need not stand in the way of every other kind of political dealmaking, sounding indeed rather more like Douglas than like Lincoln:

> On the territorial question, I am inflexible, as you see my position in the book. On that, there is a difference between you and us; and it is the only substantial difference. You think slavery is right and ought to be extended; we think it is wrong and ought to be restricted. For this, neither of us has any just occasion to be angry with the other. (2:191)

A week later, to his former Whig colleague in Congress, the soon-to-be vice president of the Confederacy Alexander Stephens, Lincoln asked, with a touch of incredulity, whether southerners actually believed that his election represented a dire threat to them: "Do the people of the South really entertain fears that a Republican administration would, *directly* or *indirectly*, interfere with their slaves, or with them, about their slaves? If they do, I wish to assure you, as once a friend, and still, I hope, not an enemy, that there is no cause for such fears" (2:194).

Lincoln went on to answer his own question, giving the answer he had given in the Cooper Union speech: southerners cannot really believe such a thing, and the whole conflict really comes down to southern insistence that northerners morally approve of slavery. But here there was an odd hesitancy in Lincoln's language. He could have meant, "We have come to morally irreconcilable positions, and persuasive engagement between us is at an end." But he could also have meant, against the usual grain of his argument, that "all that separates us is an issue of preference":

The South would be in no more danger in this respect, than it was in the days of Washington. I suppose, however, this does not meet the case. You think slavery is *right* and ought to be extended; while we think it is *wrong* and ought to be restricted. That I suppose is the rub. It certainly is the only substantial difference between us. (2:194)

Lincoln also had tried out some of the concepts, but not much of the language, of the First Inaugural, during his journey from Springfield to Washington. It is fair to say that the impromptu speeches Lincoln gave during his travels were a very mixed bag, and reflected, particularly in the early going, Lincoln's uncertainty about the proper course to take. In brief remarks at Indianapolis on February 8, Lincoln bandied words with a sympathetic audience about just what acts by the federal government against the seceders would count as coercion, arguing that retaking the federal harbor forts that the seceders had captured, or collecting the tariffs, or withdrawing the mail (especially from areas that had censored the mail) could not count as coercion. Perhaps stampeded by his own high spirits and by the sympathetic response of the crowd, Lincoln went on to jest that those who (like Buchanan) had professed love of the Union but had objected to these means of preserving it had sought only piddling measures:

It occurs to me that the means for the preservation of the Union they so greatly love, in their own estimation, is of a very thin and airy character. [Applause.] If sick, they would consider the little pills of the homœopathist as already too large for them to swallow. In their view, the Union, as a family relation, would to be anything like a regular marriage at all, but only as a sort of free-love arrangement,— [laughter,]—to be maintained on what that sect calls passionate attraction. [Continued laughter.] (2:201–202)

Lincoln went on, in an argument that is probably correct but that could not have been reassuring to what was left of the southern Unionists, to jeer at "the particular sacredness of a State":

By what principle of original right is it that one-fiftieth or one-ninetieth of a great nation, by calling themselves a State, have the right to break up and ruin that nation as a matter of original principle? Now, I ask the question—I am not deciding anything—[laughter,]—and with the request that you will think somewhat upon that subject and decide for yourselves, if you choose, when you get ready,—where is the mysterious, original right, from principle for a certain district of country with inhabitants, by merely being called a State, to play tyrant over all its own citizens, and deny the authority of everything greater than itself. [Laughter.] (2:202)

Having rattled the saber at Indianapolis, Lincoln adopted a head-in-the-sand strategy two days later at Columbus:

I have not maintained silence from any want of real anxiety. It is a good thing that there is no more than anxiety, for there is nothing going wrong. It is a consoling circumstance that when we look out there is nothing that really hurts anybody. We entertain different views upon political questions, but nobody is suffering anything. This is a most consoling circumstance, and from it we may conclude that all we want is time, patience, and a reliance on that God who has never forsaken this people. (2:205)

After this shaky start, Lincoln seemed to find himself as an orator as he moved east, settling upon a tone that was neither so conciliatory as to surrender everything nor so unyielding as to foreclose the possibility of reconciliation. Certainly the First Inaugural Address shows none of the amateurishness of the impromptu speeches at Indianapolis and Cincinnati.

The address opened with a very plain avowal that not only did Lincoln have no plan to interfere with slavery in the slave states, but he believed he both had no right to do so and had no inclination to do so. Frederick Douglass took this last point as a craven surrender, as if it meant that Lincoln had abandoned his hostility to slavery; in fact all Lincoln meant by it was that in the touchy situation in which he found himself he was not looking for an occasion to upset the applecart. Lincoln backed up this concession by quoting language from the Republican platform that not only made the same avowal but also indirectly denounced John Brown's raid "no matter under what pretext, as among the gravest of crimes." The last phrase is particularly important, since it not only disassociated the Republican Party from the raid, but disavowed the higher-law language in which even critics of the raid expressed grudging admiration for Brown.

Lincoln followed this up with two more specific pledges. The first was to give all the protection that can be given, consistently with the Constitution, to the states of any section when lawfully demanded, "as cheerfully to one section, as to another" (2:216). I take this to be a promise of federal intervention in the case of a second John Brown's raid, something that Buchanan, actually, had balked at. But it is also a promise to intervene on behalf of Unionist southern state governments in the event of a secessionist insurrection. Buchanan, it should be remembered, had argued that secession was unconstitutional but had also argued that the federal government lacked the constitutional power to resist secession by force. Lincoln probably also had in mind less dramatic forms of protection as well—such as putting the federal government behind the enforcement of the Fugitive Slave Act and against Wisconsin's attempt in the case of *Ableman v. Booth* to nullify it.

The second pledge was to recognize that the fugitive slave clause of the Constitution required him to create some machinery for the recapture of fugitive slaves. Lincoln described the controversy over the Fugitive Slave Act in a minimizing language that seemed to blunt any too-vivid sense of the stakes and to ignore the history of the enforcement of that act: "There is some difference of opinion whether this clause should be enforced by national or by state authority; but surely that difference is not a very material one. If the slave is to be surrendered, it can be of but little consequence to him, or to others, by which authority it is done" (2:216).

Lincoln spoke here as if the *Prigg* case, or the Anthony Burns affair, had never happened. It made a very large difference whether it was the state or the federal government that recaptured fugitive slaves. Indeed, the whole reason the *Prigg* case happened was to prevent Pennsylvania from taking reasonable care to assure that someone whom someone else claimed as a fugitive slave really was one. And much of the impetus behind the 1850 Fugitive Slave Act itself was to take the recapture of fugitive slaves out of the hands of presumably soft-on-slavery federal judges in the free states, who might ask the same kind of questions Pennsylvania's judges were in the habit of asking, and to deny accused fugitive slaves the ability to contest their recapture in federal court, which would not only open a host of procedural ways they could delay being remanded to slavery but also implicitly concede that they had the same due process rights other people enjoyed.

In this connection Lincoln suggested, using exceptionally temperate language, that the 1850 law was flawed, modestly asking, "In any law upon this subject ought not all the safeguards of liberty known in civilized and humane jurisprudence to be introduced, so that a free man be not in any case surrendered as a slave?" (2:216). Lincoln's tone implied that the reasonableness of his suggestion was so obvious that no decent slaveholder in his right mind would refuse these safeguards. But the whole point of the 1850 law was to tie the hands of state and federal judges on the subject of fugitive slaves, and to subvert the insistence upon due process. That is why fugitive slaves were not to be brought into state or federal courts, but before special federal commissioners who did not have to take testimony from the putative fugitive slave, and who were paid more if they remanded the accused to the putative owner than if they freed him. Lincoln here sought to offer reasoned and temperate argument about an issue that was designed from the first by slaveholders to exclude reasoned and temperate argument, and whose aim, even more than the recovery of actual fugitive slaves, was to force the politicians of the free states to accept the humiliation of bending to slave state orders.

In support of this desire to protect free blacks from enslavement, Lincoln added, with the same tone of modest reasonableness, "And might it not be well at the same time to provide by law for the enforcement of that clause in the Constitution which guarantees that 'The citizens of each state shall be entitled to all the privileges and immunities of citizens in the several States?'" (2:217). There was an edge in this, since it was precisely the idea that free blacks were entitled to national citizenship rights (as opposed to citizenship rights only in the few states that granted them) that the *Dred Scott* decision had been at such pains to deny.

Lincoln's argument here, although very indirectly and gently stated, was that by denying those who are accused of being fugitive slaves the normal rights of due process the Fugitive Slave Act violated the Constitution. In an understated way, Lincoln's sentence took aim also at the black codes of many northern states, among them Illinois. Lincoln may have have had in mind as well how the southern states often did not give the privileges and immunities of citizens to citizens from other states when those states were northern, as in the recent wave of persecutions of northern travelers in the South after John Brown's raid, or the less recent cases of the imprisonment of black sailors from Massachusetts whenever their ships would call at southern ports.[60]

Lincoln went on to promise to take the oath of office "with no mental reservations" and with no purpose to construe the Constitution or laws, by any hypercritical rules" (2:217). He meant by this to deny that he would set his own private conscience above the Constitution, and to deny that he would bring higher-law doctrines to the interpretation of the Constitution. (Lincoln's promise here anticipated the argument he would make in the Hodges letter in 1864.) Perhaps he also had in mind to disavow novel constitutional doctrines, such as Lysander Spooner's view (endorsed also by Frederick Douglass) that the Constitution, three-fifths compromise and all, is on balance so anti-slavery that slavery could be abolished by a legal decision.[61]

One thing Lincoln's phrase is unlikely to mean is that he promised only a "strict constructionist" or "literalist" reading of the constitutional text, because it is indeed "strict constructionist" readings that are most likely to resort to construing the Constitution by hypercritical rules. The interpreter who most loudly proclaims his literalism or the strictness of his construction is the one who is most likely to be pressing some loaded and counterintuitive reading of the text, as the repeated example of Calhoun should suffice to prove. The Court itself has not been immune to invoking this same doctrine in the service of perverting the Constitution, as witness the way it eviscerated the Fourteenth Amendment after the end of Reconstruction.

Lincoln's promise was not the (usually) dishonest one of fidelity to the text, but a promise of fidelity to a consensus shared by friend and foe. What he was promising was that he would not do anything that his foes would think of as strange or loaded. Now it is of course possible that the promise to remain true to a consensus is as capable of loadedness and disingenuousness as the promise to remain true to a text. But there is a difference: when one professes loyalty to a text, one professes loyalty to *one's own sense* of that text, and the text itself might not provide one with a check upon one's interpretation of it, since one reviews one's interpretations with the same preconceptions that governed one when one made the interpretation in the first place. When one professes loyalty to a consensus, by contrast, one's opponents, who share some, but not all, of one's preconceptions, are in a position to object if one strays from that consensus. But of course the value of this strategy depends upon the sturdiness of the consensus in the face of disagreements about other things, and that is something that in the 1850s had become too slender a reed to depend on. By 1860 southern partisans were ready to treat even the most obviously true claims Lincoln might have made about the Constitution as dangerously loaded innovations.

Lincoln in the same breath promised to continue to enforce even the laws that he himself thought of as unconstitutional (separating himself in this from predecessors like Andrew Jackson), preferring to argue for the repeal of those laws rather than merely to break them in the hope that the Supreme Court would declare them unconstitutional in retrospect. Since the Court he had in mind was still headed by Roger Taney, appealing to the Court to overturn unconstitutional pro-slavery laws would not have been a winning strategy anyway. But Lincoln's promise did have meaning—it meant that he would continue to enforce the Fugitive Slave Act, despite his reservations about it. Here his language harkens back to his treatment of unjust laws in the 1838 Lyceum speech, in which he argued that it is better to obey an unjust law until one has been able to secure its repeal by normal methods than to break it in the name of a higher law and risk anarchy in so doing.

These promises being made, Lincoln turned to the pressing issue of the secession of the Deep South states. He made a case against the legality of secession, using arguments that were for the most part familiar Unionist points dating back to Webster's second reply to Hayne, noting, for instance, that no organic law provides for the destruction of the state it defines. Even conceding that the United States was more an alliance than a country, itself a rather large concession, Lincoln argued that secession was at best a way to *break* the contract that made the alliance, not a way to *rescind* it. Secession, this is to say, can be a revolutionary act, but it can never be a constitutional one.[62] Acts of violence against the authority of the United States, therefore, are by nature "insurrectionary or revolutionary, according to circumstances." (Lincoln had originally written "treasonable" rather than "revolutionary.")[63] One reason that secession cannot be constitutional is that the Union preceded the Constitution, going back through the Declaration of Independence to the 1774 Articles of Association. Even the Articles of Confederation, which projected a much weaker government than the Constitution, stated that the Union it described was to be perpetual, and the Constitution, in seeking a more perfect union, would hardly have made it less perfect by making it temporary.

Lincoln's attack on the legality of secession was cursory, and, relative to the tedious defense of secession published by Jefferson Davis after the war, mercifully brief. Douglas L. Wilson argues that this reflects Lincoln's choice to use the First Inaugural to affirm his own defense of the Union rather than to rebut his opponents' arguments for secession.[64]

Having asserted the paramount value of Union, and his own categorical duty to execute the laws of that Union, Lincoln disavowed using force to resist secession unless the secessionists made doing so inevitable by using force themselves:

> In doing this there needs to be no bloodshed or violence, and there shall be none, unless it be forced upon the national authority. The power confided to me, will be used to hold, occupy, and possess the property, and places belonging to the government, and to collect the duties and imposts, but beyond what may be necessary for these objects, there will be no invasion—no using of force against, or among the people anywhere. (2:218)

These remarks elicited loud praise from Douglas, who was sitting on the dais, holding Lincoln's hat. Douglas was relieved that Lincoln did not plan immediately to retake Fort Pulaski and other harbor forts that had already fallen to the seceders. In the seceded states, these lines may have been received differently, since they meant that Lincoln would not abandon either Fort Sumter or Fort Pickens. (Seward had been advising Lincoln to abandon Fort Sumter and to concentrate on holding Fort Pickens.)[65] Despite several generations of Confederate apologists' arguments that Lincoln somehow maneuvered the South into firing the first shot, it is hard to imagine that any policy other than the one he followed would have been prudent; and Lincoln did not waltz the seceders into firing on Fort Sumter anyway, because they were itching to shoot.[66]

Lincoln tied his promise not to try to retake the forts with a promise not to use the patronage in an aggressive way against the South: "Where hostility to the United States, in any interior locality, shall be so great and so universal, as to prevent competent resident citizens from holding the Federal offices, there will be no attempt to force obnoxious strangers among the people for that object" (2:218). Lincoln had already made this promise privately to Gilmer; making it publicly meant that Lincoln was willing to forgo in the South the advantages control of the patronage would have given his party—not only as an instrument of policy (promises of patronage could keep restive local partisans in line) but also as a means of intelligence gathering (one of the reasons Douglas understood the seriousness of the secession threat better than Lincoln did is that Democratic postmasters all over the South were keeping him informed). Lincoln's promise meant that there would simply be no federal officeholders at all in the regions Lincoln described. Strangely, he sought to apply this policy only to interior locations. (Lincoln made this proviso, I think, because he did intend to appoint loyal customs officials to collect the tariffs.)

As William Freehling has pointed out, that Lincoln might use the federal patronage to undermine slavery was a serious concern in the South, both in the places where the appointees would have to be from out of state and in the places where there was a nascent Republican Party. Lincoln might not have been tempted to appoint William Lloyd Garrison the U.S. attorney for Montgomery, but he might well have wanted to give an important local post to John Minor Botts in Virginia, which had not yet seceded but which might well have been provoked to do so by such an appointment.[67]

The last half of the speech was devoted to speaking to the people of the South directly. Lincoln assumed that those "who seek to destroy the Union at all events, and are glad of any pretext to do it" (2:219), were beyond his reach, and he did not address them. But he assumed, probably correctly, that most southerners who leaned toward secession also had long cherished some feeling for the Union, and that it would be possible to reach them by engaging their mixed feelings.

Now Lincoln had said before the speech that the suspicions of the southerners had not been argued up, and therefore they would be impossible to argue down. Lincoln meant by this that he had already repeatedly made the arguments that should have persuaded southerners of his good will, and that further arguments could have no good effect on them because they had already closed themselves off to argument. He also meant something rather darker than this: that since even repeating his earlier arguments would lead his interlocutors to parse them closely for changes of stance in one direction or another, which they would proceed to blow out of proportion and turn to a destructive end, it was not worthwhile to make any statement at all. Lincoln had concluded the Cooper Union speech with the argument that the disagreement between the North and the South over the morality of slavery was so deep but also so consistently and thoroughly worked into the mind-set of each section that a split-the-difference compromise was impossible to imagine. Each side had an internally consistent position that was already hardened against all of the arguments the other side might bring. Each side had also worked themselves up into a passion that caused them to reject unheard whatever the other side might say.

But Lincoln's claims in the letters and in the Cooper Union speech to this effect do not mean that it was useless in the First Inaugural to address pro-secession southerners whose emotional ties to the Union, however embittered at the moment, were both deep and long-standing, because the strength of Lincoln's effort here was not only the validity of its arguments but also the way it presented a character with whom it would be reasonable to engage in a persuasive rather than a vituperative way. The calmness and generosity of Lincoln's tone were an appeal to the character of the speaker, what Aristotle would call an appeal to ethos, and such an appeal is capable of reaching an interlocutor who believes himself to be closed to argument but still has feelings that are more mixed than he lets on and through which he may be re-opened to persuasion by reason. Used in this way the appeal to ethos is not an attempt to use feeling to stampede reason, but an attempt to use feeling to get past an obstacle put up by a self-sealing ideology. The appeal carried out by Lincoln's choice of style, this is to say, was a version of the appeal to "the better angels of our nature" with which he closed the speech.

These southerners with unacknowledged mixed feelings "profess to be content in the Union, if all constitutional rights can be maintained" (2:219). Lincoln may have had in mind here the kind of ties to the Union in the face of anger with it he saw in his correspondence with his friend Joshua Speed during the Kansas crisis. Now Speed remained staunchly Union-loyal in 1861 despite breathing pro-secessionist threats back in 1855, and he represented the kind of person for whom the strategy of the First Inaugural was a promising one. Lincoln asked such people to "Think, if you can, of a single instance in which a plainly written provision of the Constitution has ever been denied" (2:219). Here Lincoln felt he was on strong ground, since there were not cases where the Republicans had sought to violate anything that the Constitution requires in so many words.

The rub, as Lincoln went on to say, is that opinions differ about the meaning of the Constitution concerning issues either not anticipated or not articulated by its authors. Now in such a conflict each side can claim to invoke the plain implication of the document, but in fact the implications are never quite so plain as all that:

> No organic law can ever be framed with a provision specifically applicable to every question which may occur in practical administration. No foresight can anticipate nor any document of reasonable length contain express provisions for all possible questions. Shall fugitives from labor be surrendered by national or by State authority? The Constitution does not expressly say. *May* Congress prohibit slavery in the territories? The Constitution does not expressly say. *Must* Congress protect slavery in the territories? The Constitution does not expressly say. (2:220)

One might, faced with this kind of issue, make the claim that a more rigorous method of interpretation could construe what the Constitution commands on these unarticulated or unanticipated issues. Indeed, most of jurisprudence involves making arguments of that kind, and on these very issues Justice Taney and his allies marshaled arguments that seemed rigorous to those predisposed to embrace his view of the Constitution already, and Justices McLean and Curtis marshaled arguments that seemed rigorous to those predisposed to the other side (and seem rigorous to posterity too, for that matter). Without despairing of the ability of reason to think through these kinds of questions, it is worth noting how often the *sound* of rigor is an effect not of actual rigor but of intensity of conviction, and that the ability to have one's way when one makes this kind of parade of rigor is often a function of the amount of force one has at one's disposal. Making this argument would not have served Lincoln's rhetorical purpose of talking the South out of secession anyway, since touting one's rigor in the discerning authoritative command of the Constitution about issues on which the Constitution expressly says nothing is usually a way to sharpen disagreements, not a way to assuage threatened feelings.

Lincoln shied in the First Inaugural from the close critique of the *Dred Scott* decision he had provided in his 1857 speech and during the 1858 debates, probably because he did not wish to seem to be making an argument that says, in effect, "I'm right about the Constitution, so shut up." Instead, Lincoln proposed rules for how one ought to behave in the face of intractable divisions of opinion on constitutional issues.

The guiding principle was majority rule, since unanimity is impossible and "the rule of a minority, as a permanent arrangement, is wholly inadmissible" (2:220). Now we have no reason to assume in any particular case that the majority will have right on its side, since both majorities and minorities are capable of interpreting the Constitution in loaded and self-serving ways. But we also cannot have government by the consent of the governed unless consent really is of paramount importance, and majority rule ultimately follows from that requirement. The minority cannot ask a higher tribunal to give it a permanent right to rule. It cannot use the relationships among the branches to permanently stalemate a majority, although it can use them to win time, perhaps a great deal of time, to persuade the majority about its point of view. In the final analysis, if a minority is to have its way, it can have it only through persuasion, not by the dictation of authority, although it can use the deliverances of authorities in a persuasive way. The minority's interests are safeguarded by the means Madison described in *Federalist* 10, by the fact that the majority's power is temporary, both because times change and majorities lose their cohesion and their passion and because in the course of time other issues, which will divide the people along different lines, are bound to become salient and soften the divisions about yesterday's quarrels. Furthermore, even in the short run the members of the majority are constrained by the knowledge that they will have to deal with other issues about which the line between the majority and the minority will fall in different places. Finally, if one has no faith that the majority will seek out the right course over the long haul, then one has no business with a democratic regime in the first place.

Because a conflict between minorities and majorities is a durable feature of a democratic society, secession cannot be an admissible solution to that conflict, since inevitably the seceded part will also divide into majorities and minorities, and will be tempted to solve that division by further secession. "A majority," Lincoln declares, "held in restraint by constitutional checks, and limitations, and always changing easily, with deliberate changes of popular opinions and sentiments, is the only true sovereign of a free people. Whoever rejects it, does, of necessity, fly to anarchy or to despotism" (2:220).

It is in the context of his defense of majority rule that Lincoln issued his famous attack upon the power of the Supreme Court. The main burden of the argument was considerably softer than Lincoln's arguments on the same subject in 1857 and 1858 (and considerably softer than his arguments in draft), because it was a different matter to comment about the power of the Court when one is president from what it was to comment on the same issue when one was a citizen or a candidate. Lincoln did not in so many words deny a voice to the Supreme Court in adjudicating constitutional issues in which a majority confronts a majority. But he limited the reach of their decisions to the cases in hand, and noted that the Court's decisions were "entitled to very high respect and consideration, in all parallel cases, by all other departments of the government," which is not quite the same thing as saying that the Court actually has the last word about such constitutional questions. Lincoln's critical point, relative to how he developed it in earlier speeches, was very indirectly put, and then hedged about with disclaimers, and also with a curious (and Douglas-like) attempt to take the onus of the *Dred Scott* decision off of Chief Justice Taney and to place it onto President Buchanan:

> At the same time the candid citizen must confess that if the policy of the government, upon vital questions, affecting the whole people, is to be irrevocably fixed by decisions of the Supreme Court, the instant they are made, in ordinary litigation between parties, in personal actions, the people will have ceased, to be their own rulers, having, to that extent, practically resigned their government, into the hands of that eminent tribunal. Nor is there, in this view, any assault upon the court, or the judges. It is a duty, from which they may not shrink, to decide cases properly brought before them; and it is no fault of theirs, if others seek to turn their decisions to political purposes. (2:221)

Lincoln's analysis of the central political problem was also put more softly in the First Inaugural than it was in the Cooper Union speech.

In the latter, he had treated the moral conflict over slavery as intractable, as deep-seated, and as inevitably enflaming, since at its heart was a burning wound to the moral narcissism of the slaveholders which drove them to repress democratic opposition to, or even criticism of, the peculiar institution. Furthermore, he described his party's position as hostility only to the extension of slavery, but did not mention in the First Inaugural, as he usually did, that he hoped to put slavery in the course of ultimate extinction.

Here, as in the letter to Stephens, Lincoln slightly minimized the depth of the moral conflict, and noted that on each side the people were, however grudgingly, willing to do what the common political life they shared required them to do. Lincoln treated the recent instances of the revival of the international slave trade (which Douglas had witnessed) as exceptions to the rule that trade should be suppressed, exceptions that reflected the fact that the South's acceptance of that rule was grudging. Resistance to the Fugitive Slave Act, Lincoln remarked, was again the exception, not the rule, and was no more widespread than one should reasonably expect given that the acceptance of the Fugitive Slave Act by the North was grudging. Now partisans of both sides had been inclined to treat both of these things as outrages, even as signs of a deeply laid sinister design against the interests of the other side, not as exceptions. Given what we know Lincoln to have felt about the revival of the international slave trade, his language is almost shockingly moderate:

> One section of our country believes slavery is *right*, and ought to be extended, while the other believes it is *wrong*, and ought not to be extended. This is the only substantial dispute. The fugitive slave clause of the Constitution, and the law for the suppression of the foreign slave trade, are each as well enforced, perhaps, as any law can ever be in a community where the moral sense of the people imperfectly supports the law itself. The great body of the people abide by the dry legal obligation in both cases, and a few break over in each. This, I think, cannot be perfectly cured; and it would be worse in both cases *after* the separation of the sections, than before. The foreign slave trade, now imperfectly suppressed, would be ultimately revived without restriction, in one section; while fugitive slaves, now only partially surrendered, would not be surrendered at all, by the other. (2:221)

Having so defined the key issue, Lincoln developed not the illegality but the futility of secession, arguing that even if the South were to secede, it would still face all the same issues with the North, but since it would have to resolve those issues by treaty rather than by law, it would have weaker means at its disposal to work its satisfaction. From within the Union, for example, southern masters were in a strong position to demand the return of slaves who had fled to the North; they would be in a very weak position to make such a demand were the South successful in leaving the Union. Given these difficulties, Lincoln argued, it would be more practical for the South to seek some reasonable accommodation with the North than for it to secede, and he proposed that the remedy of amending the Constitution was available, whether by individual amendments or by calling a constitutional convention.

Now of course the amendment route had been proposed by Crittenden and by the Washington Peace Conference, and the results of neither were very promising. But Lincoln went so far as to propose one of the very amendments he had rejected during the secession winter, an amendment to prevent Congress from emancipating the slaves, which amendment Thomas Corwin of Ohio, one of the founders of the Republican Party, had just shepherded through Congress. The Corwin Amendment would seem to surrender the central motivating idea of the Republican Party, the idea that slavery is wrong, and would seem to concede that there must be some portion of the United States that will forever hold slaves. Why did this concession seem less fatal to Lincoln than extending the Missouri Compromise line? Perhaps the reason is that the Corwin Amendment surrendered only something Lincoln already knew he would probably never be in a position to ask for, abolition of slavery in the slave states through ordinary legislation by Congress. The Corwin Amendment would not, like the Lecompton Constitution's language about slavery in Kansas, or like the Crittenden Compromise's version of the same amendment, put slavery beyond the power of being abolished by a constitutional amendment.[68] That said, however, the Corwin Amendment was still a large and to modern ears even a scandalous concession; it is surprising that making it had no persuasive effect at all.

Ultimately what Lincoln depended on to save the Union in this speech was not arguments about the illegality of secession, or even concessions to the slave power, but the ability to awaken a latent love of the Union that he hoped had persisted in his interlocutors beneath the clamor for disunion. To do this, Lincoln distinguished between the immediate arguments being made in focal consciousness and the charged but implicit background of allegiances, feelings, common history, and common values that exerted a kind of pull in the direction of union and reconciliation. What he had in mind was the distinction between a hot resolution in the here and now and the upshot of a hundred resolutions over almost ninety years that may be in tension with that immediate resolution. By "the better angels of our nature" Lincoln had in mind that half-conscious structure of habits and values against which our acts take their long-term meaning but that no individual act suffices to define too precisely and that individual acts sometimes contradict. "The better angels of our nature" is another name for what I have been calling the public mind, that zone of implicitness in which values take on all the complexity (and all the opacity) of living things, those identity-forming intuitions that always elude complete articulation but that inform and drive what we do articulate. To invoke the better angels of our nature is to invoke that intense but indescribable gravitational field that holds together the scraps of our acts and arguments and makes something whole and human of them, that ever-changing ground of becoming and belonging by which we are transformed into what we did not know we already were, and to which we are called back, by a shadowy kind of force, when we have bewildered ourselves. The better angels of our nature tie us back as much to what is *given* as to what is *chosen*, to the *nation* as much as to the *state*, to *America* as much as to the *United States.*

It is chiefly the fact that the majority and the minority are imbricated in a common public mind, in a common tangle of values and intuitions upon which neither has an exclusive purchase, which binds majority and minority together in one polity. Otherwise the minority's concession is mere submission, and the majority's power is merely the power of making the other side submit. The majority does not have the right to drive the minority to the wall, but the minority also does not have the right to claim that every concession is an attempt to drive it to the wall. As I cannot argue a proposition without understanding where that proposition is vulnerable and where the opposing proposition has a case, so I cannot take a position in a persuasive culture if I cannot recognize when my faction's position is a losing one or if I cannot imagine some nonsuicidal way to back down. The minority would be wise to accept the concessions it must make anyway, not merely because to do so is its duty (duty being as always a rather unattractive reason for doing something one is not inclined already to do) but also because its own purchase upon its governing values does not exhaust their meaning, and the minority therefore remains bound up with those of opposing views who, from their different point of view about shared values, may yet shed an unexpected light on their meaning. The legitimacy of the majority's rule arises not only from the fact that it for the most part values the same things the minority does but also from the fact that even where the majority's take on those values differs from that of the minority, the minority is not in a position to argue that the majority never has a point about them. One of the hallmarks of intellectual maturity is after all the recognition that sometimes the other side has a point, and that sometimes one does not see that point right away. The same considerations, the fact that the majority too has an investment in the minority's point of view, which may yet shed light on the meaning of their common values, bind the majority to a generous settlement with the minority.

It is just this background of common moral assumptions that under most circumstances links together consent and principle, the chief requirements of political legitimacy in a democratic society. These common moral assumptions and common history ground popular will in something deeper than the momentary ascendency of one party or another, and limit the damage one party can do to the other:

> Why should there not be a patient confidence in the ultimate justice of the people? Is there any better, or equal hope, in the world? In our present differences, is either party without faith of being in the right? If the Almighty Ruler of nations, with his eternal truth and justice, be on your side of the North, or on yours or the South, that truth, and that justice, will surely prevail, by the judgment of this great tribunal, the American people.
>
> By the frame of the government under which we live, this same people have wisely given their public servants but little power for mischief; and have, with equal wisdom, provided for the return of that little to their own hands at very short intervals.
>
> While the people retain their virtue, and vigilance, no administration, by any extreme of wickedness or folly, can very seriously injure the government, in the short space of four years. (2:223)

Lincoln's use of the idea of the public mind in the First Inaugural differed substantially from his use of the same idea in his political speeches from the Peoria speech to the Cooper Union speech. In the earlier speeches, he had emphasized the public mind's vulnerability. In the First Inaugural he emphasized its durability. In the political speeches he had portrayed the public mind as endangered by the recklessness of his political opponents. But in the First Inaugural it is the public mind itself that Lincoln invoked to hold far more formidable opponents within bounds.

Lincoln's key invocation of the public mind is the famous peroration of the First Inaugural. Much of the language of the peroration derived from Seward, who felt that the original ending, particularly with its ominous concluding question, "Shall it be peace, or a sword?" concluded the speech in too threatening a way. Seward may have worked from notes Lincoln wrote on the back of Orville Browning's letter to Lincoln suggesting revisions. Seward's version lacks some of Lincoln's music, and some of his argument as well:

Seward's Version

I close. We are not we must not be aliens or enemies but fellow countrymen and brethren. Although passion has strained our bonds of affection too hardly they must not, I am sure they will not be broken. The mystic chords which proceeding from so many battle fields and so many patriot graves pass through all the hearts and all the hearths in this broad continent of ours will yet again harmonize in their ancient music when breathed upon by the guardian angel of the nation.[69]

Lincoln's Version

I am loth to close. We are not enemies, but friends. We must not be enemies. Though passion may have strained, it must not break our bonds of affection. The mystic chords of memory, streching from every battle-field, and patriot grave, to every living heart and hearthstone, all over this broad land, will yet swell the chorus of the Union, when again touched, as surely they will be, by the better angels of our nature. (2:24)

Ronald White captures the stylistic ways in which Lincoln set Seward's draft to music—his use of antithesis to define the conflict, of alliteration to link together all of the stakes, and of assonance for emphasis. He also details how Lincoln removed some of the redundancies and oratorical paste gems from Seward's draft.[70]

The revision from "I close" to "I am loth to close" captures something of the pathos of Lincoln's rhetorical task. Seward's phrase merely announced that a peroration was about to begin. Lincoln's registered his fear of what will happen once that peroration ends. Lincoln was reluctant to close (but knew also that the closing was inevitable) because closing the speech meant ending the effort at persuasive engagement with the South; the sentence is a hesitant and unwilling recognition of the imminence of war.[71]

Lincoln transformed the desperate, pleading volubility of "We are not we must not be aliens or enemies but fellow countrymen and brethren" into the firm, air-clearing statement, as much command as proposition, as much performative as constative, "We are not enemies, but friends." The mawkish wishful thinking of Seward's "they [our bonds of affection] must not, I am sure they will not be broken" is transformed into an imperative, shadowed with a sense of its own futility: "Though passion may have strained, it must not break our bonds of affection." Both versions use the word "bonds" in several senses: a bond is a connection (perhaps a restraining one), but also a special kind of promise, a promise deeply seated in the moral identity.

Both versions of the final sentence offer a complex, and rather mixed, metaphor. Both turn on a half-conscious pun, in which "chords" are at the same time tightened strings (cord-like anatomical structures, perhaps versions of "our bonds of affection") and harmonized sounds (like the chords one might play on a harp). The two metaphors are linked, in that it is only the straining of the chords in the first sense of the word that makes the harmonizing music of the second sense possible. Seward's chords are somehow external and abstract, in that they "proceed" from battlefields and graves and pass *through* hearts and hearths, but do not seem to be essentially the property of those hearts. Lincoln's chords, by contrast, stretch, like living things, or like something pulled taut by a living thing, and are more directly the expressions of the inward feelings of a multitude of people, since they are "mystic chords of *memory*" (emphasis added). Lincoln's mystic chords of memory stretch *to* every heart rather than *through* them, as if each chord terminated in one living heart, connecting that heart to all of the dead hearts haunting the battlefields and the patriot graves. (That the living are bound to the dead who died on their behalf, and are obligated to fulfill what the dead gave the last full measure of devotion to but were unable to fulfill, will be, of course, the major theme of the Gettysburg Address.)

Seward seems to have imagined the mystic chords as parts of a kind of aeolian harp, which will make music when breathed on from above by a guardian angel. Lincoln's chorus of Union, as Doris Kearns Goodwin pointed out, is swelled from *within*, by the better angels *of our nature*, who *touch* the strings, but Seward's chorus of Union is harmonized from *without*, by the guardian angel of the nation, who *breathes* upon them.[72] Seward's angel is singular, a metaphorical concretion of the nation like the statue on top of the Capitol.[73] Lincoln's angels, in contrast, are plural, since they represent that part of each of us that knows better, that part that catches us by surprise even when, in the midst of our conflict, we think we have seen and heard the last things we need to see and hear, and think that we no longer have any choice but to do something we expect to regret. They are divine second thoughts, which reopen the case we have not been able to find any reason not to consider closed.

Even the kind of hope these angels represent is slightly different in Lincoln's version. Seward's angel will "yet again harmonize" the chorus of Union, as if that chorus had just a second ago stopped sounding, and will sound again momentarily. When Lincoln says that the better angels of our nature "will yet swell the chorus of the Union," he means that "yet" to have the force of "despite everything, despite all appearances, despite the fact that we ourselves have almost given up."

Both Seward and Lincoln treated their perorations as appeals to feeling, but they understood feeling in slightly different ways. Seward appealed to good feelings to heal the effects of bad ones, to heal the effects of the passions that have strained our bonds of affection too hardly. But for Lincoln, stampeding passions were only part of the problem. There was also a stampeding rationality, one that was invested in particular self-imprisoning theories of the Constitution, of states, of race, and of social order. These stampeding rationalities have reasoned those in their grip into a corner, so that they are indistinguishable from passions, as brandished rather than meditated-upon reasons, reasons that clank when they move (to use Eudora Welty's phrase), tend to become. The slaveholders, in Lincoln's view, have thought themselves into a predicament counter to the intuitions that shaped the thinking of their Revolutionary ancestors; they have alienated themselves from the democratic traditions they claim to be heirs of. They can be reconciled to the Union not just by recalling better feelings, but by reawakening deeply rooted, identity-giving feelings they have lost touch with. If they are to be persuaded, it is not simply by a change of mood, but by a revolution of feeling that restores them to themselves, a rebuke from a forgotten self, a blow from the Socratic daimon. What Lincoln hopes for, rather desperately, is not just that the secessionists will set aside their anger, but that, having closed themselves off to persuasion by means of loyalty politics and suicidally apodictic arguments, they all of a sudden come to themselves in the way people do who find themselves saying, "What could I have been thinking?" When that happens, feeling does not overrule rationality, but frees rationality from the trap it has set for itself.

But the war came. The northern Democratic papers were predictably critical, seeing the First Inaugural as the work of the loose-jointed hayseed they had already decided that Lincoln had to be. The *New York Herald*, for instance, said that this inaugural "would have caused a Washington to mourn, and would have inspired a Jefferson, Madison, or Jackson with contempt." The *Philadelphia Evening Journal* complained that the speech was "one of the most awkwardly constructed official documents we have ever inspected."[74] The responses from the southern papers, predictably, took a harsher tone, finding the First Inaugural to be no less than a declaration of war, a manifesto employing, in the *Richmond Enquirer*'s terms, "the cool, unimpassioned, deliberate language of the fanatic," in order to bring about "the dismemberment of the Government with the horrors of civil war."[75] So vituperative was the response in southern circles that the *New York Times* speculated that the responses may have been written before Lincoln's speech was even delivered.[76]

Despite this failure, the First Inaugural Address was no blunder, and its attempt at sectional reconciliation was not wholly unrealistic. Actual people's convictions are usually a little bit more mixed than their compact statements of them (frequently made in public contexts where conformity is expected) would lead one to believe. When one asserts that one is wholehearted in one's convictions and entertains them without a shred of doubt, that assertion is usually made for public consumption, and it rarely has much truth to it. To appeal to the "better angels of our nature" is not to ask feeling to stampede argument, but to ask those who make the argument to examine themselves to determine whether their feelings really are quite as resolute as they advertise them to be. The rationality that cannot resist this kind of appeal is mechanical, a kind of metal armature designed to prop up the appearance of resoluteness, not the product of a serious and unflinching examination of the sources of one's convictions, and it does not really deserve the respect of reason.

Part of reason is reasonableness, and reasonableness involves a frank recognition of the limits of one's certainties and the tentativeness of one's conclusions. From the Peoria speech forward, Lincoln never failed (well, almost never failed) to recognize that intellectual and moral maturity requires reasonableness as much as it requires rationality. It involves an acknowledgment that full humanity requires recognition on both sides of the intellectual divide of the implicitness of values and of the deep agreements in whose terms persuasive arguments, as opposed to mere screaming, must always be phrased. The failure of the First Inaugural had nothing to do with the weakness of Lincoln's arguments, because they were strong arguments, or the insufficiency of his concessions, because he conceded rather more than he should have. The failure of the First Inaugural is entirely the product of the fact that it was addressed to an audience that had been stampeded by their ideology and by their fears into a nervous rejection of the implicitness of their own convictions and a repudiation of those grounds in shared values upon which persuasive engagement always depends. The secessionists were rational, in just the way that paranoids and kooks are rational. Such people are often very rational, more rational indeed than most of the rest of us. But that is because their rationality is all that is left to them; it is a mode of their disease. The secessionist response to the First Inaugural was a failure of pragmatism, a failure of self-scrutiny, a failure of the mature detachment one expects reasonable people to engage in as a kind of second nature. What the secessionists lacked was reason, not rationality. So the war came.

CHAPTER 9

Coda: And the War Came

*T*HE GREAT THEMES OF LINCOLN'S presidential
speeches and public papers are the consequences of the great themes of
the Lincoln-Douglas debates: that the absolute cultural precondition
of political freedom is the moral equality of all people; that the problem of moral equality is fraught with conflicts so deep and so intractable that the Union, whose commitment to moral equality is compromised by hypocrisy and shadowed by self-deceit, cannot be preserved
or retain its freedom except through a struggle that risks its survival;
that emancipation is both morally and practically the necessary precondition of restoring the Union; that conflicts over moral issues are
so entangled with the weaknesses of human nature that all outcomes
are tragic and no agents are pure; that a common fallenness, a sense of
mutual complicity in evil, and a shared legacy of unending inner conflict over the issues that divided the outward belligerents ultimately
demands an un-self-righteous rapprochement with the former enemy.
The Gettysburg and Second Inaugural Addresses, in particular, return to issues that were left unsettled at the end of the 1858 debates.
Douglas's strongest argument in 1858 was that attempting to settle the
moral issue of slavery in a thoroughgoing way risked a war that the
United States might lose or that, in victory, would cost it its freedom.
Only in the two greatest speeches of his presidency did Lincoln finally
come up with satisfactory if still ambiguous answers to the arguments
Douglas had posed.

9.1 The Gettysburg Address

The verbs of the first sentence of the Gettysburg Address are drawn from organic life, and they imagine the United States as a developing child. The new nation is "conceived" (by the Fathers), "brought forth" (upon this continent), and "dedicated" to the proposition that all men are created equal. And the speech ends by projecting a "new birth" of freedom, transmuting, by means of a life-giving idea, the deaths of the men who struggled in that place into a new form of life, held in common by the entire nation, North and South, black and white. Even the date of the Declaration of Independence ("Fourscore and seven years ago") is given in terms that call to mind the biblical phrase from Psalm 90 for the length of a human life.[1]

This organic metaphor was noticed at the time by several hostile critics. The *New York World*, for instance, ridiculed the speech for representing "the 'fathers' in the stages of conception and parturition," and the *Boston Daily Courier* sneered at the "obstetric allusion."[2] But the organic metaphor plays several important purposes in the rhetoric of the speech.[3]

First, as John Channing Briggs has pointed out, if the nation grows like a child, then the Founders can beget it and nurture it, but they cannot assemble it or design it. The nation is not so much the product of a contract, something subject to strict construction, and completely subordinated to the plan of the Founders, as it is something that grows from within, in its own way, toward ends that it gropingly, and only gradually, realizes.[4] It is not put together like a machine, but develops out of its own inwardness, the offspring of its parents but not their instrument. Eric Foner points out that Lincoln never refers in the Gettysburg Address to the United States as "the Union," as he had tended to do earlier. The organic unity of the nation replaces the created unity of the Union.[5] In *Lincoln at Gettysburg* (1992), Garry Wills goes so far as to read "on this continent" as to imply that the Americans see themselves almost as children of the earth mother, autochthonous, as the Athenians saw themselves in their own national mythology. I take his point to be that the nation's development is a mysterious unfolding that one can understand only with a certain amount of negative capability, that the key values of the nation have what I have been calling implicitness. The nation demands to be understood not epistemically but intuitively, as an example of what Wittgenstein called "a form of life."

The metaphor of organic development carries with it the dual implication that the nation has a telos, and that how that telos will find its ultimate realization is unknowable in advance. A child like this one, a "dedicated" child, is born with a calling, but it must find its own way to realizing that calling, and even its parents cannot fully understand where that calling will take it, although they know where it began and how it began to take shape. The "dedication" of the young nation is not merely a covenant, but a baptism, the giving of its true name, the sign that its identity includes a destiny which, at that moment, could only be seen as in a glass darkly.

That said, I rush to add that this vision of the telos of the Republic is a vision only of its *ends*. It has nothing to say about the *means* to that end, which Lincoln always scrupulously kept within the bounds of what the Constitution allowed him to do.[6] Lincoln did, here and elsewhere, give the promises of the Declaration priority over the Constitution, reaching back four score and seven years ago to 1776, the date of the Declaration, not three score and sixteen years ago to 1787, the date of the Constitutional Convention. And Lincoln did find the Constitution to be spiritually inferior to the Declaration. But he never treated that priority as freeing him from the rule of the Constitution, and he always, to the impatience of some, limited what he did in the name of the Declaration to what he knew the Constitution would allow. He treated the Declaration, this is to say, as a statement of the *concept* of American liberty, which could be brought to realization only through the *conceptions* of the Constitution. He never treated the Declaration as a higher law that would license him to suspend the Constitution. The endless argument about whether Lincoln's sympathies were with the radicals or with the conservatives turns on whether one focuses chiefly upon his ends, which were radical, or on his means, which were conservative.[7]

A second effect of the organic metaphor of the first sentence is that it enabled Lincoln to define the nature and meaning of the Civil War in an unexpected way. If the nation is a growing child, the Civil War is an almost inevitable, life-threatening childhood trauma that either kills or transforms the child.[8] By phrasing the legacy of the Declaration as a "proposition" rather than as a self-evident truth, Lincoln implied that that legacy has to be tested, has to undergo a trial by fire before its truth can be recognized.[9] What is at stake is not the mere survival of the United States, but whether any society dedicated to equality can survive. Moreover, any society dedicated to equality must risk a similar test, and cannot authentically affirm equality until it has undergone such a test. The Republic had to survive the almost mortal test of Civil War as children had to survive the almost mortal test of disease.

When we wonder whether a nation will "endure," we wonder rather more than merely whether it will be able to continue. "Enduring" is something you *do*, something that requires stern strength of will; "surviving" is just something that happens to you. To endure is to face down suffering; indeed, it is to continue to bear the mark of that suffering past the end of suffering. Even more than "survive," the word "endure" registers a continuing struggle for life, and registers that the struggle itself is somehow transformative. Those who survive may be exhausted and emptied by the experience, but those who endure have proven something about themselves that otherwise might not have been expected. One is marked by enduring, but one is also hardened by it, like steel under the hammer.[10]

The citizens' watch over their imperiled Republic was analogous to the parents' watch over their dangerously ill children, a touchstone of nineteenth-century fiction from Little Nell to Little Eva to Beth March. Lincoln himself, during the ceremony at the Gettysburg National Cemetery, still wore the black band on his hat he put on after the death of his son Willie the previous year.[11]

In all of these novels of the death of children from *The Old Curiosity Shop* to *Little Women*, the dying children became a source of transformative wisdom to their grieving families. Eva St. Clair in *Uncle Tom's Cabin*, for instance, saw the wrong of slavery clearly, and, in dying, brought her father to recognize that wrong, something he had perhaps dimly known from the beginning but had never fully acknowledged to himself, blinded as he was by the ironies and double-binds of adulthood.[12] The care and grief of the worried parent are transformed into the wisdom given that parent by the dying child, and the direction of the action reverses itself, so that the parents, who dedicated the child, are rededicated by their dying children to a cause the children saw more clearly than their parents did. Indeed, in the final movement of the Gettysburg Address, in which the living are rededicated by the dead, only the experience of mourning their children frees the adults, as Mr. St. Clair is freed, from illusions, in the citizens' case the illusion that the aim of the war is restoration of the old Union rather than the development of equality, an illusion in which they would otherwise have been imprisoned forever.

The grief of the many thousands of parents who lost their children at Gettysburg was brutally different from the idealized forms of death rendered in nineteenth-century fiction. The suddenness; the randomness; the violation of the body's integrity, torn to pieces by shrapnel or Minié balls; the chaos that prevented many bodies from being found at all, or returned to their families if found—all of these were violations of the mid-nineteenth-century's sense of "the good death," expressed in the fiction and poetry of the age, and expressed just as much in the carefully shaped and tended landscapes of the new "rural" cemeteries such as Cambridge's Mount Auburn Cemetery, or indeed the Gettysburg National Cemetery (designed, Wills reminds us, by the same William Saunders who laid out the Oak Ridge Cemetery in Springfield where Lincoln's body would be buried after his assassination).[13]

The restraint of Lincoln's rhetoric sublimated the experience of violent death into the rebirth of the Republic. Part of what made this possible—a task so hard that most wartime elegies turn inauthentic in the face of it—was Lincoln's ability to invest his hearers in a transformative unfinished project, the completion of democracy, so that the death of their loved ones was not merely a kind of sacrifice at the altar of the state, but a way to assure the victory of a great value that the state exists to realize. But part of it was also his ability to recast the mourners in a role more familiar to nineteenth-century deathways, the parents of a mortally threatened child. If the citizens are metaphorical parents watching over the sickbed of a mortally threatened republic, they are, in the speech's final movement, rather like the parents in nineteenth-century novels, rededicated by their dying actual children.

The fiery trial of the Union differs in one crucial respect from the deaths of children in nineteenth-century fiction, and that is that a childhood disease is a random event, whereas the trial of democracy is built into the design of democracy itself. Democracy cannot develop without this trial, and what democracy becomes under pressure of this trial is more truly what democracy is than what it was beforehand: only the mortal pressure of civil war forces an honest reckoning with the problem of democracy, and without the power of violence to unde-ceive, democracy would have settled for an illusory life, a once-born life without a "new birth of freedom." Without the violence of the war, Union-loyal Americans, Lincoln included, would have settled for that oxymoron a slaveholder democracy, or, in the event of emancipation, for *herrenvolk* democracy. The war, this is to say, is a necessary episode in the becoming of democracy, without which democracy cannot come to fulfillment.

Because the war is the agent of the metamorphosis of democracy, an endangered becoming mediated and made possible by the threat of destruction, neither side stands in a position of moral privilege relative to the other: the nation must be tested, and the North and the South both have roles to play in that test. The war is not the outcome of a malign conspiracy of slaveholders seeking to confirm themselves in power. Nor is it a crusade by opponents of slavery against a signal evil. The war is a trial given to the North and the South on account of slav-ery, an unavoidable although dangerous episode in the coming to be of democracy, necessary because of their mutual complicity in slavery.

Conceiving of the war as a necessary trial of democracy also enabled Lincoln to account not only for the meaning of the war but also for why it was so violent, so long, and so inconclusive, for the Republic was given to suffer until it learned to repudiate certain corrupt values—slavery and *herrenvolk* democracy—that it not only held deeply but also felt to be constitutive of its politics; the extended slaughter of the war was necessary to disabuse both the North and the South of crippling illusions about democracy.

A third effect of Lincoln's organic metaphor was that to see America as an organic collective form of life, not just with a history but with a biography, was to see America as a nation rather than as a state. A state is a body of concrete institutions, laws, deliberative bodies, agencies of enforcement, regulation, and registration—an organization having a monopoly over the means of violence, to cite Max Weber's pungent definition of the state from "Politics as a Vocation" (1919). A nation is something muddier but deeper. To a first approximation, a nation is a people, but what makes a mass of human beings a people is hard to say.

Perhaps, according to Benedict Anderson in *Imagined Communities* (1983), the chief thing that makes a nation is a ruthless and successful practice of hype. In the nineteenth century, the role of making a mass of people into a nation was sometimes attributed to blood, and more often to blood's metaphorical cousins, culture and language.[14] Under that definition of "nation," it is hard to see that the term applies to the United States, whether in the nineteenth or in the twenty-first century. The United States has typically imagined itself, except in eras of xenophobic frenzy such as the 1920s, or the 1850s (or the present), as a nation of newcomers. Despite occasional xenophobic outbursts, the United States is still almost the only nation, not the only state, of course, but the only nation, that one can join by an act of will. Immigration can make you a citizen of France, but it cannot make you French, as France has been painfully learning.[15] Immigration cannot even make you a citizen of Japan. But immigration can make you American; indeed, since the immigrant has to choose what the native-born has been given, the immigrant is in some way the paradigmatic American.

This is not to say that American society has always practiced what its thinkers sometimes preach about assimilation. Nor is it to say that assimilation has been without cost to the assimilated. Nor is it even to say that all those who have come to the United States have sought assimilation. But it is to say that the idea, articulated by Lincoln, that immigrants who have embraced the political ideals of the Founders have as deep a share of American nationality as those whose ancestors were born in the United States is an idea, however contested, with a powerful following and a venerable history. Whether or not the United States actually *is* a culture, not merely a state, one can join by an act of will, the fact that a significant fraction of American thinkers are ashamed of its failure to become such a culture is itself testimony to the power of the ambition to create one. That ambition could not have been entertained at all if more traditional understandings of the meaning of culture and nation were not contested in the United States.

The reason immigration can make one American is, as Lincoln argued in his 1858 Chicago speech, that political traditions in America stand in the place cultural history and language and blood do in other nations.[16] To be American is not a matter of blood but a matter of an idea, said Count Adam Gurowski, who acutely if vituperatively observed Washington society during the Civil War years; American nationality is as much a matter of consent as it is of descent, to use Werner Sollors's phrase for it.[17] Nationality is usually something *given*, not something *chosen*. By founding nationality upon political values, even those for whom American nationality is given see it as something chosen, at least to the extent that they do not see it as a private cultural property, but as a possibility, opened to them perhaps by their own special history, but somehow expressive of a project in which the whole rest of the world has a stake.

It is placing these ideas at the center of American cultural *nationhood*, not merely at the center of American political traditions, that George Fletcher, following Robert Penn Warren, sees as one of the outcomes of the Civil War.[18] Fletcher, like Edmund Wilson before him, sees Lincoln as one of the great nineteenth-century forgers of nations, like Giuseppe Garibaldi, Lajos Kossuth, or Otto von Bismarck, and he sees the idea of American nationality itself as, however it might have been proclaimed in the spread-eagle Fourth of July oratory of the antebellum era, the chief cultural consequence of the Civil War, and the chief rhetorical burden of Lincoln's greatest speeches.

Fletcher sees the Civil War as the death of the first American republic, which, for all its relative cultural homogeneity and fervid patriotism, was a state, but not a nation. In making this distinction, Fletcher wishes to point out the ways in which the first republic was organized around values that sharply distinguish it from the second republic. Fletcher identifies three linked themes in the first republic: peoplehood as a voluntary association, individual freedom, and republican elitism. He contrasts these with three themes that characterize the second republic: organic nationhood, equality of all persons, and popular democracy.

The second republic, no less than the first, was the creature of certain political ideas. The difference between the two republics is not the difference between a compact founded on a deal and an organic nation founded on something else, but between a compact founded upon a deal whose meaning one seeks to bind into the narrowest compass, in the way one interprets a contract, and a society that places certain ideals at the center of its identity, ideals that themselves become, and that force the society to become as well, so that the compact is not so much a concrete deal as a troubling and challenging promise. And it is a covenant that demands the nation keep faith with it, even as both covenant and nation become in wholly unanticipated ways.

The chief object of value to the first republic was individual freedom, which the first republic saw only in what Isaiah Berlin, in his essay "Two Concepts of Liberty," would call a "negative" way, as something purely private, to be shielded from interference by public power.[19] By contrast, the chief object of value to the second republic is moral equality, something that transcends contracts, something that all people have a claim on as people, and that the state is called upon to affirm in a positive way.[20] People under the second republic are equal not in the way that members of the same club are equal; they are equal in the way that only subjects of infinite value are equal. They are not, to repeat, equal in the way we mean it when we say that hawks and chickadees are equally birds, but equal in the way we mean it when we say that black and white are equally human, or in the way that Saint Paul meant it when he said that there is neither Jew nor Greek in Christ.

Freedom and equality can be contrary values if the freedom in question is not universal freedom. Among the freedoms defended by the first republic was the freedom to own slaves, and the analogous freedom to treat workers more or less however you pleased to treat them, a freedom the business elite enjoyed until the New Deal. Among the features of the compact that established the state and defined the meaning of freedom were curbs on the ability of the state to interfere with either exploitive relationship. In *Our Secret Constitution* (2001), Fletcher argues that the tendency to see legal institutions only in the light of explicit deals and compacts, what under other circumstances we might call "strict constructionism," and what Fletcher, explicitly borrowing Robert Penn Warren's language, calls "legalism," inevitably and necessarily sees the freedom it cherishes and protects as the freedom of the strong to exploit the weak.

Lincoln defined the meaning of the strict-constructionist ideal of freedom with tolerable exactitude in a speech at the Baltimore Sanitary Fair on April 18, 1864:

> The world has never had a good definition of the word liberty, and the American people, just now, are much in want of one. We all declare for liberty; but in using the same *word* we do not all mean the same *thing*. With some the word liberty may mean for each man to do as he pleases with himself, and the product of his labor; while with others the same word may mean for some men to do as they please with other men, and the product of other men's labor. Here are two, not only different, but incompatable things, called by the

same name—liberty. And it follows that each of the things is, by the respective parties, called by two different and incompatable names— liberty and tyranny.

The shepherd drives the wolf from the sheep's throat, for which the sheep thanks the shepherd as a *liberator*, while the wolf denounces him for the same act as the destroyer of liberty, especially as the sheep was a black one. Plainly the sheep and the wolf are not agreed upon a definition of the word liberty; and precisely the same difference prevails to-day among us human creatures, even in the North, and all professing to love liberty. Hence we behold the processes by which thousands are daily passing from under the yoke of bondage, hailed by some as the advance of liberty, and bewailed by others as the destruction of all liberty. Recently, as it seems, the people of Maryland [by voting to abolish slavery] have been doing something to define liberty; and thanks to them that, in what they have done, the wolf's dictionary, has been repudiated. (1:589–590)

The connection between Fletcher's first two themes, the insistence upon the ruling instruments as a purely explicit deal and the insistence upon a purely negative idea of freedom, yields the third great theme of Fletcher's reading of the politics of the first republic, the theme of republican elitism. The classical republic, Fletcher reminds us, offers freedom only for those who are members of the political nation, only for those who have access to the polis.[21] But the freedom of the polis depends upon the subjection of the *oikos*, where the uncompensated labor of those subjected to necessity, and therefore incapable of deliberative freedom, has always been the price of the deliberative freedom of others. The members of the polis, freed from crushing dependencies upon each other by the bondage of others, can enter the space of public deliberation with each other as equals. There was no contradiction between slavery and freedom in the classical republic, because it was only the slavery of the *oikos* made possible the freedom of the polis. There was also no contradiction between slavery and equality in the classical republic, because only the slavery of the *oikos* made possible the equality of the polis. Negative freedom is not only the means of exploitation, but also the fruit of exploitation, and legalism is its scripture.

The elitism of the classical republic was not lost upon the thinkers of the first American republic. John C. Calhoun, in his 1848 speech in the Senate on the admission of Oregon, made the connections I pointed out above in yet more trenchant language than I have used, stigmatizing the Jeffersonian claim that all men are created equal as an obvious, even sophomoric, mistake—and one with dire consequences. Senator James Henry Hammond, of South Carolina, in the famous 1857 Senate oration in which he coined the phrase "Cotton is King," also argued that there has never been a free society that was not founded upon a mud-sill of subjection.[22] And when Chief Justice Roger Taney, in his 1857 opinion in the *Dred Scott* case, attributed to the Founders the view (which even he found repugnant) that the black man has no rights that the white man is bound to respect, he touched upon the key meaning of the relevance of classical republicanism to the first American republic, for it was characteristic of that republic to see possession of rights not as the inheritance of all human beings as human beings, but as a function of membership in the political community, a membership in which admission was controlled only by the explicit declaration of the community itself.

When Matthew Arnold encountered the word "proposition" in the Gettysburg Address, he is said to have reacted with disgust at the clash between the high biblical rhetoric of the opening phrase and the descent to the language of legal pettifogging at its conclusion.[23] Wills persuasively argues that the provenance of "proposition" is not the rural county-seat courthouse, but Euclid, suggesting not the details of some business arrangement, but the deeply rooted axioms of the mathematical world.[24] "Proposition" is a word that has majesty for Lincoln, because it suggests to him the principled drawing of a line, the definition of an identity-giving and life-risking moral stake. A proposition is something one might nail to a cathedral door, or put one's name to, hazarding one's life and one's sacred honor.

Whatever the provenance of the word, the contrast between the organic "bringing forth" of the new nation and the metaphysical "proposition" to which it is dedicated, captures something of the crux of the idea that something like the United States can be a nation: it is made a nation not by blood or history, but by an identity-founding commitment to a value, available to everyone but given special local salience by being tested there and then. America is the nation whose identity is created by its being in a position to test values it hopes will be found good for all nations; its uniqueness is given to it by its calling of testing a set of values which, if they stand the test, are not then to be seen as unique to it, but as universal.

The word "proposition" captures the common awareness that American identity both is and is not organic. For the immigrant, it is something chosen, but chosen in a way that has the identity-making power of something given. For the native-born, it is something given, but is taken as if it were chosen, the fruit of agency rather than agency's precondition. That is why the sentence uses the metaphor of baptism: the nation is "dedicated" to a proposition, given its identity in that proposition, called into being as a test of that proposition, discovering its meaning in piecing together the significance and the consequences of that proposition.

The aim of this dedication, the value Lincoln saw as at the heart of the prospective American character, is equality, a value in fact not achieved by the United States then or now. Lincoln's choice, like his choice of the founding moment in 1776 rather than in 1787, the sweeping promises of the Declaration rather than the painful and exacting compromises of the Constitution, was a polemical one. One could easily imagine another figure choosing self-rule, the consent of the governed, before choosing equality. Or Lincoln could have chosen the three inalienable rights, life, liberty, and the pursuit of happiness. Lincoln chose equality because it seemed to him to be somehow logically prior to all of the others, because only moral equality enables one to distinguish between self-rule as the political project of moral autonomy and self-rule as merely the habit of honor among thieves. Only equality founds self-rule in liberal respect for the human person; without equality, self-rule is little more than the privilege of exemption from service in the *oikos*.[25]

Lincoln did not say that the equality he had in mind was racial equality. But he did not have to, since class equality or gender equality or ethnic equality was not at the center of a great war. His Democratic opponents, after all, had been the major force behind the push for equality across class lines, and did not need any reminding about that subject from him. He himself, somewhat running against the grain of his Whiggish political ancestry, had brought the Republican Party to power by embracing equality across lines of national origin. Gender equality was a live issue in Lincoln's generation, but it was not the subject of a military conflict. Despite the fact that he himself had not completely embraced racial equality, despite the fact that he had not in any way committed himself to social or political equality among the races, Lincoln did in these words proclaim that what was at stake in the war was at least the basic equality of human beings across races, the right to enjoy one's own life and liberty without being subject to physical domination by another. Freedom and equality are not contrary values for Lincoln, for freedom as a political value depends upon the mutual acknowledgment of free persons *as* free persons; freedom is agency, and agency happens only among moral equals. That is why, toward the end of the speech, Lincoln imagined that the fruit of a victory in a war over moral equality will be a "new birth of freedom," the transformation of freedom into a deeper thing than the ability of the strong to exploit the weak without interference by any third party. The new birth of freedom can only be a new depth of acknowledgment, such as that later embodied in the three Reconstruction amendments to the Constitution, whose actual contents Lincoln had not yet imagined.

What the Civil War tests, Lincoln argued, is not only, as he might have said earlier, whether a government of the people would be able to preserve its stability in the face of disagreements, or whether it must ever fracture into ever smaller Confederacies whenever it faces a conflict. The issue was not even, as Lincoln had also said elsewhere, only whether a minority can contest by force the majority's fairly won power to rule, whether the minority can claim by the bullet what it had lost by the ballot. The central issue, from which all of the other issues depended, was whether any government was capable of making and keeping the promise of equality. As the issue of slavery somehow underlay the issue of the tariff, of internal improvements, and of strict or loose construction of the Constitution, so under all of the other things at stake in the war, under Union, under political stability, under majority rule, lay the issue of racial equality.[26]

Opposition newspapers were not slow to pick up the implications of Lincoln's first sentence. The editor of the *Chicago Times*, for instance, argued that Lincoln's embrace of equality and his call for a new birth of freedom "did most foully traduce the motives of the men who were slain at Gettysburg," for those men did not die for the freedom of the slave, but for the Union and the Constitution, the "old" Constitution, as the *Times* called it, three-fifths compromise, fugitive slave clause, and all:

Mr. Lincoln occupies his present position by virtue of this constitution, and is sworn to the maintenance and enforcement of these [pro-
slavery] provisions. It was to uphold this constitution, and the Union
created by it, that our officers and soldiers gave their lives at Gettysburg. How dare he, then, standing on their graves, misstate the cause
for which they died, and libel the statesmen who founded the government? They were men possessing too much self-respect to declare
negroes were their equals, or were entitled to equal privileges.[27]

Over the first four sentences of the speech, Lincoln gradually narrowed the focus of his attention, from the whole history of the Republic
and the entire continent, to the years of the Civil War and the nation,
to the Gettysburg battlefield itself, to the portion of that battlefield that
is to be dedicated as a final resting place for those who here gave their
lives that that nation might live. But as the focus narrows, the central
idea, that the nation is a living thing, and that fates of the living and the
dead are intertwined, takes on stronger prominence.

By the time the focus has narrowed to the immediate here and now
of the cemetery (described in a limiting way as "a portion of that field")
and the present ceremony, Lincoln has placed the participants in the
ceremony in a position that echoes the acts of the Fathers in a very
diminished way. The Fathers dedicated a nation to the proposition
that all men are created equal. The participants dedicate a portion of a
battlefield for those who gave their lives that that nation might live.
The concern of the paragraph narrows to the grammar of a single sentence: we dedicate a portion of this field to the dead. It is an act that
Lincoln describes with Horatian gravity, but also with a touch of be-
littlement: "It is altogether fitting and proper that we should do this."

The transformation that occurs at the beginning of the third paragraph elegantly turns the grammar of that sentence around: the brave
men, living and dead, who struggled here, have already consecrated
that land, and the true task is for the survivors to be dedicated by the
dead to the task for which they gave their lives. This transformation
is the upshot of a series of antitheses the next sentence develops, the
contrast between what the world will little note and what it cannot
forget, the contrast between words and deeds, and, finally, the contrast
between "they" and "we." The soldiers and the Founders have a metaphysical depth unavailable to the living civilians. The dead Founders

dedicated the new Republic to a proposition. The soldiers rededicate the Republic to a new birth of freedom. The living civilians, by contrast, are defined by what they cannot do.

The tricolon with which the paragraph opens, "we can not dedicate—we can not consecrate—we can not hallow," builds to a crescendo. "Dedicate" gives way to the more explicitly religious "consecrate," leading one from the Horatian world of "fitting and proper" to a more Christian set of concerns. To "dedicate" may have a religious flavor, but dedication is also commonly an act done by a public secular authority, not by a religious one, and as an abstract noun "dedication" may mean nothing more than intense seriousness of purpose. To "consecrate" is something that can be done only by a religious authority, and for a religious purpose. You can dedicate a stadium, but you cannot consecrate it. When you consecrate a cemetery, as when you consecrate a church, you mark it as a sacred place, a place where the concerns of the sacred radiate into the secular world. At the completion of the tricolon, "consecrate," with its hint of abstraction and Latinate formality, gives way to the Anglo-Saxon intimacy, concreteness, and directness of "hallow." The difference between "consecrated" and "hallowed" is roughly the difference between being legally married and being madly in love. To be consecrated is to be formally, institutionally, put into the category of sacred things and places. But to be hallowed is to feel, in the immediate here and now, and with a fierce personal urgency, the visceral chill of the absolute in manifestation. Those who can hallow, those who are hallowed, have an ontological reality unavailable to those who have come to that place to make a ritual performative utterance, an utterance the speaker debases by describing it as merely "what we say here." Deeper than what we do is the kinship between the living and the dead, between the Founders and the surviving Republic, between the living and the dead brave men who struggled at Gettysburg.

Our access to ontological gravity is mediated by our ability to participate in this exchange between the living and the dead. From the dead, who gave the last full measure of devotion to the cause, we can renew our own devotion, from their dedication of the hallowed place, echoing as it does the Founders' dedication of the nation as a whole, we can ourselves be dedicated. This exchange does not bring the dead to life in the renewed Republic; it instead enables us to participate in the dead's generosity. It makes us more like them, not them more like us.[28]

Our increased devotion is never quite the equal of their last full measure of devotion. The dead, who gave their lives to the Republic, do
not live on in mere fame, but in acts the living have not yet performed
but will perform in their name. Life and death interpenetrate each
other, not only in the way the dead gave their lives to the living and
gave their lives to continue the life of the Republic but also in that it is
only through the dead that the lives of the living have meaning, or are
real lives at all. They died not only to assure the lives of the living and
the life of their Republic, but to assure that those lives really are something worthy of being called life to begin with.

What is the "unfinished work" that "they who fought here" have so
nobly advanced? Does "they who fought here" include the Confederate as well as the Union dead? If the unfinished work is merely the
incomplete Union victory—the incomplete Union victory at Gettysburg, the incomplete Union victory in the war as a whole by November
1863—then "they who fought here" of course cannot include the Confederates. Lincoln assumed that his audience would interpret the task
this way to begin with, but he had a larger aim in mind.

One of the harsher and uglier tasks of a wartime funeral elegy is to
exhort the living, for the sake of the dead, to die and to kill in the
name of the state. It is because he senses this that Hemingway's Frederic
Henry, in *For Whom the Bell Tolls*, can no longer stomach the heightened language of wartime elegy, which reduces in his mind to wartime
propaganda. He picks out for particular scorn Lincoln's key phrase,
that "these dead shall not have died in vain," as an especially dark instance of the big words that make people so unhappy. The great reversal of field of the Gettysburg Address—we do not dedicate the field to
the dead, they dedicate us to the proposition that all men are created
equal—transforms not only the agent, revealing that it is the dead, not
us, who do the dedicating. It also transforms the aim of the dedication.
To employ the dead to exhort the living to victory is as tawdry and as
mistaken as imagining that the ultimate aim of the war is the mere
restoration of the old Union. Both are disastrous under-readings of
the meaning of the war. The "great task remaining before us" includes
but is not limited to military victory.

Lincoln develops the meaning of that unfinished work in four parallel clauses, only the last two of which make it clear that the unfinished
work is the perfection of democracy, not the survival of the Union.

The reversal of field suggests that we in the present, relative to the Founders, and relative to the dead, are impotent and inauthentic. But what Lincoln goes on to demand from his audience is not a small task appropriate to that audience's impotence, but a large task, a new birth of freedom, which both the Founders and the dead had not been in a position to complete.

First, we are to be dedicated to the task in order to ensure that from these honored dead we take increased devotion to that cause for which they gave the last full measure of devotion. "Devotion," it must be noted, is both intimate and sacred. The term does not refer so much to a feeling as to the effect upon feeling of something larger than feeling. The word has an imperative force that transcends the limitations of the individual will—it has an urgent, compulsive, demanding, trans-rational force, as for instance when we refer to someone as "devoted to destruction." It describes a compulsion that arises from and affirms some deep layer of identity beyond the mere happen-so of desire or will. It arises from our stake in being. And the language about a "full measure of devotion" sees devotion not only as something poured out—the lives, indeed the blood, of the soldiers—but also as something poured out to drink, the full cup of hemlock given to Socrates, or the cup Jesus asked to be spared, but accepted, at the Garden of Gethsemane. Briggs (2005) notes that the word draws its meaning from Matthew 7:2, where it has to do with both giving and the reward for giving: "with what measure ye mete, it shall be measured to you again."

Second, we are dedicated in order "that we here highly resolve that these dead shall not have died in vain." As Lincoln had not completely specified what the object of devotion was to which the dead gave the full measure of devotion, here he did not specify what would be the test of whether the dead have died in vain. He left open the possibility that it was only mere military victory he had in mind. But of course the series does not stop there.

It is only in the third parallel clause that Lincoln specified what the dead died for, and what, if it is not secured, will cause their deaths to be empty ones: we are to be dedicated in order "that this nation, under God, shall have a new birth of freedom." The phrase "under God," like the similar phrase in the Pledge of Allegiance, was an afterthought, not in the text from which Lincoln spoke, but added by him in later holograph copies.[29] One might at first assume that the purpose of the revision was to decorate the sentence with a whiff of pious in-cense. But to do that would be to mistake the nature of Lincoln's God. If the God he refers to here is the same one he treats in the Second In-augural Address or in the Meditation on the Divine Will (written, depending upon whom you ask, in either 1862 or 1864), one must reckon with Lincoln's standing assumption that to call upon the divine will to ratify some course of action you have already decided to embark upon is to act with a kind of moral narcissism, which that same God almost never fails to trip. The one thing Lincoln's God never allows is for mortals to imagine they have him in their back pocket, ready to use as a club on their opponents. The force of "under God," this is to say, is a rebuke: as we did not know the meaning of the war when it began, so we do not know the scope of the new birth of freedom when we commit ourselves to it, and our version of that new birth is as likely as not to turn out to be too narrow.

Lincoln did not specify the particulars of the new birth of freedom, although certainly it has something to do with the proposition that all men are created equal. The realization of a new commitment to equal-ity, not mere military victory, is the test of Union success in the war. We will not know who really won the war, Lincoln argued, until we know what kind of Union emerges out of it. Lincoln did not in so many words press the issues that were later embodied in the three Re-construction amendments, only the first of which could have been in his focal attention anyway. But the test of a new birth of freedom is a stern one, and it is not certain even to this day how close our Republic is to passing that test.

This vision of the meaning of the war is the culmination of Lincoln's thought about the meaning of the conflict over slavery going back to the "House Divided" speech. There he had treated an escalating con-flict over slavery as almost an inevitability, and argued that only by fac-ing that conflict for what it is can one affirm that the American nation has a moral identity at all. The argument of that speech was flawed, as Stephen Douglas repeatedly pointed out, by an implausible conspiracy theory, and, more, by the temptations the speech offered to the hearers of the speech to see their political conflict in morally self-righteous terms somewhat alien to Lincoln's nature. The Gettysburg Address saw in the conflict over slavery the same inevitability that Lincoln had described in the "House Divided" speech. But in the Gettysburg Address his account of that war's inevitability was purged of conspiracy theories and self-righteousness. Douglas had also argued that a violent conflict over slavery might cost the United States its democracy, but rather than, as wartime presidents tend to do, arguing only that the war was necessary for the safety of democracy and that procedural democracy would reemerge once wartime exigencies no longer put it under pressure, Lincoln also argued that the test of victory would be an extension of democracy so profound that it could only be described as a second birth.

Many readers of the Gettysburg Address have noticed the speaker's impersonality, how he seems to disappear as a particular human being, appearing to speak not from the podium but from history, as if the speech were transmitted through Lincoln rather than uttered by him.[30] Even the repeated adjective "great," applied to the Civil War, and to the battle-field, is strangely reticent, registering the momentousness of the war and the battle, but not registering its anguish, adopting an eerily cool point of view, as if seeing the action from eternity.

Part of the effect also arises from Lincoln's repeated use of "we" in the second paragraph of the speech: we are engaged in a great civil war; we are met on a great battle-field of that war; we have come to dedicate a portion of that field. Not all of those instances of "we" are equivalent to each other. The "we" who are engaged in a great Civil War presumably includes the entire Republic, civilian as much as soldier, North as much as South, since it is given to both the Union and the Confederacy to test the ability of a nation conceived and dedicated to equality to endure. The "we" who are met on the battlefield, and who have come to dedicate a portion of that field, are first of all the president and his immediate audience. But the phrase seems to include the whole civilian population of the North by proxy: the soldiers do the suffering, but the civilians as a whole do the recognizing, with the actual celebrants of the ceremony standing in for them. The purpose of a public ceremony is to fuse the "we" of the immediate audience with the "we" of the entire Union. The "we" who are to be rededicated, after the speech's great reversal of field, likewise certainly includes more than the audience. Like the "we" of those who have come to dedicate the cemetery, that "we" includes the entire population of the Union.

But the word "we" bears differently upon Republicans and Democrats. To Republicans the possibility of rededication chiefly asks that

they keep the courage of their convictions. Having painfully and gradually embraced the idea that the Union cannot be restored without
emancipation, and that the ultimate meaning of emancipation is an
affirmation of the proposition that all men are created equal, Republicans are asked not to be driven by their perfectly rational fear of the
political consequences of these acts to draw back from them.

The invitation to Democrats is somewhat sterner. Of them it asks
that they give up a conviction, *herrenvolk* democracy, which is not only
deeply held but also foundational to their sense of their party's identity. It repeats the challenge Lincoln had made three months earlier in
the Conkling letter, where he had as good as said: "You Democrats say
that you support the Union, but you have hesitated to accept Emancipation, arguing that the only aim of the war was restoration of the
Union, and if Emancipation is a sticking point for you, then for you
racial equality is something completely beyond the pale. But as a practical matter, it should be clear to you that the Union cannot be restored
without Emancipation, and, particularly in view of what we have asked
of black soldiers, the Union cannot be restored without equality either."
The convictions that separate Democrats from Republicans amount, in
the language of Lincoln's December 1862 Annual Message to Congress,
to dogmas of the quiet past, and are inadequate to the stormy present. In
asking Democrats to support emancipation, to free their thralls, he asks
them also to free themselves, to disenthrall themselves of an enslaving
illusion, the illusion that an unequal society can be a democratic one.
Only then can they save their country and nobly save the last best hope
of earth.

Does this final "we" in the Gettysburg Address also include the inhabitants of the Confederacy? Several facts argue against this possibility, chief among them of course the fact that they were at the moment
in rebellion against the government and seeking the dissolution of the
Union. Furthermore, Confederate dead were not included in the national cemetery. But Lincoln did include the southerners among the
people who are subject to the test of the Civil War: their challenge to
the Union is part of the test the idea of equality must undergo, and
their rebellion was to that extent almost a historical necessity, an implication of the idea of democracy. Nothing in the speech suggests
that Lincoln will imagine the South after its defeat as a kind of subject
province, not a full part of the Union. If the rededication Lincoln

speaks of is to bring a new birth of freedom to the Union, the former Confederacy will have two roles to play: they must give that new birth of freedom reality, by granting it to their slaves, and they must practice that freedom themselves, as citizens of the restored Union. The speech's focus is so intently upon the distinction between the living and the dead that one might for an instant lose sight of the violent distinction between supporters of the Union and supporters of the Confederacy, since Lincoln makes that distinction seem trivial beside the distinction between the living and the dead. For practical reasons the "we" who are to be dedicated by the dead of the war at Gettysburg does not include the living adherents of the Confederacy. But the speech offers an invitation to them, since they too are caught up in the moral interpenetration of the living and the dead by which the survivors are to be consecrated, and indeed the new birth of freedom Lincoln demands in the speech ultimately cannot happen without them.

The fourth parallel claim about the task to which we are to be dedicated is rendered in the speech's famous closing tricolon, "that government of the people, by the people, for the people, shall not perish from the earth." Government of the people is in Lincoln's view a government that assumes moral equality as its basis. There is a leap of faith involved in this equation, because it is not clear that if the two things are logically implicated in each other then they must also be causally connected. Self-rule logically depends upon the mutual recognition of agency among plural people, people with different needs and desires, people sometimes with different values as well. But that self-rule requires mutual acknowledgment as its logical precondition does not mean that self-rule has the power to bring acknowledgment about. Indeed, the story of American politics in the Jacksonian era is that one cannot count on majorities to grant acknowledgment to minorities. Probably the least plausible outcome of a plebiscite of white voters in the United States in 1860 would have been emancipation, let alone civil rights for black people. Indeed the contradiction between means and ends, between consent and principle, between the logical preconditions of popular rule and its actual workings, is as live an issue now as then. Only the violence of the war undeceived the people, and then only fleetingly, about the instability of a slaveholding democracy, or about a society offering government of the people while excluding many of those people from a say.

That the new birth of freedom Lincoln described may be as fleeting as it was hard won is a possibility Lincoln raised in the closing words of the speech. Lincoln did not speak of the successful outcome of the war as establishing liberal democracy as a resilient and durable form of government. He spoke only of its not perishing from the earth. To perish from the earth is not precisely the same thing as to fail. It is to fail so utterly that no trace of the attempt is to be found. It is to fail in such a way that the possibilities of future attempts are foreclosed. It is not merely to vanish, but to be extirpated. The new nation was "brought forth" on the earth of this continent. The dead who gave their lives that that nation might live have hallowed "this ground," the battlefield at Gettysburg, and the land of the United States, but a failure to secure a new birth of freedom might yet wipe this nation off of this earth, as if it had never been planted, never sprung up. What victory in the Civil War can yield, Lincoln argued, is not a secure legacy of self-rule, but only that for that moment at least the United States has not so discredited itself as to be unworthy of further sacrifice. After the Compromise of 1877, that question became more open than ever.

9.2 The Will of God Prevails

The rhetoric of the Gettysburg Address, like the rhetoric of the Second Inaugural, turns on the theme of awakening from self-deception. Lincoln argued that the forces of the Union deceived themselves if they believed that the only issue at stake between them and the Confederacy was the survival of the Union. They deceived themselves if they believed that the only issue between them was the legality of secession. They deceived themselves if they believed that the only issue between them was majority rule. They deceived themselves if they believed that the only issue between them was whether a popular government could be stable, or must always destroy itself whenever it faced a serious conflict. The war was a test of whether America or any nation would be capable of redeeming the promise of equality, a promise whose ultimate meaning was still obscure to Lincoln in 1863, a promise whose chief implications he not only did not mention in the speech but might have denied entertaining had he been asked. The Union deceived itself by not acknowledging that the chief issue of the war was slavery. And it continued to deceive itself by failing to acknowledge that the issue of slavery could not be solved without also solving the issue of racial equality. Lincoln's vision of the Union's self-deception about the central issue of the war is a vision of complicity, not only the economic complicity of the entire Union in the slave economy but also complicity between slavery and freedom in the very origins of the idea of freedom, the ways in which freedom itself was made possible only by slavery. Lincoln's insight into the entanglements of complicity was thorough. And the entangled included himself, not only as one who was reluctant to force the issue over slavery but also as one who continued to be reluctant to force the issue over racial equality.

Chase's Anecdote

Our examination of Lincoln's Second Inaugural Address, the culmination of his political thought, and his deepest, although still mysterious, treatment of the theme of moral conflict in politics begins with several theological asides, because the thinking of the Second Inaugural Address is informed by an anguish that is as much religious as political.

When after the Battle of Antietam Lincoln decided finally to issue the Emancipation Proclamation publicly, he described his act in religious language that has long puzzled commentators. What Salmon Chase described in his diary entry for September 22, 1862, looks suspiciously like a vulgar bargain with God: "You give me victory, and I'll end slavery." According to Chase, Lincoln described his decision to issue the Emancipation Proclamation this way:

> Gentlemen: I have, as you are aware, thought a great deal about the relation of this war to slavery; and you all remember that, several weeks ago, I read to you an order I had prepared on this subject, which, on account of objections made by some of you, was not issued. Ever since then my mind has been occupied with this subject, and I have thought, all along, that the time for acting on it might probably come. I think the time has come now. I wish it were a better time. I wish that we were in a better condition. The action of the army against the rebels has not been quite what I should have best liked. But they have been driven out of Maryland, and Pennsylvania is no longer in danger of invasion. When the rebel army was at Frederick, I determined, as soon as it should be driven out of Maryland, to issue

a proclamation of emancipation such as I thought most likely to be useful. I said nothing to anyone; but I made the promise to myself and (hesitating a little) to my Maker. The rebel army is now driven out, and I am going to fulfill that promise.[31]

Navy Secretary Gideon Welles described the same event this way:

He had, he said, made a vow, a covenant, that if God gave us the victory in the approaching battle (which had just been fought) he would consider it his duty to move forward in the cause of emancipation. We might think it strange, he said, but there were times when he felt uncertain how to act; that he had in this way submitted the disposal of matters when the way was not clear to his mind what he should do. God had decided this question in favor of the slave. He was satisfied it was—was confirmed and strengthened by the vow and its results; his mind was fixed, his decision made; but he wished his paper announcing his course to be as correct in terms as it could be made without any attempt to change his determination.[32]

The best students of Lincoln's religious thinking, William Wolf (1959), Stewart Winger (2003), and Allen Guelzo (2004), find this passage a little shocking, saved only from the most primitive superstitiousness by Lincoln's characteristic lack of self-righteousness. Perhaps the best way to understand Chase's anecdote is to see it as a way to account for the meaning of the event, the battle of Antietam, rather than a way to account for its outcome. Can we imagine, for instance, Lincoln deciding *not* to issue the proclamation because the Union armies had been defeated there? Yes, we can—but not because that defeat would have proven to him that God approved of slavery; Lincoln would have postponed the announcement until a later victory would have given the announcement the air of something other than desperation. If a bloody draw like Antietam will serve as enough of a victory to enable Lincoln to proclaim emancipation, then almost anything would have served. Indeed, if events are signs that God favors or disfavors one's own politics, then the fact that Lee was able to escape after the battle with most of his army back across the Potomac, living to fight not only another day but another thousand days, might count as much as the rather marginal victory at Antietam Creek did as a sign of God's will. And certainly if Antietam was a (marginal) sign of God's favor, then the Union disaster at Fredericksburg, only three months later, would count as a rather less ambiguous sign of his disfavor.

Most superstitions are metaphors made literal, and the best way to understand them is to understand the metaphor. Surely Lincoln's thinking was intended to illuminate the meaning of the battle, and the war, not just its outcome. What the anecdote seems to mean is not that Lincoln has been reading the tea leaves of the divine plan, but that he understood himself to be under a moral obligation, a transcendent obligation, to serve a historical process that he knew must unfold in time but whose local developments are unpredictable.

The Meditation on the Divine Will

It is not beyond possibility that the vow Chase and Welles recorded has something to do with Lincoln's Meditation on the Divine Will. Scholars used to date it to the period between the rout of Pope's army at Second Bull Run in the last days of August and the repulse of Lee at South Mountain and Antietam in Maryland in the middle of September. Most recent scholars date the meditation to a similarly dark period in the summer of 1864. Whether or not the meditation captures the moment of the promise Chase referred to, it certainly captures Lincoln's theological cast of mind at the period.

Here is the text of the meditation:

> The will of God prevails. In great contests each party claims to act In accordance with the will of God. Both *may* be, and one *must* be wrong. God can not be *for*, and *against* the same thing at the same time. In the present civil war it is quite possible that God's purpose is something different from the purpose of either party—and yet the human instrumentalities, working just as they do, are of the best adaptation to effect His purpose. I am almost ready to say this is probably true—that God wills this contest, and wills that it shall not end yet. By his mere quiet power, on the minds of the now contestants, He could have either *saved* or *destroyed* the Union without a human contest. Yet the contest began. And having begun He could give the final victory to either side any day. Yet the contest proceeds. (2:359)

The opening sentence might at first seem to have consolatory force, since it seems to argue that history has a shape and a purpose, and is not merely a heap of bloody contingencies. But because each party claims to act in accordance with the will of God, and one or both must be wrong about doing so, the true force of the sentence is to rebuke the folly of imagining that one has insight into God's motives and can claim to be an instrument in his hand. Claiming to act in accordance with God's will is an act not only of folly but of blasphemy, and it is such an act even if the agent is in fact acting with moral right. The argument is presented in a cool, Euclidean tone: "In great contests each party claims to act in accordance with the will of God. Both *may* be, and one *must* be wrong." Underneath that cool Euclidean tone is a trace of disdain for the idea that one might claim God for an ally. Neither saving the Union nor destroying it matters to God, because if either mattered He would have already brought victory to one side or the other in the war. What God seems to will is not victory, but continuing inconclusive slaughter for both sides. Lincoln argues not merely that God wills that the contest, which God could have headed off before it even began, shall not end yet, but that at each moment the divine will renews the killing power of the opponents against each other. In later workings out of this theme, such as the Hodges letter or the Second Inaugural Address, Lincoln guesses what God's motives might be—to punish both sides for their complicity in slavery. But God does not say that in this passage; God's purpose here is dark, and what he wills, for his own reasons, is ever-renewing bloodshed.

What precisely is the tone of the last sentences of the passage? It is charged with an eerie detachment, as if Lincoln were taking the point of view of God against himself, as if it participates not in the suffering of the combatants but in God's own dark enthrallment with death. God is not rebuked for this enthrallment: wonder, not anger, is the register of that last sentence. The sentence closes a door, and that door does not separate God and the speaker, as it at first seems, but separates God and the addressee of the passage, with the speaker moving, at the moment of that sentence, across the threshold that separates where he was at the beginning of the paragraph (with us, puzzled and bleeding) from where he is at its end (with God, coldly fascinated, determined, and opaque). The sentence forecloses something for its addressee, rules something out: here you will go no further, here you will understand nothing further. The agency that remains is not ours, and not also the agency of a traditionally moral God, but of a dark fatality that will not allow itself to be known. Lincoln adopts precisely this same tone in the darkest sentence of the Second Inaugural, in which war itself becomes the agent, sweeping away the delusions of agency cherished by both sides: "And the war came." In the midst of his grief, and without letting go of that grief, he adopts the point of view of the inflictor of that grief. He builds an altar to the Beautiful Necessity.

The Meditation on the Divine Will is often taken as a kind of rough draft of the Second Inaugural, and indeed in its rebuke to both sides it has much in common with the later speech. But the Second Inaugural makes a case for God's wisdom and justice that the meditation, which makes a case only for God's power, does not make. The bleak Gnosticism of this passage is present in the Second Inaugural, but there it is the anxiety that the speaker is trying to face down. Here it is the force the speaker is trying to render.

The Reply to the Chicago Clergymen

Only nine days before issuing the Emancipation Proclamation, Lincoln met with a two-man delegation of Chicago clergymen and gave them all of the counterarguments against the emancipation measure he did not tell them he had already resolved to issue, specifying as well the conditions under which such a proclamation would become politically possible. Accustomed to hearing arguments about the divine will from clergymen, he opened with an argument whose asperity he allowed them to register before he withdrew it:

> I am approached with the most opposite opinions and advice, and that by religious men, who are equally certain that they represent the Divine will. I am sure that either the one or the other class is mistaken in that belief, and perhaps in some respects both. I hope it will not be irreverent for me to say that if it is probable that God would reveal his will to others, on a point so connected with my duty, it might be supposed he would reveal it directly to me; for, unless I am more deceived in myself than I often am, it is my earnest desire to know the will of Providence in this matter. *And if I can learn what it is I will do it!* These are not, however, the days of miracles, and I suppose

it will be granted that I am not to expect a direct revelation. I must study the plain physical facts of the case, ascertain what is possible and learn what appears to be wise and right. The subject is difficult, and good men do not agree. (2:361)

It is hard not to hear annoyance in the opening sentences of this passage. As in the Hodges letter, and as in the Second Inaugural, the fact that people make confident pronouncements about God's deliverances on opposite sides of the same question is reason to wonder whether both sides, even the one that might be right, are merely kidding themselves, are the prisoners of a fantastic moral narcissism. The next sentence takes a somewhat harder tone: "If God really did want me to abolish slavery, don't you think he might have told *me* about it before he told *you?*" But the sentence turns on a semicolon, and takes a very different tack: Lincoln has to assume that none of the people who report God's will to him speak for God at all, but all the same he does need to know what God's will is. The counsel of faith seems to demand two opposite things: an intense skepticism about any claim about God's will, and an intense desire to know that will, a desire that almost, but not quite, balances out the skepticism.

Lincoln does not say that he knows nothing about God's will. There are some things he does know; among other things he knows that almost everything he hears on the subject must be wrong. And he knows that God cannot positively support slavery, although it does not follow from that that slaveholders are any more out of the divine protection than other sinners are. Lincoln wrote tartly to George B. Ide, James R. Doolittle, and A. Hubbell on May 30, 1864:

To read in the Bible, as the word of God himself, that "In the sweat of *thy* face shalt thou eat bread," and to preach therefrom that, "In the sweat of *other mens* faces shalt thou eat bread," to my mind can scarcely be reconciled with honest sincerity. When brought to my final reckoning, may I have to answer for robbing no man of his goods; yet more tolerable even this, than for robbing one of himself, and all that was his. When, a year or two ago, those professedly holy men of the South, met in the semblance of prayer and devotion, and, in the name of Him who said "As ye would all men should do unto you, do ye even so unto them" appealed to the christian world to aid them in doing to a whole race of men, as they would have no man do unto themselves, to my thinking, they contemned and insulted God and His church, far more than did Satan when he tempted the Saviour with the Kingdoms of the earth. The devils attempt was no more false, and far less hypocritical. But let me forbear, remembering it is also written "Judge not, lest ye be judged." (2:597)

Speaking to two ladies from Tennessee whose prisoner of war husbands he had released in December 1864, Lincoln is reported to have said:

You say your husband is a religious man; tell him when you meet him, that I say I am not much of a judge of religion, but that, in my opinion, the religion that sets men to rebel and fight against their government, because, as they think, that government does not sufficiently help *some* men to eat their bread on the sweat of *other* men's faces, is not the sort of religion upon which people can get to heaven! (2:663)

There is rather more asperity in this than in the letter to Ide, and it lacks the final qualification, perhaps because it is a secondhand report. Lincoln has a pretty clear idea of what God's will cannot be, but he holds himself back, just barely, from using that as a way to understand what God's will is.

What Lincoln would call faith is close to what other people would call doubt: anyone who claims to speak for God is probably a fool. But the doubt is not a completely skeptical doubt, because it knows well enough that not all moral views are on the table. Knowing with certainty that some things are wrong, however, does not necessarily lead one to know that other things are right, nor even does it necessarily tell one what is the best way to proceed against that wrong. The divine matters to the extent that human acts remain morally meaningful and are not to be seen merely in terms of success or failure, pleasure or pain, survival or death. But to say that acts remain morally meaningful is not to say that the divine provides a clear guide to immediate acts, and indeed all of Lincoln's thinking points to the idea that the more meaningful an act is, the less certain its course is; the higher the moral stakes, the less the moral clarity. You must, and yet you cannot, know the will of God, and when you think you know that will, you know that you have lost your way with it. The opacity of the divine will is a sign that it is in earnest.

The Gurney Letters

In October 1862, just after the transformation or evolution of Lincoln's racial thinking over the previous summer had borne fruit in the preliminary Emancipation Proclamation, Lincoln was visited by Eliza P. Gurney, the widow of a prominent Quaker leader. Lincoln commenced a correspondence with her that says a great deal about how his thinking on racial issues was bound up in his thinking about religious issues. Lincoln's correspondence with Mrs. Gurney captures the way in which the unfolding implicitness of a political ideal, against the explicit or avowed intentions of the political agents who bring it about, ties Lincoln at once to a sense of his own complicity (the way his acts both advance and betray that ideal) and to a sense of his destiny as a political agent (working through a destiny he always understands imperfectly).

One might be tempted to call this sense of destiny a vision of providence, were it not for Lincoln's awareness that every attempt to call the divine to the aid of his own political program is bound to fail, entangled as such attempts must be in the agent's complicities, self-deceits, and moral narcissism. Beyond Lincoln's own complicities, Lincoln has in view his nation's complicities, not only the involvement of the free states in many aspects of the slave economy but also the long dependence of freedom itself upon slavery.

Introduced to the president on a Sunday morning of beating rain, Mrs. Gurney began, at least in the version of it recorded in her memoirs by another member of her party, a sermon in which, rather like the Chicago clergymen who had visited him the previous summer to tell him that God had told them that the time had come to end slavery, she described herself as having been commissioned by God to her task. Where she differed from the Chicago clergymen was in the absence of self-righteousness in her address.

In Lincoln's reply, likewise recorded in Gurney's memoir, and repeated in his letter to her of October 26, 1862, gratitude and skepticism are mingled. Here is the version from the letter:

> I am glad of this interview, and glad to know that I have your sympathy and prayers. We are indeed going through a great trial—a fiery

trial. In the very responsible position in which I happen to be placed, being a humble instrument in the hands of our Heavenly Father, as I am, and as we all are, to work out his great purposes, I have desired that all my works and acts may be according to his will, and that it might be so, I have sought his aid—but if after endeavoring to do my best in the light which he affords me, I find my efforts fail, I must believe that for some purpose unknown to me, He wills it otherwise. If I had had my way, this war would never have been commenced; if I had been allowed my way this war would have been ended before this, but we find it still continues; and we must believe that He permits it for some wise purpose of his own, mysterious and unknown to us; and though with our limited understandings we may not be able to comprehend it, yet we cannot but believe, that he who made the world still governs it.[33]

Conceding that, if God orders the events of history, Lincoln has, willy-nilly, been a humble instrument in the hands of his heavenly Father—a claim that is probably as true of Jefferson Davis as of Lincoln—Lincoln argued that no matter how hard he might have tried to align his will and God's will as he understood it, he could not know whether his will and God's will were in fact aligned; indeed, he could not know whether he actually knew anything about God's will at all. If, as he attempts to do what he believes to be God's will, all of his efforts fail, then God must have some will Lincoln cannot fathom.

It does not follow from this failure, necessarily, that God approves of slavery, only that Lincoln is not privy to God's plans. But it does follow from this that it is God who makes the war, and makes it as violent and as apparently pointless as it has so far been, since neither side has had a convincing victory of more than local moment. God made the war happen, and God keeps the war inconclusive, a view that might have, or at least should have, raised an eyebrow among his interlocutors.

This dark, even fatal idea of God, however, is not entirely a morally skeptical one, since Lincoln goes on to argue that there must be some purpose, some good purpose, behind all this purposeless bloodshed, "for we cannot but believe that he who made the world still governs it." The 1862 Gurney letter adumbrates the themes of the Meditation on the Divine Will, and the themes of the Second Inaugural. Like those texts, it rebukes the idea that one can ever conceive of one's self as the sword of God. Like them it concedes that one is never quite privy to the moral meaning of one's own acts, that it making a fraught moral decision, even with the best will and the best of reasons, one is nevertheless to some extent always making a leap in the dark.

The 1862 Gurney letter, like the Meditation on the Divine Will and the Second Inaugural, also arises out of a sense of moral complicity: neither side can honestly claim moral purity about the slavery issue, and each side's sense of its own cause is intoxicated by moral narcissism. At the same time, however, Lincoln is strongly bound by a moral imperative, even if all the means are fraught, even if the outcome is uncertain, even if the meaning of the act is unclear.

A vision of entangling complicity might motivate one to take a position of moral skepticism. Or it might motivate a morally paralyzed state of impasse, in which one cannot act because one must always do so with dirty hands. But in Lincoln's case the outcome of his vision of entangling complicity is twofold. In the first place it motivates his generosity toward his enemies, his refusal to see them in a demonized way, to see them as somehow of a different moral kind from himself. In the second place, it motivates him to see his most important moral acts as a kind of wager, a kind of leap of faith taken in the face of the absurd. Crucial moral acts like emancipation are made in the face of what might be crippling doubt, in the face of a sense that one's act might be impure as to motives, as to means, and to ends, and might leave one in a world as fallen as the one in which one is already entangled. One does the right as one sees it, knowing that there will be unanticipated consequences, and that one will still have to face those down, and knowing also that that act will leave one still as human, still as fallen, as one ever was. Reinhold Niebuhr made the point very eloquently: "It was Lincoln's achievement to embrace a spiritual paradox which lies at the center of the spirituality of all Western culture: affirmation of a meaningful history along with religious reservations about the partiality and bias which human actors and agents betray in their definition of that meaning."[34]

This generous morality through complicity is what I have been trying to define all through this book as "tragic pragmatism." What faith turns out to be in this passage is not conviction about God's aims, but skepticism about despair, skepticism maintained in the face of an unflinching recognition that the grounds for despair are very strong ones. Faith does not nerve the arm for action, but chastens the mind to circumspection; it holds before it the contradiction between our own wills, even our earnest will for the right, and God's will, about which we know only that we are often mistaken, and that we often call upon it in self-serving and self-deceiving ways. Faith here is not a proposition to be advanced on the basis of the trumping authority of God's will, but a crux to be experienced; God is manifested chiefly through his absence, and faith is a way to keep one's self-possession while registering that absence.[35]

The next August, through an intermediary, the commissioner of Agriculture Isaac Newton, Lincoln renewed the correspondence. Mrs. Gurney wrote to Lincoln on August 18, 1863. Her letter picked out for special praise Lincoln's July 15, 1863, Proclamation of Thanksgiving, offered an account of the dual Union victories at Gettysburg and Vicksburg on July 4:

> I can hardly refrain from expressing my cordial approval of thy late excellent proclamation appointing a day of thanksgiving for the sparing and preserving mercies which, in the tender loving-kindness of our God and Saviour, have been so bountifully showered upon us; for though (as a religious people) we do not set apart especial seasons for returning thanks either for spiritual or temporal blessings, yet, as I humbly trust, our hearts are filled with gratitude to our Almighty Father that His delivering arm of love and power has been so manifestly round about us. And I rejoice in the decided recognition of an all-wise and superintending Providence, which is so marked a feature in the aforesaid document, as well as the immediate influence and guidance of the Holy Spirit, which perhaps never in any previous state paper has been so fully recognized before. Especially did my inmost heart respond to thy desire "that the angry feeling which has so long sustained this needless and cruel rebellion may be subdued, the hearts of the insurgents changed, and the whole nation be led through paths of repentance and submission to the Divine Will back to the perfect enjoyment of union and fraternal peace." May the Lord in His infinite compassion hasten the day! (Gurney [1884] 315)

The language of the proclamation was, considering its occasion, remarkably un-triumphant, rejoicing not in the defeat of the Confederacy, but in the fact that the victories "furnish reasonable grounds for

augmented confidence that the Union of these States will be maintained, their constitution preserved, and their peace and prosperity
permanently restored."[36] Lincoln's rejection of the triumphalism one
might expect in such a document has to do not only with his sense of
the cost of those victories in the "fearful bereavements" suffered in
"sacrifices of life, limb, health and liberty" incurred by the combatants
but also with his recognition of the "domestic affliction" that has followed in the train of the victory.

The phrase "domestic affliction" primarily refers to the grief of the
survivors, but it also probably includes a reference to the several days
of bloody rioting over the draft that took place in New York City immediately after the victories at Gettysburg and Vicksburg. These were
the worst outbreaks of civil disorder in American history, and they
strained the ability of democracy to maintain itself in wartime to the
breaking point.

What particularly drew Mrs. Gurney's interest was the sentence
she paraphrased from the proclamation, in which Lincoln called for
the people of the United States to assemble in their accustomed places
of worship to offer thanks, but even more,

> [to] invoke the influence of His Holy Spirit to subdue the anger,
> which has produced, and so long sustained a needless and cruel re-
> bellion, to change the hearts of the insurgents, to guide the counsels
> of the Government with wisdom adequate to so great a national emer-
> gency and to visit with tender care and consolation throughout the
> length and breadth of our land all those who, through the vicissi-
> tudes of marches, voyages, battles, and sieges, have been brought to
> suffer in mind, body or estate, and finally to lead the whole nation,
> through the paths of repentance and submission to the Divine Will,
> back to the perfect enjoyment of Union and fraternal peace.[37]

The point of this sentence was that the meaning of victory is not
that evildoers will be subdued, but that anger will pass, both the anger
that moved secession and the anger arrayed against it, and the influence over the Holy Spirit that Lincoln invokes is to act equally upon
the hearts of the insurgents, to enable them to return to their proper
state of mind and feeling, and upon the wisdom of the government, to
enable it to complete its victory without giving in to the spirit of retri-

bution and to give succor to those on both sides who have suffered through the war.

The proclamation is marked by the spirit of reconciliation that people celebrate in the Second Inaugural Address, and like the Second Inaugural it founded the forgiveness it offered and sought in a sense of mutual complicity and mutual fallenness shared by all parties to the war. It is not, after all, only the Confederacy, but the whole nation, that is to be led through the paths of repentance and submission to the divine will.

The passage captures one of the central themes of Lincoln's mind, and one of the great mysteries of his personality, the theme of mutual forgiveness before a divinity who sees through both sides, and the mystery of Lincoln's being able to fight a great war, a war of almost unparalleled ferocity, with an enemy he resists hating. It is a religious sense, although not precisely an orthodox religious sense, that links the sense of mutual complicity and the requirement of mutual forgiveness.

Lincoln's biographers, particularly since Wolf, have often noted a religious turn in the thinking of Lincoln's later years, but they are not in agreement about its nature. Nobody describes this turn in Lincoln's thinking as embracing New Light Calvinism, with its emphasis upon disciplined practice and conscious moral choice, since Lincoln's thinking is to the end too dark and too skeptical for the New Light, although the anti-slavery movement and Lincoln's cultural allies both in the Whig and in the Republican Parties were strongly influenced by the cluster of Second Great Awakening themes represented by the New Light. Stewart Winger (2003) persuasively notes elements of American romantic spirituality in Lincoln's thinking, particularly in the commitment to equality he shares with Parker, Emerson, and Whitman. And Richard Carwardine (2006) persuasively argues for elements of nineteenth-century liberal religion in Lincoln's thought. But Lincoln's sensibility, for all of its allegiance to progress (and for all of its pragmatism) is a tragic one, and one does not see a tragic sensibility in Emerson and his congeners.[38] Ronald C. White (2002, 2005) sees Lincoln turning to Old Light Calvinism of a traditional kind, with its emphasis upon human weakness, fallibility, and self-deceit, and its argument that human beings must be saved from the outside, by grace, because their own moral machinery is so fatally compromised.

Certainly Lincoln's God is a dark jeerer, someone who sees through the moral pretenses of all agents, good and bad. But Lincoln's God also does not really offer forgiveness through grace, as a Calvinist God would have to. Like Hawthorne, Lincoln has the Calvinist's skepticism about human nature without the Calvinist's remedy of divine grace, and, also like Hawthorne, offers only a chastened knowingness about human things where one might expect redemption. Indeed, even the figure of Jesus is hard to find anywhere in Lincoln's thinking. The softer side of Christianity is alien to him. Lincoln may himself in a way be a Man of Sorrows, but that man himself does not figure explicitly in his thought.

A dark sui generis faith, owing little to the available institutional forms of religion, but with a firm sense of tragic necessity and with a bleak version of Emerson's doctrine of compensation, in which one pays for one's illusions by living out their consequences, seems more characteristic of Lincoln. Allen C. Guelzo (2004) is right to compare Lincoln to Melville, who likewise had to improvise his own dark and uncompromising faith, a faith that looks more like skepticism than like dogmatism, in which Lincoln's youthful "doctrine of necessity" (by which he probably meant scientific materialism of Laplace's kind) becomes reborn as a doctrine of fate, an ironic, unmasking fate which sees through the pretensions, and tramples the plans, even of the good.

9.3 The Second Inaugural Address

The Second Inaugural Address opened with a demurral, almost apologizing that a speech had to be made at all. Indeed, the opening sentences of the speech are so diffident, so understated, and so indirect that they seem flat, and hardly give any indication of the great speech to come. Having noted that at the time of the First Inaugural it was "fitting and proper" to give "a statement, somewhat in detail, of a course to be pursued," Lincoln went on to concede that there was no need for such a speech on this second occasion, since "little that is new could be presented." Lincoln himself drops from the sentence: he does not so much describe himself as making an utterance, as describing the occasion on which somebody, possibly himself, made an utterance: "At this second appearing to take the oath of the presidential office, there is less occasion for an extended address than there was at the first."[39] Indeed, Lincoln almost treated four years of statements by him about the war as if they were so much tiresome bluster, so much elaboration of an unhealthy obsession, dismissing the lot as "public declarations [which] have been constantly called forth on every point and phase of the great contest which still absorbs the attention, and engrosses the energies of the nation." This is rather harsher than the modesty Lincoln had shown in the Gettysburg Address's claim "that the world will little note nor long remember what we say here." The sentence shows positive distaste for war oratory, and impatience with the responsibility of delivering it.

His remarks about the state of the great war that was only a few weeks from its conclusion were also pointedly understated: "The progress of our arms, upon which all else chiefly depends, is as well known to the public as to myself; and it is, I trust, reasonably satisfactory and encouraging to all." There is perhaps a touch of quiet pride in the statement that everyone already knows as well as Lincoln does how well the war has recently been going. Lincoln did not wish to boast, or to seem to be taking credit for an achievement that was really in his view the work of the American people as a whole. Indeed, as Hansen points out, Lincoln presents himself here not as the architect of the impending military victory but as one of the pleased spectators of that victory, more like a member of the audience than like the speaker. The modesty of "reasonably satisfactory and encouraging to all," however, seems a touch dismissive, resembling that moment in T. S. Eliot's poem "The Journey of the Magi," in which the narrator, after a tormenting odyssey, finally arrives at the Bethlehem manger, to report that they "arrived at evening, not a moment too soon / Finding the place; it was (you may say) satisfactory." I would like to attribute this modesty to Lincoln's desire to avoid triumphalism, and perhaps to a desire not to speak too soon, while the mortally wounded Confederacy still retained its power to do harm. But I hear also the impatience that Lincoln had showered upon the "public declarations constantly called forth on every point and phase of the great contest."

Lincoln's account of the political milieu of the First Inaugural was strikingly disenchanted, portraying all of the actors in 1861 as hopeless prisoners of their illusions and wishful thinking. All dreaded an impending civil war, and all sought to avert it. But nobody understood what was really driving the nation to war, and nobody understood how the war was going to develop. Or rather, everybody had dark misgivings on both subjects that they tried to put from their minds. Lincoln did not review the fatuousness of all parties with anger, but he did not treat it with sympathy either. He assumed the language of a participant in the action who has been so burned by it that he has had to see it from a rueful distance.[40] As the First Inaugural was being delivered, aimed at "*saving* the Union without war, insurgent agents were in the city seeking to *destroy* it without war." Both parties "deprecated," war, but each was committed to a course that would make war inevitable, the one refusing to allow the Union to be destroyed without war, the other insisting upon war if it could not have peaceful secession.[41]

Lincoln's word "deprecated" was pointedly formal, and it implied either illusion or bad faith in both parties. On the Union side, the word translates into something like "Well of course I don't *want* war, but I'm not afraid of it (although I have no clear idea just how imminent war is, and just how huge in scale and violence it will be)." Lincoln here seemed to criticize his own behavior during the interregnum. Harold Holzer has recently made a strong case that Lincoln during the secession winter did not underestimate the seriousness of the threat the secessionists had offered, and used with intelligence the persuasive resources available to him, although ultimately he could not have prevented war no matter what policy he followed. But Lincoln in the Second Inaugural seems rather to side with Henry Adams and a host of other critics of Lincoln since Adams's day.

Lincoln did not, however, say, and it would anyway be unfair to say, that there was some other course available to him that could have saved the Union without war. In fact, Lincoln in 1861 conceded everything he could have conceded without making a fatal sacrifice of interest and principle. Perhaps, since he also conceded a constitutional amendment forbidding the abolition of slavery by the federal government, and was willing to allow New Mexico Territory to be organized on a slaveholding basis, he conceded rather more than he should have. And clearly not just in the First Inaugural but also in the Cooper Union speech it was clear that he regarded an attempt to come to persuasive equilibrium with the slave power as the longest of long shots. But Lincoln did imply in the Second Inaugural that he had underestimated the strength of the forces arrayed against him, forces that, even had he estimated them clearly, he could not have prevented from destroying the Union. Lincoln probably did not fault his policy, but he certainly did fault his own hopefulness.

It is not completely clear who the "insurgent agents" Lincoln described were. Possibly he referred to the disloyal members of the government, such as John B. Floyd, Buchanan's corrupt secretary of war, or Supreme Court Justice John A. Campbell, who opposed secession in 1861 but later served as the Confederacy's assistant secretary of war.[42] Campbell is a particularly good candidate, because Lincoln implied that these insurgent agents were attempting to negotiate the peaceful secession of the South. Probably Lincoln's main reference is to the southern participants in the Washington Peace Conference, many of whom ultimately went over to the Confederacy. If so, the reference was somewhat unfair, since the participants in the conference were looking for some way to hold the Union together, even if their proposals pleased nobody on either side, and even if they ultimately left the Union with their states.

Whoever the "insurgent agents" were, they shared the lack of realism of everyone on all sides in 1861. When they "deprecated" war, what they meant was something like "Well, I don't *want* war. But don't try me. And don't demand anything of me. And don't hesitate to give me what I demand. And you'd better smile as you give that stuff to me too." The issues over which they argued—slavery in New Mexico Territory, the extension of the Missouri Compromise line, the Corwin Amendment, the Dual Executive, the acquisition or conquest of Cuba, the imposition of a federal slave code for the territories, and so on— were all of them trivialities, false issues, dead ends, all of them blown away like last year's leaves by the attack on Fort Sumter. Lincoln's critique here was, like so much else in this speech, tonally distanced. He surveyed the folly of the insurgent agents. But he did not see them in an entirely partisan way, as malefactors aiming to launch the wave of destruction they in fact wound up launching. Seen by Lincoln in 1865, the politics of 1861 were full of sound and fury, signifying nothing but creating slaughter as an unforeseen, or dimly foreseen, consequence.

Although the two parties were equally in the dark about the meaning of their acts and about the future they were unleashing, they are not moral equivalents. The "insurgent agents" make war, but the Union party merely "accepts" war. The distinction captures not only the fact that it was the slaveholders who fired the first shot but also that it was their aggressive intentions that drove the conflict.

Lincoln's retrospect of the secession winter ends with a blunt, dark, four-word sentence. "And the war came." This sentence seems to be spoken not by the president in 1865 but by a historian from the distant future, or maybe by a dark narrator, overheard by the reader but not by the characters.[43] The sentence has the distance, and the blunt clarity, of Lincoln's view of God, who accurately, and without a trace of pity, sees through every pretense. The political leaders were the prisoners of vanity, folly, and wishful thinking, and the only substantial agent was the war itself. Lincoln's phrase curtly dismisses the entire world of prewar politics.

The corrective account that follows is narrated by Lincoln from an extreme distance, and the imagined audience is imagined as distant too, since they needed to be reminded that not only were one eighth of the whole population colored slaves, but those slaves were localized in the southern part of the Union. Briggs points out that the circumlocution about the "southern part" of the Union is designed to avoid treating the South as a distinct region, let alone as a seceding would-be Republic. The conflict over slavery is an inner conflict in the Union itself, not a conflict between regions in the Union.[44]

Lincoln described the centrality of slavery to prewar politics with clear-eyed and understated detachment: "These slaves constituted a peculiar and powerful interest. All knew that this interest was, somehow, the cause of the war." A "peculiar and powerful interest" is something that exerts crushing pressure upon the political order, but nevertheless remains somewhat opaque, somewhat unknowable, an unspoken misgiving, an unfaced obsession. Its power is the power of a compulsion that even those in its grip do not fully comprehend. "Peculiar" here does not mean merely "unique to the South, or to the United States," as in "the Peculiar Institution" of slavery. When Americans referred to slavery as "the Peculiar Institution," they meant to imply that if you have not lived in a slave society you not only do not understand it clearly but also are not even in a position to judge it. "Peculiar" in Lincoln's use also means "mysterious, dark, unfathomable." Even those who led the slave power, the word implies, did not fully understand the forces to which they were subjected by the exigencies of slaveholding. They had been deprived not only of their moral agency—since they were the prisoners of their own mastery—but also of their intellectual clarity, since they could not analyze their compulsions even as they became more and more subjected by them. The term is forbearing to the extent that it does not treat slavery as the creature of conscious villainy. But its critical force is sharp as well.

When Lincoln went on to elaborate that all—everyone, North and South, Democrat and Republican—knew that slavery was "somehow" the cause of the war, that "somehow" captures the moral and political myopia of the generation it indicts. Lincoln's "somehow" meant that dimly everyone did know, but would not acknowledge, what the source of their conflict was. The conflict may have disguised itself in false issues or proxy struggles over the tariff, over states' rights, even over improvement of rivers and harbors, but somehow everybody always knew, "somehow," what they were really fighting about. It is not just that the combatants were dishonest about their motivations. It is that slavery had the power to cloud the minds of the contestants, to enflame them about what they obscurely knew but had to resist acknowledging. They "knew but did not know" in the way we usually know but do not know the worst things about ourselves. When the parties "deprecated" war, they were the victims of wishful thinking, but when they knew but did not face the fact that "somehow" slavery was the cause of the war, they behaved with blind narcissism. White notes also that this same "somehow" renders Lincoln's own developing awareness of the meaning and stakes of the war. He too had, from the beginning, a nagging but unacknowledged sense not only of what the real issue was but also what it would take to address that issue.[45]

Lincoln's "somehow" captures a dark version of what I have been calling the implicitness of concepts. The unacknowledged but overpowering inner compulsions emanating from the presence of slavery in a nominally democratic republic are the shadow of the acknowledged but only dimly registered intuitions that underlie a democratic culture. Both are felt obscurely, as a kind of pressure upon the public mind. Both are fraught with consequences that do not show themselves clearly in prospect but seem inevitable in retrospect. Both drive historical events but seem to transcend them. Both demand to be seen in a concrete, historically situated way, but also seem to be more than the creatures of historical exigencies. Both stand on the line that separates what one wills from what one is destined for, the line that separates what one chooses from what one cannot help but do since it arises from the same sources one's identity arises from.

Lincoln reminded his hearers that he did not enter the presidency with a design to overthrow slavery. Noting that his party claimed "no right to do more than to restrict the territorial enlargement of [slavery]," Lincoln recognized that he too shared the blindness of all the parties to the depth of the issue. At the same time, Lincoln's reminder underscored how modest the threat his side offered to slavery was, how willing the slaveholders were to push the Union over the brink in pursuit of something—slavery in New Mexico and Utah—they probably could not have succeeded at establishing anyway. The Republicans may have deceived themselves about the gravity of slavery (although they did look to its ultimate extinction), but the slaveholders were so intoxicated by slavery that they were willing to kill hundreds of thousands of Americans over a false issue rather than accept reality if that reality came with even the smallest political setback for them.

The same combination of wishful thinking and failure to acknowledge what one already dimly knew that marked the thinking of the prewar politicians marked also the conduct of the war itself. While Lincoln's account of prewar politics turned on complex antitheses (one party "would *make* war rather than let the nation survive; and the other would *accept* war rather than let it perish"), his account of the war itself binds the two parties together in a common folly, and turns on "each," "both," and "neither." Each party expected a short war, an easy war. Each party, misled by its own bluster, underestimated the courage and commitment of the other. Each party, sure of its own rightness, imagined that the fact of their rightness would give them the quick victory their virtue deserved. Each party, believing not only in the glory of war itself but also in the idea that readiness to die and to kill in war is the only undeniable index of moral seriousness, looked forward to the war as a way to cut the Gordian knot of prewar compromise and exigency politics. Each side felt dirtied and shamed by accommodation, and looked forward to being purified by violence. Each side believed it entered the war with pure motives, sullied only by the things it had had to do to prevent the conflict that, reassuringly, had become inevitable. Neither side understood that war has its own logic and that the logic of war would override their own wills, as if once war begins only the war itself had any agency. Neither side understood that war would darken their natures.[46]

Describing not the Civil War, nor even the vicious guerrilla conflict between pro-slavery and anti-slavery militias on the Kansas-Missouri border during the war years, but the friction between two Unionist factions in Missouri, Lincoln gave a grim description of the brutal inner logic of violent struggle. Writing on October 5, 1863, to Charles D. Drake and a party of Missouri Radicals who had come to the White House to remonstrate with him and to demand his intervention on their side of the quarrel, Lincoln described how conflict entrains the agency of the parties in conflict:

> At once, sincerity is questioned, and motives are assailed. Actual war coming, blood grows hot and blood is spilled. Thought is forced from old channels into confusion. Deception breeds and thrives. Confidence dies, and universal suspicion reigns. Each man feels an impulse to kill his neighbor, lest he be killed by him. Revenge and retaliation follow. And all this, as before said, may be among honest men only. But this is not all. Every foul bird comes abroad, and every dirty reptile rises up. These add crime to confusion. Strong measures deemed indispensable, but harsh at best, such men make worse by maladministration. Murders for old grudges, and murders for pelf, proceed under any cloak that will best serve for the occasion. (2:522–523)

Neither party to the war imagined that slavery itself would become the acknowledged focus of the war, rather than merely the open secret of the war. Each side sought more modest aims than the transformation the war yielded. Each side looked for "a result less fundamental and astounding." Each came to the war for a half-measure—restoration of the Union, or completion of secession. What they got was not only a titanic conflict but also a social revolution that upended the economic and political order, freeing the slaves and uprooting the southern political class. They suffered also an intellectual revolution that discredited (for a few years) both the republican elitism and the *herrenvolk* democracy that characterized the thinking of the prewar era. The logic of war overturned the very last things that either party intended to overturn.

The values each side brought to the war reduce in Lincoln's view to self-congratulation. It is easy to see the falsity of asking God's help in keeping other men in slavery. But the Unionists also called on God's help in a way that was scarcely less self-serving:

Both read the same Bible and pray to the same God, and each invokes His aid against the other. It may seem strange that any men should dare to ask a just God's assistance in wringing their bread from the sweat of other men's faces, but let us judge not, that we be not judged. The prayers of both could not be answered. That of neither has been answered fully. The Almighty has His own purposes. (2:687)

The kind of good that we cling to from desperate, angry, wounded narcissism (in the hope of redeeming ourselves from our history and identity) can never produce anything but evil. Both sides read the same Bible, drawing from it only the things that supported their own politics, both treating that great book as a set of pointed out-of-context quotations to be brandished in the face of the enemy. Both sides prayed to the same God: themselves with a louder voice and a thunderbolt ready-to-hand for anyone who stood in their way. Both sides worshipped not a God but a deus ex machina. Both sought the authority of transcendence as a way to shield themselves from criticism, and as a way to shrug off the duty to acknowledge each other. Both used the earnestness of their own moral commitments as a way to stampede their feelings and as an incitement to violence, as if the shrillness of one's professions and the amount of blood one is willing to shed in their service were the only measure of one's moral seriousness. Both proclaimed their allegiance to life as a way to further their romance with death.

When Lincoln said "let us judge not, that we be not judged," he did not mean, as Douglas meant when he quoted the same passage during the Lincoln-Douglas debates, that nobody is in a position to question the morality of slavery. What Lincoln restrained here was not his sense that slavery is wrong, but his sense of moral privilege over slaveholders, his sense that he was different in kind from them. Douglas had assumed that no actual human being is capable of making a moral distinction without transforming it into a club to wield against his enemies, and that no moral claim ever gets made without self-congratulation. But Lincoln's stricture against "judging" did not mean that nobody should judge slavery, only that nobody has a right to imagine that they are morally pure relative to their enemies.[47] "Judge not," then, does not mean that because one's hands are dirty one must adopt a position of moral neutrality. It only means that one cannot point out the mote in one's brother's eye without also reckoning with the beam in one's own.

Lincoln's revulsion against a vindictive and self-righteous moral style had deep roots, going back at least to his address to the Washington Temperance Society of 1842. In that speech, he had praised the "Washingtonians" approach, in which reformed drunkards appealed to alcoholics in a friendly and nonjudgmental way. The previous generation of temperance advocates had denounced confirmed alcoholics as "utterly incorrigible," people who "must be turned adrift, and damned without remedy, in order that the grace of temperance might abound to the temperate *then*, and to all mankind some hundred years *thereafter*." Of this kind of reformer, a type who would become even more familiar to Lincoln during the struggle over slavery, Lincoln said that there is "something repugnant to humanity," something so like "throwing fathers and brothers overboard, to lighten the boat for our security—that the noble minded shrank from the manifest meanness of the thing" (1:87). Those who attempt to drive people to goodness by force, or even by force of denunciation, not only fail to improve those they confront, but sometimes derive from that failure a covert thrill of moral narcissism, a narcissism that Lincoln describes as intoxicating in much the same way that liquor is intoxicating, except that the intoxication always has an edge of cruelty. Everyone who gets drunk on right is a mean drunk.

Historians have seen in the Temperance speech, ever since Harry Jaffa's commentary on it half a century ago, a foreshadowing of the themes of the Second Inaugural Address. Certainly it shares with the Second Inaugural its moral generosity toward fallen human beings, its moral clarity without moral pretense, its modesty without surrender. And it shares with that speech its insights into how to make bad citizens into better ones, bad democrats into better ones, for it offers the promise of moral kinship across deep dividing lines, teaching "hope to all—despair to none" (to quote the prophetic words of the earlier speech, foreshadowing as they do the famous concluding lines of the Second Inaugural) and offering a kind of moral reformation in which even the dram maker and the dram seller are invited to take part. It offers a vision of how, without self-righteousness but nevertheless with stern moral clarity, human willing can be brought back from intoxicating dependencies that compromise its own moral freedom and raise unanswerable questions about what counts as an act of will. This lesson about intoxication and how one can be patiently led away from it applies just as well to America, hung over to this day from its long intoxication with slavery and racism, and even yet no more out of the woods than any alcoholic ever is.

What makes the charity of the Temperance address not mere wishful thinking is its development of a family of themes present in the Peoria and Cooper Union speeches as well and in the great speeches of Lincoln's presidency. The first is of course the mutual imbrication of good and evil agents in each other's acts. No moral act of any consequence is available in Lincoln's world that is not rooted in a recognition of complicity: the good and the evil agent share the same fallenness and the same human nature, and the ethos of responsibility begins with the rejection of the idea that one can purify one's self by refusal of recognition of the evildoer, or, even more, by a cathartic act of violence against him. Good and evil matter intensely, but we are never allowed to know whether we are completely on the side of the angels or not, and we are bound by that recognition not to a craven surrender of our moral claims but to a magnanimous and pragmatic development of those claims.

The moral world of the Second Inaugural differs in one important particular from that of the Temperance address, for the Second Inaugural is marked by a sense of tragedy, and seeks the meaning of experience in the way tragedy does, by reflecting upon the imponderable. The Temperance address, like the earlier Lyceum speech, sought to restrain charismatic evil—the mob's thirst for revenge and the tyrant's thirst for power in the Lyceum speech, the drunkard's obsession but also the temperance fanatic's moral thrill of revulsion in the Temperance speech—by using opinion, the public mind, the never fully examined sense of "how we do things," to support a morally reasonable ethos of restraint. In the Lyceum speech, he had modeled the alternative to the tyrant as George Washington, who not only had refused to be king but also had ruled throughout with restraint and respect for the rules, always resisting the temptation to be a "man on horseback," and showing thereby a kind of charismatic anti-charisma. In the Temperance address, Washington's name and example grace the temperance association Lincoln praises. And Washington's role as a charismatic example of anti-charisma is taken in the Temperance address by Reason, which conquers both slavery by the bottle and slavery by the whip. One might look hard for a more fervid example of praise of restraint of fervidness:

Happy day, when, all appetites controled, all passions subdued, all
matters subjected, *mind*, all conquering *mind*, shall live and move the
monarch of the world. Glorious consummation! Hail fall of Fury!
Reign of Reason, all hail!

And when the victory shall be complete—when there shall be neither a slave nor a drunkard on the earth—how proud the title of that
Land, which may truly claim to be the birthplace and the cradle of
both those revolutions that shall have ended in that victory. How
nobly distinguished that People, who shall have planted, and nurtured to maturity, both the political and moral freedom of their species. (1:89–90)

The Second Inaugural does not take this turn into charismatic anti-
charisma, nor does it hail the reign of reason, nor even does it hail the
land that has nurtured freedom to maturity. Instead, it reflects upon
the unpredictable course of history and the insoluble puzzle of God's
will. And it rebukes, rather than praises, the Republic. Indeed, rueful
puzzlement in the face of a divine rebuke even of those who imagined
themselves doing God's will, not reason supported by opinion, is what
restrains destructive charisma in the Second Inaugural.

Lincoln's meditations on the way the war has overturned all sides'
thinking about its course and meaning lead him to a biblical quotation,
which Lincoln interpreted as making some sense of the senselessness of
the struggle: "Woe unto the world because of offenses; for it must needs
be that offenses come, but woe to that man by whom the offense cometh." The quotation bursts into the midst of the paragraph, as if it
were an urgent interruption by another voice. In the context of Lincoln's
cool and distant skepticism, this passage sounds like a hot denunciation,
something that bursts the shackles of iron self-restraint, something that
refuses to be held back. At the point of the prophetic interruption, Michael Leff (1995) notes, the speech shifts from the past tense to the present tense, the shift in tense corresponding to the shift in subject matter
from the causes and conduct of the war to its religious meaning. Before
the shift in tense, the speaker, like the audience, is as much a passive witness to history as an agent in it, and even his agency is blunted by his
imprisonment in illusion. After the shift in tense, the speaker is intensely present, adopting the rhetoric of prophetic denunciation, leaping
from a past tense to what Leff calls "the sacred present."

William Lee Miller (2008) points out that Lincoln's quotation from the King James version of Matthew 18:7 does not accord with what most modern scholars take it to mean. The Revised Standard Version reads that verse as "Woe to the world for temptations to sin! For it is necessary that temptations come, but woe to the man by whom the temptation comes." Jesus had, in the previous two verses of the Sermon on the Mount, argued that only those who could become like children were worthy to enter the Kingdom of God, that humility and modesty are the attributes of the saved, not ostentatious parades of virtue or assumptions of authority, the characteristic religious habits of adults. Jesus then rebukes those who might cause "one of these little ones who believe in me to sin," which I take to mean not only those who, by being "stumbling blocks" (a better translation of the word the King James Bible translates as "offenses" and the RSV as "temptations"), or bad examples, drive such children out of their state of innocence, but also those who would insist upon wielding the kind of moral authority held by the Scribes and Pharisees rather than that proper to the simplest child.

When Jesus says, "Woe to the world for temptations to sin! For it is necessary that temptations come, but woe to the man by whom the temptation comes," I take him to recognize that the innocence of childhood is passing, which is to say not only that it is in the nature of things that all of us grow up into fallen adults, but also that the spontaneity and purity of the religious sense of childhood hardens into the discredited forms of institutional religious authority Jesus saw himself as called to rebuke. The denunciation claims that everything human is fallen, but the fact that everything human is fallen is no defense for those who helped make it so.

Lincoln's reading of the passage was rather harsher than Jesus's intention. But it was not quite so harsh as what Lincoln's hearers would have assumed him to have had in mind when he said it. A more obvious use of this passage in the context of Union victory would be to justify taking a vindictive stand toward the conquered South: "for it must needs be that offenses come, but woe to that man by whom the offense cometh!" could be taken to mean "It may be true that you didn't invent slavery, and it may be true that you were powerless to end it on your own, but you were masters still and have still to pay the price for that." Lincoln did not, however, give the passage that reading. Instead he saw it as rendering the complicity of both sections in slavery, and as opening both sections to judgment and punishment, referring, as White points out, not to "Southern slavery," but to *American* slavery:

> If we shall suppose that American Slavery is one of those offenses which, in the providence of God, must needs come, but which, having continued through His appointed time, He now wills to remove, and that He gives to both North and South, this terrible war, as the woe due to those by whom the offense came, shall we discern therein any departure from those divine attributes which the believers in a Living God always ascribe to Him? Fondly do we hope—fervently do we pray—that this mighty scourge of war may speedily pass away. Yet, if God wills that it continue, until all the wealth piled by the bondman's two hundred and fifty years of unrequited toil shall be sunk, and until every drop of blood drawn with the lash, shall be paid by another drawn with the sword, as was said three thousand years ago, so still it must be said "the judgments of the Lord are true and righteous altogether." (2:687)

The God who is portrayed in this passage is both amoral and morally unforgiving. This God is amoral because slavery itself is ordained by his providence, like every other evil in this created world, whether as something He willed or as something He allowed to happen. But God's amorality does not lift the moral burden off of the shoulders of men; providence is no excuse. If the offense needs must come, yet woe to those by whom the offense came. Lincoln himself did not flinch from the implications of this view: not only the fact of the war, and not only the intense violence of the war, but also the fact that it involved years of bloody stalemate indicate that God intended the war as punishment to both the North and the South for slavery.

In the midst of a hugely destructive war, we might well pray to evade the punishment of our history, but although our prayer is fervent, our hope is fond. Lincoln means that word "fond" not only in the modern sense of "intensely earnest" but also in the archaic sense of "futile and without hope." Indeed, there may be some connection between the two senses: our hope is intense and earnest especially because it is futile and foolish. Nor did Lincoln expect mercy or forgiveness from this God, since God prolonged the war because America had it coming, and nothing that America possesses—not its wealth, not its resources, not its power—is not somehow essentially the interest on blood money.

"Fondly do we hope—fervently do we pray—that this mighty scourge of war may speedily pass away" evokes, again, the language of Jesus in the Garden of Gethsemane, but "Fondly do we hope" carries the implication that even in our version of that prayer there is a measure of self-deception and wishful thinking. The war will end when it is ready to end, and that will be only when God determines whether the United States has suffered enough. Nobody could complain of his injustice or cruelty were God to insist that the entire wealth of the nation, "all the wealth piled by the bond-man's two hundred and fifty years of unrequited toil," be sunk, or that "every drop of blood drawn with the lash shall be paid by another drawn with the sword."

The "mighty scourge of war" works on the Union in exactly the way the wishful thinking of the prewar politicians did: it is our own doing, but it is not entirely the product of our fully conscious agency. Neither side intended war, yet the war came. Neither side aimed at a prolonged stalemate that would strain the social order so powerfully as to bring about a revolutionary transformation. If this terrible war is "given to both North and South," it is to make them the instruments of their own punishment. The North did not punish the South for slavery; rather, because of their mutual imbrication in slavery, Americans killed each other by the hundreds of thousands, and Americans punished themselves.[48] And each side's folly in believing that God took their side against the other was not only one of the offenses the scourge of war was designed to punish but also itself a means of that punishment, for that folly was one of the things that allowed the violence of the war to intensify beyond the designs of the combatants. For our self-righteous folly God maddened us with conviction in that folly, and set us furiously against each other in defense of that folly.

If there is no forgiveness to be expected from God, there is at least forbearance to be expected from people. God's wrath and human forbearance, in Lincoln's rendering, have a common origin, in that both are responses to the recognition of human fallenness. That fallenness itself is the ground of human kinship. Recognition of complicity, as Robert Penn Warren famously said, is the beginning of innocence, in that it requires us to abandon that moral narcissism that enables us to imagine ourselves as uniquely clean and our opponents as uniquely soiled. The purpose of Lincoln's rendering of a wrathful, unforgiving God who sees through all of our pretenses and uses our own vanities to cause us to inflict bloody retribution upon each other is to rebuke us for seeing ourselves as the instruments rather than as the objects of God's wrath, for by seeing ourselves as the instruments of God's wrath, we ourselves became the agents of it against ourselves. We can only actually serve God by giving up the illusion that we know his will well enough to serve it in purity. As Lincoln puts it in the famous last sentence of the speech:

> With malice toward none; with charity for all; with firmness in the right, as God gives us to see the right, let us strive on to finish the work we are in; to bind up the nation's wounds; to care for him who shall have borne the battle, and for his widow, and his orphan—to do all which may achieve and cherish a just, and lasting peace, among ourselves, and with all nations. (2:687)

Lincoln's thought about God in the Second Inaugural is a version of his thought about history in his December 1862 Annual Message to Congress. Both are creatures of implicitness. And both tie together implicitness and complicity, so that nobody can finally look for justification at the bar of history, just as nobody can seek God as a political ally. History has a direction, and historical events have meaning. But we cannot know how to turn in that direction when we are in history's midst, and we cannot know which act will or will not advance what is, for Lincoln, at stake in history, will or will not, that is, advance the course of self-rule and equality. History is opaque in the way that God is. It calls us, but does not allow us to interpret that call. Yet it also holds us responsible for how we answer that call, even as no answer can be a satisfactory one.

In the midst of the Second Inaugural's call for mutual forgiveness, it is nevertheless only humans who must offer that forgiveness to each other, and then only on the basis of a mutual recognition of fallenness. God, by contrast, makes fools of everyone who believes he can unambiguously serve a moral purpose. And God forgives nothing, demanding that every drop of blood drawn by the lash be paid for by one drawn by the sword.

When Douglas charged Lincoln with harboring plans to bring not only emancipation but also racial equality to the United States, Lincoln honestly denied having such plans. But both emancipation and equal citizenship are implicitly among the consequences of the values Lincoln served, whether he chose to face it or not, and it fell to him, as he himself came to understand in the summer of 1862, to disentangle freedom from slavery, to acknowledge and begin to pay the price of those complicities that arose from the fact that freedom not only tolerated slavery but also depended upon slavery for its coming into being. Nor could freedom, as Lincoln came to understand it, maintain itself as freedom unless it treated freedom as the natural moral birthright of all human beings, since, as Lincoln argued in 1858, those who deny others freedom are beginning the process of losing it for themselves, and are not worthy of it anyway. Douglas was right that, whatever Lincoln's professions, emancipation and racial equality were in the penumbra of his intentions. Douglas was right about Lincoln because, like Jefferson, Lincoln trembled for his country when he reflected that God is just.

The harshness of Lincoln's theological argument and the generosity of his conclusion depend upon each other. Lincoln's theology is negative theology—we do not know God's will, and whenever we claim to know it, we imprison ourselves in narcissist fantasies and spring at each other's throats. But it is still theology, in that it is still a crucial matter to do God's will, to be subject to a moral demand that arises from something deeper than our own interests and needs and desires. Lincoln's negative theology resists atheist skepticism as much as it resists dogmatic narcissism. For the doubts and second thoughts that are motivated by the recognition of complicity are not versions of moral skepticism, the belief that moral questions are somewhat unreal or are disguised versions of interests or biological or economic imperatives. Moral skepticism of that kind offers no ground of recognition of other people, because it gives us a reason to reject their moral arguments against us unheard: they are merely advancing rationalized forms of their interests. I have no reason under that view of the moral world not to exploit others, since the arguments they may bring against me arise from the same kind of interests my desire to exploit them does, and they cannot claim a warrant from some deeper level of conviction. What restrains me from social Darwinist exploitation of others is my recognition of the transcendent value of the human person, a view that arises not from interest calculations, but from my sense of the logical requirements of my own sense of moral agency, demanding as it does an acknowledgment of the agency of others in order to be real. One cannot have agency for one's self so long as one sees what others do only as behavior, not as agency. But one cannot see others as possible agents, with moral selfhood and moral freedom, unless one also sees them as subject to moral imperatives that are not merely disguised versions of their desires.

Lincoln spent the 1850s arguing against the idea that there is no principle of action other than interest. Lincoln attributed this idea to Douglas. But Douglas did not actually believe that; he replaced the language of moral conflict with the language of interest conflict because he feared, and had reason to fear, a descent of the political world into the kind of crusader politics that kills what it loves, into precisely the world Lincoln rebuked as dogmatically narcissistic in the Second Inaugural Address. Lincoln was right, however, to fear that disenchanted moral skepticism might come to dominate political thought. He saw that moral skepticism already in Calhoun. And after the war, it would become the dominant strain of political thinking, embraced as an idea so obvious, so "scientific," so "modern," that alternative views seemed as archaic as believing in witchcraft. It was embraced with enthusiasm by Herbert Spencer and Oliver Wendell Holmes Jr., and with horror by Henry Adams. It has dominated the thinking of the social sciences since Durkheim and Weber, and is probably still the reigning dogma of our own day.

Douglas had a terror, and not an irrational one, of religious politics. He was wrong to imagine that that kind of politics was embraced by Lincoln. But he was not wrong to see it as a threat. In office Lincoln in fact faced the kind of thinking Douglas had feared from Lincoln, and in the Second Inaugural, Lincoln successfully makes the response to the temptation of crusader politics that had eluded both Lincoln and Douglas in the debates. Lincoln continually saw in his Radical opponents, not merely Chase and Sumner but harsher spirits like Zachariah Chandler and Henry Winter Davis, the kinds of position Douglas had attributed to Lincoln himself in 1858. In some ways, once he had won election, Lincoln was forced to replay the Lincoln-Douglas debates, this time with himself as Douglas and with the Radicals as Lincoln.

One of the reasons the Lincoln-Douglas debates seemed to be an impasse is that Lincoln and Douglas each conceived of the quarrel as offering only the alternatives of moral severity, which seemed under pressure always to be ready to descend into crusader politics, and of dealmaking, which seemed under pressure always to be ready to descend to expediency politics. Neither Lincoln nor Douglas quite represented either of these positions. But neither of them characterized their own position in such a way as to forestall the implication that, in the hurly-burly of political conflict, their position would not ultimately descend in just the way their opponents each said they might. Douglas was no amoral broker, but nothing in his position ruled out his developing into one, and the prediction that he might just bargain away all of the most important things in order to secure a peace-saving deal was not an implausible one; Lincoln was no fanatic, but nothing in his position ruled out what he might become once he had to draw a line in the sand, once he had decided that a house divided really could not stand and that the Union was under ontological threat not just from secession but from slavery.

The problem was not just a political problem turning on the differences between the Democratic and Republican Parties. Nor was it a personal problem turning on the different stances of the two men. It was a philosophical problem that has to do with the fact that political legitimacy depends upon the harmony of two forces, principle and the unforced consent of the will, which, under strain, can come apart catastrophically. Without the necessity of referring to moral absolutes, we have no reason to see our conflict with each other as anything other than a contest of force. If I cannot imagine that my opponent can launch at me a just but wholly unexpected rebuke from some deeper stratum of shared values, I have no reason not to just have my way with him by force if I think I can get away with it and have the daring to try. On the other hand, if I hold myself to the absolute, I am tempted to wield it rather than to obey it, and to treat it merely as a kind of divine permission to do anything. What, after all, is more likely to turn one demonic, to make an Ahab of Starbuck, than too deep a draft of the absolute? If the world of the moral skeptic is a world in which the good is only the will of the stronger, then the world of the dogmatic idealist, once he begins to imagine himself as having "a letter of marque from God," is also a world in which the good is only the will of the stronger. And if I abandon the attempt to seek persuasive engagement with my opponent, because our differences of principle seem too deep to be resolved or because our differences of principle make him seem to be little less than demonic to me, then I also have entered a world in which the victory goes to the strong, not to the good, even if the good turns out by chance to be the stronger.

It is this impasse, which the 1858 debates left unresolved, that Lincoln addresses and solves in the Second Inaugural Address. But the solution he proposes is slightly opaque. The combination of severity and charity in the address is not the problem, since it makes possible a generous policy of reconciliation premised upon a common recognition of complicity. The recognition of complicity reaches to both sides of the opposition Lincoln wishes to bridge: it chastens the moral narcissism of the victorious Union without excusing the sins of the defeated Confederacy. It mediates the absolute to the human, by seeing the human as held to a standard against which it can only be wanting, while preventing the absolute from being appropriated by either party by requiring us to recognize that we are never in a position to securely claim to be on the side of the angels. But although we are subject to judgment by the absolute, we do not know precisely what it demands of us. We know that it intensely matters that we do the right, but we also know that whenever we are very sure that we are doing the right we are often fooling ourselves. The charity and the severity of the Second Inaugural Address depend upon each other.

The negative theology of the Second Inaugural also makes possible a new view of the nature of the appeal to principle. First, it introduces a way to be circumspect about the application of principle without being skeptical of the reality of principle. The first thing that people learn about their moral reasoning is that they must be circumspect about its use. This of course means that moral reasoning does not work the way calculation works. Part of the difference arises from the lesser precision of ethical thought, the relative messiness of phronesis relative to *episteme*. But the necessity of circumspection is also forced upon us by the simultaneous unavailability and necessity of moral absolutes. Circumspection, that is to say, grounds itself in reason, not in understanding. We are circumspect because we know we will always be mystified by the good, that those moments when we are most on our moral high horses are the moments when we are most likely to fall off them and do evil in the name of good.

A dogmatic appeal to a commanding value is merely an appeal to an opinion that is fraught with powerful emotion, and which one is prepared to back up with violence. But there are nondogmatic ways to appeal to the absolute. Chief among these is the recognition that in our disputes with each other we may be moved to uncover a yet deeper level of conviction by which my view is to be rebuked after all. A nondogmatic vision of the absolute motivates the conviction that one must be very cautious before asserting that there is no argument that you can make that could persuade me, and that you must be very cautious before you assert the same thing about me.

The difficulty of this view of commanding values is that it requires us to frame a concrete policy in which every act of generosity must risk turning into moral surrender and every act of moral severity must risk turning into moral narcissism. At best, the strictures of the Second Inaugural rule out certain bright-line solutions to the problem of Reconstruction, ruling out vindictive score-settling but also ruling out restoring "the Union as it was." Probably it also requires what in the Gettysburg Address Lincoln had called "a new birth of freedom," since his oblique reference to "the work we are in" must certainly refer to more than merely finishing up the destruction of the Confederacy. Certainly among the things the phrase "the work we are in" picks out are the works of succor and reconciliation—to bind up the nation's wounds, but also to bind up the actual wounds of the combatants, to care for him who shall have borne the battle, and for his widow, and his orphan. It requires us to act with firmness in the right, but it also concedes that we know the right only in part; we know only so much of the right as God lets us see. But that of course leaves the problem unsolved, since God all too often lets us see the right only in completely self-serving ways.

It is a temptation to read the issues of the Reconstruction era back into the Second Inaugural Address. But the effort is complicated by the tensions between the last two paragraphs of the speech, for both the radicals and their opponents can find support in one paragraph or the other. Perhaps the tension between the two paragraphs indicates that Lincoln sought a way to thread the needle, to offer amnesty to the southern political class on condition of civil and political rights for the

Freedmen. Such a bargain may have been impossibly difficult to pull off, since it would have required the white southern political class to sign on to a new racial order, and it would have required the Republicans to hand a large measure of power over to people whom they had just heaved from their positions at the cost of hundreds of thousands of lives. It also would have required building a governing coalition between white nonslaveholders and former slaves, a coalition that, since the racism of the nonslaveholders was as a rule more bitter even than the racism of the slaveholders, would have been hard to maintain. We do know that Lincoln was prepared to offer civil and political rights to former slaves, and we do know that he sought to avoid taking a vindictive attitude toward his former enemies. We do not know what success he would have had following a policy that faced such obvious and daunting political difficulties. But he could hardly have managed worse than his successors actually did.

More generally the recognition of complicity is both the lesson and the method of the speech: we are urgently bound to the right, and just as urgently prevented from knowing whether what we seek to do really is the right or whether we are doing the right thing in the right way and for the right reasons. The recognition of complicity is also the recognition that our insight into our own motives, even into the meaning of our own acts, is limited. It requires us to see our wills as always compromised, but it also requires us to see our virtues not as ways of purifying our wills but as something we can do only in the face of the fact of our being compromised, and in the face of the fact that what we go on to do as we muddle through may also go on to compromise us a little more. That recognition can itself be grounds for generosity, although it concedes that the morality of our actions will always in some sense come down to a wager. To act with firmness in the right as God gives us to see the right is to act in the face of the understanding that one's hands are always dirty; but it is also to recognize that clean hands are better seen as Pilate's concern than as Jesus's.

The greatest difficulty of all is grasping the wisdom of complicity in the midst of a hugely violent war, since that wisdom itself can mask the temptation to moral surrender or to a retreat to a passive if worldly sense of irony. And there are circumstances under which that temptation is as dangerous as the temptation to imagine one's self as wielding the sword of God. The Second Inaugural Address asks us to thread the Scylla of moral skepticism and the Charybdis of moral narcissism, and also the Scylla of war and the Charybdis of peace. The teaching of the Second Inaugural picks out neither a peace policy nor a war policy; it leaves the concrete questions mostly unanswered, although it enlarges the sense that each of the obvious alternatives is fraught and likely wrong. Even what Lincoln articulated in the Second Inaugural could not have availed him had he still stood in the position he stood in while giving the First. It could not have prevented war. It could not have prevented the breaching of persuasive engagement that preceded war. It could not have ended slavery or have moderated the threat slavery posed to democracy. At best, given the fact of war, it might have made it easier to reestablish persuasive engagement once the killing was over. And it might have prevented the violence from descending into one of those thirty-year death spirals, one of those "wars of peoples," in which two peoples who just plain do not like each others' faces see in every event only grounds for renewing their hostility to each other, and continue killing each other until they become too sick of it to continue.

We can come to an intuitive sense of the political meaning of the Second Inaugural Address, but because it involves negotiating an intractable tension between justice and mercy, it is hard to say whether any particular policy Lincoln might have adopted then or any particular policy we are meditating now is or is not in its spirit. Because we experience our values in the tension between their concepts and their conceptions, we never have the kind of grasp upon them that would satisfy our moral vanity. But we also never see them clearly enough to satisfy them fully either, and every concrete realization of our values becomes soon enough only the next way we have betrayed them. Rationality ultimately is not fully equal to the demands of principle, yet rationality cannot be sacrificed without also sacrificing principle. When we seek to act "with firmness in the right, as God gives us to see the right," we seek to act in the face of the aporia that separates the concept from the conception. To act with firmness in the right as God gives us to see the right will always involve a leap of faith.

What we arrive at when we arrive at the end of reason is aporia. But aporia is not irrationality. It is the rebuke of a shallow rationality by a deeper one, a demand to rethink one's way to a better reason one could not have worked one's way down to from within one's starting premises. Otherwise the experience of the irony of history—the tragic po-

litical form of aporia Lincoln describes in the Second Inaugural—
motivates only value-positing or decisionism, motivates merely choosing
any value since all of them are irrational, are all "mere value judgments." But the call to recognize this aporia is not a call to abandon
reason. It is a call to rescue reason from the understanding. What happens in the moral impasse of the irony of history is a kind of leap of
faith, but that leap has to earn its reason in retrospect, in providing a
deeper grasp upon principle than a more rigid and less negatively capable method could have arrived at. We do not know how to judge it
when we make it. But we do expect to hold it to the severe judgment of
a retrospect without special pleading or self-dealing. The leap of faith
is a leap in the dark. But it is not a leap into darkness.

Notes

Note: Throughout this volume, parenthetical citations of Abraham Lincoln's works of the form (1:407) refer to the volume and page number in Lincoln, *Abraham Lincoln: Speeches and Writings*, 2 vols., ed. Don E. Fehrenbacher (New York: Library of America, 1989). All emphases in passages cited from Lincoln are in the original.

1. Introduction

1. For the idea of reflective equilibrium, see Rawls (1971).

2. The term "overlapping consensus" derives from Rawls's *Political Liberalism* (1993).

3. The distinction between purely political liberalism and cultural or comprehensive liberalism is made by Rawls in *Political Liberalism* (1993). Rawls specifically has in mind making it clear that religious believers can take part in a liberal political order without making a fatal sacrifice of their values. Rawls generalizes his case to include committed Islam—although not necessarily Qutb-style Islamic fundamentalism—in *The Law of Peoples* (1999). This last book also lays out the possibility that liberal regimes can easily coexist with certain kinds of nonliberal regimes, specifically with what Rawls calls "decent hierarchical societies."

4. Readers should note that the distinction between consent and principle is not precisely the same thing as the distinction between the fair and the good. Nor is the distinction between consent and principle precisely the same as that between deontological and teleological politics. Indeed, a politics that depends upon the harmony of principle and consent will be in some ways deontological and in some ways teleological.

5. For further arguments about the moral commitments of liberalism, see the essays in Rosenblum (1989), especially William A. Galston, "Civic Education in the Liberal State" (1989); George Kateb, "Democratic Individuality and the

Meaning of Rights" (1989); and, most trenchantly of all, Stephen Holmes, "The Permanent Structure of Antiliberal Thought" (1989). For a strongly Kantian argument on the same subject, see Burton Dreben, "On Rawls and Political Liberalism," in Samuel Freeman, *The Cambridge Companion to Rawls* (2003). Other cogent defenses of the moral commitments of liberalism include James T. Kloppenberg, *The Virtues of Liberalism* (1998), and my own essay "John Rawls and the Moral Vocation of Liberalism" (1994). For a brilliant delineation of the different varieties of liberalism in play in the antebellum era, see David Greenstone, *The Lincoln Persuasion* (1993); David Ericson, *The Shaping of American Liberalism* (1993) and the latter's *The Debate over Slavery* (2000).

6. Ackerman defines the "private citizen" in the first volume of his multivolume *We the People* (1991).

7. The most familiar form of this argument was made by Locke, but its ancestry is considerably older. King John Sigismund of Transylvania, in his 1568 Edict of Torda, guaranteeing legal protection in his realm for Catholics and several varieties of Protestants—but only bare toleration for the Greek Orthodox, Muslims, and Jews—followed essentially this logic.

8. My abbreviated account of the origins of liberalism in the ethos of toleration that arose in reaction to the Wars of Religion, and in a consequent development of a theory of moral autonomy and agency, depends upon the accounts given in Rawls's *Lectures on the History of Moral Philosophy* (2000) (views themselves adumbrated in his *Political Liberalism* [1993]). My account also follows J. B. Schneewind's argument in *The Invention of Autonomy* (1998).

9. Three starting places for this line of thinking were Bernard Bailyn's *The Ideological Origins of the American Revolution* (1967); Gordon Wood's *The Creation of the American Republic 1776–1787* (1972); and J. G. A. Pocock's *The Machiavellian Moment* (1975). All three presented a critical alternative to the traditional account of American liberalism, Louis Hartz's *The Liberal Tradition in America* (1955). See, for example, John Patrick Diggins, *The Lost Soul of American Politics* (1984); and, from the same author, *The Promise of Pragmatism* (1994). For a sympathetic but not completely committed version of the "Republican critique," see Stanley Cavell, *Conditions Handsome and Unhandsome* (1990). For how the "republicanism" thesis plays out in legal philosophy, see Mark Tushnet, *Red, White, and Blue* (1988). For a clear-eyed treatment of the "republicanism" theme generally, see Joyce Appleby, *Liberalism and Republicanism in the Historical Imagination* (1992). For a (to my mind) devastating critique of the entire enterprise, see Mark Hulliung, *Citizens and Citoyens* (2002).

10. Zarefsky's *Lincoln, Douglas, and Slavery* (1990) gives a deeply persuasive account of the way Lincoln and Douglas strove to avoid reaching an argumentative impasse with each other.

11. See George Fredrickson, *The Black Image in the White Mind* (1987).

12. Genovese's classic on this subject is his masterwork, *Roll, Jordan, Roll* (1972), but his theory is adumbrated in *The World the Slaveholders Made* (1969) and taken to its furthest limit in *The Southern Front* (1994).

2. Lincoln's Peoria Speech of 1854

1. In preparation for this speech, Lincoln had engaged in political organization against the Kansas-Nebraska Act all summer long. He encouraged Richard

Yates to run against Thomas Harris for Congress; attempted to persuade John M. Palmer, the Democrat who would have had the nomination that went to Harris had he not been proscribed for opposing the Kansas-Nebraska Act, to stick to his guns about Kansas even if he did, for party loyalty reasons, have to cast his support with Harris; and debated John Calhoun, the Douglas protégé who had once employed him and who would later play a pivotal role in the Lecompton Convention during the Bleeding Kansas struggle. Lincoln gave draft versions of his speech at Winchester on August 26, at Carrollton on August 28, and at Jacksonville on September 2 (Waugh [2007] 208). Lincoln also made important speeches at Bloomington on September 12 and 26, the latter, like the Springfield and Peoria speeches, a kind of debate with Douglas. For details about the background of the speech, see Lewis E. Lehrman, *Lincoln at Peoria* (2008).

2. Douglas gave the land for the founding of the University of Chicago. See Douglas, *The Letters of Stephen A. Douglas*, ed. Robert W. Johannsen (1961) 390. For an excellent account of Douglas's motives in many crises, see Johannsen's biography and his other studies of Douglas (1973, 1989, 1991). Wells's *Stephen Douglas* (1990) is also a moving and sympathetic account of the Little Giant. Douglas was often a hero to the "blundering generation" school, which sought to treat the Civil War as the consequence of the domination of 1850s politics by incompetent hotheads. These accounts of Douglas's motives include sympathetic biographies of Douglas by Milton (1934) and Capers (1959). Similar views inform Randall's biography of Lincoln (1945) and Roy Franklin Nichols's *The Disruption of American Democracy* (1962). And this highly sympathetic view of Douglas informs even Nevins's *The Emergence of Lincoln* (1950, 1950b), despite the fact that Douglas is pretty much the villain of Nevins's *The Ordeal of the Union* (1947a, 1947b). My own reading of Douglas is strongly influenced by Harry Jaffa's *Crisis of the House Divided* (1959), but as will be seen, I see Douglas far more sympathetically than Jaffa does. It is not my intention to revive Milton's Douglas. But I do want to see him in a more nuanced and more fair-minded way than Jaffa does. A very fair-minded recent view of Douglas's views, and how they differ from Lincoln's, is in Greenstone's *The Lincoln Persuasion* (1993).

3. Douglas organized the territories of Minnesota, Oregon, New Mexico, Utah, Washington, Kansas, and Nebraska, and brought the state constitutions of Texas, Iowa, Wisconsin, California, Minnesota, and Oregon to Congress (Douglas [1961] 470).

4. There is a nuance about this that should be developed, since the feelings among slaveholders about the expansion of slavery into the territories was actually more complicated than this, and varied by region. According to Freehling (1990), the border and upper slave states tended to favor expansion of slavery into the territories because they looked forward to the day when, like the upper North, they would be able to rid themselves of both slavery and African Americans by exporting their slaves to the new regions. The older slave states of the Eastern Seaboard, such as South Carolina and Georgia, had, until anti-slavery opposition made it an issue of sectional loyalty, mixed feelings about territorial expansion. They also had mixed feelings about letting Virginia and Kentucky off the hook through expansion, and doubted that the border South would stand with them in a crisis if the people of those states thought they could eventually shake slavery off. At the same time, without expansion into the territories, and with the border

South restive about slavery, these states also feared being "cooped up" in a diminishing area with their slaves. By contrast, entrepreneurial slaveholders of the Southwest, especially in Louisiana, had imperial ideas about expansion of slavery, embracing not only expansion into the territories but the conquest of Cuba and Nicaragua as well. And slaveholders on the western margin of the slave states, most especially in Missouri, embraced slavery expansion because they hoped it would prop up the increasingly marginal status of slavery in their home state. Missouri slaveholders in particular feared the situation in which their state would be surrounded on three sides by free states. The situation was also complicated by the demands of loyalty politics within the slaveholding region, in which politicians from some faction or region somewhat less invested in slavery's hard line (which is to say Whigs, and border South politicians generally) would take a hard line in order to prove their sectional loyalty, or those invested in a hard line would enforce it on their wavering brethren. The increasingly rigid conformity of southern politicians on the slavery issue concealed and repressed many kinds of mixed feelings and mixed motives.

5. President Taylor was not a supporter of the Wilmot Proviso, but he did favor the immediate admission of the entire Mexican Cession as states. Although he would have wished to do so on a popular sovereignty basis, functionally this position was not far different from advocating the Wilmot Proviso, and his firmness against southern pressure on these issues made him functionally the ally of Seward. For more on Taylor, see K. Jack Bauer, *Zachary Taylor* (1985).

6. See the interesting discussion of this issue in Drew McCoy's study of Madison in retirement, *The Last of the Fathers* (1989).

7. For interesting treatments of the gag rule controversy, see William Lee Miller, *Arguing about Slavery* (1996), and William Freehling's treatment of the same issue in the first volume of *The Road to Disunion* (1990). Don E. Fehrenbacher has an interesting treatment of the issue in *The Dred Scott Case* (1978).

8. Fehrenbacher notes that Calhoun's argument here raises the major issue in *Dred Scott*, and employs some of the main arguments Taney would use in order to maintain that the Missouri Compromise restriction was unconstitutional.

9. The Benjamin F. Butler mentioned here is the New York politician, Van Buren's former law partner, not the Massachusetts politician who organized for Breckinridge in 1860, commanded the Union occupation of New Orleans during the Civil War, and ran for president on the Greenback ticket afterward.

10. For Wilmot's complex motives, see Morrison (1997) 43. Until he felt the sting of Polk's betrayal, Wilmot had been very pro-southern. He had, for instance, supported the gag rule against petitions concerning slavery in the District of Columbia, and had supported Calhoun's plan, not Douglas's or Cass's, about the organization of Oregon Territory. Wilmot himself, unlike other Wilmot Proviso Democrats, also supported the Walker tariff (about this, see Wilson [1874] 17). It is also worth remembering that Wilmot, like many Wilmot Proviso Democrats, was not per se hostile to slavery. He wished to keep slavery out of the West because he saw it as a place for white independent farmers to settle, free of competition from slave labor. Wilmot, Henry Wilson noted, was all for territorial expansion, all for the annexation of Texas, all for the conquest of New Mexico and California. "If the war is not for slavery, then I do not embarrass the administration with my amendment. If it is for slavery, I am deceived in my object" (Wilson

[1874] 19). See Howe (2007) 831 for an analysis of the politics of the Wilmot Proviso.

11. For a persuasive argument to this effect, see Howe (2007) 402–403.

12. And however much he may have hedged about this later, Lewis Cass also believed in 1850 that the territorial legislatures should decide for themselves whether or not to permit slavery in the territory. In his 1859 defense of popular sovereignty in *Harper's* magazine, Douglas carefully cites Cass's language to this effect from the debates on the Compromise of 1850. Referring first to a move by the Committee of Thirteen, which wrote the "omnibus" bill combining all of the elements of the compromise, to include a provision forbidding the territorial legislatures from making any law at all on the slavery question, and second, to amendments by Jefferson Davis and Salmon Chase specifically forbidding the territorial legislatures from abolishing or permitting slavery in the territory, Cass said:

> Now with respect to the amendments. I shall vote against them both; and then I shall vote in favor of striking out the restriction in the Bill upon the power of the Territorial governments. I shall do so upon this ground. I was opposed, as the honorable Senator from Kentucky has declared he was, to the insertion of this prohibition by the committee. I consider it inexpedient and unconstitutional. I have already stated my belief that the rightful power of internal legislation in the Territories belongs to the people. (Jaffa and Johannsen [1959] 118–119)

13. Fehrenbacher (1978) notes that Douglas came very late to the idea of "constitutionalizing" popular sovereignty. Certainly during the debates over the Compromise of 1850 he held that Congress did have power over slavery in the territories, and saw popular sovereignty as a prudential matter, rather than a constitutional one (178). Cass, by contrast, was an early adopter of the constitutionalized view.

14. For Douglas's views on this, see Johannsen (1973) 255–256. Clay took the same view.

15. For the *Somerset* case, see Davis's *the Problem of Slavery in the Age of Revolution* (1975).

16. For the argument that the purported ambiguity over when the territorial population gets to exercise their popular sovereignty is a late, pro-slavery confection, see Morrison (1967) 86–91. The Oregon case is a special one, however, in that a de facto territorial government had taken root over the several years Congress spent dallying over organizing a government. Douglas may not have felt that allowing them to continue using the language of the Northwest Ordinance, which the settlers had copied from the constitution of Iowa, committed him to anything in regard to the Mexican Cession, since the latter did not have a de facto government already in place. On the other hand, Douglas from very early on had used language supporting the right of the people of Oregon Territory to forbid slavery if they wished to do so. That said, Douglas was worried that how the Oregon question was settled might provide precedents for the Mexican Cession, and thus sometimes threw his support behind the idea that Oregon should be a free territory only because it was situated north of the 36° 30′ line, and sometimes also supported for New Mexico and Utah Clayton's original

"nonintervention" position, which, far from giving those territories power over slavery, forbade them from passing any law about it, for or against. Douglas's views during the Polk administration are rather unclear; they might, in an excess of charity, be called pragmatic.

17. David Potter argues that most southerners knew that slavery could not prosper in the Mexican Cession, and were exercised by the symbolic insult of the Wilmot Proviso at least as much as by the effect admission of all those free states from the territory of the Mexican Cession might have on the balance of power between the sections in the Senate. See Potter (1976) 68.

18. *Congressional Globe*, 30th Cong., 1st sess., appendix, 366, cited in George Fort Milton, *Eve of Conflict* (1934) 64.

19. For the debate over King's and Burt's strategies, see Chaplain W. Morrison, *Democratic Politics and Sectionalism* (1967) 29–35. See also Don Fehrenbacher's account in *The Dred Scott Case* (1978).

20. The situation is actually slightly more complicated than this. Burt was a follower of Calhoun, and a believer in his joint sovereignty theory. Extending the Missouri Compromise line would seem to contradict the Calhoun theory. In 1854 other supporters of the Calhoun-Davis joint sovereignty theory lined up to support the Kansas-Nebraska Act, behavior that would also seem to contradict their arguments that the federal government was bound to affirmatively protect slavery in the territories. These contradictions are instances of the naked expediency that characteristically ruled the pro-slavery faction.

21. The text here is from Lence's edition, 521. Morrison (1967) 35–37 provides a detailed treatment of Calhoun's strategy. He notes that southern politicians embraced Calhoun's doctrine, with its threat of secession, because it was political dynamite for them, but also continued largely to support Burt's attempt to extend the Missouri Compromise line. Apparently they did not notice that not only were the two policies contradictory, but they depended upon contradictory reasoning about who should or should not have a say about slavery in the territories. The contradiction works in two directions. First, supporters of Calhoun's position would support the Missouri Compromise Line or the popular sovereignty position if it gave them traction against northern opponents. But, second, more moderate southerners, who supported these two positions, would echo Calhoun's arguments as well, if only to persuade everybody that they too knew how to wave a big stick.

22. This is from Lence's edition of the speech, in Calhoun, *Union and Liberty* (1992) 518. Notice that Calhoun, in passing, but characteristically, slights the idea of individual freedom; the only freedom that matters to Calhoun is the corporate freedom of states. This partly follows from his idea that human identity is fundamentally a socially constructed thing, inextricable from the culture that nurtured it, and thus not really capable of a point of view that transcends that culture. The concept of individuals with rights of a transcendental kind and with irreducible moral claims upon each other is completely alien to his thinking. For my own take on Calhoun's Oregon speech, see section 7.3 below.

23. The bill that Douglas, now a senator, proposed on August 5, 1848, actually tried to have it both ways, employing both the language of the Northwest Ordinance and the rationale that the territory was north of the Missouri Compromise line. Douglas said, of his language, that he wanted to make it possible for people

who agreed that Oregon Territory should be organized without slavery but did not agree about why to sign onto the same bill. This won him nothing, except denunciation as a Free Soiler by Senator Mason of Virginia, and a threat from Senator Butler of South Carolina to send his constituents to Oregon with arms in their hands and take possession of the territory (Wilson [1874] 46). Wilson believes that the secession threat that Calhoun made more explicit after Butler's speech scared more moderate southerners like Bell and Houston to support the organization of Oregon as a free territory, if only to end the debate.

24. Indeed, since Dickinson's Barnburner opponent, Silas Wright, had come out for the Wilmot Proviso, Dickinson's position certainly was, as far as New York was concerned, aimed against Van Buren's supporters. But on the national scene the same position had to play out differently, because it faced opposition not only from the Barnburners but from supporters of the Calhoun joint sovereignty position, and from more conservative northern Democrats like James Buchanan, who in his "Harvest Home" letter had come out for extending the Missouri Compromise line. Over the war years, Dickinson's convictions were transformed; from a conservative "Hard" Democrat he became a Republican, and was seriously considered for the vice presidency in 1864. The possibilities for counterfactual history offered up by Daniel Dickinson rather than Andrew Johnson succeeding Lincoln in the presidency are large ones.

25. The politics of prewar politicians do not always predict their postwar course. Samuel Tilden, who followed Martin Van Buren into Free Soil, remained a Democrat. Daniel Dickinson, who opposed reconciliation with Free Soilers when they sought to rejoin the Democratic Party, become a Republican, and was in the running to become Lincoln's vice president in 1864. And Benjamin Butler supported Breckinridge in 1860, but became a radical Republican during Reconstruction. Go figure.

26. See Johannsen's biography of Douglas for details. See also Carl Schurz's very old biography of Henry Clay for his own pointed view of the matter.

27. Clayton was about the only southern politician to ever vote for the Wilmot Proviso. For a discussion of this, see Holt (1999) 320.

28. During the Oregon debate, Reverdy Johnson, who later made the slaveholders' case in the *Dred Scott* trial before the Supreme Court, argued that if the North really succeeded in preventing slavery from entering the territories, the Union could not survive. But he also believed then that Congress had the power to enact such a prohibition, and that the Supreme Court would decide that Congress had that power too. How times change.

29. Morrison (1997) 100; Johannsen (1973) 242.

30. I count this last, as Douglas and Webster did, as part of the northern side of the bargain, although most northerners, who preferred the sure-thing outcome of the Wilmot Proviso, did not see the Utah and New Mexico provisions that way. Don Fehrenbacher, in *The Dred Scott Case* (1978), saw these provisions as concessions to the slave states, since they (barely) opened to slavery a region where it had previously been prohibited by Mexican law, and organized new territories without applying the Wilmot Proviso to them. The actual votes on the bills argue that politicians at the time tended to see it that way too: 82 percent of southerners voted for the bill, and 62 percent of northerners voted against it (Fehrenbacher [1978] 176). Pro-slavery politicians, however, almost immediately

interpreted this provision as a gross betrayal of the interests of the slave states by the free states. During the final stages of the debate over the Compromise of 1850, Representative James Seddon of Virginia tried to block the organization of a territorial government for Utah unless the territorial legislature were prohibited from preventing the immigration of citizens with "any kind of property recognized as such in any of the States of the Union" (Bordewich [2012] 344). Georgia's Robert Toombs, then a Unionist, pointed out that in fact the northern representatives had mostly opposed the provisions calling for popular sovereignty about slavery in Utah and New Mexico, and that a majority of twenty-three of the representatives of the slave states, including eight representatives from Virginia, had voted for it. Seddon's argument shows that fire-eater revision of the historical record about the Compromise of 1850 began before the compromise was even complete. See Bordewich (2012) 344–345.

31. For a close analysis of the crucial votes, see Hamilton (1964). For a general treatment of the Wilmot Proviso controversy, see Morrison (1967). For more of my own take on the collapse of the omnibus bill, see section 3.4 below.

32. Douglas described his strategy during the 1850 debates in a long letter to Charles Lanphier in August. Douglas had opposed the creation of the Committee of Thirteen on the grounds that an "omnibus" bill would simply unite the opponents of compromise (which turned out to be true). Douglas reported that the committee had taken his bills on statehood for California, and territorial governments for Utah and New Mexico, and simply united them:

> The Committee was appointed & took my two printed Bills & put a wafer between & reported them back without changing or writing a single word, except one line. This one line inserted prohibited the Territorial Legislatures from Legislating upon the subject of slavery. This amendment was voted in by the Com in opposition to the wishes of Gen'l Cass & Mr Clay, and they gave notice that they should move to strike it out in the Senate & it was stricken out. So you see that the difference between Mr. Clay's Compromise Bill & my two Bills was a wafer, & that he did not write one word of it & that I did write every word.

Curiously, Douglas's letter did not mention the Fugitive Slave Act at all. And it went on to suggest that Buchanan had whipped up the Nullifiers and the Disunionists to oppose the bill, out of jealousy of the leadership of Cass. Douglas's suspicions of Buchanan were of long standing. See Douglas (1961) 190–193.

33. Johannsen (1973) 302.

34. One of the reasons that Douglas dismissed the criticisms of northern Whigs who blamed him for disrupting the uneasy peace established by the Compromise of 1850 was that those who criticized him most harshly probably did not themselves support the compromise when it was made. Douglas dismissed Lincoln's attack on this issue as pious gas of this sort. But Douglas was probably unfair in doing so, since Lincoln went out of his way, even when he did not have to, to say that he would even be willing to abide by the Fugitive Slave Act, abominable as he thought it was. We just do not really know whether Lincoln would have stood with Taylor or with Clay had he been in Washington in the summer of 1850.

35. See Douglas's speech of March 3 (1854b) 12–25. One thing that should be noticed about this is that each side uses its political power to rescind a compro-

mise it has already made. There would not seem to be much difference between New Mexico being unable to abolish slavery but successfully keeping it out by refusing to pass the necessary police legislation—Douglas's Freeport Doctrine— and Congress understanding that Oregon as a state could either accept or reject slavery as it wished, but refusing to allow it admission unless it accepted slavery.

36. This is Nevins's view in the second volume of *The Ordeal of the Union*. For more of my take on this, see sections 2.2 and 4.2 below.

37. William Seward, then the leading anti-slavery leader in the Senate, later bragged that he himself had put Dixon up to this demand, in order to put Douglas in an impossible position. If that is true, then Seward is guilty of a scarcely credible act of double-dealing. Most historians now do not take Seward's boast seriously.

38. See my treatment of these remarks in section 6.2 below.

39. Blaine made this oft-quoted remark in his book *Twenty Years in Congress* (1884) 272. Blaine attributes the phrase to "a witty politician of the south." But I have never seen any attribution of this phrase other than to Blaine himself.

Blaine's remark was widely cited in the historical literature by historians of the "blundering generation" school exemplified by Charles W. Ramsdell, who argued, in a famous article in the October 1929 *Mississippi Valley Historical Review* about the natural limits of slavery extension, that for geographical and economic reasons slavery could not have thriven in the western territories, that for this reason the conflict over slavery in the territories was unnecessary, and that therefore the United States worked itself up into fighting a civil war over a false issue. This was Douglas's view in 1858, of course. But it has not been the prevailing view among the historians of the last century.

My own view about the Ramsdell thesis is that some of it is mistaken—its assumption that slavery was economically feeble, for instance. And, as Don Fehrenbacher pointed out—and for that matter as Lincoln himself pointed out in the Peoria speech—it was the Northwest Ordinance, not geography, that kept slavery out of Illinois while it (marginally) survived just across the Mississippi in Missouri and (somewhat more robustly) at the same latitudes across the Ohio in Kentucky, and, furthermore, there is no particular reason to believe that slavery would not have been just as strong in the eastern counties of Kansas as it was in the western counties of Missouri, the region in the latter state, in fact, where slavery had the strongest footing.

That said, there are sociological arguments, arguments about the sort of people who went to Kansas (white nonslaveholders from the border South), why they went there (to get away from competition with slaveholders), and what they expected to be able to do there (farm for themselves), that militated against the success of slavery in Kansas.

40. See Howe (2007) 273.

41. See Miller (1981); Scott (1994); Weiss (1981).

42. Whether Douglas was right about this is still a hot subject of debate. I finally believe, with Potter, that Douglas's thesis is culturally if not economically true. See Potter (1976) 68. The classic book on anti-slavery racism is Eugene Berwanger, *The Frontier against Slavery* (1967).

43. The Topeka Constitution, advanced by free state forces during the Bleeding Kansas struggle, prohibited the entry of free blacks. This constitution did

not, however, ever really become law. The Wyandotte Constitution under which Kansas was eventually admitted to the Union as a free state in 1861 had no such provision, and in fact there was considerable black emigration to Kansas. See Nell Painter, *Exodusters* (1977), for an account of this emigration.

44. Johannsen makes this claim in *The Frontier, the Union, and Stephen A. Douglas* (1989). The argument is so persuasive that I am rather surprised it had not been made before. Douglas also proposed, in 1859, a bill to establish land-grant colleges in the states, what later became the Morrill Act in 1862. (About this see Roy Morris, *The Long Pursuit* [2008] 135.) All three of the great national tasks the federal government was able to accomplish once southern obstructionists were out of the government—the transcontinental railroad, the Homestead Act, the Morrill Act—were parts of Douglas's program.

45. All of the standard histories cover the notion of a slave power conspiracy to subvert the free political institutions of the South. But an interesting account of it is also given in Davis's short book on the subject (1969).

46. Here I follow Fehrenbacher's astute reading of many of Lincoln's racist remarks in *Lincoln in Text and Context* (1987). Burlingame (2008a) also cites an 1836 anonymous letter in the *Sangamo Journal*, probably written by Lincoln, in which he ridicules the Democrats as supporters of votes for blacks, on account of Van Buren's support for black suffrage in New York. There are also accounts of Lincoln taunting Douglas in 1840 on the subject of black suffrage, again citing Van Buren's example. See Donald (1995) 80, and Burlingame (2008a) 154–155. Douglas Wilson has an interesting account of the incident in which Lincoln trapped Douglas with Van Buren's acknowledgment that he had indeed, under certain conditions, supported black suffrage. See Wilson (1998) 204–205.

47. For this detail, see Roy Franklin Nichols, *Franklin Pierce* (1958) 174.

48. The fling against Pierce in the Scott Club speech as a "political mulatto" also seems to be a retort to Douglas's usual charge that the Whigs are closet abolitionists.

49. Douglas in fact seized on the example of California as proof that popular sovereignty would lead to the admission of new free states. He wrote to Charles Lanphier and George Walker on January 7, 1850:

> My impression is that we will all be together in favor of the admission of California as a State. I started the proposition at the beginning of last Session & then predicted that the people would decide against slavery if left to settle the question for themselves. The result has verified the prediction. Gen'l Cass expressed the same opinion I believe in his Nicholson Letter & the whole Democratic Party of the North took the same ground. The Free Soilers declared that slavery would go there unless, Congress prohibited it. The result has shown that we were right & they wrong. (See Douglas [1961] 182–183.)

50. See Douglas's speech of January 30 (1854a) 13.

51. Douglas gives his own account of this speech during the debates over the Kansas-Nebraska Act in a speech on March 20, 1854.

52. See Douglas's speech of March 3 (1854b) 12–25.

53. See Douglas's speech of January 30 (1854a) 13.

54. Milton (1934) notes, for instance, that the New York legislature refused to ratify the Missouri Compromise the next year. This is particularly important

since most accounts of the Missouri Compromise see the struggle over Missouri as originating in the struggle between pro- and anti-Clintonian factions in New York.

55. Douglas, "Letter to Twenty-five Chicago Clergymen" (April 6, 1854), in Douglas (1961) 316. Lincoln, however, felt bound by the act, however distasteful he felt it to be.

56. Cited in Johannsen (1973) 406.

57. *Senate Reports*, 33/1, no. 15, 1–4, cited in Johannsen (1973) 406.

58. The distinction between an ad hoc, modus vivendi arrangement and a relationship of principled reciprocity is developed by John Rawls in *Political Liberalism* (1993).

59. The horizon of persuadability Lincoln imagined in his debates with Douglas was far narrower. Lincoln's speeches in 1858 had nothing to say to southern Democrats, nothing to say to southern Whigs, and even nothing to say to northern Democrats. His entire energy was directed toward persuading moderate northern Republicans that even though the popular sovereignty position had won out in Kansas it was still not a position that the Republican Party could afford to adopt.

60. For the role colonization played in Lincoln's thinking in the war years, see section 6.1 below.

61. Opponents of the proviso North Carolina put upon its cession of its western lands in 1790—what eventually became Tennessee—cited Jefferson's language about equality from the Declaration of Independence (Gerteis [1987] 13). It is not only Lincoln's generation that assumed that that language was incompatible with slavery.

62. Dworkin (1986), following the lead of H. L. A. Hart, uses a law's concept to describe the deep but perhaps not fully articulable value it is intended to serve. A law's conception is its concrete working-out in the political and legal institutions of a particular time and place. To see moral conflict as a conflict between concept and conception is very promising, because it means that each side is quarreling about insights into the same meaning. But it was the habit of nineteenth-century politicians to see the moral conflict as a conflict between higher law and positive law. That is a far less promising formalism, since it tempts everyone to see it as an issue between those who have moral authority and those who have only power. To see moral conflict as a conflict between concept and conception is to invite moral engagement among opponents. To see moral conflict as a conflict between higher law and positive law is to invite only civil war.

63. Freehling (1990) has a good analysis of the way in which masters were simultaneously emotionally enmeshed with their slaves and terrified of them.

64. See my discussion of this letter at section 5.3 below.

65. Lincoln was not the only Illinois politician to argue that the passage of the Kansas-Nebraska Act indicated an erosion of the sentiments of the Declaration of Independence. John M. Palmer, a Democrat whose opposition to the Kansas-Nebraska Act Lincoln encouraged while not yet asking him to leave behind his allegiance to the Democratic Party—he was one of the five anti-Nebraska Democrats whose reluctance to vote for the Whiggish Lincoln gave the 1855 Senate election to Lyman Trumbull—also saw the act as embodying Calhoun's attack on the Declaration, and cautiously rebuked Douglas's different reading

of the Declaration as well. In his autobiography, Palmer remembered the speech he gave on July 4, 1854, this way:

> I indulged in the usual glorification of our revolutionary fathers and quoted from the Declaration of Independence, as I had often done on like occasions, that "All men are created equal, and are endowed with certain inalienable rights, among which are life, liberty and the pursuit of happiness," words which Mr. John C. Calhoun [from South Carolina] had characterized as "glittering generalities," and Mr. Douglas said meant "no more than our fathers intended to claim by those words that British subjects born on this continent had the same rights that British subjects had who were born in Great Britain." I attacked Mr. Calhoun, but spoke of Mr. Douglas with the respect I really felt for him, but my remarks stirred up a storm. Before I left the ground I was convinced that the Democratic party was hopelessly divided, and that the repeal of the Missouri compromise had stirred up passions that could not be allayed, and that the country was about entering upon a struggle which would probably result in very serious consequences. (Lehrman [2008] 16, quoting John M. Palmer, *Personal Recollections of John M. Palmer: The Story of an Earnest Life* [Cincinnati: R. Clarke, 1901] 63.)

Lincoln and Theodore Parker were clearly not the first people to find in the Kansas-Nebraska Act and in the threat of the slave power more generally a threat to the values of the Declaration of Independence.

66. For more on this, see section 6.2 below. For a recent sterner view of Douglas than mine, see Graham A. Peck, "Was Stephen A. Douglas Antislavery?" (2005) 1–2.

67. See Morris (2008) 171.

68. Wells (1990) 281.

69. Johannsen (1973) 860.

70. Ibid. 867.

71. Remember, after all, that even pro-Breckinridge Democrats like Benjamin Butler and Edwin Stanton ultimately were radicalized by conflict with the secessionists.

72. Philip Paludan insightfully describes the transformation of Francis Lieber's convictions in the 1850s from a defender of local governments to a kind of nationalism that was willing to abolish slavery if slavery proved a threat to the Union. Paludan describes also the change of heart that came over northern defenders of the South as the South's insistence in the later 1850s—whether in the form of a federal slave code for the territories or in the form of the Calhoun-Davis imposition of slavery upon the territories—that slavery "receive the active protection of the federal government" became more alarming to them than the abolition rhetoric they had traditionally denounced as a threat to Union:

> Such alarm would lead them into an important new position. They would become not the defenders of an order in which slavery had its legal place, but protectors of an order which slavery seemed to be attacking. Slavery was never a proper candidate for inclusion in the national identity. At best it was something that most Americans lived with and thought about as little as they could. It was a necessary part of the constitutional compromise that made

Union possible. Since they wanted their own local governments to be respected, most Northerners were willing to respect the southern desire to maintain slavery in the South. By insisting that slavery was the South's (and not the nation's) institution, Northerners probably numbed their responsibility for it even as they espoused the nation's legal traditions. But when frightened Southerners supported the abolitionist contention that slavery was a national matter, they unleashed the wrath of the guilty even as they threatened an innovation in constitutional government.

This innovation itself received the brunt of the response of northern lawyers. Their anger revealed a fact crucial for the emancipation of the Negro: many of the natural northern supporters of the South had become that section's antagonists. Men who had argued that the Constitution protected slavery where it was and that order demanded restraint in suggesting change now turned on the South. They removed the shield of law and order from the South and turned it into a sword for attackers of slavery. This was the moment when the possibility of ending slavery began to dawn. No longer would respect for order, Union, and the Constitution protect it. (Paludan [1975] 79)

Lieber was always several steps ahead of Douglas, but they were traveling down the same road.

73. If Douglas was trying to draw a certain kind of anti-slavery politician to his side in 1858, prominent Republicans were also paying court to him, trying to draw him into their party. These Republicans included not just the mercurial Greeley but also such stalwarts as Henry Wilson, Anson Burlingame, and William H. Seward. For more on this, see Fehrenbacher (1960) 616.

74. For what Douglas thought privately about slavery, see section 6.2 below.

75. The reader should notice that I did not argue that Douglas rejected entirely the idea that liberal regimes require the support of cultural habits, only that his view of them was far less sweeping than Lincoln's was.

76. Indeed, failure to see this was an important factor in the establishment of the doctrine of "separate but equal" public accommodations for people of different races in *Plessy v. Ferguson*. The argument was that the Fourteenth and Fifteenth Amendments sought to establish formal political equality in matters like voting and jury service, but they did not establish social equality and could not be used to make people associate with others they did not like. This is why the attempt to solve deep social conflicts, such as over religion, by enforcing the boundary between a public world in which one must be fair and a private world in which one can behave in as ugly a fashion as one wishes is so often unavailing. For Democracy does have a stake in what people's private feelings are. But even so it cannot shape those feelings by outlawing the bad ones.

77. This detail suggests that the agitation on this subject by Breckinridge's supporters was more an organizing issue, a political litmus test, than a serious policy proposal. It was designed to force a humiliating submission out of northern Democrats in order to demonstrate which states were going to boss the party, but it provided the South with something, when push came to shove, it did not in fact especially want. To some extent the Kansas-Nebraska Act worked the same way. Deep southerners were not especially enthusiastic about it when it was proposed, but once it became the object of a sectional power struggle, they insisted

upon a hard line about it as a way to enforce sectional loyalty politics, and as a way to destroy the credibility of compromise-seeking Whigs in the South. Now sometimes things one adopts for symbolic reasons, in order to force waverers in line or to show them who is boss, wind up being things one winds up embracing for themselves. But even passionate supporters of slavery turned out to have mixed enough feelings about the African slave trade that when they came to power they did not seek to reopen it. William Lee Miller, in his recent, excellent *President Lincoln* (2008), recounts how even Henry Wise, known to history as the strongly proslavery governor of Virginia who presided over the trial of John Brown, had, as minister to Brazil in the 1840s, been an effective opponent of the African slave trade to Brazil, collaborating on that project with his British counterpart (242). Now, as Miller points out, as slave exporters themselves—but not as slave exporters to Brazil—Virginians had an interest in closing the African slave trade. But, Miller argues, "Nevertheless, one would not want to discount a certain amount of displaced moral revulsion even in the states whose social order still rested on the results of the trade. Perhaps if you were foreclosed from making moral judgment on the institution itself by your own involvement with it, you could compensate by being particularly fierce against the trade from which it had sprung" (242). Wise's career was full of ironies and strange turns. See the précis of his career in Freehling (2007). After the Civil War, Wise wound up a Republican, and a supporter of civil rights for African Americans. For Wise as a Republican, see Burton (2007) 299.

78. For the complex history of the persistence of American participation in the African slave trade even after the piracy statute, see Fehrenbacher (2001). For the complicity of southern federal judges, in particular the notorious Andrew Magrath in Charleston, in dismissing the cases against accused American slavers in 1859 and 1860, see Allan Nevins's account in volume 2 of *The Emergence of Lincoln* (1950b). For a detailed account of the trail of Nathaniel Gordon, the only slaver captain actually executed under the statute, see Miller (2008).

3. Lincoln's Conspiracy Charge

1. John Channing Briggs's account (2005) of the composition of the speech makes it clear not only that Lincoln was aware the speech would be controversial, but that he knew his closest political friends would be taken aback by its stark recklessness. Lincoln's law partner, William Herndon, argued in his controversial biography of Lincoln that the famous "Lost Speech" that Lincoln delivered at the state Republican Convention in Bloomington on May 29, 1856, was essentially the "House Divided" speech. That speech, delivered from notes rather than from a written text, was said to be so bold, and so eloquent, that it left its hearers too spellbound to transcribe it. But Herndon suggests another reason why the text of that Bloomington speech went missing: that pressure from other Republicans, who were taken aback by the speech's radicalism and feared it would give the party an abolitionist cast that would cost the party politically, kept the speech out of print. Lincoln's close advisors (excepting Herndon himself) had the same misgivings about the "Lost Speech" that they had about the "House Divided" speech. Since Herndon's testimony is supported by Lincoln's own 1857 statement that he had used the metaphor "a year ago," the likelihood is that Lincoln did use the "House Divided" metaphor in 1856, although Don Fehrenbacher has pro-

vided convincing evidence that the 1856 speech, which so took its hearers aback, was not the May 29, 1856, "Lost Speech" but another speech, also given in Bloomington, on September 12, 1856, with his friend T. Lyle Dickey (Fehrenbacher [1960] 635). Perhaps Lincoln also advanced what I am calling the "general" slave power conspiracy theory then too. Certainly if he did use the "House Divided" metaphor in the "Lost Speech," the idea that slavery would destabilize any democratic republic that tolerated it would have had its attractions, particularly in the very week of the sack of Lawrence and the Pottawatomie massacre in Kansas, and the assault upon Massachusetts senator Charles Sumner in the Senate chamber by South Carolina congressman Preston Brooks. But it is not likely that in either 1856 speech Lincoln developed in full detail the "special" slave power conspiracy theory, the one directed against Douglas, because a key element of that theory, the *Dred Scott* case, was not yet available.

When Lincoln previewed the 1858 speech to a gathering of friends, they were (with the exception of Herndon himself, who said that the speech would make Lincoln president) universally critical, describing it as a "d—d fool utterance," "unwise and impolitic, if not false," and one that might "drive away a good many voters fresh from the Democrats' ranks." Lincoln brushed aside their criticisms, arguing, "The time has come when these sentiments should be uttered; and if it is decreed that I should go down because of this speech, then let me go down linked to the truth—let me die in the advocacy of what is just and right." (Herndon and Weik [1930] 326, discussed by Briggs on 167. See also Wilson and Davis, *Herndon's Informants* [1998] 574–575.)

Briggs accounts for this hostility by noting that the speech treated the slavery question as incapable of solution by half-measures (although it went on to propose some), and that it contained a not very oblique prediction of civil war.

2. See Guelzo, *Lincoln and Douglas* (2008).

3. The 1856 use of the "House Divided" metaphor probably served a similar purpose, except that the trimmers at whom it was aimed were not the Bates Republicans but the Fillmore Whigs. This is the argument made by Fehrenbacher in his 1960 article on the origins and purpose of Lincoln's "House Divided" speech. Why Lincoln felt he had to draw this line against anti-Lecompton Democrats in 1858, even at the possible price of his own defeat, is the subject of section 4.4 below.

4. For my take on this speech, an essay originally written for this book, see Burt (1997).

5. These statistics and those in the next few paragraphs are from Nevins (1947b) 382.

6. That said, Lane early in the Civil War called for enlisting black troops, and the First Kansas Colored Troops, a regiment organized under his auspices, was the first black regiment to see combat.

7. See the excellent analysis of Atchison's motives in Freehling (2007).

8. For a detailed account of the kind of intimidation the self-defense associations practiced, see Etcheson (2004); Goodrich (1998); Morrison (1997), as well as more general accounts in Nichols (1962); Nevins (1947b); Potter (1976).

9. But in one of those strange turns common to Civil War–era politics, Lecompte not only remained Union-loyal during the war, but became a Republican (Malin 1953).

10. Despite the modest title, this was one of the most powerful appointments in the territory, with a great deal of patronage at its disposal. See Etcheson (2004) 152. The fact that Calhoun was Douglas's protégé naturally made people imagine that Calhoun was doing Douglas's work even when he was stabbing Douglas in the back.

11. This story is in Etcheson (2004) 50.

12. Whitfield would most likely have won the election anyway, but Atchison and his friends were taking no chances (Goodrich [1998] 29). The number of bogus votes is from Etcheson (2004) 54.

13. Goodrich (1998) 34–38.

14. Etcheson (2004) argues that the pro-slavery forces would most likely have won this election anyway.

15. Etcheson (2004) 63.

16. There is a nuance here to be noticed: the Topeka government claimed to be not a territorial government, but a state government. The pro-slavery government, by contrast, was a territorial government. This distinction does make a difference. When in 1858 Robinson was arrested on a charge of usurping the government, he defended himself by arguing that he had not usurped the territorial government because the Topeka government was not a territorial government but a state government in waiting. This did not impress the pro-slavery judge, Judge Cato, but it did win him acquittal from the jury.

17. *Congressional Globe*, 34th Cong., 1st sess., appendix, 844. Cited in Morrison (1997) 163.

18. Douglas made an interesting case, however, concerning the swarm of voters from Missouri who voted in the elections for the first territorial legislature. Many who intended to settle in Kansas in 1854 were either turned back by Indian agents, since they sought to settle on tribal land where the Indian titles had not yet been extinguished, or, staking their claims too late to build proper shelters for the winter, spent the winter in Missouri, and thus missed Reeder's census, which was taken in midwinter. Douglas understood that there had been plenty of fraud in the 1855 election, but at least some of the charges of fraud were false (see Johannsen [1973] 497).

19. For an analysis of Douglas's report, see Johannsen (1973) 492.

20. For a discussion of this see ibid. 496. This sorts oddly with his endorsement of exactly the same principle in Illinois, which he mentioned, apropos of Kansas, a few weeks later: "Our people are a white people; our State is a white State; and we mean to preserve the race pure, without any mixture with the negro" (ibid. 501).

21. See Douglas's letter on this subject to Cooper Kinderdine Watson, April 19, 1856, in Douglas (1961).

22. Johannsen (1973) 502.

23. Ibid.

24. See Douglas's letter of July 4, 1856, to J. E. Roy, a Chicago clergyman, in Douglas (1961) for his response to this charge. Sumner himself made this charge against Douglas as well. Douglas actually was not in the room when the beating occurred. He started to rush into the chamber to break up the fight, then reflected that everyone would think that he had come to join in, and did nothing until it was over.

25. For this detail see Malin (1953). On March 24, the *New York Tribune* said the following of this nonexistent utterance: "When the arch-traitor from Illinois recently vomited his rage upon the Senate in his declaration, "We intend to subdue you," he only reechoed the warwhoop which, from the beginning of things, the principle of Evil in the world has forever shouted its warfare upon the Good."

26. Etcheson (2004) 127.

27. For an account of how and when Douglas changed his mind about who had the majority in Kansas, see Johannsen (1973) 560–564.

28. Reeder had a subsequent career as a Republican. For instance, he attended the 1856 convention in Bloomington that founded the Republican Party in Illinois. See Burlingame (2008a) 418. Reeder also played a role in the 1860 Republican National Convention.

29. It was unusual for territorial legislatures to be able to override the veto of the governor, because territorial governors were appointed by the federal government and were charged with superintending the territory's maturation into statehood. A territorial governor is more like a proconsul than like a state governor. The Kansas territorial legislature was given this power at Douglas's insistence, on popular sovereignty grounds. Douglas here was hoist on his own petard.

30. The letter is cited in Etcheson (2004) 144.

31. Johannsen's ([1973] 565) point here is that Douglas's suspicions about the Lecompton Convention were long-standing, and that his ultimate opposition to the Lecompton Constitution was not an opportunist improvisation, but the reflection of settled convictions and careful observation.

32. Ibid. See also Stampp (1990) for a detailed treatment of Walker's negotiations over this issue with Buchanan, and of the rather explicit promises to Walker that Buchanan broke when his masters demanded it.

33. Smith (1975) 34.

34. Buchanan knew this about Walker when he appointed him. Walker had made his views clear in a pamphlet called "An Appeal for the Union" in the fall of 1856. For a discussion of this see Kenneth Stampp, *America in 1857* (1990) 159. Stampp also argues that even many southerners saw Kansas the way Walker did, before the loyalty-politics competition between Democratic and Native American newspapers in 1857 about which party was more true to the South made such views politically untenable.

35. See Walker's letter to Buchanan of June 28, 1857, cited in Fehrenbacher (1978) 458. Although we are in the habit of using the term "Missourians" as a shorthand expression for supporters of slavery in Kansas, many Missourians who settled in Kansas were free state Democrats.

36. Smith (1975) 36.

37. Fehrenbacher (1978) 460.

38. Ibid. 466.

39. For this story, see Stampp (1990) 261.

40. Smith (1975) 38.

41. The Topeka Constitution had also had some strange provisions concerning amendment. It could not be amended at all until 1865, and could be amended only once during the five years after that (Johannsen [1973] 474). Furthermore, the foreign-born could not vote in Kansas at all. This is perhaps about as far as the anti-slavery/nativist alliance ever went.

42. These were not the only strange features of the Lecompton Constitution, which also prohibited the state from having more than one bank, and more than two branches of that bank. See Smith (1975) 39.

43. Calhoun played a double game with Douglas throughout this period. Because Douglas had secured his appointment, he thought of Calhoun as his agent, and as his eyes, in the territory. Douglas had hoped, through Calhoun, to create a Democratic coalition in Kansas that would include both free state and pro-slavery factions, and Calhoun did unsuccessfully exert himself in 1855 to this end. Calhoun's failure caused many free state Democrats—a large faction in Kansas—to organize with the Republicans (see Johannsen [1973] 562–566). Calhoun did in fact, unsuccessfully, lobby the Lecompton Convention for true submission of the constitution to a ratification election. But his own ambitions and ties in the territory complicated whatever allegiance he had to Douglas. In fairness to both Calhoun and Martin, the not-quite-ratification strategy was a desperate improvisation, the best thing they could talk the convention majority into, not the result of a plan on their part, and certainly not anything either Douglas or Buchanan had put them up to, although enemies of both Douglas and Buchanan insisted the contrary at the time.

44. Smith (1975) 39.

45. Etcheson (2004) 164. So by the spring of 1858, the free staters controlled the Lecompton territorial legislature, the Lecompton state legislature in waiting (now meeting at Lawrence), and the Topeka state legislature in waiting. But the Buchanan administration continued to seek some way, any way, to put the region into pro-slavery hands.

46. For an analysis of this statement, see Baker (2004) 103. Baker notes, for instance, that the white population of the slave states in 1858 was closer to 20 percent than to 50 percent of the white population of the Union as a whole.

47. This conversation is in Johannsen (1973) 586–587. In Buchanan's defense, his biographer Philip Shriver Klein has argued that his position arose from a hidebound proceduralism that paid attention only to the formal legitimacy of the territorial government's call for the convention, the elections of the convention delegates, and the December 21 "ratification" election. Smith (1975) has advanced the idea that ratification might not have seemed to Buchanan to be quite the issue it seems to us, noting that thirty-three of the sixty-three antebellum state constitutions (including that of Illinois) were never subject to popular ratification, although by 1858 only nine states, eight of them southern, lived under unratified constitutions (41). More recently, Baker (2004) argued that Buchanan was the stubborn and willing prisoner of the prejudices instilled in him by decades of socializing principally with southerners. She compares his vigorous use of federal troops against the Mormons in Utah and against remote Paraguay with his passivity in the face of secession. Buchanan was not a passive, ineffectual president in Baker's view, but a stubborn pro-southern ideologue, who relied upon advisors who later joined the Confederacy (advisors who also connived with the seceded states while still in federal office), and in general came as close to treason as it is possible for a chief executive to do.

48. Etcheson (2004) 175.

49. The Wyandotte Constitution, under which Kansas was admitted to the Union, while racially a step down from the Leavenworth Constitution, allowed

black men and white women the right to vote in school elections. Both white women and black men, pitted against each other by a shrewd Democratic operation, wound up losing a fight for a more general franchise in a bitter campaign—with plenty of bitterness between the supporters of both groups—in 1867. This campaign marked a definitive, decades-long parting of the ways between the movements for black suffrage and for women's suffrage, and the wounded and wounding remarks of the great suffragists at that time still pack a sting. For an account of this election, see Eric Foner, *Reconstruction* (1988).

50. Cited in Wells (1990) 35.

51. See Etcheson (2004) 181 for a description of how English undermined Douglas's position.

52. Ibid. 184.

53. Quoted in Simon (2006) 114.

54. Ibid.

55. On the issue of whether the Court delayed the judgment in order to influence the 1856 presidential election, see Fehrenbacher (1978) 290.

56. Fisher (1866) 258.

57. For this last detail, see ibid. The sally about the Hartford Convention may have been part of a cultural attack of a kind Douglas himself engaged in to the effect that anti-slavery convictions were merely a kind of resurgence of old-fashioned blue light Hartford Convention federalism. Buchanan was probably playing to a hostile political stereotype of New Englanders, roughly in the way contemporary right-wing talk radio plays to hostile political stereotypes about opponents of the Vietnam War. For further remarks on this, see section 5.1 below.

58. The reader will notice that Buchanan, in being able to evade responsibility for the Kansas-Nebraska Act while at the same time asserting its authority, successfully pulled off the trick that poor Winfield Scott in 1852 was unable to manage about the Compromise of 1850.

59. The locus classicus of this interpretation of the idea that "the Constitution follows the flag," is Calhoun's speech of June 27, 1848, about the organization of Oregon Territory. Calhoun noted that Mexican law prohibited slavery but permitted a kind of peonage that was not much different from slavery. He argued that the law of Mexico became extinct in the Mexican Cession as soon as the Treaty of Guadalupe Hidalgo was ratified. Calhoun conceded that the law of nations allows that the Mexican municipal laws of that territory remain in force until changed "not as a matter of right, but merely of sufferance, and as between the inhabitants of territory, in order to avoid a state of anarchy, before they can be brought under our laws." By this he meant that property owners in the cession continued to own their property, and their American conquerors could not simply expropriate them. But that sufferance did not extend so far as to "exclude emigrants from the United States, because their property or religion are such as are prohibited from being introduced by the laws of Mexico," because that would "give a higher authority to the extinct power of Mexico over the territory than to our actual authority over it." Besides, Calhoun went on to point out, Mexican law also prohibited the Protestant religion, and if the Mexican law prohibiting slavery remained in force, then so did the Mexican law prohibiting Protestantism. (See Lence's edition of this speech [1992] 558–559.)

60. The evidence for the idea that word of the dissents in preparation by Justices Curtis and McLean provoked the majority into abandoning a limited case using the *Strader* decision in favor of a more sweeping decision comes from recollections of Justices Catron and Grier. But no evidence from McLean or Curtis corroborates this, and Catron and Grier could have simply been following the typical Democratic strategy of blaming everything on meddling anti-slavery types ("Look what you made me do!").

61. See the account of this turn of events in Bordewich (2012) 293–299.

62. See Gienapp (1987) for details.

63. Quoted in Fehrenbacher (1978) 477.

64. Perhaps the main reason Lincoln continued to dwell upon the speech against the *Washington Union* is that he wished to make it impossible for Douglas to mend fences with Buchanan's faction once the Senate election was over. Douglas did have in mind some ultimate rapprochement with Buchanan's followers, if not with Buchanan himself, and this led him, somewhat implausibly, to treat his attack upon the administration's organ as only an attack upon the actual editor of the *Union*, one Cornelius Wendell.

65. This defense of the Court has recently been offered by Mark Graber in *Dred Scott and the Problem of Constitutional Evil* (2006) and by William Freehling in the second volume of *The Road to Disunion* (2007).

66. See for instance Wiecek (1978) and Maltz (1992).

67. Allan Nevins and Milton Halsey Thomas, eds., *The Diary of George Templeton Strong*, 4 vols. (New York: Farrar, Straus, and Giroux, 1974) 3:57, cited in Finkelman (1981) 315.

68. Wiecek (1978) 57.

69. *Congressional Globe*, 35th Cong., 1st sess., 27, pt. 1: 547. See Zarefsky (1994) 26.

70. Lyman Trumbull, speech in Chicago, August 7, 1858, National Era (Washington), September 2, 1858. See the discussion of this speech in Burlingame (2008a) 464.

71. Finkelman (1981) sees a threat in these lines, at the very least, a threat against New York's law concerning transit with slaves. He does not quite see in these lines the threat to nationalize slavery along the lines Lincoln laid out in his arguments concerning a "second *Dred Scott* decision." But he does later sketch out just how such a threat would materialize. Those are, however, two different threats, and Nelson is, at the worst, only making the first of them in this passage.

72. That said, there is some evidence from an earlier case, which Grier heard twice, in 1850 and in 1852, *Oliver v. Kauffman et al.*, which pulls in an opposite direction. Mrs. Cecilia Oliver's slaves, en route from Arkansas to Maryland, passed through Pennsylvania after it repealed its law allowing masters six months' sojourning with their slaves. The slaves some months later fled back to Maryland, where they were aided by Daniel Kauffman and others. Kauffman was very ably defended by Thaddeus Stevens, who argued, among other things, that the slaves in question had been freed by their transit through Pennsylvania, and thus were not fugitive slaves when they reentered Pennsylvania later. Grier decided, on the basis of the recently decided *Strader* case (see section 7.1 below), that whether the slaves were free or not was for Maryland to decide, inasmuch as they had come to Pennsylvania from Maryland. Finkelman (1981) sums up Grier's charge this way:

> Grier's charge was a new and striking development in the federal adjudi-
> cation of comity cases. In Pennsylvania the law specifically declared that
> slaves brought into the state became free the moment they came under Penn-
> sylvania jurisdiction. No court action or other procedure was required to
> free a slave. Yet Grier declared that this law would not be recognized by a
> federal court sitting in a free state. The implications of this decision were
> frightening. Slaves could be brought into Pennsylvania by a master and, if
> they refused to leave, the master could simply seize them and bring them
> back to the slave state. If they later escaped into Pennsylvania, where they
> were legally entitled to freedom, the federal courts would not protect them.
> Rather, the federal courts would protect the master's right to seize them.
> The court would not "go behind the status of these people where they es-
> caped" even if they had a legitimate claim to freedom when they escaped.
> (254–255)

Grier's decision is a bad one, and an ugly one. But I am not sure it is evidence of a
conspiracy against the original emancipation of slaves in Pennsylvania. For one
thing, it is not clear that Grier's charge really does allow a slave to be brought to
Pennsylvania by a master and, were they to refuse to leave, to be seized and carried away by him. For another thing, Grier's mind seems here to be focused on
whether slavery "reattaches" to slaves upon their return to Maryland, not on
whether Pennsylvania can free slaves within its borders. (For a discussion of "reattachment" see section 7.1 below.)

   Allowing a slave to be brought to Pennsylvania by a master and, were he to refuse to leave, allowing him to be seized and carried away by the master really
were an issue raised by a later case, the famous *Passmore Williams* case (*United
States ex rel. Wheeler v. Williamson*, 28 F. Cas. [1855]), in which the federal judge,
one John K. Kane, invented a federal right to transit with slaves out of whole
cloth, and trumped up a long imprisonment for Williamson on contempt charges
as well. Charles Sumner felt that Kane's decision was a step (and *Lemmon* another)
toward the reintroduction of full-scale slavery in the free states. We will never
really know, since Passmore's case, like *Lemmon*, offered many opportunities for
dodging the bullet. A federal right to transit with slaves would have been ugly
enough, with a host of legal ramifications and consequences—what happens if a
slave escapes in transit?—but it still would not have amounted to the repeal of
emancipation in the free states.

   73. Wayne and Catron were punished for their loyalty to the Union. Wayne's
property in Georgia was confiscated. Catron was expropriated too, and expelled
from Nashville, proclaiming on his departure, "I have to punish treason, and I
will" (see Freehling [2007] 111). Freehling notes that all of the Court's southern
judges conceded the power of states to abolish slavery, which itself makes the
Lemmon scenario unlikely. Wayne in an 1854 address to the American Colonization Society had praised gradual emancipation, and argued that interference from
northern critics had made that task more difficult. Freehling sees at least Catron
and Wayne not as agents of the slave power conspiracy but as wishful-thinking
appeasers of the slave power who hoped that, if northern pressure were removed,
the South would behave itself.

   74. Fehrenbacher (1978) 395.

75. Actually, it is a little more complicated than that, since the Court actually simply refused jurisdiction over the case, and the actual slaves in the case, having escaped to Canada, were not vulnerable to "reattachment" in any case. The decision did not precisely elide the distinction between domicile and sojourning; it merely said that if a state chose to do so in a case of someone actually at the moment residing in that state, the Supreme Court would not stand in the way.

76. I am not alone in having seen this as a possible unintended consequence for the South of pressing the *Lemmon* case. In his separate concurrence in the New York Court of Appeals upholding the liberation of the Lemmon slaves, Justice William B. Wright noted that if it is "conceded that, by the exercise of any powers granted in the Constitution to the Federal Government, it may rightly interfere in the regulation of the social and civil condition of any description of persons within the territorial limits of the respective States of the Union, it is not difficult to foresee the ultimate result" (cited in Finkelman [1981] 308). Paul Finkelman sees Wright's threat the same way I do.

77. For what Lincoln meant by the "public mind," see also Zarefsky (1994).

4. Douglas's Conspiracy Charge

1. Lincoln described his avoidance of the 1854 Springfield convention during the Ottawa debate (1:509).

2. That said, Douglas's picture of Lincoln here is the one that haunted the southern mind in 1860, and twentieth-century conservatives like Willmoore Kendall have persisted in seeing Lincoln as a kind of Cromwell who united the fanatic and the tyrant. For a discussion (and principled rejection) of Kendall's view of Lincoln, see Allen C. Guelzo, "Apple of Gold in a Picture of Silver: The Constitution and Liberty" in Gabor Boritt, *The Lincoln Enigma* (2001). See also Thomas Krannawitter, *Vindicating Lincoln* (2008); Thomas Schneider, *Lincoln's Defense of Politics* (2006).

3. For accounts of Lincoln's transformation from Whig to Republican, see, among others, Allan Nevins, *The Emergence of Lincoln* (1950a, 1950b); Don E. Fehrenbacher, *Prelude to Greatness* (1962); Roy P. Basler, *A Touchstone for Greatness* (1973); David R. Potter, *The Impending Crisis* (1976); David Herbert Donald, *Lincoln* (1995); William Lee Miller, *Lincoln's Virtues* (2002); Michael Lind, *What Lincoln Believed* (2004).

4. Donald (1995) 191. Gienapp notes that Lincoln had actually attended the February 22 Republican state convention in Decatur, which adopted a conservative platform very different from the Springfield platform Douglas makes such play with. But Gienapp does not think of this convention, which was sparsely attended, as representing the beginning of the Republican Party as a state organization. See Gienapp (1987) 289.

5. For a detailed discussion of the political geography of 1850s Illinois, see Heckman (1967); Sigelschiffer (1973). For a detailed treatment of how the candidates approached the political geography of Illinois, see Allen C. Guelzo, "Houses Divided: Lincoln, Douglas, and the Political Landscape of 1858" (2007).

6. For an account of the fusion politics that put Chase and Sumner into the Senate, see Sewell (1976). For my own take on these elections, see section 4.6 below.

7. Douglas makes this argument in detail during the Jonesboro debate (1:589–591).

8. Senators were elected by state legislatures in the nineteenth century. Good accounts of this election can be found in Fehrenbacher (1962) and in the standard biographies. Donald is particularly illuminating about this, because he makes clear that Trumbull really did double-cross Lincoln and that Lincoln understood that he had done so (Donald [1995] 184).

9. Joseph Gillespie told Lincoln's law partner William Herndon, when the latter was collecting material for his Lincoln biography, that the five anti-Nebraska Democrats who supported Trumbull felt that "having been elected as Democrats they could not vote for any one but a Democrat for US Senator. . . . They stated that they had no objection to Mr Lincoln except his political antecedents but that they could not sust[ain t]hemselves at home if they were to vote for him but expressed regret that they were so circumstanced" (Joseph Gillespie to William H. Herndon, September 19, 1866, in Wilson and Davis, *Herndon's Informants* [1998] 344).

10. Matteson, notes Gienapp ([1987] 175), had opposed the repeal of the Missouri Compromise, which gave him some credibility as an anti-Nebraska candidate, although he remained a regular Democrat. Guelzo ([2008] 38) points out that although Matteson had taken no public stand about the Kansas-Nebraska Act, he had privately told the anti-Nebraska Democrats that he shared their views. Douglas himself felt that opposition to Shields, a native of Ireland, had more to do with nativism than with anti-slavery. Shields's defeat was not the product of a Know Nothing conspiracy, but nativism did have something to do with it, and indeed nativism and anti-slavery were deeply intertwined with each other in the 1850s. For more on this, see sections 4.2 and 4.3 below.

11. Indeed, Michael Burlingame renders the explanation of John M. Palmer, an anti-slavery Democrat, who voted for Trumbull despite being Lincoln's personal friend, that he had already "alienated his party by opposing the Kansas-Nebraska Act and could not vote for any candidate but a Democrat for the Senate." See Michael A. Burlingame, *The Inner World of Abraham Lincoln* (1994) 244.

12. See Lincoln's letter lobbying Trumbull on this subject of June 7, 1856 (1:366). Part of the thrust of the letter is that McLean would be more acceptable to Illinois Whigs than more radical figures. But Lincoln also was taking the occasion to remind Trumbull that the Whigs, who are most of the anti-Nebraska voters in the state anyway, were owed a chit, and would not look kindly upon the nomination for the presidency of former Democrats like Nathaniel Banks of Massachusetts.

13. Harris (2007) 91.

14. Fehrenbacher (1987) has a detailed account of this.

15. Heckman (1967) 55.

16. When Richard Hofstadter first described what he called "the paranoid style," he thought of it as a kind of deviant politics, closer to collective mental illness than to politics, expressive of an embattled cultural and political Right's sense of its waning prestige (Hofstadter 1965). Conspiracy thinking is indeed an episodic disease of American politics, and some of it is very ugly, and it has not always been confined to bad causes. (See, for instance, David Brion Davis's *The Slave Power Conspiracy and the Paranoid Style* [1969].) But it has also been one of the

ways nondiseased peoples have attempted to make sense of political events that happen at a larger-than-human scale. My sense of what conspiratorial thinking is derives from the analysis of that style in Bernard Bailyn's *The Ideological Origins of the American Revolution* (1967).

17. My use of the term "country party" (as opposed to "court party") derives of course from Bailyn, and from Lance Banning, *The Jeffersonian Persuasion* (1978). See also Marvin Meyers, *The Jacksonian Persuasion* (1957), and, in my view the most illuminating book on the whole structure of nineteenth-century politics, David Greenstone's *The Lincoln Persuasion* (1993). On the emergence not only of the second party system but also on the ideas that parties are legitimate instruments of ordinary politics rather than illegitimate conspiracies aimed at subverting politics, see Richard Hofstadter, *The Idea of a Party System* (1969). On the rise and fall of the second party system, see Michael Holt, *The Rise and Fall of the American Whig Party* (1999); Holt, *Political Parties and American Political Development from the Age of Jackson to the Age of Lincoln* (1992); Holt, *Forging a Majority* (1969). For an especially illuminating treatment of what Whigs typically believed, see Daniel Walker Howe, *The Political Culture of the American Whigs* (1979), as well as his related *The Unitarian Conscience* (1988). See also William Nisbet Chambers and Walter Dean Burnham, eds., *The American Party Systems* (1967); Ronald Formisano, *The Birth of Mass Political Parties* (1971); Paul Kleppner, *The Third Electoral System, 1853–1892* (1979); Joel Silbey, *The American Political Nation, 1838–1893* (1991); Stephen E. Maizlish and John J. Kushma, eds., *Essays on American Antebellum Politics, 1840–1860* (1982); Richard J. Ellis, *American Political Cultures* (1993). The point here is that the Whig Party is not the ideological successor of the Federalist Party, although many but not all former Federalists became Whigs. That said, many Democrats as late as the 1840s acted as though they believed the Whig Party was attempting to revive the Federalist Party.

18. David Wilmot himself, who favored the Mexican War but wished to keep slavery out of the Mexican Cession, who opposed the extension of slavery but was no particular friend of the interests of black people, is a fairly typical example of those Democrats who supported the Free Soil movement in 1848. Wilmot wished, he said, to "preserve to free white labor a fair country, a rich country, where the sons of toil, of my own race and color, can live without the disgrace which association with negro slavery brings upon free labor." (*Congressional Globe*, 29th Cong., 2nd sess., appendix, 314–318, cited in Graber [2006] 81. See also the extensive treatment of Wilmot in Nevins [1947a].) The Free Soil Party was largely an insurgent movement of Wilmot Proviso Democrats who resented the treatment of Van Buren by his party, although the party also drew upon "Conscience Whigs" such as Charles Francis Adams, whom it nominated for the vice presidency in 1848. There is of course a large overlap between those Democrats who left the party for the Free Soil Party in 1848 (returning in 1852) and those who later left the party over the Kansas-Nebraska Act after 1854. Nevins (1947a) has a very good portrait of Wilmot and racist Free Soilers like him, as does Potter (1976). For more detail, see John Mayfield, *Rehearsal for Republicanism* (1980); Chaplain W. Morrison, *Democratic Politics and Sectionalism: The Wilmot Proviso Controversy* (1967). See also Jean H. Baker, *Affairs of Party* (1983). For a reading of the kind of working class Democrat who was attracted to Free Soil, see Sean Wilentz, *Chants Democratic* (1984). Wilentz also provides an insightful, if to my mind

a little too sympathetic, account of the inner struggles of the Democratic Party in *The Rise of American Democracy* (2005).

19. For a discussion of the factional structure of the early Republican Party, see Eric Foner, *Free Soil, Free Labor, Free Men* (1977). See also Foner's *Politics and Ideology in the Age of the Civil War* (1980) and Richard Sewell, *Ballots for Freedom* (1976). For other strains of anti-slavery politics, see Lewis Perry, *Radical Abolitionism* (1973); John Mayfield, *Rehearsal for Republicanism* (1980); Louis S. Gerteis, *Morality and Utility in American Antislavery Reform* (1987); Louis Filler, *Crusade against Slavery* (1986).

20. Nativism had played a role in Federalist Party organizing as well, and shaped its 1798 Alien Act. But the Alien and Sedition Acts so discredited the party that Federalist Party nativism acquired a bad name. Federalist nativism was directed against the French, anyway. And when one speaks of "nativism" in the antebellum era, one usually means hostility to immigrants from Ireland. Nativism was really a movement about religion, not about immigration; Protestant Germans arriving after the failure of the 1848 revolution faced a different atmosphere from Catholic Germans, or, what is more, from Catholic Irish arriving during the same period, after the Potato Famine.

21. Johannsen (1973) 83.

22. The Bedini incident is described in detail by Nevins (1947b) and by Anbinder (1992) in the context of the development of nativism, and by Ahlstrom (1972) as an event in American religious history.

23. Douglas's authorship of the Kansas-Nebraska Act would seem to be the greatest blunder of the blundering generation, but historians of that school almost always idealized Douglas at the expense of the fire-eaters and, most of all, of the abolitionists.

24. To some extent the Randall school may have been driven to their views by the hardening of racial attitudes after the end of Reconstruction. They were imprisoned by the same blindness about race that motivated the Dunning school of historians of Reconstruction, rightly taken to task by Kenneth Stampp in *The Era of Reconstruction, 1865–1877* (1965). The ways in which the Confederacy, having lost the war, won the historiography of the war have been amply documented by David Blight in *Race and Reunion* (2001). But the Randall school's sense of the catastrophic effects of blunders made by limited politicians jockeying for advantage may have also owed something to their historical experience of the Sarajevo crisis of 1914.

25. Gienapp (1987) 73, citing Robert Winthrop, "The Fusion Parties in Massachusetts: A Letter to the Chairman of the Whig Executive Committee, October 15, 1855," in *Addresses and Speeches on Various Occasions*, 4 vols. (Boston, 1852–1886) 2:233–234.

26. Gienapp (1987) 38.

27. The "New Political History," which sees parties as creatures of an ethnocultural structure as much as of a political agenda, while perhaps overstating its case, nevertheless persuasively showed how ethnocultural issues entangle political ones. Whig hostility to slavery is closely tied to Whig hostility to Catholicism, and nativism, temperance, and anti-slavery run together (Howe [1979]). When Douglas whips up hostility to anti-slavery, he will link it to temperance and to nativism, and also to a religious perfectionism he has distaste for as a kind

of moral interference in everyone else's business. For ethnocultural politics see Michael Holt, *The Political Crisis of the 1850s* (1978); William Gienapp, *The Origins of the Republican Party 1852–1856* (1987); Taylor Anbinder, *Nativism and Slavery* (1992), as well as the books cited above by Formisano (1971); Holt (1969, 1992, and 1999); Silbey (1991); Kleppner (1979).

28. The large-scale political histories—Nevins (1947a, 1947b, 1950a, 1950b), Potter (1976), and more modest books like Eric Walther's *The Shattering of the Union* (2004)—cover this, as do studies with more local scope, such as Roy F. Nichols's *The Disruption of the American Democracy* (1962), Fehrenbacher's *The South and Three Sectional Crises* (1980), Avery Craven's *The Growth of Southern Nationalism* (1953), and Robert Johannsen's *Steven A. Douglas* (1973), as well as Johanssen's *The Frontier, The Union, and Stephen A. Douglas* (1989) and his *Lincoln, the South, and Slavery* (1991). See also Bradley Bond, *Political Culture in the Nineteenth-Century South* (1995); David Grimsted, *American Mobbing, 1828–1861* (1998).

29. This observation derives from Daniel Walker Howe, *The Political Culture of the American Whigs* (1979) 30.

30. Anbinder (1992) 45, citing Anson Burlingame (1854).

31. Anbinder (1992) 89.

32. Ibid. 155.

33. Ibid. 167.

34. Here I follow Nevins (1950b) and Anbinder (1992). But the observation is a commonplace among historians of the nineteenth century.

35. Goodwin (2005) 221.

36. Here I follow Holt's account in *The Rise and Fall of the American Whig Party* (1999). In an odd move for the nominal leader of an anti-Catholic party, Fillmore had sent his daughter to a Catholic school and contributed money for building cathedrals (Anbinder [1992] 203–204).

37. About this, see Morris (2008) 89.

38. Guelzo (2008) 44. Guelzo points out that the Republicans in 1856 did a particularly poor job of wooing the former Whigs in the central counties of the state, where the 1858 election would be fought out. For just how badly Lincoln did in the "Whig Belt" of central Illinois in the 1858 election, see ibid. 282–284.

39. Harris (2007) 147. Harris also points out that the commonly accepted view that Lincoln's victory was owing to Democratic gerrymandering is probably false. The reapportionment bill, after all, was passed in 1852 before the Republican Party was created, and it did not prevent Trumbull from being elected in 1855. If Lincoln lost the election, it is because he did not run as well against Douglas as Trumbull had against Shields.

40. It seems here as though I am rejecting the argument of William C. Harris in his recent, persuasive *Lincoln's Rise to the Presidency* (2007) that Lincoln's key strategy in 1858 was to appeal to conservative voters, a category that might include both the McLean-Bates wings of the Republican Party and the former Fillmore voters. Lincoln did try to take relatively conservative positions. And, two years later, this strategy gave him an advantage in the contest against Seward and Chase for the Republican nomination. But there is a shade of difference between McLean-Bates voters and Fillmore voters. Lincoln lost the latter to Douglas in 1858, partly because of Douglas's successful enlisting of John Critten-

den's support and partly because his own conspiracy politics alienated them, but Lincoln took these voters from Douglas in 1860.

41. See Heckman (1967) 65.

42. See Fehrenbacher (1962) 113–114.

43. Ibid. 114.

44. Zarefsky (1990) 94.

45. Indeed, Lincoln had declined the Republican nomination for governor in 1856, which probably would have gone to him, because he felt that William Bissell, as a former Democrat, had a better chance at statewide office. See Burlingame (1994) 245.

46. Crittenden actually had told Lincoln he would keep his views private, but his letter leaked out on the eve of the election. Harris (2007) believes that the letter did not receive enough circulation to affect the course of the election. But he also concedes that Crittenden's support of Douglas was widely known (143).

47. In his presidential race, according to William Gienapp, "Lincoln won 40 percent or more of the Fillmore vote in Indiana and Ohio; over 50 percent in New York; over 60 percent in Iowa; better than 70 percent in Illinois; and over 80 percent in Pennsylvania." See William Gienapp, "Who Voted for Lincoln" (1986) 65. In 1856 the breakdown was far different:

> Although the Republicans won the state offices, Lincoln's attempt to win the reluctant Whigs to the Republican party on national issues must be adjudged a failure, for the central Illinois Whigs divided almost evenly in the election, the proportion varying almost directly in proportion to latitude. In Henderson, Warren, McLean, and Fulton counties, for example, a three to one majority of ex-Whigs supported Frémont. In Tazewell, Coles, Hancock, and Logan counties, a little farther south, the split was more nearly even, but in Sangamon, Jersey, Macon, and Madison, a majority of former Whigs stayed with the Fillmore ticket. The Fillmore electors carried Bond, Edwards, Madison, and Piatt counties and were second in 41 other central and southern Illinois counties, in each case having received more votes than the Republican electors. In the northern part of the state fusion was so substantially achieved that few old Whigs voted for Fillmore—in 13 counties of the northern part, 50 or fewer Fillmore votes were recorded. In southern Illinois, on the other hand, Frémont received fewer than 50 votes in each of 16 counties. (Wright, *Lincoln and the Politics of Slavery* [1970] 119)

48. Douglas (1894) 87–89.

49. The classic text on this subject is Eugene Berwanger's *The Frontier against Slavery* (1967). But Allan Nevins was also fully aware of the anti-slavery racism of the people who settled Kansas, and Oregon and California for that matter. For more on this subject, see Chaplain W. Morrison, *Democratic Politics and Sectionalism* (1967); James A. Rawley, *Bleeding Kansas and the Coming of the Civil War* (1969); Michael A. Morrison, *Slavery and the American West* (1997); Thomas Goodrich, *War to the Knife* (1998); Nicole Etcheson, *Bleeding Kansas* (2004). Black people did go to Kansas from early on anyway, and they organized the First Kansas Colored Volunteer Infantry (raised by Jim Lane, the free state leader, himself) in the summer of 1862, which was the first black regiment to serve in combat alongside white troops. For the experiences of black emigrants to Kansas after the war, see Nell

Irvin Painter, *Exodusters* (1977). For the failed attempt to secure suffrage for black people during the Reconstruction era, see Eric Foner, *Reconstruction* (1988).

50. Samuel Tilden, April 12, 1848, speech to Democratic members of the New York legislature (in Tilden, *The Writings and Speeches of Samuel Tilden* [1885] 2: 569), cited in Morrison (1967) 63.

51. Readers of Berwanger's book, noticing the racist strain among Free Soilers, are in the habit of dismissing Free Soilers as *merely* racist, which is a mistake. Richard Sewell (1976) notes that, however qualified by racism, the hostility of Free Soil leaders to slavery itself was genuine, and that they were not merely motivated by negrophobia (171). Free Soilers in Massachusetts, aided by Know Nothings, even opposed racially segregated schools (184).

52. Lincoln's silence about the "Black Laws" of Illinois distinguishes him from Seward and Chase, both of whom spoke out against the Black Laws of their home states. But Seward and Chase both had more political running room to do this than Lincoln had, since Lincoln was running for office in what was arguably the most racist of the free states.

53. This is a commonplace of most treatments of Lincoln's campaign for the 1860 Republican nomination, treated in detail by Nevins and by Potter, as well as by all of Lincoln's biographers. For recent instances, for example, see Oates (1977); Donald (1995); Carwardine (2006). For the specifically German angle, see Gienapp (1986) 71. The religious crosscurrents of the antebellum era are a little more complicated than my sketch of them here. As Holt (1992) points out, some German Lutherans may have remained Democrats because they were taken aback by the anti-clericalism of prominent "1848ers" like Carl Schurz. And evangelical Protestants from Ireland and Wales may also have felt nativism to be directed against them as much as against the Catholic Irish.

54. Letter to Abraham Jonas, July 21, 1860 (2:172).

55. See the commentary on this in Miller, *Lincoln's Virtues* (2002); and in Neely, *The Last Best Hope of Earth* (1995). See also Neely, *The Fate of Liberty* (1991).

56. Heckman (1967) 135.

57. Ibid. 65.

58. Fehrenbacher (1962) 13–14.

59. This incident is from Harris (2007) 144.

60. For an analysis of the Liberal Republicans, see Foner (1988).

61. Allen Guelzo works a variation on this theme in his treatment of early Republican Party ideology in *Abraham Lincoln, Redeemer President* (1999).

62. My account of this movement follows Sydney Ahlstrom's in *A Religious History of the American People* (1972).

63. For more on this, see Daniel Walker Howe, *What Hath God Wrought* (2007).

64. For my own views, see section 9.2 below.

65. See on both of these points Doris Kearns Goodwin, *Team of Rivals* (2005).

66. Here I follow Howe's characterization of Whig economic thinking, particularly his reading of the influence of the economic ideas of Matthew C. Carey. See Howe (1979).

67. For the postwar transformation of thinking, see Louis Menand, *The Metaphysical Club* (2001). See also Robert Penn Warren, *Homage to Theodore Dreiser* (1971).

68. Foner develops this theme in detail in *Free Soil, Free Labor, Free Men* (1977).

69. See William S. McFeely, *Frederick Douglass* (1991).

70. Here I side with Foner's reading of Lincoln's economic thinking in *Free Soil, Free Labor, Free Men* (1977), and of Republican thinking generally in his *Politics and Ideology in the Age of the Civil War* (1980), *Nothing but Freedom* (1983) and *Reconstruction* (1988), against what seem to me to be more idealized readings of Lincoln's economic thinking in Allen C. Guelzo's *Abraham Lincoln* (1999). For a particularly telling critique of Lincoln's economic thinking, especially concerning the amateurishness of his thinking about the tariff, see Michael Lind, *What Lincoln Believed* (2004). For a critique of the extent to which such economic thinking was central to Lincoln's thought, see Stewart Winger, *Lincoln, Religion, and Romantic Cultural Politics* (2003).

71. Winger (2003) 10.

72. Lincoln's attacks upon slavery are for this reason immune to the evidence presented by Robert William Fogel and Stanley L. Engerman in *Time on the Cross* (1974) to the effect that slavery in the 1850s was still a profitable, economically robust institution.

73. There might be something to that aspect of the propaganda, after all: Fogel and Engerman (1974) argue that southern slaves in the 1850s had higher-calorie diets and longer life expectancies than northern industrial workers. Fogel and Engerman's conclusions have been contested, however.

74. For interesting treatments of Fitzhugh and other apologists for slavery, see Drew Faust, *The Ideology of Slavery* (1981); Faust, *The Creation of Confederate Nationalism* (1988). For other views of the ideology of slavery, see Eugene Genovese's classic, *Roll, Jordan, Roll* (1972); Genovese, *The Political Economy of Slavery* (1967). See also Genovese's *The World the Slaveholders Made* (1969). For his more recent thought on this subject, see *The Southern Front* (1994). For an interesting, if controversial, take on some of these same texts, see David F. Ericson, *The Debate over Slavery* (2000). Faust's biography of Hammond, *James Henry Hammond and the Old South* (1982), casts an interesting light on the development of his convictions, as does Carole Bleser's edition of Hammond's Diary, *Secret and Sacred* (1989). See also William J. Cooper, *The South and the Politics of Slavery, 1828–1856* (1978); Cooper, *Liberty and Slavery* (1983).

75. This was true, according to Fogel and Engerman, of the master class as well: although most slaves lived on larger plantations with masters who did not toil in the fields, most masters owned fewer than four slaves, and worked alongside them.

76. See Louis Hartz, *The Liberal Tradition in America* (1955) 111. Hartz is all too frequently under-read, particularly by those who wish to posit a "Republican" tradition in American politics that contests a "Liberal" one, as if he merely saw a kind of uniformity and staleness in American political thinking. Hartz had a keen sense of how some kinds of political arguments succeed or fail—how, for instance, the American Federalists had to fail because they could not, like the French Liberals, use the fear of a restored ancien régime to keep their more radical Republican opponents at bay. And he had a keen sense of how each political generation reacts upon and against the political arguments of the preceding one. The terms "Liberal" and "Republican" in the historiography of American historians of the 1990s

cannot be mapped onto the use of similar terms by historians of France. For a searching, and devastating, analysis of this, see Mark Hulliung, *Citizens and Citoyens* (2002).

77. See in this connection Hartz (1955) 205.

78. This is a theme in Howe (1979); Holt (1999); and in Robert Remini's fascinating biography of Henry Clay, *Henry Clay* (1991). See also Merrill D. Peterson, *The Great Triumvirate* (1987).

79. See Sewell (1976) 345.

80. The number is from Douglas's speech at Bloomington, July 16, 1858 (Douglas [1984] 58–59).

81. Kansas was finally admitted under the Wyandotte Constitution in 1861, after the southern representatives had departed. The Wyandotte Constitution, unlike the earlier anti-slavery constitution written in Topeka during the Bleeding Kansas crisis, did not prohibit the entry of black people into the state. About this, see Sewell (1976) 331.

82. *Congressional Globe*, 3rd Cong., 1st sess., appendix, 371. Cited in Jaffa (1959) 57–58.

83. Lincoln noted this at Freeport (1:543).

84. The details about the Springfield meeting, except of course Lincoln's nonattendance, are from Douglas's rejoinder at Ottawa (1:528–529).

85. Lincoln argued at Freeport that the Republican Party was not a statewide organization until the Bloomington convention of May 1856 (1:538).

86. Cited in Garry Wills, *Lincoln at Gettysburg* (1992) 91.

87. Douglas pointed this out at Freeport (1:567).

88. See for instance Douglas's interrogation of Thomas Turner at Freeport (1:564).

89. These were Robert Rantoul's arguments in the Sims case in Massachusetts. For an analysis of these arguments see Cover (1975) 177.

90. For a discussion of this case see ibid. 185. For more detail see http://www .heritagepursuit.com/Clark/Clark(1).htm.

91. About this, see Fehrenbacher (2001) 238–239:

> State and federal authority came into conflict most abrasively in certain episodes of enforcement like the Margaret Garner case. There, a state probate judge fined the United States marshal and ordered him to jail for contempt of court because he had not responded to a writ of habeas corpus issued on behalf of the fugitives. The marshal was then freed with a writ of habeas corpus by the area's federal district judge, who in doing so rejected the state judge's argument that the Fugitive Slave Act was unconstitutional.

92. For accounts of the *Ableman* case, see Cover (1975) 186; Potter (1976) 294–295; Filler (1986) 279; Burt (1992) 201; Fehrenbacher (2001) 239–244.

93. See Burt (1992) 287.

94. For an account of Lincoln's argument with Chase over this issue, see Harris (2007) 163.

95. There is extensive discussion of the Blair plan in Eric Foner's *Reconstruction* (1988). For Grant's negotiations with the Dominican Republic, see William S. McFeely, *Grant* (1981).

96. Douglas (1894) 65.

97. Ibid. 61–63.

98. Buchanan had replaced all of the postmasters loyal to Douglas, including the one in Galesburg itself, at the beginning of the campaign. For specific details about the postmasters, see Guelzo (2008) 66.

99. Harris (2007) 96.

100. In this, like their counterparts in Massachusetts, they were rather different from most Free Soil organizations, which tended to be drawn from Democratic supporters of Van Buren.

101. There is a detailed account of this transaction in Holt's *The Rise and Fall of the American Whig Party* (1999) 399–402. See also John Mayfield's account in *Rehearsal for Republicanism* (1980) 88.

102. Goodwin (2005) captures the long-term consequences of Chase's 1849 chicanery.

103. Holt (1999) 402.

104. Adams (1918) 41.

105. Douglas (1854b) 25.

106. Ibid. 26–27.

107. Ibid. 30.

108. Clement Eaton's *The Freedom-of-Thought Struggle in the Old South* (1964) is the classic on this subject. The repressive power of violence in southern politics in enforcing political conformity is strikingly illustrated in David Grimsted's *American Mobbing, 1828–1861* (1998).

109. See the account of Douglas's remarkable and outrageous "Invasion of States" resolution in 1860 in Michael T. Gilmore, "A Plot Against America: Free Speech and the American Renaissance" (2006). It is not completely clear to me whether Douglas was seriously proposing a law or engaging in hyperbole, but even as hyperbole the aim is clear enough.

110. Rawls elaborates this concept in *The Law of Peoples* (1999).

111. Douglas himself in 1860 came within an inch of not tolerating public advocacy of Republican positions, as we saw in note 108 above.

112. For a good distinction between Madison's method, which seeks to mediate among a chaotic mix of majorities and minorities on a host of issues, and Calhoun's method, which assumes that only a few durable groups are in conflict, each of which deserves formal representation, see Harry Jaffa's *A New Birth of Freedom* (2000).

113. This characterization of the politics of *Federalist* 10 depends largely upon Gordon Wood's *The Creation of the American Republic, 1776–1787* (1972), Lance Banning's *The Jeffersonian Persuasion* (1978), and Edmund Morgan's *Inventing the People* (1988). I am here using the distinction between "ordinary law" and "higher law" not in the sense I will be using it in Chapter 5—in which higher law is a transcendent source of right which trumps positive law—but in Bruce Ackerman's sense in his brilliant two-volume analysis of American lawmaking, *We the People* (1991, 1998), where the distinction is between ordinary law and constitution making. My thinking has also been informed by Akhil Reed Amar, *America's Constitution* (2005); Bernard Bailyn, *The Ideological Origins of the American Revolution* (1967); Samuel Beer, *To Make a Nation* (1993); John Patrick Diggins, *The Lost Soul of American Politics* (1984); Richard J. Ellis, *American Political Cultures* (1993); David F. Epstein, *The Political Theory of* The Federalist (1984); David F. Ericson,

The Shaping of American Liberalism (1993); Robert Ferguson "'We Hold These Truths': Strategies of Control in the Literature of the Founders" (1986); George P. Fletcher, *Our Secret Constitution* (2001); Jay Fliegelman, *Declaring Independence* (1993); Albert Furtwangler, *The Authority of Publius* (1984); Albert Furtwangler, *American Silhouettes* (1988); J. David Greenstone, *The Lincoln Persuasion* (1993); Michael Kammen, *A Machine That Would Go of Itself* (1988); Richard K. Matthews, *If Men Were Angels* (1995); Forrest McDonald, *E Pluribus Unum* (1979); Forrest McDonald, *Novus Ordo Seclorum* (1985); Edmund S. Morgan, *Inventing the People* (1988); Richard B. Morris, *Seven Who Shaped Our Destiny* (1973); Richard B. Morris, *Witnesses at the Creation* (1985); Jack N. Rakove, *Original Meanings* (1996); Robert Rutland, *James Madison* (1987); Herbert J. Storing, *What the Antifederalists Were For* (1981); Morton White, *Philosophy, The Federalist, and the Constitution* (1987); Garry Wills, *Inventing America* (1978); Garry Wills, *Explaining America* (1981); and Gordon S. Wood, *The Radicalism of the American Revolution* (1992).

114. About this, see Richard Hofstadter, *The Idea of a Party System* (1969).

115. As Robert Penn Warren put it in *The Legacy of the Civil War* (1961), "logical parties may lead logically to logical shooting" (43). For Van Buren's role, see Richard Hofstadter, *The Idea of a Party System* (1969), and Joel Silbey, *Martin Van Buren and the Emergence of American Popular Politics* (2002).

116. David Greenstone, in his brilliant *The Lincoln Persuasion* (1993), argues that Van Buren's success lies in his being able, through understanding the nature of winner-take-all politics, to transform the nature of political conflict. Multi-party conflict appears to Greenstone to be a version of the prisoner's dilemma game in which no stable solution emerges. But Van Buren's model of party conflict transforms the prisoner's dilemma game into a game of chicken: the price of defeat is so high that even substantial concessions that preserve party unity are wiser than defecting from party unity in order to adhere to the values of one's own faction.

117. See Lence's edition of Calhoun's selected writings (1992).

5. Douglas's Fanaticism Charge

1. See Gerald M. Capers, *Stephen A. Douglas* (1959) 182. Johannsen (1973) discusses this comment as well. Douglas's early public comment on the nomination of Lincoln is more generous still. Douglas had said the following of Lincoln in his Bloomington speech of July 16 (before lambasting him on all of the political issues):

> I shall have no controversies of a personal character with Mr. Lincoln. I have known him well for a quarter of a century. I have known him, as you all know him, a kind-hearted, amiable gentleman, a right good fellow, a worthy citizen, of eminent ability as a lawyer, and, I have no doubt, sufficient ability to make a good senator. The question, then, for you to decide is, whether his principles are more in accordance with the genius of our free institutions, the peace and harmony of the Republic, than those which I advocate. (Douglas [1894] 70)

2. About southwestern humor, see James H. Justus, *Fetching the Old Southwest* (2004). The reader should remember that Douglas's charge of a conspiracy

between Trumbull and Lincoln to establish the Republican Party is false. Lincoln was in fact a latecomer to the Republican Party. See Chapter 4.

3. This analysis essentially follows the reasoning C. Vann Woodward laid out in *Origins of the New South, 1877–1913* (1951).

4. Supporters of the Federalist Party, whose opposition to the War of 1812 led them to call a convention at Hartford to consider secession from the Union, were falsely accused of showing blue lights in their windows as signals to the British fleet.

5. Cited in Shelby Foote, *The Civil War*, vol. 2: *Fredericksburg to Meridian* (1974) 14.

6. For the statistics about this, see Allen Guelzo, "Houses Divided: Lincoln, Douglas, and the Political Landscape of 1858" (2007).

7. Like the golden rule itself, the thought-experiment is always best understood as source of second thoughts, directed against one's self, and used in a phronetic way, rather than as a bright-line standard, held against others and treated as if it could be a source of epistemic certainty. Understood as a bright-line standard, it lends itself, as all too many bright-line standards do, to special pleading, and it is safer to see it as having regulative than as having constitutive force. That said, unlike Michael Sandel in *Liberalism and the Limits of Justice* (1982), I find it impossible to imagine defending any variety of slaveholding from behind a veil of ignorance that would prevent me from knowing whether I would wind up being one of the slaves.

The distinction between the rational and the reasonable is made by Rawls in *Political Liberalism* (1993), although the construct of the "original position" was first developed in his much earlier *A Theory of Justice* (1971). The use of the reasonable as providing a ground of authority distinct from deductions from first principles on the one hand and from the pure happenstance of mutual agreement on the other is a theme of Rawls's *Lectures on the History of Moral Philosophy* (2000). My thinking about reasonableness as the foundation of autonomy has also been strongly influenced by J. B. Schneewind's *The Invention of Autonomy* (1998). The distinction between the reasonable and the rational will be a major theme again below, in our treatment of Lincoln's and Douglas's conflicting interpretations of the Declaration of Independence in Chapter 7 and in our treatment of Lincoln's concept of the public mind in Chapter 8.

8. Lincoln and Douglas will argue specifically about whether territories can make moral choices for themselves in the Ohio debates of 1859. See my discussion of this issue in Chapter 8.

9. The distinction between a principled compromise and a modus vivendi is made by Rawls in *Political Liberalism* (1993).

10. Douglas does not quite draw the conclusion, which seemed to be set up for him, that New England abolition in particular was driven to fanaticism by its attempt to shout down its bad conscience about its complicity in the slave trade. This was a common view among twentieth-century southerners. See for instance Robert Penn Warren's *John Brown* (1929).

11. Scott's position in 1852 was rather like that of Buchanan in 1856. Fillmore had to be jettisoned in 1852 in favor of Scott because Fillmore's measures were controversial, but Scott had to swallow Fillmore's compromise. Douglas had to be jettisoned in 1856 because he was the author of the Kansas-Nebraska Act,

which did not sully Buchanan, since he had been safely abroad as minister to England during the Pierce administration, but Buchanan was expected to uphold the Kansas-Nebraska Act anyway.

12. See Johannsen (1973) 444.

13. Ibid.

14. Douglas, "Letter to Twenty-five Chicago Clergymen" (April 6, 1854), in Douglas (1961) 301.

15. Ibid.

16. For a further discussion of this issue, see section 9.2 below.

17. Douglas, "Letter to Twenty-five Chicago Clergymen" (April 6, 1854), in Douglas (1961) 308.

18. I have perhaps bent over backward to be fair to Douglas here, because he does not in this passage explicitly grant his opponents the right to make theological arguments so long as they do so within the context of persuasive engagement. Indeed, he seems to treat all theological arguments as if they were claims to speak in the voice of God. Of course not all theological arguments are attempts to ventriloquize the divine. But nothing is really at stake in Douglas's failure to understand the difference, because the distinction that matters to him, between arguments deployed as persuasive resources and arguments deployed to foreclose persuasive engagement, is still the crucial one, even if Douglas does not understand that theological arguments can be found on both sides of the line that distinguishes the two kinds of argument. And besides, his interlocutors in the exchange at hand did indeed claim to speak for God.

19. Douglas, "Letter to Twenty-five Chicago Clergymen" (April 6, 1854), in Douglas (1961) 312.

20. Ibid. 313.

21. Stanley Cavell, in *The Claim of Reason* (1979), is the source of this particular use of the term "acknowledgment." He sees adopting that stance toward other persons as the precondition of moral engagement and moral agency on our own part.

22. The provenance of implicitness is from philosophy more than from psychology, and it owes as much to Polanyi's idea of "tacit knowledge" from *Personal Knowledge* (1962) as to H. L. A. Hart (1961) and to Ronald Dworkin's (1986) distinction between concepts and conceptions.

23. That said, Lincoln's use of negative capability was the central theme of David Herbert Donald's biography of Lincoln. Donald read the Hodges letter as I do, as an account of negative capability at work. Reviewers who took Donald to be arguing that Lincoln was indecisive, passive, or without purpose failed to understand the distinction between negative capability and dithering.

24. Lincoln (1953) 2:385.

25. In *A New Birth of Freedom* (2000), Harry Jaffa argues persuasively—to me at least—that even Jefferson's articulation of the "Rights of Englishmen" from as far back as *A Summary View of the Rights of British America* is better read as a statement about universal human rights than about the political culture of Englishmen.

26. At the same time to declare that something like equality is self-evident is to make a postulate that imaginatively expands the meaning of the concept. Arendt makes this argument in *Between Past and Future* (1968) but develops it more fully in her *Lectures on Kant's Political Philosophy* (1982).

27. The argument that the Civil War marks the transition from a moral economy shaped by republican elitism to a moral economy shaped by democratic citizenship is a familiar one in the historical literature. My version of it owes something to George Fletcher's *Our Secret Constitution* (2001).

28. For a more thorough treatment of the theme of "reverse Burkeanism," see my "Lincoln, Calhoun, and Cultural Politics" (2004).

29. For my analysis of the Lyceum speech, see my article "Lincoln's Address to the Young Men's Lyceum: A Speculative Essay" (1997).

30. Imagined characters do have a kind of freedom, since they become fully imagined only if we see them as characters whose stories are not already over, even if we do already know how their stories come out (which is a slightly different thing). We know many true things about such characters, but we do not know the truth about them, because we approach our knowledge of such characters with an eye to the further imaginative possibilities that knowledge opens, not with an eye to getting that person's number or settling that person's hash. We suffer for their mistakes—when Isabella Archer falls in love with Gilbert Osmond—and we feel mortified by their moral failings—when Kate Croy deceives Milly Theale. Somehow the fact that we know how their stories end, that we know indeed that their stories are already written and cannot be changed, does not prevent us from seeing them somehow as moral agents. Our experience as readers gives us a practical solution to the old Calvinist problem of reconciling predestination and moral agency.

31. Of course, I use the word "theological" here in a parodic sense, to capture a morally apodictic style Douglas (and for that matter Lincoln too, when he is not criticizing Douglas) finds unpalatable. Actual theology—say, Reinhold Niebuhr in *Moral Man and Immoral Society* (1932)—has rather fewer self-defeating things to say.

32. This description of political action owes a great deal to Hannah Arendt's *The Life of the Mind* (1978) and her much earlier *The Human Condition* (1958). My reading of Arendt was illuminated by George Kateb, *Hannah Arendt* (1983); Margaret Canovan, *Hannah Arendt* (1992); Maurizio d'Entrèves, *The Political Philosophy of Hannah Arendt* (1994); and Seyla Benhabib, *The Reluctant Modernism of Hannah Arendt* (1996).

33. This idea of human experience as ineluctably dual, of course, has its origins in Kant's distinction between laws of nature and laws of freedom. My development of that idea has been strongly influenced by several thinkers who for the most part do not agree with each other, by Hilary Putnam in *Reason, Truth, and History* (1981) and *Pragmatism* (1995); by Jürgen Habermas in *Knowledge and Human Interests* (1971), *Theory and Practice* (1973), and *Moral Consciousness and Communicative Action* (1990); and by Donald Davidson in *Essays on Actions and Events* (1980). The distinction between "accounting for a cause"—the language of natural law—and "giving a reason"—the language of laws of freedom—owes something to Peter Winch's *The Idea of a Social Science and Its Relation to Philosophy* (1958), and Winch himself follows an argument made by Wittgenstein in *The Blue and Brown Books* (1958).

34. For more on this, see John Burt, "Lincoln's Address to the Young Men's Lyceum" (1997).

35. Cited in Chaplain W. Morrison, *Democratic Politics and Sectionalism* (1967) 59. This passage is also discussed by Michael Morrison in *Slavery and the American West* (1997) and by Don Fehrenbacher in *The Dred Scott Case* (1978) 561.

36. Morrison (1967) 66.

37. Don Fehrenbacher, in *Prelude to Greatness* (1962), has a hilarious description of nineteenth-century elections in Illinois:

> In the typical town, come election time, banners bearing the names of parties and candidates were fastened to poles and erected in public places, often with elaborate ceremonies. The object was to raise a higher pole than the opposing party, and sometimes standards fluttered more than a hundred feet above the ground. At times, it was also necessary to guard them against enemy forays. The *State Journal* of August 8, 1860, announced that "on Monday night some miserable, infamous, low-flung, narrow-minded, ungodly, dirt-eating, cut-throat, hemp-deserving, deeply-dyed, double-distilled, concentrated miscreant of miscreants, sinned against all honor and decency by cutting and sawing down two or three Republican poles in this city." (14–15)

Robert Penn Warren's novel *World Enough and Time* (1950) includes a wonderful description of an election-cum-riot in 1820s Kentucky. Students of Edgar Allan Poe will remember that the most likely story about his death is that he was kidnapped by a political machine on Election Day, while changing trains in Baltimore, kept roaring drunk, and taken from polling place to polling place to vote until he expired from alcohol poisoning. For the details of this, see Arthur Hobson Quinn's 1941 biography of Poe.

38. We often think of these ugly kinds of war as the consequence of people's ignorance of each other. But usually the people who engage in wars of peoples actually know each other quite well and have a great deal in common with each other. They know each other well enough to see through each other's pretenses and to feel the kind of mutual contempt only a long and ugly intimacy can create.

39. See Mark Neely, *The Fate of Liberty* (1991).

40. A good general portrayal of these Democratic suspicions can be found in Jean H. Baker, *Affairs of Party* (1983). There is a great deal of interesting detail about wartime repression in Nevins's *The War for the Union* (1959–1971) and in Foote's *The Civil War* (1958–1974). The best analysis of Melville's war poetry and wartime experiences, and indeed the best analysis of the way wartime Democrats were thinking, is in Stanton Garner, *The Civil War World of Herman Melville* (1993).

41. As Stephen Cushman remarks concerning the Battle of the Wilderness in *Bloody Promenade* (2001), a few radicals cannot make a great war; it takes millions of moderates to do that.

6. Douglas's Racial Equality Charge

1. The attitude toward nonextension in the slave states is more complicated than it at first seems. Yes, extension of slavery into the territories would ultimately lead to more slave states and to a stronger position of the slave states in the Senate. At the same time, as William Freehling has shown, it was a common feeling in the upper South that extension of slavery would give those states a chance to rid themselves of slavery, and of black people, in roughly the way the states of the lower North had, by exporting their slaves to the new territories as a *post-nati* emancipation bill came into effect. This theory, called "diffusionism," was par-

ticularly attractive to the slave states of the upper South. Jefferson argued at the time of the Missouri crisis, in his famous "Fire Bell in the Night" letter to John Holmes (April 22, 1820), that diffusionism might actually make emancipation easier, since it would be easier to free slaves in places where they would make up a small minority population than it would in places where they would be a majority or a large minority. William W. Freehling discusses this attitude fully in the first volume of *The Road to Disunion* (1990). The slave states as a whole may have feared the effect of the admission of the seventeen new free states that Stephen Douglas predicted would enter the Union from the western territories. (See section 4.4 above.) But the lower South also feared a future in which they would be cooped up with their slaves behind a kind of cotton curtain. And they feared that the states of the upper South, where slavery was shakier anyway, would emancipate their own slaves if they could export them to the lower South, so that they would themselves be in a position to join the free states. Pro-slavery thinkers in New Orleans, Freehling argues (2007), sought through filibustering and imperialist expansion to find new areas for the expansion of slavery, especially in Cuba. But pro-slavery thinkers in South Carolina, fearing that the opening of new slave regions in the Caribbean would further drain the slave population of the upper South, tended to oppose such schemes.

For a very thorough treatment of the spread of slavery into the old Southwest and beyond, with particular attention to how diffusionism provided a nominally anti-slavery way to enable slavery to expand into new territories, see Adam Rothman, *Slave Country* (2005). See also Robert Forbes, *The Missouri Compromise and Its Aftermath* (2007).

2. The 1837 protest also may have been, as slavery quarrels often were, entangled with a side issue. Illinois was in the midst of a debate over whether to move its capital from Vandalia to Springfield, a move that Lincoln supported. The condemnation of abolition to which Lincoln and Stone reply was issued by Usher Linder, who was also a leading opponent of moving the capital. (Linder later was Lincoln's co-counsel in the *Matson* case, below.) Donald ([1995] 63) speculates that Linder's condemnation may have been motivated by anti-Springfield sentiment, intending to argue that Springfield would be in the orbit of the northern counties where hostility to slavery had made abolitionism less of a bugbear. Albert Beveridge long ago treated Lincoln and Stone's protest as a rather minimally anti-slavery position. Lerone Bennett Jr. (2000) takes an even dimmer view of the 1837 protest, arguing that one sees in it a Lincoln who has no particular concern about slavery and who is fundamentally a "man of the fence." William Lee Miller, I think, captures the meaning of the statement more accurately in his *Lincoln's Virtues* (2002). Eric Foner notes that the authors of the condemnation, while hostile to abolitionists, were also no friends of slavery, being for the most part colonizationists who argued, in the words of Lincoln's friend Orville Browning, who drafted the legislature's report, that abolitionist pressure had undermined the colonizationists' efforts to liberate "that unfortunate race of our fellow men" from "thraldom" and return them "to their own benighted land" ([2010] 25).

3. Lovejoy's murder and the St. Louis lynching of the mulatto James M'Intosh that was among the things that led to the murder (since Lovejoy had protested the lynching and had in consequence been driven from St. Louis across

the Mississippi to Alton) were still very much on Lincoln's mind at the time of the 1838 Lyceum speech.

4. Douglas supported the gag rule, and treated abolition as essentially a British conspiracy to weaken the United States. See Guelzo (2008) 11.

5. Waugh (2007) 80.

6. This is the letter we looked at in Chapter 4.

7. For a different view, see Foner (2010) 12.

8. Speed was among the many people who told Herndon that "Mr. Lincoln foresaw the necessity for it [the Emancipation Proclamation]—long before he issued it. He was anxious to avoid it—and came to it only when he saw that the measure would subtract from their labor and add to our army quite a number of good fighting men." (See Wilson and Davis [1998] 197.) For other testimony from Lincoln's friends, see Guelzo, *Lincoln's Emancipation Proclamation* (2004) 24. Speed's brother James, later Lincoln's second attorney general, had rather firmer antislavery convictions. Lincoln did not cite the incident in his letter to Speed, but Allen Gentry, his companion in his 1828 flatboat expedition to New Orleans, described Lincoln's revulsion at his first view of the New Orleans slave market (cited in Burlingame [2008a] 44). John Hanks reported similar feelings on Lincoln's part during their 1831 flatboat trip to New Orleans (Burlingame [2008a] 56). The Fehrenbachers cast doubt on the authenticity of Hanks's recollection of Lincoln's words, but note that Lincoln himself had described such a scene to Herndon (Fehrenbacher and Fehrenbacher [1996] 198).

9. For full details on the *Matson* slave case, see Anton-Hermann Chroust, "Abraham Lincoln Argues a Pro-Slavery Case" (1961) 299–308. Finkelman (1981) 152 also discusses this case, but, perhaps misled by the spelling of the owner's name as "Mateson" in the report, does not realize that he is speaking about the case Lincoln tried. For Finkelman the case is evidence that legal opinion was beginning to turn against slavery in Illinois, since the case not only enforced the distinction between domicile and sojourning but also held that had it been Matson's intent to stay in Illinois, he would have lost his slaves immediately. Lincoln also represented his wife's interest in a complex inheritance case that involved slaves and arranged a settlement in another case that involved transfer of ownership of a slave. He also twice, however, defended persons accused of harboring fugitive slaves. See on this Allen C. Guelzo, *Lincoln's Emancipation Proclamation* (2004) 25.

10. This anecdote is from Chroust (1961) 303–304. Ficklin's later history is interesting. Unlike most other Whigs, he became a Democrat after the demise of his party, and supported Douglas in 1858. During the Charleston debate, Lincoln noticed him on the platform and made him come forward and testify that although Lincoln had spoken out against the injustice of the Mexican War and voted against resolutions that proclaimed its justice, he never opposed necessary appropriations for the troops involved in that conflict. That Lincoln could not bring former Whigs like Ficklin to his side indicates something of the weakness of his appeal to the kind of conservative Whig who had supported Fillmore in 1856. For Ficklin's switch from the Whig to the Democratic Party in 1858, see Guelzo (2008) 189.

11. Chroust (1961) 301n, citing John J. Duff, *A. Lincoln, Prairie Lawyer* (New York: Bramhall House, 1960) 131.

12. Ohio, Indiana, and Kansas had similar "Black Laws." Paul Finkelman (1981) 88n argues that the enforcement of these laws was very lax, and that although these laws indicate the rampant negrophobia of the Midwest, these states also freed slaves in transit through them. Although Anthony Bryant would also have been liable under the Black Laws, for some reason the accounts do not mention him. Perhaps Matson knew Anthony Bryant was free and that mounting an attack on him would have risked his somewhat stronger case against the others. Matson could not, to regain control of Jane Bryant, just have charged her with being a fugitive slave from Kentucky, because he had himself brought her to Illinois, so she was not a fugitive slave from Kentucky, and she was not a fugitive slave from Illinois because legally speaking there was no slavery in Illinois. As a slave traveling through or sojourning with a master in a free state, she fell into a special category about which different states had taken different positions. Pennsylvania, for instance, had laws prohibiting the recovery of slaves who fled from masters in transit through the state. Illinois did not in 1847 actually have reliable formal legal machinery for the recovery of slaves fleeing from masters passing through or sojourning in Illinois. Illinois did have an 1827 law forbidding anyone from harboring fugitive slaves, whether slaves from out of state or the few remaining slaves in Illinois after it ended slavery in 1818. And an 1829 law prevented out-of-state slaves hired for work in Illinois from suing for their freedom, a law that would seem to apply to the Bryants' situation. On the whole, Illinois until 1847 gave a great deal of protection to masters who wished to sojourn in or travel through Illinois with their slaves. (See Finkelman [1981] 96. One of the few cases Finkelman cites in which Illinois interfered with a master's sojourning with slaves is *Bailey v. Cromwell*, although he does not notice that Lincoln was Bailey's attorney.) Precedents in Illinois after 1843 about whether slaves who escape from masters while sojourning in Illinois can be legally recovered are contradictory, but even the cases in which the slave was returned to the master were treated as sojourning cases, favoring the masters only because of the absence of positive laws prohibiting masters from sojourning with slaves, not as applications of the 1793 Fugitive Slave Law. The Illinois Supreme Court's defense of the rights of sojourning masters in its 1843 case of *Willard v. The People* (4 Scam. [Ill.] 461 [1843]) was very unpopular, and out of step with most legal opinion of the North by that time, so perhaps Linder and Lincoln did not wish to give the courts an opportunity to rethink their decision.

13. Donald (1995) 103.

14. It is interesting that Douglas did not take the more promising task of treating the racism of this speech as window-dressing, since doing so would have made Lincoln vulnerable to the more damaging charge of still favoring racial equality underneath the pretense of favoring white supremacy. Douglas treated the Charleston speech's racism as an example of what Lincoln really thought, and the Peoria speech's revulsion against racism as the window-dressing.

15. Letter to Nathaniel P. Banks, August 5, 1863 (2:486).

16. Slaves in the district were emancipated by Congress in April 1862, and the bill doing so bore a surprising resemblance to Lincoln's 1849 bill. Like Lincoln's bill, it provided for compensated emancipation. But it provided immediate rather than gradual emancipation, and did not require approval from Maryland, Virginia, or the white voters of the District of Columbia. See Guelzo, *Lincoln's*

Emancipation Proclamation (2004) 88; Richard Striner, *Father Abraham* (2006); Carl F. Wieck, *Lincoln's Quest for Equality* (2002). Lincoln did not play a part in the deliberations over the bill, but of course did sign it once it was passed.

17. Guelzo (2004) 26, citing Ralph Korngold, *Two Friends of Man: The Story of William Lloyd Garrison and Wendell Phillips and Their Relationship with Abraham Lincoln* (Boston: Little, Brown, 1950) 269. Of course, as Phillips should have remembered, not many in the South *would* have gone so far, since even discussing the issue at all would have been taken by them as an incitement to slave insurrection. This was why they imposed the infamous gag rule in the 1830s on petitions about abolishing slavery in the District of Columbia. For good accounts of the gag rule quarrel, see Freehling, *The Road to Disunion* (1990); William Lee Miller, *Arguing about Slavery* (1996). Other anti-slavery figures gave Lincoln more credit for his 1849 plan for the District of Columbia. Joshua Giddings said of it in 1860, choosing to support Lincoln for the Republican nomination over more vehement anti-slavery figures, that Lincoln "took his position with those who were laboring in the cause of humanity" (Harris [2007] 54, citing Paul H. Verduin, "Partners for Emancipation: New Light on Lincoln, Joshua Giddings, and the Push to End Slavery in the District of Columbia, 1848–49," *Papers from the Thirteenth and Fourteenth Annual Lincoln Colloquia, Galesburg, Illinois, September 26, 1998, and Springfield, Illinois, October 9, 1999* [Springfield: Lincoln Home National Historic Site and Lincoln Studies Center at Knox College, 2002] 86).

18. It is also important to see the "Fire Bell in the Night" letter as a retreat from Jefferson's earlier anti-slavery convictions as expressed in his draft of the Declaration of Independence, in *Notes on the State of Virginia*, and in the Northwest Ordinance. In his famous speech on the Oregon question on June 27, 1848, in which he went on to denounce the principles of the Declaration of Independence, Calhoun, responding to the claim that Jefferson, by penning the Northwest Ordinance, was the intellectual father of the Wilmot Proviso, cited the "Fire Bell in the Night" letter as evidence that Jefferson's later convictions were more like Calhoun's own than like those attributed to him by supporters of the Wilmot Proviso (Calhoun [1992] 553). McCoy's portrayal of the convictions of the elderly Jefferson (McCoy [1989]) leads one to believe that Calhoun was not far from the mark about this.

19. Of course, it is precisely because the position of slavery in Missouri, and especially in St. Louis, was shaky that Missouri produced its own variety of particularly insane fire-eaters, typified by such figures as David Atchison and Benjamin Stringfellow. For a discussion of just why the Border Ruffians in general, and Atchison and Stringfellow in particular, were such extremists, see Freehling (2007).

20. Cited in Lind (2004) 86.

21. Harris (2007) 64.

22. Richard Striner, in *Father Abraham* (2006), argues that Lincoln's thinking about colonization was always only strategic, intended to mislead racist whites about his intentions. As an example of the kind of thinking he argues Lincoln was invested in, he cites Pennsylvania congressman Charles Biddle, who said that "alarm [about emancipation] would spread to every man of my constituents who loves his country and his race if the public mind was not lulled and put to sleep with the word 'colonization'" (150, citing *Congressional Globe*, June 2, 1862, 37th Cong., 3rd sess., 2504). But he did give sincere if halfhearted support to coloniza-

tion some time after he no longer needed to hide his motives, such as in the December 1862 Annual Message to Congress.

23. There was, however, some black support for colonization, including such figures as Edward M. Thomas, of the Anglo African Institute for the Encouragement of Industry and Art; Henry Highland Garnet, who sought to found a colony in Yoruba regions of what is now Nigeria; Martin R. Delany, who sought a settlement in the Niger River valley; James Whitefield, who supported colonization in Central America; and James Theodore Holly, who supported colonization in the West Indies. See Burlingame (2008b) 389.

24. This claim is true to some extent of Blair as well, although Blair also felt a visceral racial hostility one does not find in Lincoln.

25. On the Blair plan, see Foner (1988). On Grant's Dominican Republic plan, see William S. McFeely, *Grant* (1981).

26. Zarefsky (2000) points out that Lincoln's arguments about colonization in this speech were a strategic misdirection, since he subverted those arguments as soon as he had made them, in order to strengthen his underlying argument for outright emancipation. In Zarefsky's reading of the speech, the concluding paragraphs seem to reach past the immediate question they were designed to answer, "embodying ideas and emotions that would resonate long after that context had been transcended," so that the speech, without making what would in context be an impractical assertion, nevertheless "opens the way for consideration of a far more radical alternative—one that could not yet be publicly proposed but for which the way could be prepared." This captures pretty well what I mean by "implicitness."

27. See Lincoln's letter to Edwin M. Stanton on the subject, 2:571.

28. Harry Jaffa's remarks on this strategy are astringent: "[Lincoln's strategy] made possible thereby the maintenance in the movement of a high moral tone, because it encouraged the feeling of moral indignation at the Negro's enslavement without interfering with the luxury of prejudice against the Negro himself" (Jaffa [1959] 61).

29. Cited in Tackach (2002) 33.

30. One of the few promises Lincoln did make during the secession winter to mollify southern views was the promise not to impose hostile federal employees on the South. The threat of Republican postmasters, who, even if they did not openly agitate against slavery would nevertheless chip away at its edges, particularly in the northernmost slave states, in which the Republican Party had a weak but nonnegligible presence, is a major theme in the second volume of William Freehling's *The Road to Disunion* (2007). It was the threat of the development of a southern Republican apparatus, more than the foreclosure of territorial expansion, Freehling argues, that most got under the skin of the fire-eaters in South Carolina.

31. That the racism of the nonslaveholders was different—more angry, more invested in the argument that black people are not quite human—than even the slaveholders' racism is one of the arguments of C. Vann Woodward's *The Origins of the New South, 1877–1913* (1951) and *The Strange Career of Jim Crow* (1955). The particularly virulent quality of nonslaveholder racism, captured by Stampp in *The Era of Reconstruction, 1865–1877* (1965), is nowhere captured more precisely than in the convictions of the southern anti-slavery writer Hinton Rowan

Helper, particularly as his racial convictions sharpened in the postwar era. See
for instance the portrait of Helper in Foner's *Reconstruction* (1988). Even the racism of the slaveholders was not precisely of a piece: those who embraced polygenesis, the theory most exemplified by Nott and Gliddon's *Types of Mankind* (1857)
that the different races were in fact different species, embraced something different from those who embraced slavery as a patriarchal economy. (For a discussion
of the different flavors of slaveholder racism, see Michael O'Brien, *Conjectures of
Order* [2004].)

32. See for instance, during the Charleston debate (1:672).

33. Guelzo (2008) 186, citing "Little Dug Entered at the State Fair," Chicago
Press & Tribune, September 18 and 20, 1858. Since the *Press & Tribune* was a pro-
Lincoln newspaper, there is some possibility that this account plays up Douglas's
racism a little. But the phrase is not really out of character.

34. See the characterization of Johnson in Stampp's *The Era of Reconstruction*
(1965). See also Trefousse's biography of Johnson, *Andrew Johnson* (1989).

35. George W. Julian, *Political Recollections, 1840 to 1872* (Miami, FL: Mnemo-
syne Publishing Company, 1969), cited in Sewell (1976) 176.

36. For a discussion of this figure, see Thurow, *Abraham Lincoln and American
Political Religion* (1976) 46. Harry Jaffa discusses this figure also in *A New Birth of
Freedom* (2000) 310. Both Thurow and Jaffa, I think, read Douglas's figure exactly
backward.

37. Exactly how nineteenth-century, pre-Mendelian writers and politicians
understood the word "race" is a subject of dispute, since without Mendelian gene-
tics the word could mean family or even culture. For an account of the development of racial, and racist, thinking in the South, with a particularly hilarious account of how it was that white people came to be called "Caucasians," see Michael
O'Brien, *Conjectures of Order* (2004).

38. Milton (1934) cites a letter of C. H. Ray to Elihu Washburne of November
22, 1858, in which Douglas is quoted making this complaint (359).

39. Douglas (1894) 72.

40. For more on this, see section 6.5 below.

41. Cited in Johannsen, *Stephen A. Douglas* (1973) 418.

42. McConnel recorded this in *Transactions of the Illinois State Historical Society
for 1900* 49, cited in Johannsen (1973) 419. Douglas's other biographers, such as
Milton (1934), Capers (1959), and Wells (1990), all cite McConnel's reflections.
Johannsen believes that although McConnel wrote down this memory long after
the event, Douglas probably did say something similar if he did not use exactly these
words. My own view is that Douglas probably did have these views, because
these were the views of most northern Democrats like him.

43. This is again McConnel, cited in Milton (1934) 122. Douglas does not
seem to understand the biology of tumors.

44. Johannsen (1973) 419.

45. Foote has a hilarious account of this event in *Casket of Reminiscences* (1874),
and is fully aware of the kind of fool he made of himself here, not for the only
time.

46. Gerald Capers discusses this incident at length in *Stephen A. Douglas*
(1959) 44. Even Harry Jaffa, who is usually reluctant to concede any moral points
to Douglas at all, argues that this statement shows that Douglas's professed moral
indifference to slavery was a pretense he adopted for the sake of keeping the

peace, and that slavery to Douglas was in fact an object of profound moral distaste (Jaffa [1959] 53).

47. Johannsen (1973) 211.

48. See Douglas (1961) 298 (February 18, 1854).

49. About this, see Paul Finkelman, *An Imperfect Union* (1981) 150.

50. See Lehrman (2008) 71.

51. For Douglas's use of this argument, see Gienapp (1987) 78ff.

52. Johannsen (1973) 233.

53. As Allen Guelzo (2008) points out, Galesburg was a rather anti-slavery venue, and perhaps Douglas here was tuning his argument to the frequency of his hearers, just as he accused Lincoln of doing.

54. Douglas (1894) 77–78.

55. See Zarefsky, *Lincoln, Douglas, and Slavery in the Crucible of Public Debate* (1990).

56. See, for instance, Allison Freehling's account of the Virginia anti-slavery debate of 1832, *Drift toward Dissolution* (1982).

57. See also John S. Wright, *Lincoln and the Politics of Slavery* (1970); Harold Holzer, *Lincoln Seen and Heard* (2000); William K. Klingaman, *Abraham Lincoln and the Road to Emancipation 1861–1865* (2001); Carl F. Wieck, *Lincoln's Quest for Equality* (2002); Richard Striner, *Father Abraham* (2006).

58. The letter is usually referred to as the Hodges letter, but it was also addressed to Kentucky governor Thomas E. Bramlette, and to the same Senator Archibald Dixon who, ten years earlier, had persuaded Stephen Douglas to press for explicit repeal of the Missouri Compromise line in the Kansas-Nebraska Act so that slavery might conceivably establish itself north of the 36° 30′ line, in Kansas Territory.

59. Wendell Phillips to William H. Herndon, undated, in Douglas L. Wilson and Rodney O. Davis, eds., *Herndon's Informants* (1998).

60. See Edmund Husserl, *Ideas* (1962).

61. Sandel makes this criticism in *Liberalism and the Limits of Justice* (1982). See also his next book, *Democracy's Discontent* (1996). For thoughtful replies, see Burton Dreben, "On Rawls and Political Liberalism" (2003); Stephen Mulhall and Adam Swift, "Rawls and Utilitarianism" (2003), both in Samuel Freeman, ed., *The Cambridge Companion to Rawls* (2003).

62. I have been influenced deeply by Rawls's views about the development of the concept of moral autonomy in the history of moral philosophy, and in particular with his treatment of some of the issues and pitfalls that inhere in that concept. On this, see his *Lectures on the History of Moral Philosophy* (2000). For a different view, and one that emphasizes the natural law theory embodied in Grotius and Pufendorf, see J. B. Schneewind, *The Invention of Autonomy* (1998).

63. This example is called "Harrington's Cake" because it was first imagined by the seventeenth-century political philosopher James Harrington, the author of *Oceana*. The principle is that the situation of deliberation *itself* provides constraints that force the process in the direction of fairness. The example is discussed in detail by a number of writers, including Banning (1978), Beer (1993), Morgan (1988), and Schneewind (1998).

64. For a development of this line of thinking, see Charles Taylor, *Hegel* (1975). For a larger-scale account of the same theme, see Taylor's *Sources of the Self* (1989). Martha Nussbaum develops a related argument, with Plato rather than

Kant as her target, in *The Fragility of Goodness* (1986). For an attempt to reconcile these points of view, and to answer Sandel's objection, see my own "Reason Also Is Choice: Reflection, Freedom, and the Euthyphro Problem" (2002).

65. There is an extensive literature about whether or in what sense the antebellum United States was a liberal society. I refer here not to the tired (and to my mind exploded) distinction between republicanism and liberalism that troubled the literature in the 1990s, but to those who, following as much as criticizing Louis Hartz, sought to tease apart the various strains of American liberalism. Of these studies much the best was David Greenstone's *The Lincoln Persuasion* (1993). Also very important was David Ericson's *The Shaping of American Liberalism* (1993) and his paradoxically titled *The Debate over Slavery: Antislavery and Proslavery Liberalism in Antebellum America* (2000).

66. Douglas Wilson ingeniously suggests that Greeley may not have intended his letter to prompt the dilatory Lincoln to issue an emancipation proclamation. Greeley may have gotten wind that such a proclamation was in the offing, and thus may have been attempting to claim credit for it. See Wilson (2006) 149. The least one can say is that Greeley and many others possibly understood Lincoln's reply as an oblique promise that an emancipation proclamation would be forthcoming. See Burlingame (2008b) 402.

67. Moncure Daniel Conway, *Autobiography, Memories and Experiences* (New York: Houghton Mifflin Company, 1904), 1:345–346, cited in Striner (2006) 153.

68. Carnahan (2007) has shown that Lincoln chose the very strong standard of military necessity, rather than the weaker standard of military expedience, in issuing the Emancipation Proclamation, because the necessity standard could better meet the legal challenges Lincoln expected emancipation to face. For my own take on how the military necessity argument grows out of traditional arguments about the law of war, and in particular how the argument Lincoln made differed from that Hunter had made, see section 7.1 below.

69. See Guelzo, *Lincoln's Emancipation Proclamation* (2004) 50 for examples. See also on this Mark E. Neely Jr., *The Last Best Hope of Earth* (1995) 7.

70. Letter to Orville Browning, September 22, 1861 (2:268–269).

71. The first draft of the proclamation was issued on July 22, but Guelzo (2004) cites evidence that it may have been composed as early as May 28, although all of the evidence for any particular date is shaky and the actual date of its composition is still unknown. In a way it does not matter, since the proclamation was not a sudden inspiration of Lincoln's in the first place and was clearly the product of a long period of maturation.

72. See Lincoln's appeal to the border state congressmen of July 12, 1862 (2:340).

73. See on this subject Lincoln's letter of January 13, 1863, to the Workingmen of Manchester (2:430–431). See also the congratulatory letter Karl Marx wrote to Lincoln celebrating the Emancipation Proclamation on the occasion of Lincoln's reelection. The text of the letter is available at http://www.marxists.org/archive/marx/iwma/documents/1864/lincoln-letter.htm.

74. There is an account of this conversation in Guelzo (2004) 112. The nuance about the border states is discussed in McPherson (2008) 108.

75. Lincoln did mention recruiting black soldiers in the final Emancipation Proclamation, but he did not mention it in the Preliminary Emancipation Procla-

mation in September. Perhaps the issue might then have seemed too volatile. Recruiting black soldiers, however, was unquestionably in his mind from the beginning and was a feature of the discussions in the Cabinet about issuing an emancipation proclamation from the beginning, as both Welles and Chase relate. For more on this, see Wilson (2006) 139. As early as July 1862, Lincoln allowed Jim Lane to raise black troops for use against secessionists in Kansas, and had, earlier than that, considered letting Lane lead an expedition against Texas in which he would not only pay slaves who came within his lines to dig fortifications but also, if necessary, arm them. Lincoln also suggested to General Dix in July 1862 that Fortress Monroe be garrisoned with black troops, and suggested to Andrew Johnson, then military governor of Tennessee, that he recruit black troops. See Burlingame (2008b) 466.

76. Lincoln's thinking about his ability to use the war powers of the presidency against slavery may have been influenced by William Whiting's 1862 pamphlet *The War Powers of the President, and the Legislative Powers of Congress in Relation to Rebellion, Treason, and Slavery.* (About this, see McPherson [2008] 107–108.) Lincoln's thinking about the recruitment of black soldiers may also partly have been shaped by George Livermore's pamphlet *An Historical Research: Opinions of the Founders of the Republic on Negroes as Slaves,* which Senator Charles Sumner sent him. Livermore noted in his pamphlet that the army during the Revolution was racially integrated, and that Washington thought highly of the quality of his black soldiers. See Neely (1995) 111. For more on the argument of military necessity, see section 7.1 below. It was a lesson the black soldiers themselves were soon to teach at Milliken's Bend, Port Hudson, and Fort Wagner.

77. Burlingame (2008b) 234.

78. Lind (2004) has argued that this turn in the argument demonstrates that Lincoln never considered black citizenship or even emancipation to be a central issue in the war, and that only the demonstration that republican governments could be stable really mattered to him. I think Lind is mistaken about this. It is true that a central issue for Lincoln was whether republics can be stable, or whether every loser in a political contest will break up the republic over it; it is not true that the stability of republics was the only issue for him, because, for one thing, what threatened the stability of the Union was the contest over slavery, and the stability of the Union could not be restored without destroying slavery. For another thing, it was natural that Lincoln should foreground the stability argument, rather than the slavery argument, when making his case to an audience of anti-emancipation Unionists, as he was doing in the Conkling letter. Finally, Lincoln made even the stability case, and to an anti-emancipation audience, in a way that foreshadows developments on the suffrage issue. If he really only wished to make the stability argument and had no thought of black suffrage, there were easier ways to make the argument than this one.

79. Richard Striner, who reads this letter somewhat more strongly even than I do, says of it, "Is it possible to read such a letter as the statement of a racist politician who intended nothing more than preservation of the Union?"(Striner [2006] 202).

80. See John Keegan, *The Second World War* (1990) 17–25.

81. Miller (2008) discusses this fantasy at some length. Lincoln was tempted to call the Democrats' bluff about this by offering the Confederacy just what the

Democrats proposed, in order to demonstrate that they would accept no such deal. But he never sent the feelers he meditated, judging, correctly, that even the hint that he might renege on emancipation would have very bad effects, and not only on the morale of emancipated soldiers, but on the sense of purpose that the Emancipation Proclamation had given to the white soldiers as well. See Miller (2008) 371–390.

82. Lincoln (1953) 7:506–508.

83. That said, Lincoln's first draft of the Preliminary Emancipation Proclamation was more tentative about it than the version he wound up publishing. Lincoln had said, "And the executive government of the United States will, during the continuance in office of the present incumbent, recognize such persons, as being free, and will do no act or acts to repress such persons, or any of them, in any efforts they may make for their actual freedom" (Wilson (2006) 132). This seems to imply that Lincoln feared he would be unable to prevent some later president from rescinding the proclamation. And it promised only to "recognize" the freedom of the emancipated slaves, not, as the final version did, after Seward prompted the revision, to "recognize and maintain" that freedom. For more on this, see Wilson (2006) 132.

84. This is a theme in Eric Foner, *Nothing but Freedom* (1983). It in developed in more detail in Foner's *Reconstruction* (1988).

85. Douglas was surprisingly uncritical of Maine and New York about this, perhaps because he took the view, in line with his popular sovereignty doctrine, that it was their business, not his. Besides, the suffrage law in New York, which replaced an earlier law with less demanding property requirements but still preserved black suffrage, was of Democratic origin.

86. Letter of August 5, 1863 (2:486). Cox (1981) treats this letter in persuasive detail.

87. Cox (1981) argues that Lincoln had made indirect proposals to this end as far back as August 1863.

88. Possibly Lincoln only meant that the former slaves would be secure Republican voters who might help keep the states of the reconstructed Confederacy in the Republican column, but it would require a little more evidence to show that Lincoln's motives here were entirely sordid. Given who the Democrats of that time and place were, however, preventing a return of repression really would require preventing a return to power of the democracy.

89. James Tackach in *Lincoln's Moral Vision: The Second Inaugural Address* (2002) notes how often Lincoln's capacity for growth is a key theme among his biographers, citing as paradigmatic Richard N. Current's remark, "The most remarkable thing about him [Lincoln] was his tremendous power of growth. He grew in sympathy, in the breadth of his humaneness, as he grew in other aspects of mind and spirit."

90. About this, see Alison Goodyear Freehling, *Drift Toward Dissolution* (1982). William W. Freehling makes a related but slightly different case in *The Road to Disunion*, vol. 1: *Secessionists at Bay, 1776–1854* (1990).

91. See Elbert B. Smith, *The Presidency of James Buchanan* (1975) 127.

92. This figure is from Robert William Fogel and Stanley L. Engerman, *Time on the Cross* (1974). Fehrenbacher, in *The Slaveholding Republic* (2001), argues that there were only 803 fugitive slaves in the North in 1860, half of them from the

four border states. William Freehling (1990) suggests, however, that about a thousand slaves escaped from the border states every year (503). (The discrepancy has to do with the difference between running away from one's master and making it successfully to the free states.)

93. This number is from Potter (1976) 119. Stanley W. Campbell's *The Slave Catchers* (1970) says that the total number of fugitive slave cases brought under the Fugitive Slave Act is a mere 332. Of these, 191 came before a federal tribunal, and of these, 157 escaped slaves were sent back to their owners. Twenty-two were rescued from federal custody, and only 1 escaped. Also there were fewer escapes in 1850–1860 in percent than at any former period: 1,011 slaves in 1850 (1 in 3,165), 803 in 1860 (out of 3,949,557 slaves, about 1 in 5,000).

94. This is Fehrenbacher's view in *The Slaveholding Republic* (2001) 232.

95. Freehling (1990) 504.

96. Holt (1999) 496.

97. This scarcely believable incident is detailed in Freehling (2007) 257. The Republicans did not have the votes to elect Sherman anyway, without the support of either some northern Democrats or border-South ex-Whigs, so what Miles was really exercised about was not the power of the Republicans but the possible disloyalty of his nominal allies. (Indeed, the crucial turn came when a southern ex-Whig, Henry Winter Davis of Maryland—later the author of the radical Wade-Davis Reconstruction Plan—agreed to support William Pennington, a Republican but not so controversial a Republican as Sherman, for Speaker.) Miles doubtless expected that his coup d'état would force the waverers into line behind him, much as the actual secession of South Carolina in fact did two years later.

98. The world of the *oikos* is the world of what, in *The Human Condition* (1958) Arendt calls "labor": repetitive, meaningless, and alienating drudgery in their service of others in exchange for the means of living; what, in the *Economic and Political Manuscripts of 1848* (1848) (in Tucker, *The Marx-Engels Reader* [1972]), Marx calls "estranged labor." Under some circumstances, the activity of the *oikos* might make room for what Arendt calls "work": skilled craftsmanship expressive of the worker's control over his or her means but limited to the ends for which the object of work is designed. The polis, on the other hand, is preeminently the world of what Arendt calls "action," an intervention in the course of history created by different human beings in persuasive engagement with each other. This reading of the distinction between the *oikos* and the polis derives of Arendt's distinction in *The Human Condition* (1958), although I read the polis rather less sympathetically than Arendt does. My thinking here also follows Jürgen Habermas, *The Philosophical Discourse of Modernity* (1987) 37. See also Arendt's *Between Past and Future* (1968) and Habermas's *The Structural Transformation of the Public Sphere* (1991). For an analysis of the meaning of the distinction between polis and *oikos* in the context of American slavery, see George P. Fletcher, *Our Secret Constitution* (2001).

99. Racialized slavery was not unique to the New World, however. David Brion Davis has discussed the extensive African slave trade in the medieval Arab world, a trade that in numbers of captured Africans may have approached the numbers taken to the New World, which was supported by a cultural apparatus familiar to students of American slavery and which involved bloody suppression of slave revolts of the kind familiar from Caribbean history (Davis, *Challenging*

the Boundaries of Slavery [2003]). Davis has also described an extensive slave-trading economy in which medieval Italian cities transported non-African slaves—Slavs—from Dalmatia, as well as Circassians, Georgians, and Armenians from the Caucasus, to Western Europe and to the Arab world. The ability to equate the line between *oikos* and polis with the line between black and white might have been more difficult to do without the one-drop rule. It is hard to test this theory, because the places that had slavery but did not use the one-drop rule also were not republics. It would also be difficult to specify which came first, racially marked republican slavery or the one-drop rule. Louisiana might provide a test case, since it adopted the one-drop rule at the moment of being absorbed into the American republic, but it may well have done so, indeed probably did so, as part of its cultural rather than its political assimilation to the United States. Still, the possibility is tantalizing.

100. They saw slavery in a context of a number of other hierarchical relationships, with whites who owed them deference as much as with blacks who owed them obedience, and they saw these relationships, with white and black alike, in terms of an economy of patronage and clienthood whose inner logic has been developed in detail by Eugene Genovese. See Genovese, *Roll, Jordan, Roll* (1972) for the classic development of the theme of patronage and clienthood. See also his *The World the Slaveholders Made* (1969). Set in the context of all of these other relationships of inequality, deference, and precedence, racial inequality might seem less of an inflamed distinction than it might seem under other circumstances. Indeed, as Gordon S. Wood argued in *The Radicalism of the American Revolution* (1992), one reason the Revolution led to an upsurge in anti-slavery feeling was not only that slavery was felt to be contrary to the political professions of the revolutionaries, in the ways that David Brion Davis documents in *The Problem of Slavery in the Age of Revolution* (1975), but also that the decline of other forms of inequality brought on by the Revolution made the stark inequality of slavery all the more salient.

101. This is why, as Daniel Walker Howe has shown in *The Political Culture of the American Whigs* (1979), the Jacksonians seem to have been so much more insistent and angry racists than the Whigs were.

102. See Fredrickson's *The Black Image in the White Mind* (1987).

103. Sean Wilentz, in *Chants Democratic* (1984), also has interesting things to say about how the class feelings of these Democrats sometimes shaped their racism and gave it an extremist edge—see particularly his discussion of the radical New York City working-class leader Mike Walsh. Wilentz treats some of the same themes in his later *The Rise of American Democracy* (2005). Daniel Walker Howe works through the same theme of the connection between radical democracy and racism both in *The Political Culture of the American Whigs* (1979) and in *What Hath God Wrought* (2007), though with rather less sympathy for the Democrats.

104. This irony is a recurrent theme in the two volumes of William Freehling's *The Road to Disunion* (1990, 2007). It is also a recurrent theme in the novels of Mark Twain and William Faulkner, who presented in Pap Finn and in Thomas Sutpen contrasting ways poor whites might respond to the class insult offered them by rich whites.

105. For Johnson's style of racism, see Kenneth M. Stampp, *The Era of Reconstruction, 1865–1877* (1965). See also Hans Trefousse, *Andrew Johnson* (1989).

106. About this, see C. Vann Woodward, *Origins of the New South, 1877–1913* (1951) and *The Strange Career of Jim Crow* (1955).

107. *Congressional Globe,* 35th Cong., 1st sess., appendix, 68–71.

108. Hammond (1858) 69. The General Lane here is Jim Lane, who led paramilitary free state forces. The Colonel Kirk was a leader of forces loyal to James II of England, called "Kirk's Lambs" because they had a representation of the Lamb of God on their banners. Kirk's Lambs went about stringing up the political opponents of King James in large numbers. Dickens mentions him in his *A Child's History of England* (1854).

109. This argument had an afterlife during the Reconstruction era, when the Radicals, the faction who supported congressional Reconstruction, were able to maintain that the proposed governments of the states of the former Confederacy were not in fact republican since they disenfranchised the former slaves.

110. David Zarefsky notes, for instance, that "neither the federal Constitution, nor the constitutions of the original thirteen states, nor those of most of the states added since, required submission. Ohio, Kentucky, Tennessee, Illinois, Alabama, Missouri, Maine, Vermont, and Wisconsin were admitted without referendum" (Zarefsky [1990] 12). Smith (1975) points out that thirty-three of the sixty-three antebellum state constitutions were not subject to popular ratification, although by 1858 only nine states, eight of them southern, still lived under unratified constitutions (41).

111. Hammond (1858) 69.

112. Ibid.

113. Ibid.

114. Hammond depends here upon seeing the Constitution as Americans do, as a formally developed basic law, rather than as the British do, as the upshot of a long history of ordinary legislation.

115. Ibid.

116. Ibid.

117. Ibid. 70.

118. Ibid. 71.

119. Ibid.

120. Ibid.

121. Ibid.

122. The text of Stephens's speech here is from Cleveland (1866) 717–729.

123. Cleveland (1866) 721.

124. Ibid.

125. Ibid. 722.

126. Ibid. 722–723.

127. Coming out for gradual emancipation in Kentucky in 1848, Clay rejected both the idea of black intellectual inferiority and the idea that slavery could be justified by claims about intellectual inferiority. If intellectual superiority justified someone in enslaving someone else, Clay argued, "then the wisest man in the world would have a right to make slaves of all the rest of mankind!" (Remini [1991] 718). Lincoln, in a fragment on slavery usually dated 1854, made a similar argument:

> If A. can prove, however conclusively, that he may, of right, enslave B.— why may not B. snatch the same argument, and prove equally, that he may enslave A?—

You say A. is white, and B. is black. It is *color*, then; the lighter, having the right to enslave the darker? Take care. By this rule, you are to be slave to the first man you meet, with a fairer skin than your own.

You do not mean *color* exactly?—You mean the whites are *intellectually* the superiors of the blacks, and, therefore have the right to enslave them? Take care again. By this rule, you are to be slave to the first man you meet, with an intellect superior to your own.

But, say you, it is a question of *interest;* and, if you can make it your *interest*, you have the right to enslave another. Very well. And if he can make it his interest, he has the right to enslave you. (1:303)

128. If one speaks of the complete economic and cultural commitment of both sides, and the intense mobilization of popular feeling, and the escalation of violence until it reached an intensity capable of breaking the society completely apart, one can call the American Civil War a "total war." But it was not a "total war" as the twentieth century has come to understand total war, which is to say war carried out by ruthless slaughter of civilians.

129. Striner (2006) treats this claim as a strategic prevarication. This is further than I am willing to go. At the same time, I do not think that this passage proves, as David Herbert Donald (1995) argued, Lincoln's essential passivity. That said, I think the vehement disagreement with Donald's book in Striner (2006) and in Carwardine (2006) somewhat misconstrues Donald's argument. Donald did not argue that Lincoln had no will, no agency, or no plans, but that much of his agency was guided by intuitions whose ultimate bearing was not fully clear to him until he followed them out. When Donald speaks of "passivity," what he really means, I think, is something like what Keats calls "negative capability." I do not think my views of Lincoln are ultimately that far removed from Donald's.

130. Wilson (2006) provides strong evidence that the Meditation on the Divine Will was written in 1864 rather than in September 1862. The principal evidence for setting the composition of the meditation in 1862 arises from Lincoln's apparent allusion to it in the context of an 1864 memory of his October 1862 meeting with Eliza Gurney (which I discuss in section 9.2), which Nicolay and Hay had wrongly dated to September. Wilson shows that the paper on which the meditation was written was probably not available in 1862. While it is true that the meditation's thinking about the meaning of the fact that the war has been dragging on, although God could have put a stop to it to at any moment, makes more sense as a thought of 1864 than of 1862, Lincoln's remarks at the time of the Emancipation Proclamation to Chase and to Welles (which I discuss in section 9.2) show that he may well have been thinking along the lines the meditation suggests even in 1862.

7. *The* Dred Scott *Case*

1. For the risks of higher-law idealism, see Robert Penn Warren, *The Legacy of the Civil War* (1961). For the ways in which different strains of the anti-slavery movement engaged or rejected higher-law idealism, see Louis Filler, *Crusade against Slavery* (1986); Louis S. Gerteis, *Morality and Utility in American Antislavery Reform* (1987); Richard H. Sewell, *Ballots for Freedom* (1976); Robert M. Cover, *Justice Accused* (1975); David F. Ericson, *The Debate over Slavery* (2000); John Mayfield, *Rehearsal for Republicanism* (1980); Lewis Perry, *Radical Abolitionism* (1973).

For recent good treatments of how Lincoln avoids the Scylla and Charybdis of higher-law idealism and expedience politics, see Allen C. Guelzo, *Lincoln's Emancipation Proclamation* (2004); William Lee Miller, *President Lincoln* (2008). See also the survey of anti-slavery thought, and of the recent historiography of anti-slavery thought, in David Brion Davis, *The Problem of Slavery in the Age of Revolution* (1975), and *Inhuman Bondage* (2006) by the same author. For an analysis of the consequences of the attempt to replace law with politics, or, more generally, to see law only in terms of conflicts of power and interest or in purely conventional views of justice rather than in terms of ideas of justice deeper than the merely conventional, see Harry V. Jaffa, *Crisis of the House Divided* (1959), and his more recent *A New Birth of Freedom* (2000). For a trenchant argument on a similar theme, see Leo Strauss, *Natural Right and History* (1953).

2. See for instance Douglas's Springfield speech of June 12, 1857.

3. See Fehrenbacher (1962). The claims about Lincoln's presidential ambitions later made by Norman Judd and others are thoroughly debunked in Fehrenbacher and Fehrenbacher (1996).

4. Finkelman (1981) argues for a narrower reading of the meaning of *Somerset*, that it prevents a slave brought into England from being removed from England by force. But *Somerset* was received in America as liberating any slave brought to England, so the distinction is moot. Finkelman also notes that there were *Somerset*-like cases in France as early as 1552 (37).

5. Mansfield's language is cited in David Brion Davis, *The Problem of Slavery in the Age of Revolution* (1975) 476.

6. Stephen Douglas would make this argument in his Ohio campaign in 1859. For an account of why Douglas would take this—for him—startlingly Mansfieldian line, see Chapter 8.

7. General Order 7, Department of the South, April 13, 1862, *Official Records*, series 2, vol. 1, 818, cited in Carnahan (2007) 100. Carnahan notes that Hunter's reasoning depends upon a natural law or Grotian understanding of the law of war, but does not extend it to Mansfield.

8. Carnahan (2007) 130.

9. This case is treated in Davis (1975) 510.

10. Ibid. 515.

11. For my own treatment of this case, see section 6.1 above.

12. See Finkelman (1981) 228–229.

13. Finkelman (1981) shows that the courts actually paid attention to a finer-grained set of distinctions, distinguishing transients from visitors, sojourners, and residents. Increasingly the northern states freed all of these categories of slave. Because some of the arguments concerning the property rights of transients overlap those of visitors and sojourners, an attack upon a state's right to free transient slaves, such as in the case of *Lemmon v. New York*, 20 N.Y. (1860), could also be used to mount an attack upon acts freeing visitors and sojourners. It is the argument of Finkelman's book, and a host of others, that the same arguments could be used to mount an attack upon emancipation itself.

14. For Shaw as the model for Captain Vere, see Robert Cover, *Justice Accused* (1975). For more detail on Melville's thought about his father in law, and about slavery generally, see Stanton Garner, *The Civil War World of Herman Melville* (1993).

15. Shaw's decision is treated in detail in Cover (1975) 94.

16. Shaw's argument is analyzed in detail in Finkelman (1981) 2. The attorneys for Med, the six-year-old enslaved girl at the center of the *Aves* case, made a rather harsher argument: Massachusetts, Ellis Gray Loring argued, was under no obligation to grant comity concerning an institution that offends its morals, contravenes its policy, and offers a pernicious example. Furthermore, Loring argued, Louisiana, Med's home state, had, along with South Carolina, Georgia, North Carolina, and Florida, forfeited the right to comity by passing laws enabling them to imprison free black seamen from Massachusetts and force them to work off heavy fines if they were so unlucky as to enter their ports as crew. Both Louisiana and South Carolina threatened the lives of the commissioners Massachusetts sent to look into the cases of such imprisoned seamen, and forced them to flee the state. For more detail, see Finkelman (1981) 108n, and Wiecek (1977) 109.

17. Finkelman (1981) 127.

18. As in Massachusetts after the *Aves* decision this law led to the odd state of affairs in which if a slave came to New York with his or her master, the slave was freed instantly, but if the slave came to New York alone, as an escapee, or even at the behest of his or her master, the slave could be returned to bondage even after decades of residence in the state. Dred Scott and his wife, it should be remembered, sometimes traveled unaccompanied to join their master at military posts; the slaves involved in the *Strader* case, discussed below, also traveled unaccompanied by their master in the free states; and the unfortunate Margaret Morgan, the center of the *Prigg* case, was given permission by her master not only to travel to Pennsylvania but also to live and marry there.

19. See Cover (1975) 94.

20. Finkelman (1981) 187.

21. Ibid. 189.

22. My discussion of this opinion is indebted to the discussion in Robert M. Spector, "The Quock Walker Cases (1781–83)—Slavery, Its Abolition, and Negro Citizenship in Early Massachusetts" (1968). The operative language in the preamble to the Massachusetts constitution was written by John Adams: "All men are born free and equal, and have certain natural, essential, and unalienable rights; among which may be reckoned the right of enjoying and defending their Lives and Liberties; that of acquiring, possessing, and protecting property; in fine, that of seeking and obtaining their safety and happiness." Many years later, this same language has been seen to require equal rights for gay people in Massachusetts as well.

23. On these figures, see Cover (1975).

24. The full text of the *Prigg* decision can be found at http://supreme.justia .com/us/41/539/case.html (accessed January 18, 2010). The full text of the *Strader* decision may be found at http://supreme.justia.com/us/51/82/case.html (accessed January 18, 2010).

25. It is slightly more complicated than this. Prigg did get a warrant from a Pennsylvania magistrate, but when he got Margaret and her family under his control, the magistrate refused the case. It is worth noting, however, that even had Margaret been a runaway slave of the traditional sort, Pennsylvania law would have liberated her children born in Pennsylvania. About this, see Finkelman (1981) 65.

26. This account of the revolting facts of the case in *Prigg* derives from Ahkil Reed Amar, *America's Constitution* (2005) 262–263.

27. On this, see Burt (1992) 176. Burt rightly points out that Story's fear is ludicrous: most northerners were not willing to make common cause with abolitionists. That said, after the Anthony Burns affair raised the stakes and the price, recapturing fugitive slaves even under the Fugitive Slave Act of 1850 became difficult enough that only about 300 fugitives were returned to slavery during the entire period of that act's operation, very few of them after 1854. For this number, see Stanley W. Campbell, *The Slave Catchers* (1970) 270.

28. Chief Justice Taney's opinion in this case misunderstood Story's argument, taking him to mean that state officials were prohibited from aiding in the rendition of fugitive slaves. And Taney argued that Story's opinion would practically speaking prohibit the recovery of fugitive slaves, because there were not enough federal judges to oversee all those recaptures. Taney's opinion in this case argued that the states had a positive, constitutionally mandated duty to help masters recover their slaves. At the same time he held that the state could not impose things like ordinary due process safeguards to make sure that the people being recovered really were fugitive slaves, since that would amount to interference with the master's right to his property. Taney's view, in short, was that the free states had to help white people from the slave states drag black people in the free states into slavery without stopping to inquire whether those black people were in fact fugitive slaves.

29. Fehrenbacher (1978) 43. Fehrenbacher notes that, as with Taney's *Dred Scott* pronouncements about the power of territorial governments over slavery, it is a genuinely open question whether Story was speaking for himself or for the Court when he said that a state did not have a positive duty to protect out-of-state slaveholders' rights to recapture their fugitive slaves. Chief Justice Taney, for instance, insisted that the state governments had a positive duty to establish mechanisms for protecting slaveholders' rights, and were only prohibited from interfering with them. Probably the majority were not with Story on this issue, but they all later behaved as if he spoke for the Court.

30. Burt (1992) 192.

31. Hearing this, one might ask why Taylor Blow did not just buy Scott and free him to begin with. The answer is that Irene refused to sell him. Why Irene Emerson fought so hard to retain an elderly slave already in poor health—he died within months of the end of the case—is something of a mystery.

32. Fehrenbacher (1978) 252–253. See also Finkelman (1981) 221.

33. Cited in Fehrenbacher (1978) 264. As for Judge Scott's implication that New England slave traders forced slavery on an unwilling South: oh, please.

34. Now, of course, one does not have to be a citizen to sue. I cannot just expropriate foreign tourists with impunity, for instance. But one does have to be a citizen to take a case to federal court, under the "diverse citizenship" clause, rather than to state court. And Scott's attorneys, having lost their case in the state supreme court, had nowhere else to go if they wanted to win his freedom.

35. Fehrenbacher (1978) 277.

36. Ibid. 300.

37. See Burt's treatment (1992) of Marshall's ruling concerning Native Americans in the case of *Johnson v. McIntosh*, in which Marshall argued that because the

usual rule about conflict, that it ultimately ends in grudging acceptance of a new political order, could not apply to Indian warfare because the United States could neither assimilate the Native Americans nor tolerate them as a separate jurisdiction, an *imperium in imperio*, therefore the only alternative was to deport them with the sword held continuously over their heads (161). Burt describes a similar hardening of attitudes about relations between white and black in the Jacksonian era, in which what he calls "softheaded Jeffersonianism" was gradually replaced by "hardhearted Jacksonianism," in which the racial ideology was one that posed the alternatives of ruthless subjugation or extermination. Burt also rightly (in my view) links this hardening of attitudes in both cases of racial conflict to the triumph of political democratization for the white lower classes and the collapse of an earlier "gentry" or noblesse oblige vision of politics.

38. Burt (1992) 122.

39. *Dred Scott v. Sandford*, 60 U.S. 393 (1857) 407.

40. The fact that the Constitution substituted "citizen" for "free inhabitants" does not mean that its authors meant to exclude blacks; in the Articles of Confederation, the two phrases were used as synonyms.

41. Fehrenbacher (1978) 363.

42. See for instance Douglas's Springfield speech of June 12, 1857.

43. Bickel (1962) 261.

44. Mansfield made this remark in *Omychund v. Barker*, 26 Eng. Rep. 15, 23 (Ch. 1744). The remarks was later made famous by Fuller's paraphrase, "The common law works itself pure and adapts itself to the needs of a new day." Cited in Fuller, *The Law in Quest of Itself* (1966) 140.

45. That legal culture evolves is no argument that precedent is meaningless. It is only proof that the upshot of precedents is capable of being reevaluated as circumstances bring new light upon the meaning of those precedents. The argument that justice evolves is not really inconsistent with "originalism," because what the meaning of an original intent is is something that has to be established by argument and by phronetic judgment. Furthermore, if Madison's testimony in the *Federalist* matters, rejecting originalism would be in line with the original intentions of the Founders, who understood very well that the meaning of their commitments would largely be something that future generations could see because only future exigencies would force them to clarify what the Founders had understood in implicit ways. On this last point, see Jack Rakove, *Original Meanings* (1996).

46. Jefferson's promises never described any actually existing legal order, only a legal order to be constantly aimed at, constantly aspired to, and constantly betrayed. Lincoln describes his aim as to restore Jeffersonian principles. But those principles themselves could come into focus only in a future shaped by evolution in their direction. They do not come into focus in any actual past filial piety may be bound to.

Even this formulation, with its air of teleological evolution, does not quite capture Lincoln's key argument. The problem is that the ultimate telos remains obscure, as each new birth of freedom opens yet another implicit entailment that the present betrays. Lincoln's thinking is teleological to the extent that he imagines the concept of democracy as unfolding, and to the extent that the next layer of implications becomes gradually clearer in the public mind. But it is not completely teleological, because the further ranges of implications of a key value always remain opaque, and even those who further the advancement of the telos usually act from mixed motives and in the dark about their own aims.

47. As we have seen, this distinction was described first by H. L. A. Hart in *The Concept of Law* (1961), but my development of the distinction owes a great deal to Ronald Dworkin's version in *Law's Empire* (1986). Like Dworkin, I am interested in the tension between the concept, the underlying moral insight behind a law, and the conception, the concrete workings-out in specific historical circumstances of the meaning of a concept. Unlike Dworkin, I see the concept as only capable of being known intuitively, and as always resisting fully explicit articulation; it is always the subject of what Michael Polanyi, in *Personal Knowledge* (1962), calls "tacit knowledge." Because I see the concept as always tacit, always partly betrayed by articulation, I see the concept as providing a way of reflecting on the moral meaning of legal experience, but not as providing an authoritative method of judicial review. The concept, like the Socratic daimon, continuously provokes unease with our settled legal doctrines; it enables the kind of critique of the existing order of things that Lincoln engages in in his own critique of the *Dred Scott* decision. But it does not enable one to produce a new law to take an old one's place that will be immune to the same kind of critique.

48. Lincoln's vision here somewhat resembles that developed by Hanna Fenichel Pitkin in *Wittgenstein and Justice* (1993), and, less formally, by Stanley Cavell in *The Claim of Reason* (1979).

49. Which is not to say, however, that principled commitments that derive from other things—religion, for instance—need have no say in a democracy. It is only to say that the adherents of those views will have to win public consent to have their way, and they cannot subvert the persuasive machinery of a democracy in order to do so. If they win, this is to say, they must win by persuading others by argument, and, having won, they are bound to the same restraints they would have asked for from their opponents had they lost.

50. Cited in Bickel (1962) 67.

51. Ibid. 68.

52. Hamilton, Madison, and Jay (1961) 229.

53. Ford's history (1854) 215 estimates that there were about 10,000 noncitizen voters in Illinois at that time, nine tenths of them Democratic. Ford, by the way, sided with Douglas in this argument. But of course he himself was also one of the judges appointed when the court was "overslaughed."

54. All this is from Johannsen (1973) 82–97.

55. This incident is discussed in Forbes (2007) 38–39. The consequence of this exchange, Forbes points out, is that from the Missouri debate onward, defenders of slavery either had to foreshorten the meaning of the Declaration or had to reject it entirely.

56. See Ross M. Lence's edition of Calhoun's writings, *Union and Liberty* (1992) (here referred to as Calhoun [1992]).

57. Ibid. 17.

58. Hofstadter (1948).

59. Calhoun (1992) 36.

60. Ibid. 42.

61. Ibid. 44–45.

62. Calhoun's attack upon the Declaration here is gratuitous, in the sense that it is not really required to make the political points he intended to advance in his speech. But he complains as well that the promises of the Declaration were equally gratuitous, in that those arguments were not required to justify the separation from England, since King George's violation of English political traditions of long standing would have sufficed to do that, and those arguments were also not required to reestablish a sovereign government on this side of the water, which were made mostly from "the old materials and on practical and well-established principles, borrowed for the most part from our own experience and that of the country from which we sprang." When Lincoln considers the promises of the Declaration, he likewise notices that they are gratuitous, but for him that gratuitousness is an index of their depth: Jefferson did not have to say such things to justify the independence of the United States, and he chose to say them, and to say them first, because they were of supreme importance, and he wanted to make sure that whenever the country he was establishing was tempted by tyranny, it would have to remember them.

63. Calhoun (1992) 565–566.

64. Ibid. 569.

65. Ibid. 570.

66. Cited in Fehrenbacher (1978) 456.

67. See Fehrenbacher (1962) 131.

68. See William W. Freehling's discussion of this dance in the second volume of *The Road to Disunion* (2007) 275–285.

69. Allen Guelzo, thinking about this passage, reflects that although Fehrenbacher's research has effectively debunked the claim that Lincoln trapped Douglas into making the Freeport Doctrine and losing the 1860 election, Lincoln still had a long-term aim beyond the 1858 election in asking the second Freeport question—not to prevent Douglas from winning the Democratic nomination, but to prevent him from winning the Republican nomination, by reminding voters of how flimsy a strategy popular sovereignty was.

70. Fehrenbacher makes this point in *Lincoln in Text and Context* (1987) 16.

71. Douglas (1961) 465.

72. The *Harper's* article will be examined in more detail in Chapter 8. Douglas's article set off a pamphlet war with Buchanan's attorney general, Jeremiah Black.

73. Note that I am not making an argument about whether or not slavery actually could have prospered in Kansas. I am making the argument that, given Douglas's belief that slavery would be economically weak in Kansas, his view that marginal legal hostility might turn the balance against it was plausible.

74. For the meaning of the distinction between Congress passing a federal slave code and the courts imposing one, see section 8.1 below.

75. This is Fehrenbacher's argument in *The Dred Scott Case* (1978).

76. Lincoln treats the Democrats here—and probably he really has Douglas himself in mind here, not just his supporters—as people who know, but do not acknowledge, that slavery is wrong. Their liminal status about slavery—they both know and do not know it is wrong, and they maintain their position only by laziness and cowardice—is not much different from Lincoln's own liminal status about racism itself.

8. Aftershocks of the Debates

1. See Guelzo (2008) 287. Douglas did particularly well, Guelzo notes, in the central Illinois "Whig Belt," the only region of the state where the two candidates were competitive, winning fourteen of the nineteen state representative districts and three of the five state senate districts that had gone for Fillmore, or for a combination of Fillmore and Frémont in 1856. On the gerrymandering charge, Wells (1990) notes that it was the Republicans, not the Democrats, who opposed reapportionment, and that Lyman Trumbull had beaten James Shields in 1855 under the old apportionment anyway (130).

2. Guelzo (2008) 285.

3. Ibid. 282.

4. Damon Wells argued that Douglas had widespread (if disorganized and halfhearted) support in the South even into 1859. He had conditional and short-lived backing from then-Unionists like Alexander Stephens and Henry Wise (who understood that the political position of the South in the Union was impossible to maintain without northern votes, which Douglas was in the most plausible position to provide), as well as tentative and harder-to-figure backing from harder-edged figures like David Atchison and James Henry Hammond. He also ran well with the German and Irish immigrant populations of St. Louis and New Orleans. Douglas had firmer support from moderate editors such as John Forsyth of the *Mobile Register*, which even defended him for opposing a federal slave code for the territories, which Forsyth called a "barren abstraction." But even Forsyth's loyalty was tentative and shallow, and could last only so long as Douglas was able to evade the tests that the fire-eaters and the Republicans continued to put to him (Wells [1990] 164–167).

5. Freehling (2007).

6. Freehling also sees the *Dred Scott* decision itself as a desperate appeasement of southern radicals, rather like Davis's move here, not an aggressive throwing down of the gauntlet by the slave power. I partly agree with this interpretation, but only about Justices Grier, Nelson, and Catron, not about Justices Daniel, Campbell, or Taney, and possibly not about Justice Wayne.

7. For this argument, see Freehling (2007) 275–281. One way to put this is to say that the secessionist radical William Lowndes Yancey, in accepting Davis's policy but treating it as a test of whether the North was willing to deliver the protection he understood it to have promised, was putting the same kind of pressure upon Davis's policy of pragmatic temporizing that Lincoln was putting upon Douglas's policy of pragmatic temporizing.

8. Johannsen (1973) 758.

9. The dark horse candidate Butler may have had in mind was the very pro-southern governor of New York, Horatio Seymour, although he cast his own ballots at Charleston for Jefferson Davis. (This is Johannsen's view [Johannsen (1973) 763].) Of all people, Jefferson Davis, according to his much-later memoirs, tried to persuade all the other anti-Republican candidates to drop out, so that a unified ticket could be put forward under Seymour. Davis says that Breckinridge and Bell were willing to drop out but that Douglas refused. Apparently the scheme involved throwing the election into the House of Representatives. Hearing of this plan, Douglas is said to have remarked, "By God, sir, the election shall

never go into the House; before it shall go into the House, I will throw it to Lincoln" (Morris [2008] 171).

10. Douglas's article is "The Dividing Line between Federal and Local Authority" (1859a). Buchanan's attorney general Jeremiah S. Black's reply is a pamphlet entitled *Observations on Senator Douglas's Views of Popular Sovereignty, as Expressed in Harpers' Magazine, for September, 1859* (1859). Both have been republished in *In the Name of the People: Speeches and Writings of Lincoln and Douglas in the Ohio Campaign of 1859* (1959), edited by Harry V. Jaffa and Robert W. Johannsen. Citations will be from this edition. Douglas's reply to Black at Wooster on September 16, 1859, is cited from the same volume. Further blasts from Douglas on this same subject are Douglas (1859c) and Douglas (1859d).

11. For the extent of Douglas's researches in the Library of Congress, see Johannsen (1973) 707.

12. Jaffa and Johannsen (1959) 58.

13. Ibid. 142.

14. Ibid. 63.

15. On this, see Robert Johannsen, *The Frontier, the Union, and Stephen A. Douglas* (1989) 130.

16. Jaffa and Johannsen (1959) 71.

17. Ibid. 100.

18. Ibid. 101–102.

19. Ibid. 102–103.

20. Ibid. 107.

21. Ibid. 121–122.

22. The text can be found in ibid. The *Constitution* replaced the *Union* as the administration organ as the fight began.

23. Ibid. 177.

24. Ibid. 179.

25. Ibid. 198.

26. For Congressman William Kellogg's effort, opposed by Lincoln, to construct a Republican version of popular sovereignty along these lines, see Johannsen (1973) 706.

27. For Johnson's view, see ibid. 711.

28. Jaffa and Johannsen (1959) 170–171.

29. For Douglas's claims about seeing 300 newly landed slaves in a pen in Vicksburg, and others in Memphis, see Johannsen (1973) 704–705.

30. For my reading of the controversy over the Toombs bill, see section 3.4 above.

31. Jaffa and Johannsen (1959) 213.

32. Ibid. 226–227.

33. I may seem here to be rather breezily ruling out a great many things that the philosophy of the twentieth century took for granted. But see my article "'Reason Also Is Choice': Reflection, Freedom, and the Euthyphro Problem" (2002).

34. Lincoln actually addressed this question during the secession crisis. He wrote to Seward on February 1, 1861, essentially reining in Seward's attempts to seek a sectional compromise that would, in Lincoln's view, surrender the very issue upon which he had just been elected, slavery in the territories. He did, how-

ever, give Seward leeway on issues about fugitive slaves and the District of Columbia, and was willing to bend about New Mexico, if further extensions of slavery were hedged against (2:197–198). New Mexico repealed its slave code in December 1861, and Congress abolished slavery in the territories in June 1862, freeing fifteen slaves in Nebraska and twenty-nine in Utah (Foner [2010] 204).

35. Jaffa and Johannsen (1959) 143.

36. Briggs (2005) 254.

37. For a detailed and illuminating analysis of the historical background of the speech, the context of Lincoln's giving it, and its role in Lincoln's coming into national prominence, see Harold Holzer, *Lincoln at Cooper Union* (2004).

38. Holzer (2004) 155.

39. About this, see Briggs (2005) 244. For Lincoln's fudging about who exactly counts as a Founder, see David Hirsch and Dan Van Haften, *Lincoln and the Structure of Reason* (2010).

40. For the difference made by narrowing the evidence to the actual votes taken by the thirty-nine, excluding their public statements on these subjects, see Briggs (2005) 245. Briggs points out that Lincoln also excludes the opinions of those delegates who refused to sign the Constitution and omits any consideration of what was said about the document by the ratifying conventions in the states (246). Lincoln also includes votes in untallied resolutions as if they were unanimous, and includes votes to introduce slavery into territories as confirmations of the idea of federal control over slavery in the territory, since even a positive vote implies that the federal government has a say. Both, Briggs remarks, are fishy arguments, the first because an untallied vote may simply have been so lopsided that the opposition did not feel it worthwhile to call for yeas and nays, the second because politicians are not bound to vote in every way consonant with their ideologies, but only in that way that serves the interest of their ideology—for instance, many who supported the joint sovereignty theory about slavery in the territories voted to extend the Missouri Compromise line, because it was the most available pro-slavery option before them in the vote at hand, although in theory they should have voted against it. The quantitative evidence, this is to say, is considerably less strong than Lincoln portrays it as being, and what holds the speech together more than its quantitative evidence is its general sense that the Founders opposed slavery even as they found themselves unable to eradicate it.

41. Note that the language refers to persons, not just to citizens, a nuance Taney always ignores since it would show that the Founders did after all think of black people as humans.

42. It is all to the good that Lincoln did not press the claim that the idea that the government could not prohibit slavery in the territories was unheard of until 1850. Calhoun had begun making his joint property case in the 1830s. But the point still stands that the Founders had no such notion.

43. Briggs (2005) 240.

44. C. Vann Woodward has a powerful essay on contemporary reactions to John Brown's raid in *The Burden of Southern History* (1960).

45. Freehling (2007) 10.

46. See ibid. 254.

47. As Briggs (2005) puts it with characteristic acuity:

The point is to forbear, even though (and because) the dispute cannot be re-solved by compromise. The Republicans will proceed with even temper in the face of severe disagreement. They will concede as much as possible with-out giving up claims that must, if necessary, be maintained in the face of war. Lincoln's appeal for peace does not make peace its highest aim. (254)

48. See Gilmore (2006).

49. Wilson (1874) 606.

50. Johannsen treats this incident as being about political point-scoring rather than about making legal threats (see Johannsen [1973] 723–729). Johannsen also notes a curious circumstance in Douglas's offering of the bill. Virginia's governor Wise had feared a conspiracy to rescue John Brown, and had appealed to Buchanan for federal troops to repel this would-be insurrection. Buchanan argued that he did not have the constitutional authority to put down insurrections within states—a position rather close to that he took during the secession crisis. Douglas intended his bill to empower the federal government to put down insurrections in the states, a power the government was very shortly to have great need of. If Douglas thought his bill was going to win him friends in the South, he should have thought again. In the very midst of the debate, a slanging match erupted between Douglas and Alfred Iverson, who denounced Douglas's popular sovereignty as the Wilmot Proviso in disguise, setting off a donnybrook that eventually involved Clement Clay of Alabama, Albert Gallatin Brown of Mississippi, and Jefferson Davis as well, who pushed competing versions of the federal slave code in Congress.

51. Holzer also develops a preliminary version of his argument in his earlier *Lincoln Seen and Heard* (2000). See also William C. Harris, *Lincoln's Rise to the Presidency* (2007), for a fresh view of the subject, also sympathetic to Lincoln's course during the secession winter.

52. Freehling (2007) 471. None of these proposals were ultimately part of Crittenden's plan.

53. Holzer (2008) 428.

54. Ibid. 438.

55. Browning's practical advice was good also: "In any conflict which may ensue between the government and the seceding States, it is very important that the traitors shall be the aggressors, and that they be kept constantly and palpably in the wrong" (ibid. 346).

56. Ibid. 439.

57. Ibid. 270. The evolution of the final paragraph is actually rather compli-cated. After receiving, during his inaugural journey, the letter from Browning in which he argued for changing the language about the forts, Lincoln sketched on the back of its third page, "Americans, all, we are not enemies, but friends—We have sacred ties of affection which, though strained by passions, let us hope can never be broken." Apparently Seward fleshed out, after a conversation with Lincoln, the ideas in this passage to produce his famous draft conclusion, which Lincoln then rewrote yet another time (see ibid. 346). Ronald C. White provides another detailed analysis of the differences between the draft and the final version in his *The Eloquent President* (2005). Seward's contributions included far more than this paragraph. Seward pressed Lincoln about the passage about reclaiming the seized forts, arguing that that passage alone might move Maryland and Virginia to

secede. Douglas Wilson captures a subtle but particularly pointed example of Seward's revisions. Lincoln had written "A disruption of the Federal Union is menaced, and, so far as can be on paper, is already effected." This sentence, Wilson argues, had a sardonic edge, treating secession essentially as a "paper rebellion." Seward's revision, although a touch high-flown, was less antagonistic: "A disruption of the Federal Union heretofore only menaced is now formidably attempted." See Wilson (2006) 61. All told, Seward suggested forty-nine changes, of which Lincoln adopted twenty-seven, almost all of them making the language of the speech less confrontational. (About this, see White [2005] 69; Fehrenbacher [1987] 285.)

58. Harris (2007) 255.

59. Freehling (2007).

60. Actually, it was rather worse than imprisonment. The captains of ships with black seamen were fined, and if the captains did not pay the fine, the seamen would be enslaved. When in 1844 Massachusetts sent Samuel Hoar as a commissioner to South Carolina to challenge this treatment of citizens of Massachusetts by South Carolina in federal court, South Carolina governor James Henry Hammond, armed with a resolution from the state legislature, expelled him from the state, and Hoar wound up having to flee the threat of mob violence.

61. For Spooner's views and related views by others, see Cover (1975) 56. See also Sewell (1976) 95.

62. This distinction is developed at length by Harry Jaffa in *A New Birth of Freedom* (2000).

63. The distinction between "insurrectionary" and "revolutionary" is opaque. It might be the distinction between resisting the agents of the United States by force, as in the Whiskey Rebellion, and attempting to set up an alternative government, as in the Dorr Rebellion.

64. See Holzer (2008) 440. See also Wilson (2006) 55.

65. There is a detailed account of the back-and-forth between Lincoln and Seward on this subject in William Lee Miller's *President Lincoln: The Duty of a Statesman* (2008) 55. See also 72–90.

66. Miller (2008), with his usual clarity and common sense, brushes aside volumes of pro-Confederate casuistry on this point.

67. These southern Republicans had played a crucial role at the 1860 Republican Convention in securing the nomination for Lincoln. Lincoln bragged afterward that he received more support from the southern element of his party than Douglas did from the southern element of his. So Lincoln owed Republicans like John Minor Botts and Cassius M. Clay something, and usually presidents repay that kind of debt with patronage.

68. Would language putting abolition beyond even the power of a constitutional amendment have sufficed? I do not think so. The Deep South was very afraid of being "bottled up" in a shrinking region of the Union with its slaves. The amendment would also have had to include language forbidding existing slave states from abolishing slavery, thus making sure that Delaware, Maryland, Kentucky, and Missouri would continue to stay in line.

69. Holzer (2008) 444.

70. White (2005) 90–91.

71. Again Briggs's formulation is pointed: "He wants to continue for the sake of peace, but he lets it be known he must stop" ([2005] 301).

72. Goodwin (2005) 326. Lucas Morel (2000) notes that the change shifts the focus from a hoped-for divine intervention to a reconsideration completely within the sphere of human agency (65).

73. A statue originally designed to be Freedom herself wearing a Liberty cap was transformed into an Indian maiden wearing a feathered headdress at the insistence of Jefferson Davis, who understood that liberty caps were worn in the classical world by emancipated slaves. That obscene evasion, which reminds the world that slaveholders were able to force the Republic to pervert the most basic of its values, still stands atop the U.S. Capitol.

74. Both citations are from White (2005) 94.

75. Ibid. 95.

76. Ibid.

9. *Coda*

1. Burlingame (2008b) points out that Galusha Grow delivered a widely read speech in Congress on July 4, 1861, which opened with "Fourscore years ago fifty-six bold merchants, farmers, lawyers, and mechanics, the representatives of a few feeble colonists, scattered along the Atlantic seaboard, met in convention to found a new empire, based on the inalienable rights of man" (570). Like Garry Wills (1992), Burlingame also connects the famous tricolon at the end of the speech to Webster's 1830 second reply to Hayne, in which Webster, apropos of the nullification crisis, speaks of "the people's government, made for the people, made by the people, and answerable to the people." Also like Wills, Burlingame alludes to two sermons by Theodore Parker, which Lincoln could have been familiar with through William Herndon's extensive correspondence with Parker; Parker's versions said that democracy is "government of all, by all, for all," and "Democracy is Direct: Self-Government, over all the people, for all the people, by all the people." See also Wills (1992) 107. For the citation to Psalm 90, see White (2005) 243.

2. Burlingame (2008b) 577.

3. Closer to our own day, the organic metaphor has also been noticed by the poet Robert Lowell, who discerned in the speech a "curious, insistent use of birth images: 'brought forth,' 'conceived,' 'created,' and finally 'a new birth of freedom'" (Wills [1992] 62, citing *Lincoln and the Gettysburg Address*, ed. Allan Nevins [Urbana: University of Illinois Press, 1964] 88).

4. Briggs (2005) puts this in a characteristically striking way: "[The Founders] 'brought forth' the new nation on that day; they did not author it. As fathers they were founders, but the sense of that founding is in its specific character obscure. They assisted in the nation's birth but did not create it" (306).

5. Foner (2010) 268.

6. On this see Farber (2003) and Neely (1991).

7. I read the meaning of the Gettysburg Address, this is to say, with Wills and Fletcher. But I read his concrete policies as Allen Guelzo does in *Lincoln's Emancipation Proclamation* (2004). The distinction between concept and conception reconciles the apparent contradiction.

8. Basler (1973) also notes that Lincoln compares the Civil War to a nearly fatal childhood disease (56).

9. Guelzo (1999) notices also that a "proposition" is not quite the same thing as "a self-evident truth." The difference may be more rhetorical than logical, since nothing that one has to *proclaim* to be a self-evident truth can really be one, for only tautologies and truisms, and certainly nothing so charged with argumentative élan as Jefferson's self-evident truths, really do go without saying. Proclaiming that something is a self-evident truth has the same ontological uncertainty that treating it as a proposition to be tested does, but it is less frank about that uncertainty.

10. Einhorn (1992) notes also that "endure" has a religious resonance that "continue" would not have had (99).

11. For this detail, see Wills (1992) 76.

12. Sadly, the Fehrenbachers have shown that Lincoln probably never did refer to Harriet Beecher Stowe as "the little woman who made this great war." See Fehrenbacher and Fehrenbacher (1996) l.

13. For the rural cemetery movement, see Wills (1992) chapter 2. For how Civil War–era Americans faced the violation of their norms about deathways brought by the war, see Faust (2008).

14. The language here is awkward, since it seems to imply that people already have fully formed individual identities and then add a social one. But of course we find our identities partly in terms of social relationships that precede us. And some of those social relations depend upon collective fictions. The question remains what those fictions are and what kinds of fiction are capable of serving the purpose. Can a fiction about inalienable human rights, for instance, serve the same purpose that a fiction about blood, language, or culture serves?

15. Britain and Canada, by contrast, have been becoming nations, not just states, one can join.

16. See section 7.3 above for a discussion of this speech.

17. See Sollors (1986).

18. See Fletcher (2001) and Warren (1961).

19. See Berlin (1969).

20. Fletcher has in mind here the political values of the Reconstruction era. These values were subverted after 1876, and it was precisely the use of contract theory and, in particular, the theory of "substantive due process," as the entering wedge of "negative liberty" in the legal culture that produced the *Slaughterhouse* and *Lochner* cases, that did the subverting. If, as James McPherson calls it, the American Civil War was a second American Revolution, the Compromise of 1877 was not only that revolution's Thermidorean reaction, but the ushering in of three quarters of a century of counterrevolution.

21. This aspect of the classical republican tradition was rather underplayed in the current revival of enthusiasm for classical politics, although Arendt understands it in *The Human Condition* (1958). Before the nineteenth century, freedom for some was always only made possible by bondage for others. In America, this point is most trenchantly made by Edmund Morgan in *American Slavery, American Freedom* (1975). Morgan's insight into how only slavery freed the poor white from his dependency upon the rich white and freed the rich white from the poor white's resentment, making possible a republican political culture among white people, has been persuasively generalized to other cases of interdependence between slavery and freedom, most of them not especially

involving race, by Orlando Patterson in *Freedom in the Making of Western Culture* (1991).

22. The text is available in Drew Faust's *The Ideology of Slavery* (1981). See also her biography of Hammond, *James Henry Hammond and the Old South* (1982). One might add dozens of such figures. The most commonly cited, however, George Fitzhugh, seems, as Eugene Genovese argued long ago, a special case.

23. See White (2005) 245, citing Louis A. Warren, *Lincoln's Gettysburg Declaration: "A New Birth of Freedom"* (Fort Wayne, IN: Lincoln National Life Foundation, 1964) 418. Robert Penn Warren once suggested that the clash in diction register here had something of the tang and eloquence of Donne, whose diction, no less than his metaphors, delighted in yoking disparate things by violence together. Indeed, the contrastive snapping back and forth between concrete, blunt Anglo-Saxon diction and abstract, distanced Latinate diction is often a self-conscious feature of prose in English from Shakespeare to Lincoln.

24. Wills (1992).

25. Willmoore Kendall, and following him, Robert Bork, famously took exception to how Lincoln here put the Declaration over the Constitution, "to wrench from it a single proposition and make that our supreme commitment" (Wills [1992] 146, citing Willmoore Kendall, *The Basic Symbols of the American Political Tradition* [Baton Rouge: Louisiana State University Press, 1970] 91).

26. Boritt (2006) argues that the opening sentence treats emancipation as the main aim of the war. But my reading differs from his in one nuance. Boritt argues that by quoting the Declaration, Lincoln had left the point about defending the Emancipation Proclamation unstated, which Lincoln could safely do because he knew that other speakers—Seward and Everett not least—would make the point as explicitly as necessary. My view is that in having the argument turn explicitly upon equality—if not on racial equality in so many words—Lincoln raises the stakes beyond mere emancipation, although he leaves it mysterious just how far he intended to go.

27. Most treatments of reaction to the Gettysburg Address cite this passage. This version is from Burlingame (2008b) 576–577. Burlingame cites many similar arguments from other Democratic newspapers around the North. Douglas Wilson captures something of the daring of Lincoln's formulation in this opening sentence. See Wilson (2006) 233.

28. In a way it is death that gives the dead their ontological gravity. It is not just that death has sealed them with the mark of sacrifice but also that death has made clear what the meaning of the sacrifice was, what it was the dead sacrificed themselves for. The living soldiers, like other living people, may have thought about the meaning of the war in mistaken ways. Death clears all contingencies from the dead, so that they fully make real the implicit things actual living people, even their living selves, only glimpse indirectly.

29. See White (2005) 251 and especially Boritt (2006) for a painstaking comparison of the holographs, and the newspaper transcripts, of the speech.

30. Richard Weaver famously argued that Lincoln gives the impression that the speaker is not he, but the voice of mankind, and that from that perspective the Civil War is only a passing thing. See also Einhorn (1992) 26 and White (2005) 255.

31. The anecdote is treated in William J. Wolf, *The Almost Chosen People* (1959). Wolf is quoting from Robert B. Warden, *An Account of the Private Life and*

Public Services of Salmon Portland Chase (Cincinnati: Wilstach, Baldwin, 1874) 481–482.

32. Wolf (1959) 19.

33. Lincoln (1953) 5:478.

34. Niebuhr (1965). See also Niebuhr (1932) and, most especially, Niebuhr (1952).

35. One of the things that moved Karl Barth to declare the absolute unknowability of God's will was his revulsion against the pious appropriation of the divine will by propagandists during World War I. The revulsion that yielded *The Epistle to the Romans* (1918) is akin to that Lincoln registers in the Second Inaugural, and has some related political consequences.

36. Lincoln (1953) 6:332–333.

37. Ibid.

38. That said, the dark poem at the end of Emerson's essay "Fate," in which we are asked to build altars to that beautiful necessity by which we are crushed, and in which the purpose of fate is to teach a fatal courage, a courage more authentic as it becomes more hopeless, comes close to Lincoln's sense of how history works.

39. For an analysis of the way Lincoln reads himself out of the first paragraph, see Hansen (2004).

40. White (2002) notes that Lincoln did not say "While I was delivering the Inaugural Address," but "While the inaugeral address was being delivered from this place." Lincoln did not exactly erase his own agency from the scene, but he put it in the background, since the moment of witnessing in the Second Inaugural matters more than the moment of agency in the First, since everyone's agency at that time was completely entangled in illusion.

41. Briggs (2005) notes that Lincoln always refers to the conflict as taking place between "parties," not between "sections," or "states." Support for and hostility to slavery, this is to say, had sectional centers of gravity, but the distinction does not cleanly divide the sections. The struggle is internal to the Union.

42. Later, Campbell was amnestied, and played a truly disgraceful political role, persuading the very Supreme Court he had treasonably betrayed to nullify all of the civil rights ambitions of Reconstruction. Campbell won back at the Supreme Court much of what the Confederacy had lost on the battlefield.

43. Briggs (2005) describes this with his usual pungency, finding in this passage "an almost inhuman distancing of the speaker from the few immediate facts he is citing" (316) and noting that Lincoln invests the war itself with a force "undeniable and obscure" (321).

44. Ibid. 319.

45. White (2002) 90.

46. Briggs (2005) notes that the "already" in "Neither party expected for the war, the magnitude, or the duration, which it has already attained" leaves open the possibility that the war may yet reach another unanticipated crescendo of violence (321).

47. Miller (2008) wisely says of Lincoln's remark that "This sentence, one would think, should never be used as defense, attack, or riposte but only as confession or self-criticism" (405).

48. Ahlstrom (1972) points out that other American theologians saw the war as Lincoln did. While Henry Ward Beecher saw the Union as wielding the hammer

of justice over the head of the slaveholder, who would have to atone not only for slavery but also for all of the deaths of the war, others, such as the Congregational theologian Horace Bushnell, himself writing during the weeks Lincoln was meditating the Second Inaugural Address, saw the war as an expiation of the sin of slavery by both North and South, an expiation that might make way at once for atonement and reconciliation. And the great Lutheran theologian Philip Schaff too not only saw mutual complicity and mutual expiation in the war but also saw the war as the condition of a redeemed sense of nationhood and a transformed sense of the meaning of freedom (684–685).

Works Cited

Ackerman, Bruce. *We the People*. Vol. 1: *Foundations*. Cambridge, MA: Belknap Press of Harvard University Press, 1991.

———. *We the People*. Vol. 2: *Transformations*. Cambridge, MA: Belknap Press of Harvard University Press, 1998.

Adams, Henry. *The Education of Henry Adams*. New York: Houghton Mifflin, 1918.

Ahlstrom, Sydney E. *A Religious History of the American People*. New Haven, CT: Yale University Press, 1972.

Amar, Akhil Reed. *America's Constitution: A Biography*. New York: Random House, 2005.

Anbinder, Tyler. *Nativism and Slavery: The Northern Know Nothings and the Politics of the 1850's*. New York: Oxford University Press, 1992.

Anderson, Benedict. *Imagined Communities: Reflections on the Origin and Spread of Nationalism*. New York: Verso, 1983.

Appleby, Joyce. *Liberalism and Republicanism in the Historical Imagination*. Cambridge, MA: Harvard University Press, 1992.

Arendt, Hannah. *The Human Condition*. Chicago: University of Chicago Press, 1958.

———. *On Revolution*. Harmondsworth: Penguin Books, 1962.

———. *The Origins of Totalitarianism*. Rev. ed. New York: Harcourt, Brace and World, 1967 (orig. 1951).

———. *Between Past and Future*. Enlarged ed. Harmondsworth: Penguin Books, 1968 (orig. 1961).

———. *The Life of the Mind*. New York: Harcourt Brace Jovanovich, 1978.

———. *Lectures on Kant's Political Philosophy*. Ed. Ronald Beiner. Chicago: University of Chicago Press, 1982.

Bailyn, Bernard. *The Ideological Origins of the American Revolution*. Cambridge, MA: Belknap Press of Harvard University Press, 1967.

Baker, Jean H. *Affairs of Party: The Political Culture of Northern Democrats in the Mid-Nineteenth Century*. Ithaca, NY: Cornell University Press, 1983.

————. *James Buchanan.* New York: Henry Holt and Company, 2004.

Banning, Lance. *The Jeffersonian Persuasion: Evolution of a Party Ideology.* Ithaca, NY: Cornell University Press, 1978.

Barth, Karl. *The Epistle to the Romans.* Trans. from the 6th ed. by Edwin C. Hoskyns. Oxford: Oxford University Press, 1933 (orig. 1918).

Basler, Roy P., ed. *A Touchstone for Greatness: Essays, Addresses, and Occasional Pieces about Abraham Lincoln.* Westport, CT: Greenwood Press, 1973.

Bauer, K. Jack. *Zachary Taylor: Soldier, Planter, Statesman of the Old Southwest.* Baton Rouge: Louisiana State University Press, 1985.

Becker, Carl. *The Declaration of Independence: A Study in the History of Political Ideas.* New York: Random House, 1942.

Beer, Samuel H. *To Make a Nation: The Rediscovery of American Federalism.* Cambridge, MA: Belknap Press of Harvard University Press, 1993.

Benhabib, Seyla. *The Reluctant Modernism of Hannah Arendt.* Thousand Oaks, CA: Sage Publications, 1996.

Bennett, Lerone, Jr. *Forced into Glory: Abraham Lincoln's White Dream.* Chicago: Johnson Publishing Company, 2000.

Bercovitch, Sacvan, ed. *Reconstructing American Literary History.* Cambridge, MA: Harvard University Press, 1986.

Berlin, Isaiah. *Four Essays on Liberty.* Oxford: Oxford University Press, 1969.

Berwanger, Eugene H. *The Frontier against Slavery: Western Anti-Negro Prejudice and the Slavery Extension Controversy.* Urbana: University of Illinois Press, 1967.

Bickel, Alexander M. *The Least Dangerous Branch: The Supreme Court at the Bar of Politics.* New Haven, CT: Yale University Press, 1962.

Black, Jeremiah S. *Observations on Senator Douglas's Views of Popular Sovereignty, as Expressed in Harpers' Magazine, for September, 1859.* Washington, DC: Thomas McGill, 1859.

Blaine, James Gillespie. *Twenty years of Congress: From Lincoln to Garfield. With a review of the events which led to the political revolution of 1860.* Norwich, CT: Henry Bill Publishing Company, 1884.

Bleser, Carol. *Secret and Sacred: The Diaries of James Henry Hammond, a Southern Slaveholder.* Columbia: University of South Carolina Press, 1989.

Blight, David W. *Race and Reunion: The Civil War in American Memory.* Cambridge, MA: Belknap Press of Harvard University Press, 2001.

Bond, Bradley G. *Political Culture in the Nineteenth-Century South: Mississippi, 1830–1890.* Baton Rouge: Louisiana State University Press, 1995.

Bordewich, Fergus M. *America's Great Debate: Henry Clay, Stephen A. Douglas, and the Compromise that Preserved the Union.* New York: Simon and Schuster, 2012.

Boritt, Gabor, ed. *The Lincoln Enigma: The Changing Faces of an American Icon.* Oxford: Oxford University Press, 2001.

————. *The Gettysburg Gospel: The Lincoln Speech That Nobody Knows.* New York: Simon and Schuster, 2006.

Briggs, John Channing. *Lincoln's Speeches Reconsidered.* Baltimore: Johns Hopkins University Press, 2005.

Burke, Edmund. *Reflections on the revolution in France, and on the proceedings in certain societies in London relative to that event. In a letter intended to have been sent to a gentleman in Paris.* London: J. Dodsley, 1790.

Burlingame, Anson. *Oration, by Hon. Anson Burlingame: Delivered at Salem, July 4, 1854*. Salem, MA: Printed at the Gazette Office, 1854.

Burlingame, Michael. *The Inner World of Abraham Lincoln*. Urbana: University of Illinois Press, 1994.

———. *Abraham Lincoln: A Life*. Vol. 1. Baltimore: Johns Hopkins University Press, 2008a.

———. *Abraham Lincoln: A Life*. Vol. 2. Baltimore: Johns Hopkins University Press, 2008b.

Burt, John. "John Rawls and the Moral Vocation of Liberalism." *Raritan* 14 (1994): 133–153.

———. "Lincoln's Address to the Young Men's Lyceum: A Speculative Essay." *Western Humanities Review* 51 (1997): 304–320.

———. "'Reason Also Is Choice': Reflection, Freedom, and the Euthyphro Problem." In Jennifer Lewin, ed., *Never Again Would Birds' Song Be the Same: New Essays on Poetry and Poetics, Renaissance to Modern*. Hanover, NH: University Press of New England, 2002, 147–189.

———. "Lincoln, Calhoun, and Cultural Politics." *Raritan* 23 (2004): 142–161.

Burt, Robert A. *The Constitution in Conflict*. Cambridge, MA: Belknap Press of Harvard University Press, 1992.

Burton, Orville Vernon. *The Age of Lincoln*. New York: Hill and Wang, 2007.

Bushnell, Horace. *Views of Christian Nurture, and of Subjects Adjacent Thereto*. Hartford: E. Hunt, 1847.

Calhoun, John C. *Union and Liberty: The Political Philosophy of John C. Calhoun*. Ed. Ross M. Lence. Indianapolis: Liberty Fund, 1992.

Campbell, Stanley W. *The Slave Catchers: Enforcement of the Fugitive Slave Law, 1850–1860*. Chapel Hill: University of North Carolina Press, 1970.

Canovan, Margaret. *Hannah Arendt: A Reinterpretation of Her Political Thought*. Cambridge: Cambridge University Press, 1992.

Capers, Gerald M. *Stephen A. Douglas: Defender of the Union*. Boston: Little, Brown, 1959.

Carnahan, Burrus M. *Act of Justice: Lincoln's Emancipation Proclamation and the Law of War*. Lexington: University Press of Kentucky, 2007.

Carwardine, Richard. *Lincoln: A Life of Purpose and Power*. New York: Alfred A. Knopf, 2006.

Cavell, Stanley. *The Claim of Reason: Wittgenstein, Skepticism, Morality, and Tragedy*. New York: Oxford University Press, 1979.

———. *Conditions Handsome and Unhandsome: The Constitution of Emersonian Perfectionism*. Chicago: University of Chicago Press, 1990.

Chambers, William Nisbet, and Walter Dean Burnham, eds. *The American Party Systems: Stages of Political Development*. New York: Oxford University Press, 1967.

Chroust, Anton-Hermann. "Abraham Lincoln Argues a Pro-Slavery Case." *American Journal of Legal History* 5, no. 4 (October 1961): 299–308.

Cleveland, Henry. *Alexander H. Stephens, in Public and Private: With Letters and Speeches, before, during, and since the War*. Philadelphia: National Publishing Company, 1866.

Cooper, William J., Jr. *The South and the Politics of Slavery, 1828–1856*. Baton Rouge: Louisiana State University Press, 1978.

———. *Liberty and Slavery: Southern Politics to 1860.* New York: Alfred A. Knopf, 1983.

Cover, Robert M. *Justice Accused: Antislavery and the Judicial Process.* New Haven, CT: Yale University Press, 1975.

Cox, LaWanda. *Lincoln and Black Freedom: A Study in Presidential Leadership.* Columbia: University of South Carolina Press, 1981.

Craven, Avery O. *The Growth of Southern Nationalism, 1848–1861.* Baton Rouge: Louisiana State University Press, 1953.

Current, Richard N. *The Lincoln Nobody Knows.* New York: Hill and Wang, 1968 (orig. 1958).

Cushman, Stephen. *Bloody Promenade: Reflections on a Civil War Battle.* Charlottesville: University of Virginia Press, 2001.

Davidson, Donald. *Essays on Actions and Events.* Oxford: Oxford University Press, 1980.

Davis, David Brion. *The Slave Power Conspiracy and the Paranoid Style.* Baton Rouge: Louisiana State University Press, 1969.

———. *The Problem of Slavery in the Age of Revolution.* Ithaca, NY: Cornell University Press, 1975.

———. *Challenging the Boundaries of Slavery.* Cambridge, MA: Harvard University Press, 2003.

———. *Inhuman Bondage: The Rise and Fall of Slavery in the New World.* Oxford: Oxford University Press, 2006.

d'Entrèves, Maurizio Passerin. *The Political Philosophy of Hannah Arendt.* New York: Routledge, 1994.

Dickens, Charles. *A Child's History of England.* New York: T. Y. Crowell, 1911 (orig. 1854).

Diggins, John Patrick. *The Lost Soul of American Politics: Virtue, Self-Interest, and the Foundations of Liberalism.* New York: Basic Books, 1984.

———. *The Promise of Pragmatism: Modernism and the Crisis of Knowledge and Authority.* Chicago: University of Chicago Press, 1994.

Donald, David Herbert. *Lincoln.* New York: Simon and Schuster, 1995.

Douglas, Stephen A. *Speech of Hon. S. A. Douglas, of Illinois, in the Senate, January 30, 1854, on the Nebraska Territory.* Washington, DC: The Sentinel Office, 1854a.

———. *Speech of Hon. S. A. Douglas, of Illinois, in the United States Senate, March 3, 1854, on Nebraska and Kansas.* Washington, DC: The Sentinel Office, 1854b.

———. *Remarks of the Honorable Stephen A. Douglas on Kansas, Utah and the Dred Scott Decision, Delivered at Springfield Illinois on June 12, 1857.* Chicago: Daily Times Book and Job Office, 1857.

———. *Speech of Senator Douglas against the Lecompton Constitution, March 22, 1858.* Washington, DC: Lemuel Towers, 1858.

———. "The Dividing Line between Federal and Local Authority: Popular Sovereignty in the Territories." *Harper's New Monthly Magazine* 19 (1859a): 519–537.

———. *Letter of Judge Douglas in Reply to the Speech of Dr. Gwin at Grass Valley, California.* Reprinted from the *San Francisco Daily National,* September 16, 1859. San Francisco: Daily National, 1859b.

———. *Popular Sovereignty in the Territories: Judge Douglas in Reply to Judge Black.* Washington, DC: n.p., 1859c.

———. *Popular Sovereignty in the Territories: Rejoinder of Judge Douglas to Judge Black*. Washington, DC: n.p., 1859d.

———. "Speech Delivered at Bloomington, Ill., by Senator S. A. Douglas, July 16, 1858." In *Complete Works of Abraham Lincoln*. Vol. 3. Ed. John G. Nicolay and John Hay. New York: Francis D. Tandy Company, 1894, 54–107.

———. *The Letters of Stephen A. Douglas*. Ed. Robert W. Johannsen. Urbana: University of Illinois Press, 1961.

Dreben, Burton. "On Rawls and Political Liberalism." In Samuel Freeman, ed., *The Cambridge Companion to Rawls*. Cambridge: Cambridge University Press, 2003, 316–346.

Dworkin, Ronald. *Law's Empire*. Cambridge, MA: Belknap Press of Harvard University Press, 1986.

Eaton, Clement. *The Freedom-of-Thought Struggle in the Old South*. New York: Harper and Row, 1964.

Einhorn, Lois J. *Abraham Lincoln the Orator: Penetrating the Lincoln Legend*. Westport, CT: Greenwood Press, 1992.

Ellis, Richard J. *American Political Cultures*. New York: Oxford University Press, 1993.

Epstein, David F. *The Political Theory of* The Federalist. Chicago: University of Chicago Press, 1984.

Ericson, David F. *The Shaping of American Liberalism: The Debates over Ratification, Nullification, and Slavery*. Chicago: University of Chicago Press, 1993.

———. *The Debate over Slavery: Antislavery and Proslavery Liberalism in Antebellum America*. New York: New York University Press, 2000.

Etcheson, Nicole. *Bleeding Kansas: Contested Liberty in the Civil War Era*. Lawrence: University Press of Kansas, 2004.

Farber, Daniel. *Lincoln's Constitution*. Chicago: University of Chicago Press, 2003.

Faust, Drew Gilpin. *The Ideology of Slavery: Proslavery Thought in the Antebellum South, 1830–1860*. Baton Rouge: Louisiana State University Press, 1981.

———. *James Henry Hammond and the Old South: A Design for Mastery*. Baton Rouge: Louisiana State University Press, 1982.

———. *The Creation of Confederate Nationalism: Ideology and Identity in the Civil War South*. Baton Rouge: Louisiana State University Press, 1988.

———. *This Republic of Suffering: Death and the American Civil War*. New York: Alfred A. Knopf, 2008.

Fehrenbacher, Don E. "The Origins and Purpose of Lincoln's 'House Divided' Speech." *Mississippi Valley Historical Review* 46 (1960): 615–643.

———. *Prelude to Greatness: Lincoln in the 1850's*. Stanford, CA: Stanford University Press, 1962.

———. *The Dred Scott Case: Its Significance in American Law and Politics*. New York: Oxford University Press, 1978.

———. *The South and Three Sectional Crises*. Baton Rouge: Louisiana State University Press, 1980.

———. *Slavery, Law, and Politics: The Dred Scott Case in Historical Perspective*. New York: Oxford University Press, 1981.

———. *Lincoln in Text and Context: Collected Essays*. Stanford, CA: Stanford University Press, 1987.

————. *The Slaveholding Republic: An Account of the United States Government's Relations to Slavery.* Completed and edited by Ward M. McAfee. Oxford: Oxford University Press, 2001.

Fehrenbacher, Don E., and Virginia Fehrenbacher. *Recollected Words of Abraham Lincoln.* Stanford, CA: Stanford University Press, 1996.

Ferguson, Robert. "'We Hold These Truths': Strategies of Control in the Literature of the Founders." In Sacvan Bercovitch, ed., *Reconstructing American Literary History.* Cambridge, MA: Belknap Press of Harvard University Press, 1986, 1–28.

Filler, Louis. *Crusade against Slavery: Friends, Foes, and Reforms, 1820–1860.* Rev. ed. Algonac, MI: Reference Publications, 1986 (orig. 1960).

Finkelman, Paul. *An Imperfect Union: Slavery, Federalism, and Comity.* Chapel Hill: University of North Carolina Press, 1981.

Fisher, George Park. *Life of Benjamin Silliman, M.D., LL.D, Late Professor of Chemistry, Mineralogy, and Geology in Yale College.* Vol. 2. New York: C. Scribner, 1866.

Fletcher, George P. *Our Secret Constitution: How Lincoln Redefined American Democracy.* Oxford: Oxford University Press, 2001.

Fliegelman, Jay. *Declaring Independence: Jefferson, Natural Language, and the Culture of Performance.* Stanford, CA: Stanford University Press, 1993.

Fogel, Robert William, and Stanley L. Engerman. *Time on the Cross: The Economics of American Negro Slavery.* Boston: Little, Brown, 1974.

Foner, Eric. *Free Soil, Free Labor, Free Men: The Ideology of the Republican Party before the Civil War.* New York: Oxford University Press, 1977 (orig. 1970).

————. *Politics and Ideology in the Age of the Civil War.* New York: Oxford University Press, 1980.

————. *Nothing but Freedom: Emancipation and Its Legacy.* Baton Rouge: Louisiana State University Press, 1983.

————. *Reconstruction: America's Unfinished Revolution, 1863–1877.* New York: Harper and Row, 1988.

————. *The Fiery Trial: Abraham Lincoln and American Slavery.* New York: W. W. Norton, 2010.

Foote, Henry Stuart. *Casket of Reminiscences.* Washington, DC: Chronicle Press, 1874.

Foote, Shelby. *The Civil War: A Narrative.* 3 vols. New York: Random House, 1958–1974.

Forbes, Robert Pierce. *The Missouri Compromise and Its Aftermath: Slavery and the Meaning of America.* Chapel Hill: University of North Carolina Press, 2007.

Ford, Thomas. *A History of Illinois from Its Commencement as a State in 1818 to 1847.* Chicago: S. C. Griggs and Co., 1854.

Formisano, Ronald P. *The Birth of Mass Political Parties: Michigan, 1827–1861.* Princeton, NJ: Princeton University Press, 1971.

Fredrickson, George. "The Search for Order and Community." In Cullom Davis, Charles B. Strozier, Rebecca Monroe Veach, and Geoffrey C. Ward, eds., *Public and Private Lincoln.* Carbondale: Southern Illinois University Press, 1979, 86–98.

Fredrickson, George M. *The Black Image in the White Mind: The Debate on Afro-American Character and Destiny, 1817–1914.* Middletown, CT: Wesleyan University Press, 1987 (orig. 1971).

Freehling, Alison Goodyear. *Drift toward Dissolution: The Virginia Antislavery Debate of 1832.* Baton Rouge: Louisiana State University Press, 1982.

Freehling, William W. *The Road to Disunion.* Vol. 1: *Secessionists at Bay, 1776–1854.* New York: Oxford University Press, 1990.

———. *The Road to Disunion.* Vol. 2: *Secessionists Triumphant, 1854–1861.* New York: Oxford University Press, 2007.

Freeman, Samuel, ed. *The Cambridge Companion to Rawls.* Cambridge: Cambridge University Press, 2003.

Fuller, Lon L. *The Law in Quest of Itself.* Boston: Beacon Press, 1966.

Furtwangler, Albert. *The Authority of Publius: A Reading of the Federalist Papers.* Ithaca, NY: Cornell University Press, 1984.

———. *American Silhouettes: Rhetorical Identities of the Founders.* New Haven, CT: Yale University Press, 1988.

Galston, William A. "Civic Education in the Liberal State." In Nancy L. Rosenblum, ed., *Liberalism and the Moral Life.* Cambridge, MA: Harvard University Press, 1989, 89–102.

Garner, Stanton. *The Civil War World of Herman Melville.* Lawrence: University Press of Kansas, 1993.

Genovese, Eugene. *The Political Economy of Slavery: Studies in the Economy and Society of the Slave South.* New York: Vintage Books, 1967 (orig. 1965).

———. *Roll, Jordan, Roll: The World the Slaves Made.* New York: Random House, 1972.

———. *The Southern Front: The Achievements and Limitations of an American Conservatism.* Cambridge, MA: Belknap Press of Harvard University Press, 1994.

Genovese, Eugene D. *The World the Slaveholders Made: Two Essays in Interpretation.* New York: Pantheon Books, 1969.

Gerteis, Louis S. *Morality and Utility in American Antislavery Reform.* Chapel Hill: University of North Carolina Press, 1987.

Gienapp, William. "Who Voted for Lincoln." In John L. Thomas, ed., *Abraham Lincoln and the American Political Tradition.* Amherst: University of Massachusetts Press, 1986, 50–77.

Gienapp, William E. *The Origins of the Republican Party, 1852–1856.* New York: Oxford University Press, 1987.

Gilmore, Michael T. "A Plot against America: Free Speech and the American Renaissance." *Raritan* 26 (2006): 90–113.

Goodrich, Thomas. *War to the Knife: Bleeding Kansas, 1854–1861.* Mechanicsburg, PA: Stackpole Books, 1998.

Goodwin, Doris Kearns. *Team of Rivals: The Political Genius of Abraham Lincoln.* New York: Simon and Schuster, 2005.

Graber, Mark A. Dred Scott *and the Problem of Constitutional Evil.* Cambridge: Cambridge University Press, 2006.

Greenstone, J. David. *The Lincoln Persuasion: Remaking American Liberalism.* Princeton, NJ: Princeton University Press, 1993.

Grimsted, David. *American Mobbing, 1828–1861: Toward Civil War.* New York: Oxford University Press, 1998.

Guelzo, Allen. *Lincoln and Douglas: The Debates That Defined America.* New York: Simon and Schuster, 2008.

Guelzo, Allen C. *Abraham Lincoln, Redeemer President.* Grand Rapids, MI: William B. Eerdmans Publishing Company, 1999.

―――. *Lincoln's Emancipation Proclamation: The End of Slavery in America.* New York: Simon and Schuster, 2004.

―――. "Houses Divided: Lincoln, Douglas, and the Political Landscape of 1858." *Journal of American History* 94 (2007): 391–417.

Gurney, Eliza Paul Kirkbride. *Memoir and Correspondence of Eliza P. Gurney.* Ed. Richard F. Mott. Philadelphia: J. B. Lippincott and Company, 1884.

Habermas, Jürgen. *Knowledge and Human Interests.* Trans. Jeremy Shapiro. Boston: Beacon Press, 1971.

―――. *Theory and Practice.* Trans. John Viertel. Boston: Beacon Press, 1973.

―――. *The Philosophical Discourse of Modernity: Twelve Lectures.* Trans. Frederick G. Lawrence. Cambridge, MA: MIT Press, 1987.

―――. *Moral Consciousness and Communicative Action.* Trans. Christian Lenhardt and Shierry Weber Nicholsen. Cambridge, MA: MIT Press, 1990 (orig. 1983 [German]).

―――. *The Structural Transformation of the Public Sphere: An Inquiry into a Category of Bourgeois Society.* Trans. Thomas Burger and Frederick Lawrence. Cambridge, MA: MIT Press, 1991.

Hamilton, Alexander, James Madison, and John Jay. *The Federalist Papers.* New York: Mentor Books, 1961.

Hamilton, Holman. *Prologue to Conflict: The Crisis and Compromise of 1850.* Lexington: University Press of Kentucky, 1964.

Hammond, James Henry. "Speech of Hon. J. H. Hammond, of South Carolina, in the Senate, March 4, 1858." *Congressional Globe,* 35th Cong., 1st sess., appendix (1858): 68–71.

Hansen, Andrew C. "Dimensions of Agency in Lincoln's Second Inaugural." *Philosophy and Rhetoric* 37 (2004): 223–254.

Harris, William C. *Lincoln's Rise to the Presidency.* Lawrence: University Press of Kansas, 2007.

Hart, H. L. A. *The Concept of Law.* Oxford: Oxford University Press, 1961.

Hartz, Louis. *The Liberal Tradition in America: An Interpretation of American Political Thought since the Revolution.* New York: Harcourt Brace Jovanovich, 1955.

Heckman, Richard Allen. *Lincoln v. Douglas: The Great Debates Campaign.* Washington, DC: Public Affairs Press, 1967.

Hegel, G. W. F. *The Philosophy of Right.* Trans. T. M. Knox. Oxford: Oxford University Press, 1952 (orig. 1821).

Helper, Hinton Rowan. *The Impending Crisis of the South: How to Meet it.* New York: Burdick Bros., 1857.

Herndon, William, and Jesse Weik. *Herndon's Lincoln.* New York: Charles Boni, 1930.

Hirsch, David, and Dan Van Haften. *Abraham Lincoln and the Structure of Reason.* El Dorado Hills, CA: Savas Beattie, 2010.

Hofstadter, Richard. *The American Political Tradition and the Men Who Made It.* New York: Alfred A. Knopf, 1948.

―――. *The Paranoid Style in American Politics, and Other Essays.* New York: Alfred A. Knopf, 1965.

―――. *The Idea of a Party System: The Rise of Legitimate Opposition in the United States, 1780–1840.* Berkeley: University of California Press, 1969.

Holmes, Oliver Wendell, Jr. *The Common Law.* Boston: Little, Brown, 1963 (orig. 1881).

Holmes, Stephen. "The Permanent Structure of Antiliberal Thought." In Nancy L. Rosenblum, ed., *Liberalism and the Moral Life.* Cambridge, MA: Harvard University Press, 1989, 227–253.

Holt, Michael F. *Forging a Majority: The Formation of the Republican Party in Pittsburgh, 1848–1860.* New Haven, CT: Yale University Press, 1969.

———. *The Political Crisis of the 1850s.* New York: Wiley, 1978.

———. *Political Parties and American Political Development from the Age of Jackson to the Age of Lincoln.* Baton Rouge: Louisiana State University Press, 1992.

———. *The Rise and Fall of the American Whig Party: Jacksonian Politics and the Onset of the Civil War.* New York: Oxford University Press, 1999.

Holzer, Harold. *Lincoln Seen and Heard.* Lawrence: University Press of Kansas, 2000.

———. *Lincoln at Cooper Union: The Speech That Made Abraham Lincoln President.* New York: Simon and Schuster, 2004.

———. *Lincoln President-Elect: Abraham Lincoln and the Great Secession Winter 1860–1861.* New York: Simon and Schuster, 2008.

Howe, Daniel Walker. *The Political Culture of the American Whigs.* Chicago: University of Chicago Press, 1979.

———. *The Unitarian Conscience: Harvard Moral Philosophy, 1805–1861.* Middletown, CT: Wesleyan University Press, 1988 (orig. 1970).

———. *What Hath God Wrought: The Transformation of America, 1815–1848.* New York: Oxford University Press, 2007.

Hulliung, Mark. *Citizens and Citoyens: Republicans and Liberals in America and France.* Cambridge, MA: Harvard University Press, 2002.

Husserl, Edmund. *Ideas: General Introduction to Pure Phenomenology.* Trans. W. R. Boyce Gibson. New York: Collier, 1962 (orig. 1913 [German]).

Jaffa, Harry V. *Crisis of the House Divided: An Interpretation of the Issues in the Lincoln-Douglas Debates.* Garden City, NY: Doubleday and Company, 1959.

———. *A New Birth of Freedom: Abraham Lincoln and the Coming of the Civil War.* Lanham, MD: Rowman and Littlefield, 2000.

Jaffa, Harry V., and Robert W. Johannsen, eds. *In the Name of the People: Speeches and Writings of Lincoln and Douglas in the Ohio Campaign of 1859.* Columbus: Ohio State University Press, 1959.

Johannsen, Robert W. *Stephen A. Douglas.* New York: Oxford University Press, 1973.

———. *The Frontier, the Union, and Stephen A. Douglas.* Urbana: University of Illinois Press, 1989.

———. *Lincoln, the South, and Slavery.* Baton Rouge: Louisiana State University Press, 1991.

Justus, James H. *Fetching the Old Southwest: Humorous Writing from Longstreet to Twain.* Columbia: University of Missouri Press, 2004.

Kammen, Michael. *A Machine That Would Go of Itself: The Constitution in American Culture.* New York: Alfred A. Knopf, 1988.

Kateb, George. *Hannah Arendt: Politics, Conscience, Evil.* Totowa, NJ: Rowman and Allenheld, 1983.

————. "Democratic Individuality and the Meaning of Rights." In Nancy L. Rosenblum, ed., *Liberalism and the Moral Life*. Cambridge, MA: Harvard University Press, 1989, 183–206.

Keegan, John. *The Second World War*. New York: Viking Penguin, 1990.

Kierkegaard, Søren. *Fear and Trembling; and The Sickness Unto Death*. Trans. Walter Lowrie. Princeton, NJ: Princeton University Press, 1968 (orig. 1843).

Klein, Philip Shriver. *President James Buchanan: A Biography*. University Park: Pennsylvania State University Press, 1962.

Kleppner, Paul. *The Third Electoral System, 1853–1892: Parties, Voters and Political Cultures*. Chapel Hill: University of North Carolina Press, 1979.

Klingaman, William K. *Abraham Lincoln and the Road to Emancipation, 1861–1865*. New York: Viking, 2001.

Kloppenberg, James T. *The Virtues of Liberalism*. Oxford: Oxford University Press, 1998.

Krannawitter, Thomas L. *Vindicating Lincoln: Defending the Politics of Our Greatest President*. New York: Rowman and Littlefield, 2008.

Leff, Michael. "Dimensions of Temporality in Lincoln's Second Inaugural." In Carl R. Burgchardt, ed., *Readings in Rhetorical Criticism*. State College, PA: Strata Publishing, 1995, 526–531.

Lehrman, Lewis E. *Lincoln at Peoria: The Turning Point: Getting Right with the Declaration of Independence*. Mechanicsburg, PA: Stackpole Books, 2008.

Lincoln, Abraham. *Complete Works of Abraham Lincoln*. 12 vols. Ed. John G. Nicolay and John Hay. New York: Francis D. Tandy Company, 1894.

————. *The Collected Works of Abraham Lincoln*. 8 vols. Ed. Roy P. Basler. New Brunswick, NJ: Rutgers University Press, 1953.

————. *Abraham Lincoln: Speeches and Writings*. 2 vols. Ed. Don E. Fehrenbacher. New York: Library of America, 1989.

Lind, Michael. *What Lincoln Believed: The Values and Convictions of America's Greatest President*. New York: Doubleday, 2004.

MacIntyre, Alasdair. *After Virtue: A Study in Moral Theory*. Notre Dame, IN: University of Notre Dame Press, 1981.

————. *Whose Justice? Which Rationality?* Notre Dame, IN: University of Notre Dame Press, 1988.

Macpherson, C. B. *The Political Theory of Possessive Individualism: Hobbes to Locke*. New York: Oxford University Press, 1962.

Maizlish, Stephen E., and John J. Kushma, eds. *Essays on American Antebellum Politics, 1840–1860*. College Station: Texas A&M University Press, 1982.

Malin, James C. "Judge Lecompte and the 'Sack of Lawrence,' May 21, 1856." *Kansas Historical Quarterly* 20 (1953): 465–494.

Maltz, Earl M. "Slavery, Federalism and the Structure of the Constitution." *American Journal of Legal History* 36 (1992): 466–498.

Matthews, Richard K. *If Men Were Angels: James Madison and the Heartless Empire of Reason*. Lawrence: University Press of Kansas, 1995.

Mayfield, John. *Rehearsal for Republicanism: Free Soil and the Politics of Antislavery*. Port Washington, NY: Kennikat Press, 1980.

McCoy, Drew R. *The Last of the Fathers: James Madison and the Republican Legacy*. New York: Cambridge University Press, 1989.

McDonald, Forrest. *E Pluribus Unum: The Formation of the American Republic, 1776–1790*. Indianapolis: Liberty Press, 1979 (orig. 1965).

———. *Novus Ordo Seclorum: The Intellectual Origins of the Constitution.* Lawrence: University Press of Kansas, 1985.

McFeely, William S. *Grant: A Biography.* New York: W. W. Norton, 1981.

———. *Frederick Douglass.* New York: W. W. Norton, 1991.

McPherson, James M. *Tried by War: Abraham Lincoln as Commander in Chief.* New York: Penguin Press, 2008.

Menand, Louis. *The Metaphysical Club.* New York: Farrar, Straus and Giroux, 2001.

Meyers, Marvin. *The Jacksonian Persuasion: Politics and Belief.* New York: Vintage Books, 1957.

Miller, Randall. "Slavery in Antebellum Southern Textile Mills." *Business History Review* 55 (1981): 471–490.

Miller, William Lee. *Arguing about Slavery: The Great Battle in the United States Congress.* New York: Alfred A. Knopf, 1996.

———. *Lincoln's Virtues: An Ethical Biography.* New York: Alfred A. Knopf, 2002.

———. *President Lincoln: The Duty of a Statesman.* New York: Alfred A. Knopf, 2008.

Milton, George Fort. *Eve of Conflict: Stephen A. Douglas and the Needless War.* Boston: Houghton Mifflin, 1934.

Morel, Lucas E. *Lincoln's Sacred Effort: Defining Religion's Role in American Self-Government.* Lanham, MD: Lexington Books, 2000.

Morgan, Edmund S. *American Slavery, American Freedom: The Ordeal of Colonial Virginia.* New York: W. W. Norton, 1975.

———. *Inventing the People: The Rise of Popular Sovereignty in England and America.* New York: W. W. Norton, 1988.

Morris, Richard B. *Seven Who Shaped Our Destiny: The Founding Fathers as Revolutionaries.* New York: Harper and Row, 1973.

———. *Witnesses at the Creation: Hamilton, Madison, Jay, and the Constitution.* New York: Holt, Rinehart, and Winston, 1985.

Morris, Roy, Jr. *The Long Pursuit: Abraham Lincoln's Thirty-Year Struggle with Stephen Douglas for the Heart and Soul of America.* New York: Smithsonian Books, 2008.

Morris, Thomas D. *Southern Slavery and the Law, 1619–1860.* Chapel Hill: University of North Carolina Press, 1996.

Morrison, Chaplain W. *Democratic Politics and Sectionalism: The Wilmot Proviso Controversy.* Chapel Hill: University of North Carolina Press, 1967.

Morrison, Michael A. *Slavery and the American West: The Eclipse of Manifest Destiny and the Coming of the Civil War.* Chapel Hill: University of North Carolina Press, 1997.

Mulhall, Stephen, and Adam Swift. "Rawls and Communitarianism." In Samuel Freeman, ed., *The Cambridge Companion to Rawls.* Cambridge: Cambridge University Press, 2003, 460–487.

Neely, Mark E., Jr. *The Fate of Liberty: Abraham Lincoln and Civil Liberties.* New York: Oxford University Press, 1991.

———. *The Last Best Hope of Earth: Abraham Lincoln and the Promise of America.* Cambridge, MA: Harvard University Press, 1995.

Nevins, Allan. *The Ordeal of the Union.* Vol. 1. New York: Scribner, 1947a.

———. *The Ordeal of the Union.* Vol. 2. New York: Scribner, 1947b.

———. *The Emergence of Lincoln.* Vol. 1. New York: Scribner, 1950a.

————. *The Emergence of Lincoln.* Vol. 2. New York: Scribner, 1950b.

————. *The War for the Union.* 4 vols. New York: Scribner, 1959–1971.

Nichols, Roy Franklin. *Franklin Pierce: Young Hickory of the Granite Hills.* Philadelphia: University of Pennsylvania Press, 1958 (orig. 1931).

————. *The Disruption of American Democracy.* New York: Collier, 1962 (orig. 1948).

Niebuhr, Reinhold. *Moral Man and Immoral Society: A Study in Ethics and Politics.* New York: Charles Scribner's Sons, 1932.

————. *The Irony of American History.* London: Nisbet, 1952.

————. "The Religion of Abraham Lincoln." *Christian Century* 82 (February 10, 1965): 172–175.

Nott, Josiah C., and George R. Gliddon. *Types of Mankind; or, Ethnological researches, based upon the ancient monuments, paintings, sculptures, and crania of races, and upon their natural, geographical, philosophical, and Biblical history. Illustrated by selections from the inedited papers of Samuel George Morton, and by additional contributions from L. Agassiz, W. Usher and H. S. Patterson.* Philadelphia: Lippincott Grambo, 1854.

Nussbaum, Martha. *The Fragility of Goodness: Luck and Ethics in Greek Tragedy and Philosophy.* New York: Cambridge University Press, 1986.

Oates, Stephen B. *With Malice toward None: The Life of Abraham Lincoln.* New York: Harper and Row, 1977.

O'Brien, Michael. *Conjectures of Order: Intellectual Life and the American South, 1810–1860.* Chapel Hill: University of North Carolina Press, 2004.

Olmsted, Frederick Law. *The Cotton Kingdom: A Traveller's Observations on Cotton and Slavery in the American Slave States: Based upon Three Former Volumes of Journeys and Investigations by the Same Author.* New York: Mason Bros., 1861.

Painter, Nell Irvin. *Exodusters: Black Migration to Kansas after Reconstruction.* New York: Knopf, 1977.

Paludan, Phillip S. *A Covenant with Death: The Constitution, Law, and Equality in the Civil War Era.* Urbana: University of Illinois Press, 1975.

Patterson, Orlando. *Freedom in the Making of Western Culture.* New York: Basic Books, 1991.

Peck, Graham A. "Was Stephen A. Douglas Antislavery?" *Journal of the Abraham Lincoln Association* 26, no. 2 (2005): 1–2.

Perry, Lewis. *Radical Abolitionism: Anarchy and the Government of God in Antislavery Thought.* Ithaca, NY: Cornell University Press, 1973.

Peterson, Merrill D. *The Great Triumvirate: Webster, Clay, and Calhoun.* New York: Oxford University Press, 1987.

Pitkin, Hanna Fenichel. *Wittgenstein and Justice: On the Significance of Ludwig Wittgenstein for Social and Political Thought.* Berkeley: University of California Press, 1993 (orig. 1972).

Pocock, J. G. A. *The Machiavellian Moment: Florentine Political Thought and the Atlantic Republican Tradition.* Princeton, NJ: Princeton University Press, 1975.

Polanyi, Michael. *Personal Knowledge: Towards a Post-Critical Philosophy.* Chicago: University of Chicago Press, 1962 (orig. 1958).

Potter, David R. *The Impending Crisis, 1848–1861.* Ed. Don E. Fehrenbacher. New York: Harper and Row, 1976.

Putnam, Hilary. *Reason, Truth, and History.* Cambridge: Cambridge University Press, 1981.

————. *Pragmatism: An Open Question.* Oxford: Blackwell, 1995.

Quinn, Arthur Hobson. *Edgar Allan Poe, a Critical Biography.* New York: Appleton Century, 1941.

Rakove, Jack N. *Original Meanings: Politics and Ideas in the Making of the Constitution.* New York: Vintage Books, 1996.

Ramsdell, Charles W. "The Natural Limits of Slavery Expansion." *The Southwestern Historical Quarterly* 33, no. 2 (October 1929): 91–111.

Randall, J. G. *Lincoln the President: Springfield to Gettysburg.* 2 vols. New York: Dodd, Mead, 1945.

Rawley, James A. *Bleeding Kansas and the Coming of the Civil War.* Lincoln: University of Nebraska Press, 1969.

Rawls, John. *A Theory of Justice.* Cambridge, MA: Belknap Press of Harvard University Press, 1971.

————. *Political Liberalism.* New York: Columbia University Press, 1993.

————. *The Law of Peoples.* Cambridge, MA: Harvard University Press, 1999.

————. *Lectures on the History of Moral Philosophy.* Ed. Barbara Herman. Cambridge, MA: Harvard University Press, 2000.

Remini, Robert V. *Henry Clay: Statesman for the Union.* New York: W. W. Norton and Company, 1991.

Rosenblum, Nancy L., ed. *Liberalism and the Moral Life.* Cambridge, MA: Harvard University Press, 1989.

Rothman, Adam. *Slave Country: American Expansion and the Origins of the Deep South.* Cambridge, MA: Harvard University Press, 2005.

Rutland, Robert. *James Madison: The Founding Father.* New York: Macmillan, 1987.

Sandel, Michael J. *Liberalism and the Limits of Justice.* Cambridge: Cambridge University Press, 1982.

————. *Democracy's Discontent: America in Search of a Public Philosophy.* Cambridge, MA: Belknap Press of Harvard University Press, 1996.

Schneewind, J. B. *The Invention of Autonomy: A History of Modern Moral Philosophy.* New York: Cambridge University Press, 1998.

Schneider, Thomas E. *Lincoln's Defense of Politics: The Public Man and His Opponents in the Crisis over Slavery.* Columbia: University of Missouri Press, 2006.

Schurz, Carl. *Henry Clay.* New York: Chelsea House, 1980 (orig. 1899).

Scott, Carole. "Why the Cotton Textile Industry Did Not Develop in the South Sooner." *Agricultural History* 68 (1994): 105–121.

Sewell, Richard H. *Ballots for Freedom: Antislavery Politics in the United States, 1837–1860.* New York: Oxford University Press, 1976.

Sigelschiffer, Saul. *The American Conscience: The Drama of the Lincoln-Douglas Debates.* New York: Horizon Press, 1973.

Silbey, Joel H. *The American Political Nation, 1838–1893.* Stanford, CA: Stanford University Press, 1991.

————. *Martin Van Buren and the Emergence of American Popular Politics.* New York: Rowman and Littlefield, 2002.

Simon, James F. *Lincoln and Chief Justice Taney: Slavery, Secession, and the President's War Powers.* New York: Simon and Schuster, 2006.

Smith, Elbert B. *The Presidency of James Buchanan.* Lawrence: University Press of Kansas, 1975.

Sollors, Werner. *Beyond Ethnicity: Consent and Descent in American Culture.* New York: Oxford University Press, 1986.

Spector, Robert M. "The Quock Walker Cases (1781–83)—Slavery, Its Abolition, and Negro Citizenship in Early Massachusetts." *Journal of Negro History* 53 (1968): 12–32.

Stampp, Kenneth. *America in 1857: A Nation on the Brink.* New York: Oxford University Press, 1990.

Stampp, Kenneth M. *The Era of Reconstruction, 1865–1877.* New York: Alfred A. Knopf, 1965.

Storing, Herbert J. *What the Anti-Federalists Were For.* Ed. Murray Dry. Chicago: University of Chicago Press, 1981.

Strauss, Leo. *Natural Right and History.* Chicago: University of Chicago Press, 1953.

Striner, Richard. *Father Abraham: Lincoln's Relentless Struggle to End Slavery.* Oxford: Oxford University Press, 2006.

Tackach, James. *Lincoln's Moral Vision: The Second Inaugural Address.* Jackson: University Press of Mississippi, 2002.

Taylor, Charles. *Hegel.* Cambridge: Cambridge University Press, 1975.

———. *Sources of the Self: The Making of the Modern Identity.* Cambridge, MA: Harvard University Press, 1989.

Thomas, John L., ed. *Abraham Lincoln and the American Political Tradition.* Amherst: University of Massachusetts Press, 1986.

Thurow, Glen E. *Abraham Lincoln and American Political Religion.* Albany: State University of New York Press, 1976.

Tilden, Samuel J. *The Writings and Speeches of Samuel J. Tilden.* 2 vols. Ed. John Bigelow. New York: Harper and Brothers, 1885.

Trefousse, Hans L. *Andrew Johnson: A Biography.* New York: W. W. Norton, 1989.

Trilling, Lionel. *Sincerity and Authenticity.* Cambridge, MA: Harvard University Press, 1971.

Tucker, Robert C., ed. *The Marx-Engels Reader.* New York: W. W. Norton, 1972.

Tushnet, Mark. *Red, White, and Blue: A Critical Analysis of Constitutional Law.* Cambridge, MA: Harvard University Press, 1988.

Tushnet, Mark V. *The American Law of Slavery 1810–1860: Considerations of Humanity and Interest.* Princeton, NJ: Princeton University Press, 1981.

Walther, Eric H. *The Shattering of the Union: America in the 1850s.* Wilmington, DE: Scholarly Resources, 2004.

Warren, Robert Penn. *John Brown: The Making of a Martyr.* New York: Payson and Clarke, 1929.

———. *World Enough and Time, a Romantic Novel.* New York: Random House, 1950.

———. *Brother to Dragons: A Tale in Verse and Voices.* New York: Random House, 1953.

———. *The Legacy of the Civil War.* New York: Random House, 1961.

———. *Homage to Theodore Dreiser, August 27, 1871–December 28, 1945, on the Centennial of His Birth.* New York: Random House, 1971.

Waugh, John C. *One Man Great Enough: Abraham Lincoln's Road to Civil War.* New York: Harcourt, 2007.

Weber, Max, "Politics as a Vocation." In H. H. Gerth and C. Wright Mills, trans. and ed., *From Max Weber: Essays in Sociology*. New York: Oxford University Press, 1946, 77–128. (Originally a speech at Munich University, 1918, published in 1919 by Duncker & Humblodt, Munich.)

Weiss, Thomas A. *A Deplorable Scarcity: The Failure of Industrialization in the Slave Economy*. Chapel Hill: University of North Carolina Press, 1981.

Weld, Theodore Dwight. *American Slavery as It Is; Testimony of a Thousand Witnesses*. New York: American Anti-slavery Society, 1839.

Wells, Damon. *Stephen Douglas: The Last Years, 1857–1861*. Austin: University of Texas Press, 1990 (orig. 1971).

White, Morton. *Philosophy*, The Federalist, *and the Constitution*. New York: Oxford University Press, 1987.

White, Ronald C. *Lincoln's Greatest Speech: The Second Inaugural*. New York: Simon and Schuster, 2002.

———. *The Eloquent President: A Portrait of Lincoln through His Words*. New York: Random House, 2005.

Wiecek, William. "Slavery and Abolition before the United States Supreme Court, 1820–1860." *Journal of American History* 65 (1978): 34–59.

Wiecek, William M. *The Sources of Antislavery Constitutionalism in America, 1760–1848*. Ithaca, NY: Cornell University Press, 1977.

Wieck, Carl F. *Lincoln's Quest for Equality: The Road to Gettysburg*. Dekalb: Northern Illinois University Press, 2002.

Wilentz, Sean. *Chants Democratic: New York City and the Rise of the American Working Class, 1788–1850*. New York: Oxford University Press, 1984.

———. *The Rise of American Democracy: Jefferson to Lincoln*. New York: W. W. Norton, 2005.

Wills, Garry. *Inventing America: Jefferson's Declaration of Independence*. New York: Vintage Books, 1978.

———. *Explaining America: The Federalist*. Garden City, NY: Doubleday, 1981.

———. *Lincoln at Gettysburg: The Words That Remade America*. New York: Simon and Schuster, 1992.

Wilson, Douglas L. *Honor's Voice: The Transformation of Abraham Lincoln*. New York: Alfred A. Knopf, 1998.

———. *Lincoln's Sword: The Presidency and the Power of Words*. New York: Alfred A. Knopf, 2006.

Wilson, Douglas L., and Rodney O. Davis, eds. *Herndon's Informants: Letters, Interviews, and Statements about Abraham Lincoln*. Urbana: University of Illinois Press, 1998.

Wilson, Henry. *History of the Rise and Fall of the Slave Power in America*. 3 vols. Boston: James R. Osgood and Company, 1872.

Winch, Peter. *The Idea of a Social Science and Its Relation to Philosophy*. London: Routledge and Kegan Paul, 1958.

Winger, Stewart. *Lincoln, Religion, and Romantic Cultural Politics*. Dekalb: Northern Illinois University Press, 2003.

Wittgenstein, Ludwig. *The Blue and Brown Books*. New York: Harper and Row, 1958.

Wolf, William J. *The Almost Chosen People: A Study of the Religion of Abraham Lincoln*. Garden City, NY: Doubleday, 1959.

Wood, Gordon S. *The Creation of the American Republic, 1776–1787.* New York: W. W. Norton, 1972.

———. *The Radicalism of the American Revolution.* New York: Alfred A. Knopf, 1992.

Woodward, C. Vann. *Origins of the New South, 1877–1913.* Baton Rouge: Louisiana State University Press, 1951.

———. *The Strange Career of Jim Crow.* Baton Rouge: Louisiana State University Press, 1955.

———. *The Burden of Southern History.* Baton Rouge: Louisiana State University Press, 1960.

Wright, John S. *Lincoln and the Politics of Slavery.* Reno: University of Nevada Press, 1970.

Zarefsky, David. *Lincoln, Douglas, and Slavery in the Crucible of Public Debate.* Chicago: University of Chicago Press, 1990.

———. "'Public Sentiment Is Everything': Lincoln's View of Political Persuasion." *Journal of the Abraham Lincoln Association* 15 (1994): 23–40.

———. "Lincoln's 1862 Annual Message: A Paradigm of Rhetorical Leadership." *Rhetoric and Public Affairs* 3 (2000): 5–14.

Index